GLOBAL HUMANITIES READER

UNIVERSITY OF NORTH CAROLINA ASHEVILLE HUMANITIES PROGRAM

The Humanities Program at University of North Carolina Asheville explores what it means to be human. We examine the experiences of our shared humanity by looking at the oral, literary, and material expressions of our orientations and convictions, values and passions, and struggles and strategies for survival and thriving. In engaging with a wide and diverse set of perspectives, we consider both their original contexts and their ongoing influence on our times. These inquiries are strengthened through an interdisciplinary approach to Humanities that draws together faculty and subject matter across disciplines currently including: Africana studies, anthropology, arts, Asian studies, biology, chemistry, classics, economics, history, Indigenous studies, languages, literature, mathematics, philosophy, physics, political science, psychology, religious studies, sociology, and women, gender and sexuality studies. Humanities helps us to make educated and ethical decisions as we strive to understand multiple perspectives on human experience, engage in culturally appropriate and community-centered problem solving, and thrive as global and local citizens of our own communities.

The *Global Humanities Reader* is a three-volume work edited by a team of faculty from UNC Asheville. The three volumes are *Volume 1 - Engaging Ancient Worlds and Perspectives, Volume 2 - Engaging Pre-Modern Worlds and Perspectives*, and *Volume 3 - Engaging Modern Worlds and Perspectives*.

Katherine C. Zubko and Keya Maitra, General Editors

Brian S. Hook, Sophie Mills, and Katherine C. Zubko, *Engaging Ancient Worlds and Perspectives*, Editors

Renuka Gusain and Keya Maitra, *Engaging Premodern Worlds and Perspectives*, Editors

Alvis Dunn and James Perkins, *Engaging Modern Worlds and Perspectives*, Editors

Cameron Barlow, Timeline and Source Preparation Editor

GLOBAL HUMANITIES READER

VOLUME II
Engaging Premodern Worlds and Perspectives

VOLUME EDITORS:
Renuka Gusain, Keya Maitra and
Katherine C. Zubko

ISBN 978-1-4696-6642-6 (paperback: alk. paper)
ISBN 978-1-4696-6643-3 (ebook)

Published by the University of North Carolina Asheville Humanities Program

Distributed by the University of North Carolina Press
www.uncpress.org

Cover photo credit: "Undergrowth with green ferns" by rebaisilvano,
licensed and used by permission of the photographer, through depositphotos
Cover Design by Cameron Barlow

CONTENTS

Contents by Chronology   vii

Acknowledgments   ix

General Editors' Welcome, Katherine C. Zubko and Keya Maitra   xiii

    Getting to Know the Elephant   xiii

    How to Use this Book   xviii

Premodern Worlds: An Historical Cross-Cultural Introduction, Tracey Rizzo   1

Comprehensive Timeline   34

AFRICA: COMMUNITIES AND CULTURES

    from *Kebra Nagast*   39

    from *Mishneh Torah* by Maimonides   63

    from *Muqaddima* by Ibn Khaldun   72

    Sunjata: A New Prose Version (Introduction only)   81

    from *The Travels* by Ibn Battuta   83

THE AMERICAS: TRADITIONS AND ENCOUNTERS

    from *The Truth About Stories: A Native Narrative* ("Sky Woman Falling")
    by Thomas King   90

    from *Popol Wuj*   102

    from *A Short Account of the Destruction of the Indies* by Bartolomé de las Casas   117

CENTRAL AND WEST ASIA: COMMUNITIES AND TRADITIONS

    from *The Babylonian Talmud*   127

    Deliverance from Error by Al-Ghazali (Introduction only)   134

    from *History of the Wars* and *The Secret History* by Procopius   138

    from *Kalila and Dimna* by Nasrullah Munshi   153

    from *Shahnameh* by Ferdowsi   166

EAST AND SOUTH ASIA: COMMUNITIES AND CULTURES

from *Administration of Akbar (A'in-i Akbari)* by Abu'l-Fazl 'Allami   171

from *Divine Stories (Divyavadana)*   185

from *A Dream of Splendors Past in the Eastern Capital (Dongjing meng hua lu)*
by Meng Yuanlao   190

from *Ganga Lahari (Waves of the Ganges River)* by Panditaraja Jagannatha   199

from *A Guide to the Bodhisattva Way of Life (Bodhicaryavatara)* by
Shantideva   205

from *The Ocean of Story (Kathasaritsagara)* by Somadeva   219

from *The Pillow Book* by Sei Shonagan   240

Poems of Kabir   252

Poems of Mirabai   258

"Song of the Lute" by Po Chü-i   263

from *Vishnu Purana* ("Krishna and Kaliya")   269

MEDITERRANEAN EUROPE: COMMUNITIES AND TRADITIONS

from *Canons and Decrees of Council of Trent*   274

"Canticle of the Creatures" by St. Francis of Assisi   284

Oration on the Dignity of Man by Pico della Mirandola   290

from *Rule of Saint Benedict* by St. Benedict of Nursia   301

from *The Spiritual Exercises* by St. Ignatius of Loyola   318

NORTHERN EUROPE: TRADITIONS AND ENCOUNTERS

from *The Book of the City of Ladies* by Christine de Pizan   325

from *The Book of Margery Kempe* by Margery Kempe   336

"Origins of Higher Education"   346

Othello by William Shakespeare (Introduction only)   356

from *Scivias* by Hildegard of Bingen   359

The Twelve Articles and *Martin Luther's Admonition to Peace*   367

Sources and Permissions   391

Tag Glossary   397

Index   403

CONTENTS BY CHRONOLOGY

1. from *Divine Stories (Divyavadana)* (3rd-4th century, India)   185

2. from *Vishnu Purana* ("Krishna and Kaliya") (4th century, India)   269

3. from *Rule of Saint Benedict* by St. Benedict of Nursia (6th century, Italy)   301

4. from *History of the Wars* and *The Secret History* by Procopius (6th century, Constantinople)   138

5. from *The Babylonian Talmud* (3rd-6th century, Rabbinic Judaism/ Tamudic Academies in Babylonia/ Iraq)   127

6. from *A Guide to the Bodhisattva Way of Life (Bodhicaryavatara)* by Shantideva (7th-8th century, India)   205

7. "Song of the Lute" by Po Chü-i (9th century, Tang dynasty, China)   263

8. from *Kalila and Dimna* by Nasrullah Munshi (10th-11th century, Persia)   153

9. from *Shahnameh* by Ferdowsi (11th century, Persia)   166

10. from *Pillow Book* by Sei Shonagan (11th century, Japan)   240

11. from *The Ocean of Story (Kathasaritsagara)* by Somadeva (11th century, India)   219

12. from *Scivias* by Hildegard of Bingen (12th century, Palatine of the Rhine)   359

13. from *A Dream of Splendors Past in the Eastern Capital (Dongjing meng hua lu)* by Meng Yuanlao (12th century, China)   190

14. from *Mishneh Torah* by Maimonides (1170–1180, Egypt)   63

15. *Deliverance from Error* by Al-Ghazali (Introduction only) (12th century, Persia)   134

16. *Sunjata: A New Prose Version* (Introduction only) (13th century, West Africa)   81

17. "Origins of Higher Education" (13th century, France)   346

18. "Canticle of the Creatures" by St. Francis of Assisi (13th century, Italy)   284

19. from *Muqaddima* by Ibn Khaldun (14th century, North Africa)   72

20. from *The Travels* by Ibn Battuta (14th century, Mali)   83

21. from *Kebra Nagast* (14th century, East Africa)   39

22. from *The Book of Margery Kempe* by Margery Kempe (15th century, England)   336

23. from *The Book of the City of Ladies* by Christine de Pizan (15th century France)   325

24. Poems of Kabir (15th century, India)   252

25. *Oration on the Dignity of Man* by Pico della Mirandola (15th century, Italy)   290

26. from *Administration of Akbar (A'in-i Akbari)* by Abu'l-Fazl 'Allami (16th century, India)   171

27. from *Popol Wuj* (precontact Mesoamerica)   102

28. "Sky Woman Falling" from *The Truth About Stories: A Native Narrative* by Thomas King (North America)   90

29. Poems of Mirabai (16th century, India)   258

30. from *A Short Account of the Destruction of the Indies* by Bartolomé de las Casas (1542, Americas)   117

31. from *Canons and Decrees of the Council of Trent* (16th century, Italy)   274

32. *The Twelve Articles* and *Martin Luther's Admonition to Peace* (16th century, Germany)   367

33. from *The Spiritual Exercises* by St. Ignatius of Loyola (16th century, Spain)   318

34. from *Ganga Lahari (Waves of the Ganges River)* by Panditaraja Jagannatha (17th century, India)   199

35. *Othello* by William Shakespeare (Introduction only) (1603, England)   356

ACKNOWLEDGMENTS

A s we sit down to compose these acknowledgments we are almost in disbelief that we have arrived at this point. We did not have a definitive roadmap when we started in 2017. Now a global pandemic later, we are at the finish line. Our student-centered approach served as our North Star. Working with many stakeholders we determined the steps of the process that brought us here. There were more than sixty people inside and outside of UNC Asheville who helped us with this project. Unfortunately, we can't name every single one of them, but to them, using the South African expression, we say *ubuntu*! "*I am because you are; we are because you are.*" This project is because you are!

This *Global Humanities Reader: Engaging Premodern Worlds and Perspectives*, would not be possible without the support of the following individuals and funding sources.

This project benefited from an amazing **Reader Support Team**. Jessica Park was the hub facilitating all connections and communications, keeping the project organized every step of the way. She often helped us reimagine what the project could be with her timely interventions and keen eye for detail. Jon Morris handled the copyright issues with such competence and precision that we never had to deal with the countless emails and loose ends with multiple publishers. Cameron Barlow, our student partner, actualized *all* the graphic timelines and envisioned and created the comprehensive timelines from the ground up, in addition to his detail-oriented primary source preparation. It is no easy feat transferring pdfs of ancient sources into a Word format, undoing diacritical marks, weird spacing, and nineteenth- and twentieth-century publishing styles—ALL CAPS! The success of this project is due to their ability and willingness to routinely go beyond the call of duty exhibiting constant and tireless enthusiasm, unparalleled professionalism, and a collaborative spirit that found solutions for every problem.

Our colleagues from the UNC Asheville Career Center, David Earnhardt and Chelsey Augustyniak, became a part of this project early on and read many of the primary sources in the process of their creative collaboration on the Beyond the Classroom feature. Tracey Rizzo agreed to compose the unique cross-cultural historical introductions for each volume, a task made even more difficult since we wanted her to tell a story that not only offered integrated contexts for our primary sources but also would inspire the reader to expand their engagement. Tracey not only delivered on our request but worked indefatigably on multiple drafts. One of our amazing art historians, Eva Hericks-Bares, curated the images for the introductions that Tracey wrote and located usable high-resolution images with the appropriate licensing requirements. Her detailed captions bring these images into clear focus in relation to the overview of history. Amanda Bell provided tremendous research support by creating surveys and analyzing faculty and student data to support the shape of the primary guiding priorities and pedagogical features in the project. Our colleague Lyndi Hewitt and her students offered support in designing the student survey instrument. We are grateful to Heather Hardy, a member of our Asheville community, for diligently fact checking all the timeline information. Finally, we are thankful to John McLeod from the UNC Press Office of Scholarly Publishing Services and his colleagues, including Lisa Stallings and her team at Longleaf Services, for helping us navigate this complex process.

We thank our various **funding sources**. The generous support from the Mellon grant allowed us to first conceive and then execute this audacious project. We thank our colleague Brian S. Hook for his crucial leadership in securing the grant and getting the project started as its first general editor. We also thank then-provost of UNC Asheville, Joseph R. Urgo, for his unwavering support for the project at its early stages. A Thomas W. Ross Fund Publishing Grant from UNC Press provided critical support that made the various design aspects possible. Finally, we thank Katherine C. Zubko, who offered unfailing and constant support through her NEH Distinguished Professor in the Humanities funds whenever a supplementary need arose.

A number of other individuals offered unhesitating support for this project at various moments and we thank them for their steadfast encouragement: our colleagues Ameena Batada, Dee James, and Melissa Himelein for providing important feedback on the General Editors' Welcome; Joevell Lee; Charlotte Smith; Steve Birkhofer; Wendy Mullis; Leah Dunn; Natalia Zubko; and peer reviewers for the cross-cultural introductions: UNCA History department colleagues, Saheed Aderinto (Western Carolina University), Steven Gerontakis (University of Florida), and Shawna Herzog (Washington State University).

Finally, we thank our **contributors,** who wrote source introductions and pedagogical features for all of the sources within this volume: Amanda Glenn-Bradley, Evan Gurney, Renuka Gusain, Grant Hardy, Eva Hericks-Bares, Lora Holland-Goldthwaite, Sam Kaplan, Doria Killian, Brenda K. Lewis, Jinhua Li, Gregory Lyon, Keya Maitra, Sophie Mills, Rodger Payne, Ellen Pearson, William Revere, Juan Sanchez-Martinez, Samer Traboulsi; Scott Williams, and Katherine C. Zubko.

In asking our contributors to craft the learning support items for each source, we asked them to do far more than simply writing a supporting introduction. Our contributors not only rose to the occasion but also revised their entries in response to the editorial feedback. Many of the contributors wrote multiple entries. Our colleague Grant Hardy modeled for us his devotion and excitement about student-centered pedagogy and thereby offered us crucial confidence to stay the course at various stages. And last, but not least, we thank our families who teased us for having too many tabs open on our computers and were patient and only mildly irritated on our behalf at times as this project took over countless hours, spilling over into many nights and weekends.

Katherine C. Zubko and Keya Maitra

PART I: GETTING TO KNOW THE ELEPHANT

Welcome to the University of North Carolina Asheville's *Global Humanities Reader: Engaging Premodern Worlds and Perspectives*. Let us begin by sharing a story about the elephant and the blind men from South Asia:

> Several blind men are brought before a king and asked to describe an elephant. An elephant is brought to them and they proceed to feel it with their hands. One, who grasps the elephant's trunk, claims that an elephant is like a snake. Another, grasping a leg, claims it is like a tree. Yet another grasps the tail and says it is like a rope; and another, feeling the elephant's side, claims it is like a wall. The blind men then argue amongst themselves about the true nature of the elephant. Who is correct?[1]

You might be familiar with a different version of this narrative. What is instructive is that not only does the setting of the story shift based on who is engaging it, including Hindus, Buddhists, and Jains, but that the lesson of the narrative changes as well. Thus, while the Buddha takes it to reflect how the men "cling" to their individual "finding," the Jain view uses it as an example of their epistemological perspectivalism (*anekantavada*) or many-sidedness.

This version of the story is instructive also in what it does not emphasize; for example, it doesn't draw our attention to the ground where the elephant stands. Engaging with this narrative, especially in the context of the United States, the land can no longer be ignored or taken for granted but is central to one's becoming aware of our erased and fractured histories and our uncomfortable collective self-understanding.

1. Anand Jayprakash Vaidya, "Making the Case for Jaina Contributions to Critical Thinking Education," *Journal of World Philosophies* 3 (2018): 61–62.

We want to acknowledge and honor that UNC Asheville is on *Anikituwag*i (Chero-kee) ancestral land and that we continue to build mutual, respectful relationships with the Eastern Band of Cherokee (EBCI) who are ongoing stewards of this area, and from whom we continue to learn. Acknowledgment is not enough, however, and it is our hope that these Readers help us put our commitment to this relationship into action.

We want to use the elephant story to remind us of insights that emanate from our understanding of UNC Asheville's Humanities Program:

- Exploration of truth and meaning is a collaborative affair involving perspectives from various cultures and occupants of different viewpoints within a single culture.
- No one discipline might have the final exclusive claim on truth, especially when it comes to enduring questions.
- The inquiry model, where asking questions is centered, is the most effective approach for fostering informed, engaged, and compassionate global citizens given its commitment to active, authentic, and open-minded learning.
- Finally, critical thinking has to be conceived in its global purview in order to open us to a wide spectrum of methodologies and epistemologies.

This welcome is primarily aimed at students so that the context for these Readers and the choices we have made may become more transparent.

Who We Are: The Humanities Program at UNC Asheville

On behalf of the editorial team—Brian S. Hook, Sophie Mills, Renuka Gusain, James Perkins, and Alvis Dunn—we are delighted to introduce three humanities primary source anthologies that have been created as the culmination of a multiyear faculty-led curricular revision process at the University of North Carolina Asheville. Our public liberal arts university's more than fifty-year-old Humanities Program consists of a four course sequence taken by all of our students.[2] The Humanities Program serves as the hub of the wheel of our liberal arts mission. The different spokes of this mission are critical thinking, interdisciplinarity, cross-cultural commitments to diverse perspectives, and inquiry-focused learning. They are held together by an integrative and open-minded sensibility embodied in its curriculum design, delivery, and student learning outcomes.

Early on in the history of this program, faculty saw the need to create their own anthologies of diverse primary sources, as no other available anthology was suitable to meet their goals. These anthologies, published as the Asheville Readers, have periodi-

---

2. Margaret Downes, "The Humanities Program at University of North Carolina at Asheville," in *Alive at the Core: Exemplary Approaches to General Education in the Humanities*, edited by Michael Nelson et al. (San Francisco: Jossey Banks, 2000), 203–24.

cally been revised over these past decades, as faculty continually engage in curricular revision. The main audience for these Readers has always been our own university students who participate in our homegrown, interdisciplinary program.

Thanks to the generosity of a Mellon grant awarded in 2017, this new iteration of the Asheville Readers—renamed *Global Humanities Readers*—are able to evolve in ways that better support the needs of our students at UNC Asheville and beyond who find themselves in a complex, interconnected, and rapidly changing world. For the first time, the Readers will be available online free of cost not only to our students but also to high school, community college, and university students across North Carolina public educational online communities. These developments very much align with our own public liberal arts mission and that of the Humanities Program out of which these Readers have emerged.

Values That Guide Our Readers: Diverse Cross-Cultural Perspectives and Inquiry Focus

Informed by surveys and discussions with faculty and students, the editorial team identified two main principles that have guided the shaping of these new Readers. The first is a commitment to placing materials from multiple, diverse perspectives in conversation with one another. Second is a focus on providing ways to cultivate our ability to ask questions—to inquire—while deepening our cross-cultural and cross-disciplinary engagements with the materials. We believe both values help you to see your own points of view as emerging from particular contexts, assumptions, and experiences, and that your own is only one of many co-existing views.

Furthermore, we are interested in promoting an openness to *your* encounters with materials. At times we have intentionally encouraged new insights by offering competing perspectives or challenging traditional viewpoints. In some ways, we want to foment intellectual chaos, uncertainty, and struggle by challenging the obvious or the given. Our goal is to enable the potential for growth and help you develop skillful facility in holding multiple perspectives. This is not to encourage a form of relativism but rather to foster a deeper understanding of context and position—whether disciplinary, cultural, and/or intersectional—that permeate your inquiry.

The Jain concept of *anekantavada* mentioned earlier speaks to these multiple co-existing perspectives, each limited to one's position and experience as exemplified in the parable of the elephant. But this story also speaks to the power of self-awareness of each perspective that in combination allows a different communal truth to emerge in contrast to a privileged preexistent ideal Truth (Elephant).

In order to acknowledge that the nature of truth is both communal and multifaceted, students must engage in this study and effort as deeply as possible. Engaging deeply permits us to penetrate typical surface comparisons and unfounded generalizations. Better still, we are not trapped in judgments that perpetuate one dominant view of the world as the highest or only way to perceive it. To accomplish this requires the strengthening of a very important skill related to critical thinking, namely, in-quiry. It becomes crucial that we ask questions such as: How might the Jain concept help formulate new questions about the assumptions around an ideal preexistent Truth and its consequences for human ways of knowing? How is knowledge charac-terized, who has access, and what might this reflect about human experience from these different worldviews? Each story, reflecting different ways of knowing, comes into sharper focus through the process of cross-cultural comparison. Take again, for example, another central concept in the study of humanities, namely, aesthetics. On the one hand, this term could be seen as having innately westernized constructs, but when we step back and ask, "How do humans create, define, and experience artistic expressions?," many possible approaches create multiple, contextualized case studies and interpretations that illuminate various underlying foundations.

The selections of primary sources included in each Reader reflect our unwavering commitment to the dual values of cross-cultural diverse perspectives and inquiry-focused engagements. We aim to course correct from some of the available humani-ties textbooks in which the defining narrative remains that of Western liberalism. For example, the ways that humanities' textbooks have treated race and indigeneity have often furthered harm by excluding multiple perspectives on the difficult lived reali-ties of what we now call racial injustices, as well as patronizing or whitewashing the experiences through stilted frameworks and terminology. In these volumes, there are, at times, gaps in source materials focused on experiences of race, slavery, and indige-neity that are curricular growth areas for the program. It is relevant to note here that in spite of coming from a large group of contributors, our selections are still reflective of the group's interests and areas of focus and we know that a different group might have come up with a different set of readings and perspectives. The choices made are a reflection of the times in which the editors and faculty contributors are living. Engaging in collaborative editing processes with faculty contributors provided us opportunities to have conversations about problematic framing, terms, and even the sources we decided to include. This process has made us aware that inclusivity need not be pitted against expertise or any of its cousins, such as rigor or standards, that are often used to police boundaries around knowledge. We don't always get it right, but we are working to bring more awareness, with honesty and humility, to correcting mistakes made in the past.

Our sincere attempt has been to anchor the framing narratives of each Reader in cross-cultural and interdisciplinary perspectives where no one single cultural ide-ology or disciplinary approach is privileged. However, it is important to acknowl-edge that each Reader is still temporally organized linearly, focused on written and primary source content, and clearly foregrounds a human-centered perspective that might be suspect from certain cultural viewpoints. These choices, especially the chronological framing of content, admittedly presuppose a linear understanding of time sometimes challenged by various cultures. Linear temporal systems value lo-cating dates for events and people based on criteria that at times exclude cultural expressions of humanity in which orality is valued as much as or sometimes more than writing. The emphasis on time has had the impact of undervaluing sources that come to us through oral means because they could not be tied to a particular origin date. We have tried to address this exclusionary tendency by including more sources from oral traditions to honor cultures' own understandings of their ancient roots by not marking particular time periods in the titles of the volumes.

At the moment of compiling the Readers, for many institutional, programmatic, and resource reasons, we moved forward with a chronological framing even though we are aware of ways of understanding time that diverge from this framing. Linda Tuhiwai Smith, for example, draws our attention to the fact that many Indigenous languages don't have a word for time. She takes this to reflect the fact that lineal or linear time does not operate as a foundational organizing principle in these cultures.[3] In order to disrupt a singular linear organizational model, we have included a second suggested grouping of sources by either theme, question, or some other category, and included sources in the Readers that are engaged across chronological time frames.

We realize that each of our decisions, however intentional about inclusivity, has blind spots. Instead of treating this realization as a paralyzing hurdle, we want to approach it as an opportunity for self-reflection that makes explicit the reasoning behind and also the implications of our selections/choices. Indeed, this self-awareness commits us to an epistemic humility that is the hallmark of a pedagogy that foregrounds process and meaningful engagement. Thus, while we are confident that this revision project makes huge strides, there is always more work to be done. For example, because of a long-standing commitment to written sources, our introductory Humanities course has struggled to expand its understanding of "primary source" to include artefacts, material cultures, and other aspects from the Global South. We do include these components, but they currently live on an online learning platform rather than in this Reader. It is our hope in the next revision that these materials will be incorporated more directly.

Finally, our ability to ask questions is often taken for granted, as a given without the need for cultivation. It is often assumed that we automatically learn how to ask questions without direct instruction on how we come to ask particular questions, in what contexts, based on what criteria, and for what purposes. The editorial team realized in talking with students that the skill of asking productive questions needed to be made more visible, with opportunities for practice, and thus decided to make it the central pedagogical focus of these Readers. The team began to test out several learning features that would support this noteworthy and transferable skill. In the following section we discuss how inquiry-based learning is embedded in the support features of the Readers.

---

3. Linda Tuhiwai Smith, *Decolonizing Methodologies: Research and Indigenous People*, 2nd ed. (New York: Zed Books, 2012), 52.

PART II: HOW TO USE THIS READER:
INTRODUCING THE LEARNING SUPPORT FEATURES

Over the past several years, faculty and staff collaborated across various disciplines, programs, and areas at UNC Asheville to globalize the content of courses that grew out of a westernized humanities model. In addition, to support effective and meaningful encounters with the ideas in these sources, faculty have embedded the insights of pedagogical research, namely creating learning environments that are culturally aware, active, inquiry-based, and draw upon best practices in cultivating reflective spaces. The editorial team, in view of these aims, realized the need to create a thoroughly interactive text that actualizes our commitments to student success.

Like no other revision process in the past, the editorial team engaged in a research-based approach utilizing our faculty's and students' feedback through surveys, focus groups, and pilot feedback cycles. The unique organization of these Readers emerged as a result of this process, and we want to specifically mention how central students were to the final product design. Thus, in addition to the brief introductions to each primary source, which was a hallmark of previous Readers, these new Readers now incorporate several intentional learning support features students overwhelmingly identified as useful to their learning process. We hope the descriptions of each of these features serve to enhance your own particular nuanced engagement with the sources in these Readers.[4]

Cross-Cultural Historical Introduction to Each Volume

One of the most unique features that you will encounter in these Readers is a cross-cultural historical introduction at the beginning of each volume. Authored by our colleague Tracey Rizzo, from the History Department, these essays provide a perspective on a larger sweep of history during each time period, identifying key moments and concepts that shape a particular chronological era. These introductions are global in focus, weaving examples from various parts of the world together in order to exemplify how humans in different cultures and times experience, shape, and respond to their worlds. In acknowledging the historical orientation of these cross-cultural introductions, we understand that other disciplinary approaches might have used their own framing questions and criteria. What types of questions and criteria might scholars from other disciplines foreground when seeking to discuss human forms of experience, such as religious movements, war, or love?

These introductions are intended to be flexible in how they are used in classrooms. You may be asked to read the essay at the beginning of a semester to provide

---

4. The description of learning support features has been edited from a document first drafted by Brian S. Hook and used to help guide faculty contributors who have written entries.

an historical disciplinary approach and contextualize the semester. You may also be directed to segments as relevant to particular entries for each week, as they provide further context in addition to each entry's dedicated introduction.

Snapshot Boxes with Tags

We have included a small box at the beginning of each entry that provides some basic contextual information, based on scholarly consensus, for reading at a glance. Specific information may vary based on what is appropriate to the source but often includes the following: language of the original document; date; location or origin; genre; national/ethnic identity; and tags.

A unique feature developed for these entries is the set of "tags" listed in the snapshot box. Tags aim to highlight connections, for example, by offering a bird's-eye view of central concepts within the course and possibly across courses. They are not places, names, and events; they also are not themes or keywords for that matter. Each course also contains a tag glossary that collects all the tags used in that course along with the readings in which they appear. We have come to think of the tags as hubs that offer an initial location for seeing, creating, and facilitating exciting new connections. We welcome you to enjoy exploring the trails that these tags help signpost and to create your own.

Introductions with Bolded Terms

Each course entry is accompanied by an introduction that invites you into the reading and offers a few navigational tools. These introductions are not SparkNotes summaries or comprehensive overviews like an encyclopedia or wikipedia article. Reading the introduction thus cannot replace reading the source itself, and much will be missed if this strategy is attempted. We also bolded a few terms to alert you to key concepts and frameworks.

We have modified the primary focus of these introductions to prioritize inquiry-based learning, and so you will note the inclusion of questions embedded directly in the introduction in order to prompt exploration of both the context and the source itself. Questions as opportunities of reflective pauses are often framed such that readers have an opportunity to make their own connections. Our aim is to provide much-needed contextual support while leaving room for you to engage a source without preemptively providing many of the interpretative possibilities. This moves away from "tell me what to think or what I should know" to "give me parameters that can guide my own productive engagement with the source."

In some cases, you will notice slightly different approaches to readings, especially if they are from typically underrepresented cultures in the curriculum. This might entail more notes to provide access to critical contextual sources, an expanded narrative timeline as part of the introduction, and/or different types of strategies for engaging the text. By allowing for differences in some of the entries, our intention is to provide more inclusive spaces for expert voices from the margins that our students have not usually heard or been able to find, and to build skills for working with multiple perspectives. It is a goal of the liberal arts and this project to put the values into practice that will foster, educate, and engage these skills as part of becoming global citizens.

Timelines

Most Reader entries include a timeline with three different types of chronological information: (1) black points relevant to the source directly; (2) orange points for comparison to other cultures during the same time period; and (3) larger historical time periods, eras, or movements relevant to the context of the source (as blue bands) or as cross-cultural comparisons (as orange bands). Timelines are a way to provide a type of context for each source, but with the important reminder of what else is going on in other parts of the world. Creating a timeline for ancient, oral, storytelling traditions that are not matched to a particular date did not seem effective but rather revealed the assumptions of linear time frames. In a few other cases, we have added a timeline with more modern-day points to raise awareness about present-day contexts that have inherited these storytelling traditions. Sometimes we have also included a more substantial narrative timeline for underrepresented cultures.

At the beginning of each volume you will find a comprehensive timeline noting important points across all the sources in one place. To create a comprehensive timeline is by its very nature an impossible task, as no amount of space or organizational strategy could possibly capture so many concepts visually. However, we hope that the choices we made bring into perspective some of the most prominent chronological points.

Pre-PARs and Post-PARs

You will find a unique feature on either side of the primary source itself: Primed and Ready (PAR) activities placed just before you begin reading (pre-PARs) and again after your first read-through (post-PARs). After getting your contextual and chronological grounding with the introduction and timeline, the pre-PARs are a way for you to pause and spend a few minutes connecting to your prior knowledge of a concept or experience (e.g., "What do you think the role of a teacher is?") or on knowledge already learned in class through previous materials (e.g., "What kinds of models for imitation are the heroes of earlier myths?").

These are not intended to involve research but rather invite you to gather your own thoughts before you start reading. There are no right or wrong answers. The goal is to encourage you to approach the readings with questions in mind and to see in the works a resemblance or distance between your own responses and those you find in the work.

At the end of the source reading, you will often find post-PARs that might ask you to revisit the brief observations noted in the pre-PARs, but through the lens of the source directly. If a pre-PAR asks you to list five ideas that you associate with the "sacred," a post-PAR might ask you to identify how the work presents the "sacred." A second type of post-PAR may ask you to briefly practice a particular skill, such as becoming attentive to a particular feature, or to consider the reading with an analytical tool in mind, to help with comprehension and clarity. Strategies might include outlining a small portion of an argument, identifying evidence, looking for assumptions, listing dominant and missing perspectives, or locating initial comparative patterns.

PARs are not discussion or essay questions, deep-level critical thinking activities, or "busy work." The purpose is to move you from more passive to more active forms of processing the information with which you are engaging so that when you come to class, you have a starting point to enter into the discussion. Faculty may select a particular pre-PAR and/or post-PAR for you to complete prior to class, however they are all available for you to use to support your engagement with the materials.

Inquiry Corners

Another feature comes at the end of most entries: The Inquiry Corner.[5] As part of our commitment to supporting an inquiry-based focus, we developed this feature as a platform to bring awareness to what different types of questions do as pathways of inquiry. It is intended as a model for how to ask more productive questions in relation to inquiry processes and goals. The questions provided are not the only types of questions that can be asked, nor do they need to be asked in any particular order.

You may want to ask what certain questions can help you to do—clarify, compare, connect, or critically engage with a topic in which you can delineate the criteria and assumptions of what that question entails. While you may end up utilizing some of these questions in class discussion or in writing prompts—especially the comparative or critical forms—the idea is that with practice, you will gain facility in formulating your own versions of these questions and other types, including those from various disciplinary contexts.

The Inquiry Corner is not a set assignment meant to "be completed" before class, but your professor may guide you to engage this feature in various ways as a part of assignments or class preparation or to practice creating your own questions or to

---

5. We are indebted to some inspirational models that supported the development of this inquiry-based learning feature, especially Keya Maitra's "Philosopher's Corner" as found at the end of each chapter in her *Philosophy of the Bhagavad Gita*. We are also grateful to Heather Laine Talley's question prompts that she used in her sociology classes and that served as a useful base for the development of this feature for our Humanities courses.

explore a source on your own. Here are some brief frameworks for the types of questions we chose to include:

- **Content Questions:** Models how to clarify an idea or term in the source, as part of close reading skills. (How is dharma being defined in the source?).
- **Comparative Questions:** Compares a topic between course materials for exploration. (How is nature viewed/depicted in the *Epic of Gilgamesh* and the *Daodejing*?)
- **Critical Questions:** Invites a source-grounded examination of a topic/subtopic with multiple possible perspectives/examples, within a source or across sources. This type of question builds analytical/interpretive/reasoning capacities utilizing evidence. (What forms of authority do leaders rely upon to support their positions of power?)
- **Connection Questions:** Bridges one's own knowledge/experience with ideas in the source; could also connect to student life experiences. (What rhetorical or aesthetic skills do you use when expressing your own authority? Your own doubts or vulnerabilities?)

Beyond the Classroom

In collaboration with colleagues from UNC Asheville's Career Center, in 20–25 percent of the entries, we have included questions that arise out of the content and approach of the reading but move into real-life, forward-looking engagement, thus allowing new contexts to explore, practice, and apply the active model of inquiry.

Maps

Maps are an important aspect of contextualizing our primary source materials. We decided that since there are rich and well-developed online map resources, it would be best to direct our students and faculty to their use, instead of trying to replicate them in not as detailed a form in these Readers. Some of the resources we recommend using are: Ancient World Mapping Center (http://awmc.unc.edu/wordpress/free-maps/), World History Encyclopedia (https://www.ancient.eu/mapselect/), and TimeMaps (https://www.timemaps.com/).

A FEW PARTING NOTES

Finally, the time has come to turn it over to you, dear reader. Our hope is that you have as much fun as we had in compiling this, and we mean all of us—more than sixty people from more than twenty departments/programs/areas were involved in making this series possible. We engaged in a unique collaborative process at every stage, including in the editing of sources that centered dialogue between editors in real time instead of an individualist approach. We have endeavored to not only bring the elephant into the classroom but to provide strategies to behold more than one aspect—the trunk, the ear, or the side—together and collectively while also becoming aware of the parts of the elephant we don't know how to see from our own cultural perspectives. May we all continue to find more perspectives to engage and respect. Enjoy!

An Historical Cross-Cultural Introduction

Tracey Rizzo

Images curated by Eva Hericks-Bares

Southernization characterizes the era of world history from at least 300 to 1600 CE. Commercial products, cultural innovations, and intellectual discoveries spread from southern climates, particularly South Asia, throughout Afroeurasia, and eventually into Europe, Africa, and South America. The diversity of natural resources in what today constitutes the Global South—lands south of the equator—enriched empires but also invited invaders whose southward migrations are another feature of Southernization. Southernization is a concept used by world historians to make sense of the diversity of experience across seven continents. World historians study the interactions between natural and built environments that determine the contours of people's experiences. For the study of the humanities, they describe local and transnational political and economic structures as frameworks for exploring arts, religion, and philosophy. There are striking similarities in how people try to make sense of the world they inherit even as they mold it into something different. Thus the study of world history is necessarily broad, offering a bird's-eye view of change over time, change that leads to the greater integration of diverse populations into something we recognize in this period as "the world." Southernization is just one lens through which to view those developments. It draws attention to the roots of a more recent division: the Global North, whose wealth rests on exploitative resource extraction from the Global South in this period.

From the fourth century CE onward, Malay sailors navigating monsoon winds spread across the Indian Ocean expanding sea lanes to include trade in Moluccan spices, Chinese porcelains, and East African gold. Merchants, conquerors, and missionaries likewise knit the three continents of Afroeurasia together by traversing the overland Silk Road through Central Asia and the caravan routes across the Sahara

Desert of North Africa. The meeting of Chinese and Muslim merchants in Southeast Asia seeded the beginnings of an increasingly unified, even global, economic system that some scholars describe as proto-capitalism. The incorporation of the Americas made this a truly global system during the fifteenth and sixteenth centuries CE. Closely tied to the availability of these products and the climates that supported them, Southernization also generally describes the movement of millions of people between 300 and 1600 CE. Whether they were Vikings, Mongols, or Chichimeca, nomadic peoples moved southward in search of better climates and resources. Even within a region's borders, abundant resources along with large populations concentrated in the South. Due to more drought-resistant Vietnamese rice cultivation, for example, China's population tripled in the southern half of the country between 700 and 1000 CE and imperial institutions followed. Furthermore, missionaries of all faiths moved in every direction but especially southward after 900 CE, especially Muslims into Africa and Catholics into South America.

Such movements produced synthetic and syncretic, or dynamically blended, cultural spheres, but conflicts were as likely as cohesion. Invasions and epidemics wreaked greater havoc on larger swaths of human communities, perhaps most notably in the Black Death that swept across Afroeurasia toward the end of this period. Greater integration through universal religions also meant that religious schisms tore communities apart: Eastern and Western Christendom, Shia and Sunni Islam, Theravada and Mahayana Buddhism, to give a few examples. Such vulnerabilities led them to adhere to large institutional religions. These systems offered ways to view one's purpose and place in life, ways to navigate choices and consequences about one's actions/behaviors, ways to create communities of fellow adherents, and finally, in some cases, ways of understanding death and afterlife through developing concepts such as salvation, liberation, reincarnation, or becoming an ancestor.

Tasked with telling the stories of how diverse peoples came to inhabit "the world," world historians focus on forces of integration, primarily the often unequal exchange of resources, movement of people, and hybridization of ideas. We note people's creativity and resilience alongside their suffering and set their cultural productions in political, economic, and environmental contexts. While comparing vastly different parts of the world, we emphasize commonalities in full knowledge that local variables and individual experiences also are worthy of study in their own right. In what follows, we pick up the story in Central Asia given our emphasis on Southernization and the movement of peoples during this time period.

Central Asia

Between 300 and 600 CE empires were in decline across the whole of Afroeurasia due to both internal and external pressures. The Han dynasty of China, the Gupta Empire of India, the Roman Empire in Europe, and the Sassanid Empire of Persia all eventually fell due to invading nomads from the North. Central Asia was the nexus

Bull's head bowl, gold, 8th century CE, part of the Treasure of Nagyszentmiklós (discovered 1799, now Kunsthistorisches Museum Vienna). (Photograph by Sandstein / license CC-BY-3.0)

This golden bowl is associated with a nomadic Eurasian group known as the Avars. A Turkic people of Central Asian origin, the Avars most likely fled West during power struggles with other nomadic tribes and settled in Eastern Europe (modern Bulgaria and Romania), where they often came into conflict with the Byzantine Empire. The bowl is part of a treasure hoard of 23 large gold objects and showcases both the economic power of the owner/s and the availability of skilled craftsmen to produce such luxury goods.

between these various civilizations, stretching from the Caspian Sea to present day Mongolia. The vast steppes of Central Asia constituted the crossroads of world history. As nomadic pastoralists, Central Asians often mediated the exchange of cultures along the Silk Road that crossed their lands while steadfastly guarding their own, which often retained a higher status for women, a reminder that patriarchal institutions most likely were developed in more urban and sedentary societies. When these nomadic clans forged confederacies, military conquest followed as they set their sights on the wealth of the cities to the south. One means of acquiring this wealth included demanding tribute payments to hold back their assault.

By the eighth century CE, Central Asians developed caravan cities to transport and display luxuries they acquired from the south, from jade to sugar. When extracting tribute payment from those they threatened, such as the T'ang dynasty in China, they acquired enslaved people and gold. Their status hierarchy became more pronounced with the most powerful warriors establishing dynasties. Literacy also increased with more durable settlements, in part spurred by contact with missionaries and merchants from the South—Turkish and South Asian, Russian and Chinese. The Sogdian script became their form of writing, derived from Persian, by the tenth century CE. Steppe bureaucracies formed and managing the army as an institution, rather than a loose confederation of clans, made it more formidable. This was a precondition for the Mongol empires to extend their reach in the thirteen and fourteenth centuries CE. They combined the warrior ethos of their forebears—sleeping in their saddles, launching their crossbows from behind—with the apparatus of an organized state. As was true with most nomadic pastoralists, assimilation, firepower, and climate change altered their distinctive way of life and impact on international relations.

South Asia

Command of riches assured the independence of autonomous kingdoms, especially in the South. Except for brief interludes, no one overarching political entity governed the Indian subcontinent. Chandragupta I established the Gupta Empire (319–543) by unifying all but the Deccan plateau and regions to the south. He established an empire in large part with the resources gained by his marriage to the Licchavi princess Kumaradevi, whose family owned rich iron mines with which to fund and arm his cavalry. The hierarchical Gupta system of administration, including efficient tax collection by provincial councils, sustained two centuries of stability. Its system of vassal kingdoms allowed a high degree of local autonomy coordinated by the imperial bureaucracy.

Political stability contributes to cultural flourishing especially in the aftermath of a period of chaos. In science, the arts, medicine, and above all religion, the Gupta Period is known as a golden age with wealth and talent concentrated in magnificent cities such as the capital Pataliputra. With the invention of zero, the astronomer Aryabhata (476–550 CE) introduced the decimal system, calculated the rotation of the Earth, and explained eclipses in scientific terms. In addition to abstractions like pi, practical applications of advanced mathematics included improved predictions of weather and seasonal change, necessary for thriving agriculture. The diversity of products traversing the Ganges River sea lanes and roads across the Hindu Kush mountains helped create a cultural synthesis. More than this, Hinduism, with its emerging central concept of *bhakti* or devotion emphasizing personalized connections between humans and their deities, steadily knit together the diverse communities of the subcontinent for nearly a millennium. Narrating histories and myths from the past, scholars, poets, and playwrights drew on the much older classical Sanskrit epics of the *Ramayana* and *Mahabharata* (with the *Bhagavad Gita* arguably its most famous part), and reveals some of the earliest attempts to foster a pan Hindu identity.

The larger than life warrior heroes of those epics underpinned a patriarchal and caste-based ordering of society rooted in the Vedic Period (1500–500 BCE). Yet the enhanced wealth of the *vaishyas* (merchant and farmers) caste under the Guptas could threaten the rule of *brahmins* (priests) and *kshatriyas* (warriors and nobles). Social stability resulted from the evolving power of *jatis* (craft guilds), which became subcastes maintained by strong identification by trade, including the organization of urban neighborhoods by trade and intermarriage within those trades. In addition to price, wage, and quality controls, the *jatis* provided mutual aid and supported orphans and the widows of guild members. Strong group identification and relative control over their families, neighborhoods, and professions generally attached people to the Gupta hierarchy long after the Gupta declined. Gupta patronage of Hinduism helped it overtake Buddhism as the most widely adopted religion. The proliferation of devotional texts known as *puranas* led to the rise of local and regional deities serving as personal gods for different groups to worship. The *puranas* relay the lineages and attributes of the gods and goddesses and highlight stories of human personal encounters with them as settings to teach religious and moral lessons. Because they emphasized a personal-divine connection and communication, they enabled worship without the intervention of a brahmin. Later *puranas* emphasized salvation through undying devotion. The Bhakti movement evolved to reflect the growing integration with influential Sufi traditions of Islam arriving in the 1000s CE focused on knowing the divine through paths of love and knowledge. Hinduism's capacity for absorbing other competing spiritualities included subsuming the Buddha into its pantheon as an *avatar* of the Hindu god Vishnu.

The Gupta Empire entered a period of decline after the death of Skandagupta in 467 CE hastened by internal conflicts between the rival kings (*rajas*) and incursions of nomadic Huns from the north. The White Huns, a branch of the Huns that invaded the Roman Empire a century before, had already pillaged Sassanid Persia before invading the Indian subcontinent. Notably, Hun converts to an ultraorthodox form of Shaivism (worshippers of Shiva) within one of the sectarian devotional branches of Hinduism persecuted Buddhist communities. Although it never recovered its dominant role in Indian spiritual life, pockets of Buddhism flourished in later centuries. Nalanda Mahavihara, a predominantly Buddhist university and arguably the world's first residential university, served as an eminent center for higher learning starting from the sixth and lasting into the thirteenth century CE. Other significant thriving civilizations in Southeast Asia include those of Srivijaya (circa 670–twelfth century CE), Khmer Empire (802–1432 CE), and the Bagan in Burma (circa 1000–1300 CE).

Southernization aptly describes the impact of Central Asian conquerors in this era of Afroeurasian history. The Gupta dynasty finally succumbed to another Hun invasion in the 550s CE, marking the end of a sense of political unity until the Delhi

Panel of "Vishnu lying on the cosmic waters," stone, 5th-6th century CE, Dashavatara Temple (Deogarh, India) (Public Domain)

One of the earliest still surviving Hindu temples, Dashavatara temple at Deogarh, features a panel showing Vishnu, as he sleeps on the coils of the serpent Ananta. His consort Lakshmi is seated at the left, massaging his right foot and calf muscle. Beautifully sculpted representations of the various avatars of the Hindu gods allowed the worshiper to engage in *darshan*— seeing the divine in its image.

Sultanate reintegrated the subcontinent's diverse regions into a syncretic Indo-Islamic culture in the thirteenth century. At the center of the maritime Silk Road, the Indian subcontinent might also be described as the most generally cosmopolitan region of the globe between 300 and 1300 CE, with a multitude of languages and devotional communities.

Regional empires formed throughout the Indian subcontinent loosely around the structure of the caste system. Because of its advanced navy, the Chola dynasty of the South, in today's Karnataka, expanded its influence into Malaysia and Sri Lanka in the eleventh century under Rajaraja I (r. 985–1014 CE). It conquered weak states militarily but secured diplomatic relations directly with the more powerful China. Their warriors wielded prized wootz steel weapons and specialized in a regionally distinct martial art, *silambam*. Women martial artists served as bodyguards and women diplomats accompanied military leadership during campaigns. Wealthy women patronized the arts and poets celebrated them by name. Men and women weavers, organized by guild, produced fine cotton and silk textiles for export but farming was an even more prestigious occupation. Irrigation projects resulted in dams and artificial lakes meant to showcase the glory of the ruling kingdoms and support agricultural popula-

Alai Darwaza (Alai Gate) and Qutb Minar at the Quwwat-ul-Islam Mosque, red sandstone & marble, 13th-14th century CE (Delhi, India) (Photograph by PlaneMad / license CC-SA-2.5)

The Minar and Gatehouse are among the first works of architecture created by the Delhi Sultanate. They combine the specific needs of a mosque structure with the local practices of construction and ornamentation. Both the technique of intricately carving stone surfaces and the use of red sandstone / white marble will turn into a signature style in Indian subcontinent architecture and continue for centuries.

tions. Efficient administration of revenue from tribute payments built a temple complex in Thanjavur and spurred a Tamil literary revival. Devoted to the Hindu god Shiva, Chola rulers patronized artists and writers who produced friezes, sculptures, and devotional literature. Despite its long duration, reaching back for one thousand years, Chola rulers were eventually overwhelmed by a rival dynasty, the Pandyan.

In another instance of Southernization, Muslim Turkic nomads reunified much of the Indian subcontinent under the rule of the Delhi Sultanate (1206–1526 CE). Although theirs was the minority religion, they generally tolerated India's religious diversity. They retained Persian as their official language, which strongly influenced but did not displace the subcontinent's many local languages. India's first woman ruler, Razia Sultana (r. 1236–1240 CE) ascended the throne as a surrogate while her father led a military campaign but ruled so ably that he named her his successor. Multiple conflicts erupted during her reign, including Mongol attacks and sectarian strife between Sunni and Shiite Muslims. Rival claimants ultimately murdered her. Although widespread conversion to Islam took place especially in Punjab and Bengal, Hinduism remained the majority religion.

The blending of South Asian, Persian, Turkish and Central Asian cultures reached its greatest extent under the Mughal Empire (1526–1761 CE) and especially with the Mughal emperor Akbar, who increasingly became influenced by Sufi mysti-

Jahangiri Mahal, red sandstone with marble inlay, 1560-1570 CE, Red Fort (Agra, India)
(Photograph by Diego Delso, delso.photo / license CC-BY-SA)

The visual and physical impact of architecture made it an ideal representative for Mughal
ideas of art and propaganda. Among the many structures built under Mughal rule are
palaces such as the Jahangiri Mahal (which was used as the principal *zenana* or palace for
the women of the royal household, particularly the Rajput wives of Akbar) and mausoleum
structures to commemorate specific rulers (for example the Taj Mahal, where the 5th Mughal ruler Shah Jahan and his wife Mumtaz Mahal are buried).

cism, an approach to Islam emphasizing personal union and knowledge of Allah,
especially through music in South Asian contexts. Akbar sponsored comparative
religion forums in his royal courts and promoted a new syncretic religion as a grand
union of all faiths. Akbar's interfaith commitment was exemplified by his marriage
to the Hindu princess Jodha Bai (circa 1542–1623 CE) known by her Mughal title
Mariam-uz-Zamani, Persian for Mary of the Age, bestowed after she gave birth to
Akbar's son and heir to the throne. Ultimately, however, Mughal rule depended on
military campaigns that annexed most of the subcontinent, doubling the size of the
empire and making administration more challenging. Moreover, a posthumous back-
lash to Akbar's syncretism by orthodox Sunni Muslims led to growing sectarian strife
as Hindu princes and peasants alike protested rule by increasingly intolerant Muslim elites. This culminated in widespread persecution of Hindus and imposition of
Muslim strictures by Emperor Aurangzeb (1618–1707 CE) that left nearly the entire
subcontinent in a state of rebellion by the end of his reign.

East Asia

China was finally reunited in 589 CE after Emperor Wen of Sui (541–604 CE) became the first ethnic Chinese since the Han era to reclaim the imperial throne in the North and swiftly moved to conquer the South. Institutional instability was tempered by Confucianism, which was embedded in the foundations of most social and political structures in Chinese society. This short-lived dynasty was succeeded by the Tang dynasty (618–907 CE) whose long duration supported China's Golden Age, spurred in part by a pilgrimage south. The monk Xuanzang (602–644 CE) went to the Indian subcontinent and returned with over six hundred Buddhist texts. Even more than simple southward migration, the term *Southernization* also describes the wide circulation of Indian cultural products. Buddhism spread through monastic communities, especially appealing to women dedicated to intellectual pursuits. Being exempt from taxation, the monasteries accumulated great wealth and lands. By the ninth century CE there were a quarter million Buddhist monks and nuns in China whose influence rivalled that of the ruling aristocracy and challenged traditional Confucianism and Daoism.

The spread of Buddhism created a common cultural sphere in East Asia even as local variations emerged in resistance to *sinocentrism*, the view of China as the cultural, political, or economic center of the world. China's dominance of East Asia included periodic colonization of Korea and Vietnam. Japan conversely was relatively isolated, separated from the mainland by more than 100 miles. However, contacts through trade and Buddhist missionaries facilitated the adaptation of Chinese culture, especially in the seventh and eighth centuries. These included an expansion of Confucianism and Legalism. This was followed by the Heian Period (794–1185 CE) and the Kamakura Period (1192–1333 CE), the latter governed under a feudal *shogun*, the military commander to which samurai pledged allegiance. Japanese elites adopted the fashions, writing, bureaucracy, and rituals of Chinese imperial courts but local samurai defended their autonomy and perpetuated a warrior ethos after 1000 CE. Because of its rocky terrain and remote location, empires rarely set their sights on Japan, nor did the Japanese develop imperial ambitions until the twentieth century CE. Thus the samurai ruled their independent territories for almost one thousand years.

China's only woman sovereign, Wu Zetian, seized the throne in 690 CE after the sickly emperor died and she executed or exiled rival claimants, including her own sons. She promoted a Buddhist prophecy that envisioned the reincarnation of Buddha Maitreya as a female monarch, commissioning statues of Maitreya in her likeness. Like many emperors, Wu Zetian waged wars and signed treaties to secure China's unstable borders even as internal dissidents were tracked by an elaborate network of spies and were subject to imprisonment, torture, exile, or assassination. At the same time, she promoted men into the bureaucracy based on merit rather than wealth, foreclosing power grabs by rival clans. She also revised taxation to ease the burden on peasants and promoted agricultural reforms that improved crop yields. By securing the borders and reopening the Silk Road after an epidemic in 682 CE, Wu and her successors fostered a new cultural flourishing due to contact with Persia,

Hanging scroll of "Chan master riding a mule," ink on paper, 13ᵗʰ century CE, China (now Metropolitan Museum of Art New York) (Public Domain)

Chan (or Zen, in Japanese) Buddhist painting documents the spread of the religion throughout East Asia and highlights local developments. The artwork itself would have been made by a Chan follower and attempts to capture the spiritual aspects of both the master depicted and the artist. In addition to the image, the work also has an inscription to clarify its message: "As rain darkens the mountain, One mistakes a mule for a horse."

the Indian subcontinent, and Central Asia, whose poetry, musical instruments, and calligraphy influenced the arts in China.

In 845, Emperor Wuzong (r. 840–846 CE) proclaimed the Great Anti-Buddhist Persecution that abolished nearly all of the 4,600 monasteries, demolished 40,000 temples and shrines, and forcibly returned 260,500 monks and nuns to secular life. Buddhism never regained a dominant position in China even as its doctrines endured in tandem with Daoism and Confucianism as the Three Great Teachings of China. With the later Tang unable to reassert order on the frontiers or quell the restive warlords, the dynasty was finally overthrown in 907 CE by one of Huang Chao's generals who had defected back into imperial service. This ushered in a new period of upheaval as five dynasties and ten kingdoms jousted to claim the Mandate of Heaven until the Song dynasty reunified China in 982 CE.

The Northern Song dynasty (960–1127 CE) reformed the civil service examination to create a bureaucracy based on skill and merit while sponsoring an array of tremendous innovations in science, technology, and engineering. Inventions included the magnetic compass, movable-type printing, a silk-reeling mechanism, hydraulic clocks, power chain devices, and odometers in addition to advancements in cartography, metallurgy, and astronomical observation. Perhaps most notably, the invention of gunpowder by 1044 CE changed the nature of warfare forever. Explosives with names like "heaven-shaking thunder crash bomb" and catapult delivery systems enabled the Song to fend off northern nomads. Following a series of conflicts, Jurchens invaders from the northeast defeated the North, establishing the Jin dynasty.

The Southern Song dynasty (1127–1279 CE) maintained its autonomy and established a new capital in the commercial port Hangzhou, described as a city of unparalleled wealth and splendor by such travelers as Marco Polo and Ibn Battuta. A favorable climate cycle throughout the Song era enabled experimentation with new crops and methods of irrigation. The spread of fast-growing Champa rice from Vietnam along with rice cultivation on terraced hillsides resulted in a dramatic rise in the Chinese population that reached 100 million by 1100 CE, notably concentrated in the South in a stunning example of Southernization: one million residents in Hangzhou alone. A greatly expanded consumer market sparked the invention of paper money called "flying cash" that fueled investment in joint stock companies by merchant houses and trade guilds. New trade routes were opened with the invention of the mariner's compass that permitted accurate navigation in open seas even through inclement weather, further fueling the growth of thirteenth-century Song dynasty commerce and industry, especially with Southeast Asia.

In 1211 CE, the Mongols under Genghis Khan (circa 1162–1227 CE) launched a twenty-three-year campaign against the northern Jin dynasty that resulted in the massacre of 20 million Chinese people. Mounting their wares, dwellings, and all weapons on draft animals, Mongol warriors would ride for days on the saddle and recock their bows while in motion. The Song dynasty gained a reprieve as Genghis Khan then turned toward Central Asia and Persia, but his grandson Kublai Khan (1215–1294 CE) finally defeated the Song in 1260, using their own siege technology to reunify China under Mongol rule and founding the Yuan dynasty (1271–1368 CE). Kublai adopted Chinese political institutions and cultural forms, with many of his Mongol subjects similarly replacing their shamanic beliefs upon Kublai's conversion to Buddhism. In contrast, his successors, confronted with rising popular discontent, stressed their Mongol heritage and rejected a Chinese culture that they believed had made them weak. The Yuan collapse was catalyzed by a series of natural disasters in the mid-fourteenth century, including plague, which stoked the Red Turban Rebellion, a peasant uprising that extended as far as Korea. Believing their various leaders to be incarnations of Maitreya, the rebels wore the red turban to distinguish themselves from the rest of their secret society, the White Lotus mystical sect of Buddhism. One of the peasant rebels proclaimed himself the Hongwu emperor and drove the Mongols back to the steppes, sealing his claim to the Mandate of Heaven and founding the new Ming dynasty (1368–1644 CE).

Rejecting the Mongol synthesis, the Ming emperors invoked Chinese cultural

Section of a Handscroll "Grooms and Horses," ink on paper, 1296-1359 CE, China (Metropolitan Museum of Art New York) (Public Domain)

Three generations of artists worked on this handscroll, which would have been unrolled and enjoyed scene by scene. As is customary in Chinese painting, the Zhao family added their artists' seals as well as numerous inscriptions that detail the making and ownership of the art object. Part of the Chinese Zodiac, the horse features prominently in art as a symbol of energy and ambition and to show status and military might.

and ethnic superiority as the means to consolidate their power, which included diversifying China's agriculture and economy to decrease reliance on foreign trade. Hongwu executed some 100,000 officials to cement the personal loyalty of the Ming bureaucracy and reorganized the entire countryside into communities of 110 households each with rotating village chiefs tasked to collect taxes and provide labor for state projects. He reorganized the military and gave competitor warlords hereditary districts to administer in peacetime. His harem included Mongol and Korean women but his wife, Empress Ma, was Chinese of humble origins like himself. Empress Ma accompanied her husband on his military campaigns and was given the emperor's first five sons to raise and educate as her own, with the fourth prevailing in a succession struggle to become the Yongle emperor (r. 1402–1424 CE).

To assert his own legitimacy, Yongle moved the capital to Beijing and conscripted a million laborers to build the Forbidden City palace compound. Yongle restored the imperial civil service exam to produce a new class of loyal Confucian scholars and built the Temple of Heaven complex where the emperor was venerated as the son of heaven who mediated between this world and the supreme reality. To project Chinese power abroad, Yongle commissioned a fleet entrusted to Admiral Zheng He (1371–1433 CE), a Muslim eunuch captured and castrated as a child before being sent to serve in the household of the future emperor. The armada of sixty-two treasure ships, each roughly half the size of a modern aircraft carrier, along with some two hundred supporting vessels carried 28,000 men on seven voyages to explore the Indian Ocean and secure the sea lanes of the South China Sea and Southeast Asia. Yet the arc of Chinese history would once again be dictated by the threat of invasion from the north, as later Ming emperors abandoned the seas to devote wealth and manpower to a massive expansion and maintenance of the Great Wall of China.

Indeed, the downfall of the Ming in 1644 CE did arrive with invaders from the north, the Manchu descendants of the Jurchen. Like all invaders from the north throughout Afroeurasia they were tempted by the climate-supported urban societies to the south. The last years of Ming rule were shaped by an economic crisis as the Thirty Years War in Europe led to a halt in shipments of silver from the Americas even as the Tokugawa Shogunate shut off Japan from nearly all trade, including China's other major supply of silver. The sudden spike in the value of silver that was the foundation of Ming currency made payment of taxes nearly impossible and soon a peasant uprising led by Li Zicheng (1606–1645 CE) erupted. The circulation of silver, mined in South America, illustrates another instance of the destabilizing impacts of Southernization. With a promise to divide the land equally and abolish grain taxes, Li rallied tens of thousands into his rebel army that proceeded to seize the capital Beijing where Li proclaimed himself emperor. Unable to suppress the uprising on their own, Ming generals allied with Manchu invaders who had seized the opportunity to cross the Great Wall, spelling doom for both the rebellion and the Ming dynasty.

Europe

After a succession of twenty-six emperors, mostly generals who seized power by means of coups, the Roman Empire proved too weak to resist escalating waves of invaders from the north. Emperor Constantine (272–337 CE) attempted to consolidate power by converting to Christianity and further separating the Eastern from the Western Roman Empires, establishing his capital at Constantinople. The purge of rival faiths by his successor, Theodosius (r. 379–395 CE), included the destruction of the Oracle at Delphi, a halt of the Olympic Games, and the disbanding of the Vestal Virgins in Rome. The arrival of nomadic Huns in Central Europe set off a wave of Germanic invasions as Goths, Vandals, and Franks fled before them, all pressing southward into Italy. Likely descendants of the same Xiongnu who sacked the Han dynasty in China a century before, the Huns fled the steppes due to the mega-drought in the third century CE. Attila the Hun (406–453 CE) invaded first the Eastern Roman Empire, and then marched on to the Western Roman Empire, extorting thousands of pounds of gold as tribute to hold back his forces from seizing Rome itself.

While the Western Roman Empire finally reached its end in 476, the Eastern Roman Empire was soon thriving under Emperor Justinian (r. 527–565 CE). Constantinople grew to a half million people and monumental architecture spread across the empire. The Justinian Code standardized Roman law and improved the status of

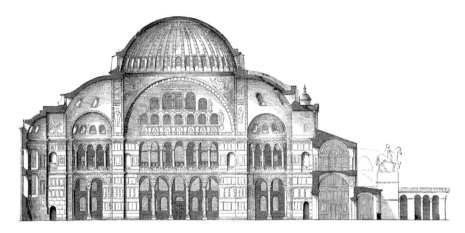

Hagia Sophia – cross-section drawing, original building 6ᵗʰ century CE, Constantinople (now Istanbul, Turkey) (Public Domain)

Designed by mathematicians (or more precisely: geometers) Isidorus of Miletus and Anthemius of Tralles, Hagia Sophia was one of the two largest dome covered buildings in the world until the early 15ᵗʰ century construction of Il Duomo in Florence, Italy. Though the first dome collapsed and had to be rebuilt within two decades, the building has since withstood numerous earthquakes, an iconoclast purge of its art and later reinstallation, and over 1500 years of different uses: from its initial designation as an Eastern Orthodox church to transforming first into a Roman Catholic church (1204), then a mosque (1453), a museum (1935), and since 2020 again a mosque.

women, children, and enslaved people by clarifying procedures for divorce, inheritance, and manumission (release from slavery) thereby influencing modern international law. He rebuilt the *Hagia Sophia* (Holy Wisdom) cathedral after it was burned in the Nika riots, erecting the architectural marvel with the second-largest dome in the world (after Rome's Pantheon) until the fifteenth century CE.

Perhaps the most far-reaching consequence of Justinian's reign was naming the emperor as head of the church, leading to a schism between Eastern Orthodoxy and Roman Catholicism in 1054. Theocracy was enforced by capital punishment for paganism or heresy. Nonetheless, to attract converts, Christians in the farthest regions of the empire assimilated pagan cultures by incorporating shrines; adapting local languages such as Egyptian Coptic for liturgical services; adopting practices/symbols such as Easter eggs; and recasting deities as Christian saints. Like Buddhists, they also formed monastic communities of celibate monks and nuns who devoted themselves to worship and study. Monasteries often came to dominate local communities, the largest monastic complexes rivalling towns as centers of trade and power.

In the West, a warrior king Charlemagne (784–814 CE) was crowned Holy Roman Emperor in 800 CE after forging a new empire, but it soon collapsed under assault by Viking marauders from the far north. The Viking Age began in 793 CE

Hagia Sophia – view of interior with original Byzantine mosaics and Islamic medallion inscriptions (Photograph by A3Camero / license CC-BY-3.0)

The half dome above the original altar area features a mosaic of the Virgin Mary as the bearer of her son Jesus (*Theotokos*). During the use of Hagia Sophia as a mosque this mosaic was plastered over, while other figural representations were covered by large calligraphic medallions containing, for example, the name of the prophet Mohammed.

with the sack of the monastery at Lindisfarne in England, possibly as retaliation for Charlemagne's forced conversion of the Saxons, many of whom sought refuge with their fellow pagans to the north. Viking assaults increased steadily in the ninth century, as their longships were designed to sail shallow rivers, dividing the Carolingian kingdoms. By the tenth century, Vikings settled into Russia, islands of the Mediterranean, and in Greenland, even reaching the coast of North America. Viking migrations eastward took them as far as Baghdad, capital of the Abbasid Caliphate, and Constantinople, where their attempt to breach the walls in 860 CE was repulsed by Greek fire, an explosive compound of petroleum and potassium. Viking women had a wide sphere of mobility as was often the case among less settled peoples, even warrior societies. Still primarily valued for birthing male heirs, they could nonetheless own property, inherit titles, and represent the family in the absence of men. Other northern nomads, the Visigoths, moved yet farther south, into southern Spain, es-

The Palatine Chapel of Charlemagne, stone, marble, and mosaics, 8-9th century CE, Aachen (Germany) (Public Domain)

Medieval European architecture often served multiple purposes. In this case, the church emphasized its Christian roots by leaning on the floor plans of famous churches in Ravenna and Jerusalem. It evoked the power of the old Roman empire by using materials taken from Roman structures, and it underlined its new central role in politics by serving as a coronation chapel for the next seven centuries.

tablishing their rule under King Roderic (688–711 CE). Muslim forces from North Africa ousted the Visigoth overlords in 711 CE, where some welcomed them as liberators. Umayyad Spain became an outpost of the Islamic world in Spain even though the majority of the population remained Christian. Although dynasties changed over seven centuries of Muslim rule, tolerance of diversity fostered stability and sparked a synthesis of arts and scholarship, including the transmission of classical Greek texts. The Caliphate of Cordoba funded monumental architecture, including some seven hundred mosques, three hundred public baths, and seventy libraries.

Knowledge from Islamic Spain traveled north along with merchants and led to what has been called by some the Renaissance or "rebirth" of classical ideals, including the polis or city-state expressed as small-scale urban government by merchant aristocracies in Italy and the Netherlands. Monastic communities had attracted religious scholars for centuries. Because they were supported by wealthy patrons, poorer Catholic men and women could pledge themselves to a life of study. As in other parts of Afroeurasia, their relative independence from the state contributed to an intellectual zone where critical thinking about power and nature, faith and reason flourished. Expanding into full-fledged universities in Paris, Oxford, Cambridge, and Salamanca, these scholastic communities gradually granted degrees that certified the completion of an advanced and diverse course of study, including the liberal arts. While some patrons sponsored the arts for the glory of the papacy and the Christian god, like Michelangelo's sculpture of David (1504 CE) or painting of the Sistine Chapel ceiling (1512 CE), others commissioned mythological figures, portraits of their own families, and even of more ordinary people such as the *Mona Lisa* by Leonardo da Vinci (1452–1519 CE).

Islamic control of Spain and the contested Holy Lands led Pope Urban II (r. 1088–1099 CE) to call for a crusade to Jerusalem. Under the pretense of protecting Christian pilgrims, Crusaders seized the city in 1099 CE and held it for nearly a century, massacring more than half the population before being removed from power. Multiple crusades followed in vain attempts to retake Jerusalem, bringing European soldiers and pilgrims to the Middle East. Millions of Crusaders traversing Afroeurasia contributed to the spread of infectious diseases, including smallpox. King Louis VII of France (1120–1180 CE) sent half a million out on a later crusade; only 1000 returned, most decimated by disease. Related instability due to crusading Christian forces and the ascent of rival Fatimid Shi'ites in North Africa led to the militarizing of Islamic Spain under the fundamentalist Almoravids and persecution of Christians. The papacy had long called for the expulsion of Muslims and allied with Christian kings to the north. The Reconquista led to the Spanish Inquisition (1478–1834 CE) even before the final reconquest of Spain in 1492 CE. Religious tribunals imposed Catholic orthodoxy, burning thousands at the stake and expelling half a million Muslims and Jews.

The aftermath of the devastating Black Death in the late fourteenth century, that is estimated to have killed between 30–60 percent of Europe's population, spurred a resurgent belief in the devil as a pervasive force in worldly affairs. In areas with the most intense religious strife, such as Germany and France, witch hunts took the lives of thousands, mostly women, as villagers sought scapegoats for inexplicable illness, natural disasters, and political instability. This period coincided with the Hundred Years War (1337–1453 CE) between England and France that also extended to Holland and Iberia. Bloody conflicts saw old rivals using religion to justify their power grabs and new claimants asserting their dominance in the midst of the chaos. One such claimant, the peasant teen Joan of Arc (1412–1431 CE), convinced the French king to give her an army. She claimed divine inspiration in the form of visions that commanded her to liberate Paris from the military occupation by the English. She won many battles but when she began to lose, enemies arrested her as a witch and burned her at the stake as a heretic.

Reformers, most notably German theologian Martin Luther (1483–1546 CE) through his *Ninety-Five Theses* published in 1517 and French theologian John Calvin (1509–1564 CE) with his theology of predestination, led a critique of the Catholic Church that came to be known as the Protestant Reformation. Reformers targeted the wealth and power of the Catholic Church in addition to its doctrines, opening a broader critique that argued all institutions could be delegitimized. Yet few rulers of any creed tolerated popular uprisings. In response to such turmoil, states consolidated their power as monarchs from England to Russia adopted variations of the ideology of the divine right of kings, claiming absolute authority granted by God to directly rule their religiously homogeneous subjects. Another means of control included the founding of the Jesuit order of priests by Pope Paul III in 1540 CE to oppose the Protestant Reformation, insist on Catholic orthodoxy, and sustain a global missionary effort that reached every continent and continues today.

Epidemics continued for centuries, destabilizing the political, economic, and social orders. The successful uprising of the English Revolution of the 1640s followed soon after the plague claimed the lives of 45,000 in London alone between 1625 and 1636 CE. Death on such a scale led survivors to demand change, and with the reduced population, men and women gained more power to force their will upon their rulers.

Islamic World

In Arabia, rival nomadic clans and merchant cities were united in the seventh century CE under the banner of the Islamic faith founded by the prophet Muhammad (570–632 CE) when he shared his visions. Muhammad preached belief in a single almighty God, or *Allah* in Arabic, one of the Five Pillars of Islam, which also included daily prayer, annual fasting, charitable giving, and recommended pilgrimage to the holy cities of Mecca and Medina. The former was the city of Muhammad's birth where he received his first prophecy in the Hira cave at a mountain on its outskirts, and the latter was the city where his early followers took refuge from persecution in 622 and where he served as both a political and religious leader. As was customary among nomads, Muhammad had multiple wives, taking care of women who had lost family protection or to forge alliances. His youngest wife, Aisha (circa 613–678 CE), was a scholar in her own right, dictating sayings of the prophet for forty-four years after his death. While the revelations of Muhammad were collected into the core Muslim scriptures of the Qur'an, his sayings were also written down as the Hadith. These were the two most important sources informing Islamic Sharia law after his death in 632 CE. Even as the four Rashidun Caliphs that succeeded Mohammad conquered the Levant, Persia, and North Africa, their reigns were marred by disputes as to the rightful successor of Muhammad: his father-in-law, Abu Bakr, or his son-in-law, Ali. Their followers fought each other until forming separate branches of Islam, the Sunni and Shia respectively. A political dispute at first, it became a religious schism over the subsequent centuries resulting in separate bodies of Sharia law and interpretations of religious practices.

Under the Umayyad Caliphate (661–750 CE) with its capital in Damascus, Is-

The Dome of the Rock (Qubbat as-Sakhra), 688-692 CE, Temple Mount (Site of the second Jewish Temple, Jerusalem, Israel) (Photograph by Andrew Shiva / license CC-SA-4.0)

One of the oldest works of Islamic architecture, the Dome of the Rock, is not a mosque, but rather encircles a stone formation associated with the prophet Mohammed's *Night Journey*. The building was inspired by and competed with existing Byzantine structures, especially the Church of the Holy Sepulchre, from which it borrowed the floor plan and interior mosaic decoration—though an inscription makes it very plain that the Dome of the Rock is a fundamentally Islamic structure.

lamic conquests stretched across Afroeurasia, reaching as far west as Spain and as far east as India. Once conquered peoples submitted, efficient administration and high degrees of tolerance for a diversity of religious and ethnic groups characterized Umayyad rule. Conquered subjects were generally permitted to retain their own customs and laws as long as they paid a special *jizya* tax imposed on non-Muslims. The routes of Islamic conquest and conversion also promoted trade, including trade in enslaved Africans. Slave labor contributed to the establishment of flourishing metropolises such as Baghdad, the capital of the Abbasid Caliphate (750–1258 CE), where the House of Wisdom became a renown center of higher learning. To support Baghdad's growing population, Iraqi landowners forced several thousand enslaved African Zanj to reclaim the salt marshes for arable land. Due to the harsh conditions, the Zanj rose up, aided by an Arab commander who armed them in order to destabilize the aristocracy and install a caliph from the Kharijite sect of Islam. While holding the egalitarian view that anyone could be caliph, members of this sect were also unyielding in proscribing luxury, gambling, music, and concubinage. The fourteen-year Zanj Rebellion (869–883 CE) as chronicled by contemporary historian Muhammad al-Tabari (839–923 CE) unfolded as a rapid succession of caliphs severely burdened with debt further undermined the legitimacy of the Abbasids. The Zanj rebels established their own capital south of Basra and even minted their own coins, while the Kharijites rewarded talented Zanj with lands and enslaved laborers. By the time the Abbasids regrouped to crush the Zanj rebels, several hundred thousand people had been killed and the infrastructure of southern Iraq was in ruins. The legacy of the Zanj Rebellion was an enduring Islamic aversion to corvée or plantation slavery. Although the Abbasid Caliphate endured for another three centuries, religious schisms made it increasingly vulnerable to invasion until it finally fell to the Mongols in 1258 CE.

Under the Abbasids, Baghdad became one of the world's most learned cities with libraries, bookstores, and an unrivalled literacy rate for both men and women. People played chess, backgammon, and checkers; pastry shops sold baklava; and massive city walls offered the illusion of security. Perhaps ironically, the spread of Islam through trade and proselytization accelerated as the Abbasid dynasty entered a period of decline. Detached from the ambitions of one family and related instability, Islam and Arabic spread throughout Afroeurasia as pilgrims to Mecca created predictable networks for the flow of goods, ideas, and technologies. Reservoirs and irrigation supported the cultivation of diverse southern products like sugarcane, eggplants, figs, and bananas in arid climates. They in turn supported the growth of large cities like Baghdad, with a population of half a million people, where scholarly debate about natural law, reason, and mysticism occurred in the House of Wisdom, an early form of university founded in 830 CE. Transmitting and augmenting knowledge traditions from across the ancient world, Muslim scholars made advances in medicine and astronomy. They developed the first hospitals and accurately described the progression of contagious diseases and developed inoculations, sometime around the year 1000. Via Muslim Spain, the accumulated learning of Afroeurasia entered Europe, influencing the development of the first European universities around 1200 CE.

The thirty-seventh caliph Al-Musta'sim (1213–1258 CE) believed Abbasid reign would last until the final Day of Judgment. However, a Mongol force, perhaps as large as 850,00 men, easily breached Baghdad's fortifications with Chinese siege engines and trebuchets that hurled rocks, alabaster, and bolts dipped in burning pitch, bringing the dynasty to an end in 1258. Hulagu Khan (1218–1265 CE) led the second Mongol attack on the Islamic world. His grandfather Genghis had already shattered Persia with the sack of Herat in 1222 CE, which resulted in the massacre of 1.6 million people. The Mongols proceeded to massacre the entire city and razed its mosques, libraries, and colleges to the ground, dumping so many books in the Tigris River that it ran black with ink. As his first wife and his mother were Nestorian Christians, a form of Christianity deemed heretical at the Council of Ephesus in 431 CE that survived by followers migrating east along the Silk Road, Hulagu placed one church off-limits as a refuge for the city's Christians. Some women survived as slaves, including the

View of the Interior of Shah Mosque, structure covered in tile, 1611-1629 CE, Isfahan (Iran) (Photograph by Amir Pashaei / license CC-SA-4.0)

The Royal Mosque was commissioned in the early 17th century by the Safavid ruler Shah Abbas, who was a great patron of the arts and known to use architecture and other visual projects to impress European diplomats and Ottoman and Mughal emissaries alike. All available surfaces of the building are covered by multi-colored tiles with floral, geometric, and calligraphic decorations and make it appear like a jewel box.

caliph's daughters who joined Hulagu's harem of five hundred seized in the conquest. Hulagu founded the Ilkhanate on the ruins of Abbasid Caliphate, but it was soon at war with another branch of Mongols that had ravaged Russia and converted to Islam. The near constant state of war between them prevented the Ilkhanids from consolidating their rule, and they finally fell in 1335 CE amid an outbreak of the Black Death.

The Mongol weakening of Islamic empires in the Levant combined with the plague enabled the rise of the Ottoman Turks as the most powerful Muslim warriors. The Ottoman Empire (1299–1923 CE) eventually extended across Afroeurasia, with Ottoman domination of both the overland Silk Road and the maritime trade of the Mediterranean, ultimately forcing European merchants to seek another route to the wealthy markets of the Indian subcontinent and China, leading Christopher Columbus to sail west into the Atlantic. In 1453 CE, the Ottomans finally achieved their centuries-long dream of conquering Constantinople, renamed Istanbul after it fell in a bloody siege as 70,000 men stormed its walls. With the conquest of Egypt in 1517 CE, the Ottoman sultans ruled a vast realm spanning three continents. Most churches including the cathedral of Hagia Sofia became mosques, and the *jizya* tax

Tughra (Insignia) of Sultan Süleiman the Magnificent, ink, watercolor and gold on paper, 1555–1560 CE, Istanbul, Turkey (now Metropolitan Museum of Art New York) (Public Domain)

This decorative signature shows the evolution of Islamic Calligraphy into an artform. Similar to carpet pages in medieval European manuscripts, no space is left undecorated, though the focus here is on interwoven flowers and other vegetal patterns known as arabesques.

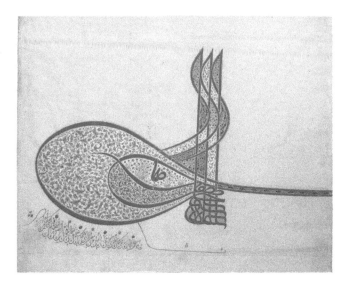

was imposed on Christians, who were otherwise tolerated so long as they refrained from proselytism. The Ottoman practice of *devshirme* conscripted Christian boys between the ages of six and fourteen, forcibly circumcised in conversion to Islam, and trained to serve in the elite Janissary corps. Over time they became one of the ruling castes of the Ottoman Empire, rivaling the Turkish aristocracy in power and influence while serving as commanders of the military and advisors to the sultans. The empire reached its height under the Sultan Suleiman (r. 1520–1566 CE), who organized its diverse laws into one coherent code and laid siege to Vienna in 1529. Extending across the Middle East, North Africa, and the Balkans, the empire's endurance for six centuries rested equally on its military and administrative skill, at the nexus of which were the Janissaries whose separation from family, language, or region ensured their personal loyalty to the sultans.

Sub-Saharan Africa

The Bantu Migration illustrates Southernization in Sub-Saharan Africa. Migrants settled across much of sub-Saharan Africa by 500 CE, spreading a related set of languages, ideas, and cultures from the central rain forests to the southern coasts. As Bantu peoples generally migrated in small clans, the transformation of Africa was more gradual than a typical conquest, with the formation of a variety of societies. The key to Bantu success was their forging of iron for weapons and farm tools, permitting them to displace or absorb hunter-gatherers and plow the land for cultivation. Some rain forest peoples like the Batwa of Central Africa adopted nearby Bantu languages but maintained their traditional lifestyle where men specialized in hunting forest game such as antelope and bush pigs and women gathered wild honey, fruits, and berries. In the grasslands of East Africa, Bantu communities cultivated grain but above all herded cattle, which they adopted from the Khoi people. Clans measured their

Bet Emanuel church, rock-hewn (volcanic tufa), 13th century CE, Lalibela (Ethiopia) (Photograph by Chuck Moravec / license CC-BY-2.0)

For thousands of years, humans used the relatively soft volcanic tufa to carve spaces into rock—for example the Ancient Egyptian tombs of the Middle Kingdom and Tumuli of the Etruscan necropolis—but they did not free the entire structure from its surroundings. The churches at Lalibela are unique as architecture-sized works of sculpture and they speak to the power and to the faith of the Christian rulers of Ethiopia who commissioned them in the 13th century.

wealth in cattle, villages were built around cattle kraals, and men paid bride price with cattle. After the maritime Silk Road reached Africa in the sixth century CE, Bantu Swahili speakers established trading post cities along the coasts of the Indian Ocean, supplying cloth and wares to market towns in the Bantu highlands, receiving ebony, gold, and ivory in return, which they in turn traded with Arab merchants for silk, porcelain, glassware, and jewelry. Kilwa and Zanzibar became cosmopolitan centers of trade between three continents.

Christianity took root south of Egypt over several centuries in the Sudanic cultures of Nubia, Kush, and then Aksum in the area of modern Eritrea and Ethiopia. The spread of religion and belief is one of the hallmarks of Southernization, in part because missionaries and ideas follow trade routes. Thanks to greater rainfall than in the Nile delta, the populations of this region engaged in herding and smaller scale agriculture enabling self-sufficient communities to thrive more than in the more arid areas of North and East Africa. Gradually they integrated into a trading network, connecting the Arabian lands across the Red Sea to the interior of Africa. The Aksumite state collected tribute from these communities and built an empire that lasted into the seventh century CE and included war elephants in its expansive army. Eventually, environmental changes, such as soil erosion, and cultural changes, such as the influence of Islam, ended the centralized rule of Aksum. Small communities built distinctive monolithic rock-hewn churches. Their paintings of biblical stories were similar to those in medieval Europe. The region continued to be ruled by Christians, culminating in the Solomonic dynasty that ruled from 1270 until the twentieth century.

Despite their dispersion, the spiritual belief systems of inland Bantu societies featured common animistic themes, centered on shamans who communed with ancestor spirits and nature forces such as the sun or sky, in order to facilitate individual and communal healing. Bantu religious specialists could be male or female, though women generally were revered as diviners for the power of their fertility. This spiritual power softened a patriarchal system where clan chiefs conveyed status by the size of their household, which included multiple wives. From the thirteenth century CE onward the most powerful chiefs established kingdoms such as the Monomotapa that ruled from the temple-fortress of Great Zimbabwe. By this time, they adopted Islam while absorbing Arab and Persian settlers following the Indian Ocean trade routes, while Swahili cities along the coasts remained independent.

The tenth-century CE arrival of Islam in West Africa, following the caravan routes across the Sahara, similarly tied that region into the circuits of Southernization and forged a new African cultural sphere quite distinct from the Bantu peoples. The hierarchical structure of Islam appealed to some African chiefs and the universalistic salvation creed appealed to converts. Conversion also had the practical advantage of facilitating trade and other peaceful relations with nearby Muslim communities. During this transition period, coexistence with and adaptation of animist beliefs helped ensure stability and continuity. In Ghana, the capital city Koumbi Saleh was divided in half by the eleventh century CE, one side fully Muslim with twelve mosques, while the other was the seat of the royal compound where a mosque for visiting merchants stood alongside a traditional temple.

Along the Niger River, a network of city-states dotted the floodplains for several centuries until around 900 CE. Jenne-jeno was among the largest, at 40,000 people. Almost uniquely in the history of settlements, these cities apparently lacked fortifications and appeared to coexist peacefully until the arrival of Muslim conquerors. West African imperial consolidation reached new heights with the conquests of Sundiata Keita (d. 1255 CE), who founded the Mali Empire in the thirteenth century. The *Epic of Sundiata*, passed down orally for centuries, traces his rise to power. Son of the ruler of a small Malinke kingdom, the young Sundiata overcame a physical disability and the massacre of his fellow princes by a rival kingdom; mastered cavalry tactics; and forged an empire to avenge his family's death. By 1240 CE, Sundiata grew strong

Detail from the Catalan Atlas Sheet 6 "Mansa Musa sitting on a throne holding a gold coin," colored inks on parchment, 1375 CE (now Bibliothèque Nationale France) (Public Domain)

This section from a Catalan Atlas shows the importance of individual, well-known figures in the larger medieval world and how these figures even functioned as "landmarks" on a map. And although the specific geographic details of Musa's empire were not fully known, there was a general understanding of places and routes the cartographer connected with known vectors.

enough to conquer the lands of the once-great Ghana Empire as the new Mali Empire spread in all directions across the West African Sahel. With control of the gold mines and salt trade that had enriched Ghana for centuries, Sundiata razed Koumbi Saleh and built his new Malian capital at Niani, which soon became the focus of the lucrative trans-Sahara trade, linked to Afroeurasia by the Arab merchants and Sufi missionaries who traveled the caravan routes. While the *Epic of Sundiata* describes him as a magician-king who adhered to traditional beliefs and rituals, his successors embraced Islam with the cities of Timbuktu and Djenne hosting universities that further integrated Mali with the Islamic world. When Emperor Mansa Musa (circa 1280–1337 CE) undertook the pilgrimage to Mecca in 1324, his entourage included 12,000 enslaved people, multiple wives and consorts, 60,000 soldiers, and a train of 80 camels each loaded with 300 pounds of gold, so much gold that it destabilized the economies around the Mediterranean for years afterward.

While Mansa Musa's slaves were dressed in Persian silk brocades to proclaim his majesty, the reality of such an extensive slave society was far more complex. Over the course of a millennium, Arab traders exported some 12 million enslaved people across the trans-Saharan caravan routes to the port markets of the Swahili Coast. They insinuated themselves into the Asian slave trade as well, especially in Southeast Asia, where conversion to Islam followed, particularly in Indonesia. For the most part war captives or convicted criminals, enslaved Africans were trafficked throughout the markets of the Islamic world from Morocco to the Indian subcontinent. While Islamic law purportedly mitigated harsh treatment and promoted manumission—release from slavery—upon conversion to Islam, the lives of enslaved people varied significantly. Women were pressed into domestic and sexual servitude, while men were commonly deployed as soldiers, guards, and sailors. In stark contrast to the chattel slavery of the Americas, slavery was seen as situational rather than an inherent racial identity based on unfounded biological interpretations of what it means to be human. Freedmen could therefore integrate into society after manumission and even ascended to rule in the Mamluk dynasties of Egypt and the Delhi Sultanate of the Indian subcontinent. Meanwhile, lighter-skinned women were often elevated to consort or concubine status, with white women from Southern Russia seen as especially valuable, many of whom mothered the sultans of the Ottoman Empire.

Slave labor built the cities of Timbuktu and Djenne, featuring grand mosques and universities with as many as 25,000 scholars in 1450 CE. The Mali Empire was governed by the Gbara Assembly, first appointed by Mansa Musa in 1235 CE, which included thirty-two representatives appointed by the Malian clans to administer the empire and check the power of the Mansa emperors. The empire's wealth enabled the payment of tribute to Tuareg nomads who threatened the borders, a system that ensured relative tranquility in urban centers. When a succession crisis weakened the empire after 1360 CE, the breakaway Songhai were able to retain autonomy and eventually prevailed to replace the Mansas with a new Songhai Empire (1468–1591 CE). Imperial Songhai continued West African administrative, intellectual, and commercial advancement, yet steadily came under strain from the south as political chaos and warfare spread across the region and into the empire itself due to the growing trans-Atlantic slave trade. Racked by civil wars and declining wealth as the Saharan trade waned in importance, the Songhai were finally conquered by an invasion force from Morocco that plundered the salt mines and looted its cities. The Moroccan Saadi dynasty was itself bankrupt and unstable, subjecting the region to Tuareg marauders who pillaged Timbuktu and Djenne nearly out of existence. The region devolved into dozens of competing kingdoms in a chronic state of instability, as European slave traders brought guns and rum.

The Americas

Mayan civilization in present-day Guatemala and southern Mexico emerged from earlier Mesoamerican settlements of complex urban and ceremonial structures dating

Temple 1 (Jaguar) on the Great Plaza, 8th century CE, Tikal (Guatemala) (Photograph by
Dennis Jarvis / license: CC-BY-SA-2.0)

Maya rulers commissioned hundreds of temples, plazas, and other structures most of which
have since been hidden by jungle. This funerary temple is associated with a ruler known
as Jasaw Chan K'awiil I (682–734 CE). He is buried deep within the structure (which was
erected over his tomb), but is brought to life in his depictions in carved panels as well as
inscriptions.

back to 2000 BCE. Extant cultural achievements are traced to around 900 CE and
include a system of calculation that enabled accurate astronomical calendars. Calendars also helped farmers and engineers terrace hillsides, drain swamps, and redirect
groundwater to support networks of towns and villages. By 750 CE, Tikal housed
50,000 residents and traded with another 50,000 people in its hinterlands. They
traded in animals and crops that would transform world history in the centuries to
come: maize, corn, potatoes, chocolate, and peanuts. Pictographic writing, carved
in stone pillars on temples or on tree bark or deerskin paper, suggests a hierarchical
society with priests and scribes above artisans and engineers. Remains of ancient
Mayan temples continued to structure spiritual life from Palenque to Chichen Itza
on the Yucatan peninsula. Their plazas included ritual ball courts and carvings of
serpents and warriors.

   The largest and grandest of all early Mesoamerican cities, at one point housing
100,000 people, was Teotihuacan located near present-day Mexico City. Its collapse

Teotihuacan Ceremonial Complex – view of the "Pyramid of the Sun and Avenue of the Dead," 100-550 CE, Mexico City (Mexico) (Photograph by *AnbyG* /license CC-SA-4.0)

Though used by the rulers of the Aztec empire, the pyramid complex was not created by them—in fact its creators predate many of the more well-known Mesoamerican civilizations. This is not unusual, since the successors generally overpower and absorb their predecessors' land, income, culture and people, but in this case the structures left behind reveal their important role and accomplishments even if their names are forgotten.

in the sixth century CE after a millennium of growth followed from a prolonged drought and possibly a volcanic eruption in 535. This fits the cyclical pattern in the Americas of stable states and cultures evolving in mild periods of predictable seasons, then expanding steadily to reach a zenith of wealth and power, only to abruptly contract or collapse due to environmental factors.

This cyclical pattern can also be used to characterize Southernization in the pre-Columbian context of the Americas. During the eighth and ninth centuries rival groups fought for dominance of the valley of Mexico. The Toltecs from the north sacked and burned Teotihuacan around 900 CE and maintained their rule for two centuries by militarizing Mesoamerica, knitting together ethnically distinct communities who paid tribute. Their wealth in turn attracted more invaders from the north; Chichimecan people migrated south and defeated the Toltecs by 1175 CE.

While much of Teotihuacan's culture endured in the smaller local communities that replaced it, they were equally vulnerable to climate change and invasion, until finally in 1428 a new empire emerged, forged by Aztec conquerors that had migrated from the northern deserts. Without metallurgy, the wheel, or draft animals, the Aztec Empire (1428–1521 CE) of Mexico achieved tremendous engineering feats, notably the *chinampas*, or floating fields, that cultivated food for the capital Tenochtitlan, a canal city of 400,000 built on islands in Lake Texcoco. Aztec god-kings reigned from its soaring temple complex, with Moctezuma II (1466–1520 CE) extending his rule across dozens of client states in an empire of 25 million at the time when Spanish conquistadors arrived on the eastern shores. Alliances cemented by marriage hinged on the relatively high status of elite women, especially among the Toltecs whose traditional prestige gave the newer Aztecs greater legitimacy. Yet, as with many empires, extensive Aztec conquests sowed resentment among subject peoples, especially with the distinct institution of mass human sacrifice believed necessary to feed the gods so that the sun would rise. Onerous demands of tribute to finance the imperial splendor of their temple-palaces and the constant waging of war to seize captives for sacrifice destabilized the empire such that when Spanish conquistador Hernán Cortes arrived in 1519 CE (and defeated the Aztecs by 1521), rivals such as the Tlaxcalans were eager to gain foreign support.

As diverse American cultures came into contact with Europeans, indigenous women facilitated alliances or conquest, especially if they had already played this role in capital cities that attracted many different languages and cultures. Most famously, La Malinche (circa 1500–1529 CE) was a Nahua woman enslaved by Mayans whose language she learned. Learning Spanish from another slave, a priest whom the Mayans held prisoner for eight years, she proved invaluable to Cortés who received her in tribute from the Maya, serving as an interpreter of her native Nahuatl, also the language of the Aztecs. La Malinche would be celebrated as the mother of Mexico for her role in bridging the Aztec and Spanish cultures and also condemned as a traitor for assisting the conquistadors in their divide-and-conquer strategy of leveraging alliances with traditional rivals of the Aztecs. Along with their possession of guns and horses, the conquistadors prevailed due to the outbreak of smallpox that felled most of the Aztec capital's defenders. Up to 90 percent of the population of the Americas was decimated due to epidemics of European diseases such as smallpox, measles, and influenza, in addition to direct colonial aggression during the sixteenth century, which enabled the worst demographic collapse the world has seen on such a scale. Those who survived were forced to work in the feudal encomienda system, which even some Spanish critics denounced as slavery, where settlers received land grants from the Spanish crown, with the right to demand goods and labor from the indigenous residents, in return for an obligation to often-forcibly convert them to Christianity.

A similar cyclical pattern of Southernization can also be seen in South America where indigenous communities in the Andes Mountains entered alliances to survive ecological vulnerability. Frosts and droughts pushed highland peoples into contact with lowland cultivators who practiced terraced farming and herded the continent's only pack animals, llamas and alpacas. Uniting highlands and lowlands into an empire that stretched 3000 miles, Inca rulers consolidated power in their capital Cuzco, a fortress city they viewed as the sacred center of the universe. Corvee laborers (*mit'a*) were used for building roads, and peasant conscripts transported cotton, cacao, maize, and potatoes, having no wheeled vehicles and unable to rely on testy llamas. The god-king Sapa Inca merged local shamanic beliefs into a new religion that worshipped the sun and legitimized his rule. The founder of the empire, Pachacuti (r. 1438–1471 CE), whose name means "cataclysm" in the Quechua language, consolidated rule in the Peruvian highland, which his successors extended along the Pacific lowlands south into Chile and Argentina and north into Ecuador and Colombia. Conquered peoples were forced to pay tribute in lives as well as wealth, but the Inca did not sacrifice war captives. In their cosmology, gods preferred elite children, especially girls, who were exposed on a mountain, such as the temple-complex at Machu Picchu, 8000 feet above sea level. Akin to the sun god himself, Inca rulers kept many wives and concubines and their sons engaged in violent succession struggles, including a civil war between rival claimants just at the moment when Spanish conquistadors arrived in 1532. A smallpox epidemic swept across the Inca Empire adding to the instability that enabled Francisco Pizarro (circa 1475–1541 CE) to seize the Inca emperor Atahualpa (circa 1502–1533 CE), whom he executed before proceeding to conquer the Inca heartland. The conquistadors were greatly aided by the Inca Empire's 25,000 miles of road, a remarkable engineering feat that extended imperial rule through inhospitable terrain while at the same time leaving imperial centers subject to easy invasion.

Further north within North America, Mississippian cultures spread throughout the south and southeast forming settlements that mixed hunting and gathering with agriculture along river banks around 1000 CE. In the Southern Appalachians, Cherokee organized their villages around platform mounds; some featured townhouse style dwellings atop them. The Cherokee population numbered in the tens of thousands by the seventeenth century and occupied 40,000 square miles. Larger towns formed with up to sixty households and might include multiple mounds. They also used the mounds for public functions, including corn festivals that held religious significance. Evidence of green corn ceremonies links Cherokee traditions to other Iroquois-language tribes, as well as with the Creek, Choctaw, Yuchi, and Seminole. Illustrating Southernization in North America, some Iroquois settled in the plains and points south from the Great Lakes area.

Some chiefdoms united in confederacies, such as the Iroquois of present-day New York and the Powhatan of present-day Virginia, to stabilize sometimes violent clashes between sedentary farmers and nomadic hunter-gatherers. These conflicts were often blood feuds and rites of passage for young men, rather than contests over access to land, which was abundant. Despite this warrior culture, chiefs did not just assume leadership through feats of arms but were often elected by acclamation. Women served as advisors and religious shamans while some clans were matrilineal. The Iroquois linguistic diaspora suggests that indigenous populations as far flung as the upper Midwest, Atlantic Seaboard, and Southern Appalachian mountains shared a common origin.

In 1567 CE the Spanish established their first outpost in the interior of North

Cherokee Burden Basket, river cane, before 1963, Cherokee, North Carolina. (Public Domain)

Baskets play an important role in Cherokee life and can be used for gathering, storing, transporting, etc. The woven pattern serves multiple purposes as well as it is both aesthetic and symbolic, and connects the object with its maker and owner. A burden basket would usually be tied to the person carrying it (on the back, with a strap around the head or chest), as it would be much too impractical to carry by hand.

America at Joara, a Native American town near Morganton, North Carolina. After one year of conflict with indigenous people the fort San Juan was destroyed. European settlers expanded their holdings, swallowing up Cherokee land and leading to sometimes violent disputes. Unlike the invading settlers, white fur traders were more likely to intermarry and assimilate into the indigenous communities with whom they traded. This gave native women among the Ojibwe of the Great Lakes, for example, considerable prestige as cultural intermediaries. With the arrival of Christian missionaries, indigenous American beliefs absorbed some Christian elements, though most customs only changed after conquest.

In the Caribbean islands, including Hispaniola where Christopher Columbus landed in 1492, the native Taino people were all but eradicated by massacres and epidemics within a generation. Yet the sugar plantations required labor, and Europeans soon found a new source across the Atlantic, launching the slave trade that forcibly relocated 12 million enslaved Africans over four centuries. The plantations swiftly grew into vast landholdings with up to a thousand enslaved laborers each, where it was deemed more profitable to brutally work enslaved people to death and simply replace them than improve their conditions. As many as 10,000 enslaved people arrived

Brimstone Hill Fortress, basalt and limestone, 17th-18th century CE, St. Christopher (now known as St. Kitts) (Photograph by Martin Falbisoner/ license CC-SA-4.0)

Brimstone Hill Fortress showcases how colonial powers combined military engineering with African enslaved labor to protect and expand their political and economic interests in the Caribbean. Built in several levels on a steep volcanic hill, the natural topography creates additional protection in conjunction with the design of thick stone walls and battlements enclosing each stage.

per year in Saint-Domingue alone, the French half of Hispaniola. As early as 1570 CE, Gaspar Yanga (b. 1545) led a slave revolt in Veracruz, Mexico, with the maroon settlement that he founded holding out in the mountains for forty years. Indeed, marronage was one of the most successful forms of resistance throughout the Caribbean. Most of the recurrent slave uprisings were swiftly crushed yet remained a constant threat within the slave system until its end in the nineteenth century.

These atrocities by Europeans, including the devastation of the native population of the Americas and the decreased population of Africa due to the slave trade, may have also had a negative impact on the environment. For example, it may have contributed to the Little Ice Age, a long period of global cooling that set in after the Mongol conquests in the thirteenth century and peaked in the seventeenth century CE. With the dramatic plunge in the American and African populations, much of its cultivated land reverted to its wild state, with thick forests and jungles to absorb CO_2 and reduce temperatures. Climate historians believe that the ash from volcanic eruptions also lowered temperatures so that the cooler, wetter weather limited food production, resulting in famines in the Northern Hemisphere. Meanwhile, drought destroyed maize crops in the Southern Hemisphere, retarding population recovery in Spanish America. Across the Pacific Ocean in China, drought ruined harvests there as well, contributing to the collapse of the Ming dynasty as Manchu horsemen descended from the north to claim the Mandate of Heaven and establish their own Qing dynasty. The civil wars that racked the Indian subcontinent in the late Mughal era as well as the near constant warfare in Europe at the time may also be linked to climate instability. World historians call this the crisis of the seventeenth century; climate change exacerbated longer standing crises of political legitimacy, unequal distribution of resources, and sectarian strife.

Conclusion

Southernization describes the process through which an array of resources entered the transregional and increasingly global economy, from Indian cotton and crystal-ized sugar to East African gold and Vietnamese rice. The concentration of wealth in cities from Constantinople to Hangzhou attracted newcomers, some of them flee-ing climatic change, some of them bent on violent conquest. The forced integra-tion of the Americas, its immense wealth attractive to conquerors from the Global North, brought more southern products and people into that economy. It created a revolution in ecological exchange that included plants, animals, people, and diseases. American silver, flooding the global economy and mined by enslaved indigenous peo-ple in Mexico and Bolivia, exacerbated wealth disparity around much of the world. It destabilized the economies that became dependent on it, such as Ming dynasty China and the Iberian empires of Europe. The new plantation system of cash crops such as sugar and cotton in the Caribbean required hard labor provided by the slave trade, resulting in a diminished African population. Only centuries later did trade in luxuries such as gold and ivory enable new empires to form in Africa, such as the Ashante of Ghana and the Benin of Nigeria. Their concentrations of wealth in turn attracted new conquerors and the process of Southernization continued.

Comprehensive Timeline

Pre-Modern Worlds Comprehensive Timeline I (300 - 700 CE)

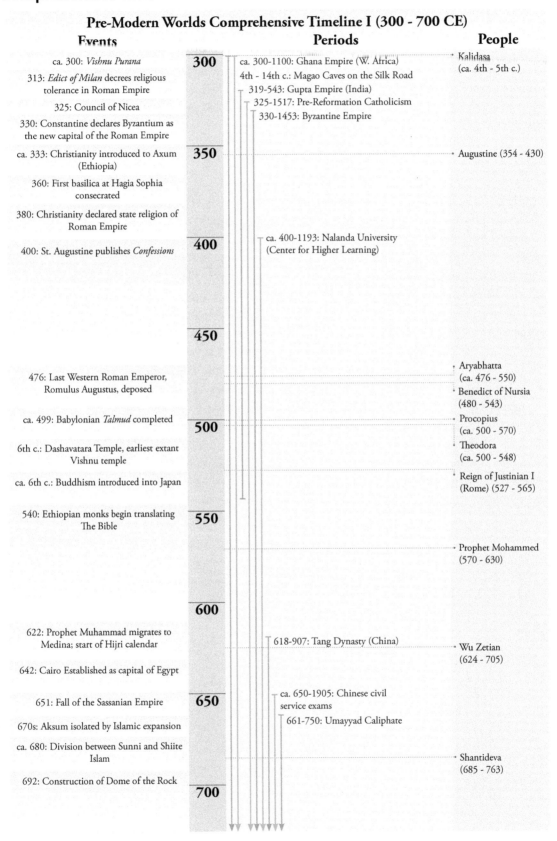

Events	Periods	People
ca. 300: *Vishnu Purana*	**300**	Kalidasa (ca. 4th - 5th c.)
	ca. 300-1100: Ghana Empire (W. Africa)	
313: *Edict of Milan* decrees religious tolerance in Roman Empire	4th - 14th c.: Magao Caves on the Silk Road	
	319-543: Gupta Empire (India)	
325: Council of Nicea	325-1517: Pre-Reformation Catholicism	
330: Constantine declares Byzantium as the new capital of the Roman Empire	330-1453: Byzantine Empire	
ca. 333: Christianity introduced to Axum (Ethiopia)	**350**	Augustine (354 - 430)
360: First basilica at Hagia Sophia consecrated		
380: Christianity declared state religion of Roman Empire		
400: St. Augustine publishes *Confessions*	**400** ca. 400-1193: Nalanda University (Center for Higher Learning)	
	450	
476: Last Western Roman Emperor, Romulus Augustus, deposed		Aryabhatta (ca. 476 - 550)
		Benedict of Nursia (480 - 543)
ca. 499: Babylonian *Talmud* completed	**500**	Procopius (ca. 500 - 570)
6th c.: Dashavatara Temple, earliest extant Vishnu temple		Theodora (ca. 500 - 548)
ca. 6th c.: Buddhism introduced into Japan		Reign of Justinian I (Rome) (527 - 565)
540: Ethiopian monks begin translating The Bible	**550**	
		Prophet Mohammed (570 - 630)
	600	
622: Prophet Muhammad migrates to Medina; start of Hijri calendar	618-907: Tang Dynasty (China)	Wu Zetian (624 - 705)
642: Cairo Established as capital of Egypt		
651: Fall of the Sassanian Empire	**650** ca. 650-1905: Chinese civil service exams	
670s: Aksum isolated by Islamic expansion	661-750: Umayyad Caliphate	
ca. 680: Division between Sunni and Shiite Islam		Shantideva (685 - 763)
692: Construction of Dome of the Rock	**700**	

Pre-Modern Worlds Comprehensive Timeline II (700 - 1050 CE)

Events	Periods	People

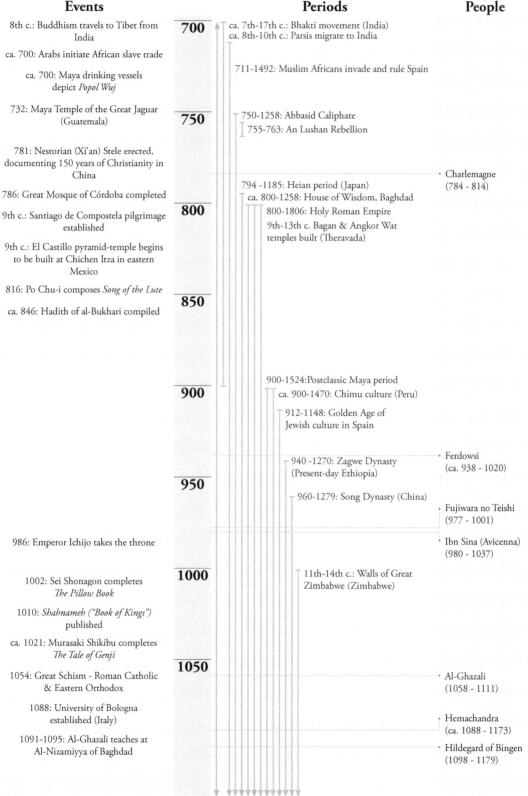

700

8th c.: Buddhism travels to Tibet from India

ca. 700: Arabs initiate African slave trade

ca. 700: Maya drinking vessels depict *Popol Wuj*

732: Maya Temple of the Great Jaguar (Guatemala)

781: Nestorian (Xi'an) Stele erected, documenting 150 years of Christianity in China

786: Great Mosque of Córdoba completed

9th c.: Santiago de Compostela pilgrimage established

9th c.: El Castillo pyramid-temple begins to be built at Chichen Itza in eastern Mexico

816: Po Chu-i composes *Song of the Lute*

ca. 846: Hadith of al-Bukhari compiled

986: Emperor Ichijo takes the throne

1002: Sei Shonagon completes *The Pillow Book*

1010: *Shahnameh ("Book of Kings")* published

ca. 1021: Murasaki Shikibu completes *The Tale of Genji*

1054: Great Schism - Roman Catholic & Eastern Orthodox

1088: University of Bologna established (Italy)

1091-1095: Al-Ghazali teaches at Al-Nizamiyya of Baghdad

750
800
850
900
950
1000
1050

ca. 7th-17th c.: Bhakti movement (India)
ca. 8th-10th c.: Parsis migrate to India

711-1492: Muslim Africans invade and rule Spain

750-1258: Abbasid Caliphate
755-763: An Lushan Rebellion

794 -1185: Heian period (Japan)
ca. 800-1258: House of Wisdom, Baghdad
800-1806: Holy Roman Empire
9th-13th c. Bagan & Angkor Wat temples built (Theravada)

900-1524:Postclassic Maya period
ca. 900-1470: Chimu culture (Peru)
912-1148: Golden Age of Jewish culture in Spain

940 -1270: Zagwe Dynasty (Present-day Ethiopia)

960-1279: Song Dynasty (China)

11th-14th c.: Walls of Great Zimbabwe (Zimbabwe)

Charlemagne (784 - 814)

Ferdowsi (ca. 938 - 1020)

Fujiwara no Teishi (977 - 1001)

Ibn Sina (Avicenna) (980 - 1037)

Al-Ghazali (1058 - 1111)

Hemachandra (ca. 1088 - 1173)

Hildegard of Bingen (1098 - 1179)

Events	Periods	People

1050

ca. 1100: City of Timbuktu
(Present-day Mali)

1107: Al-Ghazali writes
Deliverance from Error

1095-1271: The Crusades

Jutta von Sponheim
(1091 - 1136)

1100

1100-1700: Scholastic
education offered in European
Universities

1132: Hangzhou is chosen as the new
capital of Song China

1142: The Haudenosaunee / Iroquois
Confederacy of the Great Law of Peace

1127-1279: Southern Song, Jurchens rule
North China

1147: Pope Eugenius III accepted
Hildegard's visions as genuine

Maimonides
(1138 - 1204)

ca. 1150: University of Paris founded

1150

Ghengis Khan
(ca. 1160 - 1227)

1152: Hildegard of Bingen
completes *Scivias*

St. Francis of Assisi
(1182 - 1226)

1190: Maimonides writes *Guide
to the Perplexed*

1200-1650: Southeastern Ceremonial Complex
(Mississippian Indigenous cultures)

Sundiata Keita
(1190 - 1255)

1200s: Rock-hewn churches of Lalibela

1200

1206: Unification of Mongolia
under Genghis Khan

1206-1526: Delhi Sultanate (India)

1215: Signing of the Magna Carta

1238-1358: Alhambra complex
built in Granada

St. Thomas Aquinas
(1225 - 1274)

1224.: *Canticle of the Sun* composed
by St. Francis of Assissi

1240-1645: Mali Empire (West Africa)

1244: Augustinian order founded

1250

1258: Siege of Baghdad

Dante Alighieri
(1265 - 1321)

1270: Beginning of Solomonic
Dynasty (Ethiopia)

Namdev
(1270 - 1350)

1271-95 Marco Polo travels to China

1274: Mongols first attempt
to invade Japan

1300

1299-1922: Ottoman Empire

Ibn Battuta
(1304 - 1368)

Reign of Mansa Musa
(Mali)(ca. 1312-1337)

ca. 1322: *Kebra Nagast*
written

Ibn Khaldun
(1332 - 1406)

1325: Founding of Tenochtitlan

1350

Christine de Pizan
(ca. 1364 - 1430)

1346-1353: The Black Death

1368-1644: Ming Dynasty (China)

1370-1507: Timurid Empire

Zheng He
(1371 - 1435)

Margery Kempe
(1373 - 1438)

1361-1362: Boccaccio writes
On Famous Women

Kabir (ca. 15th c.)

1400

1405: Christine de Pizan's
City of Ladies

Pachacuti, Sapa Inca
(1418 - 1471)

1428-1521: Aztec Empire (Mexico)

1431: Joan of Arc captured, put on trial,
and burned at the stake

1438-1533: Incan Empire (Peru)

ca. 1440 CE: Johannes Gutenberg's
printing press

1450

Leonardo da Vinci
(1452 - 1519)

Pre-Modern Worlds Comprehensive Timeline IV (1450 - 1650 CE)

Events	Periods	People

1450

1453: Fall of Constantinople / End of Eastern Roman (Byzantine) Empire/ Silk Roads closed

1368-1644: Ming Dynasty (China)

1468-1591: Songhai Empire (West Africa)

Giovanni Pico della Mirandola (1463 - 1494)

Michelangelo (1475 - 1564)

1475

Surdas (ca. 1480 - 1580)

1493: Papal Bull by Pope Alexander VI: the Doctrine of Discovery

1493-1810: Spread of the Spanish Empire in the Americas

Martin Luther (1483 - 1546)

1494: First record of enslaved Africans forcibly transported to Hispaniola

Ignatius of Loyola (1491 - 1556)

1501-1722 Safavid Empire (Shiite-Iran)

Mirabai (ca. 1498 - 1546)

16th c:. European diseases decimate Indigenous peoples in the Americas

1500

John Calvin (1509 - 1564)

ca. 16th c.: Our Lady of Guadalupe pilgrimage established

1517-1648: Protestant Reformation

1521-1821: Viceroyalty of New Spain (Mexico)

Reign of Suleiman I (Ottoman Empire) (1520 - 1566)

1517: Martin Luther's *Ninety-Five Theses* nailed to the church door

1526-1857 Mughal Empire (India)

1522: Enslaved Africans rebel in Hispaniola

1525

Reign of Ivan (IV) the Terrible, 1st Tsar of Russia (1530 - 1584)

1524: Spanish forces claim the K'iche' land

1541: John Calvin establishes Protestant commonwealth in Geneva

Akbar (1542 - 1605)

1542: Las Casas writes *A Short Account of the Destruction of the Indies*

1550-1650: Akwamu Empire (Ghana)

1550

1545-1563: Council of Trent

Reign of Elizabeth I (1558 - 1603)

1549: St. Francis Xavier, Catholic missionary, arrives in Japan

1550s: K'iche'-Maya nobles compile the *Pop Wuj*

Panditaraja Jagannatha (1572 - 1665)

1575

1570: Gaspar Yanga leads first successful slave uprising in Mexico

Queen Nzinga Mbande (1583 -1663)

1588: Defeat of Spanish Armada by England

1600-1868: Tokugawa Shogunate (Japan)

Reign of Malik Ambar (1602 - 1626)

1600

Fasilides (1603 - 1667)

1613: Two-Row Wampum ("woven shell belt") Treaty between Iroquois and the Dutch

1616: The last remaining Moriscos expelled from Spain

Aurangzeb (1618 -1707)

1625

1637: Teatro San Cassiano, first public operahouse opens in Venice

1647-1652: The Great Plague of Seville

Matsuo Basho (1644 - 1694)

1650

Sor Juana Ines de la Cruz (1651 - 1695)

1669: First known operational reflecting telescope built by Isaac Newton

from *Kebra Nagast*

Introduction

This text is a section from a larger work known as the *Kebra Nagast* (*The Glory of Kings*). It was originally composed in Ge'ez, which was the primary language in Ethiopia, though today it is used only in religious contexts. The main story line of the *Kebra Nagast* can be traced to several sources, though maybe the most prominent of them is a passage from the Hebrew Bible, known by Christians as the Old Testament, where Queen of Sheba visits Solomon. The text was written down in the early fourteenth century, that is, a little more than 2000 years after the events it recounts were said to have transpired. It is a complex text that is neither historically factual nor entirely fictional in weaving together elements of dogma with mysticism and folklore with remarks about history. What might be some of the purposes for having a range of genres brought together in the same text?

 Two crucial events are the focus of the passages reproduced here: first, the meeting of the Queen of Sheba (known as Queen Makeda) and King Solomon, including their different interactions and her conversion; second, the queen's return to her homeland, the birth of a son, and his eventual claim of Solomonic parentage as well as birthright to the religion of his Israelite ancestors. These events are reported in detail, as if witnessed by the writer. At the same time, they are also commented on from the point of view of someone living long after the events took place. One example is the use of "Ethiopia" to refer to the realm of the queen. It would not have been given that name at the time of Queen Makeda and

SNAPSHOT BOX

LANGUAGE: Ge'ez

DATE: 14th century CE

LOCATION: Ethiopia

GENRE: Religious/ Royal Origin Myth

TAGS: Authority and Institution; Cross-Cultural Encounters; Epic; Formations and Reformations; Power Structures; Religion; Women

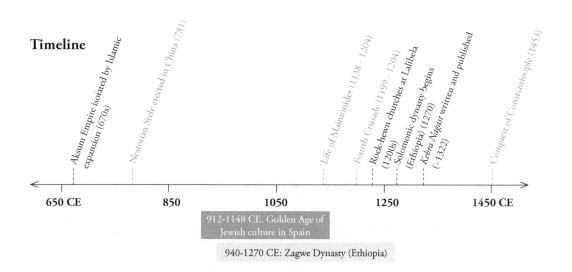

King Solomon, because it is the Greek term for the area of the Horn of Africa, and as such was first adopted locally during the reign of the Aksumite king or **Negus**, Ezana in the fourth century CE. What are some of the reasons authors have for adopting one name over another for a location?

Using the term "Ethiopia" offers further evidence for the fact that the written version of the text significantly postdates the events it describes. There is some argument over when it was compiled or recorded. Generally, the early fourteenth century is the agreed-upon date of origin for the text. It was a time of transition from one dynasty (the Zagwe) to another that was claiming Solomonic descent. What kinds of legitimacy do you think such a narrative would have lent to the new dynasty? Additionally, arguments have also been made for an origin in the sixth century, when it would have served as a means to boost the Christian ruler at the time. In addition to providing an origin story or right-to-rule for the Ethiopian kings (of any century) and an authentic conversion story and connection to Jewish and Christian monotheisms, the *Kebra Nagast* also looks back into a different time, culture, and practice and explains certain changes the reader would observe when comparing present and past practices.

A crucial aspect of the *Kebra Nagast* is that it introduces the Queen of Sheba as an equal to King Solomon: she is presented as a successful and powerful ruler in her own right, and much of the narrative focuses on her as an individual who seeks knowledge and wisdom. In the various extant narratives of the queen (ranging from local legends to national myths), she is portrayed as "an embodiment and symbol of piety, strength, and intelligence."[6] The figure of a female ruler was not originally seen as problematic—especially in Yemen, where female regents (or queens) were fairly common in the Middle Ages. However, this particular perception of the Queen of Sheba changed over the last centuries, when first nationalist and then colonialist discourses began to examine her. In the nationalist Ethiopian (and Pan-African) view, the Queen of Sheba is represented as the intellectual, economic, and political equal of King Solomon, supporting the legitimacy of a country born of her reign. This level of equality is disputed by the colonialist agenda, which uses the power of art to create the seductive and sexualized figure of the queen found in Orientalist painting, thus stripping her of the three valued characteristics of a ruler and endowing her instead with a single, devious motivation.[7]

The text fulfills different needs depending on the time, place, and motivation of the reading audience. In the original period of its creation, it would have served as a flawless justification and legitimization of the current ruler by invoking an illustrious lineage and emphasizing the authenticity of the local monotheistic belief. This gives

6. Al-Johara Hassan Al-Thani, "The Queen of Sheba in Yemeni and Ethiopian Mythology," in *Africa and the Gulf Region: Blurred Boundaries and Shifting Ties*, edited by Ragaia Mustafa Abusharaf and Dale F. Eickelman (Berlin: Gerlach Press, 2015), 27.

7. Al-Johara Hassan Al-Thani, 32–33.

both the ruler and the reader validation of their worldview. To the Ethiopian church, given its special status as custodians of one of the holiest of objects in the Judeo-Christian tradition, namely, the ark of the covenant, the *Kebra Nagast* would provide documentation for the queen's original conversion. To contemporary Ethiopians, the text gives evidence of their historic significance and defines a self-image of being God's chosen people with Aksum as the new Zion. What values might such an enduring myth with powerful individuals represent to contemporary global readers?

Eva Hericks-Bares
Department of Art and Art History

[Content Notice: non-consensual sex]

from *Kebra Nagast*

24. How the Queen made ready to set out on her Journey

And the Queen said unto them, "Hearken, O ye who are my people, and give ye ear to my words. For I desire wisdom and my heart seeketh to find understanding. I am smitten with the love of wisdom, and I am constrained by the cords of understanding; for wisdom is far better than treasure of gold and silver, and wisdom is the best of everything that hath been created on the earth. Now unto what under the heavens shall wisdom be compared? It is sweeter than honey, and it maketh one to rejoice more than wine, and it illumineth more than the sun, and it is to be loved more than precious stones. And it fatteneth more than oil, and it satisfieth more than dainty meats, and it giveth [a man] more renown than thousands of gold and silver. It is a source of joy for the heart, and a bright and shining light for the eyes, and a giver of speed to the feet, and a shield for the breast, and a helmet for the head, and chainwork for the neck, and a belt for the loins. It maketh the ears to hear and hearts to understand, it is a teacher of those who are learned, and it is a consoler of those who are discreet and prudent, and it giveth fame to those who seek after it. And as for a kingdom, it cannot stand without wisdom, and riches cannot be preserved without wisdom; the foot cannot keep the place wherein it hath set itself without wisdom. And without wisdom that which the tongue speaketh is not acceptable. Wisdom is the best of all treasures. He who heapeth up gold and silver doeth so to no profit without wisdom, but he who heapeth up wisdom—no man can filch it from his heart. That which fools heap up the wise consume. And because of the wickedness of those who do evil the righteous are praised; and because of the wicked acts of fools the wise are beloved. Wisdom is an exalted thing and a rich thing: I will love her like a mother, and she shall embrace me like her child. I will follow the footprints of wisdom and she shall protect me for ever; I will seek after wisdom, and she shall be with me forever; I will follow her footprints, and she shall not cast me away; I will lean upon her, and she shall be unto me a wall of adamant; I will seek asylum with her, and she shall be unto me power and strength; I will rejoice in her, and she shall be unto me abundant grace. For it is right for us to follow the footprints of wisdom, and for the soles of our feet to stand upon the threshold of the gates of wisdom. Let us seek her, and we shall find her; let us love her, and she will not withdraw herself from us; let us pursue her, and we shall overtake her; let us ask, and we shall receive; and let us turn our hearts to her so that we may never forget her. If [we] remember her, she will have us in remembrance; and in connection with fools thou shalt not remember wisdom, for they do not hold her in honor, and she doth not love them. The honoring of wisdom is the honoring of the wise man, and the loving of wisdom is the loving of the wise man. Love the wise man and withdraw not thyself from him, and by the sight of him thou shalt become wise; hearken to the utterance of his mouth, so that thou mayest become like unto him; watch the place whereon he hath set his foot, and leave him not, so that thou mayest receive the remainder of his wisdom. And I love him merely on hearing concerning him and without seeing him, and the whole story of him that hath been told me is to me as the desire of my heart, and like water to the thirsty man."

And her nobles, and her slaves, and her handmaidens, and her counsellors answered and said unto her, "O our Lady, as for wisdom, it is not lacking in thee, and it is because of thy wisdom that thou lovest wisdom. And as for us, if thou goest we will go with thee, and if thou sittest down we will sit down with thee; our death shall be with thy death, and our life with thy life." Then the Queen made ready to set out on her journey with great pomp and majesty, and with great equipment and many preparations. For, by the Will of God, her heart desired to go to Jerusalem so that she might hear the Wisdom of Solomon; for she had hearkened eagerly. So she made ready to set out. And seven hundred and ninety-seven camels were loaded, and mules and asses innumerable were loaded, and she set out on her journey and followed her road without pause, and her heart had confidence in God.

25. How the Queen came to Solomon the King

And she arrived in Jerusalem, and brought to the King very many precious gifts which he desired to possess greatly. And he paid her great honor and rejoiced, and he gave her a habitation in the royal palace near him. And he sent her food both for the morning and evening meal, each time fifteen measures by the kori of finely ground white meal, cooked with oil and gravy and sauce in abundance, and thirty measures by the kori of crushed white meal wherefrom bread for three hundred and fifty people was made, with the necessary platters and trays, and ten stalled oxen, and five bulls, and fifty sheep, without (counting) the kids, and deer, and gazelles and fatted fowls, and a vessel of wine containing sixty gerrât measures, and thirty measures of old wine, and twenty-five singing men and twenty-five singing women, and the finest honey and rich sweets, and some of the food which he himself ate, and some of the wine whereof he drank. And every day he arrayed her in eleven garments which bewitched the eyes. And he visited her and was gratified, and she visited him and was gratified, and she saw his wisdom, and his just judgments and his splendour, and his grace, and heard the eloquence of his speech. And she marvelled in her heart, and was utterly astonished in her mind, and she recognized in her understanding, and perceived very clearly with her eyes how admirable he was; and she wondered exceedingly because of what she saw and heard with him—how perfect he was in composure, and wise in understanding, and pleasant in graciousness, and commanding in stature. And she observed the subtlety of his voice, and the discreet utterances of his lips, and that he gave his commands with dignity, and that his replies were made quietly and with the fear of God. All these things she saw, and she was astonished at the abundance of his wisdom, and there was nothing whatsoever wanting in his word and speech, but everything that he spake was perfect.

And Solomon was working at the building of the House of God, and he rose up and went to the right and to the left, and forward and backward. And he showed the workmen the measurement and weight and the space covered [by the materials], and he told the workers in metal how to use the hammer, and the drill, and the chisel (?), and he showed the stone-masons the angle [measure] and the circle and the surface [measure]. And everything was wrought by his order, and there was none who set himself in opposition to his word; for the light of his heart was like a lamp in the darkness, and his wisdom was as abundant as the sand. And of the speech of the beasts and the birds there was nothing hidden from him, and he forced the devils to obey him by his wisdom. And he did everything by means of the skill which God gave him when he made supplication to Him; for he did not ask for victory over his enemy, and he did not ask for riches and fame, but he asked God to give him wisdom and understanding whereby he might rule his people, and build His House, and beautify the work of God and all that He had given him [in] wisdom and understanding.

26. How the King held converse with the Queen

And the Queen Makeda spake unto King Solomon, saying, "Blessed art thou, my lord, in that such wisdom and understanding have been given unto thee. For myself I only wish that I could be as one of the least of thine handmaidens, so that I could wash thy feet, and hearken to thy wisdom, and apprehend thy understanding, and serve thy majesty, and enjoy thy wisdom. O how greatly have pleased me thy answering, and the sweetness of thy voice, and the beauty of thy going, and the graciousness of thy words, and the readiness thereof. The sweetness of thy voice maketh the heart to rejoice, and maketh the bones fat, and giveth courage to hearts, and goodwill and grace to the lips, and strength to the gait. I look upon thee and I see that thy wisdom is immeasurable and thine understanding inexhaustible, and that it is like unto a lamp in the darkness, and like unto a pomegranate in the garden, and like unto a pearl in the sea, and like unto the Morning Star among the stars, and like unto the light of the moon in the mist, and like unto a glorious dawn and sunrise in the heavens. And I give thanks unto Him that brought me hither and showed thee to me, and made me to tread upon the threshold of thy gate, and made me to hear thy voice."

And King Solomon answered and said unto her, "Wisdom and understanding spring from thee thyself. As for me, [I only possess them] in the measure in which the God of Israel hath given [them] to me because I asked and entreated them from Him. And thou, although thou dost not know the God of Israel, hast this wisdom which thou hast made to grow in thine heart, and [it hath made thee come] to see me, the vassal and slave of my God, and the building of His sanctuary which I am establishing, and wherein I serve and move round about my Lady, the Tabernacle of the Law of the God of Israel, the holy and heavenly Zion. Now, I am the slave of my God, and I am not a free man; I do not serve according to my own will but according to His Will. And this speech of mine springeth not from myself, but I give utterance only to what He maketh me to utter. Whatsoever He commandeth me that I do; wheresoever He wisheth me to go thither I go; whatsoever He teacheth me that I speak; that concerning which He giveth me wisdom I understand. For from being only dust He hath made me flesh, and from being only water He hath made me a solid man, and from being only an ejected drop, which shot forth upon the ground would have dried up on the surface of the earth, He hath fashioned me in His own likeness and hath made me in His own image."

27. Concerning the Labourer

And as Solomon was talking in this wise with the Queen, he saw a certain labourer carrying a stone upon his head and a skin of water upon his neck and shoulders, and his food and his sandals were [tied] about his loins, and there were pieces of wood in his hands; his garments were ragged and tattered, the sweat fell in drops from his face, and water from the skin of water dripped down upon his feet. And the labourer passed before Solomon, and as he was going by the King said unto him, "Stand still"; and the labourer stood still. And the King turned to the Queen and said unto her, "Look at this man. Wherein am I superior to this man? And in what am I better than this man? And wherein shall I glory over this man? For I am a man and dust and ashes, who to-morrow will become worms and corruption, and yet at this moment I appear like one who will never die. Who would make any complaint against God if He were to give unto this man as He hath given to me, and if He were to make me even as this man is? Are we not both of us beings, that is to say men? As is his death, [so] is my death; and as is his life [so] is my life. Yet this man is stronger to work than I am, for God giveth power to those who are feeble just as it pleaseth Him to do so." And Solomon said unto the labourer, "Get thee to thy work."

And he spoke further unto the Queen, saying, "What is the use of us, the children of men, if we do not exercise kindness and love upon earth? Are we not all nothingness, mere grass of the field, which withereth in its season and is burnt in the fire? On the earth we provide ourselves with dainty meats, and [we wear] costly apparel, but even whilst we are alive we are stinking corruption; we provide ourselves with sweet scents and delicate unguents, but even whilst we are alive we are dead in sin and in transgressions; being wise, we become fools through disobedience and deeds of iniquity; being held in honor, we become contemptible through magic, and sorcery, and the worship of idols. Now the man who is a being of honor, who was created in the image of God, if he doeth that which is good becometh like God; but the man who is a thing of nothingness, if he committeth sin becometh like unto the Devil—the arrogant Devil who refused to obey the command of his Creator—and all the arrogant among men walk in his way, and they shall be judged with him. And God loveth the lowly-minded, and those who practise humility walk in His way, and they shall rejoice in His kingdom. Blessed is the man who knoweth wisdom, that is to say, compassion and the fear of God."

And when the Queen heard this she said, "How thy voice doth please me! And how greatly do thy words and the utterance of thy mouth delight me! Tell me now: whom is it right for me to worship? We worship the sun according as our fathers have taught us to do, because we say that the sun is the king of the gods. And there are others among our subjects [who worship other things]; some worship stones, and some worship wood (i.e., trees), and some worship carved figures, and some worship images of gold and silver. And we worship the sun, for he cooketh our food, and moreover, he illumineth the darkness, and removeth fear; we call him 'Our King,' and we call him 'Our Creator,' and we worship him as our god; for no man hath told us that besides him there is another god. But we have heard that there is with you, Israel, another God Whom we do not know, and men have told us that He hath sent down to you from heaven a Tabernacle and hath given unto you a Tablet of the ordering of the angels, by the hand of Moses the Prophet. This also we have heard—that He Himself cometh down to you and talketh to you, and informeth you concerning His ordinances and commandments."

28. How Solomon gave Commandments to the Queen

And the King answered and said unto her, "Verily, it is right that they (i.e., men) should worship God, Who created the universe, the heavens and the earth, the sea and the dry land, the sun and the moon, the stars and the brilliant bodies of the heavens, the trees and the stones, the beasts and the feathered fowl, the wild beasts and the crocodiles, the fish and the whales, the hippopotamuses and the water lizards, the lightnings and the crashes of thunder, the clouds and the thunders, and the good and the evil. It is meet that Him alone we should worship, in fear and trembling, with joy and with gladness. For He is the Lord of the Universe, the Creator of angels and men. And it is He Who killeth and maketh to live, it is He Who inflicteth punishment and showeth compassion, Who raiseth up from the ground him that is in misery, Who exalteth the poor from the dust, Who maketh to be sorrowful and Who to rejoice, Who raiseth up and Who bringeth down. No one can chide Him, for He is the Lord of the Universe, and there is no one who can say unto Him, 'What hast Thou done?' And unto Him it is meet that there should be praise and thanksgiving from angels and men. And as concerning what thou sayest, that 'He hath given unto you the Tabernacle of the Law,' verily there hath been given unto us the Tabernacle of the God of Israel, which was created before all creation by His glorious counsel. And He hath made to come down to us His commandments, done into writing, so that we may know His decree and the judgment that He hath ordained in the mountain of His holiness."

And the Queen said, "From this moment I will not worship the sun, but will worship the Creator of the sun, the God of Israel. And that Tabernacle of the God of Israel shall be unto me my Lady, and unto my seed after me, and unto all my kingdoms that are under my dominion. And because of this I have found favor before thee, and before the God of Israel my Creator, Who hath brought me unto thee, and hath made me to hear thy voice, and hath shown me thy face, and hath made me to understand thy commandment." Then she returned to [her] house.

And the Queen used to go [to Solomon] and return continually, and hearken unto his wisdom, and keep it in her heart. And Solomon used to go and visit her, and answer all the questions which she put to him, and the Queen used to visit him and ask him questions, and he informed her concerning every matter that she wished to enquire about. And after she had dwelt [there] six months the Queen wished to return to her own country, and she sent a message to Solomon, saying, "I desire greatly to dwell with thee, but now, for the sake of all my people, I wish to return to my own country. And as for that which I have heard, may God make it to bear fruit in my heart, and in the hearts of all those who have heard it with me. For the ear could never be filled with the hearing of thy wisdom, and the eye could never be filled with the sight of the same."

Now it was not only the Queen who came [to hear the wisdom of Solomon], but very many used to come from cities and countries, both from near and from far; for in those days there was no man found to be like unto him for wisdom (and it was not only human beings who came to him, but the wild animals and the birds used to come to him and hearken unto his voice, and hold converse with him), and then they returned to their own countries, and every one of them was astonished at his wisdom, and marvelled at what he had seen and heard.

And when the Queen sent her message to Solomon, saying that she was about to depart to her own country, he pondered in his heart and said, "A woman of such splendid beauty hath come to me from the ends of the earth! What do I know? Will God give me seed in her?" Now, as it is said in the Book of Kings, Solomon the King was a lover of women.[8] And he married wives of the Hebrews, and the Egyptians, and the Canaanites, and the Edomites, and the Iyobawiyan (Moabites?), and from Rif [Upper Egypt] and Kuergue, and Damascus, and Surest (Syria), and women who were reported to be beautiful. And he had four hundred queens and six hundred concubines. Now this which he did was not for [the sake of] fornication, but as a result of the wise intent that God had given unto him, and his remembering what God had said unto Abraham, "I will make thy seed like the stars of heaven for number, and like the sand of the sea."[9] And Solomon said in his heart, "What do I know? Per

---

8. 1 Kings 11, 1.
9. Genesis 22:17.

adventure God will give me men children from each one of these women." Therefore when he did thus he acted wisely, saying, "My children shall inherit the cities of the enemy, and shall destroy those who worship idols."

Now those early peoples lived under the law of the flesh, for the grace of the Holy Spirit had not been given unto them. And to those [who lived] after Christ, it was given to live with one woman under the law of marriage. And the Apostles laid down for them an ordinance, saying, "All those who have received His flesh and His blood are brethren. Their mother is the Church and their father is God, and they cry out with Christ Whom they have received, saying, 'Our Father, Who art in heaven.'" And as concerning Solomon no law had been laid down for him in respect of women, and no blame can be imputed to him in respect of marrying [many] wives. But for those who believe, the law and the command have been given that they shall not marry many wives, even as Paul saith, "Those who marry many wives seek their own punishment. He who marrieth one wife hath no sin." And the law restraineth us from the sister [-in-law], in respect of the bearing of children. The Apostles speak [concerning it] in the [Book of] Councils.

29. Concerning the Three Hundred and Eighteen [Patriarchs]

Now we ordain even as did they. We know well what the Apostles who were before us spake. We the Three Hundred and Eighteen have maintained and laid down the orthodox faith, our Lord Jesus Christ being with us. And He hath directed us what we should teach, and how we should fashion the faith.

The Narrative of Solomon and the Queen of Sheba continued

And King Solomon sent a message unto the Queen, saying, "Now that thou hast come here why wilt thou go away without seeing the administration of the kingdom, and how the meal[s] for the chosen ones of the kingdom are eaten after the manner of the righteous, and how the people are driven away after the manner of sinners? From [the sight of] it thou wouldst acquire wisdom. Follow me now and seat thyself in my splendour in the tent, and I will complete thy instruction, and thou shalt learn the administration of my kingdom; for thou hast loved wisdom, and she shall dwell with thee until thine end and forever." Now a prophecy maketh itself apparent in [this] speech.

And the Queen sent a second message, saying, "From being a fool, I have become wise by following thy wisdom, and from being a thing rejected by the God of Israel, I have become a chosen woman because of this faith which is in my heart; and henceforth I will worship no other god except Him. And as concerning that which thou sayest, that thou wishest to increase in me wisdom and honor, I will come according to thy desire." And Solomon rejoiced because of this [message], and he arrayed his chosen ones [in splendid apparel], and he added a double supply to his table, and he had all the arrangements concerning the management of his house carefully ordered, and the house of King Solomon was made ready [for guests] daily. And he made it ready with very great pomp, in joy, and in peace, in wisdom, and in tenderness, with all humility and lowliness; and then he ordered the royal table according to the law of the kingdom.

And the Queen came and passed into a place set apart in splendour and glory, and she sat down immediately behind him where she could see and learn and know everything. And she marvelled exceedingly at what she saw, and at what she heard, and she praised the God of Israel in her heart; and she was struck with wonder at the splendour of the royal palace which she saw. For she could see, though no one could see her, even as Solomon had arranged in wisdom for her. He had beautified the place where she was seated, and had spread over it purple hangings, and laid down carpets, and decorated it with *miskât* (moschus), and marbles, and precious stones, and he burned aromatic powders, and sprinkled oil of myrrh and cassia round about, and scattered frankincense and costly incense in all directions. And when they brought her into this abode, the odour thereof was very pleasing to her, and even before she ate the dainty meats therein she was satisfied with the smell of them. And with wise intent Solomon sent to her meats which would make her thirsty, and drinks that were mingled with vinegar, and fish and dishes made with pepper. And this he did and he gave them to the Queen to eat. And the royal meal had come to an end three times and seven times,[10] and the administrators, and the counsellors, and the young men and the servants had departed, and the King rose up and he went to the Queen, and he said unto her—now they were alone together—"Take thou thine ease here for love's sake until daybreak." And she said unto him, "Swear to me by thy God, the God of Israel, that thou wilt not take me by force. For if I, who according to the law of men am a maiden, be seduced, I should travel on my journey [back] in sorrow, and affliction, and tribulation."

30. Concerning how King Solomon swore to the Queen

And Solomon answered and said unto her, "I swear unto thee that I will not take thee by force, but thou must swear unto me that thou wilt not take by force anything that is in my house." And the Queen laughed and said unto him, "Being a wise man why dost thou speak as a fool? Shall I steal anything, or shall I carry out of the house of the King that which the King hath not given to me? Do not imagine that I have come hither through love of riches. Moreover, my own kingdom is as wealthy as thine, and there is nothing which I wish for that I lack. Assuredly I have only come in quest of thy wisdom." And he said unto her, "If thou wouldst make me swear, swear thou to me, for a swearing is meet for both [of us], so that neither of us may be unjustly treated. And if thou wilt not make me swear I will not make thee swear." And she

10. That is, three courses and seven courses had been consumed.

said unto him, "Swear to me that thou wilt not take me by force, and I on my part will swear not to take by force thy possessions"; and he swore to her and made her swear.

And the King went up on his bed on the one side [of the chamber], and the servants made ready for her a bed on the other side. And Solomon said unto a young manservant, "Wash out the bowl and set in it a vessel of water whilst the Queen is looking on, and shut the doors and go and sleep." And Solomon spoke to the servant in another tongue which the Queen did not understand, and he did as the King commanded, and went and slept. And the King had not as yet fallen asleep, but he only pretended to be asleep, and he was watching the Queen intently. Now the house of Solomon the King was illumined as by day, for in his wisdom he had made shining pearls which were like unto the sun, and moon, and stars [and had set them] in the roof of his house.

And the Queen slept a little. And when she woke up her mouth was dry with thirst, for the food which Solomon had given her in his wisdom had made her thirsty, and she was very thirsty indeed, and her mouth was dry; and she moved her lips and sucked with her mouth and found no moisture. And she determined to drink the water which she had seen, and she looked at King Solomon and watched him carefully, and she thought that he was sleeping a sound sleep. But he was not asleep, and he was waiting until she should rise up to steal the water to [quench] her thirst. And she rose up and, making no sound with her feet, she went to the water in the bowl and lifted up the jar to drink the water. And Solomon seized her hand before she could drink the water, and said unto her, "Why hast thou broken the oath that thou hast sworn that thou wouldst not take by force anything that is in my house?" And she answered and said unto him in fear, "Is the oath broken by my drinking water?" And the King said unto her, "Is there anything that thou hast seen under the heavens that is better than water?" And the Queen said, "I have sinned against myself, and thou art free from [thy] oath. But let me drink water for my thirst." Then Solomon said unto her, "Am I perchance free from the oath which thou hast made me swear?" And the Queen said, "Be free from thy oath, only let me drink water." And he permitted her to drink water, and after she had drunk water he worked his will with her and they slept together.

And after he slept there appeared unto King Solomon [in a dream] a brilliant sun, and it came down from heaven and shed exceedingly great splendour over Israel. And when it had tarried there for a time it suddenly withdrew itself, and it flew away to the country of Ethiopia, and it shone there with exceedingly great brightness for ever, for it willed to dwell there. And [the King said], "I waited [to see] if it would come back to Israel, but it did not return. And again while I waited a light rose up in the heavens, and a Sun came down from them in the country of Judah, and it sent forth light which was very much stronger than before." And Israel, because of the flame of that Sun entreated that Sun evilly and would not walk in the light thereof. And that Sun paid no heed to Israel, and the Israelites hated Him, and it became impossible that peace should exist between them and the Sun. And they lifted up their hands against

Him with staves and knives, and they wished to extinguish that Sun. And they cast darkness upon the whole world with earthquake and thick darkness, and they imagined that that Sun would never more rise upon them. And they destroyed His light and cast themselves upon Him and they set a guard over His tomb wherein they had cast Him. And He came forth where they did not look for Him, and illumined the whole world, more especially the First Sea and the Last Sea, Ethiopia and RÔM. And He paid no heed whatsoever to Israel, and He ascended His former throne.

And when Solomon the King saw this vision in his sleep, his soul became disturbed, and his understanding was snatched away as by [a flash of] lightning, and he woke up with an agitated mind. And moreover, Solomon marvelled concerning the Queen, for she was vigorous in strength, and beautiful of form, and she was undefiled in her virginity; and she had reigned for six years in her own country, and, notwithstanding her gracious attraction and her splendid form, had preserved her body pure. And the Queen said unto Solomon, "Dismiss me, and let me depart to my own country." And he went into his house and gave unto her whatsoever she wished for of splendid things and riches, and beautiful apparel which bewitched the eyes, and everything on which great store was set in the country of Ethiopia, and camels and wagons, six thousand in number, which were laden with beautiful things of the most desirable kind, and wagons wherein loads were carried over the desert, and a vessel wherein one could travel over the sea, and a vessel wherein one could traverse the air (or winds), which Solomon had made by the wisdom that God had given unto him.

31. Concerning the sign which Solomon gave the Queen

And the Queen rejoiced, and she went forth in order to depart, and the King set her on her way with great pomp and ceremony. And Solomon took her aside so that they might be alone together, and he took off the ring that was upon his little finger, and he gave it to the Queen, and said unto her, "Take [this] so that thou mayest not forget me. And if it happen that I obtain seed from thee, this ring shall be unto it a sign; and if it be a man child he shall come to me; and the peace of God be with thee! Whilst I was sleeping with thee I saw many visions in a dream, [and it seemed] as if a sun had risen upon Israel, but it snatched itself away and flew off and lighted up the country of Ethiopia; peradventure that country shall be blessed through thee; God knoweth. And as for thee, observe what I have told thee, so that thou mayest worship God with all thy heart and perform His Will. For He punished those who are arrogant, and He showeth compassion upon those who are humble, and He removed the thrones of the mighty, and He maketh to be honored those who are needy. For death and life are from Him, and riches and poverty are bestowed by His Will. For everything is His, and none can oppose His command and His judgment in the heavens, or in the earth, or in the sea, or in the abysses. And may God be with thee! Go in peace." And they separated from each other.

32. How the Queen brought forth and came to her own Country

And the Queen departed and came into the country of Bala Zadisareya nine months and five days after she had separated from King Solomon. And the pains of childbirth laid hold upon her, and she brought forth a man child, and she gave it to the nurse with great pride and delight. And she tarried until the days of her purification were ended, and then she came to her own country with great pomp and ceremony. And her officers who had remained there brought gifts to their mistress, and made obeisance to her, and did homage to her, and all the borders of the country rejoiced at her coming. Those who were nobles among them she arrayed in splendid apparel, and to some she gave gold and silver, and hyacinthine and purple robes; and she gave them all manner of things that could be desired. And she ordered her kingdom aright, and none disobeyed her command; for she loved wisdom and God strengthened her kingdom.

And the child grew and she called his name Bayna-Lehkem. And the child reached the age of twelve years, and he asked his friends among the boys who were being educated with him, and said unto them, "Who is my father?" And they said unto him, "Solomon the King." And he went to the Queen his mother, and said unto her, "O Queen, make me to know who is my father." And the Queen spake unto him angrily, wishing to frighten him so that he might not desire to go [to his father] saying, "Why dost thou ask me about thy father? I am thy father and thy mother; seek not to know any more." And the boy went forth from her presence, and sat down. And a second time, and a third time he asked her, and he importuned her to tell him. One day, however, she told him, saying, "His country is far away, and the road thither is very difficult; wouldst thou not rather be here?" And the youth Bayna-Lehkem was handsome, and his whole body and his members, and the bearing of his shoulders resembled those of King Solomon his father, and his eyes, and his legs, and his whole gait resembled those of Solomon the King. And when he was two and twenty years old he was skilled in the whole art of war and of horsemanship, and in the hunting and trapping of wild beasts, and in everything that young men are wont to learn. And he said unto the Queen, "I will go and look upon the face of my father, and I will come back here by the Will of God, the Lord of Israel."

33. How the King of Ethiopia travelled

And the Queen called Tamrin, the chief of her caravan men and merchants, and she said unto him, "Get ready for thy journey and take this young man with thee, for he importuneth me by night and by day. And thou shalt take him to the King and shalt bring him back hither in safety, if God, the Lord of Israel, pleaseth." And she prepared a retinue suitable to their wealth and honorable condition, and made ready all the goods that were necessary for the journey, and for presenting as gifts to the King, and all that would be necessary for ease and comfort by the way. And she made ready everything for sending him away, and she gave to the officers who were to accompany him such money as they would need for him and for themselves on the journey. And she commanded them that they were not to leave him there, but only to take him to the King, and then to bring him back again to her, when he should assume the sovereignty over her land.

Now there was a law in the country of Ethiopia that [only] a woman should reign, and that she must be a virgin who had never known man, but the Queen said [unto Solomon], "Henceforward a man who is of thy seed shall reign, and a woman shall nevermore reign; only seed of thine shall reign and his seed after him from generation to generation. And this thou shalt inscribe in the letters of the rolls in the Book of their Prophets in brass, and thou shalt lay it in the House of God, which shall be built as a memorial and as a prophecy for the last days. And the people shall not worship the sun and the magnificence of the heavens, or the mountains and the forests, or the stones and the trees of the wilderness, or the abysses and that which is in the waters, or graven images and figures of gold, or the feathered fowl which fly; and they shall not make use of them in divining, and they shall not pay adoration unto them. And this law shall abide for ever. And if there be anyone who shall transgress this law, thy seed shall judge him for ever. Only give us the fringes of the covering of the holy heavenly Zion, the Tabernacle of the Law of God, which we would embrace (or, greet). Peace be to the strength of thy kingdom and to thy brilliant wisdom, which God, the Lord of Israel our Creator, hath given unto thee."

And the Queen took the young man aside and when he was alone with her she gave him that symbol which Solomon had given her, that is to say, the ring on his finger, so that he might know his son, and might remember her word and her covenant which she had made [with him], that she would worship God all the days of her life, she and those who were under her dominion, with all [the power] which God had given her. And then the Queen sent him away in peace.

And the young man [and his retinue] made straight their way and they journeyed on and came into the country of the neighbourhood of Gaza. Now this is the Gaza which Solomon the King gave to the Queen of Ethiopia. And in the Acts of the Apostles Luke the Evangelist wrote, saying, "He was the governor of the whole country of Gaza, a eunuch of Queen Hendake, who had believed on the word of Luke the Apostle."

34. How the young man arrived in his mother's country

And when the young man arrived in his mother's country he rejoiced there in the honor [which he received], and in the gifts [that were made] to him. And when the people saw him they thought him to be the perfect likeness of Solomon the King. And they made obeisance to him, and they said unto him, "Hail, the royal father liveth!" And they brought unto him gifts and offerings, fatted cattle and food, as to their king. And [the people of] the whole country of Gaza, as far as the border of Judah, were stirred up and they said, "This is King Solomon." And there were some who said, "The King is in Jerusalem building his house"—now he had finished building the House of God—and others said, "This is Solomon the King, the son of David." And they were perplexed, and they disputed with one another, and they sent off spies mounted on horses, who were to seek out King Solomon and to find out if he were actually in Jerusalem, or if he were with them [in Gaza]. And the spies came to the watchmen of the city of Jerusalem, and they found King Solomon there, and they made obeisance to him, and they said unto him, "Hail, may the royal father live! [Our] country is disturbed because there hath come into it a merchant who resembleth thee in form and appearance, without the smallest alteration or variation. He resembleth thee in noble carriage and in splendid form, and in stature and in goodly appearance; he lacked nothing in respect of these and is in no way different from thyself. His eyes are gladsome, like unto those of a man who hath drunk wine, his legs are graceful and slender, and the tower of his neck is like unto the tower of David thy father. He is like unto thee exactly in every respect, and every member of his whole body is like unto thine."

And King Solomon answered and said unto them, "Where is it then that he wished to go?" And they answered and said unto him, "We have not enquired of him, for he is awesome like thyself. But his own people, when we asked them, 'Whence have ye come and whither do ye go?' said, 'We have come from the dominions of Hendake (Candace) and Ethiopia, and we are going to the country of Judah to King Solomon'" And when King Solomon heard this his heart was perturbed and he was glad in his soul, for in those days he had no children, except a boy who was seven years old and whose name was Iyorbe'am (Rehoboam). It happened to Solomon even as Paul stateth, saying, "God hath made foolishness the wisdom of this world," [11] for Solomon had made a plan in his wisdom and said, "By one thousand women I shall beget one thousand men children, and I shall inherit the countries of the enemy, and I will overthrow [their] idols." But [God] only gave him three children. His eldest son was the King of Ethiopia, the son of the Queen of Ethiopia, and was the firstborn of whom [God] spake prophetically, "God sware unto David in righteousness, and repented not, 'Of the fruit of thy body will I make to sit upon thy throne.'" And God gave unto David His servant grace before Him, and granted unto him that there should sit upon the throne of Godhead One of his seed in the flesh, from the Virgin, and should judge the living and the dead, and reward every man according to his work, One to whom praise is meet, our Lord Jesus Christ, for ever and ever, Amen. And He gave him one on the earth who should become king over the Tabernacle of the Law of the holy, heavenly Zion, that is to say, the King of Ethiopia. And as for those who reigned, who were not [of] Israel, that was due to the transgression of the law and the commandment, whereat God was not pleased.

---

11. Corinthians 1:20.

35. How King Solomon sent to his son the commander of his army

And Solomon the King sent the commander of his army, on whose hand he was wont to lean, with gifts and meat and drink to entertain that traveller. And the commander set out with a great number of wagons, and he came to Bayna Lehkem, and embraced him, and gave him everything that Solomon the King had sent unto him. And he said unto him, "Make haste and come with me, for the heart of the King is burnt up as with fire with the love of thee. Peradventure he will find out for himself whether thou art his own son or his brother; for in thine appearance and in thy conversation (or, manner) thou art in no way different from him. And now, rise up quickly, for my lord the King said unto me, 'Haste and bring him hither to me in honor, and comfort, and with suitable service, and in joy and gladness.' " And the young man answered and said unto him, "I thank God, the Lord of Israel, that I have found grace with my lord the King without having seen his face; his word hath rejoiced me. And now I will put my trust in the Lord of Israel that He will show me the King, and will bring me back safely to my mother the Queen, and to my country Ethiopia."

And Joas (?), the son of Yodahe, the commander of the army of King Solomon, answered and said unto Bayna Lehkem, "My lord, this is a very small matter, and thou wilt find far greater joy and pleasure with my lord the King. And as concerning what thou sayest, 'my mother' and 'my country,' Solomon the King is better than thy mother, and this our country is better than thy country. And as for thy country, we have heard that it is a land of cold and cloud, and a country of glare and burning heat, and a region of snow and ice. And when the sons of Noah, Shem, and Ham, and Japhet, divided the world among them, they looked on thy country with wisdom and saw that, although it was spacious and broad, it was a land of whirlwind and burning heat, and [therefore] gave it to Canaan, the son of Ham, as a portion for himself and his seed for ever. But the land that is ours is the land of inheritance (i.e., the promised land), which God hath given unto us according to the oath that He swore to our fathers, a land flowing with milk and honey, where sustenance is [ours] without anxiety, a land that yieldeth fruit of every kind in its season without exhausting labour, a land which God keepeth watch over continually from one year to the beginning of the revolution of the next. All this is thine, and we are thine, and we will be thine heirs, and thou shalt dwell in our country, for thou art the seed of David, the lord of my lord, and unto thee belongeth this throne of Israel."

And the headmen of the merchant Tamrin answered and said unto Benaiah, "Our country is the better. The air (i.e., climate) of our country is good, for it is without burning heat and fire, and the water of our country is good, and sweet, and floweth in rivers, moreover the tops of our mountains run with water. And we do not do as ye do in your country, that is to say, dig very deep wells [in search of] water, and we do not die through the heat of the sun; but even at noonday we hunt wild animals, namely, the wild buffaloes, and gazelles, and birds, and small animals. And in the winter God taketh heed unto us from [one] year to the beginning of the course of the next. And in the springtime the people eat what they have trodden with the foot as [in] the land of Egypt, and as for our trees they produce good crops of fruit, and the wheat, and the barley, and all our fruits, and cattle are good and wonderful. But there is one thing that ye have wherein ye are better than we are, namely wisdom, and because of it we are journeying to you."

And Joas (read Benaiah), the commander of the army of King Solomon, answered [saying], "What is better than wisdom? For wisdom hath founded the earth, and made strong the heavens, and fettered the waves of the sea so that it might not cover the earth. However, rise up and let us go to my lord, for his heart is greatly moved by love for thee, and he hath sent me to bring thee [to him] with all the speed possible."

And the son of the Queen rose up, and arrayed Joas (Benaiah), the son of Yodahe, and the fifty men who were in his retinue, in gorgeous raiment, and they rose up to go to Jerusalem to Solomon the King. And when they came nigh unto the place where the horses were exercised and trained, Joas (Benaiah), the son of Yodahe, went on in front, and came to the place where Solomon was, and he told him that [the son of the Queen] was well-favored in his appearance, and that his voice was pleasant, and that he resembled him in form, and that his whole bearing was exceedingly noble. And the King said unto him, "Where is he? Did I not send thee forth to bring him as quickly as possible?" And Joas (Benaiah) said unto him, "He is here, I will bring him quickly." And Joas (Benaiah) went and said unto the young man, "Rise up, O my master, and come"; and making Bayna Lehkem to go quickly he brought him to the King's Gate. And when all the soldiers saw him they made obeisance unto him, and they said, "Behold, King Solomon hath gone forth from his abode." And when the men who were inside came forth, they marvelled, and they went back to their places, and again they saw the King upon his throne; and wondering they went forth again and looked at the young man, and they were incapable of speaking and of saying anything. And when Joas (Benaiah), the son of Yodahe, came in again to announce to the King the arrival of the young man, there was none standing before the King, but all Israel had thronged outside to see him.

36. How King Solomon held intercourse with his son

And Joas (Benaiah), the son of Yodahe, went out and brought Bayna Lehkem inside. And when King Solomon saw him he rose up, and moved forward to welcome him, and he loosed the band of his apparel from his shoulder, and he embraced him, with his hands [resting] on his breast, and he kissed his mouth, and forehead, and eyes, and he said unto him, "Behold, my father David hath renewed his youth and hath risen from the dead." And Solomon the King turned round to those who had announced the arrival of the young man, and he said unto them, "Ye said unto me, 'He resembleth thee,' but this is not my stature, but the stature of David my father in the days of his early manhood, and he is handsomer than I am." And Solomon the King rose up straightway, and he went into his chamber, and he arrayed the young man in apparel made of cloth embroidered with gold, and a belt of gold, and he set a crown upon his head, and a ring upon his finger. And having arrayed him in glorious apparel which bewitched the eyes, he seated him upon his throne, that he might be equal in rank to himself. And he said unto the nobles and officers of Israel, "O ye who treat me with contumely among yourselves and say that I have no son, look ye, this is my son, the fruit that hath gone forth from my body, whom God, the Lord of Israel, hath given me, when I expected it not."

And his nobles answered and said unto him, "Blessed be the mother who hath brought forth this young man, and blessed be the day wherein thou hadst union with the mother of this young man. For there hath risen upon us from the root of Jesse a shining man who shall be king of the posterity of our posterity of his seed. Concerning his father none shall ask questions, and none shall say, 'Whence is his coming?' Verily he is an Israelite of the seed of David, fashioned perfectly in the likeness of his father's form and appearance; we are his servants, and he shall be our king." And they brought unto him gifts, each according to his greatness. And the young man took that ring which his mother had given him when they were alone together, and he said unto his father, "Take this ring, and remember the word which thou didst speak unto the Queen, and give unto us a portion of the fringe of the covering of the Tabernacle of the Law of God, so that we may worship it all our days, and all those who are subject unto us, and those who are in the kingdom of the Queen." And the King answered and said unto him, "Why givest thou me the ring as a sign? Without thy giving me a sign I discovered the likeness of thy form to myself, for thou art indeed my son."

And the merchant Tamrin spoke again unto King Solomon, saying, "Hearken, O King, unto the message which thy handmaiden, the Queen my mistress, sent by me: 'Take this young man, anoint him, consecrate him, and bless him, and make him king over our country, and give him the command that a woman shall never again reign [in this country], and send him back in peace. And peace be with the might of thy kingdom, and with thy brilliant wisdom. As for me, I never wished that he should come where thou art, but he urged me exceedingly that he should be allowed to come to thee. And besides, I was afraid for him lest he should fall sick on the journey, either through thirst for water, or the heat of the sun, and I should bring my grey hairs down to the grave with sorrow. Then I put my trust in the holy, heavenly Zion, the Tabernacle of the Law of God, that thou wilt not withhold it in thy wisdom. For thy nobles cannot return to their houses and look upon their children, by reason of the abundance of wisdom and food which thou givest them, according to their desire, and they say, The table of Solomon is better for us than enjoying and gratifying ourselves in our own houses. And because of this I, through my fear, sought protection so that thou might not establish him with thee, but might send him [back] to me in peace, without sickness and suffering, in love and in peace, that my heart might rejoice at having encountered thee.'"

And the King answered and said unto him, "Besides travailing with him and suckling him, what else hath a woman to do with a son? A daughter belongeth to the mother, and a boy to the father. God cursed Eve, saying, 'Bring forth children in anguish and with sorrow of heart, and [after] thy bringing forth shall take place thy return to thy husband'; with an oath He said, 'Bring forth,' and having sworn, thy return to thy husband [shall follow]. As for this my son, I will not give him to the Queen, but I will make him king over Israel. For this is my firstborn, the first of my race whom God hath given me."

And then Solomon sent unto the young man evening and morning dainty meats, and apparel of honor, and gold and silver. And he said unto him, "It is better for thee to dwell here in our country with us, where the House of God is, and where the Tabernacle of the Law of God is, and where God dwelleth." And the young man his son sent a message unto him, saying, "Gold, and silver, and [rich] apparel are not wanting in our country. But I came hither in order to hear thy wisdom, and to see thy face, and to salute thee, and to pay homage to thy kingdom, and to make obeisance to thee, and then [I intended thee] to send me away to my mother and to my own country. For no man hateth the place where he was born, and everyone loveth the things of his native country. And though thou givest me dainty meats I do not love them, and they are not suitable for my body, but the meats whereby I grow and become strong are those that are gratifying to me. And although [thy] country pleaseth me even as doth a garden, yet is not my heart gratified therewith; the mountains of the land of my mother where I was born are far better in my sight. And as for the Tabernacle of the God of Israel, if I adore it where I am, it will give me glory, and I shall look upon the House of God which thou hast builded, and I will make offering and make supplication to it there. And as for Zion, the Tabernacle of the Law of God, give me [a portion of] the fringe of the covering thereof, and I will worship it with my mother and with all those who are subject to my sovereignty. For my Lady the Queen hath already rooted out all those who served idols, and those who worshipped strange objects, and stones and trees, and she hath rooted them out and hath brought them to Zion, the Tabernacle of the Law of God. For she had heard from thee and had learned, and she did according to thy word, and we worship God." And the King was not able to make his son consent to remain [in Jerusalem] with all [his persuadings].

37. How Solomon asked His Son Questions

And again Solomon held converse with his son when he was alone, and he said unto him, "Why dost thou wish to depart from me? What dost thou lack here that thou wouldst go to the country of the heathen? And what is it that driveth thee to forsake the kingdom of Israel?"

And his son answered and said unto him, "It is impossible for me to live here. Nay, I must go to my mother, thou favoring me with thy blessing. For thou hast a son who is better than I am, namely Iyorbe'am (Rehoboam) who was born of thy wife lawfully, whilst my mother is not thy wife according to the law."

And the King answered and said unto him, "Since thou speakest in this wise, according to the law I myself am not the son of my father David, for he took the wife of another man whom he caused to be slain in battle, and he begot me by her; but God is compassionate and He hath forgiven him. Who is wickeder and more foolish than men? and who is as compassionate and as wise as God? God hath made me of my father, and thee hath He made of me, according to His Will. And as for thee, O my son, thou fearer of our Lord God, do not violence to the face of thy father, so that in times to come thou mayest not meet with violence from him that shall go forth from thy loins, and that thy seed may prosper upon the earth. My son Rehoboam is a boy six years old, and thou art my firstborn son, and thou hast come to reign, and to lift up the spear of him that begot thee. Behold, I have been reigning for nine and twenty years, and thy mother came to me in the seventh year of my kingdom; and please God, He shall make me to attain to the span of the days of my father. And when I shall be gathered to my fathers, thou shalt sit upon my throne, and thou shalt reign in my stead, and the elders of Israel shall love thee exceedingly; and I will make a marriage for thee, and I will give thee as many queens and concubines as thou desirest. And thou shalt be blessed in this land of inheritance with the blessing that God gave unto our fathers, even as He covenanted with Noah His servant, and with Abraham His friend, and the righteous men their descendants after them down to David my father. Thou seest me, a weak man, upon the throne of my fathers, and thou shalt be like myself after me, and thou shalt judge nations without number, and families that cannot be counted. And the Tabernacle of the God of Israel shall belong to thee and to thy seed, whereto thou shalt make offerings and make prayers to ascend. And God shall dwell within it for ever and shall hear thy prayers therein, and thou shalt do the good pleasure of God therein, and thy remembrance shall be in it from generation to generation."

And his son answered and said unto him, "O my lord, it is impossible for me to leave my country and my mother, for my mother made me to swear by her breasts that I would not remain here but would return to her quickly, and also that I would not marry a wife here. And the Tabernacle of the God of Israel shall bless me wheresoever I shall be, and thy prayer shall accompany me whithersoever I go. I desired to see thy face, and to hear thy voice, and to receive thy blessing, and now I desire to depart to my mother in safety."

38. How the King planned to send away his son with the children of the nobles

And then Solomon the King went back into his house, and he caused to be gathered together his councillors, and his officers, and the elders of his kingdom, and he said unto them, "I am not able to make this young man consent [to dwell here]. And now, hearken ye unto me and to what I shall say unto you. Come, let us make him king of the country of Ethiopia, together with your children; ye sit on my right hand and on my left hand, and in like manner the eldest of your children shall sit on his right hand and on his left hand. Come, O ye councillors and officers, let us give [him] your firstborn children, and we shall have two kingdoms; I will rule here with you, and our children shall reign there. And I put my trust in God that a third time He will give me seed, and that a third king will be to me. Now Baltasor, the King of Rom, wisheth that I would give my son to his daughter, and to make him with his daughter king over the whole country of Rom. For besides her he hath no other child, and he hath sworn that he will only make king a man who is of the seed of David my father. And if we rule there we shall be three kings. And Rehoboam shall reign here over Israel. For thus saith the prophecy of David my father: 'The seed of Solomon shall become three heads of kingdoms upon the earth.' And we will send unto them priests, and we will ordain laws for them, and they shall worship and serve the God of Israel under the three royal heads. And God shall be praised by the race of His people Israel, and be exalted in all the earth, even as my father wrote in his Book, saying, 'Tell the nations that God is king'; and again he said, 'Announce to the peoples His work, praise Him and sing ye unto Him'; and again he saith, 'Praise God with a new song. His praise is in the congregation of the righteous, Israel shall rejoice in his Creator.' Unto us belongeth the glory of sovereignty and we will praise our Creator. And the nations who serve idols shall look upon us, and they shall fear us, and make us kings over them, and they shall praise God and fear Him. And now, come ye, let us make this young man king, and let us send him away with your children, ye who possess wealth and position. According to the position and wealth that ye have here shall your children [rule] there. And they shall see the ordering of royalty, and we will establish them according to our law, and we will direct them and give them commands and send them away to reign there."

And the priests, and the officers, and the councillors answered and said unto him, "Do thou send thy firstborn, and we will send our children also according to thy wish. Who can resist the commandment of God and the king? They are the servants of thee and of thy seed as thou hast proclaimed. If thou wishest, thou canst sell them and their mothers to be slaves; it is not for us to transgress thy command and the command of the Lord thy God." And then they made ready to do for them (i.e., their children) what it was right to do, and to send them into the country of Ethiopia, so that they might reign there and dwell there forever, they and their seed from generation to generation.

39. How they made the Son of Solomon King

And they made ready the ointment of the oil of kingship, and the sounds of the large horn, and the small horn, and the flute and the pipes, and the harp and the drum filled the air; and the city resounded with cries of joy and gladness. And they brought the young man into the Holy of Holies, and he laid hold upon the horns of the altar, and sovereignty was given unto him by the mouth of Zadok the priest, and by the mouth of Joas (Benaiah) the priest, the commander of the army of King Solomon, and he anointed him with the holy oil of the ointment of kingship. And he went out from the house of the Lord, and they called his name David, for the name of a king came to him by the law. And they made him to ride upon the mule of King Solomon, and they led him round about the city, and said, "We have appointed thee from this moment"; and then they cried out to him, "Bah [Long] live the royal father!" And there were some who said, "It is meet and right that thy dominion of Ethiopia shall be from the River of Egypt to the west of the sun (i.e., to the setting sun); blessed be thy seed upon the earth!—and from Shoa to the east of India, for thou wilt please [the people of these lands]. And the Lord God of Israel shall be unto thee a guide, and the Tabernacle of the Law of God shall be with all that thou lookest upon. And all thine enemies and foes shall be overthrown before thee, and completion and finish shall be unto thee and unto thy seed after thee; thou shalt judge many nations and none shall judge thee." And again his father blessed him and said unto him, "The blessing of heaven and earth shall be thy blessing," and all the congregation of Israel said, "Amen." And his father also said unto Zadok the priest, "Make him to know and tell him concerning the judgment and decree of God which he shall observe there" [in Ethiopia].

Kebra Nagast: The Queen of Sheba & her only son Menyelek; being the history of the departure of God & His Ark of the covenant from Jerusalem to Ethiopia, and the establishment of the religion of the Hebrews & the Solomonic line of kings in that country, translated by E. A. Wallis (Ernest Alfred Wallis) Budge, 20–54. London, Boston, Mass. [etc.] The Medici Society, limited, 1922. https://archive.org/embed/queenof shebaherooobudgrich (accessed March 19, 2020).

POST-READING PARS

1. How did your definition of origin-myth fit with the *Kebra Nagast* as an origin-myth for the Ethiopian royal lineage?
2. Identify two ways the narrative of *Kebra Nagast* speaks to aspects of Ethiopian identity.

Inquiry Corner

Content Question:	Critical Question:
Consider the wisdom comparison metaphors — for example, wisdom is: sweeter than honey, better than gold and silver, makes one rejoice more than wine, and so forth — used in the queen's initial speech. What do they tell us about the material culture of the time and which resources were valued?	How does the author justify the events leading to Menelik I's birth?
Comparative Question:	**Connection Questions:**
Compare the Queen of Sheba's journey in search of wisdom to some of the other accounts of journeys and pilgrimages we have read about in the Reader, for example, Margery Kempe and Ibn Batutta.	Do you think knowledge and wisdom necessarily require journeys? How far would you be willing to travel in the pursuit of knowledge?

from *Mishneh Torah* by Maimonides

Introduction

Maimonides was one of the most influential and prolific Jewish thinkers of the Middle Ages. His work spanned Jewish law (**halakha**), philosophy, medicine, and astronomy. Born Moshe Ben Maimon in Cordoba, Spain, in 1135 CE, he is now more popularly known as Maimonides (the Latin form of his name). His life reflects the political and intellectual challenges and opportunities of his time that required his family to flee from Cordoba to Fez, Morocco, to finally Cairo, Egypt. In Cairo, Maimonides began his great work, the **Mishneh Torah**, that took ten years to complete. How might his experience of persecution have influenced his work as a physician, rabbi, and religious scholar?

To place the Mishneh Torah in context, it is important to understand that Rabbinic civil and religious law is rooted in the **Torah** (lit. "law"), which is comprised of five books: Genesis, Exodus, Leviticus, Numbers, and Deuteronomy. An oral tradition of how to understand, interpret, and derive general legal principles from the Torah began about 300 BCE. About a thousand years before Maimonides, Rabbi Judah HaNasi, a central Jewish leader during the Roman control of Judea, was concerned that with fewer scholars, especially under Roman persecution, it was important to record the oral tradition. Over a period of fifty years, from around 170 CE to 220 CE, Rabbi Judah HaNasi wrote down the oral tradition in a massive work called the **Mishnah** (lit. "to repeat from memory"). How might this transition and transmission from oral to written medium have influenced its content? Over the next two hundred years, rabbis added commentary to the Mishnah, called the **Gemara** (lit. "study"), which attempted to fill out underlying reasoning for decisions in

Timeline

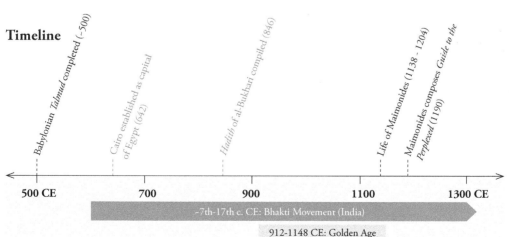

Babylonian *Talmud* completed (~500)

Cairo established as capital of Egypt (642)

Hadith of al-Bukhari compiled (846)

Life of Maimonides (1138 - 1204)

Maimonides composes *Guide to the Perplexed* (1190)

500 CE   700   900   1100   1300 CE

~7th-17th c. CE: Bhakti Movement (India)

912-1148 CE: Golden Age

the Mishnah. Together, the Mishnah and Gemara, compiled along with several more generations of commentary, are called the **Talmud**. The Talmud is a massive work of nearly two million words written in Hebrew and Aramaic that contains intergenerational debates on halakha as well as legends, biographies, ethics, and customs.

Like Rabbi Judah HaNasi, Maimonides felt he was living in a time in which Jewish scholarship was suffering. With Jewish communities experiencing persecution and forced migration, religious scholarship was on the wane. Additionally, studying Talmud takes a great deal of background knowledge and time, which these persecuted communities did not have. As Maimonides describes in the introduction to the Mishneh Torah, "In our day, severe vicissitudes prevail and all feel the pressure of hard times. . . . [The authors of the Talmud] and their compilations of laws and responses which they took care to make clear, have in our times become hard to understand."[12] So Maimonides undertook the task of extracting all of the *halakhot* (plural of *halakha*) from the Mishnah. He did not feel bound to either cite the source for any halakha nor did he obligate himself to list the *halakhot* in the order they appear in the Talmud. Each *halakha* is stated briefly and reorganized topically to create continuity and consistency. All other extraneous material, such as debates and legends, were removed. What can we infer about his intended audience and purpose here?

Called the **Mishneh Torah** (Laws of the Mishna), this library of halakhot was unlike anything found before in Jewish literature. While it did receive criticism from contemporaries who worried it might supplant the study of Talmud, the Mishneh Torah was very popular and widely distributed in the Jewish world throughout Europe, North Africa, and the Middle East. When Maimonides passed away in 1204 CE, his reputation was such that he was referred to as the "second Moses." Citations of Maimonides were so common to later generations of rabbis that they referred to him by the acronym Rambam (for Rabbi Moshe Ben Maimon).

The reading below is from the Mishneh Torah. Specifically, it is from the book **Zeraim** (seeds), the reading, taken from chapter 10, is a collection of halakha pertaining to charity and the obligations of the person asked to give to charity. In Hebrew, there is no word for charity. Rather, the word in Hebrew that has been translated as charity, **tzedakah**, literally means righteousness. Maimonides organized various legal comments and halakhot from the Talmud into ten chapters on gifts to the poor. The book addresses halakhot regarding the rights of the poor to the produce of the annual harvest as well as halakhot for farmers related to planting crops, keeping gardens, and caring for orchards. How does this larger context of the reading inform a larger or deeper interpretation of the halakhot?

The text utilizes the terms of *mitzvah* (commandment) and *mitzvot* (plural of *mitzvah*). A mitzvah is a general statement of purpose while a *halakha* is a rule,

---

12. Maimonides, *Mishneh Torah*, translated by Moses Hyamson (Jerusalem: Boys Town Jerusalem Publishers, 1962).

guide, or boundary to meet that purpose. For example, you could say that to drive safely is a mitzvah. Safe driving is a general positive social goal. The handbook of rules for drivers would be like the halakhot. They indicate how to drive safely, including what to do and what to avoid doing as a driver. Think about what the central mitzvah in the text could be.

Samuel R. Kaplan
Department of Mathematics

PRE READING PARS

1. What kinds of giving might qualify as charity?
2. How does charity relate to human dignity?

from *Mishneh Torah*: "Matnot Aniyim — Chapter 10"

Halacha 1

We are obligated to be careful with regard to the mitzvah of charity to a greater extent than all [other] positive commandments, because charity is an identifying mark for a righteous person, a descendant of Abraham, our patriarch, as [Genesis 18:19] states: "I have known him, because he commands his children... to perform charity." The throne of Israel will not be established, nor will the true faith stand except through charity, as [Isaiah 54:14] states: "You shall be established through righteousness." And Israel will be redeemed solely through charity, as [*ibid.* 1:27] states: "Zion will be redeemed through judgment and those who return to her through charity."

Halacha 2

A person will never become impoverished from giving charity. No harm nor damage will ever be caused because of charity,[13] as [ibid. 32:17] states: "And the deed of charity is peace." Everyone who is merciful evokes mercy from others, as [Deuteronomy 13:18] states: "And He shall grant you mercy and shower mercy upon you and multiply you." Whenever a person is cruel and does not show mercy, his lineage is suspect, for cruelty is found only among the gentiles, as [Jeremiah] 3:42] states: "They are cruel and will not show mercy."

The entire Jewish people and all those who attach themselves to them are as brothers, as [Deuteronomy 14:1] states: "You are children unto God your Lord." And if a brother will not show mercy to a brother, who will show mercy to them? To whom do the poor of Israel lift up their eyes? To the gentiles who hate them and pursue them? Behold their eyes are pointed to their brethren alone.

Halacha 3

Anyone who turns his eyes away from [giving] charity is described as being "rebellious" like someone who worships false divinities is described as "rebellious, as [Deuteronomy 13:14] states with regard to the worship of false divinities: "Rebellious men

---

13. On the contrary, it leads to blessing, as Proverbs 28:27 states: "He who gives to the poor will not lack."

went out." And with regard to a person who turns his eyes away from [giving] charity, [ibid. 15:9] states: "Be careful, lest a rebellious thought arise in your heart." Such a person is also called "wicked," as [Proverbs 12:10] states: "The mercies of the wicked are cruel." And he is called a sinner, as [Deuteronomy, *loc. cit.*,] states: "And he shall cry out against you to God and you will be deemed as sinning." The Holy One, blessed be He, is close to the outcry of the poor, as it is written:[14] "You hear the outcry of the poor." Therefore one must be careful with regard to their outcry, for a covenant has been established with them, as [Exodus 22:26] states: "When he will cry out to Me, I will listen, for I am compassionate."

Halacha 4

Whenever a person gives charity to a poor person with an unpleasant countenance and with his face buried in the earth, he loses and destroys his merit even if he gives him 1000 gold pieces. Instead, he should give him with a pleasant countenance and with happiness, commiserating with him about his troubles, as [Job 30:25] states: "Did I not weep for those who face difficult times; did not my soul feel sorrow for the destitute?" And he should speak to him words of sympathy and comfort, as [ibid. 29:13] states: "I would bring joy to a widow's heart."

Halacha 5

If a poor person asks one for a donation and he has nothing to give him, he should conciliate him with words. It is forbidden to scold a poor person or to raise one's voice against him while shouting, because his heart is broken and crushed, and [Psalms 51:19] states: "God will not scorn a broken and crushed heart." And [Isaiah 57:15 describes as Divine the attribute of] "reviv[ing] the spirit of the lowly and revitalize[ing] the heart of the crushed." Woe unto he who shames the poor, woe be he! Instead, one should be like a father to him, both in mercies and in words, as [Job 29:16] states: "I am a father to the destitute."

Halacha 6

A person who compels others to give charity and motivates them to do so receives a greater reward than the person who actually gives, as [alluded to by Isaiah 32:17]: "And the deed[15] of charity is peace." With regard to the collectors of charity and the

14. There is no verse that fits the wording the Rambam quotes. Commentaries have notes that Job 34:28 reads: "He hears the cry of the poor" and Psalms 22:25 states: "And when he cries out to Him, He will listen."

15. The word *ma'aseh* translated as "work" can also be interpreted as meaning "compel." In that context, the verse can be interpreted as praise for a person who compels a colleague to give charity.

like can be applied [the words of praise, Daniel 12:3]: "Those who bring merit to the many are like the stars."

Halacha 7

There are eight levels in charity, each level surpassing the other. The highest level beyond which there is none is a person who supports a Jew who has fallen into poverty [by] giving him a present or a loan, entering into partnership with him, or finding him work so that his hand will be fortified so that he will not have to ask others [for alms]. Concerning this [Leviticus 25:35] states: "You shall support him, the stranger, the resident, and he shall live among you." Implied is that you should support him before he falls and becomes needy.

Halacha 8

A lower [level] than this is one who gives charity to the poor without knowing to whom he gave and without the poor person knowing from whom he received. For this is an observance of the mitzvah for its sake alone.[16] This [type of giving was] exemplified by the secret chamber that existed in the Temple. The righteous would make donations there in secret and poor people of distinguished lineage would derive their livelihood from it in secret.

A level close to this is giving to a charity fund. A person should not give to a charity fund unless he knows that the person managing it is faithful, wise, and capable of administering it in a proper manner as Rebbe Chananya ben Tradyon was.

Halacha 9

A lower level than that is an instance when the giver knows to whom he is giving, but the poor person does not know from whom he received. An example of this were the great Sages who would go in secret and throw money into the doorways of the poor. This is a worthy way of giving charity and it is a good quality [to express] if the trustees of the charitable fund are not conducting themselves appropriately.[17]

Halacha 10

A lower level than that is an instance when the poor person knows from whom he took, but the donor does not know to whom he gave. An example of this were the

16. That is, since neither the donor nor the recipient knows the other's identity, there can be no ulterior motive involved.

17. In such an instance, it would not be desirable for a person to distribute his charity himself rather than give it to the charitable fund.

great Sages who would bundle coins in a sheet and hang them over their shoulders and the poor would come and take them so that they would not be embarrassed.

Halacha 11

A lower level than that is giving [the poor person] in his hand before he asks.[18]

Halacha 12

A lower level than that is giving him after he asks.

Halacha 13

A lower level than this is giving him less than what is appropriate, but with a pleasant countenance.

Halacha 14

A lower level than that is giving him with sadness.

Halacha 15

Great sages would give a *p'rutah* to a poor person before every prayer service and then they would pray, as [implied by Psalms 17:15]: "I will see Your countenance in righteousness."[19]

Halacha 16

A person who gives money to his sons and daughters who are past the age of majority[20] and whom he is not obligated to support in order to teach the males Torah and to direct the females in a course of upright path so that they will not become objects of derision and similarly one who gives food to his father and his mother is included among [those who give] charity. Indeed, it is a very important charity, for precedence is established on one's degree of closeness. Anyone who gives food and drink to the poor and orphans at his table,[21] he will call out to God and [God] will answer him and he will derive pleasure from Him, as [Isaiah 58:9] states: "Then you will call out and God will answer."

18. In this way, at least the poor person is not humbled by having to ask for the alms.

19. *Tzedek*, "righteousness," and *tzedakah*, "charity," share the same root.

20. Strictly speaking, this refers to children above the age of six. Today, there are many authorities who require parents to support their children until much more advanced ages.

21. That is, not only does he provide them with food, he makes them feel part of his household.

Halacha 17

Our Sages commanded that the poor and orphans should be members of a person's household rather than servants. This is preferable for him to employ these people and thus enable the descendants of Abraham, Isaac, and Jacob benefit from his possessions rather than the descendants of Cham. Whoever increases [the number of] servants in his possession adds sin and transgression to the world every day. [Conversely,] if the poor are members of one's household, at every hour he adds merits and mitzvot.

Halacha 18

A person should always construct himself and bear hardship rather than appeal to people at large and make himself a burden on the community. Our Sages commanded, saying: "Make your Sabbaths as weekdays, and do not appeal to people at large." Even a distinguished sage who becomes poor should involve himself in a profession - even a degrading one - rather than appeal to people at large. It is preferable for a person to skin the hide of animal carcasses, rather than tell people: "I am a great sage..." or "I am a priest, grant me sustenance." Our Sages commanded conducting oneself in such a manner.[22]

There were great sages who were woodchoppers, porters of beams, water-carriers for gardens, and iron-smelters and makers of charcoal, but they did not ask anything from the community, nor did they accept gifts that were given to them.

Halacha 19

Any person who does not need to take [charity] and deceives the people and takes will not reach old age and die until he requires assistance from people at large. He is among those of whom it is said [Jeremiah 17:5]: "Cursed be a person who trusts in mortals."

[Conversely,] anyone who needs to take [charity] and cannot exist unless he takes, e.g., an elderly man, sick, or beset by afflictions, but is proud and does not take is considered as a murder. He is liable for his soul and all that he has earned through his hardship is sin and guilt. But anyone who needs to take [charity], but causes himself affliction and temporarily constrains himself and lives a life of difficulty so that he will not overburden the community will not reach old age and die before he provides sustenance for others from his own means. Concerning such a person and those like him, it is stated [ibid.:7]: Blessed be a person who trusts in God."

Blessed be the Merciful One who grants assistance.

---

22. In general, the Rambam appreciated the positive dimension of earning one's livelihood through one's own efforts and not relying on others.

Maimonides. "Matnot Aniyim—Chapter 10." In *Mishneh Torah*. Translated by Eli-yahu Touger. Published and copyright by Moznaim Publications. https://www.chabad.org/library/article_cdo/aid/986711/jewish/Matnot-Aniyim-Chapter-10.htm (accessed October 10, 2020) [no page numbers on online source].

POST-READING PARS

1. Identify three levels of charitable giving outlined in the text.
2. In what ways do the halakhot address the human dignity of those experiencing poverty?

Inquiry Corner

Content Question:	**Critical Question:**
Maimonides is extracting halakhot from all over the Talmud related to charity. What might be his reasoning for placing the halakhot in the particular order in which they appear in the text?	How does the text rank different levels of charitable giving and why?
Comparative Question:	**Connection Question:**
How does the halakhot's conception of giving and receiving charity compare with views of charity, reciprocity, and generosity in some of the other traditions we encounter in this course?	If you were creating mitzvot and halakha about studying as a student, what would be the core obligation(s)?

BEYOND THE CLASSROOM

» In what ways can we show charity through the work that we choose to pursue? Must one work for a nonprofit organization in order to do this/make a difference? Why or why not?

» If giving is important to you, how could this influence or impact your career development and career decision-making? What things may you want to think about when searching for career opportunities?

from *Muqaddima* by Ibn Khaldun

SNAPSHOT BOX

LANGUAGE: Arabic

DATE: 1377 CE

LOCATION: Present-day Algeria

GENRE: Historiography

TAGS: Community; Cross-Cultural Encounters; Formations and Reformations; Historiography; Islamic World; Narrative; Power Structures; Ways of Knowing

Introduction

Wali al-Din 'Abd al-Rahman Ibn Khaldun (1332–1406) was an Arab jurist, historian, philosopher, and **Sufi** mystic who descended from a renowned family of state officials and bureaucrats. He became known as Ibn Khaldun (son of Khaldun) since he was the most famous member of the sons of the Khaldun family.

Ibn Khaldun spent his life moving between his birthplace, Tunis, and Muslim Spain, Morocco, Algeria, and Egypt in search of knowledge and power. His constant moving allowed him to study law under some of the leading Muslim jurists of the time. In larger cities, Ibn Khaldun had access to important libraries that satisfied his wide-ranging interests: from Islamic law, history, philosophy, and mysticism to numerology, divination, astrology, and magic. Ibn Khaldun's interest in this wide array of subjects illustrates a premodern approach to knowledge that embraced reason, faith, and spirituality as complementing rather than negating each other. How might this approach to knowledge differ from our contemporary approach to learning based on disciplinary boundaries?

Ibn Khaldun's itinerant life was also driven by his political ambitions. Fourteenth-century North Africa, where he would have pursued a political career, was marred by uncertainty and upheaval. This was due to a fractured political landscape of rival neighboring dynasties and the ravaging pandemic, the Great Pestilence, later known as the Black Death. Ibn Khaldun's political career suffered in these unforgiving times. His intellectual idealism along with some political missteps, drove him to leave — at times, flee — one court to serve in another.

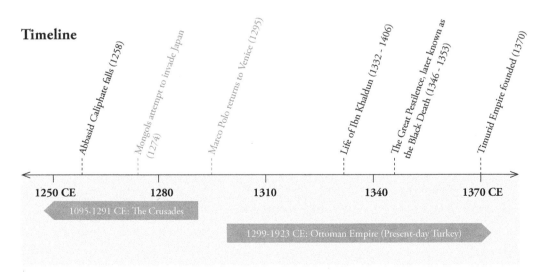

Timeline

Abbasid Caliphate falls (1258)

Mongols attempt to invade Japan (1274)

Marco Polo returns to Venice (1295)

Life of Ibn Khaldun (1332 – 1406)

The Great Pestilence, later known as the Black Death (1346 - 1353)

Timurid Empire founded (1370)

| 1250 CE | 1280 | 1310 | 1340 | 1370 CE |

1095-1291 CE: The Crusades

1299-1923 CE: Ottoman Empire (Present-day Turkey)

In 1375, Ibn Khaldun took refuge with the Berber tribe, Awlad 'Arif, in the remote mountains of Algeria. In the following four years of self-exile, he started writing *The Book of Lessons and the Record of the Causes and Consequences in the History of the Arabs, Non-Arabs, Berbers, and Their Contemporaneous Mighty Rulers*, better known as the *History of Ibn Khaldun*. It took him six years to complete his seven-volume universal history, which is an important source on the history of Muslim North Africa. Ironically, Ibn Khaldun's fame as a pioneer in the disciplines of history, sociology, and economics rests mainly on the book-long *Muqaddima* (prolegomena or introduction) to his universal history. The *Muqaddima* was a groundbreaking study of the philosophy of history that sought to understand "the causes and origins" and "the how and why of events." What do you think were some of Ibn Khaldun's reasons to begin with the philosophy of history before writing his universal history?

Ibn Khaldun thought that sound methodologies in the writing of history are necessary to form a deep and universal understanding of the past. He argued that the methodology of history, or **historiography**, required us to study the conditions and factors shaping human civilizations and social organizations. Such a study thus becomes "an independent science," which, like any other science, focuses on facts and explanations. Consequently, historians need to question inherited traditions and established accounts by examining the evidence and applying reason based on the principle of conformity with reality. After all, Ibn Khaldun argued, the rules of nature and logic apply to the past much like the present. What reasons might you give for imagining historiography as a science?

Ibn Khaldun's purpose in the study of history was to understand why states and civilizations fell. He viewed history as cyclical in nature, driven by a constant search for power. He did not distinguish the state from the civilization because people need the guidance of a ruler, who in turn derives his authority from them. Hence, the social organization with the strongest bond between the people and their leader possesses the most power. This bond is called *'asabiyya* (group feeling, solidarity), which, according to Ibn Khaldun, is strongest among desert tribes. Given his understanding of history as cyclical, he charts history through three main stages. Since the motive of *'asabiyya* is to seek power, the tribes are naturally able to take over decadent urbanized states. Once settled in the city, the tribal group feeling gradually weakens as a result of affluence and material gain. Finally, the decadent state falls to an incoming tribe with a strong group feeling. This cyclical understanding of history is a reflection of Ibn Khaldun's life experience where he witnessed the rise and fall of dynasties, the Berber tribes' takeover of urbanized states, and the ravaging effects of the Great Pestilence. Do you think Ibn Khaldun's view of history is pessimistic in nature?

Samer Traboulsi
Department of History

PRE-READING PARS

1. Identify two points to keep in mind when trying to read a text critically?
2. What are two features that a historical account should have in your opinion?

from *The Muqaddimah*

The Introduction

The excellence of historiography. An appreciation of the various approaches to history. A glimpse of the different kinds of errors to which historians are liable. Why these errors occur.

It should be known that history is a discipline that has a great number of approaches. Its useful aspects are very many. Its goal is distinguished.

History makes us acquainted with the conditions of past nations as they are reflected in their national character. It makes us acquainted with the biographies of the prophets and with the dynasties and policies of rulers. Whoever so desires may thus achieve the useful result of being able to imitate historical examples in religious and worldly matters.

The [writing of history] requires numerous sources and much varied knowledge. It also requires a good speculative mind and thoroughness, which lead the historian to the truth and keep him from slips and errors. If he trusts historical information in its plain transmitted form and has no clear knowledge of the principles resulting from custom, the fundamental facts of politics, the nature of civilization, or the conditions governing human social organization, and if, furthermore, he does not evaluate remote or ancient material through comparison with near or contemporary material, he often cannot avoid stumbling and slipping and deviating from the path of truth. Historians, Qur'an commentators and leading transmitters have committed frequent errors in the stories and events they reported. They accepted them in the plain transmitted form, without regard for its value. They did not check them with the principles underlying such historical situations, nor did they compare them with similar material. Also, they did not probe with the yardstick of philosophy, with the help of knowledge of the nature of things, or with the help of speculation and historical insight. Therefore, they strayed from the truth and found themselves lost in the desert of baseless assumptions and errors.

This is especially the case with figures, either of sums of money or of soldiers, whenever they occur in stories. They offer a good opportunity for false information and constitute a vehicle for nonsensical statements. They must be controlled and checked with the help of known fundamental facts. For example, al-Mas'udi and many other historians report that Moses counted the army of the Israelites in the desert. He had all those able to carry arms, especially those twenty years and older, pass muster. There turned out to be 600,000 or more. In this connection, al-Mas'udi forgets to take into consideration whether Egypt and Syria could possibly have held such a number of soldiers. Every realm may have as large a militia as it can hold and support, but no more. This fact is attested by well-known customs and familiar conditions. Moreover, an army of this size cannot march or fight as a unit. The whole available territory would be too small for it. If it were in battle formation, it would extend two, three, or more times beyond the field of vision. How, then, could two such parties fight with each other, or one battle formation gain the upper hand when one flank does not know what the other flank is doing! The situation at the present day testifies to the correctness of this statement. The past resembles the future more than one drop of water another.

Furthermore, the realm of the Persians was much greater than that of the Israelites. This fact is attested by Nebuchadnezzar's victory over them. He swallowed up their country and gained complete control over it. He also destroyed Jerusalem, their religious and political capital. And he was merely one of the officials of the province of Fars. It is said that he was the governor of the western border region. The Persian provinces of the two Iraqs, Khurasan, Transoxania, and the region of Derbend on the Caspian Sea were much larger than the realm of the Israelites. Yet, the Persian army did not attain such a number or even approach it. The greatest concentration of Persian troops, at al-Qadisiyyah, amounted to 120,000 men all of whom had their retainers. This is according to Sayf; who said that with their retainers they amounted to over 200,000 persons. According to 'A'ishah and al-Zuhri, the troop concentration with which Rustum advanced against Sa'd at al-Qadisiyyah amounted to only 60,000 men, all of whom had their retainers.

Then, if the Israelites had really amounted to such a number, the extent of the area under their rule would have been larger, for the size of administrative units and provinces under a particular dynasty is in direct proportion to the size of its militia and the groups that support the dynasty. Now, it is well known that the territory of the Israelites did not comprise an area larger than the Jordan province and Palestine in Syria and the region of Medina and Khaybar in the Hijaz. Also, there were only three generations between Moses and Israel, according to the best-informed scholars. Moses was the son of Amram, the son of Kohath, the son of Levi, the son of Jacob who is Israel-Allah. This is Moses' genealogy in the Torah. The length of time between Israel and Moses was indicated by al-Mas'udi when he said: 'Israel entered Egypt with his children, the tribes, and the children, when they came to Joseph numbering seventy souls. The length of their stay in Egypt until they left with Moses for the desert was two hundred and twenty years. During those years, the kings of the Copts, the Pharaohs, passed them on [as their subjects] one to the other.'

It has been assumed that this number of soldiers applied to the time of Solomon and his successors. Again, this is improbable. Between Solomon and Israel, there were only eleven generations, that is: Solomon, the son of David, the son of Jesse, the son of Obed, the son of Boaz, the son of Salmon, the son of Nahshon, the son Amminadab, the son of Ram, the son of Hezron, the son of Perez, the son of Judah, the son of Jacob. The descendants of one man in eleven generations would not branch out into such a number, as has been assumed. They might, indeed, reach hundreds or thousands. This often happens. But an increase beyond that to higher figures is improbable. Comparison with observable present-day and well-known nearby facts proves the assumption and report to be untrue. According to the definite statement of the Israelite stories, Solomon's army amounted to 12,000 men, and his horses numbered 1,400, which were stabled at his palace. This is the correct information. No attention should be paid to nonsensical statements by the common run of informants. In the days of Solomon, the Israelite state saw its greatest flourishing and their realm its widest extension.

Whenever contemporaries speak about the dynastic armies of their own or recent times, and whenever they engage in discussions about Muslim or Christian soldiers, or when they get to figuring the tax revenues and the money spent by the government, the outlays of extravagant spenders, and the goods that rich and prosperous men have in stock, they are quite generally found to exaggerate, to go beyond the bounds of the ordinary, and to succumb to the temptation of sensationalism. When the officials in charge are questioned about their armies, when the goods and assets of wealthy people are assessed, and when the outlays of extravagant spenders are looked at in ordinary light, the figures will be found to amount to a tenth of what those people have said. The reason is simple. It is the common desire for sensationalism, the ease with which one may just mention a higher figure, and the disregard of reviewers and critics. This leads to failure to exercise self-criticism about one's errors and intentions, to demand from oneself moderation and fairness in reporting, to reapply oneself to study and research. Such historians let themselves go and made a feast of untrue statements. ('They procure for themselves entertaining stories in order to lead others away from the path of God.')[23] This is a bad enough business.

It may be said that the increase of descendants to such a number would be prevented under ordinary conditions which, however do not apply to the Israelites. The increase in their case would be a miracle in accordance with the tradition which said that one of the things revealed to their forefathers, the prophets Abraham, Isaac, and Jacob, was that God would cause their descendants to increase until they were more numerous than the stars of heaven and the pebbles of the earth. God fulfilled this promise to them as an act of divine grace bestowed upon them and as an extraordinary miracle in their favor. Thus, ordinary conditions could not hinder it and nobody should speak against it.

Someone might come out against this tradition with the argument that it occurs only in the Torah which, as is well known, was altered by the Jews. The reply to this argument would be that the statement concerning the alteration of the Torah by the Jews is unacceptable to thorough scholars and cannot be understood in its plain

23. Qur'anic verse (Q 31:6).

meaning, since custom prevents people who have a revealed religion from dealing with their divine scriptures in such a manner. Thus, great increase in numbers in the case of the Israelites would be an extraordinary miracle. Custom, in the proper meaning of the word, would prevent anything of the sort from happening to other peoples.

It is true that a movement of [such a large group] would hardly be possible, but none took place, and there was no need for one. It is also true that each realm has only its particular number of militia [sic]. But the Israelites at first were no militiamen and had no dynasty. Their numbers increased that much, so that they could gain power over the land of Canaan which God had promised them and territory of which He had purified for them. All these things are miracles. God guides to the truth.

[...]

Another fictitious story of the historians, which they all report, concerns the reason for al-Rashid's destruction of the Barmakids. It is the story of al-Abbasah, al-Rashid's sister, and Ja'far bin Yahya bin Khalid, his minister. Al-Rashid is said to have worried about where to place them when he was drinking wine with them. He wanted to receive them together in his company. Therefore, he permitted them to conclude a marriage that was not consummated. Al-Abbasah then tricked Ja'far in her desire to be alone with him, for she had fallen in love with him. Ja'far finally had intercourse with her—it is assumed, when he was drunk—and she became pregnant. The story was reported to al-Rashid who flew into a rage.

This story is irreconcilable with al-Abbas's position, her religiousness, her parentage, and her exalted rank. She was a descendant of 'Abdallah bin Abbas and separated from him by only four generations, and they were the most distinguished and greatest men in Islam after him. Al-Abbaah was the daughter of Muhammad al-Mahdi, the son of Abu Ja'far Abdallah al-Mansur, the son of Muhammad al-Sajjad, the son of the Father of the Caliphs Ali. Ali was the son of Abdallah, the Interpreter of the Qur'an, the son of the Prophet's uncle, al-Abbas. Al-Abbasah was the daughter of a caliph and the sister of a caliph. She was born to royal power, into the prophetical succession [the caliphate], and was descended from the men around Muhammad and his uncles. She was connected by birth with the leadership of Islam, the light of the revelation, and the place where the angels descended to bring the revelation. She was close in time to the desert attitude of true Arabism, to that simple state of Islam still far from the habits of luxury and lush pastures of sin. Where should one look for chastity and modesty, if she did not possess them? Where could cleanliness and purity be found, if they no longer existed in her house? How could she link her pedigree with that of Ja'far bin Yahya and stain her Arab nobility with a Persian client? His Persian ancestor had been acquired as a slave, or taken as a client, by one of her ancestors, an uncle of the Prophet and noble Qurashite, and all Ja'far did was that he together with his father was drawn along [by the growing fame of] the 'Abbasid dynasty and thus prepared for and elevated to a position of nobility. And how could it be that al-Rashid, with his high-mindedness and great pride, would permit himself to become related by marriage to Persian clients! If a critical person looks at this story in all fairness and compares al-Abbasah with the daughter of a great ruler of his own time, he must find it disgusting and unbelievable that she could have done such a thing with one of the clients of her dynasty and while her family was in power. He would insist that the story be considered untrue. And who could compare with al-Abbasah and al-Rashid in dignity!

The reason for the destruction of the Barmakids was their attempt to gain control over the dynasty and their retention of the tax revenues. This went so far that when al-Rashid wanted even a little money, he could not get it. They took his affairs out of his hands and shared with him in his authority. He had no say with them in the affairs of his realm. Their influence grew, and their fame spread. They filled the positions and ranks of the government with their own children and creatures who became high officials, and thus barred all others from the positions of vizier, secretary, army commander, doorkeeper, and from the military and civilian administration. It is said that in the palace of al-Rashid, there were twenty-five high officials, both military and civilian, all children of Yahya bin Khalid. There, they crowded the people of the dynasty and pushed them out by force. They could do that because of the position of their father, Yahya, mentor to Harun both as crown prince and as caliph. Harun practically grew up in his lap and got all his education from him. Harun let him handle his affairs and used to call him 'father.' As a result, the Barmakids, and not the government, wielded all the influence. Their presumption grew. Their position became more and more influential. They became the center of attention. All obeyed them. All hopes were addressed to them. From the farthest borders, presents and gifts of rulers and amirs were sent to them. The tax money found its way into their treasury, to serve as an introduction to them and to procure their favor. They gave gifts to and bestowed favors upon the men of the Shi'a and upon important relatives of the Prophet. They gave the poor from the noble families related to the Prophet something to earn. They freed the captives. Thus, they were given praise as was not given to their caliph. They showered privileges and gifts upon those who came to ask favors from them. They gained control over villages and estates in the open and near the main cities in every province.

Eventually, the Barmakids irritated the inner circle. They caused resentment among the elite and aroused the displeasure of high officials. Jealousy and envy of all sorts began to show themselves, and the scorpions of intrigue crept into their soft beds in the government. The Qahtabah family, Ja'far's maternal uncles, led intrigues against them. Feelings for blood ties and relationship could not move or sway the Qahtabahs from the envy which was so heavy on their hearts. This joined with their master's incipient jealousy, with his dislike of restrictions and high-handedness, and with his latent resentment aroused by small acts of presumptuousness on the part of the Barmakids. When they continued to flourish, as they did, they were led to gross insubordination.

Ja'far himself paved the way for his own and his family's undoing, which ended with the collapse of their exalted position, with the heavens falling in upon them and the earth's sinking with them and their house. Their days of glory became a thing of the past, an example to later generations.

Close examination of their story, scrutinizing the ways of government and their own conduct, discloses that all this was natural and is easily explained. One understands that it was only jealousy and struggle for control on the part of the caliph and his subordinates that killed them. Another factor was the verses that enemies of the Barmakids among the inner circle surreptitiously gave the singers to recite, with the intention that the caliph should hear them and his stored-up animosity against them be aroused. These are the verses:

Would that Hind could fulfil her promise to us
And deliver us from our predicament,
And for once act on her own.
The impotent person is he who never acts on his own.

When al-Rashid heard these verses, he exclaimed: 'Indeed, I am just such an impotent person.' By this and similar methods, the enemies of the Barmakids eventually succeeded in arousing al-Rashid's latent jealousy and in bringing his terrible vengeance upon them. God is our refuge from men's desire for power and from misfortune.

The stupid story of al-Rashid's winebibbing and his getting drunk in the company of boon companions is really abominable. It does not in the least agree with al-Rashid's attitude toward the fulfilment of the requirements of religion and justice incumbent upon caliphs. He consorted with religious scholars and saints. He wept when he heard their sermons. Then, there is his prayer in Mecca when he circumambulated the Kaaba. He was pious, observed the times of prayer, and attended the morning prayer at its earliest hour. He used to go on raids [against unbelievers] one year and to make the pilgrimage to Mecca the next. He once rebuked his jester, Ibn Abi Maryam, who made an unseemly remark to him during prayer. When Ibn Abi Maryam heard al-Rashid recite: 'How is it that I should not worship Him who created me?' he said: 'Indeed, I do not know why.' 'Jokes even at prayer?' he said. 'Beware, beware of the Qur'an and Islam. Apart from that, you may do whatever you wish.'

Furthermore, al-Rashid possessed a good deal of learning and simplicity, because his epoch was close to that of his forebears who had those qualities. The time between him and his grandfather, al-Mansur, was not a long one. He was a young lad when al-Mansur died. Al-Mansur possessed a good deal of learning and religion.

His son, al-Mahdi, al-Rashid's father, experienced the austerity of al-Mansur, who would not use public funds to provide new clothes for his family. One day, al-Mahdi came to him when he was at his office discussing with the tailors the patching of his family's worn garments. Al-Mahdi did not relish that and said: 'O Commander of the Faithful, this year I shall pay for the family's clothes from my own income.' Al-

Mansur's reply was: 'Do that.' He did not prevent him from paying himself but would not permit any public Muslim money to be spent for that purpose.

Khaldūn, 'Abd al-Rahman ibn, "The Introduction." In *The Muqaddimah*, edited by N. J. Dawood, translated by Franz Rosenthal. Princeton: Princeton University Press, 1958, 1967.

POST-READING PARS

1. Identify two points Ibn Khaldun considers essential in his writing about history.
2. Identify one reason that Ibn Khaldun offers for why history is important.

Inquiry Corner

Content Questions:	**Critical Question:**
What are the important methods Ibn Khaldun urges us to use in reading and interpreting history? What is an undeniable reason Ibn Khadun gives for a person to be considered pious?	How can Ibn Khaldun be a critical scholar who relied on evidence and reason, and a devout Muslim scholar and a mystic at the same time?
Comparative Question:	**Connection Question:**
How would Ibn Khaldun evaluate Procopius's *Secret History*?	How might Ibn Khaldun's methods apply to our contemporary attempts at the retelling of history from the perspectives of the underrepresented?

BEYOND THE CLASSROOM

» What value does exaggeration play in today's society? How does hyperbole rule current discourse?
» What is the value of reflection? How does looking back at our experiences help to inform our future?

Sunjata (Introduction only)

Introduction

Sunjata is an epic narrative and an origin story that emerges from the Mande people in sub-Saharan West Africa. It tells us about events that occurred in the thirteenth century, about the birth of Sundiata Keita (circa 1216–1255), about how he overcame many obstacles and eventually established one of the greatest empires of the premodern world, the Mali Empire. *Sunjata* offers deep insight into various facets of the lives of the Mande people: their social organization, cultural and complex belief systems, kinship structures, practices of reciprocity, gender dynamics, and Indigenous epistemologies, to name a few. At the same time, this epic also offers a greater scope to understand the larger political landscape and models of governance in West Africa across centuries. In your experience, is it typical for epics to offer both an in-depth local as well as an expansive perspective?

The oral narrative of *Sunjata* has been carried, preserved, and transmitted by a lineage of storytellers and singers known as *jeli* in Manding or, more widely, as **griots**. Griots are a rich cultural voice. They are at once historians, poets, musicians, praise singers, counselors, and repositories of traditions and knowledge. Within the epic itself, griots play an important role in influencing the events and moving the plot of the narrative forward. While griots were traditionally considered to be a hereditary class with knowledge passed on only from father to son, there are female griots today as well. The epic of *Sunjata* has been passed down orally from one generation of griots to the next for several centuries

SNAPSHOT BOX
LANGUAGE: Mande
DATE: 13th century CE
LOCATION: Mali Empire
GENRE: Epic, origin narrative
Ethnic identity: Mande/Manding
CONTEXTUAL INFORMATION: variant spelling of Sunjata is Sundiata
TAGS: Agriculture, Land, and Food; Authority and Institution; Empire; Epic; Formations and Reformations; Music and Entertainment; Myth and Legend; Nature and Sacred; Orality; Poetry; Ritual and Practice

Timeline

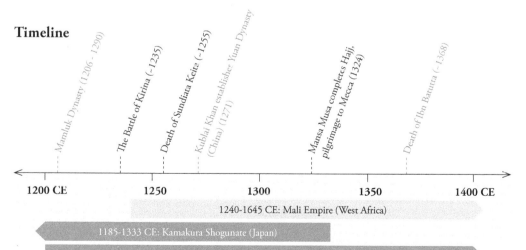

and was eventually transcribed or written down. Multiple iterations of the oral epic continue to be told today.

This epic poem is traditionally sung to the accompaniment of indigenous musical instruments, such as the *kora* (a lute-like twenty-one string instrument) and the *balafon* (a gourd-resonated xylophone). A quick internet search will give you an opportunity to listen to these instruments being played and give insight into the rich aesthetic, sensory experience that accompanies the singing and the reception of this epic. While entertaining, the music also adds texture and nuance to the narrative and becomes yet another medium for communication. For example, the music can increase in tempo and rise to a crescendo during the description of a battle scene and add to the affective/emotional responses a listener might experience. Additionally, music also aids in the memorization and transmission, and therefore the preservation of this epic. How might your experience of listening to a story be enhanced if it is narrated with musical accompaniment? Why is it easier sometimes to remember songs than orated speeches?

When sung aloud in front of an audience, this epic becomes a performance. This performance is often episodic, that is, different parts or episodes of the epic are performed at a given time. The griot may repeat certain phrases, using different names for the same historical figure depending on what part of the story is being emphasized. For instance, in various versions of this epic and even within the same version, we find Sunjata referred to as Mari Jata, Sogolon Jara, Simbon, and other praise names at different times. What do you think happens when an oral performance like this gets written down? What is added and what is lost?

There exist many versions of this epic. You can find several written versions and translations online today, both in prose/novelized and poetry forms. The version currently read at UNC Asheville is a translation based on a live oral performance by Djanka Tassey Condé (d. 1997) who was descended from a long line of griots in present-day Guinea. Since the epic has no single author, the versions we read today are often known and identified by the name of the translator or editor. This allows us to consider a host of questions especially about texts with a rich oral history: Who owns the story and who decides which version is more "authentic" than another? Whose name should appear on the published text? What do you think might be the challenges of accurately translating an epic that has such a long and complex transmission history? As readers how do we engage ethically and conscientiously with such a dynamic epic? What kind of affective and cognitive readiness do you think is required for a meaningful and deep engagement with this epic?

Renuka Gusain
Humanities Program

Source adopted at UNC Asheville:
Sunjata: A New Prose Version. Edited and translated, with an Introduction, by David C. Conrad. Hackett Publishing Company, Indianapolis, 2016.
[Content Notice: nonconsensual sex in some other translations]

from *The Travels* by Ibn Battuta

Introduction

While many of us are familiar with the name Marco Polo in the context of travel writing, the name Ibn Battuta—medieval world traveler extraordinaire—and his accounts are largely unknown. He was born in Tangier in what is today Northern Morocco, on the Straits of Gibraltar across from Spain. In his lifetime he traveled from the west coast of Africa to the east coast of China. However, even in his own era, Ibn Battuta was not as widely influential as his transmediterranean counterpart. What might be a reason for Ibn Battuta's relative obscurity?

Ibn Battuta's dictated travelogue recording his journeys spent almost half a millennium tucked away and forgotten in libraries and archives across the Near East. It was rediscovered in the nineteenth century and translated into French and German, and then English. The existence of the written record of Battuta's travels is itself a story against all odds: first, he had to survive the numerous illnesses and various dangers (including being shipwrecked) that were associated with travel in the fourteenth century. Second, as Ibn Battuta could not write himself, it was only recorded because the Sultan of Morocco, who had listened to the story, found it of merit and ordered it written down and transcribed by a young writer named Ibn Juzayy. This particular genre of travelogue is specific to the Islamic world, where it is known as **Rihla**. It combines the regular descriptive travel writing with commentary on people and practices in the many regions of **Dar al-Islam** (the house of Islam).

SNAPSHOT BOX
LANGUAGE: **Arabic**
DATE: **c. 1354 CE**
LOCATION: **Fez, North Africa**
GENRE: **Travelogue (Rihla)**
Ethnic identity: **Maghribi (North African)**
TAGS: **Agriculture, Land, and Food; Cross-Cultural Encounters; Islamic World; Narrative; Pilgrimage**

Timeline

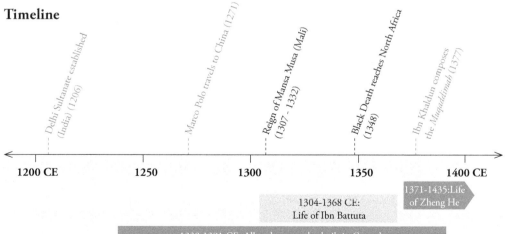

During this era, most individuals taking on the challenges of travel were motivated either by economic reasons — especially trade — or by religious ones, such as the **Hajj**. Hajj is one of the five pillars of Islam, a pilgrimage to Mecca that every able Muslim should undertake once in their lives. Ibn Battuta recounts that his initial journey was "with the intention of making the Pilgrimage." Starting from Tangier he traveled first across North Africa and spent two months in Egypt, then ventured on to explore the architectural marvels of Jerusalem and Damascus, before he joined the annual pilgrim caravan setting out for Medina and Mecca. Eventually, he made it to his destination and thus completed the religious requirement. By this time, Ibn Battuta had made acquaintances who encouraged him to continue on farther east to Asia. Given that he was only twenty-two years old at the time of his initial journey, what might have influenced him to undertake such a risk-fraught venture that he had an entire lifetime to complete?

After returning from his eastward journeys, Ibn Battuta traveled farther south on the African continent. The appeal of traveling to the east can be understood when we consider the stories told by those who traded along the Silk Road about the wonders and art of those places. However, the stories that came from the caravans trading to the south, across the Sahara Desert, did not include accounts of architectural marvels. Therefore, the interest in journeying there in 1354 had to be motivated by a different curiosity. In fact, in 1324 (or two years before Ibn Battuta originally visited Cairo), the king of Mali — Mansa Musa — had also stopped in Cairo on his pilgrimage to Mecca. He had brought with him such enormous quantities of gold, as well as an immense entourage (according to sources this included "thousands of slaves, soldiers, wives, and officials"), that the gold market was depressed for decades to come. This account of the ruler's fantastic wealth would have been impressive and compelling to Ibn Battuta. Further, the knowledge that the West African kingdom was also the supplier of other luxury items, such as ivory and ostrich feathers, could have been enough to make the now-seasoned traveler curious about the place that exported such exclusivity — even without boasting of such historic sites as he had encountered on his previous journeys.

To understand how these kinds of travel were possible in the fourteenth century, it is important to consider that there were several circumstances that aided a traveler like Ibn Battuta — including, but not limited to the well-established pilgrimage routes he could follow, the existence of a **lingua franca** (shared language — Arabic was used throughout Dar al-Islam, lands in which Muslims are free to practice their religion), diplomatic gift giving practices that were pervasive in the medieval Islamic world, as well as periods of relative peace and prosperity in the regions he explored. In the end, Ibn Battuta covered more than 75,000 miles in his thirty years of travel and recounted his experiences in an account originally titled *A Gift to Those Who Contemplate the Wonders of Cities and the Marvels of Traveling.*

Eva Hericks-Bares
Department of Art and Art History

[Content Notice: outdated racialized language]

PRE-READING PARS

1. Which place would motivate you to leave everything behind (home, family, and friends—not to mention comforts and conveniences) and set out on a journey in the excess of 4000 miles long?

2. Consider the most exciting trip you've ever taken and write down three reasons why it was so interesting.

3. List any two challenges you faced during your exciting trip and what you did to overcome them.

from *The Travels*

Ibn Battuta arrives at the city of Mali, capital of the kingdom of Mali

Thus I reached the city of Malli [Mali], the capital of the king of the blacks. I stopped at the cemetery and went to the quarter occupied by the whites, where I asked for Muhammad ibn al-Faqih. I found that he had hired a house for me and went there. His son-in-law brought me candles and food, and the next day Ibn al-Faqih himself came to visit me, with other prominent residents. I met the qadi of Malli, 'Abd ar-Rahman, who came to see me; he is a negro, a pilgrim, and a man of fine character. I also met the interpreter Dugha, who is one of the principal men among the blacks. All these persons sent me hospitality-gifts of food and treated me with the utmost generosity—may God reward them for their kindnesses!

Ten days after our arrival we ate a gruel made of a root resembling colocasia, which is preferred by them to all other dishes. We all fell ill—there were six of us—and one of our number died. I for my part went to the morning prayer and fainted there. I asked a certain Egyptian for a loosening remedy and he gave me a thing called "bay-dar," made of vegetable roots, which he mixed with aniseed and sugar, and stirred in water. I drank it off and vomited what I had eaten, together with a large quantity of bile. God preserved me from death but I was ill for two months.

Ibn Battuta meets the king of Mali

The sultan of Malli is Mansa Sulayman, "mansa" meaning [in Mandingo] sultan, and Sulayman being his proper name. He is a miserly king, not a man from whom one might hope for a rich present. It happened that I spent these two months without seeing him, on account of my illness. Later on he held a banquet in commemoration of our master [the late sultan of Morocco] Abu'l-Hasan, to which the commanders, doctors, qadi and preacher were invited, and I went along with them. Reading-desks were brought in, and the Koran was read through, then they prayed for our master Abu'l-Hasan and also for Mansa Sulayman.

When the ceremony was over I went forward and saluted Mansa Sulayman. The qadi, the preacher, and Ibn al-Faqih told him who I was, and he answered them in their tongue. They said to me, "The sultan says to you 'Give thanks to God,'" so I said, "Praise be to God and thanks under all circumstances." When I withdrew the [sultan's] hospitality gift was sent to me. It was taken first to the qadi's house, and the qadi sent it on with his men to Ibn al-Faqih's house. Ibn al-Faqih came hurrying out of his house barefooted, and entered my room saying, "Stand up; here comes the sultan's stuff and gift to you." So I stood up thinking—since he had called it "stuff"—that it consisted of robes of honor and money, and lo!, it was three cakes of bread, and a piece of beef fried in native oil, and a calabash of sour curds. When I saw this I burst out laughing, and thought it a most amazing thing that they could be so foolish and make so much of such a paltry matter.

The court ceremonial of king Sulayman of Mali

On certain days the sultan holds audiences in the palace yard, where there is a platform under a tree, with three steps; this they call the "pempi." It is carpeted with silk and has cushions placed on it. [Over it] is raised the umbrella, which is a sort of pavilion made of silk, surmounted by a bird in gold, about the size of a falcon. The sultan comes out of a door in a corner of the palace, carrying a bow in his hand and a quiver on his back. On his head he has a golden skull-cap, bound with a gold band which has narrow ends shaped like knives, more than a span in length. His usual dress is a velvety red tunic, made of the European fabrics called "mutanfas." The sultan is preceded by his musicians, who carry gold and silver guimbris [two-stringed guitars], and behind him come three hundred armed slaves. He walks in a leisurely fashion, affecting a very slow movement, and even stops from time to time. On reaching the pempi he stops and looks round the assembly, then ascends it in the sedate manner of a preacher ascending a mosque-pulpit. As he takes his seat the drums, trumpets, and bugles are sounded. Three slaves go out at a run to summon the sovereign's deputy and the military commanders, who enter and sit down. Two saddled and bridled horses are brought, along with two goats, which they hold to serve as a protection against the evil eye. Dugha stands at the gate and the rest of the people remain in the street, under the trees.

The negroes are of all people the most submissive to their king and the most abject in their behaviour before him. They swear by his name, saying "Mansa Sulayman ki" [in Mandingo, "the emperor Sulayman has commanded"]. If he summons any of them while he is holding an audience in his pavilion, the person summoned takes off his clothes and puts on worn garments, removes his turban and dons a dirty skullcap, and enters with his garments and trousers raised knee-high. He goes forward in an attitude of humility and dejection and knocks the ground hard with his elbows, then stands with bowed head and bent back listening to what he says. If anyone addresses the king and receives a reply from him, he uncovers his back and throws dust over his head and back, for all the world like a bather splashing himself with water. I used to wonder how it was they did not blind themselves. If the sultan delivers any remarks during his audience, those present take off their turbans and put them down, and listen in silence to what he says.

Sometimes one of them stands up before him and recalls his deeds in the sultan's service, saying, "I did so-and-so on such a day," or, "I killed so-and-so on such a day." Those who have knowledge of this confirm his words, which they do by plucking the cord of the bow and releasing it [with a twang], just as an archer does when shooting an arrow. If the sultan says, "Truly spoken," or thanks him, he removes his clothes and "dusts." That is their idea of good manners.

Festival ceremonial

I was at Malli during the two festivals of the sacrifice and the fast-breaking. On these days the sultan takes his seat on the pempi after the midafternoon prayer. The armour-bearers bring in magnificent arms—quivers of gold and silver, swords ornamented with gold and with golden scabbards, gold and silver lances, and crystal maces. At his head stand four amirs driving off the flies, having in their hands silver ornaments resembling saddle-stirrups. The commanders, qadi and preacher sit in their usual places.

The interpreter Dugha comes with his four wives and his slave-girls, who are about a hundred in number. They are wearing beautiful robes, and on their heads they have gold and silver fillets, with gold and silver balls attached. A chair is placed for Dugha to sit on. He plays on an instrument made of reeds, with some small calabashes at its lower end, and chants a poem in praise of the sultan, recalling his battles and deeds of valour. The women and girls sing along with him and play with bows. Accompanying them are about thirty youths, wearing red woollen tunics and white skull-caps; each of them has his drum slung from his shoulder and beats it. Afterwards come his boy pupils who play and turn wheels in the air, like the natives of Sind. They show a marvellous nimbleness and agility in these exercises and play most cleverly with swords. Dugha also makes a fine play with the sword. Thereupon the sultan orders a gift to be presented to Dugha and he is given a purse containing two hundred mithqals of gold dust and is informed of the contents of the purse before all the people. The commanders rise and twang their bows in thanks to the sultan. The next day each one of them gives Dugha a gift, every man according to his rank. Every Friday after the 'asr prayer, Dugha carries out a similar ceremony to this that we have described.

On feast-days after Dugha has finished his display, the poets come in. Each of them is inside a figure resembling a thrush, made of feathers, and provided with a wooden head with a red beak, to look like a thrush's head. They stand in front of the sultan in this ridiculous make-up and recite their poems. I was told that their poetry is a kind of sermonizing in which they say to the sultan: "This pempi which you occupy was that whereon sat this king and that king, and such and such were this one's noble actions and such and such the other's. So do you too do good deeds whose memory will outlive you." After that the chief of the poets mounts the steps of the pempi and lays his head on the sultan's lap, then climbs to the top of the pempi and lays his head first on the sultan's right shoulder and then on his left, speaking all the while in their tongue, and finally he comes down again. I was told that this practice is a very old custom amongst them, prior to the introduction of Islam, and that they have kept it up.

Ibn Battuta judges the character of the people of Mali

The negroes possess some admirable qualities. They are seldom unjust, and have a greater abhorrence of injustice than any other people. Their sultan shows no mercy to anyone who is guilty of the least act of it. There is complete security in their country. Neither traveller nor inhabitant in it has anything to fear from robbers or men of violence. They do not confiscate the property of any white man who dies in their country, even if it be uncounted wealth. On the contrary, they give it into the charge of some trustworthy person among the whites, until the rightful heir takes possession of it. They are careful to observe the hours of prayer, and assiduous in attending them in congregations, and in bringing up their children to them.

Their piety

On Fridays, if a man does not go early to the mosque, he cannot find a corner to pray in, on account of the crowd. It is a custom of theirs to send each man his boy [to the mosque] with his prayer-mat; the boy spreads it out for his master in a place befitting him [and remains on it] until he comes to the mosque. Their prayer-mats are made of the leaves of a tree resembling a date-palm, but without fruit.

   Another of their good qualities is their habit of wearing clean white garments on Fridays. Even if a man has nothing but an old worn shirt, he washes it and cleans it, and wears it to the Friday service. Yet another is their zeal for learning the Koran by heart. They put their children in chains if they show any backwardness in memorizing it, and they are not set free until they have it by heart. I visited the qadi in his house on the day of the festival. His children were chained up, so I said to him, "Will you not let them loose?" He replied, "I shall not do so until they learn the Koran by heart."

The nakedness of the women

Among their bad qualities are the following. The women servants, slave-girls, and young girls go about in front of everyone naked, without a stitch of clothing on them. Women go into the sultan's presence naked and without coverings, and his daughters also go about naked. Then there is their custom of putting dust and ashes on their heads, as a mark of respect, and the grotesque ceremonies we have described when the poets recite their verses. Another reprehensible practice among many of them is the eating of carrion, dogs, and asses.

Ibn Battuta leaves the city of Mali

The date of my arrival at Malli was 14th Jumada I, 53 [AH 753, June 28, 1352], and of my departure from it 22nd Muharram of the year 54 [AH 754, February 27, 1353].

Battuta, Ibn. "Ibn Battuta Arrives at the City of Mali, Capital of the Kingdom of Mali." In *Ibn Battúta: Travels in Asia and Africa, 1325–1354*, translated by H. A. R. Gibb, 323–35. London: Broadway House, 1929.

POST-READING PARS

1. Identify two characteristics that help us understand what kind of a traveler Ibn Battuta might have been?

2. What do you think might have been some of Ibn Battuta's expectations as he embarked on his journeys?

3. Identify one challenge that Ibn Battuta faced and how he managed to overcome it.

Inquiry Corner

Content Question:	Critical Question:
What are some of the dangers of medieval travel according to Ibn Battuta?	This is an eyewitness account written down by another person years after the original experience—which elements appear to be fact, which seem to be fiction, and which could be the result of the passage of time between the actual event and its retelling?
Comparative Question:	**Connection Question:**
How does Ibn Battuta's experiences in Mali compare to the narratives about Mali you encounter in *Sunjata*?	Consider the role played by stereotypes and bias in Ibn Battuta's account and other travel narratives of his time. Are such biases inevitable in travelogues?

from *The Truth About Stories: A Native Narrative* ("Sky Woman Falling") by Thomas King

SNAPSHOT BOX

LANGUAGE:
Iroquoian languages
/ Anishinaabemowin
/ Contemporary
English version

DATE: Pre-
Columbian / King:
2003 CE

LOCATION: Great
Lakes region and
New York State

GENRE: Storytelling

TAGS: Ethics
and Morality;
Indigeneity; Myth
and Legend;
Narrative; Orality;
Ritual and Practice;
Ways of Knowing

Introduction

What is a creation story? Thomas King whose story "Sky Woman Falling," which we are about to read, offers a great response. A creation story is one "that recounts how the world was formed, how things came to be, for contained within creation stories are relationships that help to define the nature of the universe and how cultures understand the world in which they exist."[24] The Sky Woman story is a creation story, and in order to listen to it and read it, King invites us first to agree that there are many ways (understandings) of being in the world, and that those ways are guided by different stories of kinship and relation. There is a word in English that is critical for non-Indigenous readers and researchers to appreciate the complexity of Indigenous storytelling and their diverse ways-of-being: **relationality**, or the state of being relational. "Relationality is the concept that we are all related to each other, to the natural environment, and to the spiritual world, and these relationships bring about interdependencies."[25]

King self-identifies as being of Cherokee, German, and Greek descent.[26] Continuing the multimodal material culture from pre-Colombian times, King's story is a written version in English of a trans-Indigenous and multilingual creation story that belongs to the Native nations who have inhabited for millennia the Great Lakes region and the east coast of what is known today as the United States and Canada. Even far south in North Carolina, we can find versions of this story among the Cherokee (Teuton), who also speak an Iroquoian language (Tsalagi), as the Haudenosaunee Confederacy. The Haudenosaunee, the people of the Long House, are the Six Nations (Cayuga, Mohawk, Oneida, Onondaga, Tuscarora, and Seneca). The Hiawatha Wampum Belt (woven shell belt) represents the intentional connection made through Gyanesshagowa / the Great Law of Peace, founded in righteousness, justice, health, and consensus.

As described by Potawatomi (part of Anishinaabe First Nations) writer and scholar Robin Wall Kimmerer, the Sky Woman story "is a constant star in the constellation of teachings we call the **Original Instructions**. These are not 'instructions'

---

24. Thomas King, "'You'll Never Believe What Happened' Is Always a Great Way to Start," in *The Truth About Stories: A Native Narrative* (Toronto: House of Anansi Press, 2003), 10.

25. Asma Na-hi, Antoine, Rachel Mason, Roberta Mason, Sophia Palahicky, and Carmen Rodriguez de France, "Indigenous Epistemologies and Pedagogies." BC Campus. Canada.

26. Thomas King self-identifies as Cherokee through his father's heritage, but is not an enrolled member of the Cherokee Nation.

Timeline

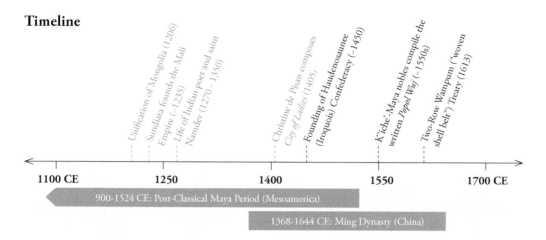

- Unification of Mongolia (1206)
- Sundiata founds the Mali Empire (~1235)
- Life of Indian poet and saint Namdev (1270 - 1350)
- Christine de Pisan composes City of Ladies (1405)
- Founding of Haudenosaunee (Iroquois) Confederacy (~1450)
- K'iche' Maya nobles compile the written Popol Wuj (~1550s)
- Two-Row Wampum ("woven shell belt") Treaty (1613)

1100 CE   1250   1400   1550   1700 CE

900-1524 CE: Post-Classical Maya Period (Mesoamerica)

1368-1644 CE: Ming Dynasty (China)

like commandments, thoughts, or rules; rather, they are like a compass: they provide an orientation but not a map. The work of living is creating that map for yourself. How to follow the Original Instructions will be different for each of us and different for every era."[27] Both the Anishinaabe and the Haudenosaunee envision North America and more broadly the Earth as "Turtle Island" — the location of their shared Sky Woman story. It is a living story, whose Original Instructions are current, and King invites us to read it as that — a story that changes each time someone tells it. Can you think of a story that is constantly shifting as you tell and retell it over time?

Let's now think about relationality and how Sky Woman's existence relates with the natural world. Since rabbit, fish, and otter speak with Sky Woman as equals, some readers may suggest the word "animism" when describing Indigenous storytelling. However, this concept may overlook Indigenous relationality and the ancestral way of coming to know that is at the center of Indigenous storytelling practices. Instead of assuming that the storyteller or writer is attributing "human characteristics" to the natural world, we should keep in mind that within the Sky Woman story — therefore the way-of-being that underlies it — all beings are relatives and have specific skills and teachings to contribute to the laws of interdependence. Knowledge therefore exists as **reciprocity-based Traditional Ecological Knowledge (TEK)** — "the ongoing accumulation of knowledge, practice and belief about relationships between living beings in a specific ecosystem that is acquired by Indigenous people over hundreds or thousands of years through direct contact with the environment, handed down through generations, and used for life-sustaining ways."[28]

---

27. Robin Wall Kimmerer, *Braiding Sweetgrass: Indigenous Wisdom, Scientific Knowledge, and the Teaching of Plants* (Canada: Milkweed, 2013), 7.

28. Traditional Ecological Knowledge vs. Western Science. National Park Service. USA.

Given dominant ways of approaching knowledge, how can we hold space appropriately in our own ways of being for TEK?

An example of TEK is the kindness and respect shown by the water animals and birds when taking care of Sky Woman, which it is interpreted by Robin Wall Kimmerer via migration, hospitality, exchange, and the teaching of becoming Indigenous: "As we consider these instructions, it is also good to recall that, when Sky-woman arrived here, she did not come alone. She was pregnant. . . . It was through her actions of reciprocity, the give and take with the land, that the original immigrant became Indigenous."[29] Indeed, she did not arrive alone, she brought within her the reciprocal forces of creating/destructing life represented as the twins. She also brought teachings about seeds and the "magic of land," as well as the dances and the songs to show gratitude. Since this story changes every time it is told, at this point it is important to remember that in a longer version of the Turtle Island story, Sky Woman brings with her the berries, the three sisters (corn, beans, and squash), and the four medicines (tobacco, sweetgrass, cedar, and white sage) that are at the foundation of TEK on the Turtle's shell/North America.

Sometimes, Indigenous ways of coming to know and TEK are also framed as **land-pedagogies**, and, according to King, the Sky Woman story is about curiosity as a creation force. Anishinaabe scholar and poet Leanne Simpson has analyzed this curiosity as a "rebellious transformation" within experiential land-pedagogy: intuition, trust, and nonhierarchical relationships allow Anishinaabe people to incarnate and revitalize the old stories in everyday life. As woman and mother, Sky Woman disrupts "the rigidity of colonial gender binaries"[30] when she opens curiously the hole-in-the-sky and leads a cosmic "revolution" between the spirit world and Turtle Island. How does curiosity serve as a storytelling strategy?

Renowned Dakota philosopher Vine Deloria Jr. reminds us that one version is not a better version of an Indigenous story:

> Tribal elders did not worry if their version of creation was entirely different from the scenario held by a neighboring tribe. People believed that each tribe has its own special relationship with the superior spiritual forces that governed the universe. The task of each tribe was to remain true to its special calling without worrying about what others were doing. Tribal knowledge was not fragmented data arranged according to rational speculation. It was simply the distilled memory of the People describing the events they had experienced and the lands they had lived in.[31]

29. Wall Kimmerer, *Braiding Sweetgrass*, 9.

30. Leane Simpson. "Land as Pedagogy: Nishnaabeg Intelligence and Rebellious Transformation," *Decolonization: Indigeneity, Education and Society* 3 (2014): 8.

31. Deloria Jr. Vine, *Red Earth, White Lies: Native American and the Myth of Scientific Fact* (Colorado: Fulcrum Publishing, 1997), 36.

In the context of Indigenous storytelling, words and stories can both heal and make us sick. King reminds us that we must be careful with what we say and envision: "For once a story is told, it cannot be called back. Once told, it is loose in the world."[32] Following this piece of advice, be conscious that after reading the Sky Woman story, these words and teachings will be loose in your world, with the power to heal and restore or harm and destroy. Therefore, if this is your first time reading a version of the Sky Woman story, please take a moment and remember that creation stories like this one are still being told for several hours or even nights when communities gather in the ceremonial houses on specific dates of the year. Imagine listening to a story for several nights, following the rhythm of the elder's words, making sure you don't miss any detail despite being tired and cold. Depending on the storyteller, the listener, the dialogue with the audience, and the spirit of the story itself, some details will resonate in some people more than in others, so open your mind, your heart, your body, and your spirit, and listen carefully to the Sky Woman story.[33]

Juan Sánchez-Martínez
Department of Languages and Literatures

32. King, "'You'll Never Believe What Happened,'" 10.
33. See also Lina Sunseri, "Sky Woman Live On: Contemporary Examples of Mothering the Nation." *Canadian Woman Studies* 26 (2008): 21–25; and Christopher B. Teuton, *Cherokee Stories of the Turtle Island Liars' Club* (Chapel Hill: University of North Carolina Press, 2012). For tribal history and appropriate terminology, see Anishinaabe Nation: Wiikwemkoong unceded Territory (Manitoulin Island), Canada; "Anishinaabe Timeline," Bemidji State University, Minnesota; and Haudenosaunee Nation, "The Haudenosaunee Guide for Educators," "The Learning Longhouse Project, New York."

The points and bands on the graphic timeline earlier in the Introduction are unable to capture the full story, so we are including an extended narrative timeline. For example, there was no way for us to capture the pre-Columbian migration, through which Sacred Migis (the little white shell) leads the Ojibwe Nations migration westward from St. Lawrence River to the place of wild rice around the Great Lakes region. Some other events not captured in our graphic timeline are as follows:

- 1610–1650: First encounters between Europeans and Ojibwe/Anishinaabe. Around 1610, the Anishinaabe establishes first contact with the French via Étienne Brûlé, who was a part of the Samuel de Champlain expeditions on Turtle Island/North America, along Georgian Bay.
- 1670: Hudson's Bay Company is created. It is one of the engines of the European colonization on Turtle Island. Fur trading is one of its biggest markets. The company still exists as HBC.
- 1756–1763: Seven Years War between the French and the English colonies for the monopoly of the fur trade.
- 1776–1871: Nation to Nation Treaty Years.
- 1871: Indian Appropriation Act. The United States declares that "no Indian nation or tribe" will be recognized "as an independent nation, tribe, or power with whom the United States may contract by treaty."
- 1876: Indian Act. Canadian government seeks to assimilate Indigenous-peoples into Canadian settler society by encouraging "enfranchisement." Indigenous matrilineal clan system is disrupted by the heteropatriarchal colonial economic system.
- 1934: Indian Reorganization Act.
- 1968: American Indian Movement—AIM is founded.
- 1969: Alcatraz Occupation.
- 1973: AIM at Wounded Knee.
- 1975: Indian Self-Determination Act and Education Assistance Act.
- 1978: Indian Freedom of Religion Act.
- 1988: Indian Gaming Regulatory Act.
- 1990: Native American Grave Protection and Repatriation Act; and Native American Language Act.
- 1990: Oka Crisis, Quebec, Canada.
- 2012: Idle No More Movement, Canada.
- 2016: Standing Rock Movement, USA.

PRE-READING PARS

1. What words would you choose to start your creation story? Why?

2. Imagine yourself writing a story about how things came to be in the universe. List four principles or instructions underlining your narrative.

3. What are two words you would use to describe your relationship with the natural world? Is there a separation between the natural world and you?

Sky Woman Falling

So you have to be careful with the stories you tell. And you have to watch out for the stories that you are told. But if I ever get to Pluto, that's how I would like to begin. With a story. Maybe I'd tell the inhabitants of Pluto one of the stories I know. Maybe they'd tell me one of theirs. It wouldn't matter who went first. But which story? That's the real question. Personally, I'd want to hear a creation story, a story that recounts how the world was formed, how things came to be, for contained within creation stories are relationships that help to define the nature of the universe and how cultures understand the world in which they exist.

And, as luck would have it, I happen to know a few. But I have a favorite. It's about a woman who fell from the sky. And it goes like this.

Back at the beginning of imagination, the world we know as earth was nothing but water, while above the earth, somewhere in space, was a larger, more ancient world. And on that world was a woman.

A crazy woman.

Well, she wasn't exactly crazy. She was more nosy. Curious. The kind of curious that doesn't give up. The kind that follows you around. Now, we all know that being curious is healthy, but being curious can get you into trouble.

Don't be too curious, the Birds told her.

Okay, she said, I won't.

But you know what? That's right. She kept on being curious.

One day while she was bathing in the river, she happened to look at her feet and discovered that she had five toes on each foot. One big one and four smaller ones. They had been there all along, of course, but now that the woman noticed them for the first time, she wondered why she had five toes instead of three. Or eight. And she wondered if more toes were better than fewer toes.

So she asked her Toes. Hey, she said, how come there are only five of you?

You're being curious again, said her Toes.

Another day, the woman was walking through the forest and found a moose relaxing in the shade by a lake.

Hello, said the Moose. Aren't you that nosy woman?

Yes, I am, said the woman, and what I want to know is why you are so much larger than me.

That's easy, said the Moose, and he walked into the lake and disappeared.

Don't you love cryptic stories? I certainly do.

Now before we go any further, we should give this woman a name so we don't have to keep calling her "the woman." How about Blanche? Catherine? Thelma? Okay, I know expressing an opinion can be embarrassing. So let's do it the way we always do it and let someone else make the decision for us. Someone we trust. Someone who will promise to lower taxes. Someone like me.

I say we call her Charm. Don't worry. We can change it later on if we want to.

So one day the woman we've decided to call Charm went looking for something good to eat. She looked at the fish, but she was not in the mood for fish. She looked at the rabbit, but she didn't feel like eating rabbit either.

I've got this craving, said Charm.

What kind of craving? said Fish.

I want to eat something, but I don't know what it is.

Maybe you're pregnant, said Rabbit. Whenever I get pregnant, I get cravings.

Hmmmm, said Charm, maybe I am.

And you know what? She was.

What you need, Fish and Rabbit told Charm, is some Red Fern Foot.

Yes, said Charm, that sounds delicious. What is it?

It's a root, said Fish, and it only grows under the oldest trees. And it's the perfect thing for pregnant humans.

Now, you're probably thinking that this is getting pretty silly, what with chatty fish and friendly rabbits, with moose disappearing into lakes and talking toes. And you're probably wondering how in the world I expect you to believe any of this, given the fact that we live in a predominantly scientific, capitalistic, Judeo-Christian world governed by physical laws, economic imperatives, and spiritual precepts.

Is that what you're thinking?

It's okay. You won't hurt my feelings.

So Charm went looking for some Red Fern Foot. She dug around this tree and she dug around that tree, but she couldn't find any. Finally she came to the oldest tree in the forest and she began digging around its base. By now she was very hungry, and she was very keen on some Red Fern Foot, so she really got into the digging. And before long she had dug a rather deep hole.

Don't dig too deep, Badger told her.

Mind your own business, Charm told him.

Okay, said Badger, but don't blame me if you make a mistake.

You can probably guess what happened. That's right, Charm dug right through to the other side of the world.

That's curious, said Charm, and she stuck her head into that hole so she could get a better view.

That's very curious, she said again, and she stuck her head even farther into the hole.

Sometimes when I tell this story to children, I slow it down and have Charm stick her head into that hole by degrees. But most of you are adults and have already figured out that Charm is going to stick her head into that hole so far that she's either going to get stuck or she's going to fall through.

And sure enough, she fell through. Right through that hole and into the sky.

Uh-oh, Charm thought to herself. That wasn't too smart.

But she couldn't do much about it now. And she began to tumble through the sky, began to fall and fall and fall and fall. Spinning and turning, floating through the vast expanse of space.

And off in the distance, just on the edge of sight, was a small blue dot floating in the heavens. And as Charm tumbled down through the black sky, the dot got bigger and bigger.

You've probably figured this part out, too, but just so there's no question, this blue dot is the earth. Well, sort of. It's the earth when it was young. When there was nothing but water. When it was simply a water world.

And Charm was heading right for it.

In the meantime, on this water world, on earth, a bunch of water animals were swimming and floating around and diving and talking about how much fun water is.

Water, water, water, said the Ducks. There's nothing like water.

Yes, said the Muskrats, we certainly like being wet. It's even better when you're under water, said the Sunfish.

Try jumping into it, said the Dolphins. And just as the Dolphins said this, they looked up into the sky.

Uh-oh, said the Dolphins, and everyone looked up in time to see Charm falling toward them. And as she came around the moon, the water animals were suddenly faced with four variables—mass, velocity, compression, and displacement—and with two problems.

The Ducks, who have great eyesight, could see that Charm weighed in at about 150 pounds. And the Beavers, who have a head for physics and math, knew that she was coming in fast. Accelerating at thirty-two feet per second per second to be precise (give or take a little for drag and atmospheric friction). And the Whales knew from many years of study that water does not compress, while the Dolphins could tell anyone who asked that while it won't compress, water will displace.

Which brought the animals to the first of the two problems. If Charm hit the water at full speed, it was going to create one very large tidal wave and ruin everyone's day.

So quick as they could, all the water birds flew up and formed a net with their bodies, and, as Charm came streaking down, the birds caught her, broke her fall, and brought her gently to the surface of the water.

Just in time.

To deal with the second of the two problems. Where to put her.

They could just dump her in the water, but it didn't take a pelican to see that Charm was not a water creature.

Can you swim? asked the Sharks.

Not very well, said Charm.

How about holding your breath for a long time? asked the Sea Horses.

Maybe for a minute or two, said Charm.

Floating? said the Seals. Can you float?

I don't know, said Charm. I never really tried floating.

So what are we going to do with you? said the Lobsters.

Hurry up, said the Birds, flapping their wings as hard as they could.

Perhaps you could put me on something large and flat, Charm told the water animals.

Well, as it turns out, the only place in this water world that was large and flat was the back of the Turtle.

Oh, okay, said Turtle. But if anyone else falls out of the sky, she's on her own.

So the water animals put Charm on the back of the Turtle, and everyone was happy. Well, at least for the next month or so. Until the animals noticed that Charm was going to have a baby.

It's going to get a little crowded, said the Muskrats.

What are we going to do? said the Geese.

It wouldn't be so crowded, Charm told the water animals, if we had some dry land.

Sure, agreed the water animals, even though they had no idea what dry land was.

Charm looked over the side of the Turtle, down into the water, and then she turned to the water animals.

Who's the best diver? she asked.

A contest! screamed the Ducks.

All right! shouted the Muskrats.

What do we have to do? asked the Eels.

It's easy, said Charm. One of you has to dive down to the bottom of the water and bring up some mud.

Sure, said all the water animals, even though they had no idea what mud was.

So, said Charm, who wants to try first?

Me! said Pelican, and he flew into the sky as high as he could and then dropped like a knife into the water. And he was gone for a long time. But when he floated to the surface, out of breath, he didn't have any mud.

It was real dark down there, said Pelican, and cold.

The next animal to try was Walrus.

I don't mind the dark, said Walrus, and my blubber will keep me warm. So down she went, and she was gone for much longer than Pelican, but when she came to the surface coughing up water, she didn't have any mud, either.

I don't think the water has a bottom, said Walrus. Sorry.

I'm sure you're beginning to wonder if there's a point to this story or if I'm just going to work my way through all the water animals one by one.

So one by one all the water animals tried to find the mud at the bottom of the ocean, and all of them failed until the only animal left was Otter. Otter, however, wasn't particularly interested in finding mud.

Is it fun to play with? asked Otter.

Not really, said Charm.

Is it good to eat? asked Otter.

Not really, said Charm.

Then why do you want to find it? said Otter.

For the magic, said Charm.

Oh, said Otter. I like magic.

So Otter took a deep breath and dove into the water. And she didn't come up. Day after day, Charm and the animals waited for Otter to come to the surface. Finally, on the morning of the fourth day, just as the sun was rising, Otter's body floated up out of the depths.

Oh, no, said all the animals, Otter has drowned trying to find the mud. And they hoisted Otter's body onto the back of the Turtle.

Now, when they hoisted Otter's body onto the back of the Turtle, they noticed that her little paws were clenched shut, and when they opened her paws, they discovered something dark and gooey that wasn't water.

Is this mud? asked the Ducks.

Yes, it is, said Charm. Otter has found the mud.

Of course I found the mud, whispered Otter, who wasn't so much dead as she was tired and out of breath. This magic better be worth it.

Charm set the lump of mud on the back of the Turtle, and she sang and she danced, and the animals sang and danced with her, and very slowly the lump of mud began to grow. It grew and grew and grew into a world, part water, part mud. That was a good trick, said the water animals. But now there's not enough room for all of us in the water. Some of us are going to have to live on land.

Not that anyone wanted to live on the land. It was nothing but mud. Mud as far as the eye could see. Great jumbled lumps of mud.

But before the animals could decide who was going to live where or what to do about the mud-lump world, Charm had her baby.

Or rather, she had her babies.

Twins.

A boy and a girl. One light, one dark. One right-handed, one left-handed.

Nice-looking babies, said the Cormorants. Hope they like mud.

And as it turned out, they did. The right-handed Twin smoothed all the mud lumps until the land was absolutely flat.

Wow! said all the animals. That was pretty clever. Now we can see in all directions.

But before the animals could get used to all the nice flat land, the left-handed Twin stomped around in the mud, piled it up, and created deep valleys and tall mountains.

Okay, said the animals, that could work.

And while the animals were admiring the new landscape, the Twins really got busy. The right-handed Twin dug nice straight trenches and filled them with water.

These are rivers, he told the animals, and I've made the water flow in both directions so that it'll be easy to come and go as you please.

That's handy, said the animals.

But as soon as her brother had finished, the left-handed Twin made the rivers crooked and put rocks in the water and made it flow in only one direction.

This is much more exciting, she told the animals.

Could you put in some waterfalls? said the animals. Everyone likes waterfalls.

Sure, said the left-handed Twin. And she did.

The right-handed Twin created forests with all the trees lined up so you could go into the woods and not get lost. The left-handed Twin came along and moved the trees around, so that some of the forest was dense and difficult, and other parts were open and easy.

How about some trees with nuts and fruit? said the animals. In case we get hungry.

That's a good idea, said the right-handed Twin. And he did.

The right-handed Twin created roses. The left-handed Twin put thorns on the stems. The right-handed Twin created summer. The left-handed Twin created winter. The right-handed Twin created sunshine. The left-handed Twin created shadows.

Have we forgotten anything? the Twins asked the animals.

What about human beings? said the animals. Do you think we need human beings?

Why not? said the Twins. And quick as they could the right-handed Twin created women, and the left-handed Twin created men.

They don't look too bright, said the animals. We hope they won't be a problem.

Don't worry, said the Twins, you guys are going to get along just fine.

The animals and the humans and the Twins and Charm looked around at the world that they had created. Boy, they said, this is as good as it gets. This is one beautiful world.

King, Thomas. Selection from "'You'll Never Believe What Happened' is always a great way to start." In *The Truth About Stories: A Native Narrative*, 10–21. Toronto: House of Anansi Press, 2003.

POST-READING PARS

1. Compare and contrast your own creation story with the Sky Woman story. What is the major difference?

2. Identify two ways in which Sky Woman can be understood as an Indigenous role model for nonpatriarchal empowered womanhood, motherhood, and/or kinship?

3. It is recommended by Indigenous educators that while you read native literatures, you learn as much as you can about the land/language/community connection from which these literatures come from. Especially given that UNC Asheville is on Cherokee land, look up two details about Cherokee land and language.

Inquiry Corner

Content Question:

What kind of storytelling strategies are used by King to engage with the reader/audience (i.e., figures of speech, repetitions, hyperbole, etc.)? Provide examples.

Critical Question:

What principles or instructions of TEK (Traditional Ecological Knowledge) are embedded in the story of Turtle Island?

Comparative Question:

How does King's Sky Woman story compare in theme and form with other creation stories you have come across (i.e., *Popol Wuj*)?

Connection Question:

If Indigenous land-pedagogy is based on principles such as respect, reciprocity, honesty, and caring, how do these principles translate in the current Indigenous resistance against the commodification of the land and transnational extractivist megaprojects?

Read the *Haudenosaunee Address*. Do you find connections between this prayer and the Sky Woman story?

How do the Original Instructions of the Haudenosaunee compare with your own ethics and belief?

from *Popol Wuj*

SNAPSHOT BOX

LANGUAGE: K'iche'-Maya

DATE: Mid-1550s CE

LOCATION: Guatemala

GENRE: Creation narrative

TAGS: Agriculture, Land, and Food; Indigeneity; Myth and Legend; Narrative; Nature and Sacred; Orality; Power Structures; Spirituality; Ways of Knowing

Introduction

In the K'iche' language the *Popol Wuj*[34] literally means the Book of the Mat, a cultural matrix woven together with many threads, a meeting place of numerous peoples. So it is no surprise that the book includes a wide range of features: a creation story (which is the focus of this excerpt), genealogies, historical records, wisdom literature, heroic narratives, instructions for divination, and much more. The *Popol Wuj* collates and preserves an array of sacred Maya stories and beliefs that circulated widely during the precontact period—in ceramic vases and stonework, in hieroglyphic texts, and especially in stories—and show the influence of varied traditions throughout Mesoamerica. These stories and beliefs continue to inform and enrich Maya culture today.

From at least 300 CE until the Spanish arrived in 1524, a diverse collection of Maya peoples flourished in a large region extending from the Yucatán peninsula of southeastern Mexico to the highlands of Guatemala. These communities, bound together loosely by language and culture, each possessed highly developed urban centers, complex economies with intricate networks of trade and tribute, and rich traditions of sculpture and monumental architecture. They were also linked by agricultural practices focused on the production of maize, which was harvested and stored to provide year-round sustenance, and its centrality to Maya society is

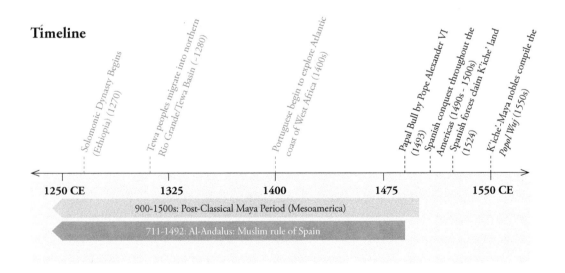

Timeline

Solomonic Dynasty Begins (Ethiopia) (1270)

Tewa peoples migrate into northern Rio Grande/Tewa Basin (~1280)

Portuguese begin to explore Atlantic coast of West Africa (1400s)

Papal Bull by Pope Alexander VI (1493)

Spanish conquest throughout the Americas (1490s – 1500s)

Spanish forces claim K'iche' land (1524)

K'iche'-Maya nobles compile the *Popol Wuj* (1550s)

| 1250 CE | 1325 | 1400 | 1475 | 1550 CE |

900-1500s: Post-Classical Maya Period (Mesoamerica)

711-1492: Al-Andalus: Muslim rule of Spain

34. The K'iche' text title has variant spellings, including *Pop Wuj*, *Popul Vuh*, and *Popol Vuh*.

illustrated by the crop's prominent role in the creation narrative of the *Popol Wuj*. Finally, the Maya were a highly literate society, having developed early in the first millennium CE a hieroglyphic script that was inscribed on pages of bark paper, which were then assembled into a unique form of screenfold codex — a book with its pages folded within like an accordion. Scribal culture was richly valued in Maya communities, largely because these written records offered "the means of seeing life clearly," as the preamble to the *Popol Wuj* states, archiving matters of sacred belief and ritual as well as issues of secular governance and ordinary life.

The text of the *Popol Wuj* is a testament to the power and resilience of scribal culture among the Maya, who adapted their manuscript tradition to meet the threat of Spanish conquest. In addition to the wars, forced labor, and spread of novel diseases initiated by the Spanish, who also severed important trade routes and tribute systems, many Catholic missionaries suppressed Indigenous religion by destroying hieroglyphic manuscripts, a perverse acknowledgment of the dangerous power a rival sacred text could pose to their efforts at Christian conversion. The destruction was hardly the result of Spanish consensus — numerous Catholic friars condemned these events and policies, for example. But the combined force of these actions resulted in what is best described as genocide: by the end of the sixteenth century, only 10–15 percent of the Maya population survived; and of the countless manuscripts from precontact Maya culture, only four are believed to have remained intact and undestroyed. In response to these persecutions, several members of the Kaweq lineage within the K'iche'-Maya nobility collated and transcribed the stories of their people during the 1550s, making use of an alphabetized form of K'iche' developed by Spanish missionaries to aid in Christian conversion. The original text of *Popul Wuj* itself is now lost to scholars in the West, and the source of this excerpt is a copy of the earlier manuscript that was transcribed at the beginning of the eighteenth century by another missionary, Francisco Ximénes, as a part of his conversion project. It is impossible, consequently, to disentangle the *Popol Wuj* from its colonial context, but the work is remarkably free of references to the Spanish, even if its preamble explicitly notes that it was composed under a newly imposed law of Christianity. The *Popol Wuj* offers its readers one of the most comprehensive surviving repositories of precontact Mesoamerican culture. With the context of Spanish colonization and oppression in mind, why might the K'iche' choose to look back to the "xe,'" the "root" or "beginning" of Maya culture, as a means of safeguarding their future?

In addition to the textual sophistication of Maya culture, the *Popol Wuj* is shaped by an oral poetics that is central to spoken narrative, music, and chanted prayer. Scholars believe the K'iche' scribes based the *Popol Wuj* on a precontact text (now lost) that was used by master storytellers to aid in recitation. The language of the *Popol Wuj* preserves this style of oral performance, capturing different registers of speech that blend together formal and conversational elements. In this way we can see the complementary and ongoing roles of oral and textual traditions, each aiding and enriching the other.

The most prominent vestige of oral tradition in the text is its use of parallel couplets, often repeating names or phrases to achieve emphasis, rhythm, and power, and then sometimes inverting these parallel structures. Understanding this parallelism can help to clarify some of the initial difficulties in reading the *Popol Wuj*. Near its beginning is a list that includes many names of gods, but most of these are parallel couplets that assign new and different titles to the same pair of gods, Xpiyacoc and Xmucane. These two creator grandparents are often invoked in gendered terms and nearly always as complementary pairs, as the Framer and the Shaper, for example, or He Who Has Begotten Sons and She Who Has Borne Children. There is another especially creative deity named Heart of Sky, who seems to be three gods in one (Thunderbolt Huracan, Youngest Thunderbolt, and Sudden Thunderbolt), embodying a form of divine consensus. As you encounter parallel couplets (and their occasional inversions) in the excerpt, think about how the pairings might represent distinct but complementary forces in the world (male and female, earth and sky, hot and cold). How might this reflect the role of mutuality and reciprocity in Maya cosmology and culture? You might look for other pairings, too—the text's surprising mixture of humor and sacred profundity, for example—and think about the implications of this coordination and balance.

The *Popol Wuj*, the Book of the Mat with many woven threads, rewards flexible and sensitive reading practices, encouraging us to consider the intertwining of historical and mythic narratives, to search for the proper role of humans in a cosmological story, and to ponder the continued lessons we can learn from the Maya people's stories of creation.

Evan Gurney
Department of English

from *Popol Wuj* (Creation Narratives)

Preamble

This is the beginning[35] *of the ancient traditions of this place called Quiché.*[36]

Here we shall write.[37] We shall begin[38] to tell the ancient stories of the beginning, the origin of all that was done in the citadel of Quiché, among the people of the Quiché nation. Here we shall gather the manifestation, the declaration, the account of the sowing[39] and the dawning by[40] the Framer[41] and the Shaper,[42] She Who Has Borne

35. The Quiché word *xe'* (root) is used here to describe the beginning or foundation of the authors' words concerning the history of the Quiché people. The subsequent narrative is thus seen as growing like a plant from this "root" (lines 4–6).

36. The authors at various times refer to the land, the nation, the capital city, and the people themselves as Quiché (K'iche' in the modern orthography of the Maya languages), meaning "many trees" or "forest." The homeland of the Quiché people in western Guatemala is mountainous and heavily forested.

37. The authors here state that they are "writing" this history. Following the Spanish conquest, Native Americans were discouraged from using their own ancient writing systems in favor of the Latin script. The manuscript of the *Popol Vuh* was thus written in the Mayan language of the Quichés, but with a European script. It is this set of circumstances that has preserved the *Popol Vuh* in a fully readable form when so many other Native American texts were either destroyed or written in an as yet incompletely decipherable glyphic form.

38. *Tikib'a'* is literally "to plant." "The beginning," also in this sentence, is therefore literally "the planting."

39. The manuscript reads *euaxibal* (obscurity, that which is hidden in darkness). This is likely a transcription error for *auaxibal* (sowing, that which is sown), a concept that is paired with "dawning" throughout the text as a metaphor for the creation.

40. The following is a long list of deities, arranged in pairs, which the Quichés believed to have participated in the creation at the beginning of time. The list consists of not only the names of separate gods but their titles and secondary names as well. It is thus difficult to distinguish how many gods are really involved.

41. *Tz'aqol* (Framer) refers to one who makes something by putting things together (i.e., a building from stone or adobe, a meal from various ingredients, or a woven cloth from individual threads).

42. *B'itol* (Shaper) refers to one who makes something by modeling (i.e., pottery from clay, or a sculpture from carved stone), thus giving shape to an otherwise amorphous substance. The Framer and the Shaper are the most frequently mentioned gods involved in the creation of the world and its inhabitants.

Children and He Who Has Begotten Sons,[43] as they are called; along with Hunahpu Possum[44] and Hunahpu Coyote, Great White Peccary[45] and Coati,[46] Sovereign and Quetzal Serpent,[47] Heart of Lake and Heart of Sea,[48] Creator of the Green Earth and Creator of the Blue Sky,[49] as they are called.

These collectively are evoked and given expression as the Midwife[50] and the Patriarch, whose names are Xpiyacoc[51] and Xmucane, the Protector and the Shelterer, Twice Midwife and Twice Patriarch, as they are called in Quiché traditions. They gave voice to all things and accomplished their purpose in purity of being and in truth.

This account we shall now write under the law of God and Christianity.[52] We shall bring it forth because there is no longer the means whereby the *Popol Vuh* may

43. These are titles for the divine couple, Xmucane and Xpiyacoc.

44. Hunahpu Possum and Hunahpu Coyote are also likely titles for the gods Xpiyacoc and Xmucane.

45. *Saqi Nima Aq* (Great White Peccary [wild pig]). The word *saqi* may be translated as "light, bright, or white." "Great White Peccary" is given as one of the names or titles of the patriarchal creator god Xpiyacoc.

46. This is another name or title for the female creator goddess Xmucane. The coati, or coatimundi, which inhabits tropical Central America is a raccoon-like animal with a long tail and a long, pointed, flexible snout.

47. Q'ukumatz may be translated as "Quetzal Serpent" or, less accurately, as "Feathered Serpent." *Q'uq'* refers to the quetzal bird that have brilliantly colored iridescent blue/green feathers on their wings, tail, and crest, while their breasts are a bright crimson. *Kumatz* is a general term for "snake" or "serpent." The serpent was a common Maya symbol for regeneration or rebirth because of its tendency to periodically shed its skin to reveal a newer and brighter one. The combination of an avian lord of the skies with a serpentine lord of the earth and underworld gave this god power over all levels of the Maya universe. He is undoubtedly related to the well-known god Quetzalcoatl (Nahua for "Quetzal Serpent) worshiped by the Aztecs of Central Mexico.

48. These are likely titles for Sovereign and Quetzal Serpent, who are associated with water. *K'ux* may refer to either "heart" or "spirit." This pair of deities thus embodies the inward powers of large, standing bodies of water. The *Popol Vuh* states that prior to the creation the world consisted of a vast expanse of placid waters from which all things emerged.

49. These are likely titles for Xpiyacoc and Xmucane. They literally mean "blue/green plate" and "blue/green bowl." The Quiché language has only one word, *räx*, for both blue and green. When distinguishing between the colors, modern Quiché people are forced to say "*räx* like the sky" for blue, or "*räx* like a tree" for green. The "blue/green plate" refers to the green surface of the earth covered with vegetation, and the arch of the sky is envisioned as an inverted "blue bowl."

50. Midwife and Patriarch are titles for Xmucane and Xpiyacoc. I'yom may be literally translated as "She Who Has Had Grandchildren," but the word is also commonly used as an affectionate title for a midwife. The title of the goddess implies that she assists in the "birth" of the world.

51. Xpiyacoc is the male deity, while Xmucane serves as the divine female principal that brings about the creation.

52. Here, the authors of the *Popol Vuh* confirm that they are compiling the ancient traditions of their people under the law of Christianity, imposed following the Spanish conquest. Surprisingly, *Dios* (God) and *Christianoil* (Christianity) are the only examples of Christian or Spanish-derived words in the *Popol Vuh* until the end of the text, where the arrival of the Spaniards is

be seen,[53] the means of seeing clearly that had come from across the sea—the account of our obscurity, and the means of seeing life clearly, as it is said. The original book exists that was written anciently, but its witnesses and those who ponder it hide their faces.[54]

Great is its performance and its account of the completion and germination of all the sky and earth—its four corners and its four sides. All then was measured and staked out into four divisions, doubling over and stretching the measuring cords of the womb of sky and the womb of earth.[55] Thus were established the four corners, the four sides, as it is said, by the Framer and the Shaper, the Mother and the Father of life and all creation, the giver of breath and the giver of heart,[56] they who give birth and give heart to the light everlasting, the child of light born of woman and the son of light born of man, they who are compassionate and wise in all things—all that exists in the sky and on the earth, in the lakes and in the sea.

The Primordial World

This is the account of when all is still silent and placid. All is silent and calm. Hushed and empty is the womb of the sky.

These, then, are the first words, the first speech. There is not yet one person, one animal, bird, fish, crab, tree, rock, hollow, canyon, meadow, or forest. All alone the sky exists. The face of the earth has not yet appeared. Alone lies the expanse of the sea, along with the womb of all the sky. There is not yet anything gathered together. All is at rest. Nothing stirs. All is languid, at rest in the sky. There is not yet anything stand-

---

described. This lack of intrusive Spanish words argues for the purity of the text as an accurate record of Precolumbian cosmology and history.

53. *Vuh* refers to Maya books, or codices painted on deerskin or bark paper. *Popol* is derived from the root *pop*, meaning "mat." Thus a literal translation would be "book that pertains to the mat." Within ancient Quiché society, a woven mat was used as a royal throne from which the king gave counsel to his people. The mat symbolized the power not only of the ruler, but also of his subjects. In this sense, the interlaced fibers of the mat represented the unity of the members within the community, linked inseparably in a common purpose. Thus Ximénez translated *popol* as "community," and the Motul Dictionary glosses *popol na* as a "community house." *Popol Vuh* might then be interpreted as "Book of the Community" or "Counsel Mat Book."

54. It is significant that this passage affirms that it is the "witness" and "ponderer" of the ancient book who "hide their faces," not the book itself. The authors of the Popol Vuh were anonymous, perhaps out of fear of persecution should the manuscript be discovered by the Spanish authorities.

55. The gods thus laid out the extent of their creation by measuring its boundaries, driving stakes to mark its four corners, and stretching a measuring cord between the stakes.

56. *K'uxlanel* (literally "heartener"). The heart is the central defining essence of a person, or what might be referred to as the soul. Thus the creators are those who ensoul living things. In addition, the Quichés use "hearten" to refer to someone who provides for, looks after, tends to, or counsels someone. The verbal form of this word also has the sense of "to remember." In English this would be "bear in mind," but for the Quichés this would be conceived as "bear in heart."

ing erect. Only the expanse of the water, only the tranquil sea lies alone. There is not yet anything that might exist. All lies placid and silent in the darkness, in the night.

All alone are the Framer and the Shaper, Sovereign and Quetzal Serpent, They Who Have Borne Children and They Who Have Begotten Sons. Luminous they are in the water,[57] wrapped in quetzal feathers and cotinga[58] feathers. Thus they are called Quetzal Serpent. In their essence, they are great sages, great possessors of knowledge. Thus surely there is the sky. There is also Heart of Sky,[59] which is said to be the name of the god.[60]

The Creation of the Earth

Then came his word. Heart of Sky arrived here with Sovereign and Quetzal Serpent in the darkness, in the night. He spoke with Sovereign and Quetzal Serpent. They talked together then. They thought and they pondered. They reached an accord, bringing together their words and their thoughts.[61] Then they gave birth, heartening one another. Beneath the light, they gave birth to humanity. Then they arranged for the germination and creation of the trees and the bushes, the germination of all life and creation, in the darkness and in the night, by Heart of Sky, who is called Huracan.

First is Thunderbolt Huracan, second is Youngest Thunderbolt, and third is Sudden Thunderbolt. These three together are Heart of Sky.[62] Then they came together with Sovereign and Quetzal Serpent. Together they conceived light and life:

57. "Quetzal Serpent," whose Quiché name is traditionally written Qucumatz in colonial documents, is associated with water in most ancient highland Maya texts. The ancient Maya generally associated standing water with the underworld. Thus, the god Quetzal Serpent combines the contrasting powers of a celestial bird with a terrestrial serpent, the darkness of deep waters with the light of the upper world. Thus he transcends all levels of existence.

58. The *räxon*, commonly known as the Lovely Cotinga, is a dovelike tropical bird with turquoise-blue plumage and a purple breast and throat.

59. *U K'ux Kaj* (Heart of Sky—also called Huracan, appears to be the principal god in the *Popol Vuh* account. He is the only deity to appear in every phase of the creation. During each creative period, Heart of Sky is the deity who first conceives the idea of what is to be formed. Other deities then carry out his will by giving it material expression.

60. *K'ab'awil* (god) refers to the general concept of deity in the *Popol Vuh*. The word is used to refer to ancient gods such as Heart of Sky, as well as to the wood or stone effigies carved to represent them. Soon after the Spanish conquest, Dominicans chose the word *k'ab'awil* to refer to the Christian "God." Franciscans, on the other hand, rejected this usage of the word because of its earlier association with Precolumbian religion.

61. The creation is described as a unified effort by a number of gods, all acting in concert with one another after careful deliberation and planning. None can act alone without the direction and assistance of other deities. In Quiché society, lack of unity is seen as one of the chief causes of misfortune and failure.

62. These three gods comprise the powers of the sky, symbolized by various aspects of the thunderbolt. Thunderstorms combine the elements of water (rain) and fire (lightning), which Quichés see as essential to all life.

"How shall it be sown? When shall there be a dawn for anyone? Who shall be a provider? Who shall be a sustainer?

"Then be it so. You are conceived. May the water be taken away, emptied out, so that the plate of the earth may be created—may it be gathered and become level. Then may it be sown; then may dawn the sky and the earth. There can be no worship, no reverence given by what we have framed and what we have shaped, until humanity has been created, until people have been made," they said.

Then the earth was created by them. Merely their word brought about the creation of it. In order to create the earth, they said, "Earth," and immediately it was created. Just like a cloud, like a mist, was the creation and formation of it.

Then they called forth the mountains from the water. Straightaway the great mountains came to be. It was merely their spirit essence,[63] their miraculous power, that brought about the conception of the mountains and the valleys. Straightaway were created cypress groves and pine forests to cover the face of the earth.

Thus Quetzal Serpent rejoiced:

"It is good that you have come, Heart of Sky—you, Huracan, and you as well, Youngest Thunderbolt and Sudden Thunderbolt. That which we have framed and shaped shall turn out well," they said.

First the earth was created, the mountains and the valleys. The waterways were divided, their branches coursing among the mountains. Thus the waters were divided, revealing the great mountains. For thus was the creation of the earth, created then by Heart of Sky and Heart of Earth, as they are called. They were the first to conceive it. The sky was set apart. The earth also was set apart within the waters. Thus was conceived the successful completion of the work when they thought and when they pondered.

The Creation of the Animals

Then were conceived the animals of the mountains, the guardians of the forest, and all that populate the mountains—the deer and the birds, the puma and the jaguar, the serpent and the rattlesnake, the pit viper and the guardian of the bushes.

She Who Has Borne Children and He Who Has Begotten Sons then asked:

"Shall it be merely solitary, merely silent beneath the trees and the bushes? It is well that there shall be guardians for them," they said.

Thus they considered and spoke together, and immediately created the deer and the birds. Having done this, they then provided homes for the deer and the birds:

"You, deer, will sleep along the courses of rivers and in the canyons. Here you will

---

63. *Nawal* also has no English equivalent. In Quiché theology, all things, both living and inanimate, have a spirit essence which they call *nawal*. This spirit essence is believed to give them power to act or communicate on a supernatural plane, for example, to transform their usual form into that of a powerful animal or force of nature. Thus the creation took place by means of the power of the gods' spirit essence or divine knowledge rather than by physical action.

be in the meadows and in the orchards. In the forests you shall multiply. You will walk on all fours, and thus you will be able to stand," they were told.

Then they established the homes of the birds, both small and great.

"You, birds, you will make your homes and your houses in the tops of trees, and in the tops of bushes. There you will multiply and increase in numbers in the branches of the trees and the bushes," the deer and the birds were told.

When this had been done, all of them received their places to sleep and their places to rest. Homes were provided for the animals on the earth by She Who Has Borne Children and He Who Has Begotten Sons. Thus all was completed for the deer and the birds.

The Fall of the Animals

Then it was said to the deer and the birds by the Framer and the Shaper, She Who Has Borne Children and He Who Has Begotten Sons:

"Speak! Call! Don't moan or cry out. Speak to one another, each according to your kind, according to your group," they were told—the deer, the birds, the pumas, the jaguars, and the serpents.

"Speak therefore our names. Honor [64] us, for we are your Mother and your Father. Say this, therefore: 'Huracan, Youngest Thunderbolt, and Sudden Thunderbolt, Heart of Sky and Heart of Earth, Framer and Shaper, She Who Has Borne Children and He Who Has Begotten Sons.' Speak! Call upon us! Honor us!" they were told.

But they did not succeed. They did not speak like people. They only squawked and chattered and roared. Their speech was unrecognizable, for each cried out in a different way.

When they heard this, the Framer and the Shaper said, "Their speech did not turn out well."

And again they said to each other:

"They were not able to speak our names. We are their Framer and their Shaper. This is not good," said She Who Has Borne Children and He Who Has Begotten Sons to each other.

They were therefore told:

"You shall be replaced because you were not successful. You could not speak. We have therefore changed our word. Your food and your sustenance, your sleeping places and your places to rest, that which belonged to you, shall be in the canyons and the forests.

"Nevertheless, because you have not been able to worship us or call upon us, there will yet be someone else who may be a worshiper. We shall now make one who will

---

64. The gods' purpose in carrying out the creation seems to be to provide beings who will be able to speak intelligibly. Only in this way could the gods be worshiped properly—through the articulation of their names with human speech.

give honor. Your calling will merely be to have your flesh eaten. Thus be it so. This must be your service," they were told. Thus were commanded the animals, both small and great, that were upon the face of the earth.

Then they wanted to test again their fate. They wanted to make another attempt. They wanted to try again to arrange for those who would honor them.

The speech of the animals could not be understood. Because of the way they were made, they were not successful. Therefore their flesh was brought low. They were made to serve. The animals that were on the face of the earth were eaten and killed.

The Creation of the Mud Person

Thus there was another attempt to frame and shape man by the Framer and the Shaper, by She Who Has Borne Children and He Who Has Begotten Sons:

"Let us try again before the first sowing, before the dawn approaches. Let us make a provider, a sustainer for us. How shall we then be called upon so that we are remembered upon the face of the earth? We have already made a first attempt with what we have framed and what we have shaped. But we were not successful in being worshiped or in being revered by them. Thus, let us try again to make one who will honor us, who will respect us; one who will be a provider and a sustainer," they said.

Then was the framing, the making of it. Of earth and mud was its flesh composed. But they saw that it was still not good. It merely came undone and crumbled. It merely became sodden and mushy. It merely fell apart and dissolved. Its head was not set apart properly.[65] Its face could only look in one direction. Its face was hidden. Neither could it look about. At first it spoke, but without knowledge. Straightaway it would merely dissolve in water, for it was not strong.

Then said the Framer and the Shaper:

"We have made a mistake; thus let this be merely a mistake. It cannot walk, neither can it multiply. Then let it be so. Let it be merely left behind as a thing of no importance," they said.

Therefore they undid it. They toppled what they had framed, what they had shaped.

Then they said again:

"How then will we truly make that which may succeed and bear fruit; that will worship us and that will call upon us?" they asked.

Then they thought again:

"We shall merely tell Xpiyacoc and Xmucane, Hunahpu Possum and Hunahpu Coyote, 'Try again a divination,[66] a shaping,'" said the Framer and the Shaper to each other.

---

65. The fact that the head was not placed apart from the body indicates that it did not have a neck with which to turn its head.

66. *Q'ijixik*, which might be translated "dayification," refers to a divinatory ceremony in which a handful of *tz'ite* beans or grains of maize are cast and then interpreted by a sequential

Then they called upon Xpiyacoc and Xmucane, and in this manner were the seers addressed: "Grandmother of Day, Grandmother of Light!" In this way, they were addressed by the Framer and the Shaper, for these are the names of Xpiyacoc and Xmucane.

The Creation of the Effigies of Carved Wood

Huracan, along with Sovereign and Quetzal Serpent, then spoke to the Master of Days[67] and the Mistress of Shaping, they who are seers:

"It shall be found; it shall be discovered how we are to create shaped and framed people who will be our providers and sustainers. May we be called upon, and may we be remembered. For it is with words that we are sustained, O Midwife and Patriarch, our Grandmother and our Grandfather, Xpiyacoc and Xmucane. Thus may it be spoken. May it be sown. May it dawn so that we are called upon and supported, so that we are remembered by framed and shaped people, by effigies and forms of people. Hearken and let it be so.

"Reveal your names, Hunahpu Possum and Hunahpu Coyote, Great She Who Has Borne Children and Great He Who Has Begotten Sons, Great Peccary and Great Coati, Jeweler and Worker in Precious Stones, Sculptor and Wood Worker, Creator of the Green Earth and Creator of the Blue Sky, Incense Maker and Master Artist, Grandmother of Day and Grandmother of Light. Thus shall you all be called by that which we shall frame and shape. Cast grains of maize and *tz'ite*[68] to divine how what we shall make will come out when we grind and chisel out its mouth and face in wood,"[69] so it was said to the Masters of Days.

Thus began the divination ceremony, the casting of grains of maize and of *tz'ite*, the revelation of days and of shaping. Then spoke the one Grandmother and the one Grandfather to them.

For this was the Grandfather, the Master of the *Tz'ite*, Xpiyacoc by name. And this was the Grandmother, the Mistress of Days and Mistress of Shaping who is at the foot, who is called Xmucane.

---

counting of the days of the Quiché ritual calendar. Thus the outcome of the creation is to be ritually determined through a divinatory "counting of days."

67. *Aj q'ij* is still the title used by Quiché priests who divine the will of deity through a ritual counting of the days in the sacred calendar. The title means literally "he/she of days," or "master of days," although modern ethnographers often refer to them as "daykeepers." Because Xmucane and Xpiyacoc assisted in the creation of the universe at the beginning of time, thus setting in motion the endless cycles of day and night, birth and death, sowing and harvest, they stand as the ideal interpreters through divination of these cycles.

68. *Tz'ite* is the bright-red beanlike seed of the coral tree. The seeds are used in divination ceremonies. Just as in the Popol Vuh manuscript, modern Quiché *aj q'ij* priests may use maize kernels or *tz'ite* seeds for such divinations.

69. Each of the first three creative attempts used a different class of material—animal (wild beasts and birds), mineral (mud), and vegetable (wood).

Thus they began to speak, to carry out their divination ceremony:

"May it be discovered. May it be found. Say it! Our ears hear you. Speak! Tell it! May the tree be found that is to be carved and chiseled out by the Framer and the Shaper. If this is to be the provider and the sustainer, then may it now be sown that the dawn may come. You, grains of maize, and you, *tz'ite*; you, days, and you, the shaping—you are called, you are summoned." Thus it was said to the grains of maize and the *tz'ite*, to the days and the shaping.

"Bring it to a conclusion, O Heart of Sky. Do not punish them further.[70] Do not cause any more suffering for Sovereign and Quetzal Serpent," they said.

Then they spoke straight to the point:

"May these effigies of wood come out well. May they speak. May they communicate there upon the face of the earth. May it be so," they said.

And when they had spoken, straightaway the effigies of carved wood were made. They had the appearance of people and spoke like people as well. They populated the whole face of the earth. The effigies of carved wood began to multiply, bearing daughters and sons.

Nevertheless, they still did not possess their hearts nor their minds. They did not remember their Framer or their Shaper. They walked without purpose. They crawled on their hands and knees and did not remember Heart of Sky. Thus they were weighed in the balance. They were merely an experiment, an attempt at people. At first they spoke, but their faces were all dried up. Their legs and arms were not filled out. They had no blood or blood flow within them. They had no sweat or oil. Their cheeks were dry, and their faces were masks.[71] Their legs and arms were stiff. Their bodies were rigid. Thus they were not capable of understanding[72] before their Framer and their Shaper, those who had given them birth and given them hearts. They were the first numerous people who have lived here upon the face of the earth.

70. The phrase *mak'ajisaj u chi', u wach* (don't grind up his mouth, his face) is a common expression meaning something like "don't punish him" or "don't teach him a hard lesson." Heart of Sky is thus being counseled not to cause Sovereign and Quetzal Serpent any more grief with further failures to successfully create beings who can honor and support them. Perhaps a bit of frustration at the gods' lack of success up to this point is evident in this address by Xpiyacoc and Xmucane to Heart of Sky.

71. Quichés consider the face to be the symbol for the personality or essence of a person. The fact that the wooden effigies had masks rather than faces implies that they were false by nature.

72. *Na'wik.* This is the capacity to understand, notice, observe, perceive. Thus it is the wooden effigies' inability to learn and grow in knowledge that destroys them. *Na'b'al* (understanding, knowledge, memory) is a uniquely human trait.

The Fall of the Effigies of Carved Wood

Then came the end of the effigies carved of wood, for they were ruined, crushed,[73] and killed. A flood was planned by Heart of Sky that came down upon the heads of the effigies carved of wood. The body of man had been carved of *tz'ite* wood by the Framer and the Shaper. The body of woman consisted of reeds according to the desire of the Framer and the Shaper. But they were not capable of understanding and did not speak before their Framer and their Shaper, their makers and their creators.

Thus they were killed in the flood. There came a great resin down from the sky.[74]

There came the ones called Chiselers of Faces, who gouged out their eyes. There came Death Knives, which cut off their heads. There came Crouching Jaguar, who ate their flesh. There came Striking Jaguar, who struck them. They smashed their bones and their tendons.

Their bones were ground up. They were broken into pieces. Their faces were ground up[75] because they proved to be incapable of understanding before the face of their mother and the face of their father, Heart of Sky, Huracan by name.

Thus they caused the face of the earth to be darkened, and there fell a black rain,[76] a rain that fell both day and night. The small and the great animals came in upon them.[77] Their faces were crushed by the trees and the stones. They were spoken to by all their maize grinders and their cooking griddles, their plates and their pots, their dogs and their grinding stones.[78] However many things they had, all of them crushed their faces.

Their dogs and their turkeys[79] said to them:

"Pain you have caused us. You ate us. Therefore it will be you that we will eat now."

Then the grinding stones said this to them:

"We were ground upon by you. Every day, every day, in the evening and at dawn,

---

73. *Q'utuxik* is "to be crushed or pulverized," generally with reference to dried vegetables like chili peppers.

74. Here the flood is composed of resin, sap, or turpentine (secretions of pine trees). Later in the text it is a watery flood caused by heavy rainfall.

75. To "grind someone's face" is a metaphor for inflicting punishment.

76. "Black" in the sense that the storm was so severe that the sky was darkened with clouds.

77. The implication is that the wild animals of the mountains entered into the houses of the wooden effigies. The Quichés believe that when a wild animal enters their home it is to deliver a message from the earth god, who is the master of the animals. In this case, the message is a foreshadowing of the destruction that is soon to come upon the wooden effigies.

78. This is the *metate*, upon which maize and other grains are ground. It is usually made from a single block of heavy volcanic stone, quadrangular in shape, and supported by three short stone legs.

79. The dog and turkey together represent those domesticated animals raised by the Quichés and thus under their direct care and supervision. The wooden effigies thus reaped the vengeance of their own animals as a result of their cruelty and thoughtlessness.

always you did *holi, holi, huki, huki*[80] on our faces. This was our service for you who were the first people. But this day you shall feel our strength. We shall grind you like maize. We shall grind up your flesh,"[81] said their grinding stones to them.

Then their dogs said this to them:

"Why was it that you didn't give us our food? All we did was look at you, and you chased us away. You threw us out. You raised sticks against us to beat us while you ate. Thus you have spoken to us. We could not speak; therefore we received nothing from you. How could you not have understood this? You did understand. We were forgotten because of you. This day, therefore, you shall try the teeth that are in our mouths. We shall eat you," said the dogs to them. Thus their faces were crushed.

Then spoke also their griddles and their pots to them:

"Pain you have caused us. Our mouths and our faces are sooty. You were forever throwing us upon the fire and burning us. Although we felt no pain, you now shall try it. We shall burn you," said all of their pots. Thus their faces were all crushed.

The stones of the hearth flattened them. They would come out from the fire, landing on their heads and causing them pain. They fled. They hurried away. They wanted to climb up on top of the houses, but the houses would fall apart beneath them and they were thrown off. They wanted to climb up to the tops of the trees, but the trees would not support them. They wanted to hide in caves, but the mouths of the caves closed up before their faces.

Thus the framed people, the shaped people, were undone. They were demolished and overthrown as people. The mouths and the faces of all of them were ruined and crushed.

It is said that the spider monkeys that are in the forest today are descendents of these people. This was their heritage because their flesh was merely wood when it was created by the Framer and the Shaper. Therefore the spider monkeys appear like people, descendents of one generation of framed and shaped people. But they were only effigies carved of wood.

Popol Vuh: The Sacred Book of the Maya, translated by Allen J. Christenson, 48–75. Norman: University of Oklahoma Press, 2007.

---

80. The phrase *holi, holi, huqui, huqui* has been translated in a variety of ways. I have chosen to leave the phrase untranslated, because I believe the authors intended the words to convey the sound that is produced when maize is ground on a *metate* stone.

81. It is poetic justice that each of the household possessions of the wooden effigies chose to punish their owners with the same torments that they had suffered previously at their hands. Thus the grinding stones grind the faces of the wooden people in the same way that their own faces had been ground upon day in and day out. The dogs who had been eaten now eat their masters. The griddles and pots, which had been placed on the fire each day, now throw their owners into the fire to be burned. The stone tools and hearthstones pound the heads of the wooden effigies as they had been beaten upon.

POST-READING PARS

1. What are two or three character traits (among gods as well as humans) that seem to be most highly prized in the *Popol Wuj* creation stories?
2. Identify one way in which this story is similar to other creation narratives that you've read, such as Gilgamesh, Purusha, or Genesis. Identify one element that seems completely new.

Inquiry Corner

Content Question:

Describe the process of creation in the *Popol Wuj*, taking care to identify each particular stage. What is the role of failure in the creation stories?

Critical Questions:

What does the creation narrative tell us about how the Maya conceived of their gods? What does it tell us about how they conceived of themselves?

Comparative Question:

How does the *Popol Wuj*'s vision of the natural world or cosmic creation compare to other works we have read, such as Francis of Assisi's Canticle or the Ganga Lahari?

Connection Question:

Where and in what context have you come across a similar emphasis on reciprocity and mutual collaboration?

from *A Short Account of the Destruction of the Indies* by Bartolome de Las Casas

Introduction

Bartolome de Las Casas was the first to expose the abuse of Indigenous peoples of the Americas by Spanish conquistadors. He was born circa 1484 to a landowning family in Sevilla, Spain. His father and uncle joined Christopher Columbus on his second journey to the Americas in 1493, and Las Casas made his first trip to Hispaniola, a Caribbean island, in 1502. During his first five years in the New World, he lived and worked in Santo Domingo, working his family's lands. He also accompanied two military expeditions, during which he observed a tragic massacre of a large group of Indigenous leaders on the island of Cuba. Las Casas was horrified at the treatment of the Indigenous peoples of Hispaniola, as Spaniards enslaved them and forced them to mine for gold. After his return to Europe he was ordained as a Dominican priest in 1507.

During his time in Europe, Las Casas advocated for the people of the Americas to the pope. When he returned to Hispaniola, he served as official catechist—a teacher of Christianity to the Indigenous Americans whom he also forced to work his family's farmland. The Dominican priests who had arrived on Hispaniola starting in 1510 challenged his abuse of indigenous Americans. Eventually after a few years Las Casas renounced his ownership of Indigenous Americans and began to preach against the abuses of the conquest. From 1515 until his death in 1566, he repeatedly petitioned the Spanish crown to end Spanish imperial practices of abuse and enslavement of the peoples of the Indies. The Spanish government, however, chose to follow economic and political interests instead of moral consid-

SNAPSHOT BOX
LANGUAGE: Spanish
DATE: 1542 (published in 1552) CE
LOCATION: Spain
National identity: Spanish Empire
TAGS: Cross-Cultural Encounters; Empire; Identity and Self; Indigeneity; Power Structures

Timeline

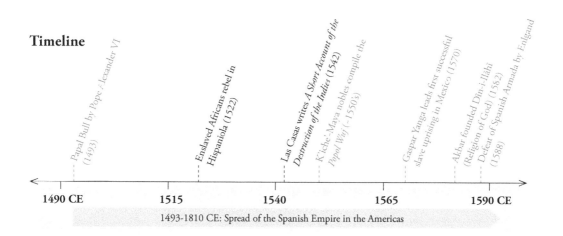

Papal Bull by Pope Alexander VI (1493)

Enslaved Africans rebel in Hispaniola (1522)

Las Casas writes *A Short Account of the Destruction of the Indies* (1542)

K'iche'-Maya nobles compile the *Popol Wuj* (~1550s)

Gaspar Yanga leads first successful slave uprising in Mexico (1570)

Akbar founded Din-i-Ilāhi (Religion of God) (1582)

Defeat of Spanish Armada by England (1588)

1490 CE   1515   1540   1565   1590 CE

1493-1810 CE: Spread of the Spanish Empire in the Americas

erations. What aspects of Las Casa's dispositions and religious sensibilities does this shift in his perspective represent?

Las Casas himself changed his rhetoric about race and enslavement over time. For example, when he first argued for the protection of the Indigenous peoples of the Indies, he advocated for the use of enslaved Africans to replace Indigenous Americans. He argued that Africans were hardier than the natives. Indigenous peoples did indeed die more quickly of European illnesses such as smallpox and malaria than did enslaved Africans, who had already been "seasoned" against European disease. Therefore, Las Casas, like all of his contemporaries, assumed that Africans were just naturally better suited for strenuous labor. In making this argument, Las Casas endorsed the idea of slavery based on race rather than the traditional concepts of enslavement as a result of war. However, he later came to regret his stance on African slavery and advocated that all slavery be abolished. But the Spanish monarchy, drawn by the potential for wealth and power that the Americas offered and convinced of the inherent "inferiority" of non-Europeans and non-Christians, continued the dehumanizing practice of slavery and refused to listen to his petitions.

Las Casas continued to advocate for Indigenous groups, drawing upon theologians and moral philosophers such as Thomas Aquinas and Aristotle to argue that the Spanish crown should allow the natives to govern themselves. While the Spanish government eventually allowed Indigenous peoples to adjudicate matters between themselves, in cases involving the Spanish government, they were required to rely on an advocate known as a "protector," who represented their interests and offered judgments based on traditional Indigenous customs that did not conflict with Christian tradition. In 1516, Las Casas was appointed the first protector under this new policy, but Spanish legal reforms did not translate into reforms of practice. His attempts to revoke *encomiendas* (Spanish royal grant of land and the right to forced labor from the Indigenous peoples living on the land) met with resistance, as Spaniards asserted that the Indians were incapable of living without supervision. Although Las Casas and his fellow Dominicans continued to chastise *encomenderos* for enslaving Indigenous peoples, he was not successful at emancipating them.

The excerpts below are drawn from Las Casas's *A Short Account of the Destruction of the Indies*, which he wrote in 1542. This documentation of the terrible abuses brought by conquest and colonization reveals much about the ways that sixteenth-century scholars used rhetoric to appeal to the king, in order to effect change. Las Casas's account was largely responsible for eventually convincing the king of Spain to make new Spanish colonial laws abolishing native slavery. Las Casas's fight against the dehumanization of Indigenous peoples that began in 1515 and resulted in these new laws show us the power and influence of a single individual's persistence and moral convictions. How might you begin to imagine being in his shoes?

Ellen Holmes Pearson
Department of History

[Content Notice: graphic violence against Indigenous peoples]

PRE-READING PARS

1. List three actions that you associate with European explorations and colonization of the New World in the late fifteenth/early sixteenth century.

2. Outline one instance where you have witnessed another individual being treated unjustly. Identify one way you have tried to address that injustice.

A Short Account of the Destruction of the Indies

Prologue of Bishop Brother Bartolomé de Las Casas, or Casaus, to the most high and most mighty Prince of Spain, our Lord the Prince Philip

Most high and most mighty Lord:

As Divine Providence has ordained that the world shall, for the benefit and proper government of the human race, be divided into kingdoms and peoples and that these shall be ruled by kings, who are (as Homer has it) fathers and shepherds to their people and are, accordingly, the noblest and most virtuous of beings, there is no doubt, nor could there in all reason be any such doubt, but that these kings entertain nothing save that which is morally unimpeachable. It follows that if the commonwealth suffers from some defect, or shortcoming, or evil, the reason can only be that the ruler is unaware of it; once the matter is brought to his notice, he will work with the utmost diligence to set matters right and will not rest content until the evil has been eradicated. This would appear to be the sense of the words of Solomon in the Bible: 'A king that sitteth in the throne of judgement scattereth away all evil with his eyes.' For, granted the innate and natural virtue of the ruler, it follows that the simple knowledge that something is wrong in his kingdom is quite sufficient to ensure that he will see that it is corrected, for he will not tolerate any such evil for a moment longer than it takes him to right it.

Contemplating, therefore (most mighty Lord), as a man with more than fifty years' experience of seeing at first hand the evil and the harm, the losses and diminutions suffered by those great kingdoms, each so vast and so wonderful that it would be more appropriate to refer to them as the New World of the Americas—kingdoms granted and entrusted by God and His Church to the Spanish Crown so that they might be properly ruled and governed, converted to the Faith, and tenderly nurtured to full material and spiritual prosperity—I am persuaded that, if Your Highness had been informed of even a few of the excesses which this New World has witnessed, all of them surpassing anything that men hitherto have imagined even in their wildest dreams, Your Highness would not have delayed for even one moment before entreating His Majesty to prevent any repetition of the atrocities which go under the name of 'conquests': excesses which, if no move is made to stop them, will be committed time and again, and which (given that the indigenous peoples of the region are naturally so gentle, so peace-loving, so humble and so docile) are of themselves iniquitous, tyrannical, contrary to natural, canon, and civil law, and are deemed wicked and are condemned and proscribed by all such legal codes. I therefore concluded that it would constitute a criminal neglect of my duty to remain silent about the enormous loss of life as well as the infinite number of human souls despatched to Hell in the course of such 'conquests,' and so resolved to publish an account of a few such outrages (and they can be only a few out of the countless number of such incidents that I could relate) in order to make that account the more accessible to Your Highness.

Thus it was that, when the then bishop of Cartagena and tutor to your Highness, the archbishop of Toledo, asked me for a copy of my *Account*, I duly gave him one and this he presented to Your Highness. But Your Highness has been fully occupied with journeys, by land and sea, as well as other pressing royal business, and it may well be that Your Highness has never found the time to read the *Account*, or has perhaps allowed it to slip to the back of your mind. Meanwhile, the boldness and the unreason of those who count it as nothing to drench the Americas in human blood and to dispossess the people who are the natural masters and dwellers in those vast and marvellous kingdoms, killing a thousand million of them, and stealing treasures beyond compare, grow by the day, and, masquerading under false colours, they do everything within their power to obtain further licence to continue their conquests (licence that cannot be granted without infringing natural and divine law and thereby conniving at the gravest of mortal sins, worthy of the most terrible and everlasting punishment). I therefore determined to present Your Highness with this *Short Account*, which is but a brief digest of the many and various outrages and depredations which could and should be recorded. I implore Your Highness to accept it and to read it in that spirit of clemency and royal benevolence with which Your Highness traditionally approaches the works of those of Your Highness's subjects and servants whose only desire is to serve the public good and the interests of the Crown. It is my fervent hope that, once Your Highness perceives the extent of the injustices suffered by these innocent peoples and the way in which they are being destroyed and crushed underfoot, unjustly and for no other reason than to satisfy the greed and ambition of those whose purpose it is to commit such wicked atrocities, Your Highness will see fit to beg and entreat His Majesty to refuse all those who seek royal licence for such evil and detestable ventures, and to put a stop once and for all to their infernal clamour in such a way that nobody will henceforth dare to make such a request nor even to mention ventures of this kind.

This, Your Royal Highness, is a matter on which action is both urgent and necessary if God is to continue to watch over the Crown of Castile and ensure its future well-being and prosperity, both spiritual and temporal. Amen.

Preface

The Americas were discovered in 1492, and the first Christian settlements established by the Spanish the following year. It is accordingly forty-nine years now since

Spaniards began arriving in numbers in this part of the world. They first settled the large and fertile island of Hispaniola, which boasts six hundred leagues of coastline and is surrounded by a great many other large islands, all of them, as I saw for myself, with as high a native population as anywhere on earth. Of the coast of the mainland, which, at its nearest point, is a little over two hundred and fifty leagues from Hispaniola, more than ten thousand leagues had been explored by 1541, and more are being discovered every day. This coastline, too, was swarming with people and it would seem, if we are to judge by those areas so far explored, that the Almighty selected this part of the world as home to the greater part of the human race.

God made all the peoples of this area, many and varied as they are, as open and as innocent as can be imagined. The simplest people in the world—unassuming, long-suffering, unassertive, and submissive—they are without malice or guile, and are utterly faithful and obedient both to their own native lords and to the Spaniards in whose service they now find themselves. Never quarrelsome or belligerent or boisterous, they harbour no grudges and do not seek to settle old scores; indeed, the notions of revenge, rancour, and hatred are quite foreign to them. At the same time, they are among the least robust of human beings: their delicate constitutions make them unable to withstand hard work or suffering and render them liable to succumb to almost any illness, no matter how mild. Even the common people are no tougher than princes or than other Europeans born with a silver spoon in their mouths and who spend their lives shielded from the rigours of the outside world. They are also among the poorest people on the face of the earth; they own next to nothing and have no urge to acquire material possessions. As a result they are neither ambitious nor greedy, and are totally uninterested in worldly power. Their diet is every bit as poor and as monotonous, in quantity and in kind, as that enjoyed by the Desert Fathers. Most of them go naked, save for a loincloth to cover their modesty; at best they may wrap themselves in a piece of cotton material a yard or two square. Most sleep on matting, although a few possess a kind of hanging net, known in the language of Hispaniola as a hammock. They are innocent and pure in mind and have a lively intelligence, all of which makes them particularly receptive to learning and understanding the truths of our Catholic faith and to being instructed in virtue; indeed, God has invested them with fewer impediments in this regard than any other people on earth. Once they begin to learn of the Christian faith they become so keen to know more, to receive the Sacraments, and to worship God, that the missionaries who instruct them do truly have to be men of exceptional patience and forbearance; and over the years I have time and again met Spanish laymen who have been so struck by the natural goodness that shines through these people that they frequently can be heard to exclaim: 'These would be the most blessed people on earth if only they were given the chance to convert to Christianity.'

It was upon these gentle lambs, imbued by the Creator with all the qualities we have mentioned, that from the very first day they clapped eyes on them the Spanish fell like ravening wolves upon the fold, or like tigers and savage lions who have not eaten meat for days. The pattern established at the outset has remained unchanged to this day, and the Spaniards still do nothing save tear the natives to shreds, murder them and inflict upon them untold misery, suffering and distress, tormenting, harrying and persecuting them mercilessly. We shall in due course describe some of the many ingenious methods of torture they have invented and refined for this purpose, but one can get some idea of the effectiveness of their methods from the figures alone. When the Spanish first journeyed there, the indigenous population of the island of Hispaniola stood at some three million; today only two hundred survive. The island of Cuba, which extends for a distance almost as great as that separating Valladolid from Rome, is now to all intents and purposes uninhabited; and two other large, beautiful and fertile islands, Puerto Rico and Jamaica, have been similarly devastated. Not a living soul remains today on any of the islands of the Bahamas, which lie to the north of Hispaniola and Cuba, even though every single one of the sixty or so islands in the group, as well as those known as the Isles of Giants and others in the area, both large and small, is more fertile and more beautiful than the Royal Gardens in Seville and the climate is as healthy as anywhere on earth. The native population, which once numbered some five hundred thousand, was wiped out by forcible expatriation to the island of Hispaniola, a policy adopted by the Spaniards in an endeavour to make up losses among the indigenous population of that island. One God-fearing individual was moved to mount an expedition to seek out those who had escaped the Spanish trawl and were still living in the Bahamas and to save their souls by converting them to Christianity, but, by the end of a search lasting three whole years, they had found only the eleven survivors I saw with my own eyes. A further thirty or so islands in the region of Puerto Rico are also now uninhabited and left to go to rack and ruin as a direct result of the same practices. All these islands, which together must run to over two thousand leagues, are now abandoned and desolate.

On the mainland, we know for sure that our fellow-countrymen have, through their cruelty and wickedness, depopulated and laid waste an area which once boasted more than ten kingdoms, each of them larger in area than the whole of the Iberian Peninsula. The whole region, once teeming with human beings, is now deserted over a distance of more than two thousand leagues: a distance, that is, greater than the journey from Seville to Jerusalem and back again.

At a conservative estimate, the despotic and diabolical behaviour of the Christians has, over the last forty years, led to the unjust and totally unwarranted deaths of more than twelve million souls, women and children among them, and there are grounds for believing my own estimate of more than fifteen million to be nearer the mark.

There are two main ways in which those who have travelled to this part of the world pretending to be Christians have uprooted these pitiful peoples and wiped them from the face of the earth. First, they have waged war on them: unjust, cruel, bloody and tyrannical war. Second, they have murdered anyone and everyone who has shown the slightest sign of resistance, or even of wishing to escape the torment to which they have subjected him. This latter policy has been instrumental in suppressing the native leaders, and, indeed, given that the Spaniards normally spare only women and children, it has led to the annihilation of all adult males, whom they habitually subject to the harshest and most iniquitous and brutal slavery that man has ever devised for his fellow-men, treating them, in fact, worse than animals. All the many and infinitely varied ways that have been devised for oppressing these peoples can be seen to flow from one or other of these two diabolical and tyrannical policies.

The reason the Christians have murdered on such a vast scale and killed anyone and everyone in their way is purely and simply greed. They have set out to line their pockets with gold and to amass private fortunes as quickly as possible so that they can then assume a status quite at odds with that into which they were born. Their insatiable greed and overweening ambition know no bounds; the land is fertile and rich, the inhabitants simple, forbearing and submissive. The Spaniards have shown not the slightest consideration for these people, treating them (and I speak from first-hand experience, having been there from the outset) not as brute animals—indeed, I would to God they had done and had shown them the consideration they afford their animals—so much as piles of dung in the middle of the road. They have had as little concern for their souls as for their bodies, all the millions that have perished having gone to their deaths with no knowledge of God and without the benefit of the Sacraments. One fact in all this is widely known and beyond dispute, for even the tyrannical murderers themselves acknowledge the truth of it: the indigenous peoples never did the Europeans any harm whatever; on the contrary, they believed them to have descended from the heavens, at least until they or their fellow-citizens had tasted, at the hands of these oppressors, a diet of robbery, murder, violence, and all other manner of trials and tribulations.

Hispaniola

As we have said, the island of Hispaniola was the first to witness the arrival of Europeans and the first to suffer the wholesale slaughter of its people and the devastation and depopulation of the land. It all began with the Europeans taking native women and children both as servants and to satisfy their own base appetites; then, not content with what the local people offered them of their own free will (and all offered as much as they could spare), they started taking for themselves the food the natives contrived to produce by the sweat of their brows, which was in all honesty little enough. Since what a European will consume in a single day normally supports three native households of ten persons each for a whole month, and since the newcomers began to subject the locals to other vexations, assaults, and iniquities, the people began to realize that these men could not, in truth, have descended from the heavens. Some of them started to conceal what food they had, others decided to send their women and children into hiding, and yet others took to the hills to get away from the brutal and ruthless cruelty that was being inflicted on them. The Christians punched them, boxed their ears and flogged them in order to track down the local leaders, and the whole shameful process came to a head when one of the European commanders raped the wife of the paramount chief of the entire island. It was then that the locals began to think up ways of driving the Europeans out of their lands and to take up arms against them. Their weapons, however, were flimsy and ineffective both in attack and in defence (and, indeed, war in the Americas is no more deadly than our jousting, or than many European children's games) and, with their horses and swords and lances, the Spaniards easily fended them off, killing them and committing all kind of atrocities against them.

They forced their way into native settlements, slaughtering everyone they found there, including small children, old men, pregnant women, and even women who had just given birth. They hacked them to pieces, slicing open their bellies with their swords as though they were so many sheep herded into a pen. They even laid wagers on whether they could manage to slice a man in two at a stroke, or cut an individual's head from his body, or disembowel him with a single blow of their axes. They grabbed suckling infants by the feet and, ripping them from their mothers' breasts, dashed them headlong against the rocks. Others, laughing and joking all the while, threw them over their shoulders into a river, shouting: 'Wriggle, you little perisher.' They slaughtered anyone and everyone in their path, on occasion running through a mother and her baby with a single thrust of their swords. They spared no one, erecting especially wide gibbets on which they could string their victims up with their feet just off the ground and then burn them alive thirteen at a time, in honor of our Saviour and the twelve Apostles, or tie dry straw to their bodies and set fire to it. Some they chose to keep alive and simply cut their wrists, leaving their hands dangling, saying to them: 'Take this letter'—meaning that their sorry condition would act as a warning to those hiding in the hills. The way they normally dealt with the native leaders and nobles was to tie them to a kind of griddle consisting of sticks resting on pitchforks driven into the ground and then grill them over a slow fire, with the result that they howled in agony and despair as they died a lingering death.

It once happened that I myself witnessed their grilling of four or five local leaders in this fashion (and I believe they had set up two or three other pairs of grills alongside so that they might process other victims at the same time) when the poor creatures' howls came between the Spanish commander and his sleep. He gave orders that the prisoners were to be throttled, but the man in charge of the execution detail, who was more bloodthirsty than the average common hangman (I know his identity and even met some relatives of his in Seville), was loath to cut short his private entertainment by throttling them and so he personally went round ramming wooden bungs into their mouths to stop them making such a racket and deliberately stoked the fire so that they would take just as long to die as he himself chose. I saw all these things for myself and many others besides. And, since all those who could do so took to the hills and mountains in order to escape the clutches of these merciless and inhuman butchers, these mortal enemies of human kind trained hunting dogs to track them down—wild dogs who would savage a native to death as soon as look at him, tearing him to shreds and devouring his flesh as though he were a pig. These dogs wrought havoc among the natives and were responsible for much carnage. And when, as happened on the odd occasion, the locals did kill a European, as, given the enormity of the crimes committed against them, they were in all justice fully entitled to, the Spanish came to an unofficial agreement among themselves that for every European killed one hundred natives would be executed.

De Las Casas, Bartolomé. Selections from "Prologue," "Preface," and "Hispaniola." In *A Short Account of the Destruction of the Indies*, translated by Nigel Griffin, 5–17. London: Penguin, 1992.

POST-READING PARS

1. Who was Las Casas's audience? Identify two rhetorical strategies he employs to get their attention?

2. Identify two of the many atrocities that Las Casas identifies that the Indigenous people suffer.

3. What tone does Las Casas use in his descriptions of the Indigenous peoples?

Inquiry Corner

Content Questions:

What are some of Las Casas's criticisms of Christians?

What were some of the dominant emotions you felt when you read Las Casas's account of the inhumane and cruel atrocities inflicted by human beings on other human beings?

Critical Questions:

What arguments did Bartolome de Las Casas make to advocate for more humane treatment of Indigenous Americans in the New World?

Critically evaluate some of the inaccurate assumptions Las Casas makes about Indigenous Americans.

Comparative Question:

Compare Las Casas's account with other instances of devout Christians (and sometimes even clergy) critiquing other Christians.

Connection Questions:

How might you compare Las Casas's report/account to a present-day whistleblower account? Is having knowledge about injustices enough to prompt action that would address the situation?

BEYOND THE CLASSROOM

» This narrative shows how people of a certain race or background can destroy the lives and livelihoods of others based on their differences and self-ascribed power over the "natives." How have you experienced, seen, or heard of racism, sexism, or other forms of oppression being present in today's workplace? How do we work toward more equitable and inclusive workplaces?

» What role do you think activism plays in the modern workforce and do you think it is enough? Too much? Not enough?

from *The Babylonian Talmud*

Introduction

The two most central texts in the Jewish tradition are known as the Torah and the Talmud. Also called the Five Books of Moses, the **Torah** (Law) consists of the biblical books Genesis, Exodus, Leviticus, Numbers, and Deuteronomy. In addition to telling the early history of the Israelites, whose descendants would become the Jewish people, the Torah also contains 613 commandments, or "mitzvot" (plural of **mitzvah**) that serve as guidelines for ethical behavior in the lives of the Jews. These commandments, while broad in the variety of subjects they address, largely lack specifics as to their application. Consequently, a huge body of legal debate and interpretation about their applications arose, which was handed down orally over the centuries. These debates came to be known as the Oral Law, which was just as sacred and authoritative to Jewish religious leaders as the Written Law of the Torah, as they believed it had been dictated by God to Moses on Mount Sinai and transmitted faithfully ever since. Combined with the commentaries of later generations, this Oral Law would eventually become the Talmud.

This method of face-to-face transmission was disrupted, however, in the first few centuries of the modern era, when Jewish civilization found itself in a period of great transition. From its dedication circa 515 BCE to its destruction some six centuries later, the Second Temple in Jerusalem had been the center of Jewish life, with

> **SNAPSHOT BOX**
>
> LANGUAGE: Hebrew
>
> DATE: c. 200 CE
>
> LOCATION: Galilee, Palestine under the Roman Empire
>
> GENRE: Jewish legal code
>
> TAGS: Agriculture, Land, and Food; Community; Ethics and Morality; Religion; Ritual and Practice

Timeline

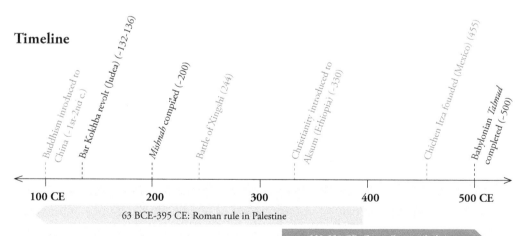

Buddhism introduced to China (~1st-2nd c.)

Bar Kokhba revolt (Judea) (~132-136)

Mishnah compiled (~200)

Battle of Xingshi (244)

Christianity introduced to Aksum (Ethiopia) (~330)

Chichen Itza founded (Mexico) (455)

Babylonian Talmud completed (~500)

100 CE   200   300   400   500 CE

63 BCE–395 CE: Roman rule in Palestine

320–550 CE: Gupta Empire (India)

priests as religious leaders and animal or agricultural sacrifice as the central religious practice. This way of life came to an end in 70 CE when the Romans destroyed the Second Temple, and any lingering hopes to reassert Jewish political autonomy in the region were definitively quashed fifty years later with the failure of the Bar Kokhba revolt circa 135 CE. What do you think happens when face-to-face transmission of knowledge breaks down in communal and religious contexts?

With the center of Jewish religious life demolished and any semblance of Jewish political power subdued, the Jewish world would have to transform itself if it were to survive. Without a temple, the synagogue and home would become the key sites of religious life. Laws and prayer would become the central religious practice, and **rabbis** (my teachers) responsible for the interpretation and transmission of Jewish law would replace the priesthood as the leaders of Jewish society. This complete restructuring of Jewish life also meant that the Oral Law could no longer be dependably transmitted face-to-face. If it were to survive, this living tradition would have to be converted into a text. Around 200 CE, a Palestinian rabbi called Judah HaNasi compiled and edited the huge corpus of Oral Law into such a text, written in Hebrew and known as the **Mishnah** (to repeat from memory). Some twenty years later, a disciple of Judah HaNasi, Rav, brought a copy of the Mishnah to Babylonia, which was rapidly becoming the center of Jewish learning at the time.

Over the next three centuries, rabbis in both Babylonia and Palestine studied the Mishnah, asked questions about it, and argued over it. These discussions, called the **Gemara** (completion), were eventually written down and codified independently of one another. Together the Gemara and the Mishnah make up the **Talmud** (learning) and, as there are two versions of the Gemara, there are also two versions of the Talmud: the Jerusalem or Palestinian Talmud and the more important Babylonian Talmud. For the next thousand years, study of the Talmud was the basis of Jewish education (male education, since Talmud study was limited to men). Why do you think the Talmud, more than the Torah, becomes central to shaping Jewish thought and observance and continues to constitute the core of Jewish religious education today?

One should not envision the Talmud as a code of law that delivers exact instructions requiring personal compliance. Rather it is a polyvocal or "many-voiced" text, which records the opinions of dozens of rabbis arguing across centuries, and in which the process of debate is just as important as the conclusion eventually reached—if one is reached at all. The Talmud addresses not only ritual and religious subjects, but also marriage and divorce, torts and contracts, commercial transactions, property, inheritance, and legal procedure. Alongside this legal material (known as **halakhah**), the Talmud contains legends and lore (known as **aggadah**).

The text below contains excerpts from a section of the Mishnah called **Zeraim** (seeds) and deals with the laws pertaining to charity. It is notable, though, that Hebrew has no word for charity. The word that is often translated to charity—*tzedakah*—literally means "justice" or "righteousness." In addition to delineating general laws of tzedakah, the reading outlines more specifically what a person is obligated to give the poor when harvesting their fields, vineyards, or trees (called *pe'ah*). As you read the entry below, think about the relationship between charity and justice.

Doria B. Killian
Center for Jewish Studies and Department of Languages and Literatures

---

PRE-READING PARS

1. Give two examples of charity and two examples of justice.
2. Do you think of charity and/or justice as matters of religion? If yes, how so? If no, why not?

"Tractate Peah": from *The Babylonian Talmud*

The Portion of the Poor (Tractate Peah)

The following have no prescribed measure: *Peah*,[82] First-Fruits, Festival-Offerings, deeds of kindness, and the study of the Law. And the following are the things the fruit of which a man enjoys in this world, hut the capital fund of which remains for him in the world to come: The honoring of father and mother, deeds of kindness, and the making of peace between one man and another, but the study of the Law is greater than any of them.

One should not leave *Peah* less than one-sixth of the field. And although there is no prescribed measure it should be fixed according to the size of the field, the number of the poor, and the need.

One may leave *Peah* in the beginning or in the middle of the field. Rabbi Simon says: As long as he leaves at the end the prescribed measure. Rabbi Yehuda says: If he leaves but one stalk at the end, he has fulfilled his obligation as to *Peah*; but if not, whatever he left at the beginning or at the end is regarded as abandoned property.

A ruling has been established as regards *Peah*: whatever is used as food, and has to be tended, and is raised from the soil, and is reaped at one time, and is brought in for storage, requires the leaving of *Peah*; and this includes grain and pulse.

Of the trees, sumach, carob, nut trees, the almond, vines, the pomegranate, the olive, and date palm are all subject to Peah.

The following serve as boundaries for a field, in all that concerns *Peah*: A river, a pond, a private road, a public road, and a public path. Also a private path that is used during the summer and during the rainy-season, uncultivated soil, fallow-land, and a different variety of crop. If one cuts the produce of one field for fodder, he makes thereby a boundary, this is according to Rabbi Meir, but the Sages say: It does not act as a boundary unless he ploughed it up.

A stream, both sides of which cannot be cut in one operation serves as a boundary, according to Rabbi Yehuda. The hills that can be ploughed by a mattock, though the oxen cannot go through them with their plough, is considered one field, and is subject to only one *Peah*.

---

82. Peah: corner of the field, the portion of the crop that must be left by the owner to the poor. See Leviticus 19:9, 23:22.

Everything serves as a boundary for a sown field, but for trees a fence only serves as a boundary, but if the branches of the trees intertwine, then the fence does not constitute a boundary, and all is subject to only one *Peah*.

From Chapter I

Peah is given from what is attached to the soil. From vines and date palms, the owner takes down some fruit and distributes it to the poor. Rabbi Simon says: This applies also to nut trees.

If ninety-nine of the poor vote that *Peah* be distributed, and one says that it should be left for them to help themselves, it is to be done according to the one because the law is in agreement with him.

But it is not so with vines and date palms; if ninetynine vote for helping themselves and one says it should be distributed, he is followed, because the law is in agreement with him.

If one took some of the *Peah* and threw it over the rest, none of it belongs to him. If he fell upon it or spread his cloak over it, it must be taken away from him. The same applies to Gleaning and to Forgotten Sheaf.

Peah must not be cut with a sickle and must not be uprooted with a hatchet, so that one will not hurt his neighbor.

If a heathen reaped his field and then became a proselyte, he is exempt from Gleaning, from Forgotten Sheaf, and from *Peah*. Rabbi Yehuda says: He is subject to the Forgotten Sheaf, because this is given at the time of binding.

What constitutes Gleaning? Whatever falls down at the time of reaping. If one cut a handful, or pulled up a handful, and a thorn pricked him and it fell from his hands to the ground, it belongs to the owner. If it fell on the inside of the hand or the inside of the sickle, it belongs to the poor; if it fell on the outside of the hand or the back of the sickle, it belongs to the owner. If it fell over the top of the hand or the top of the sickle, Rabbi Ishmael says: It belongs to the poor. Rabbi Akiba says: It belongs to the owner.

From Chapter II

From a stack of sheaves beneath which no Gleaning has been taken, everything that touches the ground belongs to the poor. If the wind scattered the sheaves from the stack, one must estimate the amount of gleanings that would be gathered from the field and give it to the poor. Rabbi Simon ben Gamaliel says: One gives in proportion to the yield of the field.

If a man sells a field the seller may take the gleanings, but the buyer must not take any. One must not hire workers with the stipulation that the worker's son shall gather the gleanings behind him. One who does not allow the poor to gather, or allows one, and does not allow another; or if he aids one of them, he is robbing the poor. Of such a one it was said: (*Proverbs* xxii, 28) *Remove not the ancient landmark which thy fathers have set.* (The *Mishna* reads the word "Olam" as "Olim" and translates the second part of the verse: for those that come up.)

From Chapter VII

A poor man who goes from one place to another should be given not less than a loaf worth one *Pandion*, and one *Selah's* worth of grain. If he stays for the night, he should be given his needs for the night. On the Sabbath he should be given three meals.

If a man has food for two meals, he should not take any food from the public kitchen. If he has food enough for fourteen meals, he should not take anything from the charity chest. Money for the charity chest is to be collected by two, and should be distributed by three.

If a man has two hundred *Zuz*, he must not take Gleanings, Forgotten Sheaf, *Peah*, and Poor-man's Tithe. But if he has two hundred less one *Denar*, even if a thousand was given to him at one time, he may still take everything that is allowed to a poor man. If his money is pledged to a debtor, or for his wife's marriage contract, he may [take(?)] of the poor man's portions. A man must not be compelled to sell his house or his tools.

If one has fifty *Zuz*, and he trades with them, he must not take of the poor man's portions. He who does not need and takes will not die of old age, until he has been compelled to seek the aid of his fellow man. But one who needs and does not take any, will not die of old age, till he shall be in a position to aid others. Of him it was said: (*Jeremiah* xvii, 7) *Blessed is the man that trusteth in the Lord, and whose hope the Lord is.* And this applies also to the judge who renders a true verdict according to the evidence. And every person who is not lame, blind or dumb, but pretends that he is; shall not die of old age before he does become like one of them, for it was said: (*Proverbs* xi, 27) *He that seeketh mischief, it shall come unto him.* And it was also said: (*Deuteronomy* xvi, 20) *That which is altogether just shalt thou follow.* A judge who accepts a bribe and perverts a decision shall not die from old age until his eyes have become blinded, for it was said: (*Exodus* xxiii, 8) *And thou shalt take no gift, for the gift blindeth the wise, and perverteth the words of the righteous.*

Auerbach, Leo. "Tractate Peah." In *The Babylonian Talmud: In Selection*, 49–53. New York: Philosophical Library, 1944.

POST-READING PARS

1. Identify two ways your conceptions of charity and justice compare with the conception presented in the Mishnah.
2. At times the rabbis present contradictory opinions. What does this tell you about the nature of authority among the rabbis?

Inquiry Corner

Content Question(s):	Critical Question(s):
Who is entitled to receive charity? What are the requirements outlined in the reading?	How do the laws governing charity in this reading work toward justice? Are there ways in which they do not?
Comparative Question(s):	**Connection Question(s):**
Compare the Mishnah's intentionally dynamic and collaborative spirit with the primarily prescriptive focus of some of the other religious texts you read in this course, for example, *The Rule of St. Benedict.*	Many of the laws outlined in this reading pertain to agriculture, as most of the civilizations at this time were largely agricultural. Human civilization is less centered around agriculture today. How could some of the laws in this reading be adapted to function in today's societies?

Deliverance from Error by al-Ghazali (Introduction only)

SNAPSHOT BOX

LANGUAGE: Arabic

DATE: 1106–1107 CE

LOCATION: Modern-day Iran

GENRE:
Autobiography, letter

Ethnic identities:
Arabic and Persian

TAGS: Devotion;
Ethics and
Morality; Islamic
World; Mysticism;
Narrative;
Philosophy; Religion;
Ways of Knowing

Introduction

Abu Hamid Muhammad, son of Mohammad, son of Muhammad, al-Ghazali (448 AH[83]/ 1056 CE–505 AH/1111 CE), henceforth "al-Ghazali," wrote the *Deliverance from Error (al-Munqidh min al-Dalal)* near the end of his life around the year 500 AH/1106 CE. This religious and philosophical classic is a letter written to a "brother in religion" in which al-Ghazali gives advice, warnings, and explanations of errors and how to avoid them. It is likely that the letter is addressed to a Muslim readership, rather than to one particular individual. Al-Ghazali narrates key events in his life and what they mean, and so the letter is like an autobiography. However, historians have shown that there are a few important historical events that al-Ghazali omits from the *Deliverance from Error*, and that al-Ghazali's reasons for these omissions help us to understand the immediate social and political context in which he wrote *Deliverance from Error*.

In *Deliverance from Error* al-Ghazali outlines his understanding of **Sufism**. Sufism is an Islamic ascetic and mystical tradition going back to at least the ninth century CE. Sufis pay close attention to the underlying motives of their every action and seek to infuse their everyday lives with

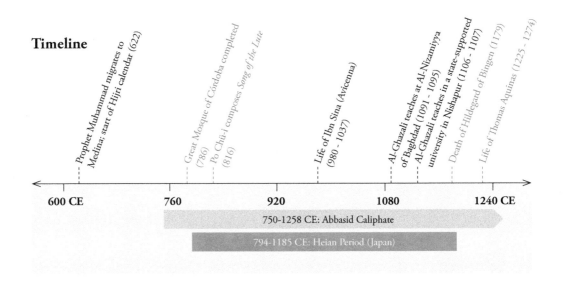

Timeline

Prophet Muhammad migrates to Medina; start of Hijri calendar (622)

Great Mosque of Córdoba completed (786)

Po Chü-i composes *Song of the Lute* (816)

Life of Ibn Sina (Avicenna) (980 - 1037)

Al-Ghazali teaches at Al-Nizamiyya of Baghdad (1091 - 1095)

Al-Ghazali teaches in a state-supported university in Nishapur (1106 - 1107)

Death of Hildegard of Bingen (1179)

Life of Thomas Aquinas (1225 - 1274)

600 CE   760   920   1080   1240 CE

750-1258 CE: Abbasid Caliphate

794-1185 CE: Heian Period (Japan)

83. "AH" is from the Islamic calendar, which is based on a lunar (as opposed to a solar) year. "AH" stands for "anno Hegirae," that is, in the year of the Hijra. This is when the Prophet Muhammad fled from Mecca to Medina and established the first Islamic community.

a deep spiritual meaning. Some early Sufis were known to be "intoxicated" with the contemplation of God, but others were known as more "sober," given that some of the former were charged with heresy because they claimed things like, "I am God!" Al-Ghazali followed the "sober" tradition, according to which mystical experience was not the ultimate goal but only an intermediate step toward God. One key thing to understand is that Sufism, as understood by al-Ghazali, is keenly focused on preparing oneself for God's judgment by means of living righteously and turning oneself wholly toward God in this life. Sufi practices involve intellectual studies that al-Ghazali understands as necessary for cultivating upright moral living and worshipping God. The turn toward God, or conversion, involves our every thought and action. Al-Ghazali exposes mistaken forms of reasoning in *Deliverance from Error* so that with correct understanding the reader will do what is right in the eyes of God.

In what follows, I give a general outline of the contents in the *Deliverance from Error* itself and then discuss the important omissions. By understanding these omissions, we can return to the *Deliverance from Error* itself in order to gain a deeper appreciation of it. Leaving things out from one's autobiography seems to be fairly common. When you become friends with someone new and tell them about yourself, what significant events in your life do you omit? Why would you leave out these events?

The *Deliverance from Error* opens with an invocation to God, followed by some official titles that al-Ghazali received through the course of his life. He was called "the most eminent and ascetic Master, the Ornament of Religion, and the Proof of Islam." The first title references al-Ghazali's adoption of, and leadership in, the moral, intellectual, and mystical tradition of Sufism within Islam. The second and third titles signal his international fame as a theologian, philosopher, and scholar of Islamic law.

The letter can be understood as divided into six sections. In section 1, al-Ghazali narrates a personal epistemological crisis having to do with whether he can really know anything (as opposed to merely having a true belief). He worries whether he can really *know* that Islam is the true religion. Importantly, he assumes that knowledge (as opposed to mere true belief) requires that one be immune to even the possibility of making a mistake. This passage has drawn the attention of many philosophers, including comparisons with the *Meditations* of the French philosopher Rene Descartes.

In section 2, al-Ghazali gives an overview of what he'll discuss next. He suggests that in his life he first studied *kalam*, which is a science having to do with interpreting and defending the Qur'an, then he studied philosophy—particularly Aristotle, al-Farabi, and Ibn Sina—then he studied an Islamic group, called the Batanites, who claimed that all knowledge comes only from an infallible Imam (a religious leader), and finally he studied Sufi texts. Historians have pointed out that al-Ghazali was introduced to Sufi texts and teachers early in his life. This suggests that the order of these four groups is not strictly based on the order in which he studied these groups, but rather the order is based on pedagogical concerns for the intended reader. It makes pedagogical sense that the last group discussed is Sufism because al-Ghazali strongly commends it to the intended readers and Sufism played a key role in defending himself against other scholars' attacks, as well as aiming to avoid severe political consequences because of his having broken his promise to the Caliph that he would teach in the university in Baghdad.

In section 3 he discusses *kalam*, pointing out its strengths and weaknesses. In section 4, which is considerably longer, al-Ghazali charts out what was considered the subdisciplines in philosophy, namely, mathematics, logic, physics, metaphysics, political science, and moral science. Al-Ghazali focuses on errors that students of these sciences might make, and how these errors connect with believing or doing what is wrong in the eyes of God.

In section 4 al-Ghazali summarizes and objects to claims made by the Batanites. It is noteworthy that al-Ghazali raises objections based on logical reasoning. He references his earlier work, *The Book of the Correct Balance*, in which he explains syllogistic logic and propositional logic, and uses examples from the Qur'an.

In section 5 al-Ghazali discusses "the way of the Sufis," with a focus on why he gave up his lucrative teaching position in Baghdad in 488 AH/1095 CE. His explanation of his departure leaves out key details. What al-Ghazali omits from his explanation in *Deliverance from Error* was the source for why he wished to stop teaching in the state-funded university in Baghdad (Al-Nizamiyya of Baghdad). In al-Ghazali's first two years of teaching there (484–486 AH), he wrote his famous text, *The Incoherence of the Philosophers*. In the subsequent two years he became deeply worried that he was arguing against others, in part, for the sake of fame and so was not preparing himself for God's judgment in the afterlife by living rightly in this life. He gives this reason in *Deliverance from Error*. But there is another crucial reason, which he omits from the letter. Historians tell us, after two years of teaching at the state university in Baghdad, al-Ghazali became morally anxious and fearful of divine judgment. Why? Because he believed that he was being paid with money that was illicitly acquired by his employer, the Seljuk Empire. According to Islamic law, as understood by al-Ghazali, being paid with illicitly acquired money puts one in jeopardy of damnation. Moreover, in *Deliverance from Error* he mentions that he visited the tomb of Abraham, but omits the fact, which he discusses in his Persian letters, that while there he made a vow to God that he would never again teach for money. He knew that Sufi teachers refused tuition payment from students in order to avoid worries about whether the tuition money was legally or illegally acquired by the students. What are some reasons for and against teachers accepting salaries?

Al-Ghazali found this Sufi practice of refusing tuition payment profoundly inspiring and freeing and promised God to follow this practice. In *Deliverance from Error* he reports that he did not tell the Caliph in Baghdad that he wanted to settle in Damascus, but he did not say why. Historians tell us that al-Ghazali wanted to stop teaching at a university that was supported by state-funding; but since he had pledged himself to the Caliph in Baghdad and did not want to be punished by him for breaking his promise to teach there, he only said that he wished to go on pilgrimage to Mecca for a few months. What really happened was that al-Ghazali quit his teaching job at Al-Nizamiyya, a state-funded university, and moved to a non-state-funded school run by Sufis in Damascus. In effect, al-Ghazali personally divested from morally questionable sources for fear of damnation. Have you ever refused money from sources that you believed were profoundly immoral? What would it be like to take a stand like this?

This information helps us better appreciate the content in section 6 of the *Deliverance from Error*. Al-Ghazali talks about how many people became lukewarm in their faith and made excuses for themselves to avoid following some Islamic laws. He reports that a godly sultan had commanded him to come teach in Nashapur (eastern Iran) in order to revive the practice of Islam. He reports that Sufis—whom he respected—claimed that God revealed to them that al-Ghazali's return to "official" teaching was commanded by God. Al-Ghazali came to believe that God commanded him to revive Islamic teaching at the beginning of a new century. Given these reasons, in 499 AH/1106 CE he accepted a new teaching position at a state university in Nashapur (in eastern Iran), after spending several years teaching at Sufi convents.

Although he returned to teaching for the state university in Nashapur, he was not consistently there, and his governmental employer sent letters to him at his Sufi convent in Tabaran, where he still spent time. This meant that although he had a government job, he avoided public disputations in public courts and preferred the more secluded Sufi school in which all students lived according to Sufi moral practices, including the renouncing of all money from illicit sources.

What all of this reveals about the *Deliverance from Error* is that the text not only offers advice, warnings, and some snapshots of al-Ghazali's life, but it also shows us an internationally respected scholar defending himself against other scholars and trying to protect himself from possible governmental retribution. What would have happened to al-Ghazali if he told the Caliph in Baghdad that the government's money was illicitly obtained? Not only is the *Deliverance from Error* a religious, philosophical, and spiritual text, and an autobiography, it is also a politically sophisticated defense that obscures as much as it reveals about al-Ghazali.

Scott M. Williams
Department of Philosophy

Adopted at UNC Asheville: *Al-Ghazali's Path to Sufism: His Deliverance from Error (al-Munqidh min al-Dalal)*, translated by R. J. McCarthy. Lexington, KY: Fons Vitae, 2000.

from *History of the Wars* and *The Secret History* by Procopius

SNAPSHOT BOX

LANGUAGE: Greek

DATE: c. 550 CE

LOCATION:
Constantinople

National identity:
Eastern Roman
Empire

TAGS: Empire;
Gender;
Historiography;
Power Structures;
Ways of Knowing

Introduction

The traditional date often given for the fall of Ancient Rome is 476 CE, but it can also be argued that it had already picked up and moved east in 330 CE, when the emperor Constantine declared the ancient, Greek-speaking city of Byzantium the new capital of the Roman Empire and renamed it New Rome. The Byzantine Empire, as it came to be known, flourished for many subsequent centuries until the fall of Constantinople and the Byzantine Empire to the Ottoman Turks in 1453 CE.

Procopius (circa 500–circa after 565) is one of the principal sources of our knowledge about the early Byzantine emperor Justinian (483–565 CE, ruled 527–565 CE). Justinian ruled from Constantinople, as New Rome came to be known, and managed a remarkable series of military victories to regain former Roman territory in the western Mediterranean. Justinian's most successful military commander was the general Belisarius (circa 500–565), and Procopius accompanied Belisarius from the beginning of his campaigns as his highly educated legal advisor. Do you think Procopius's closeness to Belisarius could have influenced his account of Justinian's reign?

Procopius would later write the *History of the Wars*, a massive work in Greek, describing not just the campaigns of Justinian's armies but also the political events back in the capital. In one of our selections, Procopius describes the Nika riots (*Nika* means "Conquer!" or "Win!"), in Constantinople in 532 CE, when rival political factions, the Blues and the Greens (originally named after the uniform colors of the

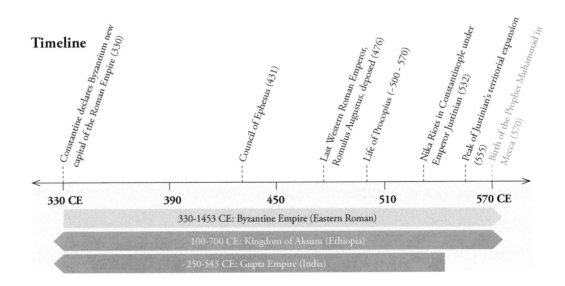

charioteer teams for which each faction cheered), teamed up against the imperial authorities to riot over corruption, high taxation, reduced civil services, and what they saw as the wrongful imprisonment of their fellow rioters. The riot began at the races in the Hippodrome (the stadium for horse racing built adjacent to the imperial palace), which Justinian himself viewed before escaping to a hiding place while half the city burned and many thousands died. In this story we are introduced to Justinian's formidable wife, the Empress Theodora.

If all the information we had of Justinian's reign were the official histories of the Byzantine Empire, including Procopius's *History of the Wars*, he would be considered one of the greatest rulers of late antiquity. Unfortunately for Justinian, though, Procopius also wrote a second, unofficial history of Justinian's reign, what we now call *The Secret History*. In this uncensored, tell-all account, we discover that Procopius passionately loathed not only the emperor Justinian and his general Belisarius, but perhaps more so their respective wives, the empress Theodora and Antonina. We do not know the extent to which this work circulated soon after Procopius wrote it, but the text was suppressed in the Byzantine Empire and remained unpublished until the seventeenth century, when a copy was found in the Vatican Library in Rome. What impact might this discovery have had on the personal reputations of Justinian and Theodora?

Our selections below come from two histories by the same author, mostly about the same people. *History of the Wars* is an officially sanctioned work, rich in political and military analysis, written in the style of classical Greek and Roman monumental histories. *The Secret History*, on the other hand, is unofficial, personal, and defamatory to the point of character assassination. Yet it belongs to another classical tradition of history writing by a political insider who seems to spare no criticism of an emperor considered to be tyrannical and personally immoral.

Both of these works by Procopius reveal a remarkably skilled writer, deeply immersed in the literary traditions of the classical Greeks and Romans. Some of these literary conventions seem odd to us in a work of history, such as the invention of speeches by historical figures where there is no recorded evidence of the exact words spoken. Yet the classical historian felt it was part of the historian's task (and art) to make a past event come alive by depicting a vivid scene that would move the imagination of the reader, thus allowing a deeper understanding of that event. While modern historians cannot get away with this invented reconstruction of the past without qualification, we still see these techniques used effectively in historical fiction and film. We must also remember that many in Procopius's audience, educated in these classical literary traditions as well, would have picked up on literary allusions that are now known only to specialists (and helpfully left in footnotes in our text by our editors). By tracing these allusions in his invented speeches, for example, we can see that even when he seems to be depicting Theodora or Justinian as praiseworthy, he may be leaving ironic hints of harsh criticism that would go unnoticed by the less informed reader.

As critical readers, we are left with some serious questions about these texts. Can these two accounts by the same author about the same persons — one seemingly positive, the other thoroughly negative — be reconciled?

Gregory Lyon
Humanities Program

[Content Notice: misogynist language]

PRE-READING PARS

1. When we are trying to evaluate the quality of historical sources, maybe we should interrogate them as if they are on the witness stand in a court case. What are two qualities of a good witness or their testimony in a court case?

2. What are two qualities in a witness or their testimony that would lead us to be skeptical?

3. In today's court of public opinion (for example, in the press or on social media), what are two examples of bad behavior that can harm the reputation of a public figure?

from *History of the Wars* and *The Secret History*

from History of the Wars

Preface: The Purpose of This Book.

Procopius of Caesarea has written the history of the wars which Justinian, Emperor of the Romans, waged against the barbarians of the East and of the West, relating separately the events of each one, to the end that the long course of time may not overwhelm deeds of singular importance through lack of a record, and thus abandon them to oblivion and utterly obliterate them. The memory of these events he deemed would be a great thing and most helpful to men of the present time, and to future generations as well, in case time should ever again place men under a similar stress. For men who purpose to enter upon a war or are preparing themselves for any kind of struggle may derive some benefit from a narrative of a similar situation in history, inasmuch as this discloses the final result attained by men of an earlier day in a struggle of the same sort, and foreshadows, at least for those who are most prudent in planning, what outcome present events will probably have. Furthermore he had assurance that he was especially competent to write the history of these events, if for no other reason, because it fell to his lot, when appointed adviser to the general Belisarius, to be an eye-witness of practically all the events to be described. It was his conviction that while cleverness is appropriate to rhetoric, and inventiveness to poetry, truth alone is appropriate to history. In accordance with this principle he has not concealed the failures of even his most intimate acquaintances, but has written down with complete accuracy everything which befell those concerned, whether it happened to be done well or ill by them.

It will be evident that no more important or mightier deeds are to be found in history than those which have been enacted in these wars, provided one wishes to base his judgment on the truth. For in them more remarkable feats have been performed than in any other wars with which we are acquainted; unless, indeed, any reader of this narrative should give the place of honor to antiquity, and consider contemporary achievements unworthy to be counted remarkable.

The Nika Riots

At this same time an insurrection broke out unexpectedly in Byzantium among the populace, and, contrary to expectation, it proved to be a very serious affair, and ended in great harm to the people and to the senate, as the following account will show. In every city the population has been divided for a long time past into the Blue and the Green factions; but within comparatively recent times it has come about that, for the sake of these names and the seats which the rival factions occupy in watching the games, they spend their money and abandon their bodies to the most cruel tortures, and even do not think it unworthy to die a most shameful death. And they fight against their opponents knowing not for what end they imperil themselves, but knowing well that, even if they overcome their enemy in the fight, the conclusion of the matter for them will be to be carried off straightway to the prison, and finally, after suffering extreme torture, to be destroyed. So there grows up in them against their fellow men a hostility which has no cause, and at no time does it cease or disappear, for it gives place neither to the ties of marriage nor of relationship nor of friendship, and the case is the same even though those who differ with respect to these colours be brothers or any other kin. They care neither for things divine nor human in comparison with conquering in these struggles; and it matters not whether a sacrilege is committed by anyone at all against God, or whether the laws and the constitution are violated by friend or by foe; nay even when they are perhaps ill supplied with the necessities of life, and when their fatherland is in the most pressing need and suffering unjustly, they pay no heed if only it is likely to go well with their "faction"; for so they name the bands of partisans. And even women join with them in this unholy strife, and they not only follow the men, but even resist them if opportunity offers, although they neither go to the public exhibitions at all, nor are they impelled by any other cause; so that I, for my part, am unable to call this anything except a disease of the soul. This, then, is pretty well how matters stand among the people of each and every city.

But at this time the officers of the city administration in Byzantium were leading away to death some of the rioters. But the members of the two factions, conspiring together and declaring a truce with each other, seized the prisoners and then straightway entered the prison and released all those who were in confinement there, whether they had been condemned on a charge of stirring up sedition, or for any other unlawful act. And all the attendants in the service of the city government were killed indiscriminately; meanwhile, all of the citizens who were sane-minded were fleeing to the opposite mainland, and fire was applied to the city as if it had fallen under the hand of an enemy. The sanctuary of Sophia and the baths of Zeuxippus, and the portion of the imperial residence from the propylaea as far as the so-called

House of Ares were destroyed by fire, and besides these both the great colonnades which extended as far as the market place which bears the name of Constantine, in addition to many houses of wealthy men and a vast amount of treasure. During this time the emperor and his consort with a few members of the senate shut themselves up in the palace and remained quietly there. Now the watchword which the populace passed around to one another was *Nika*, and the insurrection has been called by this name up to the present time. [...]

Now the emperor and his court were deliberating as to whether it would be better for them if they remained or if they took to flight in the ships. And many opinions were expressed favoring either course. And the Empress Theodora also spoke to the following effect: "As to the belief that a woman ought not to be daring among men or to assert herself boldly among those who are holding back from fear, I consider that the present crisis most certainly does not permit us to discuss whether the matter should be regarded in this or in some other way. For in the case of those whose interests have come into the greatest danger nothing else seems best except to settle the issue immediately before them in the best possible way. My opinion then is that the present time, above all others, is inopportune for flight, even though it brings safety. For while it is impossible for a man who has seen the light not also to die, for one who has been an emperor it is unendurable to be a fugitive. May I never be separated from this purple, and may I not live that day on which those who meet me shall not address me as mistress. If, now, it is your wish to save yourself, O Emperor, there is no difficulty. For we have much money, and there is the sea, here the boats. However consider whether it will not come about after you have been saved that you would gladly exchange that safety for death. For as for myself, I approve a certain ancient saying that royalty is a good burial-shroud."[84] When the queen had spoken thus, all were filled with boldness, and, turning their thoughts towards resistance, they began to consider how they might be able to defend themselves if any hostile force should come against them.

from The Secret History

Preface: The Purpose of This Book

In recording everything that the Roman people has experienced in successive wars up to the time of writing I have followed this plan—that of arranging all the events described as far as possible in accordance with the actual times and places. But from

---

84. Procopius, in this invented speech, has Theodora slightly misquoting a famous tyrant, Dionysius of Syracuse (circa 432–367 BCE), who said, "Tyranny is a good burial shroud," as he suppressed a popular uprising by using mercenary soldiers. The quote by Dionysius has a long tradition in classical literature, as related by the orator Isocrates (436–338 BCE), the historian Diodorus Siculus (circa 90–30 BCE), and the biographer Plutarch (46–119 CE). Procopius could have expected an educated reader to recognize Theodora's misquote.

now on I shall no longer keep to that method: in this volume I shall set down every single thing that has happened anywhere in the Roman Empire. The reason is simple. As long as those responsible for what happened were still alive, it was out of the question to tell the story in the way that it deserved. For it was impossible either to avoid detection by swarms of spies, or if caught to escape death in its most agonizing form. Indeed, even in the company of my nearest relations I felt far from safe. Then again, in the case of many events which in my earlier volumes I did venture to relate I dared not reveal the reasons for what happened. So in this part of my work I feel it my duty to reveal both the events hitherto passed over in silence and the reasons for the events already described.

But as I embark on a new undertaking of a difficult and extraordinarily baffling character, concerned as it is with Justinian and Theodora and the lives they lived, my teeth chatter and I find myself recoiling as far as possible from the task; for I envisage the probability that what I am now about to write will appear incredible and unconvincing to future generations. And again, when in the long course of time the story seems to belong to a rather distant past, I am afraid that I shall be regarded as a mere teller of fairy tales or listed among the tragic poets. One thing, however, gives me confidence to shoulder my heavy task without flinching: my account has no lack of witnesses to vouch for its truth. For my own contemporaries are witnesses fully acquainted with the incidents described, and will pass on to future ages an incontrovertible conviction that these have been faithfully recorded.

And yet there was something else which, when I was all agog to get to work on this volume, again and again held me back for weeks on end. For I inclined to the view that the happiness of our grandchildren would be endangered by my revelations, since it is the deeds of blackest dye that stand in greatest need of being concealed from future generations, rather than they should come to the ears of monarchs as an example to be imitated. For most men in positions of power invariably, through sheer ignorance, slip readily into imitation of their predecessors' vices, and it is to the misdeeds of earlier rulers that they invariably find it easier and less troublesome to turn. But later on I was encouraged to write the story of these events by this reflexion— it will surely be evident to future monarchs that the penalty of their misdeeds is almost certain to overtake them, just as it fell upon the persons described in this book. Then again, their own conduct and character will in turn be recorded for all time; and that will perhaps make them less ready to transgress. For how could the licentious like of Semiramis or the dementia of Sardanapalus and Nero have been known to anyone in later days, if contemporary historians had not left these things on record?[85] Apart from this, those who in the future, if so it happens, are similarly ill

85. In the Greek historical tradition, Semiranis and Sardanapalus were legendary Assyrian (Mesopotamian) rulers. Queen Semiranis was famous conquering and building cities, as well as for sleeping with her soldiers. Sardanpalus was allegedly the last Assyrian king, infamous for his extravagant spending and sexual decadence. The Roman emperor Nero (r. 54–68 CE) was already known in Procopius's time as the archetypal "bad emperor."

used by the ruling powers will not find this record altogether useless; for it is always comforting for those in distress to know that they are not the only ones on whom these blows have fallen.

That is my justification for first recounting the contemptible conduct of Belisarius, and then revealing the equally contemptible conduct of Justinian and Theodora. [...]

The Affair of Antonina

Belisarius[86] had a wife, whom I have mentioned in the earlier books. Her father and grandfather were both charioteers who had performed professionally in Byzantium and Thessalonica. Her mother, on the other hand, had been one of those types who whore themselves on the stage.[87] Before marrying Belisarius, then, this woman had lived a wanton life and had never learned to show any restraint. She had also spent time with those people from her parents' world who knew all about poisons and magic herbs and had learned from them many things that were useful to her. Later she became the lawful wife of Belisarius, though she was already the mother of many children. She had every intention of cheating on him from the start but took precautions to practice her adultery in secret, not because she felt any qualms about her habits, and certainly not because she had any fear of the man with whom she now lived given that, firstly, she never felt shame for anything that she did and, secondly, she had quite overpowered her husband with her charms and philters of seduction. No, it was because she was terrified that the empress might punish her. [...]

There was a young man from Thrace in Belisarius's household named Theodosius, who belonged, through the tradition of his ancestors, to the sect of the so-called Eunomians.[88] When the expedition was about to sail for Africa, Belisarius purified him in the holy immersion of baptism. Raising him up from the font with his own hands, he formally accepted him into his family as the son of himself and his wife, according to the custom of adoption among Christians. From that moment on Antonina, as was only to be expected, loved Theodosius for he was her son according to sacred law, and cared for him greatly, keeping him by her side. But during that voyage she quickly became immoderately infatuated with him, and was seized by an insatiable passion. She shook off all fear and respect for both human convention and divine authority and had sex with him, at first secretly but finally even before

---

86. The Greek forms of proper nouns (such as "Belisarios" and "Byzantios") have been Latinized throughout for consistency with other translations.

87. Acting was for women a dishonorable profession, overlapping with sex work.

88. Eunomians were extreme Arian Christians who believed that the substance (*ouisa*) of the Son (Jesus Christ) was different from that of God the Father. Arian Christianity was deemed heretical at the Council of Nicea (325 CE) but continued to gain adherents and challenge orthodoxy, particularly among the Germanic tribes (so-called *barbarians*) on the frontiers of the Roman Empire.

the household servants and handmaidens. Smitten with desire and obviously driven by erotic passion, she did not see any further reason why she should refrain from the deed. When Belisarius once caught them in the act when they were in Carthage, he willingly allowed his wife to pull the wool over his eyes. For even though he was furious at finding them together in a basement room, she was not overcome with shame nor even flinched at her compromising situation. "I came down here," she said, "with the boy to hide the most precious spoils of war so that the emperor doesn't find out about them." That was her excuse, and he let on that he had bought it, even though he could see that the belt around Theodosius's pants had been loosened in the part closest to his genitals. He was so infatuated with this person, his wife, that he could not bring himself to believe the evidence of his own eyes. [...]

Justinian's Physical Appearance and Character

I think that now would also be a good time to give a sense of the man's physical appearance. He was neither tall nor too short, but of medium height, not thin at all but slightly fleshy. His face was round and not unshapely. He retained a ruddy complexion even after two days of fasting. If I had to capture his whole appearance in one image I would say that he was most similar to Domitian, the son of Vespasian, whose foul character the Romans so enjoyed that their rage against him, they decided, was not satisfied even when they had hacked him into pieces, so that the Senate passed a decree that the name of this emperor should never again be carved in an inscription and no image of him should be allowed to survive.[...]

That is what he looked like. I could not, however, accurately describe his character. This man was both prone to evil and simultaneously easy to lead around by the nose, a type that they called a "fool and villain in one." On the one hand, he himself never spoke the truth to anyone in his presence, always saying and doing everything with treacherous intent; yet at the same time he was easy prey for those who wished to deceive him.[...] This emperor, then, was ironic in speech, treacherous in his intentions, a hypocrite, secretly vindictive, two-faced, a formidable man in his own way and highly accomplished at hiding his true opinion. When he cried it was not as an expression of genuine joy or sorrow at anything but a strategy to serve the needs of the moment. He was always lying but his lies were prepared. Indeed, he ratified his agreements with his signature and the most dread oaths, even when dealing with his own subjects. But he would immediately depart from what had been agreed on and sworn to, like the most contemptible of slaves who, fearing torture, confess to things that they had denied under oath. He was unreliable as an ally, treacherous as an enemy, craving murder and money like an ardent lover, stirring up strife and obsessively innovating, easily persuaded to commit evil but rejecting all counsel for the good, eager to devise base plans and implement them, a man whose ears were offended by the very mention of the good—how could words, therefore, ever suffice to describe Justinian's character? All the vices I have described along with other, even worse ones that he had seemed to exceed human capacity; it was as though nature had removed every inclination to do wrong from other people and deposited them all together into the soul of this man.

He was, in addition to all that, quite receptive to slander and eager to inflict punishment. He never once decided a matter by investigating the facts but made his decision known as soon as he had heard the slanderer. He had no qualms about writing orders for the sacking of villages, the burning of cities, and the enslavement of entire nations, and all for no good reason. So that if one wanted to weigh these things against everything that has befallen the Romans from the beginning, he would discover, it seems to me, that more people have been slaughtered by this one man than in all of past history put together. As for the money of others, he showed no hesitation in quietly appropriating it. And when he reached out to take possession of things that did not belong to him, he did not even bother to screen what he was doing behind a pretext of legality. Yet once it was his, he was quite capable of squandering it through wasteful generosity and by giving it away to the barbarians, even though there was no good reason to do so. In sum, neither did he himself ever have any money nor would he allow anyone else to have it either, as if the problem was not that he was driven by love of money but rather by envy of those who had it. Prosperity, then, migrated out of the land of the Romans because of him, while he inaugurated an era of poverty for all.

Theodora's Background

All that I am able to say about Justinian's character is as I have stated above. As for the woman he married, I will now disclose her origins and the manner of her upbringing as well as how she destroyed the Roman state root and branch after marrying this man.

There was a certain Acacius in Byzantium who kept the amphitheater beasts for the Green fan-club, his position being what they call the keeper of the bears. This man died of illness while Anastasios was emperor and left behind him three children, all girls: Comito, Theodora, and Anastasia, of whom the eldest was not yet seven years old. His widow, facing hardship, married another man and their arrangement was that he would help her in the future to provide for the household and carry on her husband's job. But the dancing-master of the Greens, a certain Asterius, was bribed by another man to remove these two from that position and, without making a fuss, appoint in their place the man who gave him the bribe. For the dancing-masters had the authority to arrange such appointments as they saw fit. So when the woman saw that the entire populace had gathered in the hippodrome, she placed garlands on her children's heads and in their hands and made them sit as suppliants. But the Greens were in no way inclined to accept the supplication. The Blues, however, appointed the woman and her daughters to the equivalent position on their side, as their keeper of the beasts had recently died as well.

When these children reached puberty, their mother immediately put them on the stage in that place, for they were beautiful to behold. They did not all enter the profession at the same time, but each whenever her mother deemed her suitably attractive. The first, Comito, was already a great success among the call girls of her age. But the second, Theodora, covered by a loose dress with sleeves, the kind that slaves wear, would follow her sister and serve her in many ways but especially by always carrying around on her shoulders the base upon which her sister perched before her audiences. At this time Theodora was hardly ripe enough to sleep with a man or to have sex with him in the way that a woman should. So she would offer herself to certain poor wretches who performed that disgusting act on her that some men do with other men. She did it even with slaves who were attending their owners at the theater and who took the opportunity to step aside for a moment and practice this pestilence. And so she spent much time selling herself in this way, specializing in that unnatural service of the body.

As soon as she reached puberty and was ripe enough, she joined the women on the stage and immediately became a call girl in her own right. She belonged to the lowest rank, which in the old days they called "basic infantry."[89] For she had no skill with the *aulos*,[90] nor could she sing or even perform in the dance troupe: all she had to offer to passing customers was her youth, and she put her whole body to work for them. Later she took up full-time with the mimes in the theater, taking part in their performances by providing backup vulgarity for the comedians. For she had an especially quick and biting wit, and soon became a star feature of the show. There was no shame at all in her, and no one ever saw her embarrassed. She would provide shameful services without the slightest hesitation and was of such a sort that if someone slapped her or even punched her full in the face she would crack a joke about it and then burst out laughing. She would strip down in front for any passers-by and then in back as well, revealing in the nude those parts which custom forbids to be shown to men. She would joke with her lovers lying around in bed with them, and, by toying with new sexual techniques, constantly managed to arouse the souls of those who were debauched. Nor did she wait for her customers to make the first pass at her; quite the contrary, she herself tempted all who came along, flirting and suggestively shaking her hips, especially if they were beardless youths. Never has there been a person so enslaved to lust in all its forms. She often went to the potluck dinner parties in the company of ten young escorts, or even more than that, all at the peak of their physical prowess and skilled at screwing, and she would bed down with her fellow diners in groups all night long. And when all were exhausted from doing this,

89. In ancient comedy, this designated the most common type of prostitute. This section on the early career of Theodora is appropriately full of language taken from the comedians.

90. The *aulos* was a wind instrument, akin to recorder or a flute. Female *aulos* players ("flute-girls") are depicted in art (on pottery) and in literature as entertainers at dinner parties—and are often linked to sex work.

she would turn to their servants, all thirty of them if that's how many there were, and couple with each of them separately—but even this would not satisfy her lust.

One time when she went to the house of a notable to entertain during drinks, they say that when the eyes of all the diners were upon her she mounted the frame of the couch by their feet and unceremoniously lifted up her clothes right there and then, not caring in the least that she was making a spectacle of her shamelessness. Even though she put three of her orifices to work she would impatiently reproach Nature for not making the holes in her nipples bigger than they were so that she could devise additional sexual positions involving them as well.[91] She was often pregnant, but by using almost all known techniques she could induce immediate abortions.

Often in the theater too, and with the entire populace as her audience, she would strip and stand naked at the very center of attention, having only a loincloth about her genitals and groin—not that she would have been ashamed to flaunt those before the whole city too, but only because it was not permitted for anyone to be entirely naked in the theater, that is without a loincloth about the groin. Wearing this outfit, then, she would lie down on her back and spread herself out on the floor whereupon certain menials, who were hired to do this very job, would sprinkle barley grains all over her genitals. Then the geese, which were trained for this purpose, pecked them off one at a time with their beaks and ate them. When she stood up again not only was she not blushing with shame but seemed rather to be proud of this performance.[92] For she was not just shameless: she was also more accomplished than anyone else at devising shameless acts. Often she would take her clothes off and stand in the middle of the stage by the mimes, alternately bending backwards or drawing attention to her rear, advertising her special brand of gymnastics both to those who had more intimate knowledge of it and to those who did not—yet. Thus did she abuse her own body licentiously, making it seem that she had genitals not in the place where nature ordained for all other women, but in her face! All who were intimate with her were instantly known, by that very fact, to be men who did not have sex according to the laws of nature, while any decent men who came across her in the marketplace would turn back and beat a hasty retreat, lest they should touch a corner of that person's clothes and feel that they had been tainted by the pollution. Those who saw her, especially early in the morning, regarded her as an ill omen. Yet she was in the habit of constantly lashing out viciously, like a scorpion, against her fellow actresses, for she was mad with envy.

91. Procopius is likely inventing this anecdote, as it references a famous ancient Greek speech which defamed a woman by saying "she plied her trade through three orifices." Procopius ups the ante for Theodora by having her wish for yet another orifice. Again, Procopius is referencing a literary tradition that many educated readers of his time would have known, even if we no longer do.

92. Theodora's performance may be recalling the popular story of Leda and the swan, where the god Zeus takes the form of a swan in order to seduce and impregnate the human Leda, who bears Zeus's children Helen (of Troy) and Pollux.

Justinian's Misgovernment.

When Justinian ascended the throne it took him a very little while to bring everything into confusion. Things hitherto forbidden by law were one by one brought into
public life, while established customs were swept away wholesale, as if he had been
invested with the forms of majesty on condition that he would change all things to
new forms. Long established offices were abolished, and new ones set up to run the
nation's business; the laws of the land and the organization of the army were treated
in the same way, not because justice required it or the general interest urged him to
it, but merely that everything might have a new look and might be associated with
his name. If there was anything which he was not in a position to transform then and
there, even so he would at least attach his own name to it.

Of the forcible seizure of property and the murder of his subjects he could never have
enough: when he had looted innumerable houses of wealthy people he was constantly on
the look-out for others, immediately squandering on one foreign tribe or another, or on
crazy building schemes, all that he had amassed by his earlier looting. And when he had
without any excuse got rid of thousands and thousands of people, or so it would seem, he
promptly devised schemes for doing the same to others more numerous still. [...]

Frequently matters agreed between Senate and Emperor ended by being settled
quite differently. The Senate sat merely as a picturesque survival, without any power
either to register a decision or to do any good, assembling for the sake of appearance
and in fulfillment of an old law, since no member of that assembly was ever permitted to utter one word. The Emperor and his consort for the most part made a show
of taking sides in the questions at issue, but victory went to the side upon which they
had already agreed. If a man had broken the law and felt that victory was not securely
his, he had only to fling more gold to this Emperor in order to obtain the passage of
a law going clean contrary to all existing statutes. Then if somebody else should call
for the first law, which had now been repealed, His Majesty was perfectly prepared
to re-enact it and substitute it for the new one. There was nothing that remained
permanently in force, but the scales of justice wandered at random all over the place,
whichever way the greater mass of gold weighing them down succeeded in pulling
them. The home of justice was the market-hall, though it had once been the Palace,
and there sale-rooms flaunted themselves in which not only the administration of
justice by the making of laws too was sold to the highest bidder. [...]

The Arrogance of the Imperial Pair

Among the innovations which Justinian and Theodora made in the conduct of official business are the following.

In previous reigns, when the Senate came into the Emperor's presence it was customary to pay homage in this way. A man of patrician rank used to salute him on the
right breast: the Emperor responded by kissing him on the head, and then dismissed

him. Everyone else bent his right knee to the Emperor and then retired. To the Empress, however, homage was never paid. But when they came into the presence of Justinian and Theodora all of them, including those who held patrician rank, had to fall on the floor flat on their faces, stretch out their hands and feet as far as they could, touch with their lips one foot of each of Their Majesties, and then stand up again. For Theodora too insisted on this tribute being paid to her, and even claimed the privilege of receiving the ambassadors of Persia and other foreign countries and of bestowing gifts of money on them, as if she were mistress of the Roman Empire—a thing unprecedented in the whole course of history.

Again, in the past persons engaged in conversation with the Emperor called him "Emperor" and his wife "Empress," and addressed each of their ministers by the title appropriate to the rank he held at the moment; but if anyone were to join in conversation with either of these two and refer to the "Emperor" or "Empress" and not call them "Master" and "Mistress," or attempted to speak of any of the ministers as anything but "slaves," he was regarded as ignorant and impertinent; and as if he had committed a shocking offence and had deliberately insulted the last person who should have been so treated; he was sent packing.

Lastly, while in earlier reigns few visited the Palace, and they on rare occasions, from the day that these two ascended the throne officials and people of every sort spent their days in the Palace with hardly a break. The reason was that in the old days the officials were allowed to do what was just and proper in accordance with their individual judgements; this meant that while carrying out their official duties they stayed in their own offices, while the Emperor's subjects, neither seeing nor hearing of any resort to force, naturally troubled him very rarely. These two, however, all the time taking everything into their own hands to the detriment of their subjects, compelled everyone to be in constant attendance exactly like slaves. Almost any day one could see all the law-courts pretty well deserted, and at the Emperor's Court an insolent crowd elbowing and shoving, and all the time displaying the most abject servility. Those who were supposed to be close friends of Their Majesties stood there right through the whole day and invariably for a considerable part of the night, getting no sleep or food at the normal times, till they were worn out completely: this was all that their supposed good fortune brought them.

When, however, they were released from all their misery, the poor wretches engaged in bitter quarrels as to where the wealth of the Romans had gone to. Some insisted that foreigners had got it all; others declared that the Emperor kept it locked up in a number of small chambers. One of these days Justinian, if he is a man, will depart this life: if he is Lord of Demons, he will lay his life aside.

Then all who chance to be still living will know the truth.

Procopius. From "History of the Wars." In *Procopious: Volume I*. Loeb Classical Library, Vol. 48, translated by H. B. Dewing, 3–5, 219–223, 231–233. Cambridge, MA: Harvard University Press, 1914.

Procopius. "Preface," "Justinian's Misgovernment," and "The Arrogance of the Imperial Pair" from *The Secret History*, translated by G. A. Williamson, 37–39, 94, 111, 192–194. New York: Penguin Classics, 1966.

Prokopius. "The Affair of Antonina," "Justinian's Appearance and Character," and "Theodora's Background," from *The Secret History*, edited and translated by Anthony Kaldellis, 5–7, 36–43. Indianapolis, IN: Hackett, 2010. Reprinted by permission of Hackett Publishing Company, Inc. All rights reserved.

POST-READING PARS

1. List one reason Procopius gives in the preface to the *History of the Wars* for why we should believe his historical reporting?

2. Now looking at the preface to *The Secret History*, does he give a different reason there for why we should believe him? How would you briefly describe the difference in tone between the two prefaces?

3. Take the four cases of Belisarius, Antonina, Justinian, and Theodora separately. In a line each, how would you describe their worst behavior and what that reveals about their character, according to Procopius? Which of these portraits did you find most believable and why? Which did you find least believable and why?

Inquiry Corner

Content Question(s):	Critical Question(s):
Find a passage that reveals something implicitly [not directly stated by Procopius] about gender roles and/ or expectations during the reign of Justinian. What about sexual attitudes?	How do these written sources compare to what the visual source of the mosaics depicting Justinian and Theodora in the Basilica of San Vitale (in Ravenna, Italy) say about the political power of these two historical figures?
Comparative Question(s):	**Connection Question(s):**
How does Procopius's description of the uses of history in the prefaces to *History of the Wars* and *The Secret History* compare to those given by Ibn Khaldun in his *Muqaddima*?	How do our tools for evaluating the sources of modern political news differ from those we use to evaluate the sources of Procopius's political reports about the late Roman (early Byzantine) Empire?

from *Kalila and Dimna* by Nasrullah Munshi

Introduction

The fables identified here as excerpted from *Kalila and Dimna* have a rich literary translation history and serve as a terrific example of the transmission of stories and cross-cultural encounters in the premodern period. These stories originated in the narrative framework of a collection known as the *Panchatantra* (Five Treatises) in South Asia around the third century BCE. Over centuries and spanning different geographical locations, this Sanskrit collection was translated into many languages within and outside of the subcontinent: Syriac, Greek, Hebrew, Persian, and Spanish, to name a few. The excerpt included here is believed to have the following trajectory of transmission and translation: Sanskrit to Middle Persian (Iran) to Syriac, to Arabic in the eighth century, to New Persian by Nasrullah Munshi who was writing in the Ghaznavid court. Nasrullah titled this translation as *Kalila u Dimna-I Bahramshahi* (Kalila and Dimna Bahram Shahi) and dedicated it to Sultan Bahram-Shah (1084–1157). What kinds of works might one dedicate to a ruler?

Kalila and Dimna is a collection of animal fables that at first glance may read as childish and playful, sometimes even bawdy. The titular characters after all, are two clever jackals who spend a lot of time in the narrative simply talking to each other, plotting and strategizing, telling one story after another to elucidate their points of view. A story can be as short as a paragraph like the one about a monkey getting his testicles smashed because he tried to imitate the carpenter or much longer, containing a story within a story told by other animals and

SNAPSHOT BOX

LANGUAGE: New Persian

DATE: 1120 CE

LOCATION: Ghazni, Ghaznavid Empire (present-day Afghanistan)

GENRE: Fables

TAGS: Authority and Institution; Cross-Cultural Encounters; Education; Ethics and Morality; Islamic World; Narrative; Orality; Ways of Knowing

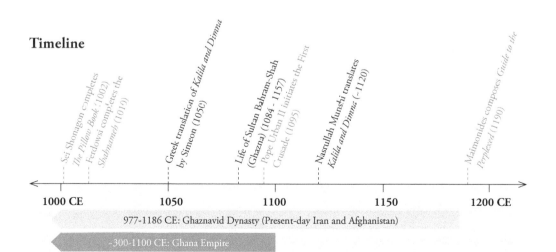

Timeline

Sei Shonagon completes *The Pillow Book* (~1002)

Ferdowsi completes the *Shahnameh* (1010)

Greek translation of *Kalila and Dimna* by Simeon (1050)

Life of Sultan Bahram-Shah (Ghazna) (1084 - 1157)

Pope Urban II initiates the First Crusade (1095)

Nasrullah Munshi translates *Kalila and Dimna* (~1120)

Maimonides composes *Guide to the Perplexed* (1190)

1000 CE   1050   1100   1150   1200 CE

977-1186 CE: Ghaznavid Dynasty (Present-day Iran and Afghanistan)

~300-1100 CE: Ghana Empire

humans. It is important, however, to remember that the multiple and far-ranging stories set in forests and villages are housed under the overarching narrative framework of the Raja of India being given counsel and advice by his brahmin minister.

All the stories told under this primary framework serve as morals, guidance, and examinations of human virtues, vices, and foibles. In his preface, Nasrullah describes the collection as "a mine of wisdom and perspicacity and a storehouse of experience and practical knowledge. By listening to it kings can learn policy for ruling a realm and ordinary people can read it and benefit from it to preserve their possessions."[93] More fittingly then, these animal fables serve as one of the earliest in the genre of the mirror for princes, a genre of instructive, advice literature for rulers on how to conduct themselves and how to maintain power. The advice to the ruler comes packaged sometimes as an extended allegory and sometimes as a pithy, idiomatic phrase. How might such advice change and be effective across various languages, religions, and cultures?

It should come as no surprise that, given the long and complex transmission history of this collection, the time and the location of a translation influences some of the reference points in the narrative. For example, even though the *Panchatantra* (that emerged in a predominantly Hindu setting) does not contain any Islamic quotes or sayings of Prophet Muhammad from the *Hadith*, this Arabic translation by Nasrullah Munshi that occurred in a Persianate Muslim empire contains verses from the Qur'an, sayings of the Prophet, and references and lines from Arabic and Persian poetry. The names of animals have been changed in places, replacing those found only on the Indian subcontinent to ones that would have been more familiar to a Ghaznavid audience. Since the caste system is not prevalent in that community, the references to brahmins and other castes have been switched. How might the cultural context and literary skill of a translator add to or take away from such collections of stories?

In his preface, Nasrullah Munshi, acknowledges some of the complex transmission history of the collection, tracing it back to India and also identifying other translators. He speaks with intellectual humility about the wisdom in these tales, describing them as "a condensation of several thousand years of wisdom."[94] As you read the following excerpt, think of the different ways that Nasrullah Munshi models some critical postures we could benefit from as careful readers, interpreters of texts, and responsible storytellers. A quick internet search of manuscripts of *Kalila and Dimna* should take you to images from various manuscripts originating in different locations and several centuries after Nasrullah. This will give you insight into the journey of this collection beyond Nasrullah.

Renuka Gusain
Humanities Program

---

93. Nasrullah Munshi, *Kalila and Dimna*, translated by Wheeler Thackston (Indianapolis, IN: Hackett, 2019), xxiv.
94. Munshi, *Kalila and Dimna*, xxvi.

PRE-READING PARS

1. List two pieces of advice you would have for a ruler/leader.
2. List two characteristics for each that you might associate with lions and rabbits.

---

from *Kalila and Dimna*

The Lion and the Bull

The Raja of India said to the Brahman, "Tell me a story of two individuals who had a friendship that was ruptured by the machinations of a treacherous schemer and turned into enmity and separation."

The Brahman said, "When an evil person comes between two friends, they will of course be parted. An example is the following."

There once was a rich merchant, and he had sons who refused to learn a trade and squandered their father's wealth. The father advised and chided them, saying, "My sons, the people of this world seek three things they cannot attain unless they have four traits. As for the three they seek, they are easy living, high status, and reward in the afterlife. The four things by which those goals can be attained are, one, the acquisition of wealth in an honest way; two, perseverance in keeping it; three, spending it to ensure a good life, the contentment of one's family, and as provision for the afterlife; and four, protecting oneself from the vicissitudes of fate insofar as possible. Anyone who neglects any one of these four things will have a veil of misfortune drawn over his goals by fate. No one who refuses to acquire wealth will be able either to make a living for himself or to provide for others. A person who acquires wealth but neglects to make it productive will soon be poverty-stricken—like collyrium: no matter how sparingly it is used, ultimately it is all used up. If you seriously put your wealth to work but spend inappropriately you will fall prey to regret and tongues will be loosed in reviling you. If you are tightfisted and do not make necessary expenditures you will be just as deprived of good things as a poor man, and additionally destiny and vicissitudes will bring about loss—like a pool that does not have outflow to match its inflow. Inevitably the water will spill over the edges or cause cracks, and all will be lost."

The merchant's sons listened to their father's advice and realized the benefits. The eldest brother went off to engage in commerce and traveled far and wide. He had two bulls. One was named Shanzaba, and the other was called Nandaba. Along the way there was a bog in which Shanzaba got stuck and scrambled out only with great difficulty. Too exhausted to go farther, he was left in the care of a man who was to feed him and bring him to the merchant when he had regained his strength. The man stayed one day and then got tired and left Shanzaba, telling the merchant the bull had died.

Shanzaba grazed for a while and wandered around in search of pasture until he came to a meadow that had all sorts of plants and herbage. Shanzaba liked it; as has been said, "When you find what you like don't go any farther." As the proverb says, "When you come to a place with grass, dismount." When he had been there for a time and grown fat, he rejoiced in his ease and comfort and mooed loudly in exhilaration.

In the vicinity of that meadow was a lion, and there were many other beasts, all of whom obeyed the lion, who was young and good-looking but rather opinionated. He had never seen a cow or heard one moo. When he heard Shanzaba's mooing he was gripped by fear, but he did not want the other beasts to know he was afraid, so he stood still and did not budge.

Among the beasts were two jackals. One was named Kalila and the other was Dimna, and both were extremely clever. Dimna, who was the greedier and worldlier of the two, asked Kalila, "Why do you think the king is fixed in place and isn't moving?"

"What is it to you," replied Kalila, "and why do you ask? We enjoy ease at the king's gate and receive scraps. We are not of the class who are honored to converse with the king or whose words are listened to by royalty. Forget it, for anyone who meddles in what does not concern him will suffer the fate of the monkey."

"How was that?" asked Dimna.

The Monkey That Pulled Out the Wedge

A monkey saw a carpenter sitting on a plank, using two wedges to split it. When he pounded one wedge in he would take out the one he had driven in previously. The carpenter went to relieve himself, and the monkey sat on the end of the plank that had been split with his testicles dangling in the gap. Before he drove the second wedge in he pulled out the one that was there, and the two sides of the plank slammed shut, mashing his testicles so hard that he fainted. When the carpenter returned he beat him until he was dead. Thus it is said that carpentry is not a job for a monkey.

"I understand," said Dimna, "but when one seeks intimacy with kings it should not be in hopes of sustenance, for the belly can be filled anywhere and with anything. The benefits of intimacy with kings are elevation of station, acquisition of friends, and confounding of enemies. Contentment indicates low expectations and a lack of manliness. Anyone whose ambition does not go beyond a morsel is reckoned a beast—like a hungry dog that is happy with a bone and a crust of bread. When a lion sees a wild ass while hunting a rabbit, it leaves the rabbit and goes after the ass. When one achieves high status, even if it is as short-lived as a flower, the wise reckon it a long life filled with good achievements and renown, while he who is content to be obscure, even if it is as long-lasting as a cypress, is of no importance in the view of the successful."

"I hear what you say," said Kalila, "but consult your own intelligence and know that every class has its station, and we are not of the class that can aspire or attempt to achieve such heights."

"The ranks of the manly and those of high ambition are open to all and hotly contested," said Dimna. "Anyone who has a noble soul will get himself from a lowly position to a high one, while he whose mind is weak will sink from lofty position to obscurity. To ascend to high status has many benefits, while to sink from a position of power has few advantages. A heavy rock may be lifted from the ground and put on one's shoulder only with great difficulty, while it can be thrown onto the ground without much exertion. Anyone who does not agree with a high-minded individual in acquiring greatness is excused since the greater the demand, the fewer are those who are fit. We who are worthy of seeking high station are not satisfied with obscurity and lowliness."

"What plan have you thought up?" asked Kalila.

"I want to get a chance to show myself to the lion while he is confused and perplexed and advise him on a way out. By this means I will achieve intimacy and status," said Dimna.

"How do you know the lion is confused?" asked Kalila.

"With my own perspicacity I can see signs of it," said Dimna. "A wise man recognizes a quality by its external signs."

"How are you going to achieve intimacy with the lion?" asked Kalila. "You have never served kings and do not know how to do it."

"When a man is wise and capable," said Dimna, "he is not shy of leaping into action or bearing a great burden. An ambitious person who is enlightened will not achieve little, and a wise person does not suffer from being alone or in exile."

"Kings do not always single out persons of excellence and virtue for honors," said Kalila, "but rather they give status to their intimates who occupy inherited positions and ranks and are devoid of all good qualities—like a grapevine, which does not go to the best and most productive tree but rather clings to whatever is nearest."

"The ruler's friends and their ancestors have not always held those positions," said Dimna. "They have acquired them over time with great effort. I seek the same, and therefore I will strive. He who joins a king's retinue will get his wish in the best possible manner provided he does the following: he must not mind being subjected to great tribulation or quaffing distasteful potions, he must quench the fire of wrath with the water of clemency, he must use an incantation of wisdom to lure the demon of passion into a bottle, he must not allow deceptive greed to overpower guiding wisdom, he must base his labor on honesty and acumen, and he must confront setbacks with calmness and resignation."

"Suppose you become intimate with the king," said Kalila. "How are you going to attract his favor and achieve high station?"

"If I can attain intimacy and learn his ways I will serve him loyally and focus my attention on carrying out his will, and I will avoid criticizing his deeds and actions. When he starts to do something that is correct and in the best interests of the kingdom I will make it seem good in his eyes and be eloquent in praising the benefits so that he will be more self-confident. If he initiates an action that would have bad results and would be harmful to the kingdom, after much reflection and contemplation I would tell him so in the gentlest of terms and with all humility and make him aware of the disastrous consequences in a way that other servants would not do. If an eloquent wise man wants to he can clothe the truth in a false garb and make falseness appear true. A clever painter can paint things that look three-dimensional even though they are flat, and he can make things appear flat when they are actually three-dimensional. When the king sees my skills he will be even eagerer to elevate me than I am to serve him."

"If you are resolved and determined to do this," said Kalila, "you must at least be aware that there is great danger. The wise say that only fools engage in three things: companionship with a ruler, testing poison, and telling secrets to women. The wise have likened a ruler to a high mountain on which are various fruits and mines but which is also home to lions, snakes, and other noxious animals that make going there difficult and tarrying there dreadful."

"It is true," said Dimna, "but he who avoids danger gets nowhere. One cannot engage in three things without lofty ambition and a strong constitution: working for rulers, commerce on the sea, and overcoming enemies. The wise say that there are two positions fit for a virtuous person: either to be honored in the service of successful kings or to be respected among contented ascetics."

"I hope you are successful in your endeavor," said Kalila, "although I am still opposed to the idea."

Dimna went off and greeted the lion. The lion asked his courtiers who he was. They told him that he was So-and-So, son of So-and-So.

"Oh, yes," he said, "I knew his father." Then he summoned Dimna forward and asked, "Where do you live?"

"I have taken up residence at the king's gate," he said, "and it is the direction in which I turn for all my needs and the focus of all my hopes. I am waiting for a job to come my way that I can accomplish with my wisdom and intelligence, for there are posts at a king's court for which underlings are necessary. No person, no matter how lowly, is devoid of the desire to repel harm and attract benefit, and even a dry twig tossed on the roadway may be of use, if only to scratch one's ear. How can a being be dismissed as useless when it has both benefit and harm and good and evil? As they say, if we cannot be made into a bouquet, at least we are good for kindling under a pot."

When the lion heard what Dimna said he was amazed and thought he would offer a piece of advice. Turning to his intimates, he said, "A skillful man with virtue, however obscure he may be and however many enemies he may have, will stand out among his peers for his intelligence and virtue, like a flame that rises up even though the kindler wants it to burn low." Dimna rejoiced at these words and knew that his charm had had an effect on the lion.

"It is incumbent upon a king's servants and members of his retinue to offer advice and make the king aware of their knowledge and understanding," said Dimna, "for unless a king knows his followers well and is aware of the limits of the acumen and loyalty of each he cannot derive benefit from their service or issue appropriate commands. So long as a seed lies hidden in the earth no one will tend it. Only when it has rent the veil of the earth and shown its face by turning the earth emerald green can it be known what it is, and consequently it will be tended and benefited from. Reliable men are useful in all respects, as is said, 'I am like the earth, and you are like the sun and the cloud. I will give forth flowers and tulips if you cultivate me.' Kings owe it to their subjects to promote each according to his skill, loyalty, and ability to advise and not to elevate or demote on a whim or to promote persons who are negligent in their tasks and devoid of skill over those who are competent and clever, for two things would be strange for kings to do: to wear a head ornament on the foot and to put a foot ornament on the head. To have a ruby or pearl set in lead or tin is not so much demeaning to the jewels as it is reprehensible for the person who has it done. Hordes of friends who are not farsighted and competent are harmful in and of themselves. Tasks are carried out by people of insight and understanding, not by crowds of henchmen and hangers-on. A person who has a ruby is not heavy-laden and can do anything he wants with it, while a person who has a rock in his purse is needlessly burdened and cannot do anything with it when need arises. A wise man does not demean a person of virtue even if he is obscure, for boughs may be raised from the dust and turned into saddles or bows and be fit for companionship with kings and nobles. It is not fitting for kings to neglect wise men simply because their ancestors were obscure and befriend the unskilled on account of their heredity when they have no skill. Rather kings' favor should be in proportion to the benefit a person will have for the kingdom, since if the unskilled are favored for their ancestors' service the kingdom will suffer and skilled people will remain undiscovered. No one is closer to humans than those of their own species, and when one of them falls ill they treat him with medicine that may be brought from far away. A mouse shares a house with humans, but when it becomes bothersome they drive it away or try to kill it. A hawk may be wild, but when it is needed it can be caught, however unwillingly, and it will sit on a king's arm."

When Dimna was finished talking the lion was even more amazed. Praising him greatly, he took to him. When he had a chance Dimna asked to speak to the lion in private and said, "For some time now I have seen the king staying in one place and not hunting or moving. What is the reason?"

The lion wanted to keep his fear hidden from Dimna, but just then Shanzaba mooed loudly, and the sound so shook the lion that he could not control himself and thus revealed his state to Dimna. "The cause is this sound you hear," said the lion. "I do not know from what direction it is coming, but I imagine its owner to be powerful in proportion to the sound. If that is the case, it would be unwise to remain here."

"Aside from this noise is the king frightened by anything else?" asked Dimna.

"No," he said.

"Then the king should not vacate his position or leave his home on this account, for it is said that the worst detriment to intelligence is boasting, the worst detriment to manliness is scoffing, and the worst detriment to a weak heart is a loud noise. It is shown in a fable that not every loud noise indicates a powerful body."

"How is that?" the lion asked.

The Fox That Tried to Eat a Drum

Once upon a time a fox went into a forest and saw a drum lying next to a tree. Every time the wind blew, a branch of the tree would hit the drum and cause a dreadful sound to reach the fox's ear. When the fox saw how enormous the body of the drum was and heard the terrible sound it made he greedily thought its innards would be as great as the sound. He strove to rip it open, but actually he found nothing but a greasy skin. Regretfully he said, "Now I realize that the larger the body and the more dreadful the sound, the less the benefit."

"I have told this fable so that the king may be enlightened and know that this sound should not trouble his mind," said Dimna.

The king found this comforting and ordered Dimna to go investigate. When Dimna was out of sight the lion reflected and, regretful at having sent him away, said to himself, "It was a bad idea to send him. A king should be very well informed of ten types of people before he sends one of them to an opponent or makes him an emissary and privy to secrets. The first is a person who has been tormented at a king's court without having committed a crime. The second is one who has suffered long, has been afflicted with poverty, and has been deprived of his possessions or status. The third is one who has been dismissed from his post. The fourth is a known troublemaker who plots sedition and does little good. The fifth is a criminal whose confederates are pardoned while he is punished, or they are punished and he receives an even harsher punishment. Sixth is someone who has done a good service with his peers and his peers are rewarded more. Seventh is one over whom a rival has been promoted. Eighth is one who is not trustworthy. Ninth is one who does something to the detriment of the king, thinking it beneficial to himself. Tenth is one who takes refuge with the king's enemy. This Dimna is farsighted and has long suffered deprivation at my court. If there is any spite lurking in his heart he may have treacherous thoughts and stir up sedition. He may find more favor with the enemy and prefer to serve him and share with him the secrets he has learned."

The lion was uneasy in these thoughts, getting up and sitting down restlessly and looking out, when suddenly Dimna appeared from afar. The lion sat down calmly. When Dimna joined him he asked, "What did you do?"

"I saw the bull whose voice the king heard," he said.

"How powerful is it?" he asked.

"I didn't see any splendor or magnificence that would indicate great power," he said. "When I got to him I spoke to him as an equal, and he did not evince any desire for humility or veneration. For my part I did not find him so awe-inspiring that great respect would be necessary."

"Nonetheless," said the lion, "that should not be attributed to weakness, and one should not be fooled, for a strong wind does not break a weak stalk while it can rip out mighty trees and fell strong buildings. The great recognize that it is not lordly to attack underlings, and unless an opponent is grand and noble a show of strength is not permissible. Everyone should be confronted according to his rank, for among the nobility equality of rank is of great importance. 'A hawk does not make a truce with locusts, and a lion does not go out to wound a jackal.' "

"The king should not attach any importance to it," said Dimna. "If so ordered I will go and bring him so the king may see what a submissive servant and obedient creature he is."

This pleased the king, and he ordered him to bring the bull. Dimna went and spoke to him without hesitation or indecision.

"The lion has sent me and ordered me to take you to him," said Dimna. "He has said that if you comply straightaway I am to offer you pardon for any shortcoming you may have committed in serving him. If you agree I will return immediately and report what has transpired."

"Who is this lion?" asked the bull.

"King of the beasts," said Dimna.

As soon as the bull heard the words "king of the beasts," he was afraid and said to Dimna, "If you assure me that I am safe from his wrath I will go with you." Dimna gave him assurance and reaffirmed what he had said, and they set out together in the direction of the lion.

When they were before him the lion asked the bull warmly, "When did you come to these parts, and what brought you here?" The bull told his story. The lion said, "Settle down here, for you will receive a full share of our compassion and bounty." The bull praised the lion and willingly entered the lion's service. The lion made him an intimate and was very kind to him. He also made an investigation into his condition and assessed the extent of his wisdom. After reflection, consultation, counsel, and auguries, he made him a confidant and privy to his secrets. The more experience he had of him, the more his confidence in his competence and understanding increased. Every day he rose in the king's opinion and received a greater share of the king's bounty until he surpassed all the army commanders and intimates.

When Dimna saw how intimate the lion had become with the bull and how he kept promoting him, jealousy and vengeful spite awoke in Dimna's heart and kept him awake. He went to Kalila and said, "Brother, do you see what a mistake I have made? I limited my ambitions to pleasing the lion and neglected to think of myself. I brought him this bull, who has been promoted to high station, and I have fallen from grace."

"The same thing happened to you that happened to the holy man," said Kalila. "What was that?" asked Dimna.

The Holy Man's Adventures

A holy man was given a magnificent suit of clothing and a robe of honor by a king. A thief saw him wearing them and craved them, so he went up to him and said, "I want to accompany you and be initiated into the rites of your order." And he became a confidant of the holy man and lived comfortably until he got a chance to steal all the clothing. When the holy man saw his clothing gone he realized who had taken it and set out for the city in search of him. Along the way he passed by two rams that were fighting, butting, and wounding each other with their horns. A fox was attracted and was lapping up their blood when suddenly the rams gored the fox and killed it.

The holy man reached the city by night and looked for a place to stay. He found the house of a madam who kept prostitutes. One of the girls was extremely beautiful and attractive. She had fallen in love with a good-looking youth, and of course he would not allow rivals to frequent her. The madam was fretting over her loss of income, and it was not long before she discovered the girl's secret and plotted to kill the youth. She had planned to do it on the very night the holy man came and was just waiting for her chance. She plied the two of them with strong drink until they both passed out. When both were asleep she put poison into a straw. One end of the straw she put in the youth's anus and the other end she put in her mouth to blow the poison into him. However, just as she took a breath the youth farted, forcing all the poison down her throat. She died on the spot, and the holy man witnessed it all.

When dawn lit the world the holy man freed himself from the degradation of those people and went out to find another place to stay. A cobbler welcomed him in as a guest and charged his wife to serve him well while he went off to visit some friends. The wife had a lover, and her go-between was the wife of a barber. She sent a message to her lover with the barber's wife telling him that her husband was not at home. The lover was just arriving that night when the cobbler returned drunk and saw him at the door. Since he had already harbored suspicions, he went in angrily, beat his wife, tied her to a post, and went to sleep. When everyone was asleep the barber's wife came and said, "Why are you keeping him waiting? If you are coming out, be quick about it. If not, tell him to come back another time."

"Sister," she said, "if you have any compassion, untie me and let me tie you up in my place. I'll apologize to my lover and return immediately. I will be obliged to you forever."

The barber's wife untied her, let herself be tied up, and sent her out. At this point the cobbler awoke and called out to her. The barber's wife was too afraid to reply lest he recognize her voice. He called out repeatedly, but she said nothing.

The cobbler's anger increased, and he took a cobbler's knife and went to the post. Cutting the woman's nose off, he handed it to her and told her to send it to her lover as a gift.

When the cobbler's wife returned and saw her go-between with her nose cut off she grieved and apologized. Then she untied her and tied herself back to the post. The barber's wife went home with her nose in her hand. All this the holy man saw and heard.

When the cobbler's wife had calmed down she lifted her hands in prayer and said, "O Lord, if you know that my husband has falsely accused me, forgive him and give me back my nose."

"You worthless witch," the cobbler said, "what's all this talk?"

"Get up, you tyrant," she replied, "and see how the Creator in his justice and mercy has given me back my nose in return for the cruelty I have suffered when it was clear that I was innocent. He did not let me remain mutilated and disgraced."

The cobbler got up, lit a lamp, and saw his wife whole and her nose intact. He immediately apologized, confessed his wrongdoing, and asked her forgiveness, promising never again to do such a thing without proof, not to harm a righteous woman on the say-so of evil informants, and never to do anything contrary to the will of a woman whose prayers were answered.

Meanwhile the barber's wife went home with her nose in her hand, wondering how she was going to explain it to her husband and neighbors. What was she to say if they asked? Just then the barber woke up and called out for his instruments because he was going to the house of a nobleman. The wife dallied for a while and then gave him only his razor. In the darkness of the night the barber threw it away, knocked his wife down, and yelled, "Your nose! Your nose!" The barber was utterly perplexed. The neighbors came running and blamed him.

When morning lit the sky the wife's relatives gathered and took the barber before the judge.

"For no obvious fault or known crime why did you mutilate this woman?" asked the judge.

Baffled, the barber had no excuse to offer. The judge sentenced him to retribution and punishment, but the holy man rose and said, "The judge must reflect on this case. The thief did not steal my clothes. The fox was not killed by the rams. The madam was not killed by poison. The barber did not cut off his wife's nose. We have all brought these things upon ourselves."

The judge let the barber go and turned to the holy man for an explanation. The holy man said, "If I had not been so desirous of having many disciples and a large following and not been deceived by the thief's drivel, he wouldn't have had an opportunity to steal. If the fox had not been so greedy and not licked up the blood it wouldn't have been harmed by the rams. If the madam had not tried to kill the young man she wouldn't have lost her life. If the barber's wife had not encouraged and abetted adultery she wouldn't have been mutilated."

"I have told this story," Kalila said, "that you may know that you have brought this misery upon yourself by being negligent of the consequences."

"It is as you say," said Dimna. "It was my own doing. Now, what do you see as a means of saving myself?"

"What do you propose?" Kalila asked.

"I think I may be able to reach this goal through subterfuge and cunning and try by whatever means possible to get rid of him. In the code of zeal neglect and shortcoming are not allowed, and if I am negligent I will be subjected to blame by the manly, and furthermore I will not be able to find a new position or get a promotion because I will be accused of greed and cupidity. There are five goals allowed by the intelligent in which any amount of wile and cunning are allowed: to regain past status and position, to avoid harm of which one has experience, to maintain a benefit one has, to get oneself out of a present calamity, and to attract benefit and ward off harm in the future. Since I am hopeful of regaining my position, the way to do it is to lie in wait until the bull departs this earth, for that would be the best thing for the lion since he has gone so far in preferring the bull that he can be accused of being addlebrained."

"I can find no fault in the lion for befriending and promoting the bull," said Kalila.

"He has gone too far," said Dimna. "He has been contemptuous of his other advisors to the point that they are complaining that they have been deprived of the benefits of his service. They say six things are disastrous for a king: deprivation, sedition, lust, reversal of fortune, ill temper, and ignorance. Deprivation means depriving oneself of well-wishers and leaving people of good counsel and experience in despair. Sedition means that unexpected battles and unplanned-for affairs happen and enemies' swords are drawn. Lust means a burning desire for women, hunting, singing, wine, and the like. Reversal of fortune means plague, drought, flood, fire, and such like. Ill temper means an excess of wrath and abhorrence and overdoing punishments. Ignorance means using appeasement when hostility would be more appropriate and engaging in dispute instead of cajolery."

"I see," said Kalila, "but how can you make an attempt on the bull's life? He is much stronger than you are and has more friends."

"You shouldn't worry about such things," said Dimna. "Things are not accomplished through strength and helpers alone. It is said that strategy comes before a show of bravery. That which can be done by strategy and cunning cannot be done by strength of arm. Have you not heard that the crow destroyed the snake by cunning?"

"How was that?" asked Kalila.

The Crow That Killed a Snake

Once upon a time a crow had its nest on top of a tree on a mountain. In the vicinity was a snake's hole. Every time the crow had a chick the snake would eat it.

When this had gone on for a long time the crow grew desperate and complained to its friend the jackal, saying, "I think I will rid myself of this murderous tyrant."

"In what way are you going to do it?" asked the jackal.

"When the snake is asleep I will attack and pluck out its eyes so that in the future my dear children will be safe from its depredation," said the crow.

"This is not a wise plan," said the jackal. "A wise person attacks his enemy in a way that poses no danger. Beware lest you do like the heron that tried to kill the crab."

"How was that?" the crow asked.

Munshi, Nasrullah. "The Lion and the Bull." Selections from *Kalila and Dimna*, translated by Wheeler Thackston, 3–15. Indianapolis, IN: Hackett, 2019.

POST-READING PARS

1. Identify two pieces of advice for a ruler in *Kalila and Dimna*.
2. List two ways these stories depict the characteristics of lions and rabbits.

Inquiry Corner

Content Question(s):	Critical Question(s):
What is the teaching or moral of "The Monkey That Pulled out the Wedge" story?	Critically evaluate the merits and shortcomings of Dimna's ideas about social organization and thoughts about who should hold power and serve the king.
Comparative Question(s):	**Connection Question(s):**
Compare the animal imagery/use of animals in *Kalila and Dimna* with others you have encountered in this course?	Think of the fables you have encountered in your childhood (books, plays, movies). Do any of them have resonances with the stories in *Kalila and Dimna*? Were they intended to be instructive in the ways these fables are?

from *Shahnameh* by Ferdowsi

Introduction

Persia is the Anglicized name for the country situated between Iraq (ancient area of Mesopotamia) to the west and Turkmenistan, Afghanistan, and Pakistan to the east. In 1935, Shah Reza Khan changed its name from Persia to Iran (Aryan land) in an effort to modernize the country, but many modern Iranians still refer to themselves as Persians. Arabic has heavily influenced modern Farsi (a name derived from the Arabic word for Parsi "Persian" — the letter "f" does not occur in Persian except in words borrowed from Arabic), but Iranians are not Arabs, a Semitic people whose language is related to Hebrew and Aramaic. Persians are descended from the same Aryan ancestors as arguably some of the peoples of India and Europe, referred to linguistically as Indo-Europeans. And the Persian languages belong to the Indo-Iranian branch of this huge family tree. After the Muslim conquest (651 CE), the Arabic script began to be used for writing the Persian language, and it is still used today. The Parsis or Parsee of the Indian subcontinent are ethnoreligious Persians who fled persecution during the Muslim conquest, and who still practice Zoroastrianism, an ancient religion of Persia, revealed by the prophet Zoroaster.

About three hundred years after the Muslim conquest, a Persian poet named Abdolqasem Ferdowsi (932–1025 CE) was among those concerned that the imposition of Islamic culture in Persia would soon cause the loss of knowledge about indigenous Persian mythology and history. So, he joined in with those intent on preserving the ancient stories, spending many years gathering written and oral sources.

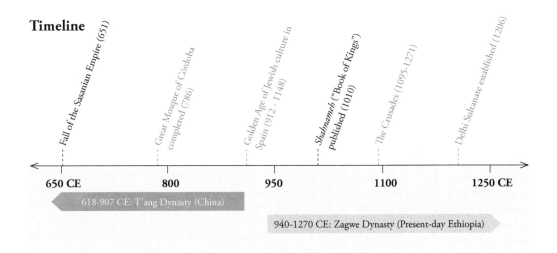

Timeline

Fall of the Sasanian Empire (651)

Great Mosque of Córdoba completed (786)

Golden Age of Jewish culture in Spain (912 - 1148)

Shahnameh ("Book of Kings") published (1010)

The Crusades (1095-1271)

Delhi Sultanate established (1206)

650 CE   800   950   1100   1250 CE

618-907 CE: T'ang Dynasty (China)

940-1270 CE: Zagwe Dynasty (Present-day Ethiopia)

He recast them in about 50,000 rhyming couplets, using almost no words of Arabic origin even though he was using the Arabic writing system. The arrangement of the stories is loosely chronological as a history of the world, beginning with the first shah, Kayumars, and continuing through the historical era of Alexander the Great and other kings until the end of the Sassanian era in the mid-seventh century CE. It includes many stories of the fabulous, such as tales of huge talking birds, giant worms, and other beasts, kings and queens, heroes and heroines, love stories, tragic events — in short, all of Persian history, myth, and legend. Ferdowsi published his poem in 1010 CE as the *Shahnameh* (*Book of Kings*), and it became an instant classic, still beloved and considered to be a national epic in Iran today. What features in your opinion might elevate an artwork to be considered a national treasure?

Shahnameh uses 1261 verses to tell the story, more than a millennium after the event occurred, of Alexander the Great's conquest of Persia (Sekandar or Iskandar in Persian). It reveals a unique Persian understanding of Alexander and his legacy, which is at odds with the more commonly known Greek accounts. According to the Greek historians, Alexander was the son of King Philip II of Macedon in northern Greece. His mother, Olympias, was a Greek princess from western Greece. The Greek biographer Plutarch relates some rumors and stories about Alexander's birth, including one that his mother was already pregnant with him when she married Philip II, and that his real father was the god Zeus. The *Shahnameh* asserts that he was actually of Persian royal blood but raised in Greece as Philip's adopted son. All the sources agree that Alexander married Persian princesses while in Persia. Even Alexander's superhuman ability to defeat his foes and his transformation into a civilizing hero has much in common with other great heroes of the *Shahnameh*, such as Rostam. How and why might a local culture adapt aspects of a conquering culture's narrative?

Lora Holland Goldthwaite
Department of Classics

PRE-READING PARS

1. Think of two reasons why cultures cherish stories of fabulous adventures and fantastic creatures.
2. Think of two features of an imagined land in an epic story and its geography.

from *Shahnemah*

Sekandar Reaches a Land Where the Men Have Soft Feet and Kills a Dragon

They reached a land where men have soft feet; the host of inhabitants was beyond numbering, and each man was as tall as a cypress tree, but they had neither horses nor armor nor swords nor maces. Their war cry was like the roll of thunder, and they attacked naked, as if they were devils. Against Sekandar's army they hurled a hail of rocks, which rained down like an autumn wind bowing trees before it. But the army advanced with arrows and swords, and the day seemed to turn to night with the dust. When there were only a few of the soft-footed warriors remaining, Sekandar rested, and then led his army forward again.

They quickly reached a city that seemed limitless; the inhabitants courteously and kindly came out to welcome them, bringing with them carpets, clothes, and food as gifts. Sekandar questioned them and treated them respectfully, and a sufficient area for his army's camp was set aside. Tents were set up on the plain, and the army made no attempt to enter the city. Nearby there was an enormous mountain, which seemed almost to touch the skies. The few people on the mountain's slopes didn't stay there at night. Sekandar asked them the best way forward and by which paths he should lead his army. They made their obeisance before him and greeted him as the world's king, and then said:

A path exists around this mountainside
But first you'll have to find a willing guide;
Beyond the crest there lies a dragon's lair,
His poison sickens birds that venture there.
The noxious vapors reach the moon, there's no
Safe route by which your warriors could go.
His massive maw breathes fire, and he could snare
An elephant with his two locks of hair;
Our city doesn't have the strength to fight.
We have to take up five cows, every night,
For him to feed on; and how fearfully
We place them on the rocks for him to see,

Afraid that if he finds us he'll come down
And, piece by piece, destroy us and our town.

Sekandar said, "Tomorrow, see that no one takes him any food." When the time for his meal had passed, the dragon stood on the mountain slope breathing fire, and Sekandar ordered his troops to shoot a storm of arrows against him. The foul dragon exhaled fire and caught a few men in the blast. Sekandar had the war drums beaten, and the dragon drew back in fear from the echoing drums.

The sun rose in Taurus, and the meadows resounded with the song of larks. When it was again time for the dragon to be fed, the king chose a number of men from his army and gave them money to buy five cows. He killed the cows and skinned them, leaving the hide attached to their heads. The hides were then filled with poison and oil and inflated; prayers were said and the cows were passed from hand to hand up the mountainside. The king approached the dragon and saw that he was like a huge dark cloud: his tongue purple, his eyes blood red, and fire issuing continuously from his maw. The soldiers rolled the cows down toward the dragon, their hearts anxious to see what he would do. Immediately, the dragon descended on the carcasses like the wind. He ate them, and the poison spread throughout his body, bursting his intestines and forcing its way even into his brain and feet. For a long time he beat his head against the rocks in desperation, and the army released a hail of arrows against him. The mountainous monster sank to his feet, and his body finally succumbed to the arrows. Leaving the creature's body where it lay, Sekandar quickly led his troops out of that area.

The adventurous hero led his men to another mountainous area, where he saw an astonishing sight. Perched on a summit sharp as a sword blade, far removed from all humanity, was a golden throne. On the throne was a dead man, and even after death he radiated *farr* and glory. He was wrapped in a brocade cloak, and on his head was a crown encrusted with jewels. So much gold and silver was scattered around him that no one could approach the throne, and anyone who went up the mountain hoping to take some of the dead man's wealth would tremble in terror and die, and eventually rot there. Sekandar ascended the mountain and, as he stared at the man, and at the gold and silver, he heard a great voice that said, "O king, you have lived long enough in the world. You have destroyed so many thrones and raised your head up to the heavens, and you have laid low so many friends and enemies, but now the way of the world has changed." Sekandar's face glowed like a lamp, and he descended the mountain sick at heart.

Ferdowsi. "Sekandar Reaches a Land Where the Men Have Soft Feet and Kills a Dragon." In *Stories from the Shahnameh of Ferdowsi: Sunset of Empire*, translated by Dick Davis, 87, 91–95. Odenton, MD: Mage Publishers, 2004.

POST-READING PARS

1. Make a bullet list of the events that are narrated in this excerpt. Do any of them seem real or possible?
2. List two new pieces of information you learned about Alexander the Great after reading these Persian stories.
3. List the animals that have a role in this excerpt. How do they compare to reality, or to other medieval conceptions of animals you have encountered in this course?

Inquiry Corner

Content Question(s):	Critical Question(s):
How does Alexander learn that he will die young?	The women of Harum are what the Greeks called Amazons. Are the characteristics and traits attributed to them in this excerpt consistent with the treatment and stereotypes of strong and independent women in other course readings? How or how not?
How does Alexander communicate with the women of Harum?	
Comparative Question(s):	**Connection Question(s):**
Think about how Alexander is characterized in comparison with other kings and conquerors you have encountered in this course.	If you created an adventure game based on this excerpt, what kind of ethics and morals would you give this Persian Alexander, that is, what kind of hero would he be?

from *Administration of Akbar (A'in-i Akbari)* by Abu'l-Fazl 'Allami

Introduction

Ain-i-Akbari (*Administration of Akbar*) is a multivolume text composed by Abul Fazl 'Allami as a part of his *Akbarnama* (*Book of Akbar*), a comprehensive chronicle of Akbar's life. Abul Fazl was the renowned historian in the court of emperor Abu'l-Fath Jalal-ud-din Muhammad Akbar (r. 1556–1605 CE), the third Mughal emperor, and was one of the "Nine jewels," referring to nine high officials of Akbar's royal court comprising his trusted inner circle. *Akbarnama*, commissioned by Akbar, took several years to complete (1589–1598) and included over a hundred illustrations. Unlike some of the other Mughal emperors, Akbar didn't leave a memoir, most likely because he never learned to read or write. Abul Fazl's texts therefore offer us a unique insight into the life of Akbar. They outline how Emperor Akbar expanded and consolidated the empire considerably not only by winning numerous battles but also by creating a complex administrative machinery and championing his overall values of tolerance and pluralism. What might be the circumstances where values of tolerance and pluralism allow for an effective administration?

Islam had arrived in the Indian subcontinent not long after the establishment of Islam as an organized religion in the Arabian Peninsula. The first Muslim rule of the subcontinent was established with the founding of the Delhi Sultanate in the early 1200s. The Mughal Empire, founded in 1526 CE by Akbar's grandfather, Babur, was the longest lasting Muslim empire of the subcontinent. Sufism accompanied the arrival of Islam.

SNAPSHOT BOX

LANGUAGE: Persian

DATE: 16th century CE

LOCATION: South Asia

GENRE: Administrative report

Ethnic identity: Mughal Empire

TAGS: Agriculture, Land, and Food; Authority and Institution; Education; Empire; Formations and Reformations; Historiography; Humanism; Islamic World; Philosophy; Power Structures; Women

Timeline

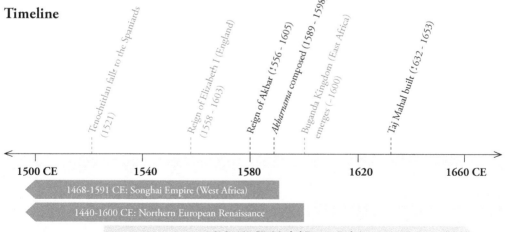

Tenochtitlan falls to the Spaniards (1521)

Reign of Elizabeth I (England) (1558 - 1603)

Reign of Akbar (1556 - 1605)

Akbarnama composed (1589 - 1598)

Buganda Kingdom (East Africa) emerges (~1600)

Taj Mahal built (1632 - 1653)

| 1500 CE | 1540 | 1580 | 1620 | 1660 CE |

1468-1591 CE: Songhai Empire (West Africa)

1440-1600 CE: Northern European Renaissance

1526-1857 CE: Mughal Empire (India)

Developed as a mystical tradition within Islam, Sufism was initially conceived as a world-renouncing movement focusing on self-purification and personal union with Allah, especially by arousing the intuitive and spiritual faculties. While a number of Sufi orders developed within the subcontinent, a number of major Sufi orders were also brought into such as the Chisti order in 1190. While elsewhere Sufism flourished as an intellectual tradition, as outlined in al Ghazali's *Deliverance from Error* (see page 134), the Chisti mystics believed in the spiritual value of music as a means of devotion. Akbar became a close disciple of Sufi saints and his overall perspective seemed to have been deeply influenced by Sufism. As you read the selection below, try to identify marks in Akbar's administration that might reflect a clear influence of Sufi sensibilities.

Akbar is considered one of the most important Mughal emperors. As the first Mughal emperor to have been born in the Indian subcontinent, he was also the first Muslim ruler of the subcontinent who seemed to be aware of the fact that he was a Muslim ruler of a Hindu majority. Unlike the other Mughal emperors who at best worked from a weak sense of tolerance, Akbar reflected a real curiosity for the diverse worldviews of the subjects of his ever-expanding empire. It is conceivable that Akbar realized that genuine tolerance could only be located in true understanding. Even though he initially convened a religious assembly with only Muslim religious experts, he soon invited in leaders who represented a wide variety of religious perspectives including Hindu, Parsi, Jain, and Christian experts. This comparative engagement inspired Akbar to initiate a new religion, ***din-i-ilahi*** (the religion of god/Divine faith), influenced by Abul Fazl's idea that common elements of truth are discernible in all the different religions. This exercise most likely resulted in Akbar's conceiving the nature of a ruler as a illumination of divine. How might these religious experimentations have been viewed by different segments of Akbar's court?

Akbar expanded the Sufi principle, *Sulh-i-kul* (universal peace) beyond its given meaning of religious harmony to reflect his overall governing ethos. This included his efforts to introduce personal laws that applied to all of his subjects irrespective of their individual faith. He thus repealed the *jizya* (poll tax) and the pilgrimage taxes that non-Muslims had to pay within a few years of becoming emperor. Commenting on the values of tolerance and pluralism in Akbar's court, Wendy Doniger, an Indologist (one who studies all things Indian) and scholar of religion, writes, "Giordano Bruno [Italian Dominican friar supporting the Copernican model] was burned at the stake in Rome in 1600, just as Akbar was preaching tolerance of all religions in Agra."[95] Akbar invited artists, musicians, dancers, performers, and philosophers to his court. He was especially interested in the Hindu philosophical school of *Vedanta*, which maintained that a single principle of truth undergirds our entire reality. Abul Fazl's admiration for Akbar clearly colors the account he offers. For example, while

95. Wendy Doniger, *The Hindus: An Alternate History* (New York: Viking Penguin, 2009), 533.

he extols Akbar's universal kindness to everyone without cruelty toward anyone, historians have noted Akbar's moments of cruelty, such as in his treatment of war prisoners. What are some of the critical reading strategies you could use to detect occasions where Abul Fazl's account most likely overshoots reality?

Keya Maitra
Department of Philosophy

PRE-READING PARS

1. Write down two or three features that you might use to characterize a harem.
2. Write down two or three virtues that you imagine are necessary in a ruler who values virtue.
3. When composing a memorandum, what are two features you need to mention?

Selections from *Administration of Akbar (A'in-i Akbari)*

The Imperial Harem

His Majesty is a great friend of good order and propriety in business. Through order the world becomes a meadow of truth and reality; and that which is but external, receives through it a spiritual meaning. For this reason, the large number of women—a vexatious question even for great statesmen—furnished his Majesty with an opportunity to display his wisdom, and to rise from the low level of worldly dependence to the eminence of perfect freedom. The imperial palace and household are therefore in the best order.

His Majesty forms matrimonial alliances with princes of Hindustan, and of other countries; and secures by these ties of harmony the peace of the world.

As the sovereign, by the light of his wisdom, has raised fit persons from the dust of obscurity, and appointed them to various offices, so does he also elevate faithful persons to the several ranks in the service of the seraglio. Short-sighted men think of impure gold, which will gradually turn into pure gold; but the far-sighted know that his Majesty understands how to use elixirs and chemical processes. Any kind of growth will alter the constitution of a body; copper and iron will turn to gold, and tin and lead to silver; hence it is no matter of astonishment, if an excellent being changes the worthless into men. "The saying of the wise is true that the eye of the exalted is the elixir for producing goodness." Such also are the results flowing from the love of order of his Majesty, from his wisdom, insight, regard to rank, his respect for others, his activity, his patience. Even when he is angry, he does not deviate from the right path; he looks at every thing with kindly feelings, weighs rumors well, and is free from all prejudice; he considers it a great blessing to have the good wishes of the people, and does not allow the intoxicating pleasures of this world to overpower his calm judgment.

His Majesty has made a large enclosure with fine buildings inside, where he reposes. Though there are more than five thousand women, he has given to each a separate apartment. He has also divided them into sections, and keeps them attentive to their duties. Several chaste women have been appointed as *daroghahs* (officers in charge), and superintendents over each section, and one has been selected for the duties of writer. Thus, as in the imperial offices, every thing is here also in proper order. The salaries are sufficiently liberal. Not counting the presents, which his Majesty most generously bestows, the women of the highest rank receive from 1610 to 1028 Rs. *per mensem*. Some of the servants have from 51 to 20, others from 40 to 2 Rs. Attached to the private audience hall of the palace, is a clever and zealous writer, who superintends the expenditure of the Harem, and keeps an account of the cash and the stores. If a woman wants anything, within the limit of her salary, she applies to one of the *Tahwildars* (cash-keepers) of the seraglio. The Tahwildar then sends a memorandum to the writer, who checks it, when the General Treasurer makes the payment in cash, as for claims of this nature no checks are given.

The writer also makes out an estimate of the annual expenditure, writes out summarily a receipt, which is countersigned by the ministers of the state. It is then stamped with a peculiar Imperial seal, which is only used in grants connected with the Harem, when the receipt becomes payable. The money itself is paid by the cash-keeper of the General Treasury to the General Tahwildar, who on the order of the writer of the Harem, hands it over to the several Sub-Tahwildars for distribution among the servants of the seraglio. All monies are reckoned in their salaries at the current rate.

The inside of the Harem is guarded by sober and active women; the most trustworthy of them are placed about the apartments of his Majesty. Outside of the enclosure the eunuchs are placed; and at a proper distance, there is a guard of faithful *Rajputs*, beyond whom are the porters of the gates. Besides, on all four sides, there are guards of Nobles, Ahadis, and other troops, according to their ranks.

Whenever *Begums*, or the wives of nobles, or other women of chaste character, desire to be presented, they first notify their wish to the servants of the seraglio, and wait for a reply. From thence they send their request to the officers of the palace, after which those who are eligible are permitted to enter the Harem. Some women of rank obtain permission to remain there for a whole month.

Notwithstanding the great number of faithful guards, his Majesty does not dispense with his own vigilance, but keeps the whole in proper order.

The Imperial Kitchen

His Majesty even extends his attention to this department, and has given many wise regulations for it; nor can a reason be given why he should not do so, as the equilibrium of man's nature, the strength of the body, the capability of receiving external and internal blessings, and the acquisition of worldly and religions advantages, depend ultimately on proper care being shown for appropriate food. This knowledge distinguishes man from beasts, with whom, as far as mere eating is concerned, he stands upon the same level. If his Majesty did not possess so lofty a mind, so comprehensive an understanding, so universal a kindness, he would have chosen the path of solitude, and given up sleep and food altogether; and even now, when he has taken upon himself the temporal and spiritual leadership of the people, the question, "What dinner has been prepared today?" never passes over his tongue: In the course of twenty-four hours his Majesty eats but once, and leaves off before he is fully satisfied; neither is there any fixed time for this meal, but the servants have always things so far ready, that in the space of an hour, after the order has been given, a hundred dishes are served up. The food allowed to the women of the seraglio commences to be taken from the kitchen in the morning, and goes on till night.

Trustworthy and experienced people are appointed to this department; and all good servants attached to the court, are resolved to perform well whatever service they have undertaken. Their head is assisted by the Prime Minister himself. His Majesty has entrusted to the latter the affairs of the state, but especially this important department. Notwithstanding all this, his Majesty is not unmindful of the conduct of the servants. He appoints a zealous and sincere man as *Mir Bakawal,* or Master of the Kitchen, upon whose insight the success of the department depends, and gives him several upright persons as assistants. There are also treasurers for the cash and the stores, several tasters, and a clever writer. Cooks from all countries prepare a great variety of dishes of all kinds of grains, greens, meats; also oily, sweet and spicy dishes. Every day such dishes are prepared as the nobles can scarcely command at their feasts, from which you may infer how exquisite the dishes are which are prepared for his Majesty.

In the beginning of the year the Sub-treasurers make out an annual estimate, and receive the amount; the money bags and the door of the storehouse being sealed with the seals of the *Mir Bakawal* and the writer; and every month a correct statement of the daily expenditure is drawn up, the receipt for which is sealed by the same two officers, when it is entered under the head of the expenditure. At the beginning of every quarter, the *Diwan i buyutat*[96] and the *Mir Bakawal,* collect whatever they think will be necessary; e.g. *Sukhdas* rice from Bharaij, *Dewzirah* rice from Gwaliar, *Jinjin* rice from Rajori and Nímlah, *ghi* from *Hicr Fíruzah*; ducks, water-fowls, and certain vegetables from Kashmir. Patterns are always kept. The sheep, goats, berberies, fowls, ducks, &c., are fattened by the cooks; fowls are never kept longer than a month. The slaughter-house is without the city or the camp, in the neighborhood of rivers and tanks, where the meat is washed, when it is sent to the kitchen in sacks sealed by the cooks. There it is again washed, and thrown into the pots. The water-carriers pour the water out of their leather bags into earthen vessels, the mouths of which are covered with pieces of cloth, and sealed up; and the water is left to settle before it is used. A place is also told off as a kitchen garden, that there may be a continual supply of fresh greens. The *Mir Bakawal* and the writer determine the price of every eatable, which becomes a fixed rule; and they sign the day-book, the estimates, the receipts for transfers, the list of wages of the servants, etc., and watch every transaction. Bad

96. Superintendent of the stores, workshops, etc.

characters, idle talkers, unknown persons are never employed; no one is entertained
without security, nor is personal acquaintance sufficient.

The victuals are served up in dishes of gold and silver, stone and earthenware;
some of the dishes being in charge of each of the Sub-Bakawals. During the time of
cooking, and when the victuals are taken out, an awning is spread, and lookers-on
kept away. The cooks tuck up their sleeves, and the hems of their garments, and hold
their hands before their mouths and noses when the food is taken out; the cook and
the Bakawal taste it, after which it is tased by the *Mir Bakawal*, and then put into the
dishes. The gold and silver dishes are tied up in red cloths, and those of copper and
china in white ones. The *Mir Bakawal* attaches his seal, and writes on it the names
of the contents, whilst the clerk of the pantry writes out on a sheet of paper a list
of all vessels and dishes, which he sends inside, with the seal of the *Mir Bakawal*,
that none of the dishes may be changed. The dishes are carried by the Bakawals, the
cooks, and the other servants, and macebearers precede and follow, to prevent people
from approaching them. The servants of the pantry send at the same time, in bags
containing the seal of the Bakawal, various kinds of bread, saucers of curds piled up,
and small stands containing plates of pickles, fresh ginger, limes, and various greens.
The servants of the palace again taste the food, spread the table cloth on the ground,
and arrange the dishes; and when after some time his Majesty commences to dine,
the table servants sit opposite him in attendance: first, the share of the derwishes[97]
is put apart, when his Majesty commences with milk or curds. After he has dined,
he prostrates himself in prayer. *Mir Bakawal* is always in attendance. The dishes are
taken away according to the above list. Some victuals are also kept half ready, should
they be called for.

The copper utensils are tinned twice a month; those of the princes, etc., once;
whatever is broken is given to the braziers, who make new ones.

The Manner in Which His Majesty Spends His Time

The success of the three branches of the government, and the fulfilment of the
wishes of the subjects, whether great or small, depend upon the manner in which
a king spends his time. The care with which His Majesty guards over his motives,
and watches over his emotions, bears on its face the sign of the Infinite, and the
stamp of immortality; and though thousands of important matters occupy, at one
and the same time, his attention, they do not stir up the rubbish of confusion in the
temple of his mind, nor do they allow the dust of dismay to settle on the vigor of his
mental powers, or the habitual earnestness with which His Majesty contemplates the
charms of God's world. His anxiety to do the will of the Creator is ever increasing;
and thus his insight and wisdom are ever deepening. From his practical knowledge,
and capacity for everything excellent, he can sound men of experience, though rarely

97. Most likely means Sufi dervishes (editors' note).

casting a glance on his own ever extending excellence. He listens to great and small, expecting that a good thought, or the relation of a noble deed, may kindle in his mind a new lamp of wisdom, though ages have past without his having found a really great man. Impartial statesmen, on seeing the sagacity of His Majesty, blotted out the book of their own wisdom, and commenced a new leaf. But with the magnanimity which distinguishes him, and with his wonted zeal, he continues his search for superior men, and finds a reward in the care with which he selects such as are fit for his society.

Although surrounded by every external pomp and display, and by every inducement to lead a life of luxury and ease, he does not allow his desires, or his wrath, to renounce allegiance to Wisdom, his sovereign—how much less would he permit them to lead him to a bad deed! Even the telling of stories, which ordinary people use as a means of lulling themselves into sleep, serves to keep His Majesty awake.

Ardently feeling after God, and searching for truth, His Majesty exercises upon himself both inward and outward austerities, though he occasionally joins public worship, in order to hush the slandering tongues of the bigots of the present age. But the great object of his life is the acquisition of that sound morality, the sublime loftiness of which captivates the hearts of thinking sages, and silences the taunts of zealots and sectarians.

Knowing the value of a lifetime, he never wastes his time, nor does he omit any necessary duty, so that in the light of his upright intentions, every action of his life may be considered as an adoration of God.

It is beyond my power to describe in adequate terms His Majesty's devotions. He passes every moment of his life in self-examination or in adoration of God. He especially does so at the time, when morning spreads her azure silk, and scatters abroad her young, golden beams; and at noon, when the light of the world-illuminating sun embraces the universe, and thus becomes a source of joy for all men; in the evening, when that fountain of light withdraws from the eyes of mortal man, to the bewildering grief of all who are friends of light; and lastly at midnight, when that great cause of life turns again to ascend, and to bring the news of renewed cheerfulness to all who, in the melancholy of the night, are stricken with sorrow. All these grand mysteries are in honor of God, and in adoration of the Creator of the world; and if dark-minded, ignorant men cannot comprehend their signification, who is to be blamed, and whose loss is it? Indeed, every man acknowledges that we owe gratitude and reverence to our benefactors; and hence it is incumbent on us, though our strength may fail, to show gratitude for the blessings we receive from the sun, the light of all lights, and to enumerate the benefits which he bestows. This is essentially the duty of kings, upon whom, according to the opinion of the wise, this sovereign of the heavens sheds an immediate light. And this is the very motive which actuates His Majesty to venerate fire and reverence lamps.

But why should I speak of the mysterious blessings of the sun, or of the transfer of his greater light to lamps? Should I not rather dwell on the perverseness of those weak-minded zealots, who, with much concern, talk of His Majesty's religion as of a deification of the Sun, and the introduction of fire-worship? But I shall dismiss them with a smile.

The compassionate heart of His Majesty finds no pleasure in cruelties, or in causing sorrow to others; he is ever sparing of the lives of his subjects, wishing to bestow happiness upon all.

His Majesty abstains much from flesh, so that whole months pass away without his touching any animal food, which, though prized by most, is nothing thought of by the sage. His august nature cares but little for the pleasures of the world. In the course of twenty-four hours, he never makes more than one meal. He takes a delight in spending his time in performing whatever is necessary and proper. He takes a little repose in the evening, and again for a short time in the morning; but his sleep looks more like waking.

His Majesty is accustomed to spend the hours of the night profitably; to the private audience hall are then admitted eloquent philosophers, and virtuous Sufis, who are seated according to their rank, and entertain His Majesty with wise discourses. On such occasions His Majesty fathoms them, and tries them on the touch-stone of knowledge. Or the object of an ancient institution is disclosed, or new thoughts are hailed with delight. Here young men of talent learn to revere and adore His Majesty, and experience the happiness of having their wishes fulfilled, whilst old men of impartial judgment see themselves on the expanse of sorrow, finding that they have to pass through a new course of instruction.

There are also present in these assemblies, unprejudiced historians, who do not mutilate history by adding or suppressing facts, and relate the impressive events of ancient times. His Majesty often makes remarks wonderfully shrewd, or starts a fitting subject for conversation. On other occasions matters referring to the empire and the revenue, are brought up, when His Majesty gives orders for whatever is to be done in each case.

About a watch before day-break, musicians of all nations are introduced, who recreate the assembly with music and songs, and religious strains; and when four *gharis* are left till morning, His Majesty retires to his private apartments, brings his external appearance in harmony with the simplicity of his heart, and launches forth into the ocean of contemplation. In the meantime, at the close of night, soldiers, merchants, peasants, tradespeople, and other professions, gather round the palace, patiently waiting to catch a glimpse of His Majesty. Soon after day-break, they are allowed to make the *kornish* (salutation). After this, His Majesty allows the attendants of the Harem to pay their compliments. During this time various matters of worldly and religious import are brought to the notice of His Majesty. As soon as they are settled, he returns to his private apartments, and reposes a little.

The good habits of His Majesty are so numerous, that I cannot adequately describe them. If I were to compile dictionaries on this subject, they would not be exhaustive.

Regulations for Admission to Court

Admittance to Court is a distinction conferred on the nation at large; it is a pledge that the three branches of the government are properly looked after, and enables subjects personally to apply for redress of their grievances. Admittance to the ruler of the land is for the success of his government, what irrigation is for a flower-bed; it is the field, on which the hopes of the nation ripen into fruit.

His Majesty generally receives twice in the course of twenty-four hours, when people of all classes can satisfy their eyes and hearts with the light of his countenance. *First*, after performing his morning devotions, he is visible, from outside the awning, to people of all ranks, whether they be given to worldly pursuits, or to a life of solitary contemplation, without any molestation from the mace-bearers. This mode of showing himself is called, in the language of the country, *darsan* (view); and it frequently happens that business is transacted at this time. The second time of his being visible is in the State Hall, whither he generally goes after the first watch of the day. But this assembly is sometimes announced towards the close of day, or at night. He also frequently appears at a window which opens into the State Hall, for the transaction of business; or he dispenses there justice calmly and serenely, or examines into the dispensation of justice, or the merit of officers, without being influenced in his judgment by any predilections, or any thing impure and contrary to the will of God. Every officer of government then presents various reports, or explains his several wants, and is instructed by His Majesty how to proceed. From his knowledge of the character of the times, though in opposition to the practice of kings of past ages, His Majesty looks upon the smallest details as mirrors capable of reflecting a comprehensive outline; he does not reject that which superficial observers call unimportant, and counting the happiness of his subjects as essential to his own, never suffers his equanimity to be disturbed.

Whenever His Majesty holds court, they beat a large drum, the sounds of which are accompanied by Divine praise. In this manner, people of all classes receive notice. His Majesty's sons and grandchildren, the grandees of the Court, and all other men who have admittance, attend to make the *kornish*, and remain standing in their proper places. Learned men of renown and skilful mechanics pay their respects; the Daroghahs and Bitikchis (writers) set forth their several wants; and the officers of justice give in their reports. His Majesty, with his usual insight, gives orders, and settles everything in a satisfactory manner. During the whole time, skilful gladiators and wrestlers from all countries hold themselves in readiness, and singers, male and female, are in waiting. Clever jugglers, and funny tumblers also are anxious to exhibit their dexterity and agility.

His Majesty, on such occasions, addresses himself to many of those who have been presented, impressing all with the correctness of his intentions, the unbiasedness of his mind, the humility of his disposition, the magnanimity of his heart, the excellence of his nature, the cheerfulness of his countenance, and the frankness of his manners; his intelligence pervades the whole assembly, and multifarious matters are easily and satisfactorily settled by his truly divine power.

This vale of sorrows is changed to a place of rest: the army and the nation are content. May the empire flourish, and these blessings endure!

Regulations Regarding the Wa'qi'ahnawis[98]

Keeping records is an excellent thing for a government; it is even necessary for every rank of society. Though a trace of this office may have existed in ancient times, its higher objects were but recognized in the present reign. His Majesty has appointed fourteen zealous, experienced, and impartial clerks, two of whom do daily duty in rotation, so that the turn of each comes after a fortnight.[99] Some other suitable men are selected as supernumeraries, each of whom is appointed for one day; and if any of the fourteen be detained by an important business, this additional person acts for him. Hence they are called *kotal* (supernumeraries).

Their duty is to write down the orders and the doings of His Majesty and whatever the heads of the departments report; what His Majesty eats and drinks; when he sleeps, and when he rises; the etiquette in the State hall; the time His Majesty spends in the Harem; when he goes to the general and private assemblies; the nature of hunting-parties; the slaying of animals;[100] when he marches, and when he halts; the acts of His Majesty as the spiritual guide of the nation; vows made to him; his remarks; what books he has read out to him; what alms he bestows; what presents he makes; the daily and monthly exercises[101] which he imposes on himself; appointments to mansabs; contingents of troops; salaries; jagirs; *Irmas* money ; *sayurghals* (rent-free land); the increase or decrease of taxes; contracts; sales; money transfers; *peshkash* (tribute receipts); dispatch; the issue of orders; the papers which are signed by His Majesty; the arrival of reports; the minutes thereon; the arrivals of courtiers; their departures; the fixing of periods; the inspection of the guards; battles, victories, and peace; obituaries of well-known persons; animal fights and the bettings on them; the dying of horses; capital punishments; pardons granted by His Majesty; the proceedings of the general assemblies; marriages, births; *chaugan* games; chaupar (possibly a dice game), nard (game pieces), chess, card games, etc.; extraordinary phenomena; the harvests of the year; the reports on events.

After the diary has been corrected by one of His Majesty's servants, it is laid before the emperor, and approved by him. The clerk then makes a copy of each report, signs it, and hands it over to those who require it as a voucher, when it is also signed by the

98. From *waqia'h* an event, and *nawis* a writer.

99. Hence the arrangement must have been as follows—first day, first and second writers; second day, second and third writers; third day, third and fourth writer, and so on.

100. Akbar wished to restrict the slaying of animals.

101. Especially fasts.

Parwanchi, by the *Mir'Arz* , and by that person who laid it before His Majesty. The report in this state is called *yaddasht*, or memorandum.

Besides, there are several copyists who write a good hand and a lucid style. They receive the *yaddasht* when completed, keep it with themselves, and make a proper abridgment of it. After signing it, they return this instead of the *yaddasht*, when the abridgement is signed and sealed by the *Waqi'ahnawis*, and the *Risalahdar*, the *Mir'Arz*, and the *Darogah*. The abridgment, thus completed, is called *Ta'liqah*, and the writer is called *Ta'liqahnawis*.

The *Ta'liqah* is then signed, as stated above, and sealed by the ministers of State.

His Majesty's object is, that every duty be properly performed; that there be no undue increase, or decrease in any department; that dishonest people be removed, and trustworthy people be held in esteem; and that active servants may work without fear, and negligent and forgetful men be held in check.

Regulations Regarding Marriages

Every care bestowed upon this wonderful tie between men is a means of preserving the stability of the human race, and ensuring the progress of the world; it is a preventive against the outbreak of evil passions, and leads to the establishment of homes. Hence His Majesty, inasmuch as he is benign, watches over great and small, and imbues men with his notions of the spiritual union and the equality of essence which he sees in marriage. He abhors marriages which take place between man and woman before the age of puberty. They bring forth no fruit, and His Majesty thinks them even hurtful; for afterwards, when such a couple ripens into manhood, they dislike having connection, and their home is desolate.

Here in India, where a man cannot see the woman to whom he is betrothed, there are peculiar obstacles; but His Majesty maintains that the consent of the bride and bridegroom, and the permission of the parents, are absolutely necessary in marriage contracts.

Marriage between near relations His Majesty thinks highly improper. He says, "The fact that, in ancient times even, a girl was not given to her twin brother, ought to silence those who are fond of historical proofs. Marriage between first cousins, however, does not strike the bigoted followers of Muhammad's religion as wrong; for the beginning of a religion resembles, in this regard, the beginning of the creation of mankind."

His Majesty disapproves of high dowries; for as they are rarely ever paid, they are mere sham; but he admits that the fixing of high dowries is a preventive against rash divorces. Nor does His Majesty approve of everyone marrying more than one wife; for this ruins a man's health, and disturbs the peace of the home. He censures old women that take young husbands, and says that doing so is against all modesty.

He has also appointed two sober and sensible men, one of whom enquires into the circumstances of the bridegroom, and the other into those of the bride. These two officers have the title of *T'uibegi*, or masters of marriages. In many cases, the duties are performed by one and the same officer. His Majesty also takes a tax from both parties, to enable them to show their gratitude. The payment of this tax is looked upon as auspicious. Mansabdars commanding from five to one thousand, pay 10 Muhurs; do. from one thousand to five hundred, 4 *M.*; do. to Commanders of one hundred, 2 *M.*; do. to Commanders of forty, 1 *M.*; do. to Commanders of ten, 4 *R.* The latter fee is also paid by rich people. The middle classes pay l *R.*, and common people 1 *dam*. In demanding this tax, the officers have to pay regard to the circumstances of the father of the bride.

Regulations Regarding Education

In every country, but especially in Hindustan, boys are kept for years at school, where they learn the consonants and vowels. A great portion of the life of the students is wasted by making them read many books. His Majesty orders that every school boy should first learn to write the letters of the Alphabet, and also learn to trace their several forms. He ought to learn the shape and name of each letter, which may be done in two days, when the boy should proceed to write the joined letters. They may be practiced for a week, after which the boy should learn some prose and poetry by heart, and then commit to memory some verses to the praise of God, or moral sentences, each written separately. Care is to be taken that he learns to understand everything himself; but the teacher may assist him a little. He then ought for some time be daily practiced in writing a hemistich or a verse, and will soon acquire a current hand. The teacher ought especially to look after five things: knowledge of the letters; meanings of words; the hemistich; the verse; the former lesson. If this method of teaching be adopted, a boy will learn in a month, or even in a day, what it took others years to understand, so much so that people will get quite astonished. Every boy ought to read books on morals, arithmetic, the notation peculiar to arithmetic, agriculture, mensuration, geometry, astronomy, physiognomy, household matters, the rules of government, medicine, logic, the *tabi'i, riyazi,* and *ilahi,* sciences,[102] and history; all of which may be gradually acquired.

In studying Sanskrit, students ought to learn the Bayakaran, Niyai, Bedanta, and Patanjal. No one should be allowed to neglect those things which the present time requires.

These regulations shed a new light on schools, and cast a bright lustre over Madrasahs.

---

102. This is the three-fold division of sciences. *Ilahi,* or *divine,* sciences comprise everything connected with theology and the means of acquiring a knowledge of God. *Riyazi* sciences treat of quantity, and comprise mathematics, astronomy, music, mechanics. *Tabi'i* sciences comprehend physical sciences.

Abu'l-Fazl 'Allami (ibn Mubārak). Selections from *The Ain I Akbari*, translated by H. Blochmann, M.A., 44–45, 56–59, 153–56, 258–59, 277–79. Calcutta: Baptist Mission Press, G. H. Rouse, 1873.

POST-READING PARS

1. Write down two or three main features of Emperor Akbar's harem.
2. Consult your response to Pre-PAR #2. Does Akbar reflect the virtues you think necessary in a ruler?
3. Identify three or four elements that become parts of a memorandum in Akbar's court.

Inquiry Corner

Content Question(s):

List some of the food items and practices that Abul Fazl describes while reporting on Akbar's imperial kitchen.

Historians believe that Akbar could not read or write. What evidence can you find for this claim?

Critical Question(s):

Critically evaluate the arguments that Akbar offers against child marriage.

How would you evaluate Akbar's leadership style?

Comparative Question(s):

In outlining Akbar's regulations regarding education, Abul Fazl describes a comprehensive curriculum. Compare this curriculum of study with a curriculum adopted at another educational institution that you read as a part of this course.

Connection Question(s):

Think of concrete examples from various regulations from Akbar that might apply in our contemporary contexts. How might they be effective?

from *Divine Stories (Divyavadana)*

Introduction

"The Story of the Two Parrot Chicks" is part of a compilation of stories from the early Buddhist literary genre, *avadana*. These are stories written in Sanskrit that the Buddha narrates about a particular character by revealing how their past lives have impacted their current life. While many of these compilations have been around since the early centuries of the common era, the version of the story you are about to read comes from a collection called *Divyavadana* (*Divine Stories*), compiled most likely in the seventeenth century. These stories often highlighted foundational concepts of Buddhism, namely, *dharma* (the main tenets of Buddhism) and *karma* (the principle that determines one's next station in the cycle of rebirth). Who, in your opinion, might have been the target audience for these stories?

In the context of Hinduism, the Sanskrit term *dharma* refers to one's duties depending on one's caste and stage in life. The teachings of the historical Buddha (circa 563 BCE to 483 BCE) offer critical responses to many of the dominant Hindu doctrines. In the process, he adapted some of the concepts of Hinduism by using them with a different meaning. Thus, he repurposed the term, **dharma** (in the language of Pali *dhamma*) to refer to his core teachings: the four noble truths, the notions of karma and rebirth, and nirvana or freedom or enlightenment. They are also often referred to as the *Dhammacakka* or the "Wheel of the Dhamma," a doctrine that the Buddha set in motion that would remain so forever. What do you think might be the significance of the wheel imagery?

> **SNAPSHOT BOX**
>
> LANGUAGE: Sanskrit
>
> DATE: Early centuries CE
>
> LOCATION: South Asia
>
> GENRE: Narrative, legends
>
> Religious identity: Buddhist
>
> TAGS: Education; Myth and Legend; Nature and Sacred; Religion; Spirituality

Timeline

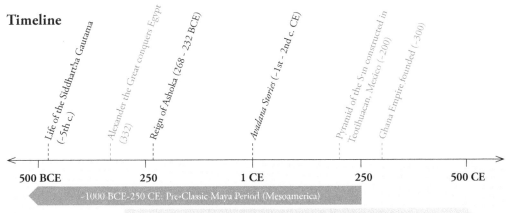

The notion of **karma** plays a pivotal role in the Buddhist worldview: it is the idea that every voluntary action—action done for a desired outcome—during a lifetime leaves a residue that cumulatively shapes one's future rebirths. Using this concept, the Buddha introduces the **four noble truths**. While the first noble truth states "all is suffering," or more accurately, the unenlightened life is suffering, the second noble truth offers a causal analysis of suffering in terms of desire and ignorance. This causal explanation of the aggregate of misery also shows the cessation of misery as contained in the third noble truth. The fourth noble truth offers a step-by-step guide to eradicating ignorance and, as a result, eradicating desire and the endless cycle of rebirth and suffering. The Buddha clarifies that it is this cessation that constitutes enlightenment, freedom (*nirvana*), and genuine contentment and when one attains this state one becomes a buddha or the awakened one. How might a cessation of desire result in contentment?

The stories compiled in *Divyavadana* involve a wide range of characters, including animals and humans, kings and beggars, monks and prostitutes, and god and hell beings. Many of these stories, including "The Story of the Two Parrot Chicks," share a few distinct elements: how the characters come to meet the Buddha and learn about his dharma in this present life and how their present circumstances are a result of their karmic past. Finally, the Buddha, as the omniscient narrator, identifies the characters in the story of the past with those in the story of the present while also predicting their ultimate freedom. Many of these stories also include two important features of Buddhist understanding of morality: the five precepts (*pancasila*) of no killing, no stealing, no sexual misconduct, no lying, and no taking of any intoxicants; and the triple refuge that a Buddhist takes in the Buddha, the community (*sangha* or monastery), and the Dharma.

By the early centuries of the common era, *sangha* (monastery) emerged to be an inseparable part of Buddhism. Most monasteries were built on the outskirts of towns and villages. The role of the sangha for Buddhism has sometimes been explained in terms of the necessary dependence that music has on musical instruments. Monasteries also came to include the lay community that supported it and with whom it developed a symbiotic relationship: while the lay community provides physical support by providing food and shelter, giving alms and so forth, the monks and nuns helped by bestowing merits on the lay community. Given the role of these stories in exemplifying central cultural and moral values, these stories are often compared with the *Purana* (ancient) stories of Hinduism (see page 269). They also had a canonical influence on Buddhist art of this period and representations of these stories are found across Asia from Kizil in China to Sanchi in India to Borobodur in Indonesia. How might these stories be used for moral education in the monastic and lay contexts?

Keya Maitra
Department of Philosophy

The Story of Two Parrot Chicks

Sukapotaka-Avadana

This incident occurred in Sravasti. One day the householder Anathapinda (Alms-giver to the Poor) acquired two parrot chicks. He brought them home, then taught them to speak, reared and nourished them, and instructed them in the language of humans. The venerable Ananda frequently visited these two parrot chicks and gave them a discourse on the dharma that penetrated the four noble truths—namely, this is suffering, this is the origin of suffering, this is the cessation of suffering, and this is the path that leads to the cessation of suffering. The most senior monks would also approach the householder Anathapinda's home, such as Sariputra, Maudgalyayana, Kasyapa, Ananda, and Raivata. As those senior monks approached time and again, those parrot chicks learned their names.

One time the venerable Sariputra arrived at the householder Anathapinda's home. The two parrot chicks saw the venerable Sariputra, and at the sight of him, they addressed the members of the household: "Friends, the elder Sariputra is coming! Prepare a seat for him." They also did the same when they saw the venerable Maha-maudgalyayana, Kasyapa, and Raivata. And when they saw the venerable Ananda, they said, "Our teacher Ananda is coming! Prepare a seat for him."

One time the Blessed One arrived at the householder Anathapinda's home. The two parrot chicks saw the Blessed One coming from a distance. He instilled faith and was worthy of faith, he was restrained at heart and in his senses, his mind was possessed of extreme tranquility, and he blazed with splendor like a golden pillar. At the sight of him, they quickly addressed the members of the household. "Friends," they cooed in a sweet and pleasing voice, "the Blessed One is coming! Prepare a seat for him."

Then, to do a good deed for the two parrot chicks, the Blessed One entered that house and sat down in the seat specially prepared for him. After sitting down, the Blessed One gave a discourse on the Dharma that penetrated the four noble truths and established those two parrot chicks in the taking of the refuges as well as in the precepts. Then the Blessed One, having instructed, incited, inspired, and delighted the two parrot chicks and the members of the household with this discourse on the Dharma, got up from his seat and went out.

Afterward, as the members of the household were wandering about, the two parrot chicks were acting carelessly and were seized by a cat. With looks of pain on their faces as their vital points were pierced and their joints were broken, they said, "Praise to the Buddha! Praise to the dharma! Praise to the community!" And with that said, they died and were reborn among the gods of Caturmaharajika (Four Groups of the Great Kings).

Meanwhile, in a certain place, the Blessed One smiled. The venerable Ananda saw the Blessed One manifesting his smile, and at the sight of the Blessed One, he said this to him: "Perfectly awakened tathagata arhats do not manifest a smile, Bhadanta, without proper cause and reason. Bhadanta, what is the proper cause and reason for your manifesting a smile?"

"It is like this, Ananda. It is like this. Perfectly awakened tathagata arhats do not manifest a smile without proper cause and reason. Ananda, did you see those two parrot chicks?"

"Yes, Bhadanta. I saw them."

"As soon as I left, Ananda, those two parrot chicks were killed by a cat. With their awareness focused on the Buddha, the dharma, and the community, they died and were reborn among the Caturmaharajika gods."

That same morning many monks got dressed, took their bowls and robes, and entered Sravasti for alms. As those many monks were wandering in Sravasti for alms, they heard those two parrot chicks in the householder Anathapinda's home saying "Praise to the Buddha! Praise to the dharma! Praise to the community!" as they were killed by a cat. Having heard this, after wandering in Sravasti for alms and after finishing their meals and returning from their alms rounds, they put away their bowls and robes, washed their feet, and then approached the Blessed One. Having approached, they venerated with their heads the feet of the Blessed One and then sat down at a respectful distance. Sitting down at a respectful distance, those many monks said this to the Blessed One: "Bhadanta, all of us here [were wandering in Sravasti for alms, when we heard] those two parrot chicks in the householder Anathapinda's home saying 'Praise to the Buddha! Praise to the dharma! Praise to the community!' as they were killed by a cat. Bhadanta, what is their destiny? What kind of rebirth will they have? What will be their future?"

"Monks," the Blessed One said, "those two parrots, as a result of taking refuge, will be reborn thirty-six times among the Caturmaharajika gods, and they will be reborn thirty-six times among the gods of Trayastrimsa (Thirty-Three), Yama (Free from Conflict), Tusita (Content), Nirmanarati (Delighting in Creation), and Paranirmitavasavartin (Masters of Others' Creations). After being reborn again and again as beings among the gods in the six spheres of desire, in their last life, their last existence, their last incarnation, they will take human form. Then they will attain awakening as solitary buddhas and become the solitary buddhas Dharma and Sudharma (Good Dharma). In just this way, monks, listening to the dharma has great results and great benefits, what to say of discoursing on the dharma or clearly understanding the dharma? So then, monks, this is to be learned: 'We shall be devoted to listening to the dharma.' It is this, monks, that you should learn to do." This was said by the Blessed One. With their minds uplifted, the monks welcomed the words of the Blessed One.

So ends the *Sukapotaka-avadana*, the sixteenth chapter in the glorious *Divyavadana*.

"The Story of Two Parrot Chicks." In *Divine Stories: Divyāvadāna*, translated by Andy Rotman, Vol. 1, 333–36. Boston: Wisdom Publications, 2008.

POST-READING PARS

1. Identify two or three main characteristics of *dharma* as they emerge from your reading of "Two Parrot Chicks."
2. How is enlightenment or freedom depicted in the story?

Inquiry Corner

Content Question(s):	Critical Question(s):
How do the two parrot chicks die in the story? What happens to them after they die?	What are the three refuges (declarations of one's commitment to the Buddha) according to the Buddha? Critically evaluate their possible effectiveness in attaining enlightenment and freedom.
Comparative Question(s):	**Connection Question(s):**
Compare and contrast the means to ultimate freedom the Buddha offers in this story with other accounts of freedom you have read in this course.	Do you remember a story from your childhood that emphasized a moral message? What were some of its defining features? What could function as such a story in our contemporary multicultural society?

from *A Dream of Splendors Past in the Eastern Capital* (*Dongjing meng hua lu*) by Meng Yuanlao

Introduction

In 1147, Meng Yuanlao wrote *A Dream of Splendors Past in the Eastern Capital* (*Dongjing meng hua lu*) describing the hustle and bustle of the city that is today known as Kaifeng, on the banks of the Yellow River in Henan Province. Meng described Kaifeng during the last years of the Northern Song dynasty (960–1127), when the imperial court was located there, just before the Jurchens, a federation of non-Chinese peoples living northeast of China, conquered north China and forced the court to flee south. He was writing retrospectively, remembering the glory days of the old capital, while he himself was experiencing war, social chaos, and economic devastation. We do not know much about his life, only that he had lived in Kaifeng between the ages of thirteen and twenty-seven, when he fled the war, and that his memoir was written in an unpolished rather than literary style. Meng's account circulated in manuscript form for several decades and was finally published in 1189. After the fall of Kaifeng, the Chinese were able to retain control of their territories around the Yangzi River and southward, and they established a new capital at Hangzhou. Despite continuing military tensions with the Jurchens, Chinese society again flourished under the Southern Song dynasty until 1279, when the Mongols invaded and took over all of north and south China.

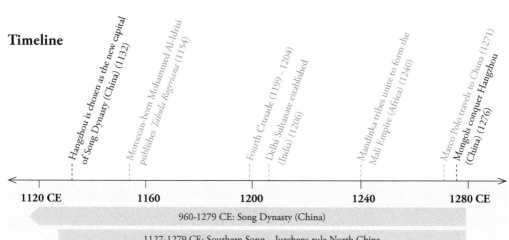

Timeline

Hangzhou is chosen as the new capital of Song Dynasty (China) (1132)

Moroccan-born Mohammed Al-Idrisi publishes *Tabula Rogeriana* (1154)

Fourth Crusade (1199 – 1204)

Delhi Sultanate established (India) (1206)

Mandinka tribes unite to form the Mali Empire (Africa) (1240)

Marco Polo travels to China (1271)

Mongols conquer Hangzhou (China) (1276)

| 1120 CE | 1160 | 1200 | 1240 | 1280 CE |

960-1279 CE: Song Dynasty (China)

1127-1279 CE: Southern Song – Jurchens rule North China

Kaifeng was an administrative as well as an economic and cultural capital (as if New York and Washington, D.C. were rolled into one), with between 600,00 and 700,000 inhabitants, probably the largest city in the world at a time when the greatest cities of Europe had at most 50,000 residents. As the administrative center of a vast empire, whose taxes, luxury goods, and talented men all flowed into the capital, it was a venue of astonishing wealth and contained a diversity of dialects, religions, and occupations. Not only were there specialty shops but also entire specialty markets that included numerous competing vendors dealing in the same types of merchandise. At all hours of the day and night, throughout the year, there were exciting things to see and do. Indeed, this memoir is an important source for the history of Chinese food, clothing, and performance. In capturing an individual's intimate perspective, how might memoirs offer ways to expand the purview of history?

Because we know so little about its author, the document has to be analyzed on its own terms. Outlining a few questions might help in this analysis. What is the function of all the lists? Who would have most appreciated the details of pricing, how to order, and how to recognize different types of establishments and specific recommendations? As you study this account of busy city life, try to figure out why it is organized the way it is, and who might have been its intended readers. What would this account have meant to people who had once lived in Kaifeng? To people who had only heard of its splendors? Or to people who knew the new capital of Hangzhou and wondered how it might have compared? When we attempt to answer any of these questions using our own experiences with cities, we become aware of the multitude of answers.

For a visual counterpart to this description of urban life in the Song dynasty, look online for reproductions of a hand scroll painted by Zhang Zeduan (1085–1145) titled *Along the River During the Qingming Festival*, which features hundreds of people in a panorama of street scenes from Kaifeng before the Jurchens took over. As you read these brief excerpts from Meng Yuanlao's ten-chapter memoir, keep in mind that some scholars have suggested that Meng may have hidden a moral message in his account: although Hangzhou today might be as splendid as Kaifeng once was, it too may soon come to an end.

Grant Hardy
Department of History

PRE-READING PARS

1. What is the biggest city you've ever visited? List two or three things that most impressed you.

2. If a friend were visiting Asheville for the first time, what would you recommend as "must see" sights or "must do" activities? Would you include any specific warnings?

3. Think for a minute about how language can mark someone as an insider or an outsider. Give two examples of when you might have tried to use specific language to seem more knowledgeable and experienced.

---

from *A Dream of Splendors Past in the Eastern Capital*

Avenues and Alleys at the Eastern Gate of Xiangguo

(Supporting the State) Monastery

Along the Monastery East Gate Avenue are to be found shops specializing in cloth caps with pointed tails, belts and waist-wraps, books, caps, and flowers as well as the vegetarian meal of the Ding family. South of the monastery are the brothels of Managers Alley.[103] The nuns and the brocade workers live in Embroidery Alley. On the north is Small Sweetwater Alley.[104] There are a particularly large number of southern restaurants inside the alley, as well as a plethora of brothels.

---

103. The term "managers" (*lushi*) derived from the old practice of feting new Advanced Scholar graduates during the Tang. One person would be appointed to oversee all of the banquet activities and supervise drinking games, including doling out wine tallies and meting out appropriate punishments. [All notes are from the translator.]

104. So named because of the sweet water wells there. Most other wells in Kaifeng produced water laden with mineral salts.

Shops and Stalls along Horse Guild Avenue[105]

North, along Horse Guild Avenue and outside Old Hill-Investiture Gate,[106] on the Angled Road of the Zoroastrian Temple, lies the Prefect-north Pleasure District. In addition to the household gates and shops that line the two sides of New Fengqiu Gate Street,[107] military encampments of the various brigades and columns of the Imperial Guard are situated in facing pairs along approximately ten tricents[108] of the approach to the gate. Other wards, alleys, and confined open spaces criss-cross the area, and are counted in the tens of thousands—no one knows their real number. In every single place, the gates are squeezed up against each other, each with its own tea wards, wineshops, stages, and food and drink.

Normally, the small-business households of the marketplace simply purchase prepared food and drink at food stores; they do not cook at home. For northern food there are the Shi Feng-style dried meat cubes[109] and the various stewed items of the House of Duan and the House of Li the Fourth, all found in front of Alum Tower. For southern food, then the Jin House located south of Xiangguo Monastery Bridge, and the House of Zhou at Nine bends are acknowledged to be the finest.

The night markets close after the third watch (11 P.M.-1 A.M.) only to reopen at the fifth (3–5 A.M.). The more boisterous places stay open until dawn. Normally, even night markets in outlying, quiet places have such items as baked sesame buns stuffed with either sour bean filling or pork tenderloin, mixed-vegetable buns, the flesh of the badger and wild fox, stews of fruit slices, blood sausages,[110] and fragrant

105. From a contemporary source:
The world is troubled by mosquitoes and blackflies, and Horse Guild Avenue alone, of all places in the capital, has no mosquitoes or blackflies. Horse Guild Avenue is a place where night markets and wine houses are extremely abundant. Now mosquitoes and blackflies hate oil (i.e., smoke from oil lamps), and Horse Guild is always raucous and afloat with people and animals. Lamp fires illuminate the heavens. They are extinguished only after the fourth drum, so the place is always void of mosquitoes and blackflies. Because the road is lined for tens of tricents by herbal simples shops and since most of the owners are physicians to the state and are all extremely rich, on the five nights of the First Prime (at the beginning of the year) the lamps are a particularly overwhelming sight, and the music and acting are absolutely extraordinary. So poets often speak of the lamp fires of Horse Guild Avenue, as well.

106. The older gate of the inner wall of the city. It got its name, Old Hill-Investiture (Fengqiu), because the road that led to Fengqiu district exited through it.

107. At the newer outer wall.

108. A Chinese unit of distance equaling about a third of a mile.

109. One recipe for a similar meat cube reads: "Slice both lean and fat pork into three-inch long slices in the shape of counters and let sit overnight in a mixture of granular sugar and fagara powder. Mix thoroughly in equal portions of sugar, powder, and spices. Dry in the sun and then steam until cooked thoroughly."

110. One recipe for these blood sausages states: "Thoroughly wash out the large and small intestines of a fat sheep. Mix cool water and fresh blood together thoroughly, half a ladle each at a time; then fill the intestines as one would for normal sausage. The fresh blood must be quickly

candied fruit. Night markets are held even in the worst snowstorms and on darkest
rainy days of the winter. Found there are such items as meat strips with ginger and
fermented bean-paste, minced tripe with blood-paste, crystal fish-paste, fried fresh
liver, clams, and crabs; walnuts, malt-sugar wheat gluten from Zezhou, cross-hatch
beans, goose pears, pomegranates, Japanese quince, Chinese quince, steamed glutinous rice balls, and soup made from salted fermented bean curd (i.e., Japanese *miso*).
Only after the third watch do tea-sellers appear bearing their pots, seeking to satisfy
those people of the capital, both privately employed and government workers, who
get off late and are able to go home only deep in the night.

Avenues and Alleys at the Southeastern Tower

Eastward from the Tower of Proclaiming Virtue is the Southeastern (literally, "South
Corner") Tower, which is at the southeast corner of the Imperial City. Crossroads
Avenue runs southward from here through the ginger guild; Highhead Avenue runs
north, following the silk guild to the Gate of Eastern Florescence, the Gate of Morning's Radiance, to the Palace of the Precious Phylactery, and straight through to the
Old Sour Jujube Gate.[111] This is where shops and vendors' displays are most bustling
and boisterous. During the Xuanhe reign (1119–1125), they expanded the official
roadway that lined the wall of the Forbidden City on both sides.

East from the Southeastern Tower is the Avenue of Pan's Loft. South of the avenue
is an area called "Raptor Inn," which is reserved as a place where traders in eagles and
hawks lodge. The rest of this area south of the street is occupied by stores and displays
of true pearls, of bolts of cloth and silk, and of incense. One alleyway runs directly
through to the south: it is called "Alley of the Altar for Restricting the Self." This is
where gold, silver, and colored silks are traded or bartered. The buildings and their
grounds are overwhelmingly impressive, and the faces of the gates are deep and broad.
They appear to the eye as a dense forest. Each transaction involves thousands or even
tens of thousands of strings of cash. It dazzles a person's perception.

Further to the east and north of the avenue is a site called the Wineshop of Pan's
Loft. Beneath it, at the fifth watch every morning, a market forms for buying and
selling clothing, books, paintings, valuable baubles,[112] rhinoceros horn, and jade.[113]
At dawn appear sheeps' heads, entrails, liver, kidney and sweetbreads, udders, plain
and honeycombed tripe, quail, rabbit, rock dove, pigeons, wild game, crabs, clams,
and the like. Only after this session has ended do the various craftsmen come to
market to buy and sell a motley of small materials. After the breakfast period, food

---

and precisely matched. It cannot be too large a portion. If too much, it congeals and cannot be
poured into the intestines."

111. Inner-wall gate through which the road to Suanzao (Sour Jujube) Prefecture ran.

112. Luxury items such as antiques, jewelry, etc.

113. This is usually understood as rhinoceros horn and jade; however, it could also mean horn
that had been burnished to a jadelike luster.

and drink appear at the market—for instance, honey-crisp, jujube-stuffed steamed dumplings, balls of finely ground sweet bean paste, fruit cooked in scented honey, and flowered designs soaked and cooked in honey. Toward evening, hair ornaments, caps, combs, scarves and bodices, valuable baubles, tools, and the like, all of inferior quality, are put out for sale.

Further to the east and on the north is the Xu Family Calabash Stew Shop; south of the avenue is the Sang Family Pleasure Precinct.

Nearby and to the north is the Middle Pleasure Precinct and next in line the Interior Pleasure Precinct. Of the fifty or more theaters within these pleasure precincts, the Lotus Flower Theater and the Peony Theater of the Middle Pleasure Precinct and the Elephant and Yaksa (Demon) theaters of the Central Pleasure Precinct are the largest. They can hold several thousand people. From the generation of Ding Xianxian, Wang Tuanzi, and Seventh Sage Zhang,[114] people of later times were allowed to perform here. Inside the pleasure precincts one finds many purveyors of medicinal simples, sellers of hexagram fortunes, hawkers of old clothes, those who barter and wager on food and drink, silhouette cutters, singers of ditties, and the like. One can stay here the whole day without being aware of the approach of nightfall.

Streets and Alleys Outside of the Gate of the Vermilion Bird [Excerpt]

On the western side, south of Dragonford Bridge, is the residence of Military Privy Counselor Deng;[115] further south is the Alley of the Military School; inside is the residence of Songster Zhang[116] and the Temple to the King Whose Military Might Brought Completion.[117] South of this is the Zhang Family Restaurant for Fried Dough as well as the residence of the Empress of Lustrous Integrity.[118]

Going west one comes to a large street called Large Alley Intersection and further west is the wineshop of the Loft of Cool Breezes. In the summer, people of the capital enjoy the coolness here. Further west is the Old Crow Alley Intersection, the Number One Armory, and finally the Number One Bridge.

Southward from the Large Alley Intersection is the Taoist Temple for Receiving

114. All famous players in the Court Entertainment Bureau.

115. This was a reward for Deng Xunwu, who had been appointed in 1116 to be Military Commissioner for Protection of the Grand Army, at which time he was also appointed Co-Commissioner of Military Affairs; he was given this residence by the emperor in 1121 as a reward for being one of the prime movers behind the return of an influential minister to the capital.

116. One of the numerous entertainers and jesters favored by Emperor Huizong (r. 1100–1125), the reigning monarch.

117. Originally a site to honor Lü Shang, who helped King Wen wrest control of China in the Zhou, this was to become the major temple for honoring military heroes. By the end of the Song, some seventy-two (a Eurasian magical number) generals and military figures from the historical past were enfeoffed here as objects of sacrifice.

118. One of Huizong's concubines; originally a woman of the wineshops, her beauty captured the eye of one of Huizong's lackeys, who presented her to the emperor.

Realized Ones. The Taoist citizens from the four quadrants are all received here. Further south and going west into Small Alley Intersection is the Monastery of Three Emulations, and going further west one comes directly to the Yinan Bridge.

South from the Small Alley Intersection is the Gate of Southern Infusion. The funeral vehicles of ordinary citizens and people of worth are not able to go through this gate to exit the city—it is said to be so because it directly faces the [major entrance] to the Great Inner [Imperial] City. It is precisely here that the pigs that citizens lead to slaughter enter the capital. Every day, until late in the evening, herds of tens of thousands of pigs, driven by no more than ten or so persons, enter the capital. There are none that run amok (all march in perfect order).

Restaurants

Generally, the largest restaurants were called "partial-tea [food shops]." They served such things as head stew, stalactite stew, pressed meat, baked sesame buns, lamb kid, large and small bones, kidneys in reduced sauce, brass-skin noodles; broad-cut noodles with ginger, twice-cooked noodles(?), cold-noodles, chess-piece pastas, and baked flour products. If one were to make it a "full tea" meal, then one added a head stew of pickled vegetables.

There were also Sichuan restaurants that served noodles with meat, noodles with preserved meat, noodles with various forms of meat or vegetable topping, stewed meat, fried giblets of fowl, and rice served with toppings both raw and cooked.

There were also southern restaurants, which had "fish pockets," cooked minced meat with brass-skin noodles, and rice with fried fish.

In addition, calabash stew shops erected a scaffolding of heavy lintels and flowered posts that were bound together like "mountain platforms." On top of these they hung out sides of pork and mutton, twenty or thirty to the span. Just inside, the door fronts and shutters were decorated with vermilion and green; these were called "gates of pleasure."

Each of these restaurants had a courtyard with eastern and western corridors that were designated as seating compartments. When the guests sat down, a single person holding chopsticks and paper[119] then asked all of the seated guests for their orders. People of the capital were extravagant and unrestrained, and they would demand a hundred different things—some hot, some cold, some warm, some room temperature, some icy cold, as well as toppings of both lean and fat meats. Each person demanded something different. The waiter took their orders, then stood in line in front of the kitchen and, when his turn came, sang out his orders to those in the kitchen. Those who were in charge of the kitchen were called "pot masters" or were called "controllers of the preparation tables." This came to an end in a matter of moments, and the waiter—his left hand supporting three dishes and his right arm stacked from

---

119. This could also mean paper to wipe the chopsticks with.

hand to shoulder with some twenty dishes, one on top of the other—distributed them in the exact order in which they had been ordered. Not the slightest error was allowed. Even the slightest mistake was reported by the guests to the head of the restaurant, who would then curse the waiter, or dock his salary, or, in extreme cases, drive him from the place.

When my kind went into a restaurant, then we used first-class ceramic bowls with shallow rims that were called "lapis bowls." Or we called it "first-class stew." Particularly fine vegetable dishes were also called "first-class pickled vegetables." Each bowl was ten wen (cash). If meat and noodles made up half the meal, it was called "combined stew." There was also an "individual stew," which was a half-portion. In the old days we used only spoons, but nowadays they use chopsticks.

Wine, Food, and Fruits

For the most part the cooks who sell snacks are called "Learned Ones of Fine Meals and Wine Measures." All of the young waiters in the wineshops are inclusively called "Uncle." There are also women from the neighborhood whose waists are wrapped with blue-flowered scarves and whose hair is coiled up in a precarious bun. They change the hot water for heating wine and pour out wine for the drinking party. They are commonly called "warmers of dregs." And there are common folk who come into the wineshops and who, spying young playboys drinking, attentively provide them services. They are dispatched to buy things or to go summon singsong girls, and to do things like fetch and send money and other items. They are called "idlers."

And there are others who come forward to change the hot water used to warm wine, pour wine, or sing, and sometimes even offer fruit or incense. They are called "riff-raff." And there are low-class singsong girls, who, without being summoned, come to sing in front of the tables. At the appropriate time they are given a little cash or some small item, and then they leave. This is called "petitioning the customers" or "hitting the wine seats." And there are those who sell medicinal herbs or things like fruit and radishes. They do not bother to ask if the customer is going to buy them or not, but pass them around to each of the seated guests and then collect money later. This is called "Temporarily Passing Out [the Goods]."

Such phenomena occur everywhere, except at Charcoal Zhang's and Yoghurt Zhang's near Zhoubridge, where people of the above categories are not allowed to enter. These two places also do not sell wine snacks. They provide only fine pickled vegetables and sell only the best category of wine.

Merchants sell hair ornaments cut from silk and feathers in the shape of jade plums, moths, bees, snowy willows, and bodhi-tree leaves; they sell small balls of pea flour in the shape of tadpoles, and flattened fried glutinous rice balls. It is precisely these fried-glutinous-rice-ball sellers who erect green umbrellas on their bamboo racks, on top of which they fix small plum-red lamps fretted with gold. They hang lamps on the front and back of the racks and, keeping time to the beat of a drum, they twirl the racks round and round as they walk along. This is called "making it whirl."

From "Recollections of the Northern Song Capital." In *Hawai'i Reader in Traditional Chinese Culture*, edited by Victor H. Mair, Nancy S. Steinhardt, and Paul R. Goldin, 408–12, 420–21. Honolulu: University of Hawai'i Press, 2005.

POST-READING PARS

1. Mention two aspects of city life that are not covered in the excerpts from the memoir.
2. Give two examples of when the writer offers personal opinions, as opposed to reporting straight facts.
3. Give two examples of slang and insider lingo in this account.

Inquiry Corner

Content Question(s):	Critical Question(s):
Amid the rapturous descriptions of the wonders of life in Kaifeng, the author notes in passing several dangers. Can you find them? Were they more likely to threaten residents or visitors?	What role did women play in the economic and cultural life of the capital? One paragraph begins "When my kind went into a restaurant . . ." What can we surmise about the author and "his kind" of people?
Comparative Question(s):	**Connection Question(s):**
How does this source compare with travel writings that we read in this course?	Food is obviously necessary to sustain life, but when have you experienced eating as a form of entertainment?

from *Ganga Lahari (Waves of the Ganges River)* by Panditaraja Jagannatha

Introduction

The *Ganga Lahari* is a poem of praise to the Ganges River that was composed by the Hindu poet Jagannatha (1572–1665 CE) under the patronage of the Mughal emperor Shah Jahan who honored him with the title Panditaraja (king of the wise). The Mughal courts of Akbar (see page 171) and also of his grandson Shah Jahan were marked by an openness to learning about various religious ideas and expressions, and it is well documented that they provided patronage to a variety of artists, poets, musicians, and scholars. It is no surprise then that Jagannatha, a Hindu brahmin born into the highest priestly caste level from the south of the Indian subcontinent, found a home in the cosmopolitan Delhi court. Besides the approval of a ruler, what other conditions might foster open exchange of diverse ideas and expressions in a society?

Jagannatha created fifty-two verses in Sanskrit dedicated to describing and praising the qualities of the divine river that was considered by Hindus to be a form of a goddess. This tradition of tracing themes back to the Vedas, one of the earliest oral sources of Hindu religious knowledge (1500–500 BCE), often recognizes nature — including the sun, moon, mountains, and rivers — as divine. Jagannatha's poem carries on this tradition as part of ***bhakti***, or devotion, that emphasized personal relationships between humans and gods and goddesses. The Ganges holds a special role for many practicing Hindus. Its waters are believed to be able to erase karmic consequences arising from human mistakes and can also release one from

Timeline

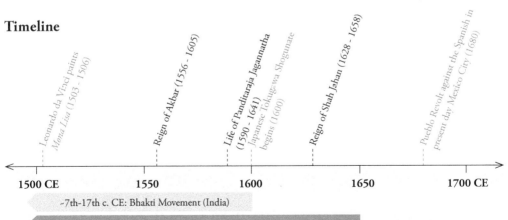

the cycles of rebirth, as explained below by the story of how the Ganges River appeared on the Earth.

According to Hindu sacred history, the Ganges River originally flowed only in the heavenly realms before it was redirected to descend and flow on the Earth as an eventual consequence of human pleading with the divine. One way that human beings could petition the gods to do certain things on their behalf was to engage in rigorous forms of **asceticism**, practices of mental and physical self-denial, like fasting, that would create *tapas*, a ritual heat. Tapas could be used in multiple ways to clear karma, heal, and clarify knowledge, as well as be used as the mechanism by which gods become obligated to fulfill requests. What other forms of asceticism come to mind and what purposes do they serve?

In the story of the Ganges River, Bhagiratha, an ascetic, spent eons standing on one foot, arms in the air, in order to create the tapas needed to be granted the divine favor of having the Ganges River flow on Earth. The primary reason for bringing the divine river to the earthly realm was for her water to run over the bones of Bhagiratha's ancestors to release them from this earthly cycle of existence and give access to any others in need of her purifying waters. While Bhagiratha was successful in his generation of tapas and subsequent request, the main problem was that the Ganges was too powerful to descend directly to Earth, as she would shatter the ground with her force. The Hindu god Shiva volunteered to allow the river to fall onto his head first, breaking her fall by winding her way through his ascetic dreadlocks. Images of Shiva include a water spout or mermaid-like figure in his hair to indicate his connection with the Ganges. This closeness to the Ganges often makes Shiva's wife Parvati jealous, as will be mentioned in one of the verses excerpted below.

Contemporary Hindus still chant this poem to express their devotion to the goddess and to request assistance in the removal of the negative effects of karmic actions as a way to create a clean slate for any perceived mistakes. This may have been true personally for Jagannatha as well. According to some accounts about the origin of the *Ganga Lahari*, Jagannatha may have composed this poem in order to rectify his exile from his own Hindu priestly community for falling in love with a Muslim woman at court. How might this specific story about the origins of the poem enhance the popularity of devotion to the Ganges?

Katherine C. Zubko
Department of Religious Studies

from *Ganga Lahari (Waves of the Ganges River)*

Namah sri-gangayai: Salutation to Goddess Ganga!

1: May your water, which is the indescribable abundant good fortune of the whole earth, which consists of the great excellence of Lord Shiva who has created this universe playfully and who possesses an axe for cutting, which is the wealth of all Vedas, and which is the merit incarnate of the gods, and which has the purity of nectar, remove our misfortune.[120]

2: May this stream of your waters, which upon reaching one's eyesight removes at once the affliction of the poor and the karmic mistakes of persons whose hearts are full of bad inclinations, which is also the spiritual teacher here on earth that immediately fells the tree of all-around ignorance, grant us unlimited prosperity.

3: May the waves be instrumental in destroying our karmic mistakes and fears; those waves which are born of the body of Ganga, which are very high, which are swirling on the head of Lord Shiva, and which have a moment of fear born from the casting of a sidelong glance by Parvati—a side-long glance half-manifest, half-hidden, like the rising sun.[121]

4: Oh mother Bhagirathi![122] On account of me causing offense to the gods, if now hereafter you take recourse to indifference, due to no small arrogance on my part, then tell me, alas, before whom shall I cry, having no other support than you?

5: Your form, possessing water deserving of worship by all the gods, which upon reading the memory even of persons who have not performed any good acts, removes mental dullness, like a beam of moonlight removes darkness; may this form take away my internal suffering and also my threefold karmic transgressions (of body, speech and mind).

---

120. The format of the verses has the main noun in the beginning and verb at the end, thus the main point here is "May your water remove our misfortune." All other statements qualify the main noun, in this case "your water."

121. Parvati, the wife of Shiva, is casting a jealous glance at the goddess Ganges for being close to Shiva, and Ganges is rightfully a bit afraid.

122. The honorific of Bhagirathi is a feminine form of address referring to the river brought down by the ascetic actions of Bhagiratha.

6: Oh mother! [The happiness of those people] who, spontaneously having given up even their well established kingdoms, have reached your bank where cane plants are moving to and fro, who are drinking to their full satisfaction an abundance of your water, more tasteful than nectar, the happiness of those people makes a mockery of the state of *nirvana*.[123]

7: Oh mother! The moment the musk, present on the bodies of the beloved wives of kings, mixes with your waters while they are bathing in the morning, instantaneously the deer, possessing charming bodies, are overwhelmed by the scent and enter at their own will into the heavenly Nandana garden.

8: The word Ganga, which remembered even once, makes one's mind instantaneously peaceful; when pronounced respectfully, removes quickly the misdeeds and suffering of the world, this word Ganga, sweet to hear, may it sound indeed in my lotus-like mouth with my very last breath.

9: Your bank on which the crows play, full of abundant satisfaction, their minds not desirous of the abode of the lord of heaven;[124] that bank which is instrumental in removing the suffering of birth and death of human beings, may your bank be capable of giving rest to our fatigue.

10: Oh river of the gods! That reality, which is not directly ascertained even through the Vedas which reject dualism, in which the function of mind and speech of individual living beings is not effective, which is formless, eternal, perfectly pure, having removed ignorance by its own greatness, you are that [reality], and not an ordinary object.

11: Please tell us, that abode of lord Vishnu, which is not to be achieved even by making great gifts, by various meditations, by various kinds of sacrifices, and even by perfectly pure severe penances, which is beyond imagination, you are granting that abode [here on earth] without discrimination to all, therefore tell us with whom you are to be compared here.

12: Who in this world can express the greatness of your form, which is instrumental in removing human beings' fear of the world even by casting a mere glance; that form which is auspicious, which Lord Shiva keeps on his head constantly, having turned down the fervent request of Parvati the daughter of the mountain king [to remove you], who was dejected due to her anger [at you].

123. The suggestion here is that people who interact with Ganga are in a more blissful state than those who have attained release from worldly existence. Hindus and Buddhists use this term in this time period.

124. The crows are not thinking of being in the heavens because being on the bank of the river is just as good, or even better.

13: The misdeeds of many people, which are to be criticized even by intoxicated persons, which are to be avoided by down-fallen persons, are not to be mentioned by outcastes, and which are to be discarded with horripilation[125] even by backbiters, because you are not fatigued ever while removing constantly such karmic mistakes, therefore you alone in the whole universe indeed excel all others.

14: Oh mother! Since slipping down from the region of heaven for removing the grief experienced by the people on the surface of the earth, you have been restrained by Lord Shiva in the knot of his tresses, freeing people from their greed.

15: Oh mother! Humans who are blind, lame, deaf since birth, mute and tortured by planets,[126] humans who lack all means for the removal of karmic transgressions, who have fallen into hell and have been rejected even by gods, you are the best medicine for protecting such humans in this world.

16: Oh mother! This greatness of your water, which is pure and cold by nature, is unlimited and indescribable and excels in the world. Even today, after the sons of Sagara[127] who maintain stainless luster and deeply manifest horripilation from happiness, sing about [your greatness] with joy.

17: Oh mother! To redeem persons who have committed minor crimes and thereafter quickly repent, different groups of sacred places are present on the surface of the three worlds;[128] but to take away from the crimes of persons whose conduct is beyond the path of [being able to alleviate the karmic effects], you, the incomparable, excel all others.

18: Your body, which is the treasure house of merits, which is somewhat indescribable, a creator of renewed joys, which is the chief of all sacred places, which is the stainless lower garment of the three worlds, which is a solution to the confused mind, and which is indeed instrumental in concealing erroneous thinking, which is instrumental in established different types of prosperity, may your body remove our suffering.

. . .

23: If you the mother who fulfills all desires, are awakened in the world, then let the creator, Brahma, enter into endless concentration without worry, let Lord Vishnu sleep pleasantly on the serpent Sesha, let Lord Shiva dance constantly; if you are awakened, then it is useless to perform expiations, penances, gifts and sacrifices.

24: This child, I, an orphan, has come to you, the mother who has extreme love, this child who missed the approach to heaven, has come to you who grants a meritorious destination, this child falling, has come to you who lifts up the whole universe out of

125. Horripilation is a term referring to the hairs of one's arms standing on end, an involuntary bodily reaction akin to goosebumps.

126. Being tortured by planets is a reference to unfavorable astrological influences.

127. These are some of Bhagiratha's ancestors who were released by Ganga's water.

128. "The three worlds" is a way to indicate the entire universe.

its misery, this child weakened by disease, has come to you who is the expert medical practitioner, this child having his mind extremely uneasy on account of thirst has come to you who is the ocean of nectar, this child has come to you, mother, please do here what is appropriate.

Adapted and excerpted from *Panditaraja Jagannatha's Gangalahari*, translated by Irma Schotsman. Delhi: NAG Publishers, 1999 [not giving page numbers because translation embedded in word-for-word breakdown and commentaries that we are not using].

POST-READING PARS

1. Identify two or three qualities about the Ganges that are praised by Jagannatha and compare to your phrases.
2. Identify two characteristics of divinity in Jagannatha's poem.

Inquiry Corner

Content Question(s):	**Critical Question(s):**
Identify two or three different types of relationships that the devotee-poet Jagannatha invokes in relating to and addressing the river Ganges/goddess Ganga?	In what ways are nature and the sacred interconnected in Jagannatha's poem? What are some of the benefits in thinking of nature and the sacred as interconnected?
Comparative Question(s):	**Connection Question(s):**
In what ways does Jagannatha's approach and petitions to the goddess Ganga compare and contrast to what other religious poets and seekers focus on and ask for from their god(s)? (For example, consider Hildegard, Kempe, St. Francis of Assisi, Mirabai.)	How might the divine nature of the river and its relationship to devotees be both beneficial and an obstacle to contemporary activism to halt river pollution in India?

from *A Guide to the Bodhisattva Way of Life (Bodhicaryavatara)* by Shantideva

Introduction

The *Bodhicaryavatara* (typically translated as *A Guide to the Bodhisattva Way of Life*) is a foundational text for Buddhism. It is viewed as *the* guide to cultivating qualities, like compassion, wisdom, and insight, that are essential for a Buddhist. Its author, Shantideva (685–763 CE), was a Buddhist monk and a renowned teacher at Nalanda University. Specific details about Shantideva's life are sparse but there are a number of legends about his life. Many of these legends have Shantideva performing extraordinary acts. For example, given his nonorthodox manners, where he appeared to other monks as simply lazing around doing nothing—"just eating, sleeping and defecating,"—his fellow instructors planned to humiliate him publicly by exposing his ignorance. So they invited him to give a recitation (a lecture) on Buddhist scripture before the entire Nalanda community. They built a seat for him to lecture from too high so that he would not be able to reach it. But, according to legend, he lowered the seat with one hand and climbed on it without any trouble and proceeded to ask whether the monks wanted him to recite from something old or something new. When requested to offer something new, he recited the entire *Bodhicaryavatara*! What might this legend tell you about Shantideva's significance for a Buddhist?

In addition to being one of the greatest achievements in world literature, Shantideva's *Bodhicaryavatara* articulates one of the most important philosophical ac-

SNAPSHOT BOX

LANGUAGE: Sanskrit

DATE: c. 700 CE

LOCATION: Present-day India

GENRE: Poetry

Religious identity: Buddhist

TAGS: Asceticism; Body; Community; Ethics and Morality; Humanism; Identity and Self; Philosophy; Religion; Ritual and Practice

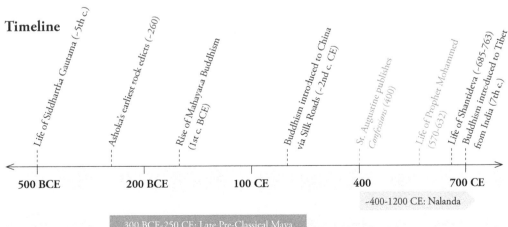

Timeline

Life of Siddhartha Gautama (~5th c.)

Ashoka's earliest rock edicts (~260)

Rise of Mahayana Buddhism (1st c. BCE)

Buddhism introduced to China via Silk Roads (~2nd c. CE)

St. Augustine publishes *Confessions* (400)

Life of Prophet Mohammed (570–632)

Life of Shantideva (~685–763)

Buddhism introduced to Tibet from India (7th c.)

500 BCE   200 BCE   100 CE   400   700 CE

~400–1200 CE: Nalanda

300 BCE–250 CE: Late Pre-Classical Maya

100 BCE–500 CE: Hopewell Cultures (N. America)

counts of the Mahayana school of Buddhism. In philosophy it is often argued that understanding something requires looking deeper and therefore going beyond what meets the eyes or other senses. The historical Buddha's primary project was to understand suffering—its abiding prevalence in sentient lives and ways of overcoming it. The Buddhist insight in this regard is to accept impermanence as a fundamental feature of our reality in spite of the appearance of permanence. How might you think suffering could result from permanence?

While no one is likely to argue with change being a constant factor in our everyday experience, the Buddhist proposal extends this to our individual selves. What we take to be fixed, constant, and permanent turns out to be an ever-changing bundle of five aggregates. A Buddhist takes these five aggregates to be physical form, sensations, conception or perception, mental activities or formations, and consciousness. According to this view, you or I don't have a permanent or fixed self. Rather, you are a series of causally connected aggregates of conditions, events, and experiences that constitute your life. I too am nothing more than such a series. It is the continuity of these series that makes us expect that there is an essential unchanging self behind the series. An interconnectedness of conditions follows. The realization of this foundational interdependence of our reality constitutes freedom from suffering in this Buddhist framework that is also embodied in the wisdom of enlightenment or **nirvana.**

The first set of verses excerpted here are from a chapter titled "The Perfection of Meditation." Here after laying out specific instructions on meditation practices Shantideva outlines his arguments for radical compassion. Since self in this Buddhist understanding is an "identityless bundle," any argument for preferring one's own suffering over that of others loses its reasonableness. Therefore, Shantideva argues, morality requires us to work equally toward the alleviation of everyone's suffering. How is this idea of radical compassion applicable in our world?

The second set of verses comes from the chapter titled "The Perfection of Wisdom" and contains the philosophical core of the *Bodhicaryavatara*. Verses in this chapter capture the fast pace of the tradition of competitive scholastic debates that took place daily in universities like Nalanda and were an integral part of the training of an aspiring monk. Shantideva's defense of **Madhyamaka** philosophy is outlined as a refutation of arguments of other Buddhist and Hindu philosophical schools holding a range of positions on what ultimately exists. For example, the earlier Buddhist atomism argues that everything can be viewed as aggregates of impartite (that which cannot be divided any further) units or atoms. Shantideva would argue that no such atoms exist. Similarly, his debate with Yogacara, another Buddhist school of thought, focuses on the cognitive and moral implications of not acknowledging the real existence of consciousness.

The most important distinction Shantideva introduces is between conventional truth and ultimate truth. Conventional truth is what is discernible through the use of our senses. For example, conventional truth about water might include things like: it is a liquid, it can quench thirst, and it is the substance that fills the oceans on Earth. Ultimate truth about water would be what is ultimately true about water. Scientists might say what is ultimately true of water is that its chemical formula is H_2O. According to Shantideva, the ultimate truth of Mahayana Buddhist philosophy is the idea of **emptiness**. Things are in reality empty of their characterization as independent, fixed, and with an essence. So, conventionally speaking, the coffee cup on the desk in your study exists whether you are in your study or not. However, none of us would argue that it exists independently or inherently. After all, it was made most likely by a potter and it can be destroyed. It was created because we need cups to hold our coffee. Shantideva wants us to consider that such is the case with *everything*! Nothing—including especially our individual self—has inherent, independent, or absolute existence. Reality is empty of such possibilities. To assume otherwise is to fall for mere illusion.

Shantideva argues that this illusion is the root cause of our grasping and attachment to our sense of unitary and permanent selves. This results in our failure to see the ultimate emptiness of our reality, which creates suffering. Meditation plays a central role in enabling us to behold the interdependent nature of our reality. This marks a defining feature of Shantideva's central argument: our ability to appreciate the ultimately empty nature of things as well as to act from selflessness and with radical compassion requires that we develop a sustained meditative practice, that is, become a contemplative. How might this emphasis on meditation shape the nature of Shantideva's philosophy?

Keya Maitra
Department of Philosophy

PRE-READING PARS

1. Find a quiet spot and sit with a stable posture. Now set a timer for three minutes, close your eyes, and bring your attention to your breath as it enters and leaves your body. When you notice your attention wandering from your breath, gently without judgment bring it back to your breath. After the timer goes off, write down two or three things you noticed during your three minutes of quiet sitting.

2. Select an item from your immediate surroundings and list two things you consider to be conventionally true of it and two things that you take to be ultimately true of it.

from *A Guide to the Bodhisattva Way of Life (Bodhicaryavatara)*

Chapter VIII: The Perfection of Meditation

[...]

89. After meditating on the advantages of solitude in this and other ways,[129] having one's discursive thoughts calmed, one should cultivate the Spirit of Awakening.

90. One should first earnestly meditate on the equality of oneself and others in this way: "All equally experience suffering and happiness, and I must protect them as I do myself."

91. Just as the body, which has many parts owing to its division into arms and so forth, should be protected as a whole, so should this entire world, which is differentiated and yet has the nature of the same suffering and happiness.

92. Although my suffering does not cause pain in other bodies, nevertheless that suffering is mine and is difficult to bear because of my attachment to myself.

93. Likewise, although I myself do not feel the suffering of another person, that suffering belongs to that person and is difficult [for him] to bear because of his attachment to himself.

94. I should eliminate the suffering of others because it is suffering, just like my own suffering. I should take care of others because they are sentient beings, just as I am a sentient being.

95. When happiness is equally dear to others and myself, then what is so special about me that I strive after happiness for myself alone?

---

129. In verse 87 of this chapter Shantideva lists empty dwelling, foot of a tree or caves as examples of forms of solitude (editors' footnote).

96. When fear and suffering are equally abhorrent to others and myself, then what is so special about me that I protect myself but not others?

97. If I do not protect them because I am not afflicted by their sufferings, why do I protect my body from the suffering of a future body, which is not my pain?

98. The assumption that "it is the same me even then" is false; because it is one person who has died and quite another who is born.

99. If one thinks that the suffering that belongs to someone is to be warded off by that person himself, then why does the hand protect the foot when the pain of the foot does not belong to the hand?

100. If one argues that even though it is inappropriate, it happens because of grasping onto a self, our response is: With all one's might, one should avoid that which is inappropriate, whether it belongs to oneself or to another.

101. The continuum of consciousness, like a series, and the aggregation of constituents, like an army and such, are unreal. Since one who experiences suffering does not exist, to whom will that suffering belong?

102. All sufferings are without an owner, because they are not different. They should be warded off simply because they are suffering. Why is any restriction made in this case?

103. Why should suffering be prevented? Because everyone agrees. If it must be warded off, then all of it must be warded off; and if not, then this goes for oneself as it does for everyone else.

[...]

Chapter IX: The Perfection of Wisdom

1. The Sage taught this entire system for the sake of wisdom. Therefore, with the desire to ward off suffering, one should develop wisdom.

2. This truth is recognized as being of two kinds: conventional and ultimate. Ultimate reality is beyond the scope of the intellect. The intellect is called conventional reality.

3. In the light of this, people are seen to be of two types: the contemplative and the ordinary person. The ordinary folks are superseded by the contemplatives.

4. Due to the difference in their intelligence, even contemplatives are refuted by successively higher ones by means of analogies accepted by both parties, regardless of what they aim to prove.

5. Ordinary people see and imagine things as real and not illusory. It is in this respect that there is disagreement between the contemplatives and the ordinary people.

6. Even the objects of direct perception, such as form and the like, are established by consensus and not by verifying cognition. That consensus is false, as is the general agreement that pure things are impure, for example.

7. The Protector taught things in order to bring people to understanding.

[Qualm:] If these things are not ultimately, but only conventionally, momentary, this is inconsistent.

8. [Madhyamika:] There is no fault in the conventional truth of the contemplatives. In contrast to ordinary people, they see reality. Otherwise, ordinary people would invalidate the perception of women as impure.

9. [Qualm:] How can there possibly be merit due to the Jina[130] who is like an illusion, as is the case if he is truly existent? If a sentient being is like an illusion, why is he born again after he dies?

10. [Madhyamika:] Even an illusion lasts for as long as the collection of its conditions. Why should a sentient being truly exist merely because its continuum lasts a long time?

11. [Yogacarin:[131]] If consciousness does not exist, there is no sin in killing an illusory person.

[Madhyamika:] On the contrary, when one is endowed with the illusion of consciousness, vice and merit do arise.

12. [Yogacarin:] An illusory mind is not possible, since mantras and the like are unable to produce it.

[Madhyamika:] Diverse illusions originate on account of diverse conditions. Nowhere does a single condition have the ability to produce everything.

13. [Yogacarin:] If one could be ultimately emancipated and yet transmigrate conventionally, then even the Buddha would transmigrate. So what would be the point of the Bodhisattva way of life?

14. [Madhyamika:] When its conditions are not destroyed, an illusion does not cease either. Due to a discontinuity of its conditions, it does not originate even conventionally.

---

130. A Buddha (editors' footnote).

131. The *Yogacara* school is a Mahayana Buddhist philosophical school that defends a kind of idealism—the Cittamatra view, that argues that only minds are real. The Yogacara theory about consciousness is called the self-intimation theory, according to which, a conscious state illuminates itself in illuminating its object. See, for example, verse 18 below (editors' footnote).

15. *[Yogacarin:]* When even a mistaken cognition does not exist, by what is an illusion ascertained?

16. *[Madhyamika:]* If for you an illusion itself does not exist, what is apprehended? Even if it is an aspect of the mind itself, in reality it exists as something different.

17. *[Yogacarin:]* If the mind itself is an illusion, then what is perceived by what?

[Madhyamika:] The Protector of the World stated that the mind does not perceive the mind. Just as a sword cannot cut itself, so it is with the mind.

18. *[Yogacarin:]* It illuminates itself, as does a lamp.

[Madhyamika:] A lamp does not illuminate itself, for it is not concealed by darkness.

19. *[Yogacarin:]* A blue object does not require something else for its blueness, as does a crystal. So something may or may not occur in dependence on something else.

20. *[Madhyamika:]* As in the case of non-blueness, blue is not regarded as its own cause. What blue by itself could make itself blue?

21: *[Yogacarin:]* It is said that a lamp illuminates once this is cognized with awareness. The mind is said to illuminate once this is cognized with what?

22. *[Madhyamika:]* If no one perceives whether the mind is luminous or not, then there is no point in discussing it, like the beauty of a barren woman's daughter.

23: *[Yogacarin:]* If self-cognizing awareness does not exist, how is consciousness recalled?

[Madhyamika:] Recollection comes from its relation to something else that was experienced, like a rat's poison.[132]

24. *[Yogacarin:]* It illuminates itself, because the mind endowed with other conditions perceives.

[Madhyamika:] A jar seen due to the application of a magical ointment is not the ointment itself.

25. The manner in which something is seen, heard, or cognized is not what is refuted here, but the conceptualization of its true existence, which is the cause of suffering, is rejected here.

26. If you fancy that an illusion is neither different from the mind nor non-different, then if it is a really existing thing, how can it not be different? If it is not different, then it does not really exist.

---

132. The analogy here refers to an animal, such as a bear, which while sleeping is bitten and infected by a rat. Although the bear is not conscious of being poisoned at the time it is bitten, it "recalls" this upon waking up and sensing the inflammation of the bite (abridged original footnote).

27. Just as an illusion can be seen even though it does not truly exist, so it is with the observer, the mind.

[Yogacarin:] The cycle of existence has its basis in reality or else it would be like space.

28. *[Madhyamika:]* How can something that does not exist have any efficacy by being based on something real? You have approached the mind as being an isolated unity.

29. If the mind were free of any apprehended object, then all beings would be Tathagatas.[133] Thus, what good is gained by speculating that only the mind exists?

30. *[Yogacarin:]* Even when the similarity to illusion is recognized, how does a mental affliction cease, since lust for an illusory woman arises even in the one who created her?

31. *[Madhyamika:]* Because her creator's imprints of mental afflictions toward objects of knowledge have not been eliminated, when seeing her, his imprint of emptiness is weak.

32. By building up the imprints of emptiness, the imprint of existence is diminished; and after accustoming oneself to the fact that nothing truly exists, even that diminishes.

33. *[Yogacarin:]* If it is conceived that a phenomenon that does not really exist cannot be perceived, then how can a non-entity, which is without basis, stand before the mind?

34. *[Madhyamika:]* When neither an entity nor a non-entity remains before the mind, then since there is no other possibility, having no objects, it becomes calm.

35. Just as a wish-fulfilling gem or a wish-granting tree satisfies desires, so the image of the Jina is seen, because of his vow and his disciples.

36. When a charmer against poisons dies after completing a pillar, that pillar neutralizes poisons and the like, even a long time after his death.

37. Likewise, the pillar of the Jina, completed in accordance with the Bodhisattva way of life, accomplishes all tasks, even when the Bodhisattva has passed into *nirvana.*

38. *[Hinayanist:[134]]* How could worship offered to something that has no consciousness be fruitful?

[Madhyamika:] Because it is taught that it is the same whether he is present or has passed into *nirvana.*

133. "Tathagata," another name for the historical Buddha, means one who is enlightened (editors' footnote).

134. Hinayana is the earliest Buddhist school, often also referred to as Theravada (editors' footnote).

39. According to the scriptures, effects of worship do exist, whether conventionally or ultimately, in the same way that worship offered to the true Buddha is said to be fruitful.

40. *[Hinayanist:]* Liberation comes from understanding the [Four Noble] Truths,[135] so what is the point of perceiving emptiness?

[Madhyamika:] Because a scripture states that there is no Awakening without this path.

41. *[Hinayanist:]* The Mahayana is certainly not authenticated.

[Madhyamika:] How is your scripture authenticated?

[Hinayanist:] Because it is authenticated by both of us.

[Madhyamika:] Then it is not authenticated by you from the beginning.

42. Apply the same faith and respect to the Mahayana as you do to it. If something is true because it is accepted by two different parties, then the *Vedas* and the like would also be true.

43. If you object that the Mahayana is controversial, then reject your own scripture because it is contested by heterodox groups and because parts of your scriptures are contested by your own people and others.

44. The teaching has its root in the monkhood, and the monkhood is not on a firm footing. For those whose minds are subject to grasping, *nirvana* is not on a firm footing either.

45. If your objection is that liberation is due to the elimination of mental afflictions, then it should occur immediately afterward. Yet one can see the power of karma over those people, even though they had no mental afflictions.

46. If you think that as long as there is no craving there is no grasping onto rebirth, why could their craving, even though free of mental afflictions, not exist as delusion?

47. Craving has its cause in feeling, and they have feeling. The mind that has mental objects has to dwell on one thing or another.

48. Without emptiness, the mind is constrained and arises again, as in non-cognitive meditative equipoise. Therefore, one should meditate on emptiness.

49. If you acknowledge the utterances that correspond to the *sutras* as the words of the Buddha, why do you not respect the Mahayana, which for the most part is similar to your *sutras*?

135. Four noble truths: all (unenlightened) life is suffering; twelve-link causes of suffering; there is cessation of suffering; the way to cessation (the eight-fold path) (editors' footnote).

50. If the whole is faulty because one part is not acceptable, why not consider the whole as taught by the Jina because one part is similar to the *sutras*?

51. Who will not accept the teachings not fathomed by leaders such as Mahakasyapa, just because you have failed to understand them?

52. Remaining in the cycle of existence for the sake of those suffering due to delusion is achieved through freedom from attachment and fear. That is a fruit of emptiness.

53. Thus, no refutation is possible with regard to emptiness, so one should meditate on emptiness without hesitation.

54. Since emptiness is the antidote to the darkness of afflictive and cognitive obscurations, how is it that one desiring omniscience does not promptly meditate on it?

55. Let fear arise toward something that produces suffering. Emptiness pacifies suffering. So why does fear of it arise?

56. If there were something called "I," fear could come from anywhere. If there is no "I," whose fear will there be?

57. Teeth, hair, and nails are not I, nor am I bone, blood, mucus, phlegm, pus, or lymph.

58. Bodily oil is not I, nor are sweat, fat, or entrails. The cavity of the entrails is not I, nor is excrement or urine.

59. Flesh is not I, nor are sinews, heat, or wind. Bodily apertures are not I, nor, in any way, are the six consciousnesses.

60. If the awareness of sound were I, then sound would always be apprehended. But without an object of awareness, what does it cognize on account of which it is called awareness?

61. If that which is not cognizant were awareness, a piece of wood would be awareness. Therefore, it is certain there is no awareness in the absence of its object.

62. Why does that which cognizes form not hear it as well?

[Samkhya:[136]] Because of the absence of sound, there is no awareness of it.

63. [Madhyamika:] How can something that is of the nature of the apprehension of sound be the apprehension of form? One person may be considered as a father and as a son, but not in terms of ultimate reality,

136. Samkhya is a Hindu philosophical school that asserts a permanent self in addition to accepting three gunas (properties or ingredients), namely, sattva, rajas, and tamas, that this school takes to constitute our everyday world of experience (editors' footnote).

64. Since *sattva, rajas,* and *tamas* are neither a father nor a son. Moreover, its nature is not seen as related to the apprehension of sound.

65. If it is the same thing taking another guise, like an actor, he too is not permanent. If he has different natures, then this unity of his is unprecedented.

66. If another guise is not the true one, then describe its natural appearance. If it were the nature of awareness, then it would follow that all people would be identical.

67. That which has volition and that which has no volition would be identical, because their existence would be the same. If difference were false, then what would be the basis for similarity?

68. That which is not conscious is not "I," because it lacks consciousness, like a cloth and the like. If it were conscious because it has consciousness, then it would follow that when it stops being conscious of anything, it would vanish.

69. If the Self is not subject to change, what is the use of its consciousness? Thus, this implies that space, which lacks consciousness and activity, has a Self.

70. *[Objection:]* Without the Self, the relationship between an action and its result is not possible, for if the agent of an action has perished, who will have the result?

71. *[Madhyamika:]* When both of us have agreed that an action and its result have different bases and that the Self has no influence in this matter, then there is no point in arguing about this.

72. One who has the cause cannot possibly be seen as being endowed with the result. It is pointed out that the existence of the agent and the experiencer of the consequences depends on the unity of their continuum of consciousness.

73. The past or future mind is not "I," since it does not exist. If the present mind were "I," then when it had vanished, the "I" would not exist any more.

74. Just as the trunk of a plantain tree is nothing when cut into pieces, in the same way, the "I" is non-existent when sought analytically.

75. *[Qualm:]* If no sentient being exists, for whom is there compassion?

[Madhyamika:] For one who is imagined through delusion, which is accepted for the sake of the task.

76. *[Qualm:]* If there is no sentient being, whose is the task?

[Madhyamika:] True. The effort, too, is due to delusion. Nevertheless, in order to alleviate suffering, delusion with regard to one's task is not averted.

77. However, grasping onto the "I," which is a cause of suffering, increases because of the delusion with regard to the Self. If this is the unavoidable result of that, meditation on identitylessness is the best.

78. The body is not the feet, the calves, nor the thighs. Nor is the body the hips, the abdomen, the back, the chest, or the arms.

79. It is not the hands, the sides of the torso, or the armpits, nor is it characterized by the shoulders. Nor is the body the neck or the head. Then what here is the body?

80. If this body partially exists in all of these and its parts exist in their parts, where does it stand by itself?

81. If the body were located in its entirety in the hands and other limbs, there would be just as many bodies as there are hands and so forth.

82. The body is neither inside nor outside. How can the body be in the hands and other limbs? It is not separate from the hands and the like. How, then, can it be found at all?

83. Thus, the body does not exist. However, on account of delusion, there is the impression of the body with regard to the hands and the like, because of their specific configuration, just as there is the impression of a person with regard to a pillar.

84. As long as a collection of conditions lasts, the body appears like a person. Likewise, as long as it lasts with regard to the hands and the like, the body continues to be seen in them.

85. In the same way, since it is an assemblage of toes, which one would be a foot? The same applies to a toe, since it is an assemblage of joints, and to a joint as well, because of its division into its own parts.

86. Even the parts can be divided into atoms, and an atom itself can be divided according to its cardinal directions. The section of a cardinal direction is space, because it is without parts. Therefore, an atom does not exist.

87. What discerning person would be attached to form, which is just like a dream? Since the body does not exist, then who is a woman and who is a man?

88. If suffering truly exists, why does it not oppress the joyful? If delicacies and the like are a pleasure, why do they not please someone struck by grief and so forth?

89. If it is not experienced because it is overpowered by something more intense, how can that which is not of the nature of experience be a feeling?

90. *[Objection:]* Surely there is suffering in its subtle state while its gross state is removed.

[Madhyamika:] If it is simply another pleasure, then that subtle state is a subtle state of pleasure.

91. If suffering does not arise when the conditions for its opposite have arisen, does it not follow that a "feeling" is a false notion created by conceptual fabrication?

92. Therefore, this analysis is created as an antidote to that false notion. For the meditative stabilizations that arise from the field of investigations are the food of contemplatives.

93. If there is an interval between a sense-faculty and its object, where is the contact between the two? If there is no interval, they would be identical. In that case, what would be in contact with what?

94. One atom cannot penetrate another, because it is without empty space and is of the same size as the other. When there is no penetration, there is no mingling; and when there is no mingling, there is no contact.

95. How, indeed, can there be contact with something that has no parts? If partlessness can be observed when there is contact, demonstrate this.

96. It is impossible for consciousness, which has no form, to have contact; nor is it possible for a composite, because it is not a truly existent thing, as investigated earlier.

97. Thus, when there is no contact, how can feeling arise? What is the reason for this exertion? Who could be harmed by what?

98. If there is no one to experience feeling and if feeling does not exist, then after understanding this situation, why, O craving, are you not shattered?

99. The mind that has a dreamlike and illusion like nature sees and touches. Since feeling arises together with the mind, it is not perceived by the mind.

100. What happens earlier is remembered but not experienced by what arises later. It does not experience itself, nor is it experienced by something else.

101. There is no one who experiences feeling. Hence, in reality, there is no feeling. Thus, in this identityless bundle, who can be hurt by it?

102. The mind is not located in the sense faculties, nor in form and other sense-objects, nor in between them. The mind is also not found inside, nor outside, nor anywhere else.

103. That which is not in the body nor anywhere else, neither intermingled nor somewhere separate, is nothing. Therefore, sentient beings are by nature liberated.

Santideva. Selections from "Perfection of Meditation" and "The Perfection of Wisdom." In *A Guide to the Bodhisattva Way of Life (Bodhicaryavatara)*, translated by Vesna A. Wallace and B. Alan Wallace, 100–102, 115–27. Ithaca, NY: Snow Lion Publications, 1997.

POST-READING PARS

1. Please repeat the quiet sitting exercise outlined in Pre-PAR #1. Do you experience this exercise differently after reading Shantideva's verses?

2. Look back to your responses to the Pre-PAR #2. After reading Shantideva's distinction between conventional truth and ultimate truth, how might you adjust your earlier response?

Inquiry Corner

Content Question(s):	Critical Question(s):
What are some of the arguments Shantideva offers while defending his position that we should try to alleviate others' suffering as much as we work to alleviate our own suffering?	Critically evaluate the arguments Shantideva offers for his view that everything is devoid of essential properties.
Comparative Question(s):	**Connection Question(s):**
Compare Shantideva's conception of two kinds of truth with another account of two kinds or levels of truth that you read in this course.	How might the concept of radical compassion that Shantideva outlines in the *Bodhicaryavatara* help us address some of the systemic injustices plaguing our contemporary realities?

BEYOND THE CLASSROOM

» Often, business founders are defined by their businesses. The proprietor puts all their effort, money, and identity into making that business successful and are defined by it (JP Morgan, JC Penny, and the Belk Family are examples). With that in mind, reflect on Chapter 9, verse 18–19. Can the owner be both the business and themselves? What is the right way to operate a business philosophically and ethically?

from *The Ocean of Story* (*Kathasaritsagara*) by Somadeva

Introduction

The story "Alankaravati" comes from the compendium of stories, the *Kathasaritsagara* (typically translated as *The Ocean of the Sea of Story* or *The Ocean of Story*) whose eighteen books with 66,000 lines make it the largest collection of Indian tales. Many of the stories in this popular Sanskrit text "rank with the *Arabian Nights* and Grimms fairy tales," "both of which have likely borrowed from the *Kathāsaritsāgara*."[137] So it is evident that these stories traveled far from their native Kashmir in present-day north India. This collection was believed to have been compiled and parts of it composed by Somadeva, a Kashmiri brahmin, a member of the priest caste, who most likely lived during the eleventh century. According to legend, he composed it around 1070 CE for Queen Suryamati, wife of the Hindu ruler of Kashmir, Anantadeva, in whose court Somadeva served as a poet. How might this legend involving the queen impact the reception of these stories?

While these stories definitely reflect Somadeva's distinct marks—for example, the prevalence of the Hindu god Shiva throughout "Alankaravati," given that he was a Shaivite, that is, a devotee of god Shiva—the stories themselves were in circulation long before Somadeva collected them together. Somadeva himself claims to have adapted them from an even bigger no longer extant compendium, "Great

SNAPSHOT BOX

LANGUAGE: Sanskrit

DATE: c. 1070 CE

LOCATION: Kashmir, South Asia

GENRE: Legend, folklore, stories

TAGS: Ethics and Morality; Gender; Orality; Pilgrimage

Timeline

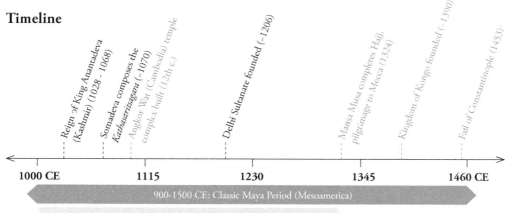

137. Arshia Sattar, *Tales from the Kathasaritsagara* (New York: Penguin Classics, 2000), xv.

Tale," many versions of which were written and rewritten possibly by multiple authors over centuries. Indeed, a short version of the ancient Sanskrit epic, *Ramayana* (the text of which is believed to have been compiled between fourth century BCE and fourth century CE), shows up as a part of "Alankaravati." Most of the stories of the *Kathasaritsagara* are adventures of Prince Naravahanadatta who is a **vidyadhara**. A vidyadhara literally stands for a holder of knowledge and is imagined to be a sky-dweller with magical powers like flying and changing its shape and form, and is known for their interaction with humans. While this offers the outer structure of the main narrative, each story often contains many layers of other stories nesting within, thereby challenging our typical assumption regarding the linearity of time or story lines. What might be the purpose of nesting stories within a larger story line?

The "Alankaravati" is a Hindu story because of its use of various Hindu concepts and themes of dharma, rebirth, karma, various Hindu gods and goddesses, the Hindu caste system, and the Hindu view of stages of life. It draws on the ubiquitous Hindu notion of rebirth, which maintains that after death a being is born again in another form to live out the consequences of the choices they have made in this and previous lives. Somadeva also uses the notion of **dharma,** primarily to refer to one's duty and to define righteousness. Interestingly, however, a Hindu can have different duties based on their caste and stage of life. The Hindu caste system is a hierarchical system dividing the population into four castes, namely, *brahmin* or priest, *kshatriya* or warrior, *vaisya* or business, and *sudra* or servant. Different duties of value are assigned to members of different castes, for example, performance of sacrificial rituals for brahmins or trading and farming for vaisyas. How do you think the different castes could become hierarchical?

Duties not only varied according to one's caste but also according to the four goals of a human life as well as one's given stage in life. The four goals that many Hindu texts outline are *dharma* or duties, *artha* or means to material prosperity, *kama* or fulfillment of desire, and *moksa* or freedom from cycle of rebirths. Additionally, Hindus believe that a typical human life goes through four stages, namely, being a student, followed by becoming a house-holder when one has a family and earns a living. Then one retires. But given the final goal of *moksha*, one does not stick around in the everyday world but leaves for a quieter social environment of a forest. This provides more opportunity for reflection and getting ready for the final stage of complete renunciation. Traditionally the forest is also the location of **aashramas**, where ascetics live renouncing their caste and other duties to commit to a life of celibacy, physical and mental austerities, and penance. While reading "Alankaravati," try to discern the various ways its main characters employ and subvert their prescribed duties based on one's caste, particular stage of life, as well as the goal of one's life.

A characteristic feature of the stories in the *Kathasaritsagara* is their internal diversity—of themes, characters, flavors, perspectives, and moral lessons. They employ many of the prominent tropes that appear in other South Asian stories, namely, predestined lovers having to go through hardships and separation only to be united in the end, or having pivotal roles of fate and destiny in the story line. However, the uniqueness and enduring values of Somadeva's stories follow from the fact that a range of emotions are expressed by almost all characters — by brahmins or sudras, devout housewives or courtesans equally — that humanizes them all.

Keya Maitra
Department of Philosophy

PRE-READING PARS

1. Identify two or three things you remember most readily about a story within a story you heard in your childhood.

2. Write down two or three ideas that come to mind when you think of fate and destiny.

3. Write down two or three characteristics of what you understand to be righteousness.

"Alankaravati" from *The Ocean of Story* (*Kathasaritsagara*)

We bow to Ganesa before whom even the mountains bow
when he dances for they stoop with the weight of Nisumbha.[138]

Naravahanadatta Falls In Love With Alankaravati

Naravahanadatta, the son of the king of Vatsa, lived in his father's palace and listened with amazement to the tales of the vidyadharas. One day, while he was hunting, he sent back his entourage and entered a vast forest with Gomukha as his only companion. His right eye began to flutter, indicating good fortune and soon, he heard singing and the sound of the vina. He proceeded in the direction of the music and not far away, he came upon a Siva[139] temple. He tethered his horse and entered the temple. He saw a celestial woman inside, surrounded by her attendants, praising Siva with her music. The moment he set eyes on her, Naravahanadatta's mind was disturbed as the waters of the ocean are disturbed by the reflection of the moon. Despite her natural modesty, the young woman returned his gaze with passion and love and as a result, she was unable to play another note on her vina.

Gomukha understood what was passing through Naravahanadatta's mind and asked one of the attendants who the young woman was. At that very moment, an older Vidyadhari[140] who resembled the younger woman in looks, descended from the skies preceded by a ray of red-gold light. She sat down beside the younger woman who rose and touched her feet. The older woman blessed her and said, 'May you obtain a husband who will be a king of the vidyadharas.' Naravahanadatta approached the older woman and bowed before her. After she had blessed him, he asked softly, 'Mother, who is this girl?' and the older woman replied, 'Listen and I will tell you.'

---

138. Nisumbha was one of the two demon brothers who were eventually killed by the goddess Durga. They had attained great powers by performing penances and austerities in the mountains. In fact, the mountains trembled and bowed with the sheer might of the brothers' ascetic practices.

139. Alternate spelling: Shiva (editors' footnote).

140. A female Vidyadhara (editors' footnote).

Alankaravati's Story

'On a mountain as high as Himavat, there is a city named Sundarapura where the *vidyadhara* king Alankarasila used to live. That generous and virtuous king had a wife named Kancanaprabha. When a son was born to them, the goddess Parvati told the king in a dream that the boy should be named Dharmasila because he would be devoted to righteousness. In time, the prince grew into a young man. The king taught him all the sciences and anointed him the crown prince. The prince was so righteous that his subjects loved him even more than they had loved his father.

'Then Kancanaprabha became pregnant again and this time, she gave birth to a daughter. When the child was born, a voice spoke, "She will be the queen of Narava-hanadatta, the ruler of the three worlds." The child was named Alankaravati and as time passed, she grew into a young woman as beautiful as the new moon. When she was old enough, her father taught her all the arts and sciences himself. She was devoted to Siva and wandered from temple to temple worshipping him. Meanwhile, her brother, Dharmasila, even though he was still young, grew disinterested in worldly matters. He said to his father, "These worldly pleasures are impermanent and do not appeal to me. Is there anything in the world that does not turn bitter at the end? Have you heard a sage's words on this subject, 'All created things are destroyed, all that is raised high falls, all unions end in separation, all life ends in death.' How can the wise enjoy momentary pleasures? Neither wealth nor earthly pleasures are of any use in the world beyond. Only righteousness stays as a friend, every step of the way. I am going into the forest to perform penances and austerities until I attain the highest truth."

'Alankarasila was deeply disturbed by his son's words. With his eyes full of tears, he said to the boy, "My son, why are you so convinced of this even though you are so young? Good people desire a life of peace and solitude after they have enjoyed their youth. This is the time for you to be married and to rule the kingdom justly and enjoy worldly pleasures, not renounce the world." In reply to his father's entreaty, Dharmasila said, "Age does not determine periods of abstinence or periods of enjoyment. Even a child can attain self-control if he is favored by the gods, but no evil person, even though he is old, can aspire to the same peace. I have no interest in the kingdom or in taking a wife. I have only one purpose in life and that is to please Siva with austerities."

'When Dharmasila said this, the king realized that whatever efforts he made, the boy would not change his mind. Weeping, he said, "My son, you display total detachment even though you are so young. Why shouldn't I, who am so much older, also take refuge in the forest?" The *vidyadhara* king went into the world of mortals and gave away huge quantities of gold and jewels to Brahmins and to the poor. Then he returned to his own city and said to his wife Kancanaprabha "I order you to stay in our city and look after our daughter Alankaravati. The auspicious time for her marriage will be on this very day, a year from now. Then I will give her to Naravahanadatta. Our son-in-law will come to our city and rule the three worlds." The king made his wife take an oath that she would abide by his wishes. Though she wept, he sent her back with their daughter, and went into the forest with his son.

'Kancanaprabha lived in the city with her daughter, for which virtuous wife would ignore her husband's wishes? Meanwhile, Alankaravati went from one Siva temple to another and her mother accompanied her out of affection. One day, the science of *prajnapti* directed Alankaravati thus: "Go and worship Siva at Svayambhu in Kashmir and you will easily obtain Naravahanadatta, king of the *vidyadharas*, as a husband." Alankaravati went to Kashmir with her mother and worshipped Siva at all the holy places, Nandiksetra, Mahadevagiri, Amaraparvata, the Suresvari mountains, Vijaya and Kapatetsvara. After they had completed this pilgrimage, Alankaravati and her mother returned home.

'Fortunate one, know that this girl is that same Alankaravati and that I am her mother Kancanaprabha. She came to this Siva temple today without telling me but through the science of *prajnapti*, I knew that she was here and I also knew that you would arrive here. Accept my daughter in marriage as ordained by the gods. Tomorrow is the day appointed for her wedding by her father. Return to your city Kausambi today. We shall also leave and tomorrow, when king Alankarasila returns from the *asrama*,[141] he will himself give you his daughter in marriage.' *Alankaravati and Naravahanadatta were very upset when they heard this. Their eyes filled with tears for they could not bear to be separated even for a night, like cakravaka birds at the end of the day. When Kancanaprabha saw their distress, she said, 'Why are you so upset at the idea of being separated for one night? Those of firm resolve are able to bear indefinite separation. Listen to the story of Rama and Sita.*

Sita's Banishment

'Long ago, King Dasaratha of Ayodhya had a son named Rama who was the older brother of Laksmana, Satrughna and Bharata. Rama was the incarnation of a part of Visnu[142] and was born for the destruction of Ravana. Rama's wife was Sita, the daughter of King Janaka and she was dearer to him than life. Bound by destiny, Dasaratha bestowed the kingdom on Bharata and sent Rama into the forest with Sita and Laksmana. Ravana abducted Rama's beloved Sita with his magic powers and took her away to Lanka, his own city, killing Jatayu along the way. The bereaved Rama killed Vali and made an alliance with Sugriva. Then he sent Hanuman to fetch news of his wife. When Hanuman found Sita imprisoned on the island of Lanka, Rama crossed the ocean by building a bridge over it and killed Ravana. He left Lanka

141. Alternate spelling: *aashrama* (editors' footnote).

142. Visnu is the only god of the Hindu pantheon who is supposed to come down to Earth in various forms to free the world of mortals from the evil doers. Rama was, among nine others, an incarnation of Visnu and is often referred to as "incarnating a part of Visnu." In this case, Rama's brothers too incarnate other parts of Visnu. However, it is rarely ever made clear which part of Visnu is incarnated in whom and why.

in the care of Vibhisana and brought Sita back with him. He returned to Ayodhya from the forest and while he was ruling the kingdom that Bharata bestowed upon him, Sita became pregnant.

'One day, Rama was wandering through the city with a small entourage so that he could learn what the people wanted. He saw a man throwing his wife out of the house because she had been with another man. The woman wailed, "Lord Rama did not reject his wife even though she had been in the house of a *raksasa* (demon). My husband is superior to him since he is throwing me out for having been in the house of a relative!" When Rama heard the woman say this to her husband he was very disturbed and returned to his palace. Fearing the people's gossip, Rama abandoned Sita in the forest. To a successful man, the pain of separation is preferable to infamy.

'Burdened by her pregnancy, Sita reached the *asrama* of the sage Valmiki. He comforted her and persuaded her to stay there. The other sages at the *asrama* said to each other, "Sita must be guilty otherwise her husband would not abandon her like this. We are becoming polluted by being with her all the time. But Valmiki will not ask her to leave the *asrama* out of pity. He overcomes the pollution of her presence by the power of his austerities. We had better go to another *asrama*." Valmiki understood what was happening and said, "Have no fear. I have seen with my meditative powers that this woman is pure and innocent."

'Even after this assurance the other sages were still doubtful and so Sita said to them, "Test my chastity by any means you like and if I prove to be guilty you can cut off my head." The sages felt sorry for her and said, "There is a lake named Tittibhasara in this great forest. In the old days, a woman named Tittibhi was falsely accused by her husband of having an affair with another man. She called upon the Earth and the *lokapalas* and they created this lake to prove her innocence. Let Rama's wife prove her chastity there."

'Sita went with the sages to the lake and, on its shores, the chaste woman said, "Mother Earth, if I have never thought about another man even in a dream, let me reach the other side of the lake!" and entered the waters. The Earth appeared and lifted Sita onto her lap and carried her to the other side. The sages honored Sita when they saw that and wanted to curse Rama for abandoning her. But Sita, who was a devoted wife, said to them, "Do not think ill of my husband. Curse me instead for I am the wicked one!" The sages were pleased with her and blessed her with the birth of a son. She continued to live at the hermitage and in time, she gave birth to a boy. Valmiki named him Lava.

'One day, Sita took the child with her when she went to bathe. When Valmiki saw the empty hut, he was worried. "Sita always leaves the child here when she goes to bathe. Where can he be? He must have been carried away by a wild animal. I had better create another child or Sita will die of grief when she returns from her bath." Valmiki took a blade of *kusa* grass and created an infant that looked exactly like Lava and left him in the hut. When Sita came back and saw the child, she asked the sage, "My child is with me. Where did this one come from?" Valmiki told her what had happened. "Accept this second child also, for I made him from a blade of *kusa* grass with my powers." Sita brought up both the boys, Lava and Kusa, and Valmiki performed all the sacred ceremonies for them. The two Ksatriya boys learned the martial arts and all the sciences from Valmiki.

'Once, the two boys killed a deer that belonged to the *asrama* and ate its flesh. On another occasion, they made a toy out of a *lingam* that Valmiki used for worship. The sage was angry but Sita interceded on their behalf and Valmiki allowed the boys to perform a penance to make up for their misdeeds. "Let Lava bring golden lotuses from Kubera's lake as well as some of the *mandara* flowers that grow in Kubera's garden. When both the brothers have worshipped the *lingam* by offering these flowers they will have atoned for their bad behavior." Lava, though still a boy, went to Kailasa and entered Kubera's garden and his lake. He killed the *yaksas* who were there and picked the lotuses and the flowers. On his way back, he was tired and rested under a tree along the path. Meanwhile, Laksmana came by looking for a man with all the auspicious marks for Rama's human sacrifice. He challenged Lava to fight according to Ksatriya custom and after stunning him with a stupefying arrow, he tied him up and carried him to Ayodhya.

'At the *asrama*, Sita was worried about Lava's absence but Valmiki comforted her. He knew what had happened and said to Kusa, "Lava has been captured by Laksmana and taken to Ayodhya. Go there and free him after you have defeated Laksmana with these," and he gave Kusa divine weapons. Kusa laid siege to the sacrificial grounds at Ayodhya and defeated Laksmana in single combat with the divine weapons. When Rama advanced to meet him, he found that he, too, could not defeat the boy who had Valmiki's power. Rama asked him who he was and why he had come there.

'Kusa said, "Laksmana has captured my older brother and brought him here. I have come to set him free. Our mother Sita has told us that we, Lava and Kusa, are the sons of Rama," and he related her story. Rama broke into tears and had Lava brought before him. He embraced both the boys, saying, "I am that wicked Rama." The citizens gathered and when they saw the two boys, they praised Sita. Rama acknowledged the boys as his sons. He had Sita brought to Ayodhya from Valmiki's *asrama* and after handing over the responsibilities of the kingdom to his sons, he lived happily with her.

'Resolute people can endure long separations like this. How is it that the two of you cannot bear it for even one night?' said Kancanaprabha to Naravahanadatta and her daughter Alankaravati who was eager to be married.

She rose into the air with her daughter and promised to return the next day. Naravahanadatta went back to Kausambi with a heavy heart.

The very next day, Naravahanadatta and Alankaravati were married in a grand ceremony with all the vidyadharas in attendance. Naravahanadatta went and spent some time in his father-in-law's city, Sundarapura, and then returned with his new wife to Kausambi.

One day, Gomukha told Naravahanadatta the following story.

The Princess Who Refused To Marry

'There is a city on earth appropriately named Surapura it is the dwelling place of heroes. King Mahavaraha, destroyer of his enemies, ruled there. Because he had propitiated Parvati, his wife Padmarati bore him a daughter named Anangarati. As Anangarati grew up, she became proud of her beauty and though many kings asked for her hand, she refused to get married. She said, "I will only marry a man who is courageous and handsome and accomplished in at least one thing." 'Four young men from the south, who had heard about Anangarati and had the qualities that she desired, arrived in Surapura to seek her hand. They were announced by the door-keeper and in Anangarati's presence, Mahavaraha asked them, "What are your names and what are your backgrounds? What are your skills?" The first one said, "I am a Sudra named Pancapattika and I can weave five sets of garments every day. I give one to a Brahmin, the second I offer to Siva the third I wear myself, the fourth I would give to my wife if I had one and the fifth I sell and live off the proceeds."

'The second one said, "I am a Vaisya named Bhasajna and I know all the languages of all the birds and animals." The third one said, "I am a Ksatriya named Khadgadhara and no one wields a sword better than I." The fourth one said, "I am a Brahmin named Jivadatta and by the grace of the goddess, I can bring a dead woman back to life." Then the Sudra, the Vaisya and the Ksatriya praised their own courage, good looks and skill but the Brahmin praised only his courage and his skill, saying nothing about his looks. The king told the door-keeper to take the four young men to his house so that they could rest.

'Mahavaraha asked Anangarati, "Daughter, which of these four young men do you like?" and she replied that she did not like any of them. She said, "One is a Sudra and a weaver. What is the use of his virtues? The second is a Vaisya. Of what value is the knowledge of the language of birds and others? I am a high born Ksatriya woman, how can I be given to him? The third one, the Ksatriya, is equal to me in rank but he is poor and lives by selling his services. I am a princess, how can I marry him? The fourth one, the Brahmin Jivadatta, I do not like at all. He is ugly and he is unrighteous. He has fallen from his exalted position because he has rejected the Vedas. You should punish him instead of offering me to him as a wife! As a king, you are the protector of the four castes and the four stages of life. A king who upholds righteousness is far better than a king who wins battles. The king who upholds righteousness will rule over thousands of heroic kings who win battles." The king sent his daughter back to her chambers and went to have a bath.

'The next day, the four young men wandered around the city, satisfying their curiosity. Just then, a vicious elephant named Padmakabala broke out of the stables and ran amok, trampling the people who came in his way. When the great elephant saw the four young men, he charged towards them to kill them and they in turn advanced towards him with their weapons ready. Khadgadhara, the only Ksatriya among them, went ahead of the others and attacked the elephant alone. With a single blow, he cut off the trumpeting elephant's trunk as easily as if it were a lotus stalk. He displayed his swiftness by escaping between the elephant's feet and dealt him another blow from the back. With the third blow, he cut off the elephant's feet and the animal fell down with a groan and died. The townspeople were amazed at this display of courage and the king was very impressed when he heard about it.

'The next day, the king went out hunting with Khadgadhara and the other young men. The king and his entourage killed tigers, deer and boars. Angry lions rushed towards them when they heard the trumpeting of elephants, but Khadgadhara split a lion that attacked them in half with a single blow of his sharp sword. He killed a second lion by grasping it by the foot with his left hand and smashing it onto the ground. Bhasajna, Jivadatta and Pancapattika also killed a lion each by dashing it to the ground. The four young men killed lions and tigers with ease even though they were on foot, and the, king was full of admiration for them. When the hunt was over, he returned to his city and the young men went to the door-keeper's house.

'The king reached his chambers and, even though he was tired, he summoned his daughter and told her about the accomplishments of the four young men. She was suitably impressed so the king said to her, "If Pancapattika and Bhāasajna are low caste and Jivadatta, even though he is a Brahmin, is ugly and dabbles in forbidden practices, what is wrong with the Ksatriya Khadgadhara? He is handsome and noble and he is known for his strength and courage. He killed the mad elephant, he takes lions by the foot and dashes them to the earth and kills other lions with a single stroke of his sword. If you find fault with him for being poor and serving others, I can make him into a man served by others. Please, daughter, choose him as your husband."

'Anangarati said, "Bring the men here and ask the astrologer what he thinks." The king had the young men summoned and in their presence, he asked the astrologer, "Find out whose horoscope matches Anangarati's and set an auspicious time for the wedding." The astrologer asked the young men what stars they had been born under and after considering the matter for a long time, he said to the king, "If you will not be angry with me, I will tell you the truth. None of these men suit your daughter. Nor will she be married here. She is a Vidyadhari who is on earth because of a curse. The curse will end in three months. Let these men wait here for three months and if she does not return to her own world, the wedding can take place." They all accepted the astrologer's advice and waited.

'When the three months had passed, the king called the four young men, the astrologer and Anangarati. Mahavaraha saw that his daughter had grown more beautiful and he was very pleased but the astrologer felt sure that the time of her death had arrived. As the king was asking the astrologer what should be done now that the three months had passed, Anangarati remembered her previous birth and covering her face with her upper garment, she gave up her human body. "Why is she doing this?" thought the king, but when he uncovered her face, he saw that she was dead, like a frost-bitten lotus. Her eyes, which had been like black bees, had ceased to move, her flower-like face was pale and her sweet voice was silenced like the song of a swan. Overcome with grief, the king fell to the ground, like the mountains which fell when Indra had clipped their wings.[143] The queen also fainted and as her ornaments fell from her body like blossoms, she seemed like a flowering tree felled by an elephant. The courtiers wailed loudly and the four young men were very upset.

'When King Mahavaraha recovered his senses, he said to Jivadatta, "This is your moment. None of the others have the appropriate skill. You declared that you could bring a dead woman back to life. Revive my daughter and I will give her to you in marriage." Jivadatta sprinkled the princess with water over which he had read some mantras and chanted the following verse. "Camunda, goddess who laughs loudly and wears a garland of skulls, you who are not to be looked at, help me!" Despite all his efforts, the princess remained lifeless and Jivadatta was overcome with despair. He said, "This skill that was bestowed upon me by the goddess has proved fruitless. Since I am now an object of scorn, I have no interest in living." He got ready to cut off his head with a sword when a voice spoke from the sky. "Wait, Jivadatta! Do not act in haste! Listen! This young woman is a *Vidyadhari* who has been a mortal for so long because of her celestial father's curse. Now she has renounced her human body and returned to her realm in her own body. Go back and worship the goddess. You will win back this noble *Vidyadhari* through her favor. Neither you nor the king should grieve for her because she is enjoying celestial pleasures." The king performed the funeral rites for his daughter and his wife got over their sorrow. The other three young men returned to where they had come from.

Jivadatta Wins the Vidyadhari

'Jivadatta felt somewhat reassured and went to worship and propitiate the goddess with austerities. She appeared to him in a dream and said, "I am pleased with you! Get up and listen to what I have to say. In the city of Virapura in the Himalayas, there is a *vidyadhara* king called Samara. His queen Anangavati gave birth to a daughter named Anangaprabha. Anangaprabha was so proud of her youth and beauty that she refused to take a husband. Her parents were very angry and cursed her: 'You shall become a mortal and not experience the joys of marriage even in that state. When you are sixteen years old, you will give up your human body and return here. A mortal who is ugly because he was cursed for falling in love with a *muni's* daughter and who has a magic sword will take you back to the world of humans against your will. You will be unfaithful to him and will be separated from your husband. Because your husband took away the wives of eight men in his previous birth, he will experience

143. There was a time when all mountains had wings and could fly around wherever and whenever they so desired. But after a while they became a menace to gods and humans alike as a result of which Indra cut off their wings with his thunderbolt. They then fell to the ground and have been stationary ever since.

enough sorrow for eight births. You will lose your memory and take many human husbands because you persisted in rejecting the husband chosen for you. You rejected Madanaprabha who wanted to marry you and was equal to you in birth. He shall also be born as a human king and shall become your husband. Then you shall be freed from your curse and return to your own world and you shall marry a suitable man.'

"Anangarati was that *Vidyadhari* who was cursed by her father. She has now returned to her parents and is Anangaprabha once again. Go to Virapura and obtain that girl for a bride by defeating her father in battle even though he is protected by his skills and his heritage. Take this sword that will make you fly through the air and invincible in battle." After saying so, the goddess vanished and when Jivadatta awoke, he saw that the magic sword was in his hand. Jīvadatta was very happy and praised the goddess. By the nectar of her grace, the fatigue from his long austerities disappeared and he was refreshed. He flew around the Himalayas with the sword in his hand till he reached Virapura, the city of the *vidyadhara* Samara.

'Jīvadatta defeated Samara in battle and then married his daughter Anangaprabha and lived in Virapura, enjoying celestial pleasures. After he had lived there for some time, he said to his father-in-law and to his beloved Anangaprabha, "Let both of us visit the human world. I long for it. The land of one's birth is always the dearest, even if it is inferior." Samara agreed, but the prescient Anangaprabha was persuaded to go with great difficulty. Jivadatta took Anangaprabha into his arms and descended to the human world from the sky. Anangaprabha was tired and when she saw a pleasant mountain, she said, "Let us rest here," and Jivadatta alighted there with her. He produced food and drink with his magic powers. Impelled by his destiny, Jivadatta said to Anangaprabha, "Beloved, sing me a sweet song." She began to sing a hymn of praise to Siva and Jīvadatta fell asleep as he listened.

Jivadatta Wakes Up

'Just then, a king named Harivara came that way, tired from his hunt and in search of some water. He was drawn to the singing as if he were a deer and leaving his chariot, he walked in the direction of the song. His right eye fluttered so he knew that something good was going to happen and then he saw Anangaprabha, shining like the brightness of the god of love. While his heart was held by Anangaprabha's voice and her beauty, the god of love pierced it with an arrow. Anangaprabha, too, was deeply attracted to this handsome man and said to herself, "Who is this man? Is he the god of love without his flowery bow? Or is he Siva's grace incarnate because the god is pleased with my song?" She asked him in a voice that quivered with passion, "Who are you? Why have you come to this forest?" Harivara told her how he had come there. He then asked her who she was and who it was that slept beside her. She replied, "I am a *Vidyadhari* and this is my husband who has a magic sword. But I fell in love with you the moment I saw you so let us leave this place quickly before he wakes up. Then I will tell you my story in detail." Harivara was so delighted, it was as if he had gained the sovereignty of the three worlds!

'Anangaprabha wanted to take Harivara in her arms and fly to her celestial world, but at the very moment, she was stripped of her magic powers because she had betrayed her husband. Then she remembered her father's curse and was very upset. Harivara noticed that she was disturbed and said "This is not the time for grief. Your husband may wake up. Besides, you should not grieve over something like this which is a matter of destiny. Who can escape the shadow of one's own head or the course of one's fate? Let us go!" Anangaprabha agreed and Harivara picked her up in his arms as happy as if he had found a great treasure and carried her to his chariot. His entourage welcomed him joyfully. He reached his city in his chariot which travelled as swiftly as thought. When his subjects saw him with a woman, they were filled with curiosity. Harivara dwelt in the city named after himself, enjoying celestial pleasures in the company of Anangaprabha. Anangaprabha stayed there happily with him, having forgotten all her powers because of the curse.

'Meanwhile, Jivadatta awoke alone on the mountain and saw that Anangaprabha and his sword were both missing. "Where is Anangaprabha? Where is my sword? Could she have gone away with it? Have they both been carried off by someone?" he wailed. As he tried to understand what had happened, he searched all over the mountain for three days burning in the fires of love. Then he came down and wandered in the forest for ten days but he could not find her anywhere. "Oh cruel fate! You gave me both the sword and Anangaprabha with such difficulty and now you have carried them both away!" He wandered around thus, wailing, without food or water until he reached a village and entered the imposing house of a Brahmin. When the beautiful lady of the house, Priyadatta, saw him, she immediately ordered her maidservants, "quickly, wash Jivadatta's feet. This is the thirteenth day that he has gone without food or water grieving over the separation from his beloved." Jivadatta was amazed when he heard this and thought to himself, "Is Anangaprabha here or is this woman a witch?" When his feet had been washed and he had eaten, he humbly asked Priyadatta, "Tell me how you knew all that had happened to me? And then tell me, where are my sword and my beloved?"

'Priyadatta, who was a devoted wife, said, "There is no one in my heart, not even in my dreams, except for my husband. I see all other men either as sons or as brothers and no one leaves my house without hospitality. Because of this, I have the power to know the past, the present and the future. Anangaprabha was carried off by a king named Harivara. While you were asleep, he passed by, drawn by fate and attracted by her song. He lives in a city named after himself and you cannot get Anangaprabha back because he is very strong. But that promiscuous woman will leave him for another man. The sword was given to you by the goddess only so that you could obtain Anangaprabha. Since that task is over, the sword has returned to the goddess by its own power and the woman has been carried away. Have you forgotten what the goddess told you in a dream about Anangaprabha? Why are you so upset about something that was bound to happen? Renounce this series of acts that lead again and again to grief! What use is that woman to you who is now attached to another man and who has lost all her powers because of her infidelity?"

'Jivadatta was now disgusted by Anangaprabha's behavior and lost all interest in her. He said, "My attachment to Anangaprabha has been destroyed by your words of wisdom, for who would not benefit by associating with good people? All this has happened to me because of my previous misconduct. So I will go to the holy pilgrimage spots and wash away my past. Why should I be hostile to others because of Anangaprabha? One who conquers anger conquers the world." While Jivadatta was saying this, Priyadatta's hospitable and righteous husband came home. He, too, welcomed Jivadatta and helped him forget his grief. After Jivadatta had rested he bade them goodbye and left on his pilgrimage.

Jivadatta Is Released

'In the course of time, Jivadatta visited all the pilgrimage centres on earth, enduring many difficulties and living on fruits and roots. Then he went to the shrine of the goddess and performed severe penances, going without food and sleeping on a bed of *kusa* grass. The goddess was pleased and manifested herself to him and said, "Rise, my son, for you are my fourth *gana*, Vikatavadana. The other three are Pancamula, Caturvaktra and Mahodaramukha. Once, you all went to the banks of the Ganga to enjoy yourselves and while you were there, you saw Capalekha, the daughter of the *muni* Kapilajata, having a bath. All of you fell in love with her and begged for her attention. She replied, 'I am a virgin. Go away!' Your three companions fell silent, but you grabbed her by the arm and she cried, 'father, save me!' Her father, who was nearby, came there in a rage and you let go of her hand when you saw him. Still, he cursed all of you. 'Be born as humans, you evil fellows!' You asked him when the curse would end and he said, 'When you have asked for princess Anangaprabha in marriage and when you have gone to the world of the *vidyadharas*, then the three of you will be free of your curse. But you, Vikatavadana, will win Anangaprabha when she becomes a *Vidyadhari* and lose her again and then endure great suffering. When you have propitiated the goddess for a long time, then your curse will end. This will happen to you because you touched Capalekha's hand and because you have taken the wives of so many others.'

"You four *ganas* who had been cursed by the sage were born as four young men Bhasajna, Pancapattika, Khadgadhara in the southern region. When Anangarati returned to her world, the other three came here and were released from their curse by me. Now that you have propitiated me, your curse is also at an end. Consume your earthly body with this fiery meditation and rid yourself of the bad acts that otherwise would take eight births to wear off." The goddess disappeared and Jivadatta burned up his mortal body and all his bad actions. He was at last freed from his curse and became the best among the *ganas*. Even the gods have to suffer for being attracted to other men's wives. Why should inferior beings not suffer for the same thing?

Anangaprabha's Adventures Continue

'Anangaprabha, meanwhile, had become Harivara's chief queen and lived happily in his city. The king was with her day and night and left the affairs of the kingdom to his minister Sumantra. Once, a new dancing teacher named Labdhavara came to Harivara's kingdom from Madhyadesa. When the king saw his skill in music and dance, he appointed him teacher to the ladies in the harem. Labdhavara made Anangaprabha into such a good dancer that even her rival queens expressed their admiration. Anangaprabha fell in love with her teacher because she spent so much time with him and also because she enjoyed his teaching. The dancing teacher, attracted by her youth and beauty, suddenly learned a new kind of dance from the god of love.

'One day, desperately in love, Anangaprabha went to the dancing teacher when he was alone and said, "I am deeply in love with you and cannot live a moment longer without you. The king will not tolerate this if he finds out. Let us leave this place and go to where he will not find us. The king has given you gold, horses and camels because he was pleased with your dancing and I have my jewels. Let us go quickly to a place where we can live without fear!" The dancing teacher was pleased with her attentions and agreed to the plan. Anangaprabha put on a man's clothes and went to the dancing teacher's house, accompanied only by a woman servant who was completely devoted to her.

'They left the city on horseback with all their wealth strapped onto a camel. First Anangaprabha gave up the glories of being a *Vidyadhari*, then she rejected the pleasures of royalty and then she took refuge in the fortunes of a dancer! Truly, women are fickle! Anangaprabha and the dancing teacher reached the distant city of Viyogapura where they lived together happily. The dancing teacher felt that by being with Anangaprabha, his name, Labdhavara, 'one who has attained a prize,' had been justified.

'When Harivara found out that Anangaprabha had left, he wanted to die of grief. But the minister Sumantra consoled him and said, "Why don't you understand this? Think it over yourself. Anangaprabha left her husband, who had obtained the powers of a *vidyadhara* by means of a sword, the moment she saw you. Why would a woman like that stay with you? She has left for something trivial because she does not desire the good, like someone who is enamored of a blade of grass believing it to be a heap of jewels. She has definitely gone with the dancing teacher for he is nowhere to be seen and I heard that they were in the dance hall together in the morning. Since you know all this, why are so you attached to her? A promiscuous woman is like the sunset which has a moment of glory every evening."

'The king mulled over what the minister had said and thought to himself, "This wise man has spoken the truth. A relationship with a promiscuous woman can never be lasting for she changes every moment. In the end, such a relationship leads to revulsion. A wise man never submits to the current of a river or to the power of a woman for both will drown him even as they playfully continue on their way. Those who are detached from pleasure, who are not interested in material wealth and who face danger bravely, they are the ones who have conquered the world." So Harivara renounced his grief and lived happily in the company of his other wives.

'Meanwhile, Anangaprabha lived with the dancing teacher in Viyogapura for some time. As fate would have it, the dancing teacher struck up a friendship with a young gambler named Sudarsana. The gambler managed to take away all the dancing teacher's remaining wealth from under Anangaprabha's very nose. Anangaprabha pretended to be angry because of that and left the dancing teacher who was now penniless and went away with Sudarsana. The dancing teacher had lost his wife and his wealth. Disgusted with the world, he matted his hair and went to perform austerities on the banks of the Ganga. But Anangaprabha, who kept taking new lovers, stayed with the gambler.

'One night, Sudarsana was robbed of all his wealth by thieves who entered his house. When Sudarsana noticed that Anangaprabha was upset about their poverty, he said, "Let us go to my friend Hiranyagupta. He is a wealthy merchant and we can borrow something from him." Impelled by destiny, the gambler went with Anangaprabha to ask Hiranyagupta for a loan. When the merchant and Anangaprabha saw each other, they fell in love. "Tomorrow I will give you the money, but today, you must eat here," said the merchant. But Sudarsana sensed the bond between the other two and said, "I did not come here today to dine with you." The merchant replied, "Do as you wish, my friend, but let your wife eat here since this is the first time she has come to my house." Sudarsana was silent and the merchant went into his house with Anangaprabha.

Hiranyagupta and Anangaprabha ate and drank and made merry together, for she was relaxed with all the wine that she had drunk. Sudarsana waited for his wife outside the house but a servant came and gave him a message from the merchant. "Your wife has eaten and left. Why are you still waiting here? You must not have seen her leave. Go home!" Sudarsana told the servant that he knew Anangaprabha was still inside the house and that he would not leave. The merchant's servants drove him from the gate with kicks and blows. Sudarsana was very dejected as he left, and he thought to himself, "Can this merchant, who is my friend, have taken my wife away from me? Or am I reaping the fruits of my actions in this birth itself? What I did to another man has been done to me. How can I be angry with the merchant when my own actions must have elicited the same feeling? I will end this chain of actions right here so that I am not humiliated further." Sudarsana renounced his anger and went to Badarika and performed severe penances.

Anangaprabha was as pleased as a bee on a flower to have found such a handsome husband in Hiranyagupta. In the course of time, she gained complete control over the wealth and the heart of the merchant who was deeply in love with her. King Virabahu, even though he knew that this beautiful woman lived in his city and was deeply attracted to her, did not carry her off and remained within the bounds of virtue. Slowly, the merchant's wealth began to decrease, for in the house of a promiscuous woman, neither prosperity nor virtue have a place. One day, Hiraṇyagupta put together some goods and went to the island of Suvarnabhumi to trade. He took Anangaprabha with him because he did not want to be separated from her. They reached the city of Sagarapura where Hiraṇyagupta made friends with a local fisherman named Sagaravira who lived near the sea. Anangaprabha and the merchant travelled with Sagaravira to the seashore where they boarded a boat to set sail for the island.

'As they were sailing along, a terrible cloud appeared with lightning that flashed as if it were its eyes and it filled the travelers with dread. Rain poured down, the wind rose and the ship began to sink beneath the waves. All the passengers started wailing and crying and Hiraṇyagupta, as the ship shattered like his hopes, girded his loins. He gazed at Anangaprabha and cried, "Dear one, where are you?" and plunged into the water. He managed to swim along and as luck would have it, he saw another trading ship and climbed onto it. Meanwhile, Sagaravira had tied some planks together with rope and placed Anangaprabha on them. He climbed onto the raft and he paddled with his arms as he comforted the terrified Anangaprabha. As soon as the ship had been destroyed, the cloud disappeared and the sea was calm like a man after his anger has passed. Hiranyagupta's ship was pushed by the wind as if it were destiny and reached the shore in five days. He was depressed at being separated from his beloved but he realized that he could not fight fate. He went slowly back to his own city and because he was a resolute man, he regained his composure, made some more money and lived happily.

'Anangaprabha was brought to the shore in one day on the planks paddled by Sagaravira. He comforted her and took her to his own house in Sagarapura. Anangaprabha treated Sagaravira like a hero for saving her life. He was also wealthy, good looking and in the prime of his life and he fulfilled all her wishes. She decided to marry him. A promiscuous woman does not distinguish between high- and low-born men. So Anangaprabha lived happily with Sagaravira, enjoying the wealth that he gave her. One day, from the roof of her house she saw a handsome young Ksatriya named Vijayavarma walking down the street. Attracted by his good looks, she went to him and said, "I was drawn to you the moment I saw you. Make love to me!" Vijayavarma was elated when he heard this invitation from an exceedingly beautiful woman who had approached him of her own accord and he took her back to his house. Sagaravira was very upset when he learned that his beloved had left him and went to the banks of the Ganga to renounce his body through ascetic practices. His grief was great, but how could such a low-born man have held on to a *Vidyadhari*?

Anangaprabha's Last Husband

'Anangaprabha continued to live in the same town, enjoying herself with Vijaya-varma. One day, King Sagaravarma toured his city mounted on an elephant. As he was admiring the beautiful city that was named after him, he went past Vijayavarma's house. Anangaprabha knew that the king was coming that way and she climbed up onto the roof to see him. The moment she set eyes on the king, she fell in love with him and boldly asked the elephant driver, "I have never ridden an elephant. Give me a ride on yours so that I can know what it is like." The elephant driver turned to the king. The king noticed Anangaprabha who was so beautiful it was as if she were the moon come down to earth. He gazed at her as if he were a *cakora* bird and knowing that he could have her, said to the elephant driver, "Take the elephant over there and gratify her desire. Let this beautiful woman sit on the elephant." The driver did as he was told and as soon as the elephant was close enough, Anangaprabha threw herself into the king's lap. How could it be that this woman, who had shown such an aversion to the idea of a husband, now had an insatiable appetite for them? Her father's curse must have brought about this change in her.

'Anangaprabha clung to the king's neck as though she were afraid of falling and he was delighted by her touch. Dying to kiss her, he carried that woman, who had approached him through artifice, off to the palace. The king placed her in the harem and made her his chief queen after she told him her story and revealed that she was a *Vidyadhari*. When Vijayavarma found out that Anangaprabha had been taken away by the king, he came and attacked the king's servants outside the palace. He fought bravely and died there, for men of honor do not suffer insults because of women. Vi-jayavarma was lifted out of the world of humans by celestial women who said to him, "What do you need this awful woman for? Come to Nandana with us!"

'Now that she was with the king, Anangaprabha strayed no further, as rivers come to rest in the ocean. She believed herself lucky to have found such a husband and the king felt that his life's goal had been accomplished when he got her for a wife. Soon, Anangaprabha became pregnant and gave birth to a son. The king named him Samudravarma and gave a great feast to celebrate his birth. The boy grew into a fine young man, known for his strength and courage, and the king anointed him crown prince. Soon, the prince brought Kamalavati, the daughter of king Samaravarma, to court in order to marry her. When he got married, his father bestowed his kingdom upon the prince because he was impressed with his virtues. Samudravarma knew his duties as a Ksatriya, so when his father gave him the kingdom, he bowed to him and said,

"Father, let me go and conquer the earth, for a king who does not conquer is as effeminate as a woman. The only prosperity and fortune that are genuine are those won by the conquest of other kingdoms. What use is kingship to those rulers who oppress the poor? They eat their subjects like greedy cats who eat their offspring."

'Sagaravarma said to his son, "You have just become king. Establish yourself here first, for there is nothing wrong with ruling your own subjects well. Also, a king should not seek battle before estimating his own strength. You are courageous and your army is mighty, but fortune in battle is fickle and you cannot be assured of victory." Even though his father used this and other similar arguments, Samudra-varma convinced him to let him go. In time, he conquered the four directions and established his rule over neighboring kings. He came back to his city with elephants and horses and all the wealth given to him as tribute. He fell at his parents' feet and honored them with precious stones from various countries. Obeying their instructions, the prince gave horses and elephants and gold and jewels to Brahmins as well. He also gave wealth to his servants and to his subjects so that the word "poor" became meaningless in his kingdom. When the old king who lived with Anangaprabha saw his son's success, he felt that his life had been fulfilled.

'While they were celebrating, the king said to his son in the presence of all his ministers, "I have done what I had to do in this life. I have enjoyed the pleasures of kingship, I have remained unconquered and now I have seen you invested with sovereignty. I have nothing left to strive for so I will go to an *asrama* while I still have the strength. The roots of age whisper in my ear, 'Why do you still live in your house when this body will soon be destroyed?'" Even though his son protested, Sagaravarma went with his beloved Anangaprabha to Prayaga, for all his goals had been fulfilled. His son escorted them there and returned to the city where he ruled wisely and well.

Anangaprabha's Curse Is Finally Over

'Sagaravarma and Anangaprabha worshipped Siva in Prayaga. Siva appeared in a dream to Sagaravarma and said, "I am pleased with the penances that you and your wife have performed. Listen. Both you and Anangaprabha are *vidyadharas*. Tomorrow your curse will end and you will return to your own world." Sagaravarma woke up and learned that Anangaprabha had the same dream. Anangaprabha was very happy and said, "I remember everything about my past birth. I was the daughter of the *vidyyadhara* king Samara in Virapura and my name was Anangarati. My father cursed me and I lost my powers. I was born a mortal woman and forgot my *Vidyadhari* nature but now I remember it all."

'As she was speaking, her father descended from the sky. Sagaravarma welcomed him with honor and Samara said to his daughter, "Take back your powers, for your curse has ended. You have suffered the pain of eight lives in one life!" He took her onto his lap and restored her powers to her. He said to Sagaravarma, "You are a *vidyadhara* prince named Madanaprabha. I am Samara and Anangaprabha is my daughter. Earlier, when she was of marriageable age, she had many suitors but she refused to take a husband because she was proud of her looks. You, who are her equal in virtues, were keen to marry her but she refused you as well. Because of that, I cursed her to be born in the world of humans. But you were in love with her and begged Siva that she be your wife in the human world. You gave up your *vidyadhara* body by your magic powers and became a man and Anangaprabha became your wife. Now, both of you can return to your own world as a couple."

'Sagaravarma then remembered his previous birth, renounced his body in Prayaga and became Madanaprabha. Anangaprabha recovered her brightness with the restoration of her powers and when she became a *Vidyadhari*, her body shone brighter than ever. Madanaprabha and Anangaprabha were attracted to each other in their celestial bodies and were very happy. Along with Samara, they flew into the air and went to Virapura. Samara married his daughter to Madanaprabha with all the appropriate rites. Madanaprabha took his beloved, whose curse had now ended, to his own city and they lived there in peace.

'Thus, celestial beings can fall to earth because of curses. Their misconduct brings them to the world of humans and after they have suffered the consequences, they return to their own world because of their previous merit.'

When Naravahanadatta heard this story from Gomukha, he and Alankaravati were very pleased and proceeded with the tasks for the day.

Naravahanadatta continued to live in happiness with his wives. One day, when he was out hunting, he reached a great forest. Soon after, four celestial men arrived and carried him away to meet Visnu who sent Naravahanadatta to retrieve four apsarases that Indra had taken from him. When Naravahanadatta had accomplished the task, Visnu gave the four apsarases to him as wives. Naravahanadatta stayed with his four new wives for some time, enjoying the celestial delights that they presented him with and then he returned with them to his earthly kingdom. His family was glad to see him after so long and welcomed his new wives warmly.

"Alankaravati." In *Somadeva: Tales from the Kathasaritsagara*, translated by Arshia Sattar, 106–30. London: Penguin, 1994.

POST-READING PARS

1. Identify any two layers of stories that are nested within the larger story of "Alankaravati."

2. Identify two or three main ways fate and destiny play pivotal roles in the story lines as well as character developments of "Alankaravati."

3. Identify two or three characters who were portrayed as righteous in "Alankaravati."

Inquiry Corner

Content Question(s):

What do you think is the goal of human life? Do different characters of "Alankaravati" take different things as the ultimate goal of their lives? Compare, for example, the goal of Dharmasila and his father, Alankarasila.

Critical Question(s):

Critically evaluate the claim that "Alankaravati" is not a Hindu "religious" text given its focus on the joys and sorrows, trials and triumphs of all human life on earth.

Comparative Question(s):

Compare and contrast the role that fate and destiny play in "Alankaravati" with other readings for this course, for example, *Sunjata* or *Othello*.

Connection Question(s):

In "Alankaravati" a wife's deep devotion enables her to see the future. Does a particular person's experience and skill, or their marginalized navigation of their world, for example, offer them a special insight into their reality?

from *The Pillow Book* by Sei Shonagon

SNAPSHOT BOX

LANGUAGE:
Vernacular Japanese

DATE: 993–1002 CE

LOCATION: Heian,
Japan (Kyoto)

GENRE: Prose

NATIONAL/ETHNIC
IDENTITY: Japanese

TAGS: Aesthetics;
Empire; Gender;
Narrative; Women

Introduction

Sei Shonagon (966–1017/1025 CE) is not the first woman writer of the Japanese prose genre of ***zuihitsu*** (lit. "follow the brush, commonly translated as "miscellany" or "miscellaneous essay"). However, she almost single-handedly elevated the seemingly casual, private, and gendered writing style to a treasured literary canon that became the foundation of Japanese cultural aestheticism and its particular sensibilities. Her masterpiece *The Pillow Book* inspired numerous later works and literary genres such as *Essay in Idleness* (or *Tsurezuregusa*, by Yoshida Kenko), and the "I novel" in twentieth-century Japanese literature. Poets are still using her descriptions of the four seasons centuries later. What gives Shonagon's *The Pillow Book* such brilliant literary legacies, and how does Shonagon contribute to the vitality and tenacity of this literary genre?

Shonagon illustrates elegance, wittiness, good taste, and minute attention to details of the life of aristocrats in her *Pillow Book*, which consists mainly of catalogues of nature, such as the names of mountains, rivers, flowers, birds, and so forth, and things that interest her. These lists of things might not seem the most intriguing subject matter to modern readers, but it is through humor, irony, frankness, and remarkable psychological depth that Shonagon transforms these inconsequential anecdotes into fresh vignettes of life itself, whose small pleasures and daily discontents have resonated with readers for more than a thousand years. As readers across time and space smile and nod over her prose, we are compelled to wonder, why might we find the millennium-old ideas familiar? What features stand out as resonating with our contemporary sensibilities?

Timeline

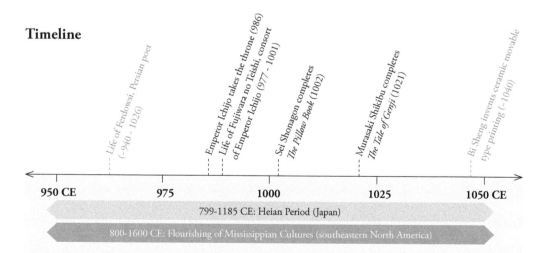

It remains uncertain whether these notes in *The Pillow Book* were meant for public circulation or only for the empress whom Shonagon served in court, as Shonagon explained in the accidental discovery of these notes by one of the court officials. But it is unquestionable that Shonagon's lucid writing style and her unique choice of subject matters fashioned a literary gender identity that impresses readers as quick-witted, learned, refined, and graceful, always candid, even to the point of acerbic in her observations and comments, and most importantly, psychologically sophisticated and insightful. This self-narrated identity conjures up an image of a stranger-friend, whose sincerity in her observations and remarks are almost therapeutic, in the sense that they reflect who we are as humans.

Such quick-wittedness and astute observations that are characteristic of Shonagon's style may be a result of her life in court and her position as lady-in-waiting to Empress Teishi. As a court lady, Shonagon's primary duty was to entertain Empress Teishi with her intellectual superiority, literary and artistic talents, and witty conversations. Ultimately the skillful capacities of court ladies added to the reputation of their respective empress's refined cultural taste. This intellectual entertainment was politically significant because Emperor Ichijō had two consorts, Empress Teishi and Empress Shoshi, and each endeavored to impress the emperor with the most culturally distinguished court. Such rivalry eventually is reflected in the competition between Sei Shonagon, who served Empress Teishi, and Murasaki Shikibu, the author of *The Tale of Gengi*, who served Empress Shoshi. *The Pillow Book* and *The Tale of Gengi* are therefore often compared and contrasted as two of the greatest literary achievements in Heian period Japan.

The unifying elements that give *The Pillow Book*'s loosely connected notes lyricism and internal logic are Shonagon's vernacular language, a narrative tone that conveys a sense of familiarity, and above all her extraordinary insight into the human psyche. As readers across centuries read about Shonagon's thoughts on "Hateful Things" or musings over a season's best moments, they are immersed in the full force of a brilliant conversationalist. Shonagon's enduring reputation is precisely because of her inimitability, as her personality comes to life so vividly that it becomes inseparable from her writing.

Jinhua Li
International Studies and Asian Studies

PRE-READING PARS

1. What do you imagine the life of a court lady to be like? Brainstorm a list of qualities and skill sets that might be expected of her?

2. In what ways does private writing differ from public writing (e.g., diary vs. social media posts)?

3. *The Pillow Book* has been compared to episodes from reality TV and modern vloggers. List two or three defining features of these forms of media.

from The Pillow Book

1. In Spring It Is the Dawn

In spring it is the dawn that is most beautiful. As the light creeps over the hills, their outlines are dyed a faint red and wisps of purplish cloud trail over them.

In summer the nights. Not only when the moon shines, but on dark nights too, as the fireflies flit to and fro, and even when it rains, how beautiful it is!

In autumn the evenings, when the glittering sun sinks close to the edge of the hills and the crows fly back to their nests in threes and fours and twos; more charming still is a file of wild geese, like specks in the distant sky. When the sun has set, one's heart is moved by the sound of the wind and the hum of the insects.

In winter the early mornings. It is beautiful indeed when snow has fallen during the night, but splendid too when the ground is white with frost; or even when there is no snow or frost, but it is simply very cold and the attendants hurry from room to room stirring up the fires and bringing charcoal, how well this fits the season's mood! But as noon approaches and the cold wears off, no one bothers to keep the braziers alight, and soon nothing remains but piles of white ashes.

5. Different Ways of Speaking

A priest's language.

The speech of men and of women.

The common people always tend to add extra syllables to their words.

6. That Parents Should Bring Up Some Beloved Son

That parents should bring up some beloved son of theirs to be a priest is really distressing. No doubt it is an auspicious thing to do; but unfortunately most people are convinced that a priest is as unimportant as a piece of wood, and they treat him accordingly. A priest lives poorly on meagre food, and cannot sleep without being criticized. While he is young, it is only natural that he should be curious about all sorts of things, and, if there are women about, he will probably peep in their direction (though, to be sure, with a look of aversion on his face). What is wrong about that? Yet people immediately find fault with him for even so small a lapse.

The lot of an exorcist is still more painful. On his pilgrimages to Mitake, Kumano, and all the other sacred mountains he often undergoes the greatest hardships. When people come to hear that his prayers are effective, they summon him here and there to perform services of exorcism: the more popular he becomes, the less peace he enjoys. Sometimes he will be called to see a patient who is seriously ill and he has to exert all his powers to cast out the spirit that is causing the affliction. But if he dozes off, exhausted by his efforts, people say reproachfully, 'Really this priest does nothing but sleep.' Such comments are most embarrassing for the exorcist, and I can imagine how he must feel.

That is how things used to be; nowadays priests have a somewhat easier life.

11. The Sliding Screen in the Back of the Hall

The sliding screen in the back of the hall in the north-east corner of Seiryo Palace is decorated with paintings of the stormy sea and of the terrifying creatures with long arms and long legs that live there. When the doors of the Empress's room were open, we could always see this screen. One day we were sitting in the room, laughing at the paintings and remarking how unpleasant they were. By the balustrade of the veranda stood a large celadon vase, full of magnificent cherry branches; some of them were as much as five foot long, and their blossoms overflowed to the very foot of the railing. Towards noon the Major Counsellor, Fujiwara no Korechika, arrived. He was dressed in a cherry-coloured Court cloak, sufficiently worn to have lost its stiffness, a white under-robe, and loose trousers of dark purple; from beneath the cloak shone the pattern of another robe of dark red damask. Since His Majesty was present, Korechika knelt on the narrow wooden platform before the door and reported to him on official matters.

A group of ladies-in-waiting was seated behind the bamboo blinds. Their cherry-coloured Chinese jackets hung loosely over their shoulders with the collars pulled back; they wore robes of wistaria, golden yellow, and other colours, many of which showed beneath the blind covering the half-shutter. Presently the noise of the attendants' feet told us that dinner was about to be served in the Daytime Chamber, and we heard cries of 'Make way. Make way.'

The bright, serene day delighted me. When the Chamberlains had brought all the dishes into the Chamber, they came to announce that dinner was ready, and His Majesty left by the middle door. After accompanying the Emperor Korechika returned to his previous place on the veranda beside the cherry blossoms. The Empress pushed aside her curtain of state and came forward as far as the threshold. We were overwhelmed by the whole delightful scene. It was then that Korechika slowly intoned the words of the old poem,

The days and the months flow by,
But Mount Mimoro lasts forever.

Deeply impressed, I wished that all this might indeed continue for a thousand years. As soon as the ladies serving in the Daytime Chamber bad called for the gentlemen-in-waiting to remove the trays, His Majesty returned to the Empress's room. Then he told me to rub some ink on the inkstone. Dazzled, I felt that I should never be able to take my eyes off his radiant countenance.

Next he folded a piece of white paper. 'I should like each of you,' he said, 'to copy down on this paper the first ancient poem that comes into your head.'

'How am I going to manage this?' I asked Korechika, who was still out on the veranda.

'Write your poem quickly,' he said, 'and show it to His Majesty. We men must not interfere in this.' Ordering an attendant to take the Emperor's inkstone to each of the women in the room, he told us to make haste. 'Write down any poem you happen to remember,' he said. 'The Naniwazu or whatever else you can think of.'

For some reason I was overcome with timidity; I flushed and had no idea what to do. Some of the other women managed to put down poems about the spring, the blossoms, and such suitable subjects; then they handed me the paper and said, 'Now it's your tum.' Picking up the brush, I wrote the poem that goes,

The years have passed
And age has come my way.
Yet I need only look at this fair flower
For all my cares to melt away.

I altered the third line, however, to read, 'Yet I need only look upon my lord.'

When he had finished reading, the Emperor said, 'I ask you to write these poems because I wanted to find out how quick you really were.

'A few years ago,' he continued, 'Emperor Enyu ordered all his courtiers to write poems in a notebook. Some excused themselves on the grounds that their handwriting was poor; but the Emperor insisted, saying that he did not care in the slightest about their handwriting or even whether their poems were suitable for the season. So they all had to swallow their embarrassment and produce something for the occasion. Among them was His Excellency, our present Chancellor, who was then Middle Captain of the Third Rank. He wrote down the old poem,

Like the sea that heats
Upon the shores of Izumo
As the tide sweeps in,
Deeper it grows and deeper—
The love I bear for you.

But he changed the last line to read, "The love I bear my lord!," and the Emperor was full of praise.'

When I heard His Majesty tell this story, I was so overcome that I felt myself perspiring. It occurred to me that no younger woman would have been able to use my poem and I felt very lucky. This sort of test can be a terrible ordeal: it often happens that people who usually write fluently are so overawed that they actually make mistakes in their characters.

Next the Empress placed a notebook of *Kokin Shu* poems before her and started reading out the first three lines of each one, asking us to supply the remainder. Among them were several famous poems that we had in our minds day and night; yet for some strange reason we were often unable to fill in the missing lines. Lady Saisho, for example, could manage only ten, which hardly qualified her as knowing her *Kokin Shu*. Some of the other women, even less successful, could remember only about half a dozen poems. They would have done better to tell the Empress quite simply that they had forgotten the lines; instead they came out with great lamentations like 'Oh dear, how could we have done so badly in answering the questions that Your Majesty was pleased to put to us?'—all of which I found rather absurd.

When no one could complete a particular poem, the Empress continued reading to the end. This produced further wails from the women: 'Oh, we all knew that one! How could we be so stupid?'

'Those of you,' said the Empress, 'who had taken the trouble to copy out the Kokin Shu several times would have been able to complete every single poem I have read. In the reign of Emperor Murakami there was a woman at Court known as the Imperial Lady of Senyo Palace. She was the daughter of the Minister of the Left who lived in the Smaller Palace of the First Ward, and of course you have all heard of her. When she was still a young girl, her mother gave her this advice: "First you must study penmanship. Next you must learn to play the seven-string zither better than anyone else. And also you must memorize all the poems in the twenty volumes of the *Kokin Shu*.'

'Emperor Murakami,' continued Her Majesty, 'had heard this story and remembered it years later when the girl had grown up and become an Imperial Concubine. Once, on a day of abstinence, he came into her room, hiding a notebook of *Kokin Shu* poems in the folds of his robe. He surprised her by seating himself behind a curtain of state; then, opening the book, he asked, "Tell me the verse written by such-and-such a poet, in such-and-such a year and on such-and-such an occasion." The lady understood what was afoot and that it was all in fun, yet the possibility of making a mistake or forgetting one of the poems must have worried her greatly. Before beginning the test, the Emperor had summoned a couple of ladies-in-waiting who were particularly adept in poetry and told them to mark each incorrect reply by a go stone. What a splendid scene it must have been! You know, I really envy anyone who attended that Emperor even as a lady-in-waiting.

'Well,' Her Majesty went on, 'he then began questioning her. She answered without any hesitation, just giving a few words or phrases to show that she knew each poem. And never once did she make a mistake. After a time the Emperor began to resent the lady's flawless memory and decided to stop as soon as he detected any error or vagueness in her replies. Yet, after he had gone through ten books of the *Kokin Shu*, he had still not caught her out. At this stage he declared that it would be useless to continue. Marking where he had left off, he went to bed. What a triumph for the lady!

'He slept for some time. On waking, he decided that he must have a final verdict and that if he waited until the following day to examine her on the other ten volumes, she might use the time to refresh her memory. So he would have to settle the matter that very night. Ordering his attendants to bring up the bedroom lamp, he resumed his questions. By the time he had finished all twenty volumes, the night was welt advanced; and still the lady had not made a mistake.

'During all this time His Excellency, the lady's father, was in a state of great agitation. As soon as he was informed that the Emperor was testing his daughter he sent his attendants to various temples to arrange for special recitations of the Scriptures. Then he turned in the direction of the Imperial Palace and spent a long time in prayer. Such enthusiasm for poetry is really rather moving.'

The Emperor, who had been listening to the whole story, was much impressed. 'How can he possibly have read so many poems?' he remarked when Her Majesty had finished. 'I doubt whether I could get through three or four volumes. But of course things have changed. In the old days even people of humble station had a taste for the arts and were interested in elegant pastimes. Such a story would hardly be possible nowadays, would it?'

The ladies in attendance on Her Majesty and the Emperor's own ladies in waiting who had been admitted into Her Majesty's presence began chatting eagerly, and as I listened I felt that my cares had really 'melted away.'

14. Hateful Things

One is in a hurry to leave, but one's visitor keeps chattering away. If it is someone of no importance, one can get rid of him by saying, 'You must tell me all about it next time'; but, should it be the sort of visitor whose presence commands one's best behaviour, the situation is hateful indeed.

One finds that a hair has got caught in the stone on which one is rubbing one's inkstick, or again that gravel is lodged in the inkstick, making a nasty, grating sound...

Someone has suddenly fallen ill and one summons the exorcist. Sinca he is not at home, one has to send messengers to look for him. After one has had a long fretful wait, the exorcist finally arrives, and with a sigh. of relief one asks him to start his incantations. But perhaps he has been exorcizing too many evil spirits recently; for hardly has he installed himself and begun praying when his voice becomes drowsy. Oh, how hateful!

A man who has nothing in particular to recommend him discusses all sorts of subjects at random as though he knew everything.

An elderly person warms the palms of his hands over a brazier and stretches out the wrinkles. No young man would dream behaving in such a fashion; old people can really be quite shameless. I have seen some dreary old creatures actually resting their feet on the brazier and rubbing them against the edge while they speak. These are the kind of people who in visiting someone's house first use their fans to wipe away the dust from the mat and, when they finally sit on it, cannot stay still but are forever spreading out the front of their hunting costume or even tucking it up under their knees. One might suppose that such behaviour was restricted to people of humble station; but I have observed it in quite well-bred people, including a Senior Secretary of the Fifth Rank in the Ministry of Ceremonial and a former Governor of Suruga.

I hate the sight of men in their cups who shout, poke their fingers in their mouths, stroke their beards, and pass on the wine to their neighbours with great cries of 'Have some more! Drink up!' They tremble, shake their heads, twist their faces, and gesticulate like children who are singing, 'We're off to see the Governor.' I have seen really well-bred people behave like this and I find it most distasteful.

To envy others and to complain about one's own lot; to speak badly about people; to be inquisitive about the most trivial matters and to resent and abuse people for not telling one, or, if one does manage to worm out some facts, to inform everyone in the most detailed fashion as if one had known all from the beginning—oh, how hateful!

One is just about to be told some interesting piece of news when a baby starts crying.

A flight of crows circle about with loud caws.

An admirer has come on a clandestine visit, but a dog catches sight of him and starts barking. One feels like killing the beast.

One has been foolish enough to invite a man to spend the night in an unsuitable place—and then he starts snoring.

A gentleman has visited one secretly. Though he is wearing a tall, lacquered hat, he nevertheless wants no one to see him. He is so flurried, in fact, that upon leaving he bangs into something with his hat. Most hateful! It is annoying too when he lifts up the Iyo blind that hangs at the entrance of the room, then lets it fall with a great rattle. If it is a head-blind, things are still worse, for being more solid it makes a terrible noise when it is dropped. There is no excuse for such carelessness. Even a head-blind does not make any noise if one lifts it up gently on entering and leaving the room; the same applies to sliding-doors. If one's movements are rough, even a paper door will bend and resonate when opened; but, if one lifts the door a little while pushing it, there need be no sound.

One has gone to bed and is about to doze off when a mosquito appears, announcing himself in a reedy voice. One can actually feel the wind made by his wings and, slight though it is, one finds it hateful in the extreme.

A carriage passes with a nasty, creaking noise. Annoying to think that the passengers may not even be aware of this! If I am travelling in someone's carriage and I hear it creaking, I dislike not only the noise but also the owner of the carriage.

One is in the middle of a story when someone butts in and tries to show that he is the only clever person in the room. Such a person is hateful, and so, indeed, is anyone, child or adult, who tries to push himself forward.

One is telling a story about old times when someone breaks in with a little derail that he happens to know, implying that one's own version is inaccurate — disgusting behaviour!

Very hateful is a mouse that scurries all over the place.

Some children have called at one's house. One makes a great fuss of them and gives them toys to play with. The children become accustomed to this treatment and start to come regularly forcing their way into one's inner rooms and scattering one's furnishings and possessions. Hateful!

A certain gentleman whom one does not want to see visits one at home or in the Palace, and one pretends to be asleep. But a maid comes to tell one and shakes one awake, with a look on her face that says, 'What a sleepyhead!' Very hateful.

A newcomer pushes ahead of the other members in a group; with a knowing look, this person starts laying down the law and forcing advice upon everyone—most hateful.

A man with whom one is having an affair keeps singing the praises of some woman he used to know. Even if it is a thing of the past, this can be very annoying. How much more so if he is still seeing the woman! (Yet sometimes I find that it is not as unpleasant as all that.)

A person who recites a spell himself after sneezing. In fact I detest anyone who sneezes except the master of the house.

Fleas, too, are very hateful. When they dance about under someone's clothes, they really seem to be lifting them up....

The sound of dogs when they bark for a long time in chorus is ominous and hateful.

I cannot stand people who leave without closing the panel behind them.

How I detest the husbands of nurse-maids! It is not so bad if the child in the maid's charge is a girl, because then the man will keep his distance. But, if it is a boy, he will behave as though he were the father. Never letting the boy out of his sight, he insists on managing everything. He regards the other attendants in the house as less than human, and, if anyone tries to scold the child, he slanders him to the master. Despite this disgraceful behaviour, no one dare accuse the husband; so he strides about the house with a proud, self-important look, giving all the orders....

I hate people whose letters show that they lack respect for worldly civilities, whether by discourtesy in the phrasing or by extreme politeness to someone who does not deserve it. This sort of thing is, of course, most odious if the letter is for oneself; but it is bad enough even if it is addressed to someone else.

As a matter of fact, most people are too casual, not only in their letters but in their direct conversation. Sometimes I am quite disgusted at noting how little decorum people observe when talking to each other. It is particularly unpleasant to hear some foolish man or woman omit the proper marks of respect when addressing a person of quality; and, when servants fail to use

honorific forms of speech in referring to their masters, it is very bad indeed. No less odious however are those masters who, in addressing their servants, use such phrases as 'When you were good enough to do such-and-such' or 'As you so kindly remarked.' No doubt there are some masters who, in describing their own actions to a servant, say, 'I presumed to do so-all-so'!

Sometimes a person who is utterly devoid of charm will try to create a good impression by using very elegant language; yet he only succeeds in being ridiculous. No doubt he believes this refined language to be just what the occasion demands, but, when it goes so far that everyone bursts out laughing, surely something must be wrong.

It is most improper to address high-ranking courtiers, Imperial Advisers, and the like simply by using their names without titles or marks of respect; but such mistakes are fortunately rare.

If one refers to the maid who is in attendance on some lady-in-waiting as 'Madam' or 'that lady,' she will be surprised, delighted, and lavish in her praise.

When speaking to young noblemen and courtiers of high rank, one should always (unless their Majesties are present) refer to them by their official posts. Incidentally, I have been shocked to hear important people use the word 'I' while conversing in Their Majesties' presence. Such a breach of etiquette is really distressing, and I fail to see why people cannot avoid it.

A man who has nothing in particular to recommend him but who speaks in an affected tone and poses as being elegant.

An inkstone with such a hard, smooth surface that the stick glides over it without leaving any deposit of ink.

Ladies-in-waiting who want to know everything that is going on.

Sometimes one greatly dislikes a person for no particular reason—and then that person goes and does something hateful.

A gentleman who travels alone in his carriage to see a procession or some other spectacle. What sort of a man is he? Even though he may not be a person of the greatest quality, surely he should have taken along a few of the many young men who are anxious to see the sights. But no, there he sits by himself (one can see his silhouette through the blinds), with a proud look on his face, keeping all his impressions to himself.

A lover who is leaving at dawn announces that he has to find his fan and his paper. 'I know I put them somewhere last night,' he says. Since it is pitch dark, he gropes about the room, bumping into the furniture and muttering, 'Strange! Where on earth can they be?' Finally he discovers the objects. He thrusts the paper into the breast of his robe with a great rustling sound; then he snaps open his fan and busily fans away with it. Only now is he ready to take his leave. What charmless behaviour! 'Hateful' is an understatement.

Equally disagreeable is the man who, when leaving in the middle of the night, takes care to fasten the cord of his headdress. This is quite unnecessary; he could perfectly well put it gently on his head without tying the cord. And why must he spend time adjusting his cloak or hunting costume? Does he really think someone may see him at this time of night and criticize him for not being impeccably dressed?

A good lover will behave as elegantly at dawn as at any other time. He drags himself out of bed with a look of dismay on his face. The lady urges him on: 'Come, my friend, it's getting light. You don't want anyone to find you here.' He gives a deep sigh, as if to say that the night has not been nearly long enough and that it is agony to leave. Once up, he does not instantly pull on his trousers. Instead he comes close to the lady and whispers whatever was left unsaid during the night. Even when he is dressed, he still lingers, vaguely pretending to be fastening his sash.

Presently he raises the lattice, and the two lovers stand together by the side door while he tells her how he dreads the coming day, which will keep them apart; then he slips away. The lady watches him go, and this moment of parting will remain among her most charming memories.

Indeed, one's attachment to a man depends largely on the elegance of his leave-taking. When he jumps out of bed, scurries about the room, tightly fastens his trouser-sash, rolls up the sleeves of his Court cloak, over-robe, or hunting costume, stuffs his belongings into the breast of his robe and then briskly secures the outer sash—one really begins to hate him.

Shonagon, Sei. From *The Pillow Book of Sei Shonagon*, translated by Ivan Morris, 21, 25–26, 34–39, 44–50. New York: Columbia University Press, 1967, 1991.

POST READING PARS

1. Compare your ideas of a court lady's life with what *The Pillow Book* tells us.

2. What features indicate that Sei Shonagon's writing was intended for a private or public audience?

3. How does Sei Shonagon's writing compare to your description of reality TV or modern vloggers?

Inquiry Corner

Content Question(s):	Critical Question(s):
What are the defining features of the literary genre of an essay?	Is writing gendered? Argue for or against this statement using Sei Shonagon's essay.

Comparative Question(s):	Connection Question(s):
How does *The Pillow Book* compare in style and subject matter with other essays that you are familiar with, for example, Montaigne's "On the Education of Children" or Ban Zhao's "Lessons for Women"? How does the treatment of nature compare and contrast to other sources that feature nature prominently?	In what ways can writing engage in a process of self-discovery and self-expression, such as reflecting on one's experiences of class, race, culture, and/or gender?

BEYOND THE CLASSROOM

» Shonagon employs a very useful tool in her writing: reflection. She reflected on her observations and wrote about them so she could revisit them at a later time, be that about her day, her interactions with people, or even how different people talk. Internships require reflection as well—considerations of how you enjoy the work, what is it about the environment that you dislike, how you see yourself in a similar role in the future, and so forth. What is an experience you've had where you used reflection?

Poems of Kabir

SNAPSHOT BOX

LANGUAGE:
Vernacular Hindi

DATE: c. 15th century
CE

LOCATION: South
Asia

GENRE: Poetry

TAGS: Asceticism;
Authority and
Institution; Body;
Devotion; Music
and Entertainment;
Mysticism;
Orality; Poetry;
Power Structures;
Spirituality

Introduction

Kabir is one of the most well-known mystical poet-saints in the north Indian **Bhakti movement**, a period of increased personal devotion to various gods and goddesses. We do not know the exact dates of his birth and death but most historians agree that he lived during the 1400–1500s in the north Indian city of Benaras (Varanasi) when a large part of the subcontinent was under the control of the Muslim dynasties of the Delhi Sultanate. How might this social context shape Kabir's poetry?

The name Kabir itself (meaning "the great") has Arabic roots and is a Quranic title of Allah, the Arabic term for god. There are numerous legends and stories about his life, some claiming that he was born into a family that recently converted to Islam and others claiming that he was born to a brahmin (Hindu priestly caste) unwed mother and grew up as a weaver who belonged to a lower caste. Some scholars of Hindi literature categorize Kabir as a *sant* (the closest translation for that word is "saint") of the *nirguna* (without attribute, form, describable qualities) persuasion within the Bhakti movement. Since *nirguna bhakti* considers the idea of God/Ram (a very popular name for God in Hinduism) to be nonimagistic, God/Ram is rendered more abstractly, without taking a specific form or having particular qualities that can be described. Consequently, Kabir is also identified as an iconoclast, a vocal critic, especially within Hindu communities that worship Ram as part of **saguna bhakti** (the opposite of nirguna and thus known as having numerous attributes and specific qualities). So, while a nirguna approach to

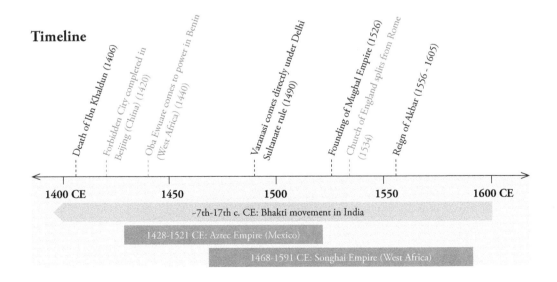

Timeline

Death of Ibn Khaldun (1406)
Forbidden City completed in Beijing (China) (1420)
Oba Ewuare comes to power in Benin (West Africa) (1440)
Varanasi comes directly under Delhi Sultanate rule (1490)
Founding of Mughal Empire (1526)
Church of England splits from Rome (1534)
Reign of Akbar (1556 - 1605)

1400 CE   1450   1500   1550   1600 CE

~7th-17th c. CE: Bhakti movement in India

1428-1521 CE: Aztec Empire (Mexico)

1468-1591 CE: Songhai Empire (West Africa)

Ram would avoid any description as it would not come close to capturing the power and presence of the divine, a saguna approach would note Ram's weapons, actions to save devotees, and glorified physical attributes.

The saguna poetic mode is much more common in Hindu devotional poetry because of all the specificity of divine forms of Hindu gods and types of affectionate relationships with devotees that can be developed. As Kabir's poems are grounded in the nirguna mode, his poetry features a strong critique of and disdain for the ritualism and ritual authority found in Hinduism that is often focused on specific gods as well as devotional and ritual practices that demarcate Muslim identity and authority. In other words, Kabir calls out anything that gets in the way of just focusing on God, especially practices that create human distinction between religious paths or impose social hierarchies (for example, class and caste) as barriers to religion.

Despite this attempt at shedding any particular religious association, both Hindu and Muslim communities have tried to claim Kabir for themselves. For some, he is placed alongside Sufi mystical poets while for others he is considered to be a precursor to Guru Nanak, the founding guru of **Sikhism**, a monotheistic religion that emerged in north India in the late fifteenth century, and his poems are included in the *Adi Granth*, or Sikh scriptures. There is also a contemporary religious community called the Kabir Panth that is focused on the teachings of Kabir. The example of Kabir, thus, allows us to wonder: what qualities enable a person to cross social and religious boundaries?

It is challenging to pin down biographical information and precise authorial intent from Kabir's poetry directly. In part this is because all of his poetry was transmitted orally for almost a century until it was first transcribed in manuscript form in the 1600s. The language in which we encounter Kabir's poetry today is a mix of several dialects of Hindi, one of twenty-two official languages spoken by a majority of the population across much of present-day India and its diasporic populations. Moreover, Kabir's name and words continue to be adapted, appropriated, and recycled in popular culture and in support of various movements against social injustice. Kabir's words live on not just because hundreds of his poems are a part of multiple Hindu, Muslim, and Sikh religious communities, but because Kabir's colloquial authorial signature "kehat Kabir" ("Kabir says") has become almost an idiomatic expression to preface or conclude pithy words of wisdom.

Renuka Gusain
Humanities Program

PRE-READING PARS

1. What three associations come to mind when you think of religion and its relationship to the body?

2. Write down three rituals or practices rooted in religion that you find personally meaningful, regardless of whether you practice them or not.

3. In what ways do people find religious meaning in their everyday lives?

Poems and Epigrams of Kabir

Go naked if you want,
Put on animal skins.
    What does it matter till you see the inward Ram?
If the union yogis seek
Came from roaming about in the buff,
    every deer in the forest would be saved.
If shaving your head
Spelled spiritual success,
    heaven would be filled with sheep.
And brother, if holding back your seed
Earned you a place in paradise
    eunuchs would be the first to arrive.
Kabir says: Listen brother,
Without the name of Ram
    who has ever won the spirit's prize?
[KG *pad* 174]

That master weaver, whose skills
            are beyond our knowing,
            has stretched his warp
                    through the world.
He has fastened his loom
            between earth and sky,
            where the shuttlecocks are the sun
                    and moon.
He fills the shuttle with the thread
            of easy spontaneity,
            and weaves and weaves
                    an endless pattern.
But now, says Kabir, that weaver!
            He breaks apart his loom

and tangles the thread
                in thread.
[KG *pad* 150]

Pundit, so well-read, go ask God
            who his teacher is
            and who he's taught.
He alone knows what shape he has
            and he keeps it to himself,
            alone.
Child of a childless woman,
            a fatherless son,
            someone without feet who climbs trees,
A soldier without weaponry,
            no elephant, no horse,
            charging into battle with no sword,
A sprout without a seed,
            a tree without a trunk,
            blossoms on a tree without a branch,
A woman without beauty,
            a scent without a flower,
            a tank filled to the top without water,
A temple without a god,
            worship without leaves,
            a lazy bee that has no wings.
You have to be a hero to reach that highest state;
            the rest, like insects,
            burn like moths in the flame—
A flame without a lamp,
            a lamp without a flame,
            an unsounded sound that sounds without end.
Those who comprehend it,
            let them comprehend.
            Kabir has gone off into God.
[KG *pad* 119]

The lean doe
Avoids the greens
Beside this pond.
Numberless hunters,
Only one life.

How many arrows
      can she dodge?
[KG *sakhi* 16.3]

Scorches by the forest fire,
The wood still stands
      and wails:
"Don't let me fall to the smith!
Don't let me burn again!"
[KG *sakhi* 16.2]

They burn:
The bones like tinder,
      hair like straw.
And seeing the world
      in flames, Kabir
      turns away.
[KG *sakhi* 15.7]

Kabir:
My mind was soothed
When I found the boundless knowledge,
And the fires
      that scorch the world
To me are water cool.
[KG *sakhi* 17.1]

Kabir. "Poems and Epigrams of Kabir." In *Songs of the Saints of India*, translated by John Stratton Hawley and Mark Juergensmeyer, 52–59. New York: Oxford University Press, 1988.

POST-READING PARS

1. Compare and contrast your ideas of the relationship between religion and body to Kabir's views.
2. List two of the rituals and practices that Kabir tells his listeners not to perform and the reasons for that. Do you think these practices could have value in a secular, social context?
3. List the different layers of meanings that emerge from the extended imagery of the weaver and weaving in the second poem. (Hint: who is the weaver? Is there more than one possibility?)

Inquiry Corner

Content Question(s):	Critical Question(s):
What claims do these poems make about Ram? What literary features or themes make Kabir's poetry relatable?	How does Kabir's form of expression contribute to or hinder social critique?
Comparative Question(s):	**Connection Question(s):**
How does Kabir's poetry compare in theme and form with other mystical writings you have read, for example, by Hildegard of Bingen or Margery Kempe?	How many disciplinary perspectives (e.g., rhetoric, history, sociology, religious studies, etc.) did you use to engage with and critically evaluate Kabir's poems?

BEYOND THE CLASSROOM

» Consider the proverb "clothes make the man" as it relates to someone's appearance, and our judgments about them. Kabir would say that clothing and ritual have nothing to do with the person, or their ability to know God or be spiritual. Do you think you would react the same way if your superior or co-worker was unkempt as you would if they were well coiffed? What about the custodial staff? What are your assumptions about the relationship between competence, appearance, and professionalism?

» You might spend up to a third of your life at work after you graduate from college. What do you think Kabir would say about working in a job that doesn't align with your career goals, or being fearful to try for a bigger goal?

Poems of Mirabai

SNAPSHOT BOX

LANGUAGE:
vernacular dialect of
Hindi

DATE: c. 16th century
CE

LOCATION: South
Asia

GENRE: Religious
poetry

TAGS: Asceticism;
Body; Devotion;
Music and
Entertainment;
Poetry; Religion;
Ritual and Practice;
Spirituality; Women

Introduction

Mirabai (circa 1498–1546 CE) is known widely across north India as a Bhakti (devotional) poet-saint, mystic, and devotee of the Hindu god, Krishna. There are no contemporaneous historical records about Mirabai so her biography presents certain challenges. Consequently, the story of her life and her **hagiography** (writing on the life of a saint) is pieced together by using several secondary sources, popular legends, and manuscripts, the earliest of which dates back to about a century after the dates she is said to have lived. The narratives about her life that have been developed over centuries continue to be perpetuated and adapted in popular culture, social reform and Indian feminist discourses, and even in traditional religious contexts (e.g., in a temple setting where people are singing her songs). In the absence of primary sources, what might we rely on to rebuild and reimagine the life of a historical figure like Mirabai?

Mirabai's life and her poems/devotional songs (*bhajans*) are often understood in the context of what has retroactively been labeled as the Bhakti movement. This movement spanned across centuries, languages, ethnicities, and gods and goddesses on the Indian subcontinent and therefore was localized and decentralized. It is reductive and also not productive to try to pinpoint its one organizing principle. In its broadest and most common sense, the Bhakti movement represented a turn to an intimate relationship with one's god(s) and a belief that this individual devotion mattered far more than a strict adherence to rituals and conventional practices prescribed by mainstream Hinduism. This also fomented ideas about all human beings being equal in the eyes of god and thus

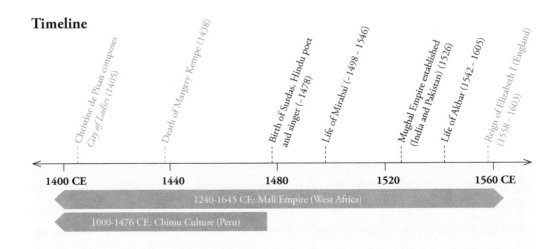

Timeline

Christine de Pisan composes *City of Ladies* (1405)

Death of Margery Kempe (1438)

Birth of Surdas, Hindu poet and singer (~1478)

Life of Mirabai (~1498 - 1546)

Mughal Empire established (India and Pakistan) (1526)

Life of Akbar (1542 - 1605)

Reign of Elizabeth I (England) (1558 - 1603)

1400 CE   1440   1480   1520   1560 CE

1240-1645 CE: Mali Empire (West Africa)

1000-1476 CE: Chimu Culture (Peru)

became one of the major avenues through which the rigid hierarchies of the caste system were challenged and rejected.

It is in this context of the Bhakti movement that we can begin to understand Mirabai's hagiography. The narrative presents Mirabai as a Rajput (high caste, lit. "descendent of royalty") born into nobility in north India. Beginning in her childhood, she was a devotee of Lord Krishna and claimed to be his bride in professing her deep love. Even after her marriage to a local king, Bhojraj Singh Sisodia, she continued her worship of Krishna who was not the god associated with the Sisodia family. Thereby, she rejected the typical practice of adopting the gods and goddesses of one's husband's family. Historians estimate 1516 as the date of her marriage, which was primarily a political alliance. There are multiple, competing narratives about their marriage. While one narrative depicted the marriage as being friendly and the king (*rana*) building a temple for her to worship Krishna, another narrative includes the husband trying to poison her because she refused to worship his family god. Part of the hagiography is that the poison gets converted to sweet elixir when it touches her lips. After her husband's death in a battle in 1526, Mirabai is said to have rejected committing **sati** (practice of self-immolation on a dead husband's funeral pyre) insisting that her husband, Lord Krishna, was still alive and that she had no reason to commit sati. How might a personal, intimate relationship with the divine be at odds with socially accepted behaviors and practices?

After the passing of her husband, Mirabai started living the life of an ascetic, giving up her royal comforts. Her songs tell us that she wore ankle bells and danced in the streets, entranced in her devotion to Krishna. Many of the themes of Mirabai's poetry correspond with that of the poetry of other Bhakti saints such as Surdas who was also a devotee of Krishna. Devotion, prayer, deep longing, and ecstatic love for the divine were some of these recurrent themes. Several poems attributed to Mirabai are imbued with both spirituality and eroticism, at once longing for a union with the divine but also describing her relationship to god using sensual imagery. Why might this kind of poetry be viewed as both transgressive and devotional?

The content of many of her poems contains references to her life and describe herself. Most of her poems carry lines that are best described as authorial signatures: "Mira wore ankle bells and danced," "Mira's lord, Girdhar (mountain-bearer, another name for Krishna)." The earliest manuscripts that claim to include her voice attribute around two hundred poems to her. Over several centuries, however, more than a thousand poems have been attributed to Mirabai. They are composed in her voice and carry her various authorial signatures. Even today, old songs are adapted and new songs emerge with her signature in a wide range of contexts: religious, entertainment (pop music, movies, TV series, graphic novels), and social protests. Why is it possible that centuries after her death, this poet-saint's voice is still alive and vibrant even outside of the strict context of religion?

Renuka Gusain
Humanities Program

Poems of Mirabai

I'm colored with the color of dusk, oh *rana*,
    colored with the color of my Lord.
Drumming out the rhythm on the drums, I danced,
    dancing in the presence of the saints,
        colored with the color of my Lord.
They thought me mad for the Maddening One,
    raw for my dear dark love,
        colored with the color of my Lord.
The *rana* sent me a poison cup:
    I didn't look, I drank it up,
        colored me with the color of my Lord.
The clever Mountain Lifter is the lord of Mira.
    Life after life he's true—
        colored with the color of my Lord.
             [Caturvedi, no. 37]

Life without Hari is no life, friend,
And though my mother-in-law fights,
    my sister-in-law teases,
    the *rana* is angered,
A guard is stationed on a stool outside,
    and a lock is mounted on the door,
How can I abandon the love I have loved
    in life after life?
Mira's Lord is the clever Mountain Lifter:
    Why would I want anyone else?
             [Caturvedi, no. 42]

Today your Hari is coming,
my friend,
to play the game of Spring.
The harbinger crow in the courtyard speaks,

my friend,
an omen of good times ahead.
All the cowherds have gathered in the garden,
    my friend,
      where the basil grows:
I hear the sound of tambourines and drums,
    my friend.
      Why sleep? Wake up and go!
There's water and betel-leaf, mats and sheets,
    my friend.
      Go greet him: touch his feet.
Mira's Lord is the clever Mountain Lifter,
    my friend,
      the best blessing you could have.
                [Sekhavat, no. 76]

I saw the dark clouds burst,
          dark Lord,
Saw the clouds and tumbling down
In black and yellow streams
          they thicken,
Rain and rain two hours long.
See –
    my eyes see only rain and water,
    watering the thirsty earth green.
Me –
    my love's in a distant land
    and wet, I stubbornly stand at the door,
For Hari is indelibly green,
          Mira's Lord,
And he has invited a standing,
          stubborn love.
              [Caturvedi, no. 82]

Mirabai. "Poems of Mirabai." In *Songs of the Saints of India*, edited by J. S. Hawley and Mark Jeurgensmeyer, 134–35. New York: Oxford University Press, 1988.

POST-READING PARS

1. Identify two or three phrases that Mirabai uses to describe Lord Krishna?
2. List two adjectives that you might use to describe Mirabai.

Inquiry Corner

Content Question(s):	Critical Question(s):
What are some of the different feelings and sensations Mirabai experiences in the poems you read?	In what ways are the spiritual and physical/sensual dimensions of Mirabai's devotion connected?
Comparative Question(s):	**Connection Question(s):**
How does Mirabai envision her relationship to the divine? How does that compare and contrast with other religious poets and seekers we have read?	How can a deeply personal and intimate relationship with the divine inspire a secular commitment to social justice?

"Song of the Lute" by Po Chü-i

Introduction

Po Chü-i (772–846 CE), whose name is often romanized as Bai Juyi, lived in the middle of the Tang dynasty—a time when the powerful Chinese empire was recovering after the An Lushan Rebellion, a devastating civil war that began when general An Lushan declared war on the Tang emperor. Born into an impoverished but scholarly family, Po passed the prestigious *jinshi* examination, which qualified him to serve as an official, at the age of twenty-eight. Thereafter, he had a long and checkered career in government. At times he held important posts at the capital, present-day Xi'an, though he was repeatedly demoted and sent to the provinces. (His passion for social reform did not endear him to everyone.) He wrote more than 2800 poems, of which "Song of the Lute" (*pipa* is the name of the instrument in Chinese) is one of the most famous.

During a period of imperial disfavor, when Po Chü-i had been serving far from the capital in an insignificant position as marshal of the city of Chiu-chiang for more than a year, he had a chance encounter that would become the basis for this poem. Seeing off a friend with a farewell party on a boat on the Yangtze River, they heard music from a neighboring boat that seemed so refined and expert as to be foreign to the region. What followed was a musical performance and a life story that allowed Po to reflect deeply on art, memory, home, disappointment, loss, and the consolation of human connections. Particularly noteworthy is that even though men and women lived very different lives in medieval China, Po was still able to identify strongly with the feelings of the female lute player. What is it about the nature of art and aesthetics that enables such transcending of conventional social norms?

SNAPSHOT BOX

LANGUAGE: Chinese

DATE: 816 CE

LOCATION: China

GENRE: Poetry

TAGS: Aesthetics; Gender; Identity and Self; Music and Entertainment; Women

Timeline

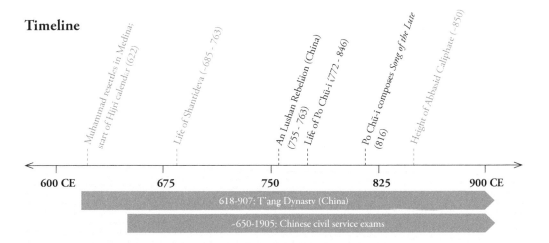

The lute player had been a singing girl in the capital, or a **courtesan**. While most Chinese women at the time had arranged marriages In their teens, some young girls were sold to businesses that would educate and train them in music, poetry, and dance to provide entertainment and female companionship for men in social situations. Intimate relations with customers sometimes occurred, but they were not necessarily expected. A courtesan as talented and in demand as the lute player would have to be wooed over time with many gifts, and she probably had several affairs in her career. Despite the opportunities to cultivate their talents and be in the limelight, options to maintain their lives as courtesans were very limited. When she aged out of her profession, her best option was to become a **concubine**, that is, a secondary wife, to a wealthy man — in this case a merchant who turned out to be inattentive and often spent a lot of time away from home. A courtesan could never hope to become a primary wife, with full rights and protections. How do you think such economic and social realities might have shaped the artistic process?

"Song of the Lute" is considered a fairly long poem by Chinese standards, containing eighty-eight lines of seven characters each, arranged into rhyming couplets. "Ambush from Ten Sides" is an example of a traditional pipa melody, several versions of which can be found on YouTube.

Grant Hardy
Department of History

PRE-READING PARS

1. Why is it so difficult to describe music in words?
2. What sorts of first encounters lead to people with very different lives finding common ground?

Song of the Lute

Preface and Poem

In the tenth year of the Yüan-ho era (815), I was exiled to the district of Chiu-chiang [Jiujiang] with the post of marshal. In the autumn of the following year, I was seeing a visitor off at the P'en River landing when I heard someone on one of the boats playing a p'i-p'a lute in the night. Listening to its tone, I could detect a note of the capital in its clear twanging. When I inquired who the player was, I found it was a former singing girl of Ch'ang-an who had once studied the lute under two masters named Mu and Ts'ao. Later, when she grew older and her beauty faded, she had entrusted herself to a traveling merchant and became his wife.

I proceeded to order wine and lost no time in requesting her to play a few selections. After the selections were over, she fell into a moody silence, and then told us of the happy times of her youth and of her present life of drifting and deprivation, moving about here and there in the region of the Yangtze and the lakes.

Two years had passed since I was assigned to this post, and I had been feeling rather contented and at ease. But this evening, moved by her words, I realized for the first time just what it means to be an exile. Therefore I have written this long song to present to her. It contains a total of 612 characters and is entitled "Song of the Lute."

Hsün-yang on the Yangtze, seeing off a guest at night;
maple leaves, reed flowers, autumn somber and sad:
the host had dismounted, the guest already aboard the boat,
we raised our wine, prepared to drink, though we lacked flutes and strings.
But drunkenness brought no pleasure, we grieved at the imminent parting;
at parting time, vague and vast, the river lay drenched in moonlight.
Suddenly we heard the sound of a lute out on the water;
the host forgot about going home, the guest failed to start on his way.
We traced the sound, discreetly inquired who the player might be.
The lute sounds ceased, but words were slow in coming.
We edged our boat closer, inviting the player to join us,
poured more wine, turned the lamps around, began our revels again.
A thousand pleas, ten thousand calls, and at last she appeared,
but even then she held the lute so it half hid her face.

She turned the pegs, brushed the strings, sounding two or three notes—
before they had formed a melody, already the feeling came through.
Each string seemed tense with it, each sound to hold a thought,
as though she were protesting a lifetime of wishes unfulfilled.
Eyebrows lowered, hand moving freely, she played on and on,
speaking of all the numberless things in her heart.
Lightly she pressed the strings, slowly plucked, pulled and snapped them,
first performing "Rainbow Skirts," then "Waists of Green."
The big strings plang-planged like swift-falling rain;
the little strings went buzz-buzz like secret conversations;
plang-plang, buzz-buzz mixed and mingled in her playing
like big pearls and little pearls falling on a plate of jade,
or the soft call of warbler voices resonant under the blossoms,
the hidden sobbing of springs and rills barely moving beneath the ice.
Then the icy springs congealed with cold, the strings seemed to freeze,
freeze till the notes no longer could pass, the sound for a while cut off;
now something different, hidden anguish, dark reproaches taking form—
at such times the silence was finer than any sound.
Then a silver vase would abruptly break, water come splashing forth,
iron-clad horsemen would suddenly charge, swords and halberds clanging.
As the piece ended, she swept the plectrum in an arc before her breast,
and all four strings made a single sound, like the sound of rending silk.
In the boat to the east, the boat to the west, stillness, not a word;
all we could see was the autumn moon white in the heart of the river.

Lost in thought, she put down the plectrum, tucked it among the strings,
straightened her robes, rose, put on a grave expression,
told us she had once been a daughter of the capital,
living in a house at the foot of Toad Barrow.
By the age of thirteen she had mastered the lute,
was famed as a member of the finest troupe of players.
Whenever a piece was over, her teachers were enthralled;
each time she donned full makeup, the other girls were filled with envy.
Young men from the five tomb towns vied to give her presents;[144]
one selection won her she knew not how many red silks.
Silver hair pins set with inlay—she beat time with them till they broke;
blood-colored gauze skirts—she stained them with overturned wine.
This year brought joy and laughter, next year would be the same;
autumn moons, spring breezes—how casually she let them pass!

144. The tomb towns, sites of imperial graves, were suburbs of the capital where wealthy families lived.

"Then my younger brother ran off to the army, the woman I called 'mother' died;
and as evenings went and mornings came, my looks began to fade.
My gate became still and lonely, few horses or riders there;
getting on in years, I gave myself as wife to a traveling merchant.
But merchants think much of profit and little of separation;
last month he went off to Fou-liang to buy tea.
Since coming here to the river mouth, I've guarded my boat alone;
in the bright moonlight that encircles the boat, the river waters are cold.
And when night deepens, suddenly I dream of those days of youth,
and my dream-wept tears, mixed with rouge, come down in streams of crimson."

Earlier, when I heard her lute, already I felt sad;
listening to her story, I doubled my sighs of pity.
Both of us hapless outcasts at the farther end of the sky;
meeting like this, why must we be old friends to understand each other?
Since last year when I left the capital,
I've lived in exile, sick in bed, in Hsün-yang town.
Hsün-yang is a far-off region—there's no music here;
all year long I never hear the sound of strings or woodwinds.
I live near the P'en River, an area low and damp,
with yellow reeds and bitter bamboo growing all around my house.
And there, morning and evening, what do I hear?
The cuckoo singing his heart out, the mournful cry of monkeys.
Blossom-filled mornings by the spring river, nights with an autumn moon,
sometimes I fetch wine and tip the cup alone.
To be sure, there's no lack of mountain songs and village pipes,
but their wails and bawls, squeaks and squawks are a trial to listen to.
Tonight, though, I've heard the words of your lute,
like hearing immortal music—for a moment my ears are clear.
Do not refuse me, sit and play one more piece,
and I'll fashion these things into a lute song for you.

Moved by these words of mine, she stood a long while,
then returned to her seat, tightened the strings, strings sounding swifter than ever,
crying, crying in pain, not like the earlier sound;
the whole company, listening again, forced back their tears.
And who among the company cried the most?
This marshal of Chiu-chiang, wetting his blue coat.

Po Chü-i. "Song of the Lute." In *The Columbia Book of Chinese Poetry: From Early Times to the Thirteenth Century*. Translated and edited by Burton Watson, 249–52. New York: Columbia University Press, 1984.

POST READING PARS

1. Think about the power of art, in this case music, to evoke feelings and memories. What does it mean that "the silence was finer than any sound?"
2. How did the mood of the farewell party change when the woman started playing?

Inquiry Corner

Content Question(s):

Reconstruct the biography of the lute player. Note all the allusions to seasons in the poem. What do they convey? Where are the two references to the moon on the river? What has changed in between? Why are both references to the moon's reflection rather than to the moon itself?

Critical Question(s):

How is being trained in the Confucian Classics, in order to take tests and write government documents, similar to being trained in music to entertain strangers?

Comparative Question(s):

Exile is a common theme in world literature. Compare this poem to another reading or art form on this theme.

Connection Question(s):

Some of the themes of this poem are homesickness and failed ambition. Is it a poem particularly suited for middle-aged persons (Po was forty-five when he wrote it), or might it apply equally well to other seasons of life?

from *Vishnu Purana* ("Krishna and Kaliya")

Introduction

The Hindu texts known as the *Puranas* (circa 300–1000 CE) highlight a turn toward **bhakti**, or personal devotion to a particular god or goddess, thereby marking a defining characteristic of Hinduism during the middle period of South Asian history. A *Purana* is typically a compilation of oral narratives (*smriti* or "that which is remembered") about the manifestations and actions of a god or goddess and is considered sacred by communities dedicated to that particular god or goddess. This excerpt comes from the *Vishnu Purana* (circa fourth century CE), a collation of stories about the god Vishnu, who is especially known for taking ten **avatars** or incarnations on Earth. According to legends, when the world becomes imbalanced or overrun by a particularly clever **rakshasa**, or demon, Vishnu appears in the form of one of these avatars. This becomes necessary because many of the demons accrued specialized forms of immunity from being killed by gods through their own ascetic practices. Avatars of Vishnu often take the form that locates the loophole in the immunity that was granted and thus will be successful at being able to rid the world of the destructive being.

The god Krishna is one of the most popular of these ten avatars and is well known for his appearance as the charioteer and friend who reveals his all-encompassing universal form to Arjuna in the *Bhagavad Gita*. However, he is just as popular because of the stories from his youth in which his divine power and playful mischievousness exist simultaneously. In the story we are about to read, Krishna is still a

SNAPSHOT BOX
LANGUAGE: Sanskrit
DATE: c. 300 CE
LOCATION: South Asia
GENRE: *Purana* (ancient stories)
TAGS: Devotion; Epic; Myth and Legend; Nature and Sacred; Religion; Spirituality

Timeline

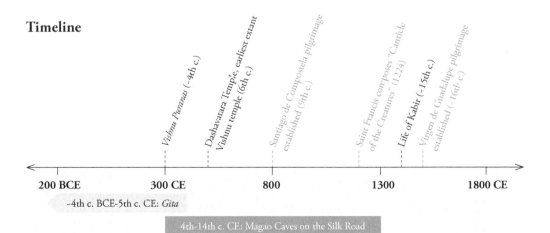

young boy living among cowherders. He identifies a threat to the people of his village, a snake named Kaliya who is poisoning the nearby river, and responds through his divine play. The notion of divine play, or **lila**, is woven through many of the stories from Krishna's youth even when the subject matter is serious. How might this idea of play enhance or detract from a human understanding of divinity? How might stories from Krishna's youth impact how Krishna is encountered by devotees in the *Bhagavad Gita*, or vice versa?

The larger movement within Hinduism centered on bhakti—the Bhakti movement (circa seventh–seventeeth century CE)—saw an increase in the building of temples supported by the resources of kings and wealthy landowners and merchants. Practices of worship, or **puja**, that involve making offerings of food, water, flowers, light (flame), and other items of hospitality to the god, and the practice of visual exchange or **darshan** (to see and be seen by the god) were also developed during this time. Wandering poet-saints increased the reputation of local deities by singing the praises of these gods, describing the landscapes in which the gods performed their divine actions, and detailing interactions with human devotees who take on the role of parent, friend, servant, or lover of the god. How might these roles increase the affection one has for a god?

Many stories about gods are read on multiple levels by practicing Hindus. For example, contemporary environmentalists in India employ this Krishna and Kaliya story as a metaphor, viewing industrial businesses that pollute the river as the new Kaliya to subdue. What are some of the religious or secular messages that might be communicated through narratives like this?

Katherine C. Zubko
Department of Religious Studies

PRE-READING PARS

1. List two qualities of a person that elicit both your affection and respect.

The Story of Krishna and Kaliya

Once Krishna went into the woods unaccompanied by his elder brother, Balarama. Radiant with a garland of forest flowers, he roved about in the company of cowherd friends. Then he came upon the river Yamuna, whose waves were tossing about as if she were laughing, throwing patches of foam on the banks. But in the water he saw a dreadful sight—it was the hideous pool of the snake Kaliya, whose water was mixed with a fiery poison! The trees on the bank nearby, splashed by the burning poison, had been scorched while the birds were singed by sprays of that poisoned water tossed aloft in the wind.

Witnessing this sight, horrible as the maw of death, Krishna thought to himself, "This must be the dwelling place of the vile Kaliya, whose weapon is poison, that wicked serpent who abandoned the ocean when I defeated him there once before. Now the entire Yamuna river is polluted by him, all the way to the sea, so that neither cows nor humans suffering from thirst are able to use it. I must tame this kind of snake so that the inhabitants of the nearby village of Vraj can move around happily, without fear. I have descended into the world for this purpose, to pacify those corrupt ones whose domain is immoral. Let me now climb this broad-branched tree nearby and fall into the pool of this snake who feeds on the wind!" So thinking, and tightly tucking up his garment, Krishna dived at once into the pool of the serpent king.

So roiled up by the force of Krishna's fall was the vast pool that it flooded even huge trees growing far away. They burst at once into flame, smitten by the wind that carried water burning with that snake's evil fiery poison.

Then, in the serpent's pool, Krishna slapped his arm defiantly.[145] Hearing the sound, the serpent king rapidly approached, his eyes coppery-red with rage. He was surrounded by other venomous wind-feeding snakes with mouths full of fiery poison, accompanied by their snake wives by the hundreds adorned with fetching necklaces, who were beautiful with jangling bracelets that trembled when their bodies moved.

Then the snakes encircled Krishna, making fetters of their coils, and bit him with their poison-filled mouths. When the cowherds saw that he had fallen into the pool and was being crushed by the serpents' coils, they fled to Vraj. Wholly overcome with grief, they cried aloud, "Krishna, distracted, has gone and fallen into Kaliya's pool where he is being eaten alive by the snake king! Come and see!"

The cowherds and their wives, thunderstruck at these words, hurried immediately to the pool, with Krishna's adopted mother, Yashoda ahead of them. "Oh oh,

---

145. This gesture is typical of warriors going into battle to signal the beginning of a fight.

where is he?" cried the agitated crowd of cowherd women as they hastened, confused and stumbling, along with Yashoda. The cowherders Nanda and Balarama, of wondrous valor, also sped to the Yamuna determined to see Krishna. There they saw him at the mercy of the serpent king, rendered powerless, wrapped in the coils of the snake. Staring at the face of his adopted son, the cowherd Nanda was immobilized, and so was his mother Yashoda. The other cowherds, too, disheartened with grief, looked on while weeping, stammering with fear, beseeching Krishna with love [. . .]

When Krishna was called to mind by the cowherds, the petals of his lips blossomed into a smile, and he split open that snake, freeing his own body from the coils. Using his two hands to bend over the middle head of that serpent with curving hoods, the wide-striding Krishna mounted that head and began to dance on it. The serpent's hood expanded with his life's breath as it was pounded by Krishna's feet. Wherever the snake's head swelled up, Krishna trod it down again. Squeezed in this manner by Krishna, the snake fainted away with a quiver, vomiting blood because of the blows of Krishna's staff.

When his wives saw the serpent king with his neck and head arched over, the blood streaming from his mouth, they went to Krishna and said piteously, "Overlord of the gods, you are known to be omniscient, without equal, the ineffable light supernal of which the supreme lord is but a portion. You are he whom the gods themselves are not able to praise fully. How then can I, a mere creature, describe you? [. . .] Please forgive this creature, you who are eminent among the forgiving! You are the support of the whole world; this is but a feeble snake. Crushed by your foot, he will soon die! How can this weak, lowly snake compare with you, the refuge of all beings? Both hate and love are within the province of the superior, O imperishable one.[146] Therefore be gracious to this snake who is sinking fast, O master of the world. Our husband is dying! O lord of creation, grant us his life as alms! [. . .]

Then Kaliya himself begged for mercy: "I am not capable of honoring nor of praising you, overlord of the gods, but please take pity on me, O god whose sole thought is compassion! The race of snakes into which I was born is a cruel one; this is its proper nature. But I am not at fault in this matter, Krishna, for it is you who pour forth and absorb the whole world; classes, forms and natures have been assigned by you, the creator. [. . .] Now I am powerless, having lost my poison. You have subdued me, Krishna; now spare my life! Tell me what to do!"

"Leave the waters of the Yamuna river, snake, and return to the ocean, along with your children and wives. And in the sea, O serpent, when the eagle Garuda, enemy of snakes, sees my footprints on your head, he will not harm you." So speaking, Krishna released the serpent king, who bowed to Krishna and returned to the ocean.

In the sight of all creatures, Kaliya abandoned his pool, along with his children and wives. When the snake had gone, the cowherds embraced Krishna like one re-

146. This is the same Krishna who counsels Arjuna in the *Bhagavad Gita* later in his adult life. The snake wives are praising the more majestic qualities of Krishna as a god.

turned from the dead and lovingly drenched his head with tears. Other happy cowherds with minds amazed, sang praises to Krishna, who is unwearied by action, when they saw the river water safe. Praised by the cowherd women and men for the fine deed he had done, Krishna returned to the village of Vraj.

From *Vishnu Purana* 5.7.1−25; 43−49; 54−7; 70−2; 76−83.

Adapted from C. Dimmitt and J. A. B. van Buitenen, eds. and trans. *Classical Hindu Mythology: A Reader in the Sanskrit Puranas*, 114−16. Philadelphia: Temple University Press, 1978.:

POST-READING PARS

1. How do Krishna's qualities and actions in the story compare to your list about what creates affection and respect?

Inquiry Corner

Content Question(s):	Critical Question(s):
How does Krishna approach Kaliya in a way that is powerful, compassionate, and also playful? What specific aspects of the story indicate Krishna as powerful? As playful? As compassionate?	How would you describe the relationship between religion and nature in this narrative? Critically evaluate the role of nature, animals, or other environmental aspects in this story.
Comparative Question(s):	**Connection Question(s):**
How do the qualities and actions of Krishna compare to gods and their interactions with humans from other materials we have read?	What types of relationship to nature did you grow up with? What are the secular, religious, or other frameworks you draw from in your engagements with nature?

from *Canons and Decrees of the Council of Trent*

SNAPSHOT BOX

LANGUAGE:
Ecclesiastical Latin

DATE: **1564 CE**

LOCATION: **Northern Italy**

CONTEXTUAL INFORMATION: **Official documents of the Roman Catholic Church**

TAGS: **Authority and Institution; Formations and Reformations; Identity and Self; Religion**

Introduction

In 325 CE, the Roman emperor Constantine summoned the first **Ecumenical** (worldwide) Council of Christian bishops and other leaders to settle a controversy over the relationship between the human and divine nature of Jesus Christ. Meeting in the Asian city of Nicaea (contemporary Iznik, Turkey)—the council produced a statement of belief (the Nicene Creed) that sought agreement about the Church's teaching on this issue. Although the dual nature of Christ continued to be the subject of highly contested debate, Constantine's council had established a model for responding to any critical issues that faced the early Christian community. Over subsequent centuries, emperors continued to follow his example of summoning councils when confronted with critical religious decisions. With the seventh such council—also held in Nicaea in 787 CE—Christian leaders in the Later Roman (Byzantine) Empire declared that the period of **conciliar** legislation had ended and that the entirety of the **Orthodox** (correct) Christian faith had been determined. Nothing else could be added or adjudicated.

In the early twelfth century, however, Christians in western Europe (Roman Catholic Christianity) revived the conciliar tradition under the authority of the pope, the bishop of Rome, rather than the emperor. In addition to determining questions about Catholic faith and practice, these councils often considered issues of clerical "discipline" as well, that is to say issues regarding the responsibilities of bishops, priests, and other church leaders. In fact, the Council

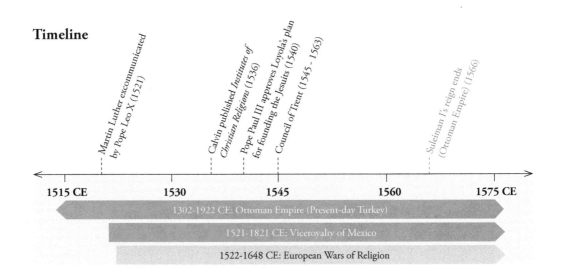

Timeline

Martin Luther excommunicated by Pope Leo X (1521)

Calvin published *Institutes of Christian Religion* (1536)

Pope Paul III approves Loyola's plan for founding the Jesuits (1540)

Council of Trent (1545 - 1563)

Suleiman I's reign ends (Ottoman Empire) (1566)

1515 CE   1530   1545   1560   1575 CE

1302-1922 CE: Ottoman Empire (Present-day Turkey)

1521-1821 CE: Viceroyalty of Mexico

1522-1648 CE: European Wars of Religion

of Constance (1414–1418 CE) was summoned by the political leaders of western Europe to settle a particularly difficult issue of discipline. Through a series of political fights over power, two and later three men claimed to be the legitimate pope — one reigned in Rome, one in Avignon, France, and one in Pisa, Italy. To end this **Great Western Schism**, the political leaders at the Council of Constance deposed all three popes and further decreed that councils were thereby superior to popes. This made future popes very reluctant to summon councils that might override their power, even as issues regarding both doctrine and discipline became very problematic again by the early sixteenth century. The failure of the popes to address needed reforms through a council was one of the reasons that Martin Luther's objections to the granting of **indulgences** (certificates forgiving sins) sparked the religious and political upheaval that became the Protestant Reformation.

Luther's *Ninety-Five Theses* of 1517 CE invited Church authorities to debate only the issue of indulgences, which he believed appropriated the prerogative of God alone to forgive sins, but other challenges immediately arose. Luther based his arguments on his interpretation of the Bible and rejected the Church's argument that Sacred Tradition was equal to the Sacred Scriptures; this became the Protestant idea of *sola scriptura* (authority based on "scripture alone"). On the issue of forgiveness, or the "justification" of sinful humans in the eyes of God, Luther proposed that God's "grace alone" (*sola gratia*) was sufficient, and that human beings could do nothing to influence God's decision. Such an idea would end not only the granting of indulgences in exchange for donations to the Church but also devotional practices such as pilgrimage, praying to departed saints or in the presence of their relics, or any activity intended to impress God with one's righteousness.

Not until 1545 CE did a pope finally summon a council to address the serious challenge that the Protestant Reformation — which now extended far beyond Luther — had brought to the Roman Catholic Church. With political states throughout central and western Europe adopting a variety of Christian beliefs and practices proposed by numerous other reformers who followed Luther's basic arguments, the council opened its sessions in the imperial city of Trent in the Italian Alps. The council itself was in part a response to sola scriptura; as it had done many times in the past the Catholic Church would rely on the teachings and traditions established by previous councils to supplement and extend biblical teachings. On the issue of justification, the council fathers agreed that grace was ultimately a gift bestowed by God at his own pleasure but also argued that God nevertheless had established certain actions (such as the seven sacraments or pious acts such as pilgrimage) that helped one to accept such grace. Is it possible to retain the idea of divine sovereignty (i.e., that God has complete control over all things) with the ability of humans to act freely? If human beings have no free will, how will they be held responsible for their actions?

Rodger Payne
Department of Religious Studies

from *Canons and Decrees at the Council of Trent*

Decree Concerning Justification

Introduction

Since there is being disseminated at this time, not without the loss of many souls and grievous detriment to the unity of the Church, a certain erroneous doctrine concerning justification, the holy, ecumenical and general Council of Trent, lawfully assembled in the Holy Ghost, . . . intends, for the praise and glory of Almighty God, for the tranquility of the Church and the salvation of souls, to expound to all the faithful of Christ the true and salutary doctrine of justification, which the Sun of justice, Jesus Christ, the author and finisher of our faith taught, which the Apostles transmitted and which the Catholic Church under the inspiration of the Holy Ghost has always retained; strictly forbidding that anyone henceforth presume to believe, preach or teach otherwise than is defined and declared in the present decree.

Chapter I:
The Impotency of Nature and of the Law to Justify Man

The holy council declares first, that for a correct and clear understanding of the doctrine of justification, it is necessary that each one recognize and confess that since all men had lost innocence in the prevarication of Adam, having become unclean, and, as the Apostle [Paul] says, by nature children of wrath, as has been set forth in the decree on original sin, they were so far the servants of sin and under the power of the devil and of death, that not only the Gentiles by the force of nature, but not even the Jews by the very letter of the law of Moses, were able to be liberated or to rise therefrom, though free will, weakened as it was in its powers and downward bent, was by no means extinguished in them.

Chapter II:
The Dispensation and Mystery of the Advent of Christ

Whence it came to pass that the heavenly Father, the Father of mercies and the God of all comfort, when the blessed fullness of the time was come, sent to men Jesus

Christ, His own Son, who had both before the law and during the time of the law[147] been announced and promised to many of the holy fathers, that he might redeem the Jews who were under the law, and that the Gentiles who followed not after justice might attain to justice, and that all men might receive the adoption of sons. Him has God proposed as a propitiator[148] through faith in his blood for our sins, and not for our sins only, but also for those of the whole world.

Chapter III: Who Are Justified Through Christ

But though He died for all yet all do not receive the benefit of His death, but those only to whom the merit of His passion is communicated; because as truly as men would not be born unjust, if they were not born through propagation of the seed of Adam, since by that propagation they contract through him, when they are conceived, injustice as their own, so if they were not born again in Christ, they would never be justified, since in that new birth there is bestowed upon them, through the merit of His passion, the grace by which they are made just. For this benefit the Apostle [Paul] exhorts us always to give thanks to the Father, who hath made us worthy to be partakers of the lot of the saints in light, and hath delivered us from the power of darkness, and hath translated us into the kingdom of the Son of his love, in whom we have redemption and remission of sins.

[...]

Chapter V: On the Necessity of Preparation for Justification in Adults, and Whence it Proceeds

It is furthermore declared that in adults the beginning of that justification must proceed from the predisposing grace of God through Jesus Christ, that is, from His vocation, whereby, without any merits on their part, they are called; that they who by sin had been cut off from God, may be disposed through His quickening[149] and helping grace to convert themselves to their own justification by freely assenting to and cooperating with that grace; so that, while God touches the heart of man through the illumination of the Holy Ghost, man himself neither does absolutely nothing while receiving that inspiration, since he can also reject it, nor yet is he able by his own free will and without the grace of God to move himself to justice in His sight. . . .

[...]

147. "Law" here means the Jewish Torah which, according to the Bible, came from God through Moses.

148. One who appeases or placates a deity.

149. Bringing to life; vitalizing.

*Chapter VII: In What the Justification of the Sinner Consists,
and What are its Causes*

This disposition or preparation is followed by justification itself, which is not only a remission of sins but also the sanctification[150] and renewal of the inward man through the voluntary reception of the grace and gifts whereby an unjust man becomes just and from being an enemy becomes a friend, that he may be an heir according to hope of life everlasting. The causes of this justification are: the final cause is the glory of God and of Christ and life everlasting; the efficient cause is the merciful God who washes and sanctifies gratuitously, signing and anointing with the holy Spirit of promise, who is the pledge of our inheritance; the meritorious cause is His most beloved only begotten, Our Lord Jesus Christ, who, when we were enemies, for the exceeding charity wherewith he loved us, merited for us justification by His most holy passion on the wood of the cross and made satisfaction for us to God the Father, the instrumental cause is the sacrament of baptism, which is the sacrament of faith, without which no man was ever justified; finally, the single formal cause is the justice of God, not that by which He Himself is just, but that by which He makes us just, that, namely, with which we being endowed by Him, are renewed in the spirit of our mind; and not only are we reputed but we are truly called and are just, receiving justice within us, each one according to his own measure, which the Holy Ghost distributes to everyone as He wills, and according to each one's disposition and cooperation.[151] For though no one can be just except he to whom the merits of the passion of Our Lord Jesus Christ are communicated, yet this takes place in that justification of the sinner, when by the merit of the most holy passion, the charity of God is poured forth by the Holy Ghost in the hearts of those who are justified and inheres in them; whence man through Jesus Christ, in whom he is ingrafted, receives in that justification, together with the remission of sins, all these infused at the same time, namely, faith, hope and charity. For faith, unless hope and charity be added to it, neither unites man perfectly with Christ nor makes him a living member of His body. For which reason it is most truly said that faith without works is dead....

    [...]

*Chapter VIII: How the Gratuitous Justification of the Sinner
by Faith is to be Understood*

But when the Apostle [Paul] says that man is justified by faith and freely, these words are to be understood in that sense in which the uninterrupted unanimity of the Catholic Church has held and expressed them, namely, that we are therefore said to be justified by faith, because faith is the beginning of human salvation, the foundation and root of all justification, without which it is impossible to please God

---

150. Making holy or sacred.
151. Note the influence of Aristotle on these "causes."

and to come to the fellowship of His sons; and we are therefore said to be justified gratuitously, because none of those things that precede justification, whether faith or works, merit the grace of justification. For, if by grace, it is not now by works, otherwise, as the Apostle [Paul] says, grace is no more grace.

[...]

Chapter X: On the Increase of Justification Received

Having, therefore, been thus justified and made the friends and domestics of God, advancing from virtue to virtue, they are renewed, as the Apostle [Paul] says, day by day, that is, mortifying the members of their flesh, and presenting them as instruments of justice unto sanctification, they, through the observance of the commandments of God and of the Church, faith cooperating with good works, increase in that justice received through the grace of Christ and are further justified. . . .

Chapter XI: On Keeping the Commandments, and on the Necessity and Possibility Thereof

But no one, however much justified, should consider himself exempt from the observance of the commandments; no one should use that rash statement, once forbidden by the Fathers under anathema,[152] that the observance of the commandments of God is impossible for one that is justified. For God does not command impossibilities, but by commanding admonishes thee to do what thou canst and to pray for what thou canst not, and aids thee that thou mayest be able. His commandments are not heavy, and his yoke is sweet and burden light. For they who are the sons of God love Christ, but they who love Him, keep His commandments, as He Himself testifies; which, indeed, with the divine help they can do. For though during this mortal life, men, however holy and just, fall at times into at least light and daily sins, which are also called venial, they do not on that account cease to be just, for that petition of the just, forgive us our trespasses, is both humble and true; for which reason the just ought to feel themselves the more obliged to walk in the way of justice, for being now freed from sin and made servants of God, they are able, living soberly, justly and godly, to proceed onward through Jesus Christ, by whom they have access unto this grace. For God does not forsake those who have been once justified by His grace, unless He be first forsaken by them. Wherefore, no one ought to flatter himself with faith alone, thinking that by faith alone he is made an heir and will obtain the inheritance, even though he suffer not with Christ, that he may be also glorified with him. . . .

152. Formal condemnation.

Chapter XII: Rash Presumption of Predestination is to be Avoided

No one, moreover, so long as he lives this mortal life, ought in regard to the sacred mystery of divine predestination, so far presume as to state with absolute certainty that he is among the number of the predestined, as if it were true that the one justified either cannot sin any more, or, if he does sin, that he ought to promise himself an assured repentance. For except by special revelation, it cannot be known whom God has chosen to Himself.

[...]

Chapter XVI: The Fruits of Justification, that is, the Merit of Good Works, and the Nature of that Merit

Therefore, to men justified in this manner, whether they have preserved uninterruptedly the grace received or recovered it when lost, are to be pointed out the words of the Apostle [Paul]: Abound in every good work, knowing that your labor is not in vain in the Lord. For God is not unjust, that he should forget your work, and the love which you have shown in his name; and, Do not lose your confidence, which hath a great reward. Hence, to those who work well unto the end and trust in God, eternal life is to be offered, both as a grace mercifully promised to the sons of God through Christ Jesus, and as a reward promised by God Himself, to be faithfully given to their good works and merits. . . .

[...]

Decree Concerning Purgatory

Since the Catholic Church, instructed by the Holy Ghost, has, following the sacred writings and the ancient tradition of the Fathers, taught in sacred councils and very recently in this ecumenical council that there is a purgatory, and that the souls there detained are aided by the suffrages of the faithful and chiefly by the acceptable sacrifice of the altar,[153] the holy council commands the bishops that they strive diligently to the end that the sound doctrine of purgatory, transmitted by the Fathers and sacred councils, be believed and maintained by the faithful of Christ, and be everywhere taught and preached. The more difficult and subtle questions, however, and those that do not make for edification and from which there is for the most part no increase in piety, are to be excluded from popular instructions to uneducated people. Likewise, things that are uncertain or that have the appearance of falsehood they shall not permit to be made known publicly and discussed. But those things that tend to a certain kind of curiosity or superstition, or that savor of filthy lucre,[154] they shall prohibit as scandals and stumbling blocks to the faithful. The bishops

153. The Eucharist (Holy Communion).
154. Money obtained through dishonest or immoral means.

shall see to it that the suffrages of the living, that is, the sacrifice of the mass, prayers, alms and other works of piety which they have been accustomed to perform for the faithful departed, be piously and devoutly discharged in accordance with the laws of the Church, and that whatever is due on their behalf from testamentary bequests or other ways, be discharged by the priests and ministers of the Church and others who are bound to render this service not in a perfunctory manner, but diligently and accurately.

On the Invocation, Veneration, and Relics of Saints, and on Sacred Images

The holy council commands all bishops and others who hold the office of teaching and have charge of the *cura animarum* ["cure of souls"] that in accordance with the usage of the Catholic and Apostolic Church, received from the primitive times of the Christian religion, and with the unanimous teaching of the holy Fathers and the decrees of sacred councils, they above all instruct the faithful diligently in matters relating to intercession and invocation of the saints, the veneration of relics, and the legitimate use of images, teaching them that the saints who reign together with Christ offer up their prayers to God for men, that it is good and beneficial suppliantly to invoke them and to have recourse to their prayers, assistance and support in order to obtain favors from God through His Son, Jesus Christ Our Lord, who alone is our redeemer and saviour; and that they think impiously who deny that the saints who enjoy eternal happiness in heaven are to be invoked, or who assert that they do not pray for men, or that our invocation of them to pray for each of us individually is idolatry, or that it is opposed to the word of God and inconsistent with the honor of the one mediator of God and men, Jesus Christ, or that it is foolish to pray vocally or mentally to those who reign in heaven. Also, that the holy bodies of the holy martyrs and of others living with Christ, which were the living members of Christ and the temple of the Holy Ghost, to be awakened by Him to eternal life[155] and to be glorified, are to be venerated by the faithful, through which many benefits are bestowed by God on men, so that those who maintain that veneration and honor are not due to the relics of the saints, or that these and other memorials are honored by the faithful without profit, and that the places dedicated to the memory of the saints for the purpose of obtaining their aid are visited in vain, are to be utterly condemned, as the Church has already long since condemned and now again condemns them. Moreover, that the images of Christ, of the Virgin Mother of God, and of the other saints are to be placed and retained especially in the churches, and that due honor and veneration is to be given them; not, however, that any divinity or virtue is believed to be in them by reason of which they are to be venerated, or that something is to be asked of them, or that trust is to be placed in images, as was done of old by the Gentiles who

155. Bodily resurrection.

placed their hope in idols; but because the honor which is shown them is referred to the prototypes which they represent, so that by means of the images which we kiss and before which we uncover the head and prostrate ourselves, we adore Christ and venerate the saints whose likeness they bear. That is what was defined by the decrees of the councils, especially of the Second Council of Nicaea, against the opponents of images. Moreover, let the bishops diligently teach that by means of the stories of the mysteries of our redemption portrayed in paintings and other representations the people are instructed and confirmed in the articles of faith, which ought to be borne in mind and constantly reflected upon; also that great profit is derived from all holy images, not only because the people are thereby reminded of the benefits and gifts bestowed on them by Christ, but also because through the saints the miracles of God and salutary examples are set before the eyes of the faithful, so that they may give God thanks for those things, may fashion their own life and conduct in imitation of the saints and be moved to adore and love God and cultivate piety. But if anyone should teach or maintain anything contrary to these decrees, let him be anathema. If any abuses shall have found their way into these holy and salutary observances, the holy council desires earnestly that they be completely removed, so that no representation of false doctrines and such as might be the occasion of grave error to the uneducated be exhibited. And if at times it happens, when this is beneficial to the illiterate, that the stories and narratives of the Holy Scriptures are portrayed and exhibited, the people should be instructed that not for that reason is the divinity represented in picture as if it can be seen with bodily eyes or expressed in colors or figures.

Furthermore, in the invocation of the saints, the veneration of relics, and the sacred use of images, all superstition shall be removed, all filthy quest for gain eliminated, and all lasciviousness[156] avoided, so that images shall not be painted and adorned with a seductive charm, or the celebration of saints and the visitation of relics be perverted by the people into boisterous festivities and drunkenness, as if the festivals in honor of the saints are to be celebrated with revelry and with no sense of decency. Finally, such zeal and care should be exhibited by the bishops with regard to these things that nothing may appear that is disorderly or unbecoming and confusedly arranged, nothing that is profane, nothing disrespectful, since holiness becometh the house of God. That these things may be the more faithfully observed, the holy council decrees that no one is permitted to erect or cause to be erected in any place or church, howsoever exempt, any unusual image unless it has been approved by the bishop; also that no new miracles be accepted and no relics recognized unless they have been investigated and approved by the same bishop, who, as soon as he has obtained any knowledge of such matters, shall, after consulting theologians and other pious men, act thereon as he shall judge consonant with truth and piety. But if any doubtful or grave abuse is to be eradicated, or if indeed any graver question concerning these matters should arise, the bishop, before he settles the controversy,

---

156. Sexual desire; lust.

shall await the decision of the metropolitan[157] and of the bishops of the province in a provincial synod; so, however, that nothing new or anything that has not hitherto been in use in the Church, shall be decided upon without having first consulted the most holy Roman pontiff.

[...]

Selections from "Decree on Justification" and "Decree Concerning Purgatory." In *Dogmatic canons and decrees: Authorized translations of the dogmatic decrees of the Council of Trent, the decree on the Immaculate Conception, the Syllabus of Pope Pius IX, and the decrees of the Vatican Council*, 21–27, 29–33, 35–40, 45–46, 165–72. New York: Devin-Adair Company, 1912. Internet Archive.

POST-READING PARS

1. Identify two ways a non-Catholic or an atheist or a secularist might relate to these teachings.
2. After reading the text, identify two ways your definition of any one of the following terms changed: faith, grace, justification, original sin, merit, good works.

Inquiry Corner

Content Question(s):	Critical Question(s):
How does the council defend the use of images and the relics of the saints?	What is the view of human nature expressed in these documents? Would you describe it as pessimistic? Optimistic?
Comparative Question(s):	**Connection Question(s):**
Compare the council's understanding of good works to those expressed in Tractate Pe'ah in the Babylonian Talmud. How are they similar? How do they differ?	Does every consideration of human identity have to include a relationship to God?

---

157. An archbishop, usually one with ecclesiastical jurisdiction over a large city and/or a "province" of several subordinate dioceses.

"Canticle of the Creatures" by St. Francis of Assisi

SNAPSHOT BOX

LANGUAGE: Italian

DATE: 1225 CE

LOCATION: Italy

GENRE: Hymn

TAGS: Formations and Reformations; Mysticism; Nature and Sacred; Poetry; Ritual and Practice; Spirituality

Introduction

The man who would become Saint Francis (circa 1182–1226), one of the most widely admired figures of the western Middle Ages, was not born to the poverty he would later espouse as a radical ideal. The son of a successful merchant family, Francesco di Bernadone was born in the town of Assisi, in the region of Umbria in central Italy. As a young man Francis (as he is called by English speakers) enjoyed poetry, wore fashionable clothing, and spent money with friends. Assisi in Francis's youth was caught up in fierce jurisdictional disputes between the Holy Roman Empire and the papacy as well as internal class conflict between a newly powerful group of merchants and an older landed aristocracy. A merchant's son, Francis had upwardly mobile social ambitions of becoming a knight. At around twenty years old, he joined a losing battle with the forces of Assisi against a rival Italian city. Francis's subsequent experience as a prisoner of war for a year, including bouts of illness that he began suffering at this time, initiated what would prove to be a series of profound changes in his life.

After experiencing an unsettling dream while traveling to join a battle in 1205 CE, Francis finally abandoned his military pursuits altogether. When he returned to Assisi, he began giving away his possessions and withdrawing from his customary social circles. He took up a new life of Christian **penance**, a sacrament that for Francis involved active religious works like prayer, almsgiving, and charitable service, especially among lepers and beggars. Francis also refused money and personal property as an expression of his commitment to a way of life modeled on that of Jesus and

Timeline

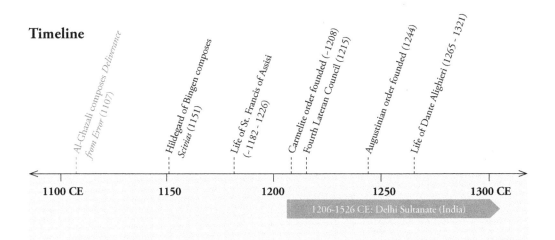

the early Christian apostles (the exact terms of this demanding commitment would be the subject of much dispute in the history of the religious order Francis founded). He accordingly renounced his inheritance rights by stripping publicly and returning the clothes off his back to his cloth merchant father. He began attracting a growing group of followers, and after an initial verbal approval from Pope Innocent III in 1209 CE, by 1215 CE, Francis and his "little brothers" were an officially recognized religious order, the Franciscans (or Order of Friars Minor). Francis's example of voluntary poverty, itinerant begging, public preaching, and service among the sick and outcast likewise appealed to Clare of Assisi (d. 1253 CE), who founded a second Franciscan order of women (the "Poor Clares" or Order of St. Clare).

In the several early biographies (*vitae*, "lives") that have been handed down to us about Francis, he is said to have fostered strikingly intimate relationships with the natural world. In one story, Francis wanders off from his colleagues on the road to preach to a group of birds, who, reportedly, listen eagerly. Other stories relate how Francis rescued trapped or displaced animals, unhooking caught fish and releasing captured rabbits and counseling them to avoid getting caught again, or moving worms off the road so they would not be trampled. Francis and his followers also sought to learn from animals, for example how they foraged for food, or how they received it when it was given to them. Francis seems to have recognized a limit to human cultivation and use of the natural world, counseling gardeners to leave the edges of their plots undisturbed, so as to allow for the growth of wild flowers and grasses. One story gives us a playful sense of Francis's imagination for nonhuman perspectives: in the live manger scene he famously organized to restage the birth of Jesus (a tradition he is credited with inventing), he is said to have personally bleated out the word "Bethlehem" in his best dramatic imitation of a sheep.

As you approach Francis's "Canticle of the Creatures" (sometimes also called the "Canticle to Brother Sun"), consider how different aspects of Francis's biography, including his sensitivity to nature, might be at work in the poem. Note in particular how the poem, in the form of a hymn or prayer, gives expression to the idea of a "sibling" relationship to and conversation with nature. Franciscans referred to one another as "brothers": here, sun, moon, stars, wind, water, fire, and earth are addressed in similar terms. Given alternative images of natural relationships available to Francis (for example, a hierarchy of created beings), why might this choice of language matter for the poem's broader vision of human and nonhuman life? The poem's language of composition, Francis's spoken Italian **vernacular** rather than the more established literary languages of Latin or French, likewise suggests the intimacies of personal, even family, conversation. (The poem is credited with inaugurating the Italian literary tradition, perhaps among the reasons the fourteenth-century poet Dante Alighieri, likewise writing in his Italian vernacular, finds so exalted a place for Francis in canto 11 of his *Paradiso*: Dante compares Francis's birth to a rising sun over an Italian hillside.) As the "Canticle" was also apparently composed in three stages while Francis was in declining health, up to the final days of his life, note too how the poem attends to weakness, vulnerability, and death as defining aspects of life. Francis's storied affection for nature can sometimes be sentimentalized, but as you read the "Canticle," reflect on whether the poem moves beyond tender sentiment alone. Foraging like birds, begging for alms like cows being given hay in the winter, and taking shelter in caves and wooded places, Francis and his early companions were a ragged bunch. Yet in their poverty and works of charity, they sought to imitate a working relational economy that they glimpsed in the natural world. What are the insights and tensions of such an "economic" vision? What ethical, ecological, and spiritual or theological questions does this poem, which has attracted a diverse range of readers and admirers since its composition, raise for you?

William Revere
Department of English

PRE-READING PARS

1. Think of two or three popular books or movies that are in some way about the natural world. What do these stories tell us about what nature means for us now and how we imagine our place in it?

2. Would you say nature has "spiritual" or "sacred" dimensions for you? Why or why not?

"Canticle of the Creatures"

1 Most High, all-powerful, good Lord,

    Yours are *the praises, the glory,* and *the honor,* and all *blessings,*

2 To You alone, Most High, do they belong,

    and no human is worthy to mention Your name.[158]

3 Praise be to You, my *Lord,* with all *Your creatures,*

    especially Sir Brother Sun,

    Who is the day and through whom You give us light.[159]

4 And he is beautiful and radiant with great splendor;

    and bears a likeness to You, Most High One.

5 *Praised* be You, my Lord, through Sister *Moon* and *the stars,*

    in heaven You formed them clear and precious and beautiful.[160]

6 Praised be You, my Lord, through Brother Wind,

    and through the air, cloudy and serene, and every kind of weather,

    through whom You give sustenance to Your creatures.

7 *Praised* be You, my Lord, through Sister *Water,*

    who is very useful and humble and precious and chaste.

158. It would seem that in these first nine verses Francis envisioned this as a song of God's creatures in which human beings, because of sin, had no part, a theme about which he hints in other writings, e.g. [other works by Francis]. While the first verse directs praise glory, honor and blessings to God alone, a sentiment underscored in the first part of this second verse, its second part is quite clear in denying any role to a human being.

159. In Francis's use of the passive voice, "Praised be you...", and his linking the praise of the Lord with that of creatures, this verse provides many insights into the interpretation of the entire Canticle. While the sun, moon and stars, wind, water, fire, and earth may be seen as instruments of praise or as reasons for praise, praising them also implies praising the God Who created them and acknowledging that they are symbols of their Creator. Thus Francis's poetic use of adjectives is important to comprehend his images of God.

160. *Per* suggests a variety of meanings: (a) a corruption of the Latin *per,* (b) the French *pour,* or (c) the developing Italian *par.* Thus it may be translated "for" offering an attitude of thanksgiving; "by," expressing a sense of instrumentality; or "through," suggesting instrumentality and, at the same time, a deeper sense of praising God's presence in the creatures mentioned. This translation follows the last possibility based on verse 3, "Praised be you, my Lord, with all your creatures..."

8 *Praised* be You, my Lord, through Brother *Fire,*
  through whom *You light the night,*
  and he is beautiful and playful and robust and strong.
9 *Praised* be You, my Lord, through our Sister Mother *Earth,*
  who sustains and governs us,
  and who produces various *fruit* with colored flowers and *herbs.*
10 Praised be You, my Lord, through those who give pardon for Your love,
  and bear infirmity and tribulation.[161]
    11 Blessed are those who endure in peace
    for by You, Most High, shall they be crowned.
12 Praised be You, my Lord, through our Sister Bodily Death,
  from whom no one living can escape.[162]
    13 Woe to those who die in mortal sin.
    Blessed are those whom death will find in Your most holy will,
       for *the second death* shall do them no harm.[163]
14 *Praise* and *bless* my *Lord* and give Him thanks
  and serve Him with great humility.

"The Canticle of the Creatures (1225)." In *Francis of Assisi: The Early Documents*, Vol. 1, edited by Regis J. Armstrong, J. A. Wayne Hellmann, and William J. Short, 113–14. Hyde Park, NY: New City Press, 1999.

POST-READING PARS

1. Why might poetry or song be a powerful medium for exploring our relationship to the natural world?
2. What particular features of this poem's spiritual perspective stand out to you?

---

161. The second section of the Canticle introduces humanity into the praise of God. However, such praise is only achieved through identifying with the suffering Servant of God, Jesus, who endured weakness and tribulation in peace. In this way, reconciliation is achieved in light of the Paschal Mystery.

162. These two verses, 12 and 13, composed in Francis's last hours, indicate an understanding of death much different from that of [other works by Francis]. Rather than fearing death, Francis greets it as yet another expression of God's presence.

163. Fulgentius of Ruspe comments on these verses in his treatise on forgiveness: "Here on earth they are changed by the first resurrection, in which they are enlightened and converted, thus passing from death to life, sinfulness to holiness, unbelief to faith, and evil actions to holy life. For this reason the second death has no power over them... As the first resurrection consists of the conversion of the heart, so the second death consists of unending torment." (cf. Fulgentius of Ruspe, *On Forgiveness*, Liber 2, 11, 1–2,1. 3–4; *Corpus Christianorum* 91A, 693–695).

Inquiry Corner

Content Question(s):

What effect does the welcome of "Sister Bodily Death" have in a poem of praise and admiration for the natural world? Is the theme of death at odds with these other aspects of the poem, or does it in some way complement them?

Critical Question(s):

How might the "Canticle" reflect positive or negative ways in which religious traditions have shaped human relationships to the natural world?

Comparative Question(s):

Choose a text from another cultural tradition in our period that represents the natural world in some way (for example, Jagannātha's poem on the river Ganges, the "Ganga Lahari"). How does this text compare to Francis's "Canticle" in its ideas, questions, and assumptions about human relationships to nature?

Connection Question(s):

Take a look at the 2015 papal encyclical by Pope Francis, *Laudato Si': On Care for our Common Home*, which takes its title and inspiration from Francis's "Canticle". How might the "Canticle" and encyclical speak to each other and address contemporary ecological concerns?

Oration on the Dignity of Man by Giovanni Pico della Mirandola

SNAPSHOT BOX

LANGUAGE: Latin

DATE: 1486 CE

LOCATION: Italy

GENRE: Philosophy

ETHNIC IDENTITY: Italian

TAGS: Humanism; Identity and Self; Mysticism; Orality; Philosophy; Religion; Ways of Knowing

Introduction

The *Oration on the Dignity of Man* by Giovanni Pico della Mirandola (1463–1494 CE), commonly referred to as Pico, is the most well-known philosophical work of the Italian Renaissance, although it was not published during its author's tragically short life. Pico wrote the oration in 1486 CE, at the age of twenty-three, intending to deliver it as the opening speech of a conference in Rome, in front of the most learned theologians and philosophers of western (Latin) Christendom. Pico intended to fund this gathering himself, as he was a wealthy young nobleman. The goal of the conference, as introduced in the *Oration*, was to show how the ancient philosophical traditions of the world (as he knew it) — despite their seeming contradictions and often mysterious meanings — contained ancient wisdom in harmony with Christianity.

Pico's method was rooted in the scholarly practice now known as ***Renaissance humanism***, which historian Peter Burke has defined as the movement to recover, interpret, and assimilate the language, literature, learning, and values of ancient Greece and Rome. The humanists, beginning in fourteenth-century Italy, looked back to the ancient Roman Republic and found its civilization — its political power, civic virtue, and artistic production — superior to Italy in their time in all ways but one: the Roman Republic had lacked the light of Christianity. To revive the spirit of ancient Rome (**Renaissance** literally means rebirth), these humanists called for a new form of education based on the studies of humanity (*studia humanitatis*),

Timeline

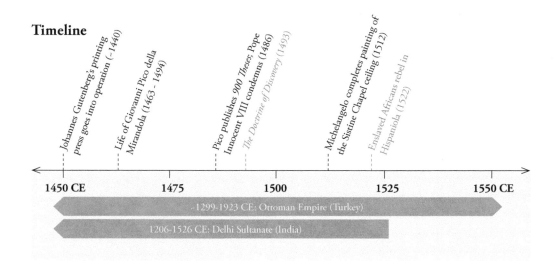

emphasizing five subjects: grammar (the study of languages), rhetoric, poetry, history, and moral philosophy (ethics). These subjects would form the core of what we now call the **humanities**. How does this compare with your understanding of the humanities?

Pico had studied in many of the greatest universities in Europe: Bologna (the oldest university in Europe), Padua, Pavia, and Paris. There he learned the practice of **disputation** (organized, public academic debate on a set topic) and mastered the fundamental scholastic texts by Thomas Aquinas (1225–1274 CE) and others who had attempted to reconcile Christian theology with the ancient Greek (and pagan) philosopher Aristotle (384–322 BCE) and his Arabic-language (mostly Muslim) commentators.

Pico added Renaissance humanist practices to his methods of philosophical studies. Renaissance humanism based its hermeneutic practice on the principle of "back to the sources" (*ad fontes*, in Latin). This meant that in order to truly understand a text, one must read it in its original language and place it within its historical context. Whereas Aquinas and other late-medieval scholastics worked with ancient Greek and later Arabic texts only in Latin translation, Pico set out to learn Greek and Arabic so that he could read these texts in their original languages. He was also one of the first Christian intellectuals since late antiquity to learn Hebrew, which he did by seeking out Jewish teachers—who were excluded from all levels of Christian education. How might your understanding shift if you were able to read a text in its original language?

In 1484, Pico traveled to Florence and met the philosopher Marsilio Ficino (1433–1499), the leader of the Platonic Academy, an advanced circle of humanists reviving the language and literature of ancient Greece. The Academy was funded by Lorenzo de' Medici, the political leader of Florence, who befriended Pico and became his protector. Ficino introduced Pico to the **prisca theologia** (ancient theology), the doctrine that there is a single, true theology that God revealed to humanity through the mystical writings of the ancient religions. These texts are the sources of many of the obscure references Pico cites throughout his *Oration*. These references include Hermes Trismegistus (a Greek source reflecting Egyptian wisdom they thought was older than Moses), the Chaldean Oracles (which they associated with the ancient Persians and Zoroaster), and the Greek philosophers and gods (including Pythagoras, the Delphic Oracles, Socrates, Plato, and the later Neoplatonists). Most novel, however, is Pico's use of *Kabbalah*, the tradition of Jewish mysticism, which we can see reflected in his elaboration of the celestial hierarchy of angels.

Pico's ambitious conference proposal, however, was not well received by Pope Innocent VIII, who called off the conference and summoned inquisitors to judge the orthodoxy of Pico's work. Pico spent his remaining years defending himself against charges of heresy and continuing his philosophical studies. He died suddenly in Florence, in 1494 CE, at the age of thirty-one, under mysterious circumstances. In 2007 his exhumed body revealed that he was poisoned by arsenic.

Despite the obscure references in the *Oration*, at least three related themes resonate to this day and deserve close inspection. The first is in the famous title, which would be translated more accurately — and notably less gendered — as *Oration on Human Dignity*. What defines human dignity? The second is humanity's place on the Chain of Being. What makes humanity special and distinct from the rest of creation? And third is the concept of "self-fashioning," the process of self-consciously creating one's identity, which scholar Stephen Greenblatt has identified as a hallmark of Renaissance culture — as one may see reflected in the characters of Shakespeare. As you read Pico's *Oration*, consider the limits on your ability to "fashion thyself."

Gregory Lyon
Humanities Program

PRE-READING PARS

1. List two characteristics that make a human being special and distinct from other creatures.

2. List two phrases you would use to describe what "human dignity" means.

3. What are a couple of ways that each of us "fashions" our identity—that is, how we might present or reveal our "self" to others?

Oration on the Dignity of Man

I have read in the records of the Arabians, reverend Fathers, that Abdala the Saracen,[164] when questioned as to what on this stage of the world, as it were, could be seen most worthy of wonder, replied: "There is nothing to be seen more wonderful than man." In agreement with this opinion is the saying of Hermes Trismegistus: "A great miracle, Asclepius, is man."[165] But when I weighed the reason for these maxims, the many grounds for the excellence of human nature reported by many men failed to satisfy me—that man is the intermediary between creatures, the intimate of the gods, the king of the lower beings, by the acuteness of his senses, by the discernment of his reason, and by the light of his intelligence the interpreter of nature, the interval between fixed eternity and fleeting time, and (as the Persians say) the bond, nay, rather, the marriage song of the world, on David's testimony but little lower than the angels.[166] Admittedly great though these reasons be, they are not the principal grounds, that is, those which may rightfully claim for themselves the privilege of the highest admiration. For why should we not admire more the angels themselves and the blessed choirs of heaven? At last it seems to me I have come to understand why man is the most fortunate of creatures and consequently worthy of all admiration and what precisely is that rank which is his lot in the universal chain of Being—a rank to be envied not only by brutes but even by the stars and by minds beyond this world. It is a matter past faith and a wondrous one. Why should it not be? For it is on this very ac-

164. The identity of this "Abdala the Saracen" and the source of Pico's story about him remain a topic of scholarly debate.

165. Hermes Trismegistus (Thrice-Great Hermes) was thought to be the Greek name for the Egyptian god Thot (Mercury in Latin), the inventor of writing, the god of occult philosophy and sciences (such as alchemy, astrology, and magic), and a contemporary of Moses whose works revealed the *prisca theologia* (ancient theology) and prefigured the coming of Christ. In the Hermetic texts, Asclepius is one of Hermes's students and shares a name with the Greek god of medicine.

166. David is the traditional author of many of the Psalms. See Psalms 8:3–7: "When I consider thy heavens, the work of thy fingers, the moon and the stars, which thou hast ordained; What is man, that thou art mindful of him? and the son of man, that thou visitest him? For thou hast made him a little lower than the angels, and hast crowned him with glory and honor" (KJV).

count that man is rightly called and judged a great miracle and a wonderful creature indeed.

But hear, Fathers, exactly what this rank is and, as friendly auditors, conformably to your kindness, do me this favor. God the Father, the supreme Architect, had already built this cosmic home we behold, the most sacred temple of His godhead, by the laws of His mysterious wisdom. The region above the heavens He had adorned with Intelligences,[167] the heavenly spheres He had quickened with eternal souls, and the excrementary and filthy parts of the lower world He had! filled with a multitude of animals of every kind. But, when the work was finished, the Craftsman kept wishing that there were someone to ponder the plan of so great a work, to love its beauty, and to wonder at its vastness. Therefore, when everything was done (as Moses and Timaeus bear witness),[168] He finally took thought concerning the creation of man. But there was not among His archetypes that from which He could fashion a new offspring, nor was there in His treasure-houses anything which He might bestow on His new son as an inheritance, nor was there in the seats of all the world a place where the latter might sit to contemplate the universe. All was now complete; all things had been assigned to the highest, the middle, and the lowest orders. But in its final creation it was not the part of the Father's power to fail as though exhausted. It was not the part of His wisdom to waver in a needful matter through poverty of counsel. It was not the part of His kindly love that he who was to praise God's divine generosity in regard to others should be compelled to condemn it in regard to himself.

At last the best of artisans ordained that that creature to whom He had been able to give nothing proper to himself should have joint possession of whatever had been peculiar to each of the different kinds of being.[169] He therefore took man as a creature of indeterminate nature and, assigning him a place in the middle of the world, addressed him thus: "Neither a fixed abode nor a form that is thine alone nor any function peculiar to thyself have we given thee, Adam, to the end that according to thy longing and according to thy judgment thou mayest have and possess what abode, what form, and what functions thou thyself shalt desire. The nature of all other beings is limited and constrained within the bounds of laws prescribed by Us. Thou, constrained by no limits, in accordance with thine own free will, in whose hand We have placed thee, shalt ordain for thyself the limits of thy nature. We have set thee at the world's center that thou mayest from thence more easily observe whatever is in the world. We have made thee neither of heaven nor of earth, neither mortal nor immortal, so that with freedom of choice and with honor, as though the maker and

167. The idea that the celestial spheres were moved by divine Intelligences can be traced back to Aristotle. In the Christian tradition these Intelligences become identified with the angels.

168. Here Pico cites the creation stories in both the biblical book of Genesis (attributed to Moses) and Plato's dialogue, *Timaeus*.

169. Pico here is describing man as the *microcosm*, containing within himself a reflection of all creation outside himself (the *macrocosm*). Pico's contemporary, Leonardo da Vinci, sketched this idea of humanity in the microcosm-macrocosm analogy with his *Vitruvian Man* (circa 1490).

molder of thyself, thou mayest fashion thyself in whatever shape thou shalt prefer. Thou shalt have the power to degenerate into the lower forms of life, which are brutish. Thou shalt have the power, out of thy soul's judgment, to be reborn into the higher forms, which are divine."

O supreme generosity of God the Father, O highest and most marvelous felicity of man! To him it is granted to have whatever he chooses, to be whatever he wills. Beasts as soon as they are born (so says Lucilius)[170] bring with them from their mother's womb all they will ever possess. Spiritual beings, either from the beginning or soon thereafter, become what they are to be forever and ever. On man when he came into life the Father conferred the seeds of all kinds and the germs of every way of life. Whatever seeds each man cultivates will grow to maturity and bear in him their own fruit. If they be vegetative, he will be like a plant. If sensitive, he will become brutish. If rational, he will grow into a heavenly being. If intellectual, he will be an angel and the son of God. And if, happy in the lot of no created thing, he withdraws into the center of his own unity, his spirit, made one with God, in the solitary darkness of God, who is set above all things, shall surpass them all. Who would not admire this our chameleon? Or who could more greatly admire aught else whatever? It is man who Asclepius of Athens, arguing from his mutability of character and from his self-transforming nature, on just grounds says was symbolized by Proteus in the mysteries. Hence those metamorphoses renowned among the Hebrews and the Pythagoreans.[171]

For the occult theology of the Hebrews sometimes transforms the holy Enoch into an angel of divinity whom they call "Mal'akh Adonay Shebaoth," and sometimes transforms others into other divinities.[172] The Pythagoreans degrade impious men into brutes and, if one is to believe Empedocles, even into plants. Mohammed, in imitation, often had this saying on his tongue: "They who have deviated from divine law become beasts,"[173] and surely he spoke justly. For it is not the bark that makes the plant but its senseless and insentient nature; neither is it the hide that makes the beast of burden but its irrational, sensitive soul; neither is it the orbed form that makes the heavens but its undeviating order; nor is it the sundering from body but his spiritual intelligence that makes the angel. For if you see one abandoned to his appetites crawling on the ground, it is a plant and not a man you see; if you see one blinded by

---

170. Gaius Lucilius (circa 180–circa 103 BCE) was an early Roman satiric poet, whose works survive only in fragments quoted by later Latin writers.

171. Within two sentences Pico has brought together four sources of *prisca theologia* (ancient theology) regarding man's ability to transform into any creature in the Chain of Being: the Hermetic texts ("Asclepius"), the Orphic Hymns ("Proteus"), Kabbalah or Jewish mysticism ("Hebrews"), and occult numerology ("Pythagoreans," via Neoplatonic philosophers).

172. Pico is referring to Kabbalah or Jewish mysticism in this passage, but his source remains unidentified.

173. Pico had been learning Arabic and had recently borrowed a Latin translation of the Qur'an from his friend Marsilio Ficino.

the vain illusions of imagery, as it were of Calypso, and, softened by their gnawing allurement, delivered over to his senses, it is a beast and not a man you see.[174] If you see a philosopher determining all things by means of right reason, him you shall reverence: he is a heavenly being and not of this earth. If you see a pure contemplator, one unaware of the body and confined to the inner reaches of the mind, he is neither an earthly nor a heavenly being; he is a more reverend divinity vested with human flesh.

Are there any who would not admire man, who is, in the sacred writings of Moses and the Christians, not without reason described sometimes by the name of "all flesh," sometimes by that of "every creature," inasmuch as he himself molds, fashions, and changes himself into the form of all flesh and into the character of every creature? For this reason the Persian Euanthes,[175] in describing the Chaldaean theology, writes that man has no semblance that is inborn and his very own but many that are external and foreign to him; whence this saying of the Chaldaeans: "Hanorish tharah sharinas," that is, "Man is a being of varied, manifold, and inconstant nature." But why do we emphasize this? To the end that after we have been born to this condition—that we can become what we will—we should understand that we ought to have especial care to this, that it should never be said against us that, although born to a privileged position, we failed to recognize it and became like unto wild animals and senseless beasts of burden but that rather the saying of Asaph the prophet should apply: "Ye are all angels and sons of the Most High,"[176] and that we may not, by abusing the most indulgent generosity of the Father, make for ourselves that freedom of choice He has given into something harmful instead of salutary. Let a certain holy ambition invade our souls, so that, not content with the mediocre, we shall pant after the highest and (since we may if we wish) toil with all our strength to obtain it.

Let us disdain earthly things, despise heavenly things, and, finally, esteeming less whatever is of the world, hasten to that court which is beyond the world and nearest to the Godhead. There, as the sacred mysteries relate, Seraphim, Cherubim, and Thrones hold the first places;[177] let us, incapable of yielding to them, and intolerant

174. In Homer's *Odyssey*, Calypso enchants Odysseus with her singing and compels him to stay with her for seven years.

175. Pico had also been learning Aramaic—which he erroneously calls Chaldaean (also spelled "Chaldean")—when he wrote the *Oration*. His source Euanthes and the quotation remain unidentified. The "Chaldaean theology" may refer to the so-called *Chaldean Oracles*, a fragmentary collection in Greek of Babylonian or Persian theosophical poems of unknown origin. Pico and other Renaissance humanists typically conflate this tradition with that of the Persian Zoroaster.

176. Asaph is one of the Psalmists. See Psalms 82:6: "I have said, Ye are gods; and all of you are children of the most High" (KJV).

177. The traditional Christian hierarchy of the angels was developed by the mystical theologian Pseudo-Dionysius the Areopagite (late 5th century to early 6th century CE) from Aristotle's and later Neoplatonic philosophers' theories of the divine Intelligences. There are nine ranks of angels, grouped into three orders (from highest to lowest): Seraphim, Cherubim, Thrones; Dominions, Virtues, Powers; Principalities, Archangels, and Angels.

of a lower place, emulate their dignity and their glory. If we have willed it, we shall be second to them in nothing.

[...]

Then let us fill our well-prepared and purified soul with the light of natural philosophy, so that we may at last perfect her in the knowledge of things divine. And lest we be satisfied with those of our faith, let us consult the patriarch Jacob, whose form gleams carved on the throne of glory. Sleeping in the lower world but keeping watch in the upper, the wisest of fathers will advise us. But he will advise us through a figure (in this way everything was wont to come to those men) that there is a ladder extending from the lowest earth to the highest heaven, divided in a series of many steps. with the Lord seated at the top, and angels in contemplation ascending and descending over them alternately by turns.[178]

11. If this is what we must practice in our aspiration to the angelic way of life, I ask: "Who will touch the ladder of the Lord either with fouled foot or with unclean hands?" As the sacred mysteries have it, it is impious for the impure to touch the pure. But what are these feet? What these hands? Surely the foot of the soul is that most contemptible part by which the soul rests on matter as on the soil of the earth, I mean the nourishing and feeding power, the tinder of lust, and the teacher of pleasurable weakness. Why should we not call the hands of the soul its irascible power, which struggles on its behalf as the champion of desire and as plunderer seizes in the dust and sun what desire will devour slumbering in the shade? These hands, these feet, that is, all the sentient part whereon resides the attraction of the body which, as they say, by wrenching the neck holds the soul in check, lest we be hurled down from the ladder as impious and unclean, let us bathe in moral philosophy as if in a living river. Yet this will not be enough if we wish to be companions of the angels going up and down on Jacob's ladder, unless we have first been well fitted and instructed to be promoted duly from step to step, to stray nowhere from the stairway, and to engage in the alternate comings and goings. Once we have achieved this by the art of discourse or reasoning, then, inspired by the Cherubic spirit, using philosophy through the steps of the ladder, that is, of nature, and penetrating all things from center to center, we shall sometimes descend, with titanic force rending the unity like Osiris into many parts, and we shall sometimes ascend, with the force of Phoebus collecting the parts like the limbs of Osiris into a unity, until, resting at last in the bosom of the Father who is above the ladder, we shall be made perfect with the felicity of theology.[179]

[...]

16. But indeed not only the Mosaic and Christian mysteries but also the theology

178. Pico is tying the biblical story of Jacob's ladder (Genesis 28:10–17) to his theory of man's relationship ro the angels on the Chain of Being.

179. Pico is recalling the story of Osiris, the Egyptian god of the dead, who was killed and cut into pieces by his brother Set. Isis, his wife, found his body and wrapped the pieces back together, enabling him to come back to life. Pico mixes myths by inserting Phoebus (also known as Apollo), the Greek sun god.

of the ancients show us the benefits and value of the liberal arts, the discussion of which I am about to undertake. For what else did the degrees of the initiates observed in the mysteries of the Greeks mean? For they arrived at a perception of the mysteries when they had first been purified through those expiatory sciences, as it were, moral philosophy and dialectic. What else can that perception possibly be than an interpretation of occult nature by means of philosophy? Then at length to those who were so disposed came that *epopteia*,[180] that is to say, the observation of things divine by the light of theology. Who would not long to be initiated into such sacred rites? Who would not desire, by neglecting all human concerns, by despising the goods of fortune, and by disregarding those of the body, to become the guest of the gods while yet living on earth, and, made drunk by the nectar of eternity, to be endowed with the gifts of immortality though still a mortal being? Who would not wish to be so inflamed with those Socratic frenzies sung by Plato in the *Phaedrus*, that, by the oarage of feet and wings escaping speedily from hence, that is, from a world set on evil, he might be borne on the fastest of courses to the heavenly Jerusalem? Let us be driven, Fathers, let us be driven by the frenzies of Socrates, that they may so throw us into ecstasy as to put our mind and ourselves in God. Let us be driven by them, if we have first done what is in our power. For if through moral philosophy the forces of our passions have by a fitting agreement become so intent on harmony that they can sing together in undisturbed concord, and if through dialectic our reason has moved progressively in a rhythmical measure, then we shall be stirred by the frenzy of the Muses and drink the heavenly harmony with our inmost hearing. Thereupon Bacchus, the leader of the Muses, by showing in his mysteries, that is, in the visible signs of nature, the invisible things of God to us who study philosophy, will intoxicate us with the fulness of God's house, in which, if we prove faithful, like Moses, hallowed theology shall come and inspire us with a doubled frenzy. For, exalted to her lofty height, we shall measure therefrom all things that are and shall be and have been in indivisible eternity; and, admiring their original beauty, like the seers of Phoebus, we shall become her own winged lovers. And at last, roused by ineffable love as by a sting, like burning Seraphim rapt from ourselves, full of divine power we shall no longer be ourselves but shall become He Himself Who made us.

17. If anyone investigates the holy names of Apollo, their meanings and hidden mysteries, these amply show that that god is no less a philosopher than a seer; but, since Ammonius has sufficiently examined this subject,[181] there is no reason why I should now treat it otherwise. But, Fathers, three Delphic precepts may suggest themselves to your minds, which are very necessary to those who are to go into the most sacred and revered temple, not of the false but of the true Apollo, who lights

180. *Epopteia* is the Greek term for the mystical vision (literally "the seeing") that is the highest stage of initiation into the ancient Greek religious cult known as the Eleusinian Mysteries.

181. Ammonius was the teacher of Plutarch (46–after 119 ce), the Greek biographer, essayist, and Platonic philosopher whose dialogue "On the *E* at Delphi" is Pico's source for the remainder of this section. Plutarch spent the last thirty years of his life as a priest at Delphi.

every soul as it enters this world.[182] You will see that they give us no other advice than that we should with all our strength embrace this threefold philosophy which is the concern of our present debate. For the saying, "Nothing too much,"[183] prescribes a standard and rule for all the virtues through the doctrine of the Mean, with which moral philosophy duly deals. Then the saying, "Know thyself," urges and encourages us to the investigation of all nature, of which the nature of man is both the connecting link and, so to speak, the "mixed bowl." For he who knows himself in himself knows all things, as Zoroaster first wrote, and then Plato in his *Alcibiades*. When we are finally lighted in this knowledge by natural philosophy, and nearest to God are uttering the theological greeting, "Thou art," we shall likewise in bliss be addressing the true Apollo on intimate terms.

Pico della Mirandola, Giovanni. "Introduction" and excerpts from "Oration on the Dignity of Man." In *The Renaissance Philosophy of Man*, translated by Elizabeth Livermore Forbes and edited by Ernst Cassirer, Paul Oskar Kristeller, and John Herman Randall, 223–27, 229–30, 233–35. Chicago: University of Chicago Press, 1948.

POST-READING PARS

1. According to Pico, what makes humans different from other creatures in the Chain of Being?

2. According to Pico, what gives human beings dignity?

3. According to Pico, if we have the ability to fashion our own identity, what identity do you think Pico is most encouraging us to become?

---

182. Pico here is quoting John 1:9, thus reassuring his readers that the "true Apollo" is the God of the Christian New Testament: "That was the true Light, which lighteth every man that cometh into the world" (KJV).

183. For each of the three sayings of the oracle of Apollo at Delphi, Pico provides the original Greek followed by a translation into Latin.

Inquiry Corner

Content Question(s):	Critical Question(s):
According to Pico, what creatures are at the top of the Chain of Being? And which are at the bottom?	The European Renaissance is said to usher in a secular, modern worldview (with emphasis on humanity in this world), as opposed to a religious medieval worldview (with emphasis on God's role in this world). In what ways does Pico's *Oration* confirm and/or refute this description?
Comparative Question(s):	**Connection Question(s):**
How does Pico value authorities (sources) from cultures different from his own? Name another author we have read who evaluates authorities (sources) from cultures different from their own?	Take a look at the concept of "human dignity" articulated in the 1948 Universal Declaration of Human Rights (UDHR). How might Pico view the UDHR?

from *Rule of Saint Benedict* by St. Benedict of Nursia

Introduction

In about the year 480, St. Benedict was born in the Italian town of Nursia (contemporary Norcia). He would go on to become one of the most well-known Christian ascetics. Ascetics — from the Greek word áskesis, meaning "to train" for an athletic contest — abstain from physical comforts and pleasures, often in pursuit of some sort of spiritual or religious benefit. Various types of ascetic practices can be found in many religions and cultures around the world.

Even the gospel accounts depict Jesus as a wandering teacher who claimed no possessions and often retreated into the wilderness. Some early Christians took this image of an abstinent Jesus to be their exemplar of the Christian life and ventured into the Syrian and Egyptian deserts in order to practice rigorous austerity amid a hostile natural environment. No one knows the name of the first Christian who decided to adopt this lifestyle. Many of these **anchorites** or **monks** (from the Greek words "to withdraw" and "solitary" respectively) sought to outdo one another in the severity of their practices, some by chaining themselves to rocks and others by constantly standing in the sun atop the columns of ruined buildings. In an effort to inhibit such exorbitant activities, a few Church leaders wrote short "rules" for the desert ascetics. Such rules were designed to encourage monks to live together in a "common life" in loosely structured communities, where they might encourage one another without feeling the need

> **SNAPSHOT BOX**
>
> LANGUAGE:
> Vernacular Latin
>
> DATE: Sixth century CE
>
> LOCATION: Central Italy
>
> CONTEXTUAL INFORMATION:
> Monastic rule
>
> TAGS: Asceticism; Body; Community; Education; Ethics and Morality; Formations and Reformations; Religion; Spirituality

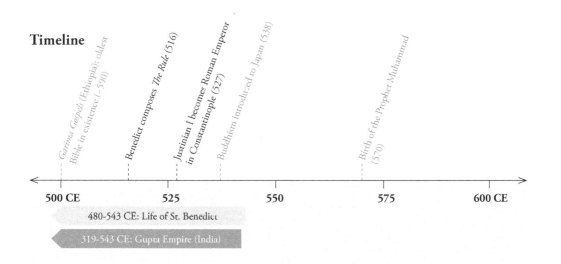

Timeline

Garima Gospels (Ethiopia): oldest Bible in existence (~590)

Benedict composes *The Rule* (516)

Justinian I becomes Roman Emperor in Constantinople (527)

Buddhism introduced to Japan (538)

Birth of the Prophet Muhammad (570)

500 CE   525   550   575   600 CE

480-543 CE: Life of St. Benedict

319-543 CE: Gupta Empire (India)

to resort to such excessive physical mortifications. What other ways might rules or structures help create balance in approaching life?

As an adult, Benedict initially adopted the solitary life of a hermit living alone in a cave outside the city of Rome. The numerous disciples who began to gather around him, however, led him to realize the need for a more structured community. He therefore organized the monks into small groups and appointed over each an experienced **abbot** (father) to whom the "brothers" vowed absolute obedience. In 529, Benedict founded his famous monastery of Montecassino on a high hill between Rome and Naples. *The Rule of St. Benedict* probably received its final form shortly after Benedict arrived at Montecassino.

The *Rule* was not fully an original work; Benedict utilized earlier monastic rules in its composition, but the balance he achieved between individual asceticism and community collaboration proved so popular that the *Rule* became the foundation for all monastic life in the Christian West. Tradition states that his (twin?) sister, St. Scholastica, even adapted the *Rule* for women who wanted to live the monastic life. Both brothers and sisters took vows of poverty, chastity, and obedience and spent their waking hours either in manual labor or in the chanting of communal prayers (known as the Liturgy of the Hours or the Divine Office). During meals, they ate in silence while a lector read from instructive texts.

Benedictine monasteries spread rapidly and were instrumental in fashioning the Christian culture of early medieval western Europe, especially after Charlemagne, in the ninth century, promoted the adoption of the *Rule* in all the monasteries within his empire. What factors might have made the monasteries so important in the spread and consolidation of Christianity in western Europe? Some 20,000 Benedictine men and women continue to live according to the *Rule* today.

Why might the lifestyle outlined in the *Rule* have been so attractive to men and women for so many centuries?

Rodger Payne
Department of Religious Studies

PRE-READING PARS

1. What three associations come to mind when you think of religion and its relationship to the body?

2. Think of ways that our contemporary culture approves or disapproves of denying physical comforts (e.g., abstinence from certain foods, sexual mores, wealth, and possessions)? Is this a type of asceticism? Why or why not?

3. Give two examples of regulations you think are necessary for some sort of communal life today.

---

from *Rule of Saint Benedict*

Prologue

Jan. 1 — May 2 — Sept. 1

Listen, my son, to your master's precepts, and incline the ear of your heart. Receive willingly and carry out effectively your loving father's advice, that by the labor of obedience you may return to Him from whom you had departed by the sloth of disobedience.

To you, therefore, my words are now addressed, whoever you may be, who are renouncing your own will to do battle under the Lord Christ, the true King, and are taking up the strong, bright weapons of obedience.

And first of all, whatever good work you begin to do, beg of Him with most earnest prayer to perfect it, that He who has now deigned to count us among His sons may not at any time be grieved by our evil deeds. For we must always so serve Him with the good things He has given us, that He will never as an angry Father disinherit His children, nor ever as a dread Lord, provoked by our evil actions, deliver us to everlasting punishment as wicked servants who would not follow Him to glory.

Jan. 2 — May 3 — Sept. 2

Let us arise, then, at last, for the Scripture stirs us up, saying, "Now is the hour for us to rise from sleep." Let us open our eyes to the deifying light, let us hear with attentive ears the warning which the divine voice cries daily to us, "Today if you hear His voice, harden not your hearts." And again, "He who has ears to hear, let him hear what the Spirit says to the churches." And what does He say? "Come, My children, listen to Me; I will teach you the fear of the Lord. Run while you have the light of life, lest the darkness of death overtake you."

Jan. 3 — May 4 — Sept. 3

And the Lord, seeking His laborer in the multitude to whom He thus cries out, says again, "Who is the man who will have life, and desires to see good days?" And if, hearing Him, you answer, "I am he," God says to you, "If you will have true and everlasting life, keep your tongue from evil and your lips that they speak no guile. Turn away from evil and do good; seek after peace and pursue it. And when you have done these things, My eyes shall be upon you and My ears open to your prayers; and before you call upon Me, I will say to you, 'Behold, here I am.'"

What can be sweeter to us, dear brethren, than this voice of the Lord inviting us? Behold, in His loving kindness the Lord shows us the way of life.

Jan. 4 — May 5 — Sept. 4

Having our loins girded, therefore, with faith and the performance of good works, let us walk in His paths by the guidance of the Gospel, that we may deserve to see Him who has called us to His kingdom.

For if we wish to dwell in the tent of that kingdom, we must run to it by good deeds or we shall never reach it.

But let us ask the Lord, with the Prophet, "Lord, who shall dwell in Your tent, or who shall rest upon Your holy mountain?"

After this question, brethren, let us listen to the Lord as He answers and shows us the way to that tent, saying, "He who walks without stain and practices justice; he who speaks truth from his heart; he who has not used his tongue for deceit; he who has done no evil to his neighbor; he who has given no place to slander against his neighbor."

It is he who, under any temptation from the malicious devil, has brought him to naught by casting him and his temptation from the sight of his heart; and who has laid hold of his thoughts while they were still young and dashed them against Christ.

It is they who, fearing the Lord, do not pride themselves on their good observance; but, convinced that the good which is in them cannot come from themselves and must be from the Lord, glorify the Lord's work in them, using the words of the Prophet, "Not to us, O Lord, not to us, but to Your name give the glory." Thus also the Apostle Paul attributed nothing of the success of his preaching to himself, but said, "By the grace of God I am what I am." And again he says, "He who glories, let him glory in the Lord."

Jan. 5 — May 6 — Sept. 5

Hence the Lord says in the Gospel, "Whoever listens to these words of Mine and acts upon them, I will liken him to a wise man who built his house on rock. The floods came, the winds blew and beat against that house, and it did not fall, because it was founded on rock."

Having given us these assurances, the Lord is waiting every day for us to respond by our deeds to His holy admonitions. And the days of this life are lengthened and a truce granted us for this very reason, that we may amend our evil ways. As the Apostle says, "Do you not know that God's patience is inviting you to repent?" For the merciful Lord tells us, "I desire not the death of the sinner, but that he should be converted and live."

Jan. 6—May 7—Sept. 6

So, brethren, we have asked the Lord who is to dwell in His tent, and we have heard His commands to anyone who would dwell there; it remains for us to fulfil those duties.

Therefore we must prepare our hearts and our bodies to do battle under the holy obedience of His commands; and let us ask God that He be pleased to give us the help of His grace for anything which our nature finds hardly possible. And if we want to escape the pains of hell and attain life everlasting, then, while there is still time, while we are still in the body and are able to fulfil all these things by the light of this life, we must hasten to do now what will profit us for eternity.

Jan. 7—May 8—Sept. 7

And so we are going to establish a school for the service of the Lord. In founding it we hope to introduce nothing harsh or burdensome. But if a certain strictness results from the dictates of equity for the amendment of vices or the preservation of charity, do not be at once dismayed and fly from the way of salvation, whose entrance cannot but be narrow. For as we advance in the religious life and in faith, our hearts expand and we run the way of God's commandments with unspeakable sweetness of love. Thus, never departing from His school, but persevering in the monastery according to His teaching until death, we may by patience share in the sufferings of Christ and deserve to have a share also in His kingdom.

[...]

Chapter 2 What Kind of Man the Abbot Ought to Be

Jan. 9—May 10—Sept. 9

An Abbot who is worthy to be over a monastery should always remember what he is called, and live up to the name of Superior. For he is believed to hold the place of Christ in the monastery, being called by a name of His, which is taken from the words of the Apostle: "You have received a Spirit of adoption as sons, by virtue of which we cry, 'Abba—Father!'"

Therefore the Abbot ought not to teach or ordain or command anything which is against the Lord's precepts; on the contrary, his commands and his teaching should be a leaven of divine justice kneaded into the minds of his disciples.

Jan. 10 — May 11 — Sept. 10

Let the Abbot always bear in mind that at the dread Judgment of God there will be an examination of these two matters: his teaching and the obedience of his disciples. And let the Abbot be sure that any lack of profit the master of the house may find in the sheep will be laid to the blame of the shepherd. On the other hand, if the shepherd has bestowed all his pastoral diligence on a restless, unruly flock and tried every remedy for their unhealthy behavior, then he will be acquitted at the Lord's Judgment and may say to the Lord with the Prophet: "I have not concealed Your justice within my heart; Your truth and Your salvation I have declared. But they have despised and rejected me." And then finally let death itself, irresistible, punish those disobedient sheep under his charge.

Jan. 11 — May 12 — Sept. 11

Therefore, when anyone receives the name of Abbot, he ought to govern his disciples with a twofold teaching. That is to say, he should show them all that is good and holy by his deeds even more than by his words, expounding the Lord's commandments in words to the intelligent among his disciples, but demonstrating the divine precepts by his actions for those of harder hearts and ruder minds. And whatever he has taught his disciples to be contrary to God's law, let him indicate by his example that it is not to be done, lest, while preaching to others, he himself be found reprobate, and lest God one day say to him in his sin, "Why do you declare My statutes and profess My covenant with your lips, whereas you hate discipline and have cast My words behind you?" And again, "You were looking at the speck in your brother's eye, and did not see the beam in your own."

Jan. 12 — May 13 — Sept. 12

Let him make no distinction of persons in the monastery. Let him not love one more than another, unless it be one whom he finds better in good works or in obedience. Let him not advance one of noble birth ahead of one who was formerly a slave, unless there be some other reasonable ground for it. But if the Abbot for just reason think fit to do so, let him advance one of any rank whatever. Otherwise let them keep their due places; because, whether slaves or freemen, we are all one in Christ and bear an equal burden of service in the army of the same Lord. For with God there is no respect of persons. Only for one reason are we preferred in His sight: if we be found better than others in good works and humility. Therefore let the Abbot show equal love to all and impose the same discipline on all according to their deserts.

Jan. 13 — May 14 — Sept. 13

In his teaching the Abbot should always follow the Apostle's formula: "Reprove, entreat, rebuke"; threatening at one time and coaxing at another as the occasion may require, showing now the stern countenance of a master, now the loving affection of a father. That is to say, it is the undisciplined and restless whom he must reprove rather sharply; it is the obedient, meek and patient whom he must entreat to advance in virtue; while as for the negligent and disdainful, these we charge him to rebuke and correct.

And let him not shut his eyes to the faults of offenders; but, since he has the authority, let him cut out those faults by the roots as soon as they begin to appear, remembering the fate of Heli, the priest of Silo. The well-disposed and those of good understanding let him correct with verbal admonition the first and second time. But bold, hard, proud and disobedient characters he should curb at the very beginning of their ill-doing by stripes and other bodily punishments, knowing that it is written, "The fool is not corrected with words," and again, "Beat your son with the rod and you will deliver his soul from death."

Jan. 14 — May 15 — Sept. 14

The Abbot should always remember what he is and what he is called, and should know that to whom more is committed, from him more is required. Let him understand also what a difficult and arduous task he has undertaken: ruling souls and adapting himself to a variety of characters. One he must coax, another scold, another persuade, according to each one's character and understanding. Thus he must adjust and adapt himself to all in such a way that he may not only suffer no loss in the flock committed to his care, but may even rejoice in the increase of a good flock.

Jan. 15 — May 16 — Sept. 15

Above all let him not neglect or undervalue the welfare of the souls committed to him, in a greater concern for fleeting, earthly, perishable things; but let him always bear in mind that he has undertaken the government of souls and that he will have to give an account of them.

And if he be tempted to allege a lack of earthly means, let him remember what is written: "First seek the kingdom of God and His justice, and all these things shall be given you besides." And again: "Nothing is wanting to those who fear Him."

Let him know, then, that he who has undertaken the government of souls must prepare himself to render an account of them. Whatever number of brethren he knows he has under his care, he may be sure beyond doubt that on Judgment Day he will have to give the Lord an account of all these souls, as well as of his own soul.

Thus the constant apprehension about his coming examination as shepherd concerning the sheep entrusted to him, and his anxiety over the account that must be given for others, make him careful of his own record. And while by his admonitions he is helping others to amend, he himself is cleansed of his faults.

Chapter 3 On Calling the Brethren for Counsel

Jan. 16—May 17—Sept. 16

Whenever any important business has to be done in the monastery, let the Abbot call together the whole community and state the matter to be acted upon. Then, having heard the brethren's advice, let him turn the matter over in his own mind and do what he shall judge to be most expedient. The reason we have said that all should be called for counsel is that the Lord often reveals to the younger what is best.

Let the brethren give their advice with all the deference required by humility, and not presume stubbornly to defend their opinions; but let the decision rather depend on the Abbot's judgment, and all submit to whatever he shall decide for their welfare.

However, just as it is proper for the disciples to obey their master, so also it is his function to dispose all things with prudence and justice.

Jan. 17—May 18—Sept. 17

In all things, therefore, let all follow the Rule as guide, and let no one be so rash as to deviate from it. Let no one in the monastery follow his own heart's fancy; and let no one presume to contend with his Abbot in an insolent way or even outside of the monastery. But if anyone should presume to do so, let him undergo the discipline of the Rule. At the same time, the Abbot himself should do all things in the fear of God and in observance of the Rule, knowing that beyond a doubt he will have to render an account of all his decisions to God, the most just Judge.

But if the business to be done in the interests of the monastery be of lesser importance, let him take counsel with the seniors only. It is written, "Do everything with counsel, and you will not repent when you have done it."

[...]

Chapter 5 On Obedience

Jan. 22—May 23—Sept. 22

The first degree of humility is obedience without delay. This is the virtue of those who hold nothing dearer to them than Christ; who, because of the holy service they have professed, and the fear of hell, and the glory of life everlasting, as soon as any-thing has been ordered by the Superior, receive it as a divine command and cannot suffer any delay in executing it. Of these the Lord says, "As soon as he heard, he obeyed Me." And again to teachers He says, "He who hears you, hears Me."

Such as these, therefore, immediately leaving their own affairs and forsaking their own will, dropping the work they were engaged in and leaving it unfinished, with the ready step of obedience follow up with their deeds the voice of him who com-mands. And so as it were at the same moment the master's command is given and the disciple's work is completed, the two things being speedily accomplished together in the swiftness of the fear of God by those who are moved with the desire of attaining life everlasting. That desire is their motive for choosing the narrow way, of which the Lord says, "Narrow is the way that leads to life," so that, not living according to their own choice nor obeying their own desires and pleasures but walking by another's judgment and command, they dwell in monasteries and desire to have an Abbot over them. Assuredly such as these are living up to that maxim of the Lord in which He says, "I have come not to do My own will, but the will of Him who sent Me."

Jan. 23 — May 24 — Sept. 23

But this very obedience will be acceptable to God and pleasing to men only if what is commanded is done without hesitation, delay, lukewarmness, grumbling, or objec-tion. For the obedience given to Superiors is given to God, since He Himself has said, "He who hears you, hears Me." And the disciples should offer their obedience with a good will, for "God loves a cheerful giver." For if the disciple obeys with an ill will and murmurs, not necessarily with his lips but simply in his heart, then even though he fulfil the command yet his work will not be acceptable to God, who sees that his heart is murmuring. And, far from gaining a reward for such work as this, he will incur the punishment due to murmurers, unless he amend and make satisfaction.

Chapter 6 On the Spirit of Silence

Jan. 24 — May 25 — Sept. 24

Let us do what the Prophet says: "I said, 'I will guard my ways, that I may not sin with my tongue. I have set a guard to my mouth.' I was mute and was humbled, and kept silence even from good things." Here the Prophet shows that if the spirit of silence ought to lead us at times to refrain even from good speech, so much the more ought the punishment for sin make us avoid evil words.

Therefore, since the spirit of silence is so important, permission to speak should rarely be granted even to perfect disciples, even though it be for good, holy, edifying conversation; for it is written, "In much speaking you will not escape sin," and in another place, "Death and life are in the power of the tongue."

For speaking and teaching belong to the master; the disciple's part is to be silent and to listen. And for that reason if anything has to be asked of the Superior, it should be asked with all the humility and submission inspired by reverence.

But as for coarse jests and idle words or words that move to laughter, these we condemn everywhere with a perpetual ban, and for such conversation we do not permit a disciple to open his mouth.

Chapter 7 On Humility

Jan. 25—May 26—Sept. 25

Holy Scripture, brethren, cries out to us, saying, "Everyone who exalts himself shall be humbled, and he who humbles himself shall be exalted." In saying this it shows us that all exaltation is a kind of pride, against which the Prophet proves himself to be on guard when he says, "Lord, my heart is not exalted, nor are mine eyes lifted up; neither have I walked in great matters, nor in wonders above me." But how has he acted? "Rather have I been of humble mind than exalting myself; as a weaned child on its mother's breast, so You solace my soul."

Hence, brethren, if we wish to reach the very highest point of humility and to arrive speedily at that heavenly exaltation to which ascent is made through the humility of this present life, we must by our ascending actions erect the ladder Jacob saw in his dream, on which Angels appeared to him descending and ascending. By that descent and ascent we must surely understand nothing else than this, that we descend by self-exaltation and ascend by humility. And the ladder thus set up is our life in the world, which the Lord raises up to heaven if our heart is humbled. For we call our body and soul the sides of the ladder, and into these sides our divine vocation has inserted the different steps of humility and discipline we must climb.

Jan. 26—May 27—Sept. 26

The first degree of humility, then, is that a person keep the fear of God before his eyes and beware of ever forgetting it. Let him be ever mindful of all that God has commanded; let his thoughts constantly recur to the hell-fire which will burn for their sins those who despise God, and to the life everlasting which is prepared for those who fear Him. Let him keep himself at every moment from sins and vices, whether of the mind, the tongue, the hands, the feet, or the self-will, and check also the desires of the flesh.

Jan. 27 — May 28 — Sept. 27

Let a man consider that God is always looking at him from heaven, that his actions are everywhere visible to the divine eyes and are constantly being reported to God by the Angels. This is what the Prophet shows us when he represents God as ever present within our thoughts, in the words "Searcher of minds and hearts is God" and again in the words "The Lord knows the thoughts of men." Again he says, "You have read my thoughts from afar" and "The thoughts of men will confess to You."

In order that he may be careful about his wrongful thoughts, therefore, let the faithful brother say constantly in his heart, "Then shall I be spotless before Him, if I have kept myself from my iniquity."

Jan. 28 — May 29 — Sept. 28

As for self-will, we are forbidden to do our own will by the Scripture, which says to us, "Turn away from your own will," and likewise by the prayer in which we ask God that His will be done in us. And rightly are we taught not to do our own will when we take heed to the warning of Scripture: "There are ways which to men seem right, but the ends of them plunge into the depths of hell"; and also when we tremble at what is said of the careless: "They are corrupt and have become abominable in their wills."

And as for the desires of the flesh, let us believe with the Prophet that God is ever present to us, when he says to the Lord, "Every desire of mine is before You."

Jan. 29 — May 30 — Sept. 29

We must be on our guard, therefore, against evil desires, for death lies close by the gate of pleasure. Hence the Scripture gives this command: "Go not after your concupiscences."[184]

So therefore, since the eyes of the Lord observe the good and the evil and the Lord is always looking down from heaven on the children of men "to see if there be anyone who understands and seeks God," and since our deeds are daily, day and night, reported to the Lord by the Angels assigned to us, we must constantly beware, brethren, as the Prophet says in the Psalm, lest at any time God see us falling into evil ways and becoming unprofitable; and lest, having spared us for the present because in His kindness He awaits our reformation, He say to us in the future, "These things you did, and I held My peace."

Jan. 30 — May 31 — Sept. 30

The second degree of humility is that a person love not his own will nor take pleasure in satisfying his desires, but model his actions on the saying of the Lord, "I have come not to do My own will, but the will of Him who sent Me." It is written also, "Self-will has its punishment, but constraint wins a crown."

184. Lustful desires

Jan. 31 — June 1 — Oct. 1

The third degree of humility is that a person for love of God submit himself to his Superior in all obedience, imitating the Lord, of whom the Apostle says, "He became obedient even unto death."

Feb. 1 — June 2 — Oct. 2

The fourth degree of humility is that he hold fast to patience with a silent mind when in this obedience he meets with difficulties and contradictions and even any kind of injustice, enduring all without growing weary or running away. For the Scripture says, "He who perseveres to the end, he it is who shall be saved"; and again, "Let your heart take courage, and wait for the Lord!"

And to show how those who are faithful ought to endure all things, however contrary, for the Lord, the Scripture says in the person of the suffering, "For Your sake we are put to death all the day long; we are considered as sheep marked for slaughter." Then, secure in their hope of a divine recompense, they go on with joy to declare, "But in all these trials we conquer, through Him who has granted us His love." Again, in another place the Scripture says, "You have tested us, O God; You have tried us as silver is tried, by fire; You have brought us into a snare; You have laid afflictions on our back." And to show that we ought to be under a Superior, it goes on to say, "You have set men over our heads."

Moreover, by their patience those faithful ones fulfil the Lord's command in adversities and injuries: when struck on one cheek, they offer the other; when deprived of their tunic, they surrender also their cloak; when forced to go a mile, they go two; with the Apostle Paul they bear with false brethren and bless those who curse them.

Feb. 2 — June 3 — Oct. 3

The fifth degree of humility is that he hide from his Abbot none of the evil thoughts that enter his heart or the sins committed in secret, but that he humbly confess them. The Scripture urges us to this when it says, "Reveal your way to the Lord and hope in Him," and again, "Confess to the Lord, for He is good, for His mercy endures forever." And the Prophet likewise says, "My offense I have made known to You, and my iniquities I have not covered up. I said: 'I will declare against myself my iniquities to the Lord'; and 'You forgave the wickedness of my heart.'"

Feb. 3 — June 4 — Oct. 4

The sixth degree of humility is that a monk be content with the poorest and worst of everything, and that in every occupation assigned him he consider himself a bad and worthless workman, saying with the Prophet, "I am brought to nothing and I am without understanding; I have become as a beast of burden before You, and I am always with You."

Feb. 4 — June 5 — Oct. 5

The seventh degree of humility is that he consider himself lower and of less account than anyone else, and this not only in verbal protestation but also with the most heartfelt inner conviction, humbling himself and saying with the Prophet, "But I am a worm and no man, the scorn of men and the outcast of the people. After being exalted, I have been humbled and covered with confusion." And again, "It is good for me that You have humbled me, that I may learn Your commandments."

Feb. 5 — June 6 — Oct. 6

The eighth degree of humility is that a monk do nothing except what is commended by the common Rule of the monastery and the example of the elders.

Feb. 6 — June 7 — Oct. 7

The ninth degree of humility is that a monk restrain his tongue and keep silence, not speaking until he is questioned. For the Scripture shows that "in much speaking there is no escape from sin" and that "the talkative man is not stable on the earth."

Feb. 7 — June 8 — Oct. 8

The tenth degree of humility is that he be not ready and quick to laugh, for it is written, "The fool lifts up his voice in laughter."

Feb. 8 — June 9 — Oct. 9

The eleventh degree of humility is that when a monk speaks he do so gently and without laughter, humbly and seriously, in few and sensible words, and that he be not noisy in his speech. It is written, "A wise man is known by the fewness of his words."

Feb. 9 — June 10 — Oct. 10

The twelfth degree of humility is that a monk not only have humility in his heart but also by his very appearance make it always manifest to those who see him. That is to say that whether he is at the Work of God, in the oratory, in the monastery, in the garden, on the road, in the fields or anywhere else, and whether sitting, walking or standing, he should always have his head bowed and his eyes toward the ground. Feeling the guilt of his sins at every moment, he should consider himself already present at the dread Judgment and constantly say in his heart what the publican in the Gospel said with his eyes fixed on the earth: "Lord, I am a sinner and not worthy to lift up my eyes to heaven"; and again with the Prophet: "I am bowed down and humbled everywhere." Having climbed all these steps of humility, therefore, the monk will presently come to that perfect love of God which casts out fear. And all those precepts which formerly he had not observed without fear, he will now begin to keep by reason of that love, without any effort, as though naturally and by habit. No longer will his motive be the fear of hell, but rather the love of Christ, good habit and delight in the virtues which the Lord will deign to show forth by the Holy Spirit in His servant now cleansed from vice and sin.

[...]

Chapter 23 On Excommunication for Faults

Feb. 28 (29)—June 30—Oct. 30

If a brother is found to be obstinate, or disobedient, or proud, or murmuring, or habitually transgressing the Holy Rule in any point and contemptuous of the orders of his seniors, the latter shall admonish him secretly a first and a second time, as Our Lord commands. If he fails to amend, let him be given a public rebuke in front of the whole community. But if even then he does not reform, let him be placed under excommunication, provided that he understands the seriousness of that penalty; if he is perverse, however, let him undergo corporal punishment.

Chapter 24 What the Measure of Excommunication Should Be

Mar. 1—July 1—Oct. 31

The measure of excommunication or of chastisement should correspond to the degree of fault, which degree is estimated by the Abbot's judgment.

If a brother is found guilty of lighter faults, let him be excluded from the common table. Now the program for one deprived of the fellowship of the table shall be as follows: In the oratory he shall intone neither Psalm nor antiphon nor shall he recite a lesson until he has made satisfaction; in the refectory he shall take his food alone after the community meal, so that if the brethren eat at the sixth hour, for instance, that brother shall eat at the ninth, while if they eat at the ninth hour he shall eat in the evening, until by a suitable satisfaction he obtains pardon.

[...]

Chapter 33 Whether Monks Ought to Have Anything of Their Own

Mar. 11—July 11—Nov. 10

This vice especially is to be cut out of the monastery by the roots. Let no one presume to give or receive anything without the Abbot's leave, or to have anything as his own—anything whatever, whether book or tablets or pen or whatever it may be—since they are not permitted to have even their bodies or wills at their own disposal; but for all their necessities let them look to the Father of the monastery. And let it be unlawful to have anything which the Abbot has not given or allowed. Let all things be common to all, as it is written, and let no one say or assume that anything is his own.

But if anyone is caught indulging in this most wicked vice, let him be admonished once and a second time. If he fails to amend, let him undergo punishment.

[...]

Chapter 48 On the Daily Manual Labor

Mar. 28—July 28—Nov. 27

Idleness is the enemy of the soul. Therefore the brethren should be occupied at certain times in manual labor, and again at fixed hours in sacred reading. To that end we think that the times for each may be prescribed as follows.

From Easter until the Calends[185] of October, when they come out from Prime[186] in the morning let them labor at whatever is necessary until about the fourth hour, and from the fourth hour until about the sixth let them apply themselves to reading. After the sixth hour, having left the table, let them rest on their beds in perfect silence; or if anyone may perhaps want to read, let him read to himself in such a way as not to disturb anyone else. Let None[187] be said rather early, at the middle of the eighth hour, and let them again do what work has to be done until Vespers.[188]

And if the circumstances of the place or their poverty should require that they themselves do the work of gathering the harvest, let them not be discontented; for then are they truly monks when they live by the labor of their hands, as did our Fathers and the Apostles. Let all things be done with moderation, however, for the sake of the faint-hearted.

185. First day.
186. The first hour of daily prayer in the Divine Office; varied with the season.
187. The ninth hour of prayer, not to be confused with the ninth hour of the day.
188. Evening prayer.

Mar. 29 — July 29 — Nov. 28

From the Calends of October until the beginning of Lent,[189] let them apply themselves to reading up to the end of the second hour. At the second hour let Terce[190] be
said, and then let all labor at the work assigned them until None. At the first signal
for the Hour of None let everyone break off from his work, and hold himself ready
for the sounding of the second signal. After the meal let them apply themselves to
their reading or to the Psalms.

On the days of Lent, from morning until the end of the third hour let them apply
themselves to their reading, and from then until the end of the tenth hour let them
do the work assigned them. And in these days of Lent they shall each receive a book
from the library, which they shall read straight through from the beginning. These
books are to be given out at the beginning of Lent.

But certainly one or two of the seniors should be deputed to go about the monastery at the hours when the brethren are occupied in reading and see that there be no
lazy brother who spends his time in idleness or gossip and does not apply himself to
the reading, so that he is not only unprofitable to himself but also distracts others. If
such a one be found (which God forbid), let him be corrected once and a second time;
if he does not amend, let him undergo the punishment of the Rule in such a way that
the rest may take warning.

Moreover, one brother shall not associate with another at unseasonable hours.

Mar. 30 — July 30 — Nov. 29

On Sundays, let all occupy themselves in reading, except those who have been appointed to various duties. But if anyone should be so negligent and shiftless that he
will not or cannot study or read, let him be given some work to do so that he will
not be idle.

Weak or sickly brethren should be assigned a task or craft of such a nature as to
keep them from idleness and at the same time not to overburden them or drive them
away with excessive toil. Their weakness must be taken into consideration by the
Abbot.

Abbot of Monte Cassino Benedict of Nursia. "St. Benedict's Rule for Monasteries,"
translated by Leonard J. Doyle, 1–9, 13–20, 33–34, 41–42, 55–56. Project Gutenberg.
Collegeville, MN: The Liturgical Press, St. John's Abbey. https://www.gutenberg.org
/files/50040/50040-h/50040-h.html (accessed March 13, 2020).

---

189. The forty days of penitence and fasting before Easter.
190. The third hour of prayer.

POST READING PARS

1. Compare and contrast your ideas on the relationship between religion and body to Benedict's views.

2. What do you think attracted women and men to the Benedictine lifestyle? Would the *Rule* offer similar attractions today — why or why not?

3. Imagine that you are a Benedictine monk or nun living in early medieval Europe. What parts of the *Rule* would you think might be the most difficult to follow? What would an ideal Benedictine brother or sister be like?

Inquiry Corner

Content Question(s):

How would you describe Benedict's view of human nature as expressed in the *Rule*?

Does the *Rule* present a negative valuation of the body?

Critical Question(s):

In what ways might such radical experiments in living provide a catalyst for social change?

If you could single out one idea or practice from the *Rule* that would be of benefit to contemporary society, what would that be?

Comparative Question(s):

In which other texts have you encountered a demand for absolute obedience to the leader? How does that compare to the absolute obedience to the abbot that the *Rule* demands?

Connection Question(s):

Does the *Rule* provide universal values and prescriptions for ascetic practices, or is it culturally bound to western Europe in the early medieval period?

BEYOND THE CLASSROOM

» Do you think organizations should be allowed to control the behavior of their employees based on their convictions?

» What value do we associate with people who can work and do work? Conversely, what value do we associate with those who choose not to work, or who cannot work?

» If you did not have to work, what would you do with your time?

from *The Spiritual Exercises* by St. Ignatius of Loyola

SNAPSHOT BOX

LANGUAGE: Spanish

DATE: c. 1522–1528 CE

LOCATION: France

CONTEXTUAL
INFORMATION:
Regulations

TAGS: Authority
and Institution;
Education; Identity
and Self; Power
Structures; Religion

Introduction

Ignatius was born in 1491 CE in the Basque town of Loyola in today's northeast Spain. As a young man, he joined a militia and was gravely wounded in his right leg during a battle. While convalescing at his family estate, he asked for some books on chivalry and warfare, but his family could offer him only books on the life of Christ and the lives of the saints. By the time he had recovered (never completely; he walked with a limp the rest of his life), Ignatius had decided to pledge himself as a "soldier for Christ" and made a pilgrimage to a Benedictine monastery in Montserrat, Spain, where he hung his sword on an altar dedicated to the Virgin Mary. What might this gesture symbolize?

Subsequently, Ignatius began his formal education, eventually becoming a student at the University of Paris, where he and six companions took vows together, including the traditional monastic vows of poverty and chastity, but adding a third vow to travel to the Holy Land and preach to the Muslims there. They envisioned their group as the "Company of Jesus," in which the term "company" was meant to be understood in military fashion. Ignatius also termed them "contemplatives in action" and developed a series of meditations and visualizations that he entitled *The Spiritual Exercises* to guide their religious formation. In 1539 CE, he and some of the members of his company traveled to Rome to present their plans to the pope and to obtain his blessing on their endeavors. What were they seeking by asking for the pope's blessing?

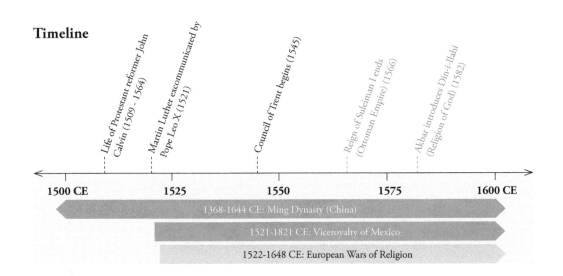

Timeline

Life of Protestant reformer John Calvin (1509 - 1564)

Martin Luther excommunicated by Pope Leo X (1521)

Council of Trent begins (1545)

Reign of Suleiman I ends (Ottoman Empire) (1566)

Akbar introduces Din-i-Ilahi (Religion of God) (1582)

1500 CE   1525   1550   1575   1600 CE

1368-1644 CE: Ming Dynasty (China)

1521-1821 CE: Viceroyalty of Mexico

1522-1648 CE: European Wars of Religion

Pope Paul III was receptive to their ideas, but before he approved the formation of a new religious order, he suggested that the vow to go to the Holy Land be substituted for a vow of direct obedience to the pope. No doubt Paul understood the value of such a group with ultimate loyalty to the pope rather than being subject to a local bishop like others religious orders were. Indeed, as the expansion of the Protestant Reformation continued to destroy the unity of the Christian faith in western Europe, the utility of having a well-educated and scrupulously loyal group of "soldiers" to do his bidding gave the pope a tremendous advantage in the struggle for religious allegiance. Thus, with this small change, Paul officially approved the Company of Jesus in 1540, with Ignatius its first Father General. The Society of Jesus, the name by which they subsequently came to be known in English, does not reflect this original military emphasis. They are popularly known as the **Jesuits**.

Paul's hunch about the value of the Jesuit order was correct. Within a few years, the Company of Jesus had become the largest religious order in the Catholic Church, surpassing many other older established groups such as the Benedictines, the Franciscans, and the Dominicans. New orders of religious women, such as the Sisters of Loretto, based their spiritual formation on *The Spiritual Exercises* and became pioneers in women's education. The Jesuits participated energetically in the various sessions of the Council of Trent (1545–1563 CE), the gathering of Catholic leaders from all over western Europe that sought to reform the Church and respond to the radical changes urged by Protestant groups. Adopting the doctrines established by the council as obligatory for the Christian faith, the Jesuits opened schools and academies throughout Europe to teach this **Tridentine** (from Trent) form of the religion in what scholars have labeled the **Catholic Reformation** of the sixteenth century. Thus, they became the great educators for the early modern Roman Catholic Church, a vocation that continues until today. What do you think might be the reasons for their enduring influence on education?

Within the decade following their papal endorsement, the Jesuits became influential as missionaries in the areas that had moved toward breaking away from the Catholic Church. Their efforts to regain areas already lost to Protestantism and to halt its further spread became known as the **Counter Reformation**. They also were among the first Christian missionaries during what Europeans called the "age of discovery" (circa 1500–1700 CE) to travel to Asia and the Americas. Their efforts to learn native languages resulted in their production of manuals that imposed Western conceptual frameworks onto native traditions. For example, they produced the initial grammar and dictionaries of many Native American languages that supported their expansionist project. While their linguistic efforts helped to preserve native languages, ultimately these colonial and imperialist endeavors resulted in the destruction of many of these Indigenous cultures.

Ignatius probably composed what is popularly called his "Rules for Thinking with the Church" while he was still a student at the University of Paris, although they were probably revised several times before they reached this final form. They are often included as an appendix in *The Spiritual Exercises*, but most are intended for all Catholics, not just Jesuits.

Rodger Payne
Department of Religious Studies

PRE-READING PARS

1. Name two things that come to mind when you think of the Roman Catholic Church.

2. Look up the meanings of any two of the following terms: faith, grace, salvation, merit, predestination.

---

from *The Spiritual Exercises*

To Have the True Sentiment Which We Ought to Have in the Church Militant

Let the following Rules be observed.

First Rule. All judgment laid aside, we ought to have our mind ready and prompt to obey, in all, the true Spouse of Christ our Lord, which is our holy Mother the Church Hierarchical.

Second Rule. To praise confession to a Priest, and the reception of the most Holy Sacrament of the Altar[191] once in the year, and much more each month, and much better from week to week, with the conditions required and due.

Third Rule. To praise the hearing of Mass often, likewise hymns, psalms, and long prayers, in the church and out of it; likewise the hours set at the time fixed for each Divine Office and for all prayer and all Canonical Hours.

Fourth Rule. To praise much Religious Orders, virginity and continence, and not so much marriage as any of these.

Fifth Rule. To praise vows of Religion, of obedience, of poverty, of chastity and of other perfections of supererogation.[192] And it is to be noted that as the vow is about the things which approach to Evangelical perfection,[193] a vow ought not to be made in the things which withdraw from it, such as to be a merchant, or to be married, etc.

Sixth Rule. To praise relics of the Saints, giving veneration to them and praying to the Saints; and to praise Stations, pilgrimages, Indulgences, pardons, Cruzadas,[194] and candles lighted in the churches.

---

191. Holy Communion.
192. Good works above and beyond what is required or expected.
193. The typical monastic vows of poverty, chastity, and obedience.
194. Crusades or wars of religion (e.g., against the "heretics" in Europe).

Seventh Rule. To praise Constitutions about fasts and abstinence, as of Lent, Ember Days, Vigils, Friday and Saturday; likewise penances, not only interior, but also exterior.

Eighth Rule. To praise the ornaments and the buildings of churches; likewise images, and to venerate them according to what they represent.

Ninth Rule. Finally, to praise all precepts of the Church, keeping the mind prompt to find reasons in their defence and in no manner against them.

Tenth Rule. We ought to be more prompt to find good and praise as well the Constitutions and recommendations as the ways of our Superiors. Because, although some are not or have not been such, to speak against them, whether preaching in public or discoursing before the common people, would rather give rise to fault-finding and scandal than profit; and so the people would be incensed against their Superiors, whether temporal or spiritual. So that, as it does harm to speak evil to the common people of Superiors in their absence, so it can make profit to speak of the evil ways to the persons themselves who can remedy them.

Eleventh Rule. To praise positive and scholastic learning. Because, as it is more proper to the Positive Doctors, as St. Jerome, St. Augustine and St. Gregory, etc., to move the heart to love and serve God our Lord in everything; so it is more proper to the Scholastics, as St. Thomas, St. Bonaventure, and to the Master of the Sentences,[195] etc., to define or explain for our times the things necessary for eternal salvation; and to combat and explain better all errors and all fallacies. For the Scholastic Doctors, as they are more modern, not only help themselves with the true understanding of the Sacred Scripture and of the Positive and holy Doctors, but also, they being enlightened and clarified by the Divine virtue, help themselves by the Councils, Canons and Constitutions of our holy Mother the Church.

Twelfth Rule. We ought to be on our guard in making comparison of those of us who are alive to the blessed passed away, because error is committed not a little in this; that is to say, in saying, this one knows more than St. Augustine; he is another, or greater than, St. Francis; he is another St. Paul in goodness, holiness, etc.

Thirteenth Rule. To be right in everything, we ought always to hold that the white which I see, is black, if the Hierarchical Church so decides it, believing that between Christ our Lord, the Bridegroom, and the Church, His Bride, there is the same Spirit which governs and directs us for the salvation of our souls. Because by the same Spirit and our Lord Who gave the ten Commandments, our holy Mother the Church is directed and governed.

195. Peter Lombard, whose work was a systematic compilation of biblical commentary and theology.

Fourteenth Rule. Although there is much truth in the assertion that no one can save himself without being predestined and without having faith and grace; we must be very cautious in the manner of speaking and communicating with others about all these things.

Fifteenth Rule. We ought not, by way of custom, to speak much of predestination; but if in some way and at some times one speaks, let him so speak that the common people may not come into any error, as sometimes happens, saying: Whether I have to be saved or condemned is already determined, and no other thing can now be, through my doing well or ill; and with this, growing lazy, they become negligent in the works which lead to the salvation and the spiritual profit of their souls.

Sixteenth Rule. In the same way, we must be on our guard that by talking much and with much insistence of faith, without any distinction and explanation, occasion be not given to the people to be lazy and slothful in works, whether before faith is formed in charity or after.

Seventeenth Rule. Likewise, we ought not to speak so much with insistence on grace that the poison of discarding liberty be engendered. So that of faith and grace one can speak as much as is possible with the Divine help for the greater praise of His Divine Majesty, but not in such way, nor in such manners, especially in our so dangerous times, that works and free will receive any harm, or be held for nothing.

Eighteenth Rule. Although serving God our Lord much out of pure love is to be esteemed above all; we ought to praise much the fear of His Divine Majesty, because not only filial fear is a thing pious and most holy, but even servile fear—when the man reaches nothing else better or more useful—helps much to get out of mortal sin. And when he is out, he easily comes to filial fear, which is all acceptable and grateful to God our Lord: as being at one with the Divine Love.

"To Have the True Sentiment Which We Ought to Have in the Church Militant." In *The Spiritual Exercises of St. Ignatius Loyola*, translated from *The Autograph* by Father Elder Mullan, 39. New York: P.J. Kenedy & Sons, 1914.

POST-READING PARS

1. Describe two main features of the Catholic Church that Loyola presents here.
2. How does the text define some of these terms: faith, grace, salvation, merit, predestination?

Inquiry Corner

Content Question(s):	**Critical Question(s):**
According to Ignatius's Rule #13: "we ought always to hold that the white which I see, is black, if the Hierarchical Church so decides it." What defense does Ignatius offer for this claim?	Imagine yourself a Catholic peasant being instructed by a visiting Jesuit about how to "think with the Church." How might you respond to these Rules?
Comparative Question(s):	**Connection Question(s):**
Compare the devotional attitudes and practices in the Rules with the devotional practices described in Mirabai or the mystical experiences of Hildegard of Bingen and Margery Kempe. How do these rules of Ignatius compare to the *Rule of St. Benedict*? How do their historical contexts differ?	How might Ignatius's understandings of faith and work be applicable or not in today's multicultural, democratic societies?

from *The Book of the City of Ladies* by Christine de Pizan

Introduction

Christine de Pizan (henceforth "Christine")[196] was born in Venice in 1364 CE. She is perhaps the first female professional writer in Europe, meaning that she was paid by various patrons to write her texts. Moreover, she had control over the production of copies of her text, including all editorial decisions; this was somewhat unheard of at the time, both for male or female authors. Christine was deeply concerned about the readers' reception of texts, particularly any moral effects on the reader. She wrote over forty texts in many different genres, including poetry, epistles, essays, allegories, proverbs, dialogues, orations, and meditations. *The Book of the City of Ladies* combines philosophical treatise with a catalogue of saints and moral heroes, along with autobiographical and allegorical elements. The complexity of this text, along with what we know of her life, reveals someone intellectually sophisticated, creative, and resilient despite many personal and social tragedies.

SNAPSHOT BOX

LANGUAGE: Middle French

DATE: 1405 CE

LOCATION: France

TAGS: Education; Ethics and Morality; Gender; Identity and Self; Philosophy; Ways of Knowing; Women

Timeline

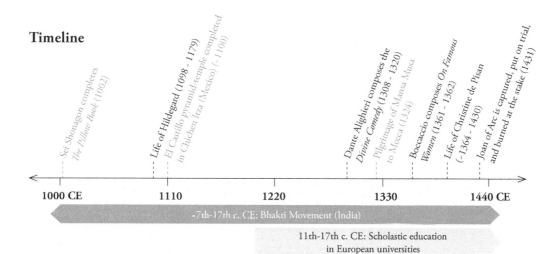

196. As "de Pizan" is a place name and not a surname, scholars use "Christine." In the introduction of the Hackett volume, p. ix, note 3, it says: "Medieval writers are often referred to by distinguishing place names, which ought not to be taken as surnames as we know them. Hence, while some medieval writers are now known more popularly by their place of origin (Aquinas, Ockham), it is more common, when employing a shorter version of the name, to refer to figures by their given names (hence Giles of Rome is "Giles," Marsilius of Padua is "Marsilius," and Christine de Pizan is "Christine)." Pizan is also spelled as Pisan.

Christine's father, Thomas de Pizan, a medical physician, was appointed to the court of the French king, Charles V, which resulted in her family's move to Paris. In 1379 CE, Christine married Etienne du Castel who was a court secretary. They had three children together. Around 1384–1389 CE, Thomas de Pizan died and, in 1389 CE, Etienne died from an epidemic, leaving the family nearly financially destitute with Christine needing to support her three children, her mother, and a niece. Christine decided that instead of trying to remarry (in order to get financial security) she would become a professional writer.

Christine credits her father along with other benefactors like Charles V and Jean Gerson for her education. Her early writings include poems on love and chivalry. Christine became embroiled in a public debate over the purported misogyny found in the thirteenth-century poem *The Romance of the Rose*. She was deeply concerned that this popular French allegorical poem had adverse effects on its male readership by perpetuating negative perceptions about women's morality thereby leading men to mistreat women. In this public dispute over this popular poem, Christine found an ally in the chancellor of the University of Paris, Jean Gerson, who when writing about Christine spoke of "the sharpness of her reasoning" and concluded that this "remarkable lady" won the debate.

In *City of Ladies*, Christine expands her critique by targeting every common false assertion or accusation about "the feminine sex." What are some of these false assertions or accusations? What argumentative strategies does Christine use in response? What are some ways that Christine uses her opponents' own beliefs against them? In Part 2, chapter 36 (and in Part 1, chapter 27), Christine reports her father's role in her own education and uses this in response to a false assertion about whether women should have the opportunity for an academic education. How does Christine use her first-person experience, here and elsewhere, to respond to these accusations?

In the nineteenth and twentieth centuries some scholars have claimed that Christine was an early "feminist." She would be one "if being a feminist means thinking about women and feeling that they deserve better in the world."[197] As you read her writing, what elements or strategies in Christine's arguments can you characterize as supporting feminist approaches or perspectives that would resonate today?

Scott Williams
Department of Philosophy

---

197. Beatrice Gottlieb, "The Problem of Feminism in the Fifteenth Century," in *The Selected Writings of Christine de Pizan*, edited by Renate Blumenfeld-Kosinski (New York: Norton), 274–97; 294.

from *The Book of the City of Ladies*

1. Here Begins the Book of the City of Ladies Whose First Chapter Tells Why and for What Purpose this Book was Written.

Following the practice that has become the habit of my life, namely the devoted study of literature, one day as I was sitting in my study, surrounded by books on many different subjects, my mind grew weary from dwelling at length on the weighty opinions of authors whom I had studied for so long. I looked up from my book, deciding then to leave subtle questions in peace and to read some lyric poetry for pleasure. With this intention, I searched for some small book, and by chance a strange volume came into my hands, not one of my own but one which had been given to me for safekeeping along with some others. When I held it open and saw from its title page that it was by Mathéolus, I smiled, for though I had never seen it before, I had often heard that like other books it discussed respect for women. I thought I would browse through it to amuse myself. I had not been reading for very long when my good mother called me to refresh myself with some supper, for it was evening. Intending to look at it the next day, I put it down. The next morning, again seated in my study as was my habit, I remembered wanting to examine this book by Mathéolus. I started to read it and went on for a little while. Because the subject seemed to me not very pleasant for people who do not enjoy lies, and of no use in developing virtue or manners, given its lack of integrity in diction and theme, and after browsing here and there and reading the end, I put it down in order to turn my attention to more elevated and useful study. But just the sight of this book, even though it was of no authority, made me wonder how it happened that so many different men—and learned men among them—have been and are so inclined to express both in speaking and in their treatises and writings so many devilish and wicked thoughts about women and their behavior.

Not only one or two and not even just this Mathéolus (for this book had a bad name anyway and was intended as a satire) but, more generally, judging from the treatises of all philosophers and poets and from all the orators—it would take too long to mention their names—it seems that they all speak from one and the same mouth. They all concur in one conclusion: that the behavior of women is inclined to and full of every vice. Thinking deeply about these matters, I began to examine my character and my conduct as a natural woman, and, similarly, I discussed this with other women whose company I frequently kept, princesses, great ladies, women of the middle and lower classes in great numbers, who graciously told me of their private experiences and intimate thoughts, in order to know in fact—judging in good conscience and without favor—whether the testimony of so many famous men could be true. To the best of my knowledge, no matter how long I confronted or dissected the problem, I could not see or realize how their claims could be true when compared to the natural behavior and character of women. Yet I still argued vehemently against women, saying that it would be impossible that so many famous men—such solemn scholars, possessed of such deep and great understanding, so clear-sighted in all things, as it seemed—could have spoken falsely on so many occasions that I could hardly find a book on morals where, even before I had read it in its entirety, I did not find several chapters or certain sections attacking women, no matter who the author was. This reason alone, in short, made me conclude that, although my intellect did not perceive my own great faults and, likewise, those of other women because of its simpleness and ignorance, it was however truly fitting that such was the case. And so I relied more on the judgment of others than on what I myself felt and knew. I was so transfixed in this line of thinking for such a long time that it seemed as if I were in a stupor. Like a gushing fountain, a series of authorities, whom I recalled one after another, came to mind, along with their opinions on this topic. And I finally decided that God formed a vile creature when He made woman, and I wondered how such a worthy artisan could have deigned to make such an abominable work which, from what they say, is the vessel as well as the refuge and abode of every evil and vice. As I was thinking this, a great unhappiness and sadness welled up in my heart, for I detested myself and the entire feminine sex, as though we were monstrosities in nature. And in my lament I spoke these words:

"Oh, God, how can this be? For unless I stray from my faith, I must never doubt that Your infinite wisdom and most perfect goodness ever created anything which was not good. Did You yourself not create woman in a very special way and since that time did You not give her all those inclinations which it pleased You for her to have? And how could it be that You could go wrong in anything? Yet look at all these accusations which have been judged, decided, and concluded against women. I do not know how to understand this repugnance. If it is so, fair Lord God, that in fact so many abominations abound in the female sex, for You Yourself say that the testimony of two or three witnesses lends credence, why shall I not doubt that this is true? Alas, God, why did You not let me be born in the world as a male, so that I would not stray in anything and would be as perfect as a male is said to be? But since Your kindness has not been extended to me, then forgive my negligence in your service, most fair Lord God, and may it not displease You, for the servant who receives fewer gifts from his lord is less obliged in his service." I spoke these words to God in my lament and a great deal more for a very long time in sad reflection, and in my folly I considered myself most unfortunate because God had made me inhabit a female body in this world.

2. Here Christine Describes How Three Ladies Appeared to Her and How the One Who Was in Front Spoke First and Comforted Her in Her Pain.

So occupied with these painful thoughts, my head bowed in shame, my eyes filled with tears, leaning my cheek on my hand, elbow propped on the pommel of my chair's armrest, I suddenly saw a ray of light fall on my lap, as though it were the sun. I shuddered then, as if wakened from sleep, for I was sitting in a shadow where the sun could not have shone at that hour. And as I lifted my head to see where this light was coming from, I saw three crowned ladies standing before me, and the splendor of their bright faces shone on me and throughout the entire room. Now no one would ask whether I was surprised, for my doors were shut and they had still entered. Fearing that some phantom had come to tempt me and filled with great fright, I made the Sign of the Cross on my forehead.

Then she who was the first of the three smiled and began to speak, "Dear daughter, do not be afraid, for we have not come here to harm or trouble you but to console you, for we have taken pity on your distress, and we have come to bring you out of the ignorance which so blinds your own intellect that you shun what you know for a certainty and believe what you do not know or see or recognize except by virtue of many strange opinions. You resemble the fool in the prank who was dressed in women's clothes while he slept; because those who were making fun of him repeatedly told him he was a woman, he believed their false testimony more readily than the certainty of his own identity. Fair daughter, have you lost all sense? Have you forgotten that when fine gold is tested in the furnace, it does not change or vary in strength but becomes purer the more it is hammered and handled in different ways? Do you not know that the best things are the most debated and the most discussed? If you wish to consider the question of the highest form of reality, which consists in ideas or celestial substances, consider whether the greatest philosophers who have lived and whom you support against your own sex have ever resolved whether ideas are false and contrary to the truth. Notice how these same philosophers contradict and criticize one another, just as you have seen in the *Metaphysics* where Aristotle takes their opinions to task and speaks similarly of Plato and other philosophers. And note, moreover, how even Saint Augustine and the Doctors of the Church have criticized Aristotle in certain passages, although he is known as the prince of philosophers in whom both natural and moral philosophy attained their highest level. It also seems that you think that all the words of the philosophers are articles of faith, that they could never be wrong. As far as the poets of whom you speak are concerned, do you not know that they spoke on many subjects in a fictional way and that often they mean the contrary of what their words openly say? One can interpret them according to the figure of grammar called *antiphrasis*, which means, as you know, that if you call something bad, in fact, it is good, and also vice versa. Thus I advise you to profit from their works and to interpret them in the manner in which they are intended in those passages where they attack women.

[...]

8. Here Christine Tells How, Under Reason's Command and Assistance, She Began to Excavate the Earth and Lay the Foundation.

Then Lady Reason responded and said, "Get up, daughter! Without waiting any longer, let us go to the Field of Letters. There the City of Ladies will be founded on a flat and fertile plain, where all fruits and freshwater rivers are found and where the earth abounds in all good things. Take the pick of your understanding and dig and clear out a great ditch wherever you see the marks of my ruler, and I will help you carry away the earth on my own shoulders."

I immediately stood up to obey her commands and, thanks to these three ladies, I felt stronger and lighter than before. She went ahead, and I followed behind, and after we had arrived at this field I began to excavate and dig, following her marks with the pick of cross-examination. And this was my first work:

"Lady, I remember well what you told me before, dealing with the subject of how so many men have attacked and continue to attack the behavior of women, that gold becomes more refined the longer it stays in the furnace, which means the more women have been wrongfully attacked, the greater waxes the merit of their glory. But please tell me why and for what reason different authors have spoken against women in their books, since I already know from you that this is wrong; tell me if Nature makes man so inclined or whether they do it out of hatred and where does this behavior come from?"

Then she replied, "Daughter, to give you a way of entering into the question more deeply, I will carry away this first basketful of dirt. This behavior most certainly does not come from Nature, but rather is contrary to Nature [...]. [...] But just as you have said elsewhere, if these writers had only looked for the ways in which men can be led away from foolishness and could have been kept from tiring themselves in attacking the life and behavior of immoral and dissolute women—for to tell the straight truth, there is nothing which should be avoided more than an evil, dissolute, and perverted woman, who is like a monster in nature, a counterfeit estranged from her natural condition, which must be simple, tranquil, and upright—then I would grant you that they would have built a supremely excellent work. But I can assure you that these attacks on all women—when in fact there are so many excellent women—have never originated with me, Reason, and that all who subscribe to them have failed totally and will continue to fail. So now throw aside these black, dirty, and uneven stones from your work, for they will never be fitted into the fair edifice of your City.

"Other men have attacked women for other reasons: such reproach has occurred to some men because of their own vices and others have been moved by the defects of their own bodies, others through pure jealousy, still others by the pleasure they derive in their own personalities from slander. Others, in order to show they have read many authors, base their own writings on what they have found in books and repeat what other writers have said and cite different authors.

"Those who attack women because of their own vices are men who spent their youths in dissolution and enjoyed the love of many different women, used deception in many of their encounters, and have grown old in their sins without repenting, and now regret their past follies and the dissolute life they led. But Nature, which allows the will of the heart to put into effect what the powerful appetite desires, has grown cold in them. Therefore they are pained when they see that their 'good times' have now passed them by [...].

27. Christine Asks Reason Whether God Has Ever Wished to Ennoble the Mind of Woman with the Loftiness of the Sciences; and Reason's Answer.

After hearing these things, I replied to the lady who spoke infallibly: "My lady, truly has God revealed great wonders in the strength of these women whom you describe. But please enlighten me again, whether it has ever pleased this God, who has bestowed so many favors on women, to honor the feminine sex with the privilege of the virtue of high understanding and great learning, and whether women ever have a clever enough mind for this. I wish very much to know this because men maintain that the mind of women can learn only a little."

She answered, "My daughter, since I told you before, you know quite well that the opposite of their opinion is true, and to show you this even more clearly, I will give you proof through examples. I tell you again—and don't fear a contradiction—if it were customary to send daughters to school like sons, and if they were then taught the natural sciences, they would learn as thoroughly and understand the subtleties of all the arts and sciences as well as sons. And by chance there happen to be such women, for, as I touched on before, just as women have more delicate bodies than men, weaker and less able to perform many tasks, so do they have minds that are freer and sharper whenever they apply themselves."

"My lady, what are you saying? With all due respect, could you dwell longer on this point, please. Certainly men would never admit this answer is true, unless it is explained more plainly, for they believe that one normally sees that men know more than women do."

She answered, "Do you know why women know less?"

"Not unless you tell me, my lady."

"Without the slightest doubt, it is because they are not involved in many different things, but stay at home, where it is enough for them to run the household, and there is nothing which so instructs a reasonable creature as the exercise and experience of many different things."

"My lady, since they have minds skilled in conceptualizing and learning, just like men, why don't women learn more?"

She replied, "Because, my daughter, the public does not require them to get involved in the affairs which men are commissioned to execute, just as I told you before. It is enough for women to perform the usual duties to which they are ordained. As for judging from experience, since one sees that women usually know less than men, that therefore their capacity for understanding is less, look at men who farm the flatlands or who live in the mountains. You will find that in many countries they seem completely savage because they are so simpleminded. All the same, there is no doubt that Nature provided them with the qualities of body and mind found in the wisest and most learned men. All of this stems from a failure to learn, though, just as I told you, among men or women, some possess better minds than others. Let me tell you about women who have possessed great learning and profound understanding and treat the question of the similarity of women's minds to men's."

[...]

19. The End of the Book: Christine Addresses the Ladies.

My most honored ladies, may God be praised, for now our City is entirely finished and completed, where all of you who love glory, virtue, and praise may be lodged in great honor, ladies from the past as well as from the present and future, for it has been built and established for every honorable lady. And my most dear ladies, it is natural for the human heart to rejoice when it finds itself victorious in any enterprise and its enemies confounded. Therefore you are right, my ladies, to rejoice when it finds itself victorious in any enterprise and its enemies confounded. Therefore you are right, my ladies, to rejoice greatly in God and in honest mores upon seeing this new City completed, which can be not only the refuge for you all, that is, for virtuous women, but also the defense and guard against your enemies and assailants, if you guard it well. For you can see that the substance with which it is made is entirely of virtue, so resplendent that you may see yourselves mirrored in it, especially in the roofs built in the last part as well as in the other parts which concern you. And my dear ladies, do not misuse this new inheritance like the arrogant who turn proud when their prosperity grows and their wealth multiplies, but rather follow the example of your Queen, the sovereign Virgin, who, after the extraordinary honor of being chosen Mother of the Son of God was announced to her, humbled herself all the more by calling herself the handmaiden of God. Thus, my ladies, just as it is true that a creature's humility and kindness wax with the increase of its virtues, may this City be an occasion for you to conduct yourselves honestly and with integrity and to be all the more virtuous and humble.

And you ladies who are married, do not scorn being subject to your husbands, for sometimes it is not the best thing for a creature to be independent. This is attested by what the angel said to Ezra: Those, he said, who take advantage of their free will can fall into sin and despise our Lord and deceive the just, and for this they perish. Those women with peaceful, good, and discrete husbands who are devoted to them, praise God for this boon, which is not inconsiderable, for a greater boon in the world could not be given them. And may they be diligent in serving, loving, and cherishing their husbands in the loyalty of their heart, as they should, keeping their peace and praying to God to uphold and save them. And those women who have husbands neither completely good nor completely bad should still praise God for not having the worst and should strive to moderate their vices and pacify them, according to their conditions. And those women who have husbands who are cruel, mean, and savage should strive to endure them while trying to overcome their vices and lead them back, if they can, to a reasonable and seemly life. And if they are so obstinate that their wives are unable to do anything, at least they will acquire great merit for their souls through the virtue of patience. And everyone will bless them and support them.

So, my ladies, be humble and patient, and God's grace will grow in you, and praise will be given to you as well as the Kingdom of Heaven. For Saint Gregory has said that patience is the entrance to Paradise and the way of Jesus Christ. And may none of you be forced into holding frivolous opinions nor be hardened in them, lacking all basis in reason, nor be jealous or disturbed in mind, nor haughty in speech, nor outrageous in your acts, for these things disturb the mind and lead to madness. Such behavior is unbecoming and unfitting for women.

And you, virgin maidens, be pure, simple, and serene, without vagueness, for the snares of evil men are set for you. Keep your eyes lowered, with few words in your mouths, and act respectfully. Be armed with the strength of virtue against the tricks of the deceptive and avoid their company.

And widows, may there be integrity in your dress, conduct, and speech; piety in your deeds and way of life; prudence in your bearing; patience (so necessary!), strength, and resistance in tribulations and difficult affairs; humility in your heart, countenance, and speech; and charity in your works.

In brief, all women—whether noble, bourgeois, or lower-class—be well-informed in all things and cautious in defending your honor and chastity against your enemies! My ladies, see how these men accuse you of so many vices in everything. Make liars of them all by showing forth your virtue, and prove their attacks false by acting well, so that you can say with the Psalmist, "the vices of the evil will fall on their heads." Repel the deceptive flatterers who, using different charms, seek with various tricks to steal that which you must consummately guard, that is, your honor and the beauty of your praise. Oh my ladies, flee, flee the foolish love they urge on you! Flee it, for God's sake, flee! For no good can come to you from it. Rather, rest assured that however deceptive their lures, their end is always to your detriment. And do not believe the contrary, for it cannot be otherwise. Remember, dear ladies, how these men call you frail, unserious, and easily influenced but yet try hard, using all kinds of strange and deceptive tricks, to catch you, just as one lays traps for wild animals. Flee, flee, my ladies, and avoid their company—under these smiles are hidden deadly and painful poisons. And so may it please you, my most respected ladies, to cultivate virtue, to flee vice, to increase and multiply our City, and to rejoice and act well. And may I, your servant, commend myself to you, praying to God who by His grace has granted me to live in this world and to persevere in His holy service. May He in the end have mercy on my great sins and grant to me the joy which lasts forever, which I may, by His grace, afford to you. Amen

Here ends the third and last part of the Book of the City of Ladies.

de Pizan, Christine. Selections from *The Book of the City of Ladies*, translated by Earl Jeffrey Richards, 3–7, 16, 18, 62–64, 254–257. New York: Persea, 1998.

POST-READING PARS

1. List two or three major false accusations that men have traditionally made against women, according to Christine de Pizan.

2. List two or three main reasons that Christine gives for why men have historically made such accusations against women.

Inquiry Corner

Content Question(s):	**Critical Question(s):**
What things does Christine de Pizan lament, and how does Lady Reason, Lady Rectitude, and Lady Justice respond to her lamentations?	Does Christine de Pizan's advice to married women at the end of *The Book of the City of Ladies* undermine her arguments earlier in the text? Are there ways that her arguments about navigating married life align with her other arguments?
Comparative Question(s):	**Connection Question(s):**
Compare and contrast Christine de Pizan's understanding of women, with the way in which women are presented or understood in other readings you have encountered, for example, *Sunjata*, *Kebra Nagast*, or "Alankaravati."	How do Lady *Reason*, Lady *Rectitude* (or righteousness of will), and Lady *Justice* help Christine to build a city that defends women against so many false accusations? How would reason, rectitude of will (or righteousness), and justice help us to build a well-functioning society today?

BEYOND THE CLASSROOM

» To this day, there still remains a wage gap between men and women in the workforce. Why is this so? What are some concrete ways of addressing this situation?

» Think of some examples of women leading just as effectively as men, if not more effectively than men. How are such women viewed by society today?

from *The Book of Margery Kempe* by Margery Kempe

SNAPSHOT BOX

LANGUAGE: English

DATE: 1435 CE

LOCATION: England

GENRE: Spiritual autobiography

TAGS: Authority and Institution; Education; Gender; Mysticism; Pilgrimage; Ritual and Practice; Spirituality; Women

Introduction

The prosperous daughter of an English mayor, Margery Kempe married at age twenty or soon after and gave birth to fourteen children. As a young woman she personally owned a brewery and then a grain mill, and much later convinced her husband to enter a celibate marriage with her, in part by agreeing to pay off her husband's debts. Unable to read, Kempe had access to spiritual classics read by others and eventually commissioned different clerics to write down her biography. What might have been some of the reasons for her inability to read?

Kempe's "Book" describes lifelong experiences of visions and **mystical** encounters. At the time of her first pregnancy, she reported a time when she was "plagued by evil spirits" and "devils," each urging her to behaviors harmful to herself and others. This time of torment ended with an appearance by "our merciful Lord Jesus Christ." Kempe reported visions from God across her lifetime that she said included inside information about other people and future events and commandments for her own actions and decisions.

Kempe made multiple pilgrimages, traveling to Jerusalem and the Holy Land, Rome, Spain, and Poland. Her descriptions of her travels focused largely on her own spiritual experiences. She also described repeated episodes of rejection by her traveling companions, at times leading to abandonment and increased personal danger. Even as Kempe described her visions and conversations with God, she openly described the negative reactions of other people in all areas of her life. She noted

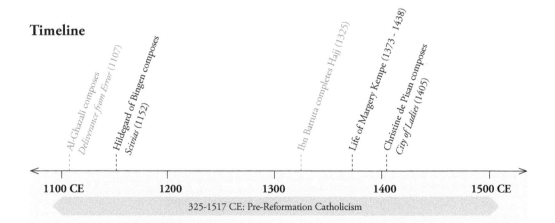

Timeline

Al-Ghazali composes *Deliverance from Error* (1107)

Hildegard of Bingen composes *Scivias* (1152)

Ibn Battuta completes Hajj (1325)

Life of Margery Kempe (1373 - 1438)

Christine de Pisan composes *City of Ladies* (1405)

1100 CE   1200   1300   1400   1500 CE

325-1517 CE: Pre-Reformation Catholicism

in particular the reactions of clergy in the Church, described here as doctors and masters of divinity, clerics, canons, and archbishops. For clergy and lay people alike, most reactions stemmed from disapproval of Kempe's wardrobe and her emotional behavior in church. Early in the book Kempe stated, "Many people said she was a false hypocrite, and wept when in company for advantage and profit."

Kempe argued that the very behaviors that brought her into disfavor with many were a direct result of the divine revelation and command that she received. She reported that wearing only white was "commanded . . . in her soul by revelation." She also described her tendency to weep and sob in church as "a gift of God, and that she could not have it but when God would give it, nor could she withstand it when God would send it."

Some clergy, including her trusted confessors, believed and supported Kempe, affirming the role of divine inspiration in her life. Others classified her as a **heretic**, specifically naming a key controversy of her time: the **Lollard** movement associated with John Wycliffe. While controversial in her behavior, Kempe did not espouse any of the pre-Reformation beliefs of the Lollard movement. In particular, the Lollard movement criticized the Catholic understanding of sacraments and the role of the priesthood and rejected other **orthodox** practices, including pilgrimage.

In her dictation of her autobiography in the midst of fifteenth-century England, Margery Kempe referred to herself as "Kempe" only one time. Rather than calling herself by her name, she made almost five hundred references to herself as the "creature." Since Kempe wrote approximately four hundred years prior to the publication of Mary Shelley's *Frankenstein* in 1818, the word "creature" lacked its modern monstrous connotations, reflecting instead the original meaning of "created one."

Kempe never articulated her reasoning for identifying herself primarily as a created one but instead left the reader to ponder the ways in which this term might signify humility or authority. How did the term "creature" level the playing field with the clergy who opposed Kempe? How did it either grant her authority or absolve her from responsibility for her actions and the reactions of other people?

Brenda K. Lewis
Humanities Program

PRE-READING PARS

1. Have you ever been on a pilgrimage?

2. Do you have experience of something that could be described as mystical? Perhaps a dream that informed your perspective, or an experience of inspiration in a creative exercise?

3. Beyond the ability to read and write, what makes a person religiously or culturally literate?

from *The Book of Margery Kempe*

Chapter 51

Another time a great cleric came to her asking how these words should be understood: *Crescite et multiplicamini.*[198]

She answering said, 'Sir, these words are not only to be understood as applying to the begetting of children physically, but also to the gaining of virtue, which is spiritual fruit, such as by hearing the words of God, by giving a good example, by meekness and patience, charity and chastity, and other such things- for patience is more worthy than miracle-working.' And she, through the grace of God, so answered that cleric that he was well pleased. And our Lord, of his mercy, always made some men love her and support her.

And so in this city of York, there was a doctor of divinity, Master John Aclom, also a canon of the Minster, Sir John Kendale, and another priest who sang by the Bishop's tomb– these were her good friends among the ecclesiastics.

So she stayed in that city for fourteen days, as she had said before, and somewhat more, and on Sundays she received communion in the Minster with much weeping, violent sobbing, and loud crying, so that many people wondered very much what was wrong with her. So afterwards there came a priest- a worthy cleric he seemed- and said to her, 'Woman, you said when you first came here that you would only stay fourteen days.'

'Yes, sir, with your leave, I said that I would stay here fourteen days, but I did not say that I should neither stay here more nor less. But now, sir, I tell you truly that I am not leaving yet.'

Then he set her a day, commanding her to appear before him in the Chapter-house. And she said that she would obey his injunction with a good will.

She went then to Master John Aclom, the said doctor of divinity, begging him to be there on her side. And so he was, and he found great favor amongst them all. Another master of divinity had also promised her to be there with her, but he drew back till he knew how the cause should go, whether with her or against her.

---

198. Genesis 1:22 ('Be fruitful, and multiply...'); held by some heretics to justify free love.

There were many people that day in the Chapterhouse of the Minster to hear and see what would be said or done to the said creature. When the day came, she was all ready in the Minster to come and answer for herself. Then her friends came to her and urged her to be cheerful. Thanking them, she said that so she would.

And immediately a priest came and very kindly took her by the arm to help her through the press of people, and brought her before a worthy doctor, the one who had ordered her to appear before him in the Chapterhouse on this day in York Minster. And with this doctor sat many other very reverend and worthy clerics, of whom some had great love for the said creature.

Then the worthy doctor said to her, 'Woman, what are you doing here in this part of the country?'

'Sir, I come on pilgrimage to offer here at St William's shrine.'[199]

Then he went on, 'Do you have a husband?'

She said, 'Yes.'

'Do you have a letter recording his permission?'

'Sir,' she said, 'my husband gave me permission with his own mouth. Why do you proceed in this way with me more than you do with other pilgrims who are here, and who have no letter any more than I have? Sir, them you let go in peace and quiet, and undisturbed, and yet I may not be left alone amongst you. And sir, if there be any cleric here amongst you all who can prove that I have said any word otherwise than as I ought to do, I am ready to put it right very willingly. I will neither maintain error nor heresy, for it is my will entirely to hold as Holy Church holds, and fully to please God.'

Then the clerks examined her in the articles of the faith and on many other points, as they pleased, to all of which she answered well and truly, so that they might have no occasion in her words to harm her, thanks be to God.

And then the doctor who sat there as a judge summoned her to appear before the Archbishop of York- and told her what day- at a town called Cawood, commanding her to be kept in prison till the day of her appearing came.

Then the secular people answered for her, and said she should not go to prison, for they would themselves undertake for her and go to the Archbishop with her. And so the clerics said no more to her at that time, for they rose up and went wherever they wanted, and let her go wherever she wanted- worship be to Jesus!

And soon after there came a cleric to her- one of the same that had sat against her- and said, 'Woman, I beg you not to be annoyed with me, though I sat with the doctor against you; he kept on at me so, that I dared not do otherwise.'

And she said, 'Sir, I am not annoyed with you for that.'

Then he said, 'I pray you then, pray for me.'

'Sir,' she said, 'I will, very readily.'

---

199. William Fitzherbert, Archbishop of York (d. 1154 CE); he was canonized in 1227 CE and miracles were reported at his tomb. There was a strong cult of the saint at York.

Chapter 52

There was a monk who was going to preach in York, and who had heard much slander and much evil talk about the said creature. And when he was going to preach, there was a great crowd of people to hear him, and she present with them. And so when he was launched into his sermon, he repeated many matters so openly that people saw perfectly well it was on account of her, at which her friends who loved her were very sorry and upset because of it, and she was much the merrier, because she had something to try her patience and her charity, through which she trusted to please our Lord Christ Jesus.

When the sermon was over, a doctor of divinity who had great love for her, together with many other people as well, came to her and said, 'Margery, how have you got on today?'

'Sir,' she said, 'very well indeed, God be blessed. I have reason to be very happy and glad in my soul that I may suffer anything for his love, for he suffered much more for me.'

Shortly afterwards, a man who was also devoted to her came with his wife and other people, and escorted her seven miles from there to the Archbishop of York, and brought her into a fair

chamber, where there came a good cleric, saying to the good man who had brought her there, 'Sir, why have you and your wife brought this woman here? She will steal away from you, and then she will have brought shame upon you.'

The good man said, 'I dare well say she will remain and answer for herself very willingly.'

On the next day she was brought into the Archbishop's chapel, and many of the Archbishop's household came there scorning her, calling her 'Lollard' and 'heretic,' and swore many a horrible oath that she should be burned. And she, through the strength of Jesus, replied to them, 'Sirs, I fear you will be burned in hell without end, unless you correct yourselves of your swearing of oaths, for you do not keep the commandments of God. I would not swear as you do for all the money in this world.'

Then they went away, as if they were ashamed. She then, saying her prayers in her mind, asked for grace to behave that day as was most pleasure to God, and profit to her own soul, and good example to her fellow Christians. Our Lord, answering her, said that everything would go well.

At last the said Archbishop[200] came into the chapel with his clerics, and he said to her abruptly, 'Why do you go about in white clothes? Are you a virgin?'

She, kneeling before him, said, 'No, sir, I am no virgin; I am a married woman.'

He ordered his household to fetch a pair of fetters and said she should be fettered, for she was a false heretic, and then she said, 'I am no heretic, nor shall you prove me one.'

---

200. Henry Bowet, Archbishop of York 1407–1423 CE; he showed zeal against the Lollards.

The Archbishop went away and left her standing alone. Then for a long while she said her prayers to our Lord God Almighty to help her and succour her against all her enemies both spiritual and bodily, and her flesh trembled and quaked amazingly, so that she was glad to put her hands under her clothes so that it should not be noticed.

Afterwards the Archbishop came back into the chapel with many worthy clerics, amongst whom was the same doctor who had examined her before, and the monk who had preached against her a little while before in York. Some of the people asked whether she were a Christian woman or a Jew; some said she was a good woman, and some said not.

Then the Archbishop took his seat, and his clerics too, each according to his degree, many people being present. And during the time that people were gathering together and the Archbishop was taking his seat, the said creature stood at the back, saying her prayers for help and succour against her enemies with high devotion, and for so long that she melted all into tears. And at last she cried out loudly, so that the Archbishop, and his clerics, and many people, were all astonished at her, for they had not heard such crying before.

When her crying was passed, she came before the Archbishop and fell down on her knees, the Archbishop saying very roughly to her, 'Why do you weep so, woman?'

She answering said, 'Sir, you shall wish some day that you had wept as sorely as I.'

And then, after the Archbishop had put to her the Articles of our Faith- to which God gave her grace to answer well, truly and readily, without much having to stop and think, so that he could not criticize her- he said to the clerics, 'She knows her faith well enough. What shall I do with her?'

The clerics said, 'We know very well that she knows the Articles of the Faith, but we will not allow her to dwell among us, because the people have great faith in her talk, and perhaps she might lead some of them astray.' Then the Archbishop said to her: 'I am told very bad things about you. I hear it said that you are a very wicked woman.'

And she replied, 'Sir, I also hear it said that you are a wicked man. And if you are as wicked as people say, you will never get to heaven, unless you amend while you are here.'

Then he said very roughly, 'Why you!... What do people say about me?'

She answered, 'Other people, sir, can tell you well enough.'

Then a great cleric with a furred hood said, 'Quiet! You speak about yourself, and let him be.'

Afterwards the Archbishop said to her; 'Lay your hand on the book here before me, and swear that you will go out of my diocese as soon as you can.'

'No, sir,' she said, 'I pray you, give me permission to go back into York to take leave of my friends.'

Then he gave her permission for one or two days. She thought it was too short a time, and so she replied, 'Sir, I may not go out of this diocese so hastily, for I must stay and speak with good men before I go; and I must, sir, with your leave, go to Bridlington and speak with my confessor, a good man, who was the good Prior's confessor, who is now canonized.'[201]

Then the Archbishop said to her, 'You shall swear that you will not teach people or call them to account in my diocese.'

'No, sir, I will not swear,' she said, 'for I shall speak of God and rebuke those who swear great oaths wherever I go, until such time that the Pope and Holy Church have ordained that nobody shall be so bold as to speak of God, for God Almighty does not forbid, sir, that we should speak of him. And also the Gospel[202] mentions that, when the woman had heard our Lord preach, she came before him and said in a loud voice, "Blessed be the womb that bore you, and the teats that gave you suck." Then our Lord replied to her, "In truth, so are they blessed who bear the word of God and keep it." And therefore, sir, I think that the Gospel gives
me leave to speak of God.'

'Ah, sir,' said the clerics, 'here we know that she has a devil in her, for she speaks of the Gospel.'[203]

A great cleric quickly produced a book and quoted St Paul for his part against her, that no woman should preach.[204] She, answering to this, said, 'I do not preach, sir; I do not go into any pulpit. I use only conversation and good words, and that I will do while I live.'

Then a doctor who had examined her before said, 'Sir, she told me the worst tale about priests that I ever heard.'

The Archbishop commanded her to tell that tale.

'Sir, by your reverence, I only spoke of one priest, by way of example, who, as I have learned it, went astray in a wood- through the sufferance of God, for the profit of his soul- until night came upon him. Lacking any shelter, he found a fair arbour in which he rested that night, which had a beautiful pear-tree in the middle, all covered in blossom, which he delighted to look at. To that place came a great rough bear, ugly to behold, that shook the pear-tree and caused the blossoms to fall. Greedily this horrible beast ate and devoured those fair flowers. And when he had eaten them, turning his tail towards the priest, he discharged them out again at his rear end.

'The priest, greatly revolted at that disgusting sight and becoming very depressed for fear of what it might mean, wandered off on his way all gloomy and pensive. He happened to meet a good-looking, aged man like a pilgrim, who asked the priest the reason for his sadness. The priest, repeating the matter written before, said he felt great fear and heaviness of heart when he beheld that revolting beast soil and devour

---

201. St. John of Bridlington (d. 1379 CE), combined his official duties with a life of fervent prayer, and had the gift of tears. Miracles were reported at his tomb, and he was canonized in 1401 CE.

202. Luke 11:27–8.

203. I.e. that like various contemporary Lollard women, Margery has been studying scripture.

204. I Corinthians 14:34–35.

such lovely flowers and blossoms, and afterwards discharge them so horribly at his rear end in the priest's presence- he did not understand what this might mean.

'Then the pilgrim, showing himself to be the messenger of God, thus addressed him, "Priest, you are yourself the pear-tree, somewhat flourishing and flowering through your saying of services and administering of sacraments, although you act without devotion, for you take very little heed how you say your matins and your service, so long as it is babbled to an end. Then you go to your mass without devotion, and you have very little contrition for your sin. You receive there the fruit of everlasting life, the sacrament of the altar, in a very feeble frame of mind. All day long afterwards, you spend your time amiss: you give yourself over to buying and selling, bartering and exchanging, just like a man of the world. You sit over your beer, giving yourself up to gluttony and excess, to the lust of your body, through lechery and impurity. You break the commandments of God through swearing, lying, detraction and backbiting gossip, and the practice of other such sins. Thus, through your misconduct, just like the loathsome bear, you devour and destroy the flowers and blossoms of virtuous living, to your own endless damnation and to the hindrance or many other people, unless you have grace for repentance and amending."'

Then the Archbishop liked the tale a lot and commended it, saying it was a good tale. And the cleric who had examined her before in the absence of the Archbishop, said, 'Sir, this tale cut me to the heart.'

The said creature said to the cleric, 'Ah, worthy doctor, sir, in the place where I mostly live is a worthy cleric, a good preacher, who boldly speaks out against the misconduct of people and will flatter no one. He says many times in the pulpit: "If anyone is displeased by my preaching, note him well, for he is guilty." And just so, sir,' she said to the clerk, 'do you behave with me, God forgive you for it.'

The cleric did not know what he could say to her, and the same cleric came to her and begged her for forgiveness that he had been so against her. He also asked her specially to pray for him.

And then afterwards the Archbishop said, "Where shall I get a man who could escort this woman from me?'

Many young men quickly jumped up, and every one of them said, "My lord, I will go with her."

The Archbishop answered. 'You are too young: I will not have you.'

Then a good, sober man of the Archbishop's household asked his lord what he would give him if he would escort her. The Archbishop offered him five shillings, and the man asked for a noble.[205] The Archbishop answering said, 'I will not spend so much on her body.'

'Yes, good sir,' said this creature, 'Our Lord shall reward you very well for it.'

Then the Archbishop said to the man, 'See, here is five shillings, and now escort her fast out of this area.'

205. I.e. six shillings and eightpence.

She, kneeling down on her knees, asked his blessing. He, asking her to pray for him, blessed her and let her go.

Then she, going back again to York, was received by many people, and by very worthy clerics, who rejoiced in our Lord. who had given her—uneducated as she was—the wit and wisdom to answer so many learned men without shame or blame, thanks be to God.

Kempe, Margery. Chapters 51 and 52. In *The Book of Margery Kempe*, translated by B. A. Windeatt, 159–67. New York: Penguin Classics, 1985.

POST READING PARS

1. What are the conditions that allowed Kempe's pilgrimages? How did the experience of pilgrimage amplify or reinterpret her mystical experience?
2. When you read of the encounters between Kempe and various leaders in the Church, would you say the conflicts arose from religious or cultural sources?
3. How did Kempe demonstrate religious literacy?

Inquiry Corner

Content Question(s):	Critical Question(s):
Members of the clergy questioned Margery Kempe using the Articles of Faith. Did they find any actual heretical beliefs when they tested her on these articles?	In what ways do institutional traditions, social norms, and gender roles interact with each other in Kempe's experiences?
Comparative Question(s):	**Connection Question(s):**
How do Kempe's experiences and behaviors compare to other mystics we have studied?	What disciplinary perspectives provide insight into *The Book of Margery Kempe*? How do literary criticism, gender studies, economics, and religious history bring different questions to the discussion?

BEYOND THE CLASSROOM

» Consider a leader in contemporary life who inspires passionate resistance and support. Why do you think they are able to inspire such loyalty from some, and such disdain from others? What is it about their rhetoric that makes it powerful and effective for some?

"Origins of Higher Education"

SNAPSHOT BOX

LANGUAGE:
Medieval Latin

DATE: 1215–1254 CE

LOCATION: Paris,
Rome

GENRE: Regulations

TAGS: Authority
and Institution;
Education;
Philosophy; Religion;
Ways of Knowing

Introduction

In the Northern Hemisphere, the idea of a university originated in twelfth-century western Europe. The concept of "higher education," however, has precedents in many different civilizations. Some of these include Plato's Academy and Aristotle's Lyceum (both founded in the fourth century BCE in Athens), which provide examples from the Classical Greco-Roman world; institutions for training government officials in Confucianism and classical literature that were operating in China as early as the third century CE; and in India, the great Nalanda Mahavihara, a Buddhist center for higher learning—founded during the fifth century CE—that drew scholars from all over south and east Asia. In the Islamic world, the great madrassa (Islamic academy) al-Qarawiyyin in Fes, Morocco, is considered by many to be the oldest continuously functioning institution of higher education in the world at some 1200 years old. Does this diversity of cultural contexts support an argument that higher education was valued universally?

Note that what distinguished all of these centers of higher learning was their emphasis on philosophy and religion as the means to understand better the human condition, since these disciplines pondered existential questions such as the purpose of the cosmos and the meaning of human life. It also indicates that "higher" education—which might be defined as any learning beyond what was required for satisfying basic needs—was a pursuit primarily for those of wealth, or those who

Timeline

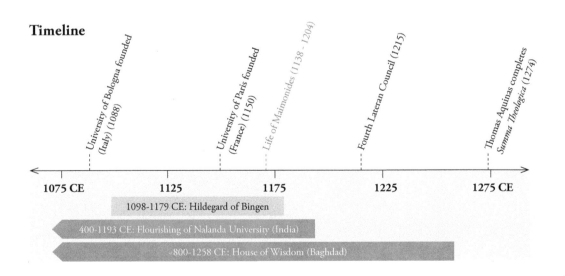

had received the necessary prior training as a monk or religious scholar. Marginalized communities, including people in bondage and women, were usually barred from participating in education considered unnecessary for their "station" in life.

The unsettled political situation leading to the twelfth century in western Europe meant that any educational opportunities were sporadic and usually confined to the local monastery. Education consisted primarily of learning information from the past rather than attempting to generate new knowledge in the monasteries and attached monastery schools. In your opinion, what is the most important function of education: to pass along acquired knowledge from the past or to generate new knowledge? or to challenge new ways of thinking? By the early twelfth century, the increase in wealth and the growth of urban populations saw an increase in monastery schools and in the creation of similar schools at some of the great cathedrals of western Europe.

While education in the monastic schools remained centered on monastic practices such as meditation and contemplation, the cathedral schools became places where a new method of learning emerged. This method of the "schoolmen" came to be called **scholasticism**, and it was a method based upon **dialectic** argumentation in which scholars debated contrary positions. The philosophy of the Greek philosopher Aristotle had been largely forgotten in western Europe but was reintroduced in the twelfth century from the Islamic world. As some of these documents illustrate, this reintroduction of Aristotelian ways of thinking about the world could be very challenging to students, or even dangerous in the eyes of Church authorities.

Students would travel to these cathedral schools to hear scholars debate the meaning of a text or resolve a seeming contradiction. As cities filled with rival scholars and bands of rowdy students, friction would often develop between these groups and the townspeople. In an attempt to rein in the excesses of student behavior, the first "universities" were officially organized not as institutions with buildings and campuses but as a type of trade guild where membership could be controlled and protected. Like guild apprentices, students were trained by experts who controlled the requirements for appropriate certification of achievement, but rather than train for a specific trade or artistic pursuit, university students were prepared for positions of professional service. Students and faculty at a university were not only recognized as clerics and thus subject only to church law, not local statutes, but students also gained the power to deny payment to inferior teachers!

Eventually, a system of instruction similar to our own began to take shape. Entering the university at about the age of fourteen, bachelor students (and as clerics, only men were enrolled) learned the seven liberal arts as a foundation for further study that might lead to a master's degree, which allowed one to teach (from the Latin *magister*, teacher). Professional degrees would be granted in theology, law, or medicine, and some schools became known for their superior instruction in these fields, such as the University of Bologna (law) and the University of Paris (theology).

Medical study was highly influenced by developments in the Islamic world where anatomical knowledge and surgical practices were much superior to those in western Europe. Students completing a course of study in one of these three fields would become "**doctors**" from the Latin term meaning "religious teacher."

Rodger Payne
Department of Religious Studies

PRE-READING PARS

1. What are two features that come to mind when you think of the words "university" and "higher education"?

2. What are two ways you would characterize the nature of a typical student-faculty relationship?

Origins of Higher Education

Rules of the University of Paris, 1215

Robert, servant of the cross of Christ by divine pity cardinal priest of the tide, St. Stephen in Mons Caelius, legate of the apostolic see,[206] to all the masters and scholars of Paris eternal greeting in the Lord. Let all know that, since we have had a special mandate from the Pope to take effective measures to reform the state of the Parisian scholars for the better, wishing with the counsel of good men to provide for the tranquility of the scholars in the future, we have decreed and ordained in this wise:

No one shall lecture in the arts at Paris before he is twenty-one years of age, and he shall have heard lectures for at least six years before he begins to lecture, and he shall promise to lecture for at least two years, unless a reasonable cause prevents, which he ought to prove publicly or before examiners. He shall not be stained by any infamy, and when he is ready to lecture, he shall be examined according to the form which is contained in the writing of the lord bishop of Paris, where is contained the peace confirmed between the chancellor and scholars by judges delegated by the pope, namely, by the bishop and dean of Troyes and by P., the bishop and J., the chancellor of Paris approved and confirmed. And they shall lecture on the books of Aristotle on dialectic old and new in the schools ordinarily and not *ad cursum*.[207] They shall also lecture on both Priscians[208] ordinarily, or at least on one. They shall not lecture on feast days except on philosophers and rhetoric and the quadrivium and *Barbarismus* and ethics, if it please them, and the fourth book of the *Topics*. They shall not lecture on the books of Aristotle on metaphysics and natural philosophy or on summaries of them or concerning the doctrine of master David of Dinant or the heretic Amaury or Mauritius of Spain.

In the *principia* and meetings of the masters and in the responsions or Oppositions of the boys and youths there shall be no drinking. They may summon some friends or associates, but only a few. Donations of clothing or other things as has been customary, or more, we urge should be made, especially to the poor. None of the mas-

206. The ecclesiastical jurisdiction of Rome, the leader of which was the pope.
207. Quickly.
208. The standard texts on Latin grammar by Priscian (circa 500 C.E.).

ters lecturing in arts shall have a cope[209] except one round, black and reaching to the ankles, at least while it is new. Use of the pallium[210] is permitted. No one shall wear with the round cope shoes that are ornamented or with elongated pointed toes. If any scholar in arts or theology dies, half of the masters of arts shall attend the funeral at one time, the other half the next time, and no one shall leave until the sepulture[211] is finished, unless he has reasonable cause. If any master in arts or theology dies, all the masters shall keep vigils, each shall read or cause to be read the Psalter, each shall attend the church where is celebrated the watch until midnight or the greater part of the night, unless reasonable cause prevent. On the day when the master is buried, no one shall lecture or dispute.

We fully confirm to them the meadow of St. Germain in that condition in which it was adjudicated to them.

Each master shall have jurisdiction over his scholar. No one shall occupy a class-room or house without asking the consent of the tenant, provided one has a chance to ask it. No one shall receive the licentiate from the chancellor or another for money given or promise made or other condition agreed upon. Also, the masters and schol-ars can make both between themselves and with other persons obligations and con-stitutions supported by faith or penalty or oath in these cases: namely, the murder or mutilation of a scholar or atrocious injury done a scholar, if justice should not be forthcoming, arranging the prices of lodging, costume, burial, lectures and disputa-tions, so, however, that the university be not thereby dissolved or destroyed.

As to the status of the theologians, we decree that no one shall lecture at Paris before his thirty-fifth year and unless he has studied for eight years at least, and has heard the books faithfully and in classrooms, and has attended lectures in theology for five years before he gives lectures himself publicly. And none of these shall lecture before the third hour on days when masters lecture. No one shall be admitted at Paris to formal lectures or to preachings unless he shall be of approved life and science. No one shall be a scholar at Paris who has no definite master.

Moreover, that these decrees may be observed inviolate, we by virtue of our lega-tine authority have bound by the knot of excommunication[212] all who shall contu-maciously presume to go against these our statutes, unless within fifteen days after the offense they have taken care to emend their presumption before the university of masters and scholars or other persons constituted by the university. Done in the year of Grace 1215, the month of August. [...]

---

209. A cape worn by priests.
210. A wool collar presented by the pope to indicate a cleric with jurisdictional authority.
211. Burial or entombment.
212. Expulsion from the Catholic Church and thus, potentially, a condemnation to hell.

Proclamation of the Official of the Episcopal Court of Paris against Clerks and Scholars Who Go about Paris Armed by Day and Night and Commit Crimes: January 11, 1269.

The official of the court of Paris to all the rectors of churches, masters and scholars residing in the city and suburb of Paris, to whom the present letters may come, greeting in the Lord. A frequent and continual complaint has gone the rounds that there are in Paris some clerks and scholars, likewise their servants, trusting in the folly of the same clerks, unmindful of their salvation, not having God before their eyes, who, under pretense of leading the scholastic life, more and more often perpetrate unlawful and criminal acts, relying on their arms: namely, that by day and night they atrociously wound or kill many persons, rape women, oppress virgins, break into inns, also repeatedly committing robberies and many other enormities hateful to God. And since they attempt these and other crimes relying on their arms, we...do excommunicate in writing clerks and scholars and their servants who go about Paris by day or night armed, unless by permission of the reverend bishop of Paris or ourselves. We also excommunicate in writing those who rape women, break into inns, oppress virgins, likewise all those who have banded together for this purpose [...]

But inasmuch as some clerks and scholars and their servants have borne arms in Paris, coming there from their parts or returning to their parts, and likewise certain others, knowing that clerks, scholars and their servants have borne arms in Paris, fear that for said reasons they have incurred the said penalty of excommunication we do declare herewith that it neither is nor was our intention that those clerks, scholars and their servants should be liable to the said sentence who, coming to Paris for study and bearing arms on the way, on first entering the city bear the same to their lodgings, nor, further, those, wishing to return home or setting out on useful and honest business more than one day's journey from the city of Paris, who have borne such arms going and returning while they were outside the city. [...] Given in the year 1268 A.D., the Friday following Epiphany.

On the Vices of Masters by Alvarus Pelagius[213]

The first [vice] is that, although they be unlearned and insufficiently prepared, they get themselves promoted to be masters by prayers and gifts [...]. And when they are called upon to examine others, they admit inept and ignorant persons to be masters.

Second, moved by envy, they scorn to admit well-prepared subordinates to professorial chairs, and, full of arrogance, they despise others and censure their utterances unreasonably....

Third, they despise simple persons who know how to avoid faults of conduct better than those of words....

213. Alvarus Pelagius (circa 1280–1352 CE) was a canon lawyer (i.e., the laws governing the Catholic Church).

Fourth, they teach useless, vain, and sometimes false doctrines, a most dangerous course in doctrine of faith and morals, yet one especially characteristic of doctors of theology. These are fountains without water and clouds driven by whirlwinds and darkening the landscape....

Fifth, they are dumb dogs unable to bark, as Isaiah inveighs against them, 66:10. Seeing the faults of peoples and lords, they keep silent lest they displease them, when they ought to argue at least in secret–which they also sometimes omit to do because they are involved in like vices themselves....

Sixth, they retain in their classes those who have been excommunicated, or do not reprove scholars who are undisciplined and practice turpitudes publicly. For they ought to impress morality along with science.

Seventh, although receiving sufficient salaries, they avariciously demand beyond their due or refuse to teach the poor unless paid for it, and want pay whether they teach on feast days or not, or fail to lecture when they should, attending to other matters, or teach less diligently.

Eighth, they try to say what is subtle, not what is useful, so that they may be seen of men and called rabbis, which is especially reprehensible in masters of theology. And in this especially offend, remarks the aforesaid Alvarus, the masters of Paris and those in England at Oxford, secular as well as regular, Dominicans as well as Franciscans, and others, of whom the arrogance of some is inexplicable. In their classes not the prophets, nor the Mosaic law, nor the wisdom of the Father, nor the Gospel of Christ, nor the doctrine of the apostles and holy doctors are heard, but Reboat, the idolatrous philosopher, and his commentator, with other teachers of the liberal arts, so that in classes in theology not holy writ but philosophy is taught. Nay more, now doctors and bachelors do not even read the text of the *Sentences* in class but hurry on to curious questions which have no apparent connection with the text.

Method of Lecturing in the Liberal Arts Prescribed, Paris, December 10, 1355

In the name of the Lord, amen. Two methods of lecturing on books in the liberal arts having been tried, the former masters of philosophy uttering their words rapidly so that the mind of the hearer can take them in but the hand cannot keep up with them, the latter speaking slowly until their listeners can catch up with them with the pen; having compared these by diligent examination, the former method is found the better. Wherefore, the consensus of opinion warns us that we imitate it in our lectures. We, therefore, all and each, masters of the faculty of arts, teaching and not teaching, convoked for this specially by the venerable man, master Albert of Bohemia, then rector of the university, at St. Julien le Pauvre, have decreed in this wise, that all lecturers, whether masters or scholars of the same faculty, whenever and wherever they chance to lecture on any text ordinarily or cursorily in the same faculty, or to dispute any question concerning it, or anything else by way of exposition, shall observe the former method of lecturing to the best of their ability, so speaking forsooth as if no one was taking notes before them, in the way that sermons and recommendations are made in the university and which the lectures in other faculties follow. Moreover, transgressors of this statute, if the lecturers are masters or scholars, we now deprive henceforth for a year from lecturing, honors, offices and other advantages of our faculty. Which if anyone violates, for the first relapse we double the penalty, for the second we quadruple it, and so on. Moreover, listeners who oppose the execution of this our statute by clamor, hissing, noise, throwing stones by themselves or by their servants and accomplices, or in any other way, we deprive of and cut off from our society for a year, and for each relapse we increase the penalty double and quadruple as above.

The condemnation of 1210: Banning of Aristotle's Works

[...]

Neither the books of Aristotle on natural philosophy nor their commentaries are to be read at Paris in public or secret, and this we forbid under penalty of excommunication.

[...]

Gregory IX on Books Offensive to the Catholic Faith, 1231

Since other sciences ought to render service to the wisdom of holy writ, they are to be in so far embraced by the faithful as they are known to conform to the good pleasure of the Giver, so that anything virulent or otherwise vicious, by which the purity of the Faith might be derogated from, be quite excluded. [...]

But since, as we have learned, the books on nature which were prohibited at Paris in provincial council are said to contain both useful and useless matter, lest the useful be vitiated by the useless, we command your discretion, in which we have full faith in the Lord, firmly bidding by apostolic writings under solemn adjuration of divine judgment, that, examining the same books as is convenient subtly and prudently, you entirely exclude what you shall find there erroneous or likely to give scandal or offense to readers, so that, what are suspect being removed, the rest may be studied without delay and without offense. Given at the Lateran, April 23, in the fifth year of our pontificate.

Courses in Arts, Paris

In the year of the Lord 1254. Let all know that we, all and each, masters of arts by our common assent, no one contradicting, because of the new and incalculable peril which threatens in our faculty—some masters hurrying to finish their lectures sooner than the length and difficulty of the texts permits, for which reason both masters in lecturing and scholars in hearing make less progress—worrying over the ruin of our faculty and wishing to provide for our status, have decreed and ordained for the common utility and the reparation of our university to the honor of God and the church universal that all and single masters of our faculty in the future shall be required to finish the texts which they shall have begun on the feast of St. Remy at the times below noted, not before....

The *Physics* of Aristotle, *Metaphysics*, and *De animalibus* on the feast of St. John the Baptist; *De celo et mundo*, first book of *Meteorology* with the fourth, on Ascension day; *De anima*, if read with the books on nature, on the feast of the Ascension, if with the logical texts, on the feast of the Annunciation of the blessed Virgin; *De generatione* on the feast of the Chair of St. Peter; *De causis* in seven weeks; *De sensu et sensato* in six weeks; *De sompno et vigilia* in five weeks; *De plantis* in five weeks; *De memoria et reminiscentia* in two weeks; *De differentia spiritus et animae* in two weeks; *De morte et vita* in one week. Moreover, if masters begin to read the said books at another time than the feast of St. Remy, they shall allow as much time for lecturing on them as is indicated above. Moreover, each of the said texts, if read by itself, not with another text, can be finished in half the time of lecturing assigned above. It will not be permitted anyone to finish the said texts in less time, but anyone may take more time.

Selections from *University Records and Life in the Middle Ages*, edited by Lynn Thorndike, 26–30, 39–40, 64–65, 78–80, 171–72, 237. New York: Columbia University Press, 1944.

POST-READING PARS

1. Articulate two points you can infer about the behaviors of students from the documents regulating student life.
2. List two things from these documents about the behaviors of students and the practices of the faculty that might lead to tensions between them.

Inquiry Corner

Content Question(s):

How would you describe the relationship between faculty and students at the University of Paris? Given the rules for faculty and students, describe what it might have been like to be a student in a "classroom" in medieval Paris.

Critical Question(s):

Why do you think that some of the works of Aristotle were censored by Catholic authorities? What do you know about Aristotelian thought that might make it appear so dangerous to Church leaders?

Comparative Question(s):

Compare the regulations for students and faculty to *The Rule of St. Benedict*. What monastic practices provided the foundations for education in western Europe? In what ways might Western higher education have been different without this monastic influence?

Connection Question(s):

Can censorship of books and ideas on a university curriculum be justified? Should contemporary universities intentionally suppress some types of speech (written, oral, or digital)?

BEYOND THE CLASSROOM

» Data is playing a larger role in the way prospective students and their families evaluate the value of higher education. For example, there are statistics for how many students complete their program of study in four years. Other organizations collect data and compile the average starting salary of graduates within the first five years of their degree completion. What do you see as positive or negative about gathering and publishing this kind of information?

Othello by William Shakespeare (Introduction only)

SNAPSHOT BOX

LANGUAGE: English

DATE: 1603 CE

LOCATION: England

GENRE: Play, tragedy

TAGS: Authority and Institution; Cross-Cultural Encounters; Ethics and Morality; Formations and Reformations; Humanism; Identity and Self; Music and Entertainment; Narrative; Religion; Ways of Knowing

Introduction

Othello is a play by playwright, actor, and poet William Shakespeare and was most likely completed in 1603 CE. The first performance took place in November 1604 CE at Whitehall Palace in London where it was called "The Moor of Venis" and attributed to "Shaxberd" (a variant spelling of "Shakespeare"); the second performance took place at the Globe Theatre in 1610 CE. Since then, and over a period of more than five hundred years, *Othello* has been translated into several languages and performed in different cultural contexts. This play has also been adapted to and inspired other genres and mediums—opera, music, films, painting, and even board games and desserts. In the midst of all these creative and innovative adaptations, *Othello* continues to be performed in its original language on stages designed to replicate the playhouses of the seventeenth century. As you read *Othello*, think about the reasons for its broad appeal and ongoing popularity.

In Shakespeare's own time in London, his plays had a broad appeal across different demographics, social classes, and literacy levels. There were several forms of entertainment competing for business in Shakespeare's London: bearbaiting and bullbaiting in arenas; cockfighting in theaters known as cockpits; brothels; and gambling that took place in gambling dens as well as in theaters. It was in close proximity to all these activities that playgoing took place and the price of admission for most of these activities was comparable. From commoners to nobility, almost every social class partook in one or more of these forms of en-

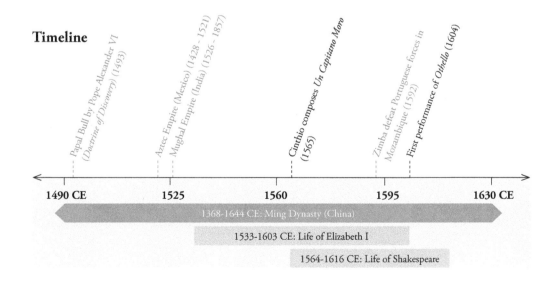

tertainment. Queen Elizabeth I (1533–1603 CE) herself was known to be a big fan of bearbaiting. Given the range of these activities that plays were competing with, it should come as no surprise that many of Shakespeare's plays had something of interest for different social strata. After all, playwriting and playacting were also commercial enterprises and they needed to attract and appeal to a wide audience. What do you think might be some of the themes that appeal to and connect with such varied audiences from the seventeenth century to the present?

At its core, *Othello* is a tragedy that revolves around intimate human relationships: the formation and fashioning of the self and the other; a couple's married life and love; and the devolution of those relationships due to jealousy, passion, misunderstandings, and manipulations. These are enduring themes that audiences over centuries have connected with in the play. The titular character is a Moorish general of most likely North African descent in a predominantly white Venetian and Christian environment. The backdrop on which the intimacies between characters play out is one of war with the Muslim Turks, which places the events of the play between 1570 CE and 1573 CE. In this, and through the many stories signaled to about Othello's heritage and adventures, *Othello* offers us a glimpse of worlds beyond the finite geographical space of Venice or the small island of Cyprus where the latter half of the play unfolds. Different worlds and cultures, real and imagined, intersect in this play. What might have been Shakespeare's inspiration in his writing of a play that is at once intimate and also expansive in its scope?

The themes and plot of *Othello* were inspired by several other works Shakespeare had access to in translation. Giambattista Giraldi (Cinthio)'s *De gli Hecatommithi* (1565 CE), a collection of short tales, is believed to have been Shakespeare's inspiration for *Othello*'s primary plot. It is possible that *A Geographical Historie of Africa* (1600 CE) by North African diplomat Leo Africanus, influenced the character of Othello, especially the details for his heritage and life prior to the events of the play. Philemon Holland's translation of Pliny's *Historie of the World* (1601 CE) is another possible source that could have informed Shakespeare's play. Consider the wide range of sources that Shakespeare drew on to write this play. Then consider the many adaptations of the play that are composed and created even today. How might Shakespeare's multilayered inspirations and influences contribute to the richness of the tradition of interpreting and adapting the play?

Different adaptations have different emphasis, and therefore can be appreciated and interpreted differently. For instance, some productions might focus more on the husband-wife dynamic, some more on issues of race and religion, and some on the nature of meaning-making or the motivation for evil. The setting of the play in a different cultural context can also change how the play is interpreted, for instance, if the play is set in India, the issue of race often gets replaced by caste and colorism.

The actors who play the various characters also influence the reception of the play. Imagine Othello, a "black Moor," being played by a white actor using stage makeup to darken their skin. Or consider a gender reversal in casting. This is a far cry from Shakespeare's London where all the roles in professional theater were played by men with boys playing the female parts. It was only in a 1660 CE performance of *Othello* that a woman, possibly actress Margaret Hughes, acted the part of Desdemona, making it one of the first professional roles to be played by a woman.

There are many scholarly resources available online that will direct you to the performance history and collections of archived images and recordings of performances over the years. Take a look at these images of actors, costumes, and various stages. Listen to some recordings of actors reciting these Shakespearean lines. As you read the text of the play, remember that these lines were meant to be spoken and heard in a large group. Playgoing was after all, a communal and social engagement. What intentionality needs to be invited to facilitate an embodied experience of this play? What might be the merits of reading the play in solitude? What is the value of memorizing some of the play's words?

Renuka Gusain
Humanities Program

Adopted at UNC Asheville: Shakespeare, William. *Othello*, edited by Barbara A. Mowat and Paul Werstine. New York: Simon & Schuster, 2017.

from *Scivias* by Hildegard of Bingen

Introduction

Hildegard of Bingen (1098–1179 CE) was one of the greatest early medieval woman monastics. From the age of three, she had mystic visions of bright lights or sometimes falling stars, accompanied by acute ill-health. When she was eight, her family sent her to live in a Benedictine monastery with Jutta, another charismatic visionary, in modern-day Germany. Thus began her life as an **anchoress,** a monastic devoted to prayer and asceticism and entirely secluded from the outside world. At first, only Jutta, Hildegard's teacher, and eventually Volmar, a monk who also taught her and remained close to her all her life, knew about her visions, but when she was forty-two and had become head of the monastery after Jutta died, she received a message from God that it was time to reveal her visions to the world. Though initially hesitant to do so, she received the blessing of St. Bernard of Clairvaux and the pope, and the rest of her life saw her flourishing as a writer, thinker, and public figure. How might the approval of these church fathers have influenced her agency?

Hildegard's mystical power and writing as God's mouthpiece brought her an agency in the world that was deeply unusual for a woman at this time, and the relationship between her mystical and worldly lives could be complex. For example, when she wished to start a new monastery and her abbot refused, she became ill with a paralyzing sickness that she claimed was caused by God's unhappiness at her inability to follow his orders. When the abbot eventually backed down, her health returned. Was she somehow manipulating the abbot to achieve the advancement of

SNAPSHOT BOX

LANGUAGE: Latin

DATE: 1141–52 CE

LOCATION: Germany

TAGS: Asceticism; Authority and Institution; Body; Mysticism; Spirituality; Ways of Knowing; Women

Timeline

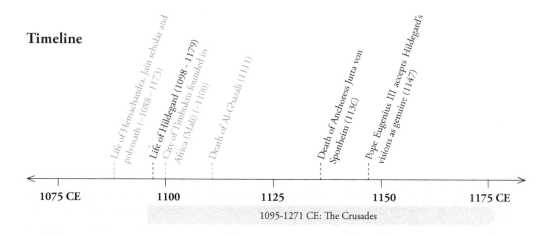

Life of Hemachandra, Jain scholar and polymath (~1088 - 1173)

Life of Hildegard (1098 - 1179)

City of Timbuktu founded in Africa (Mali) (~1100)

Death of Al-Ghazali (1111)

Death of Anchoress Jutta von Sponheim (1136)

Pope Eugenius III accepts Hildegard's visions as genuine (1147)

1075 CE   1100   1125   1150   1175 CE

1095-1271 CE: The Crusades

her plans in the world, or was her illness beyond rational understanding, a physical manifestation of Hildegard's sense of her closeness to God? Hildegard documented her visions in her first major work, *Scivias* (an abbreviation for the Latin *Sci Vias Domini*, "Know the Ways of the Lord"). She also wrote extensively on theology, medicine, and science; gave speaking tours around Germany; and became an influential and admired advisor (and sometimes critic) of many important figures in the medieval world, both religious and secular. Hildegard was also a composer and considered music a way of connecting with the joy and beauty of heaven. Her music is admired and is recorded to this day, and it is still possible to visit her convent at Eibingen. Hildegard resembles other women mystics of the time, such as Julian of Norwich and Margery Kempe, in combining spiritual vision and physical sickness. Is it possible to speculate on the reasons for this connection and its apparently gendered nature?

In *Scivias*, Hildegard first describes each of her visions and then interprets its theological significance—how it conforms to biblical teaching and illustrates the life and redemptive power of the Church. The book also contains thirty-five images illustrating these visions. How far Hildegard herself was involved in creating these illustrations remains uncertain but she may have played some part in their production. Hildegard speaks like a prophet from the Hebrew Bible and connections between the language of her visions and those of Ezekiel and Jeremiah are often drawn. Her visions are intensely physically detailed, and she explains their complex symbolism to her audience. Her conception of God is optimistic, arguing that God is essentially benevolent if human beings are obedient to divine law. Hildegard emphasizes *viriditas* (greenness or growth, fertility, vitality) as a central part of God's power to animate and nurture the world: physical creation is a proof of the unseen God. Hildegard herself was a naturalist, writer, and practitioner of herbal medicine. Just as the church (gendered as female) is the way to God, as mediator between humans and God, so Hildegard herself mediates between God and the people on Earth for whom she acts as a spiritual counselor.

A frequently observed paradox about Hildegard is her combination of confidence and extreme humility, drawing attention to her inferior education and intelligence, even as she channels the voice of God to admonish powerful men. Similarly, though she can be seen as progressive for her time, by celebrating the female in her spiritual writings through praise of female allegorical figures such as *Sapientia* (wisdom) and others, she maintains firmly traditional positions on priestly celibacy, extramarital sexuality (though she praises marital sex as part of God's plan for human beings), and even the inferiority of women, and their innate unsuitability for the priesthood. Along with a generous, nature-centered view of God, her visions are sometimes apocalyptic and violently hostile to those whom she condemns as sinners. As you read through the text below consider how you might negotiate interpreting these apparent paradoxes?

Sophie Mills
Department of Classics

[Content Notice: Problematic racialized imagery]

from *Scivias*

Vision Three: The Church, Bride of Christ and Mother of the Faithful

After this I saw the image of a woman as large as a great city, with a wonderful crown on her head and arms from which a splendor hung like sleeves, shining from Heaven to earth. Her womb was pierced like a net with many openings, with a huge multitude of people running in and out. She had no legs or feet, but stood balanced on her womb in front of the altar that stands before the eyes of God, embracing it with her outstretched hands and gazing sharply with her eyes throughout all of Heaven. I could not make out her attire, except that she was arrayed in great splendor and gleamed with lucid serenity, and on her breast shone a red glow like the dawn; and I heard a sound of all kinds of music singing about her, "Like the dawn, greatly sparkling."

And that image spreads out its splendor like a garment, saying, "I must conceive and give birth!" And at once, like lightning, there hastened to her a multitude of angels, making steps and seats within her for people, by whom the image was to be perfected.

Then I saw black children moving in the air near the ground like fishes in water, and they entered the womb of the image through the openings that pierced it. But she groaned, drawing them upward to her head, and they went out by her mouth, while she remained untouched. And behold, that serene light with the figure of a man in it, blazing with a glowing fire, which I had seen in my previous vision, again appeared to me, and stripped the black skin off each of them and threw it away; and it clothed each of them in a pure white garment and opened to them the serene light saying to them one by one:

"Cast off the old injustice, and put on the new sanctity. For the gate of your inheritance is unlocked for you. Consider, therefore, how you have been taught, that you may know your Father Whom you have confessed. I have received you, and you have confessed Me. Now, therefore, behold the two paths, one to the East and the other to the North. If you will diligently contemplate Me with your inner vision, as in faith you have been taught, I will receive you into My kingdom. And if you love Me rightly, I will do whatever you shall wish. But if you despise Me and turn away from Me, looking backward and not seeking to know or understand Me, Who am recalling you by pure penitence though you are filthy with sin, and if you run back to the

Devil as to your father, then perdition will take you; for you will be judged according to your works, since when I gave you the good you did not choose to know Me."

But the children who had passed through the womb of the image walked in the splendor that surrounded her. And she, benignly gazing on them, said in a sad voice, "These children of mine will return again to dust. I conceive and bear many who oppress me, their mother, by heretical, schismatic and useless battles, by robberies and murders, by adultery and fornication, and by many such errors. Many of these rise again in true penitence to eternal life, but many fall in false obduracy to eternal death.

And again I heard the voice from Heaven saying to me: "The great edifice of living souls, which is constructed in Heaven from living stones, is adorned with the immense beauty of its children's virtues, encircling them as a great city encircles its immense throngs of people, or as a wide net does a multitude of fishes; and however much the work of the faithful thrives in the Christian name, by so much does it blossom with celestial virtues."

I. The building of the Church, who redeems her children by Spirit and water

Wherefore now *you see the image of a woman as large as a great city,* this designates the Bride of My Son, who always bears her children by regeneration in the Spirit and in water, for the strong Warrior founded her on a wide base of virtue, that she might hold and perfect the great crowd of His elect; and no enemy can conquer or storm her. She expels unbelief and expands belief, by which it should be understood that in the mortal world each faithful is an example to his neighbor, and so they do great works of virtue in Heaven. And when the just, one by one, shall come to join the children of light, the good they have worked will appear in them, which cannot be seen here among mortal ashes, concealed as it is by the shadow of trouble.

II. The Church in her origin was adorned by apostles and martyrs

She has a wonderful crown on her head; for at her origin, when she raised up by the blood of the Lamb, she was fittingly adorned with apostles and martyrs, and thus betrothed with true betrothal to My Son, since in His blood she faithfully formed herself into a firm edifice of holy souls.

III. The Church is adorned by the priesthood and almsgiving

And from her arms a splendor hangs like sleeves, shining from Heaven to earth. This is the work of power done by priests, who with purity of heart and hands and in the strength of good works offer the holiest of sacrifices upon the holy altar in the sacrament of the body and blood of their Savior. And the most glorious of their works is to show mercy, always offering generous help for every grief and distributing alms to the poor with a gentle heart while saying with their whole soul, "This is not my property, but that of Him Who created me." And this work, inspired by God, is before His eyes in Heaven, when by the teaching of the Church it is done among the faithful on earth.

IV. On the maternal kindness of the Church

Her womb is pierced like a net with many openings with a huge multitude of people running in and out; that is, she displays her maternal kindness, which is so clever at capturing faithful souls by diverse goads of virtue, and in which the trusting peoples devoutly lead their lives by the faith of their true belief. But He Who casts the net to capture the fishes is My Son, the Bridegroom of His beloved Church, whom He betrothed to Himself in His blood to repair the fall of lost humanity.

V. The Church, not yet perfected, will be brought to perfection near the end

She does not yet have legs or feet, for she has not yet been brought to the full strength of her constancy or the full purity of her fulfillment; for when the son of perdition comes to delude the world she will suffer fiery and bloody anguish in all her members from his cruel wickedness. By this calamity, with bleeding wounds, she will be brought to perfection; then let her run swiftly into the heavenly Jerusalem, where she will sweetly rise anew as a bride in the blood of My Son, entering into life with ardor in the joy of her offspring.

VI. How the Church devoutly offers up her children in purity

But she stands balanced on her womb in front of the altar that stands before the eyes of God, embracing it with her outstretched hands; for she is always pregnant and procreating children of hers by the true ablution, and offering them devoutly to God by the purest prayers of the saints and the sweet fragrance of chosen virtues both hidden and manifest; which are plain to the clear understanding of the mind's eye when all stain of falsity and all noises of human praise are removed, as incense is purged of a noxious stench that corrupts its smell. This good work is in God's sight the sweetest sacrifice, at which the Church constantly labors, striving with her whole desire for heavenly things in bringing virtues to fruition, and by increase of such fruit thirtyfold, sixtyfold and a hundredfold building the high tower of the celestial walls.

VII. No wickedness of devilish art can obscure the Church

And she gazes sharply with her eyes throughout all of Heaven; for her purpose, which she devoutly keeps to in the heavenly places, can be obscured by no wickedness: no persuasion of devilish art, nor error of a wavering people, nor storms over the various countries in which madmen tear themselves to pieces in the fury of their unbelief.

VIII. The human mind cannot fully understand the secrets of the Church

You cannot make out her attire, which is to say that the human intellect, weighed down by fragile weakness, cannot fully understand her secrets; *except that she is arrayed in great splendor and gleams with lucid serenity*, for the True Sun shines everywhere around her by the bright inspiration of the Holy Spirit and her most becoming adornments of virtue.

IX. On the virginity of Mary

And on her breast shines a red glow like the dawn; for the virginity of the Most Blessed Virgin when she brought forth the Son of God glows with the most ardent devotion in the hearts of the faithful. *And you hear a sound of all kinds of music singing about her, "Like the dawn, greatly sparkling"*; for, as you are now given to understand, all believers should join with their whole wills in celebrating the virginity of that spotless Virgin in the Church.

X. On the expansion of the sacrament of the true Trinity

And that image spreads out its splendor like a garment, saying that she has to conceive and give birth, which means that in the Church the sacrament of the true Trinity will more widely expand, for it is her garment in which to shelter the faithful peoples, through whom she grows by the building up of the living stones, who are washed white in the pure font; thus she herself affirms that it is necessary to salvation that she conceive children in blessing and bring them forth in cleansing, by regeneration in the Spirit and water.

XI. The ministry of angels is at hand for each of the faithful

And at once, like lightning, there hasten to her a multitude of angels, making steps and seats within her for people, by whom the image is to be perfected; because for each of the faithful there is at hand a fearsome and desirable ministry of blessed spirits; they are building stairs of faith and seats of sovereign quiet for those faithful souls, in whom that happy mother, the Church, will attain to her full beauty.

XII. Those regenerated by the Church their mother in the faith of the Trinity

Then you see black children moving in the air near the ground like fishes in water; and they enter the womb of the image through the openings that pierce it. This signifies the blackness of those foolish people who are not yet washed in the bath of salvation, but love earthly things and run about doing them, building their dwelling on their unsteadiness; they come at last to the mother of holiness, contemplate the dignity of her secrets and receive her blessing, by which they are snatched from the Devil and restored to God. Thus they enter the confines of the churchly order in which the faithful person is blessed by salvation, when he says within himself, "I believe in God," and the rest of the articles of faith.

But she groans, drawing them upward to her head, and they go out by her mouth, while she remains untouched. For this blessed mother sighs inwardly when baptism is celebrated by the sacred anointing of the Holy Spirit, because the person is renewed by the true circumcision of the Spirit and water, and thus offered to the Supreme Beatitude Who is the Head of all, and made a member of Christ, regenerated unto salvation by invocation of the Holy Trinity. But in this that mother suffers no hurt, for she will remain forever in the wholeness of virginity, which is the Catholic faith; for she arose in the blood of the true Lamb, her intimate Bridegroom, Who was born of the untouched Virgin without any corruption of integrity. So too that Bride will remain untouched, so that no schism can corrupt her.

She will often, however, be bothered by the wicked, but with the help of her Bridegroom she will always most strongly defend herself, like a virgin who is often assailed by the cravings of desire through the Devil's art and the arguments of men, but pours out her prayers to God and is forcibly liberated from their temptations and her virginity preserved. So also the Church resists her wicked corrupters, the heretical errors of Christians, Jews and pagans, who infest her and try to corrupt her virginity, which is the Catholic faith. She resists them strongly, lest she be corrupted, for she was and is and will remain a virgin; the true faith which is her virginity keeps its wholeness against all error, so that her honor as a chaste virgin remains uncorrupted by any touch of lust in the modesty of her body.

And thus the Church is the virginal mother of all Christians, since by the mystery of the Holy Spirit she conceives and bears them, offering them to God so that they are called the children of God. And as the Holy Spirit overshadowed the Blessed Mother, so that she miraculously conceived and painlessly bore the Son of God and yet remained a virgin, so does the Holy Spirit illumine the Church, happy mother of believers, so that without any corruption she conceives and bears children naturally, yet remains a virgin. How is this?

XIII. Analogy of the balsam, onyx and diamond

As balsam oozes from a tree, and powerful medicines pour from an onyx vessel in which they are stored, and bright light streams without impediment from a diamond, so the Son of God, unopposed by corruption, was born of the Virgin; and so too the Church, His Bride, brings forth her children without being opposed by error, yet remains a virgin in the integrity of her faith.

Hildegard of Bingen. Excerpt from *Hildegard of Bingen: Scivias*, edited and translated by Mother Columba Hart and Jane Bishop, 169–74. New York: Paulist Press, Abbey of Regina Laudis, 1990.

POST-READING PARS

1. What would you say was the most striking or memorable image that Hildegard uses in this passage?

2. How do you think Hildegard knew she was channeling the word of God?

Inquiry Corner

Content Question(s):

Hildegard gives her readers her own interpretation of the opening image of the woman balanced on her womb. Are there other interpretations that we as modern readers could make?

Critical Question(s):

In what ways might Hildegard's gender be significant in interpreting her vision of the divine?

Comparative Question(s):

How does Hildegard's vision of God or her religion compare with those of Mirabai or Margery Kempe?

Connection Question(s):

In 2012, Hildegard was named Doctor of the Church by Pope Benedict XVI in recognition of "her holiness of life and the originality of her teaching." How might gender and authority have been a factor in this decision?

The Twelve Articles and Martin Luther's Admonition to Peace

Introduction

Germany, as we define it today, did not exist until 1871 and was at the time of the official adoption of the Twelve Articles a part of the Holy Roman Empire. The Upper Swabian Peasants' Group, a coalition of peasants and artisans formed in response to poor working and living conditions under the Swabian League, officially adopted the Twelve Articles in late March 1525 CE, and the Admonition to Peace edict from Martin Luther followed in mid-April. To say that the early sixteenth century was a time of change in what we now define as Germany would be selling its historical and cultural significance short. These German-speaking regions were divided sharply by religious and political differences. Emperor Maximilian I's reign over the Holy Roman Empire brought renewed hope of a reunified Kingdom of Germany, yet his rule centered largely on his own House of Hapsburg and their dynastic legacy. The hopes then fell upon Charles I, his grandson and direct heir, who ascended to the throne in 1519 CE.

This burgeoning tension created conditions that foregrounded the need for religious reformation. Displeasure for the Roman Catholic Church's more secular business and financial dealings had already led to reform reflecting the social, religious, and political turbulence prevalent in the region. An Augustinian friar had spoken out against **indulgences** (monetary payments toward salvation) being used for increasingly commercial purposes, among other issues, by nailing a series of ninety-five theses to a door in Wittenberg. Martin Luther never intended to become a poster

SNAPSHOT BOX

LANGUAGE: German

DATE: 1525 CE

LOCATION: Modern-day Germany

GENRE: Treatise and response

TAGS: Revolutions; Reformation; Power Structures; Renaissance; Social and Political Institutions

Timeline

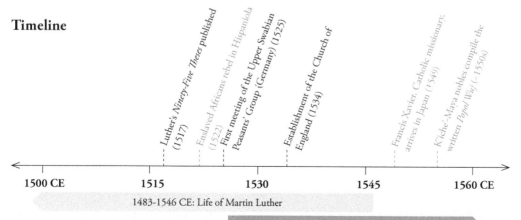

child for any political, theological, or social revolution, yet his words and writings propelled him to this role as a central figure in the Protestant Reformation. What other times can you think of where the written or spoken word propelled someone to the center of a revolution?

In response, Pope Leo X used a papal bull—the official decree from the pope, usually in the form of a letter, charter, or patent—to censure Martin Luther. In this **Exurge Dominae** ("Arise, O Lord") **papal bull**, promulgated in June 1520 CE, he censured forty-one of Luther's ninety-five theses. It also decried other speeches by Luther and threatened him with excommunication from the Catholic Church unless he recanted. Rather than acquiescing, Luther burned a copy of the papal bull and continued his work speaking out against the Church and was subsequently excommunicated in 1521 CE. The same year Emperor Charles met with the other Germanic estates at the **Diet of Worms**, which was the assembly of all of the associated states of the Holy Roman Empire. The Diet opened back up the case of the recently excommunicated Luther, allowing him to speak. Luther refused to back down from his position, asserting individual responsibility in faith rather than the ultimate authority of the pope. His words reached the German populace in pamphlets spread far and wide, and they embraced him as a beacon of hope against their social and religious stagnation and inspired their movement to improve their station in life.

This social revolution began to come to a head in 1524 CE, sparking the **Deutscher Bauernkrieg** (German Peasants' Revolt/War). The lower classes, inspired by Martin Luther and emboldened by what they viewed as Luther's support for changing their lot in life, began to refuse to work for the upper echelons of society. Countess of Lupfen had ordered the serfs under her purview to gather snail shells so she could use them as thread spools. Over 1,200 peasants gathered together and organized under a banner, electing officers and creating a detailed list of grievances. Frederich Engels was to later identify this as the event that sparked the peasant's revolt. This spirit of revolt and revolution spread across the Swabian estates, modern-day central-south Germany, the catalyst of Lupfen igniting a tinderbox of discontent spread by the winds of change. Do you think there is a pattern of events that often functions as the last thing to ignite the tinderbox of discontents in a revolution?

The first entry in this section, the *Twelve Articles*, arose from a meeting of opposing groups of the ruling-class Swabian League and representatives of the Upper Swabian Peasants Group. In the articles, the peasants group enumerates a series of demands and changes to improve their lot in life, utilizing scripture to justify their assertions. The second entry, *The Admonition to Peace*, was Martin Luther's reply to the rebellion, swiftly undercutting their intent and siding solidly with the ruling class. Luther first addressed the ruling class, urging them to respond to the rebellion rapidly while also showing equanimity and tolerance to the lower classes. Then, addressing the peasants, Luther tries to diffuse the situation while also admonishing them for using scripture as a tool in their arsenal. Finally, taking both groups to task, he warns them both against sinning against God. How might this framework of responses reflect the complexity of Luther's position?

Amanda Glenn-Bradley
Ramsey Library

PRE-READING PARS

1. Give two examples of written or spoken words that have impacted social and/or political movements.
2. Identify two key characteristics often shared by most political, social, and religious movements.

The Twelve Article of the Peasants and Martin Luther's Admonition to Peace

The Twelve Articles

Peace to the Christian reader and the grace of God through Christ:

There are many evil writings put forth of late which take occasion, on account of the assembling of the peasants, to cast scorn upon the gospel, saying "Is this the fruit of the new teaching, that no one should obey but that all should everywhere rise in revolt, and rush together to reform, or perhaps destroy altogether, the authorities, both ecclesiastic and lay?" The articles below shall answer these godless and criminal fault-finders, and serve, in the first place, to remove the reproach from the word of God and, in the second place, to give a Christian excuse for the disobedience or even the revolt of the entire peasantry.

In the first place, the gospel is not the cause of revolt and disorder, since it is the message of Christ, the promised Messiah; the word of life, teaching only love, peace, patience, and concord. Thus all who believe in Christ should learn to be loving, peaceful, long-suffering, and harmonious. This is the foundation of all the articles of the peasants (as will be seen), who accept the gospel and live according to it. How then can the evil reports declare the gospel to be a cause of revolt and disobedience? That the authors of the evil reports and the enemies of the gospel oppose themselves to these demands is due, not to the gospel, but to the devil, the worst enemy of the gospel, who causes this opposition by raising doubts in the minds of his followers, and thus the word of God, which teaches love, peace, and concord, is overcome.

In the second place, it is clear that the peasants demand that this gospel be taught them as a guide in life, and they ought not to be called disobedient or disorderly. Whether God grants the peasants (earnestly wishing to live according to his word) their requests or no, who shall find fault with the will of the Most High? Who shall meddle in his judgments or oppose his majesty?

Did he not hear the children of Israel when they called upon him and save them out of the hands of Pharaoh? Can he not save his own today? Yea, he will save them and that speedily. Therefore, Christian reader, read the following articles with care and then judge. Here follow the articles:

The First Article. First, it is our humble petition and desire, as also our will and desire, that in the future we should have power and authority so that each community should choose and appoint a pastor, and that we should have the right to depose him should he conduct himself improperly. The pastor thus chosen should teach us the gospel pure and simple, without any addition, doctrine, or ordinance of man.

The Second Article. According as the just tithe is established by the Old Testament and fulfilled in the New, we are ready and willing to pay the fair tithe of grain. The word of God plainly provides that in giving rightly to God and distributing to his people the services of a pastor are required. We will that for the future our church provost, whomsoever the community may appoint, shall gather and receive this tithe. From this he shall give to the pastor, elected by the whole community, a decent and sufficient maintenance for him and his, as shall seem right to the whole community. What remains over shall be given to the poor of the place, as the circumstances and the general opinion demand. Should anything further remain, let it be kept, lest anyone should have to leave the country from poverty. The small tithes, whether ecclesiastical or lay, we will not pay at all, for the Lord God created cattle for the free use of man. We will not, therefore, pay further an unseemly tithe which is of man's invention.

The Third Article. It has been the custom hitherto for men to hold us as their own property, which is pitiable enough, considering that Christ has delivered and redeemed us all, without exception, by the shedding of his precious blood, the lowly as well as the great. Accordingly it is consistent with Scripture that we should be free and should wish to be so. Not that we would wish to be absolutely free and under no authority. God does not teach that we should lead a disorderly life in the lusts of the flesh, but that we should love the Lord our God and our neighbor. We would gladly observe all this as God has commanded us in the celebration of the communion. He has not commanded us not to obey the authorities, but rather that we should be humble, not only towards those in authority, but towards everyone. We are thus ready to yield obedience according to God's law to our elected and regular authorities in all proper things becoming to a Christian. We therefore take it for granted that you will release us from serfdom as true Christians, unless it should be shown from the gospel that we are serfs.

The Fourth Article. In the fourth place, it has been the custom heretofore that no poor man should be allowed to touch venison or wild fowl, or fish in flowing water, which seems to us quite unseemly and unbrotherly as well as selfish and not agreeable to the word of God. In some places the authorities preserve the game to our great annoyance and loss, recklessly permitting the unreasoning animals to destroy to no purpose our crops, which God suffers to grow for the use of man; and yet we must submit quietly. This is neither godly nor neighborly; for when God created man he gave him dominion over all the animals, over the birds of the air and the fish in the water. Accordingly it is our desire, if a man holds possession of waters, that he should prove from satisfactory documents that his right has been unwittingly [unwissenlich] acquired by purchase. We do not wish to take it from him by force, but his rights should be exercised in a Christian and brotherly fashion. But whosoever cannot produce such evidence should surrender his claim with good grace.

The Fifth Article. In the fifth place, we are aggrieved in the matter of woodcutting, for the noble folk have appropriated all the woods to themselves alone. If a poor man requires wood, he must pay. [...] It is our opinion that in regard to a woods which has fallen into the hands of a lord, whether spiritual or temporal, that unless it was duly purchased it should revert again to the community. It should, moreover, be free to every member of the community to help himself to such firewood as he needs in his home.

The Sixth Article. Our sixth complaint is in regard to the excessive services which are demanded of us and which are increased day to day. We ask that this matter be properly looked into, so that we shall not continue to be oppressed in this way, but that some gracious consideration be given us, since our forefathers were required only to serve according to the word of God.

The Seventh Article. Seventh, we will not hereafter allow ourselves to be further oppressed by our lords, but will let them demand only what is just and proper according to the word of the agreement between the lord and the peasant. The lord should no longer try to force more services or other dues from the peasant without payment, but permit the peasant to enjoy his holding in peace and quiet. The peasant should, however, help the lord when it is necessary, and at proper times, when it will not be disadvantageous to the peasant, and for a suitable payment.

The Eighth Article. In the eighth place, we are greatly burdened by the holdings which cannot support the rent exacted from them. The peasants suffer loss in this way and are ruined; and we ask that the lords may appoint persons of honor to inspect these holdings, and fix a rent in accordance with justice, so that the peasant shall not work for nothing, since the laborer is worthy of his hire.

The Ninth Article. In the ninth place, we are burdened with a great evil in the constant making of new laws. We are not judged according to the offense, but sometimes with great ill-will, and sometimes much too leniently. In our opinion, we should be judged according to the old written law, so that the case shall be decided according to its merits, and not with partiality.

The Tenth Article. In the tenth place, we are aggrieved by the appropriation by individuals of meadows and fields which at one time belonged to a community. These we will take again into our own hands. It may, however, happen that the land was rightfully purchased. When, however, the land has unfortunately been purchased in this way, some brotherly arrangement should be made according to circumstances.

The Eleventh Article. In the eleventh place, we will entirely abolish the due called "heriot," and will no longer endure it, nor allow widows and orphans to be thus shamefully robbed against God's will.

Conclusion. In the twelfth place, it is our conclusion and final resolution that if any one or more of the articles here set forth should not be in agreement with the word of God, as we think they are, such article we will willingly retract if it is proved really to be against the word of God by a clear explanation of the Scripture. Or if articles should now be conceded to us that are hereafter discovered to be unjust, from that hour they shall be dead and null and without force. Likewise, if more complaints should be discovered which are based upon truth and the Scriptures and relate to offenses against God and our neighbor, we have determined to reserve the right to present these also, and to exercise ourselves in all Christian teaching. For this we shall pray to God, since he can grant our demands, and he alone. The peace of Christ abide with us all.

Martin Luther, Admonition to Peace

A Reply to the Twelve Articles of the Peasants in Swabia

The peasants who have now banded together in Swabia have formulated their intolerable grievances against the rulers in twelve articles, and have undertaken to support them with certain passages of Scripture. Now they have published them in printed form. The thing about them that pleases me most is that, in the twelfth article, they offer to accept instruction gladly and willingly, if there is need or necessity for it, and are willing to be corrected, to the extent that it can be done by clear, plain, undeniable passages of Scripture. And it is indeed right and proper that no one's conscience should be instructed or corrected except by Holy Scripture.

Now if that is their serious and sincere meaning—and it would not be right for me to interpret it otherwise, because in these articles they come out into the open and do not shy away from the light—then there is good reason to hope that things will be well. Since i have a reputation for being one of those who deal with the Holy Scriptures here on earth, and especially as one whom they mention and call upon by name in the second document, I have all the more courage and confidence in openly publishing my instruction. i do this in a friendly and Christian spirit, as a duty of brotherly love, so that if any misfortune or disaster comes out of this matter, it may not be attributed to me, nor will I be blamed before God and men because of my silence. But if this offer of theirs is only pretense and show (without a doubt there are some people like that among them for it is impossible for so big a crowd all to be true Christians and have good intentions; a large part of them must be using the good intentions of the rest for their own selfish purposes and seeking their own advantage) then without doubt it will accomplish very little, or, in fact, it will contribute to their great injury and eternal ruin.

This, then, is a great and dangerous matter. It concerns both the kingdom of God and the kingdom of the world. If this rebellion were to continue and get the upper hand, both kingdoms would be destroyed and there would be neither worldly government nor word of God, which would ultimately result in the permanent destruction of all Germany. Therefore it is necessary for us to speak boldly and to give advice without regard to anyone. It is also necessary that we be willing to listen and allow things to be said to us, so that we do not now–as we have done before–harden our hearts and stop our ears, and so that God's wrath not run its full course. For the many terrible signs that are seen both in heaven and earth point to a great disaster and a mighty change in Germany. Sad to say, however, we care little about it. Nevertheless, God goes on his way, and someday he will soften our hardheadedness.

To the Princes and Lords

We have no one on earth to thank for this disastrous rebellion, except you princes and lords, and especially you blind bishops and mad priests and monks, whose hearts are hardened, even to the present day. You do not cease to rant and rave against the holy Gospel, even though you know that it is true and that you cannot refute it. In addition, as temporal rulers you do nothing but cheat and rob the people so that you may lead a life of luxury and extravagance. The poor common people cannot bear it any longer. The sword is already at your throats, but you think that you sit so firm in the saddle that no one can unhorse you. This false security and stubborn perversity will break your necks, as you will discover. I have often told you before to beware of the saying, in Psalm 107[:40], "*Effundit contemptum super principes*," "He pours contempt upon princes." You, however, keep on asking for trouble and want to be hit over the head. And no warning or exhortation will keep you from getting what you want.

Well, then, since you are the cause of this wrath of God, it will undoubtedly come upon you, unless you mend your ways in time. The signs in heaven and the wonders on earth are meant for you, dear lords; they bode no good for you, and no good will come to you. A great part of God's wrath has already come, for God is sending many false teachers. and prophets among us, so that through our error and blasphemy we may richly deserve hell and everlasting damnation. The rest of it is now here, for the peasants are banding together, and, unless our repentance moves God to prevent it, this must result in the ruin, destruction, and desolation of Germany by cruel murder and bloodshed.

For you ought to know, dear lords, that God is doing this because this raging of yours cannot, will not, and ought not be endured for long. You must become different men and yield to God's word. If you do not do this amicably and willingly, then you will be compelled to do it by force and destruction. If these peasants do not compel you, others will. Even though you were to defeat them all, they would still not be defeated, for God will raise up others. It is his will to defeat you, and you will be defeated. It is not the peasants, dear lords, who are resisting you; it is God himself, to visit your raging upon you. Some of you have said that you will stake land and people on exterminating the Lutheran teaching. What would you think if you were to turn out to be your own prophets, and your land and people were already at stake? Do not joke with God, dear lords! The Jews, too, said, "We have no king" [John 19:15], and they meant it so seriously that they must be without a king forever.

To make your sin still greater, and guarantee your merciless destruction, some of you are beginning to blame this affair on the Gospel and say that it is the fruit of my teaching. Well, well, slander away, dear lords! You did not want to know what I taught or what the Gospel is; now the one who will soon teach you is at the door, unless you change your ways. You, and everyone else, must bear witness that I have taught with all quietness, have striven earnestly against rebellion, and have energetically encouraged and exhorted people to obey and respect even you wild and dictatorial tyrants. This rebellion cannot be coming from me. Rather the murder-prophets, who hate me as they hate you, have come among these people and have gone about among them for more than three years, and no one has resisted and fought against them except me.

Therefore, if God intends to punish you and allows the devil through his false prophets to stir up the people against you, and if it is, perhaps, God's will that I shall not be able to prevent it any longer, what can I or my Gospel do? Not only have we suffered your persecution and murdering and raging; we have also prayed for you and helped to protect and maintain your rule over the common people. If I desired revenge, I could laugh up my sleeve and simply watch what the peasants are doing or even join in with them and help make matters worse; may God keep me from this in the future as he has in the past.

Therefore my dear lords—whether you are my enemies or friends—as a loyal subject I humbly beg you not to despise my faithfulness, though I am a poor man. I beseech you not to make light of this rebellion. It is not that I think or fear that the rebels will be too strong for you or that I want you to be afraid of them for that reason. Rather fear God and respect his wrath! If he wills to punish you as you have deserved (and I am afraid that he does), then he will punish you, even though the peasants were a hundred times fewer than they are. He can make peasants out of stones and slay a hundred of you by one peasant, so that all your armor and your strength will be too weak to save you.

If it is still possible to give you advice, my lords, give way a little to the will and wrath of God. A cartload of hay must give way to a drunken man-how much more ought you to stop your raging and obstinate tyranny and not deal unreasonably with the peasants, as though they were drunk or out of their minds! Do not start a fight with them, for you do not know how it will end. Try kindness first, for you do not know what God will do to prevent the spark that will kindle all Germany and start a fire that no one can extinguish. Our sins are before God [Ps. 90:8]; therefore we have to fear his wrath when even a leaf rustles [Lev. 26:36], let alone when such a multitude sets itself in motion. You will lose nothing by kindness; and even if you did lose something, the preservation of peace will pay you back ten times. But if there is open conflict you may lose both your property and your life. Why risk danger when you can achieve more by following a different way that is also the better way?

The peasants have just published twelve articles, some of which are so fair and just as to take away your reputation in the eyes of God and the world and fulfil what the

Psalm [107:40] says about God pouring contempt upon princes. Nevertheless, almost all of the articles are framed in their own interest and for their own good, though not for their best good. Of course, I would have formulated other articles against you that would have dealt with all Germany and its government.

I did this in my book *To the German Nobility*, when more was at stake; but because you made light of that, you must now listen to and put up with these selfish articles. It serves you right for being a people to whom nothing can be told.

In the first article they ask the right to hear the Gospel and choose their pastors. You cannot reject this request with any show of right, even though this article does indeed make some selfish demands, for they allege that these pastors are to be supported by the tithes, and these do not belong to the peasants. Nevertheless, the basic sense of the article is that the preaching of the Gospel should be permitted, and no ruler can or ought to oppose this. Indeed, no ruler ought to prevent anyone from teaching or believing what he pleases, whether it is the Gospel or lies. It is enough if he prevents the teaching of sedition and rebellion.

The other articles protest economic injustices, such as the death tax. These protests are also right and just, for rulers are not appointed to exploit their subjects for their own profit and advantage, but to be concerned about the welfare of their subjects. And the people cannot tolerate it very long if their rulers set confiscatory tax rates and tax them out of their very skins. What good would it do a peasant if his field bore as many gulden as stalks of wheat if the rulers only taxed him all the more and then wasted it as though it were chaff to increase their luxury, and squandered his money on their own clothes, food, drink, and buildings? Would not the luxury and the extravagant spending have to be checked so that a poor man could keep something for himself? You have undoubtedly received further information from the peasants' tracts, so that you are adequately aware of their grievances.

To the Peasants

So far, dear friends, you have learned only that I agree that it is unfortunately all too true that the princes and lords who forbid the preaching of the Gospel and oppress the people unbearably deserve to have God pull them down from their thrones [Luke 1:52] because they have sinned so greatly against both God and man. And they have no excuse. Nevertheless, you, too, must be careful that you take up your cause justly and with a good conscience. If you have a good conscience, you have the comforting advantage that God will be with you, and will help you. Even though you did not succeed for a while, or even suffered death, you would win in the end, and you would preserve your souls eternally with all the saints. But if you act unjustly and have a bad conscience, you will be defeated. And even though you might win for a while and even kill all the princes, you would suffer the eternal loss of your body and soul in the end. For you, therefore, this is no laughing matter. The eternal fate of your body and soul is involved. And you must most seriously consider not merely how strong you are and how wrong the princes are, but whether you act justly and with a good conscience.

Therefore, dear brethren, I beg you in a kindly and brotherly way to look carefully at what you are doing and not to believe all kinds of spirits and preachers [I John 4:1]. For Satan has now raised up many evil spirits of disorder and of murder, and filled the world with them. Just listen attentively, as you offer many times to do. I will not spare you the earnest warning that I owe you, even though some of you have been so poisoned by the murderous spirits that you will hate me for it and call me a hypocrite. That does not worry me; it is enough for me if I save some of the goodhearted and upright men among you from the danger of God's wrath. The rest I fear as little as they despise me much; and they shall not harm me. I know One who is greater and mightier than they are, and he teaches me in Psalm 3[:6], "I am not afraid of ten thousands of people who have set themselves against me round about." My confidence shall outlast their confidence; that I know for certain.

In the first place, dear brethren, you bear the name of God and call yourselves a "Christian association" or union, and you allege that you want to live and act according to divine law. Now you know that the name, word, and titles of God are not to be assumed idly or in vain, as he say; in the second commandment, "Thou shalt not take the name of the Lord your God in vain," and adds, "for the Lord will not hold him guiltless who takes his name in vain" [Deut. 5:11]. Here is a clear, plain text, which applies to you, as to all men. It threatens you, as well as us and all others, with God's wrath without regard to your great numbers, rights, and terror. God is mighty enough and strong enough to punish you as he here threatens if his name is taken in vain, and you know it. So if you take his name in vain, you may expect no good fortune but only trouble. Learn from this how to judge yourselves and accept this friendly warning. It would be a simple thing for God, who once drowned the whole world with a flood [Gen. 7:17–24) and destroyed Sodom with fire [Gen. 19:24–28], to kill or defeat so many thousands of peasants. He is an almighty and terrible God.

Second, it is easy to prove that you are taking God's name in vain and putting it to shame; nor is there any doubt that you will, in the end, encounter all misfortune, unless God is not true. For here is God's word, spoken through the mouth of Christ, "All who take the sword will perish by the sword" [Matt. 26:52]. That means nothing else than that no one, by his own violence, shall arrogate authority to himself; but as Paul says, "Let every person be subject to the governing authorities with fear and reverence" [Rom. 13:1].

How can you get around these passages and laws of God when you boast that you are acting according to divine law, and yet take the sword in your own hands, and revolt against "the governing authorities that are instituted by God?" Do you think that Paul's judgment in Romans 1 [:2] will not strike you, "He who resists the authorities will incur judgment"? You take God's name in vain when you pretend to be seeking divine right, and under the pretense of his name work contrary to divine right. Be careful, dear sirs. It will not turn out that way in the end.

Third, you say that the rulers are wicked and intolerable, for they will not allow us to have the Gospel; they oppress us too hard with the burdens they lay on our property, and they are ruining us in body and soul. I answer: The fact that the rulers are wicked and unjust does not excuse disorder and rebellion, for the punishing of wickedness is not the responsibility of everyone, but of the worldly rulers who bear the sword. Thus Paul says in Romans 1 [:4] and Peter, in I Peter 3 [2:14], that the rulers are instituted by God for the punishment of the wicked. Then, too, there is the natural law of all the world, which says that no one may sit as judge in his own case or take his own revenge. The proverb is true, "Whoever hits back is in the wrong." Or as it is said, "It takes two to start a fight." The divine law agrees with this, and says, in Deuteronomy 32[:35], "Vengeance is mine; I will repay, says the Lord." Now you cannot deny that your rebellion actually involves you in such a way that you make yourselves your own judges and avenge yourselves. You are quite unwilling to suffer any wrong. That is contrary not only to Christian law and the Gospel, but also to natural law and all equity.

If your cause is to prosper when the divine and Christian law of the Old and New Testaments and even the natural law are all against you, you must produce a new and special command of God, confirmed by signs and wonders, which commands you to do these things. Otherwise God will not allow his word and ordinance to be broken by your violence. On the contrary, because you boast of the divine law and yet act against it, he will let you fall and be punished terribly, as men who dishonor his name. Then he will condemn you eternally, as was said above. For the word of Christ in Matthew 7[:3] applies to you; you see the speck in the eye of the rulers, but do not see the log in your own eye. The word of Paul in Romans 3[:8] also applies, "Why not do evil that good may come? Their condemnation is just." It is true that the rulers do wrong when they suppress the Gospel and oppress you in temporal matters. But you do far greater wrong when you not only suppress God's word, but tread it underfoot, invade his authority and law, and put yourselves above God. Besides, you take from the rulers their authority and right, indeed, everything they have. What do they have left when they have lost their authority?

I make you the judges and leave it to you to decide who is the worse robber, the man who takes a large part of another's goods, but leaves him something, or the man who takes everything that he has, and takes his life besides. The rulers unjustly take your property; that is the one side. On the other hand, you take from them their authority, in which their whole property and life and being consist. Therefore you are far greater robbers than they, and you intend to do worse things than they have done. "Indeed not," you say, "we are going to leave them enough to live on." If anyone wants to believe that, let him! I do not believe it. Anyone who dares to go so far as to use force to take away authority, which is the main thing, will not stop at that, but will take the other, smaller thing that depends upon it. The wolf that eats a whole sheep will also eat its ear. And even if you permitted them to keep their life and some property, nevertheless, you would take the best thing they have, namely, their authority, and make yourselves lords over them. That would be too great a robbery and wrong. God will declare you to be the greatest robbers.

Can you not think it through, dear friends? If your enterprise were right, then any man might become judge over another. Then authority, government, law, and order would disappear from the world; there would be nothing but murder and bloodshed. As soon as anyone saw that someone was wronging him, he would begin to judge and punish him. Now if that is unjust and intolerable when done by an individual, we cannot allow a mob or a crowd to do it. However, if we do permit a mob or a crowd to do it, then we cannot rightly and fairly forbid an individual to do it. For in both cases the cause is the same, that is, an injustice. What would you yourselves do if disorder broke out in your ranks and one man set himself against another and took vengeance on him? Would you put up with that? Would you not say that he must let others, whom you appointed, do the judging and avenging? What do you expect God and the world to think when you pass judgment and avenge yourselves on those who have injured you and even upon your rulers, whom God has appointed?

Now in all this I have been speaking of the common, divine, and natural law which even the heathen, Turks, and Jews have to keep if there is to be any peace or order in the world. Even though you were to keep this whole law, you would do no better and no more than the heathen and the Turks do. For no one is a Christian merely because he does not undertake to function as his own judge and avenger but leaves this to the authorities and the rulers. You would eventually have to do this whether you wanted to or not. But because you are acting against this law, you see plainly that you are worse than heathen or Turks, to say nothing of the fact that you are not Christians. What do you think that Christ will say about this? You bear his name, and call yourselves a "Christian association," and yet you are so far from being Christian, and your actions and lives are so horribly contrary to his law that you are not worthy to be called even heathen or Turks. You are much worse than these, because you rage and struggle against the divine and natural law, which all the heathen keep.

See, dear friends, what kind of preachers you have and what they think of your souls. I fear that some prophets of murder have come among you, who would like to use you so they can become lords in the world, and they do not care that they are endangering your life, property, honor, and soul, in time and eternity. If, now, you really want to keep the divine law, as you boast, then do it. There it stands! God says, "Vengeance is mine; I will repay" [Rom. 12:19], and, "Be subject not only to good lords, but also to the wicked" [I Pet. 2:18]. If you do this, well and good; if not, you may, indeed, cause a calamity, but it will finally come upon you. Let no one have any doubts about this! God is just, and will not endure it. Be careful, therefore, with your liberty, that you do not run away from the rain and fall in the water. Beware of the illusion that you are winning freedom for your body when you are really losing your body, property, and soul for all eternity. God's wrath is there; fear it, I advise you! The devil has sent false prophets among you; beware of them!

And now we want to move on and speak of the law of Christ, and of the Gospel, which is not binding on the heathen, as the other law is. For if you claim that you are Christians and like to be called Christians and want to be known as Christians, then you must also allow your law to be held up before you rightly. Listen, then, dear Christians, to your Christian law! Your Supreme Lord Christ, whose name you bear, says, in Matthew 6 [5:39–41], with him "Do not resist one who is evil. If anyone forces you to go a mile, go with him two miles. If anyone wants to take your coat, let him have your cloak too. If anyone strikes you on one cheek, offer him the other too." Do you hear this, O Christian association? How does your program stand in light of this law? You do not want to endure evil or suffering, but rather want to be free and to experience only goodness and justice. However, Christ says that we should not resist evil or injustice but always yield, suffer, and let things be taken from us. If you will not bear this law, then lay aside the name of Christian and claim another name that accords with your actions, or else Christ himself will tear his name away from you, and that will be too hard for you.

In Romans 12[:19] Paul says, "Beloved, never avenge yourselves, but leave it to the wrath of God." In this same sense he praises the Corinthians for gladly suffering if someone hits or robs them, II Corinthians 11[:20]. And in I Corinthians 6[:1–2] he condemns them for going to court for the sake of property rather than suffering injustice. Indeed, our leader, Jesus Christ, says in Matthew 7[5-44] that we should bless those who insult us, pray for our persecutors, love our enemies, and do good to those who do evil to us. These, dear friends, are our Christian laws.

Now you can see how far these false prophets have led you astray. They still call you Christians, although they have made you worse than heathen. On the basis of these passages even a child can understand that the Christian law tells us not to strive against injustice, not to grasp the sword, not to protect ourselves, not to avenge ourselves, but to give up life and property, and let whoever takes it have it. We have all we need in our Lord, who will ot leave us, as he has promised [Heb. 13:5]. Suffering! Suffering! Cross! Cross! This and nothing else is the Christian law! But now you are fighting for temporal goods and will not let the coat go after the cloak, but want to recover the cloak. How then will you die and give up your life, or love your enemies and do good to them? O worthless Christians! Dear friends, Christians are not so commonplace that so many can assemble in one group. A Christian is a rare bird! Would to God that the majority of us were good, pious heathen, who kept the natural law, not to mention the Christian law!

I will give you some illustrations of Christian law so that you may see where the mad prophets have led you. Look at St. Peter in the garden. He wanted to defend his Lord Christ with the sword, and cut off Malchus' ear [John 18:10]. Tell me, did not Peter have great right on his side? Was it not an intolerable injustice that they were going to take from Christ not only his property, but also his life? Indeed, they not only took his fife and property, but in so doing they entirely suppressed the Gospel by which they were to be saved and thus robbed heaven. You have not yet suffered such a wrong, dear friends. But see what Christ does and teaches in this case. however great the injustice was, he nevertheless stopped St. Peter, bade him put up his sword, and would not allow him to avenge or prevent this injustice. In addition, he passed a sentence of death upon him, as though upon a murderer, and said, "He who takes the sword will perish by the sword" [Matt. 26:52]. This should help us understand that we do not have the right to use the sword simply because someone has done us an injustice and because the law and justice are on our side. We must also have received power and authority from God to use the sword and to punish wrong. Furthermore, a Christian should also suffer it if anyone desires to keep the Gospel away from him by force. It may not even be possible to keep the Gospel from anyone, as we shall hear.

A second example is Christ himself. What did he do when they took his life on the cross and thereby took away from him the work of preaching for which God himself had sent him as a blessing for the souls of men? He did just what St. Peter says. He committed the whole matter to him who judges justly, and he endured this intolerable wrong [I Pet. 2:23]. More than that, he prayed for his persecutors and said, "Father, forgive them, for they know not what they do" [Luke 23:34].

Now, if you are genuine Christians, you must certainly act in this same way and follow this example. If you do not do this, then give up the name of Christian and the claim that Christian law is on your side, for then you are certainly not Christians but are opposing Christ and his law, his doctrine, and his example. But if you do follow the example of Christ, you will soon see God's miracles and he will help you as he helped Christ, whom he avenged after the completion of his passion in such a way that his Gospel and his kingdom won a powerful victory and gained the upper hand, in spite of all his enemies. He will help you in this same way so that his Gospel will rise with power among you, if you first suffer to the end, leave the case to him, and await his vengeance. But because of what you are doing, and because you do not want to triumph by suffering, but by your fists, you are interfering with God's vengeance and you will keep neither the Gospel nor your fists.

I must also give you an illustration from the present. Pope and emperor have opposed me and raged against me. Now what have I done that the more pope and emperor raged, the more my Gospel spread? I have never drawn a sword or desired revenge. I began neither conspiracy nor rebellion, but so far as I was able, I have helped the worldly rulers—even those who persecuted the Gospel and me—to preserve their power and honor. I stopped with committing the matter to God and relying confidently at all times upon his hand. This is why God has not only preserved my life in spite of the pope and all the tyrants—but he has made my Gospel grow and spread. Now you interfere with what I am doing. You want to help the Gospel and yet you do not see that what you are doing hinders and suppresses it most effectively.

I say all this, dear friends, as a faithful warning. In this case you should stop calling yourselves Christians and stop claiming that you have the Christian law on your side. For no matter how right you are, it is not right for a Christian to appeal to law, or to fight, but rather to suffer wrong and endure evil; and there is no other way, I Corinthians 6[:1–8]. Yourselves confess in the preface to your articles that "all who believe in Christ become loving, peaceful, patient, and agreeable." Your actions, however, reveal nothing but impatience, aggression, anger, and violence. Thus you contradict your own words. You want to be known as patient people, you who will endure neither injustice nor evil, but will endure only what is just and good. That is a fine kind of patience! Any rascal can practice it! It does not take a Christian to do that! So again I say, however good and just your cause may be, nevertheless, because you would defend yourselves and are unwilling to suffer either violence or injustice, you may do anything that God does not prevent. However, leave the name Christian out of it. Leave the name Christian out, I say, and do not use it to cover up your impatient, disorderly, un-Christian undertaking. I shall not let you have that name, but so long as there is a heartbeat in my body, I shall do all I can, through speaking and writing, to take that name away from you. You will not succeed, or will succeed only in ruining your bodies and souls.

In saying this it is not my intention to justify or defend the rulers in the intolerable injustices which you suffer from them. They are unjust, and commit heinous wrongs against you; that I admit. If, however, neither side accepts instruction and you start to fight with each other—may God prevent it!—I hope that neither side will be called Christian. Rather I hope that God will, as is usual in these situations, use one rascal to punish the other. If it comes to a conflict—may God graciously prevent it!—I hope that your character and name will be so well known that the authorities will recognize that they are fighting not against Christians but against heathen; and that you, too, may know that you are not fighting Christian rulers but heathen. Christians do not fight for themselves with sword and musket, but with the cross and with suffering, just as Christ, our leader, does not bear a sword, but hangs on the cross. Your victory, therefore, does not consist in conquering and reigning, or in the use of force, but in defeat and in weakness, as St. Paul says in II Corinthians I[10:4]. "The weapons of our warfare are not material, but are the strength which comes from God," and, "Power is made perfect in weakness" [II Cor. 12:9].

Your name and title ought therefore to indicate that you are people who fight because they will not, and ought not, endure injustice or evil, according to the teaching of nature. You should use that name, and let the name of Christ alone, for that is the kind of works that you are doing. If, however, you will not take that name, but keep the name of Christian, then I must accept the fact that I am also involved in this struggle and consider you as enemies who, under the name of the Gospel, act contrary to it, and want to do more to suppress my Gospel than anything the pope and emperor have done to suppress it.

I will make no secret of what I intend to do. I will put the whole matter into God's hands, risk my neck by God's grace, and confidently trust in him—just as I have been doing against the pope and the emperor. I shall pray for you, that God may enlighten you, and resist your undertaking, and not let it succeed. For I see well that the devil, who has not been able to destroy me through the pope, now seeks to exterminate me and swallow me up by means of the bloodthirsty prophets of murder and spirits of rebellion that are among you. Well, let him swallow me! I will give him a bellyful, I know. And even if you win, you will hardly enjoy it! I beg you, humbly and kindly, to think things over so that I will not have to trust in and pray to God against you.

For although I am a poor, sinful man, I know and am certain that my concern in this matter is right and just, for I fight in behalf of the name Christian and pray that it not be put to shame. I am sure, too, that my prayer is acceptable to God and will be heard, for he himself has taught us to pray, in the Lord's Prayer, "Hallowed be thy name" [Matt. 6:9], and in the second commandment he has forbidden that it be put to shame [Deut. 5:11]. Therefore I beg you not to despise my prayer and the prayer of those who pray along with me, for it will be too mighty for you and will arouse God against you, as St. James says, "The prayer of the righteous man who prays persistently has great effects, just as Elijah's prayer did" [James 5:16–17]. We also have many other comforting promises of God that he will hear us, such as John, "If you ask anything in my name I will do it" [John 14:14], and, "If we ask anything according to his will he hears us" [I John 5:14]. You cannot have such confidence and assurance in prayer because your own conscience and the Scriptures testify that your enterprise is heathenish, and not Christian, and, under the name of the Gospel, works against the Gospel and brings contempt upon the name Christian. I know that none of you has ever once prayed to God or called upon him in behalf of this cause. You could not do it! You dare not lift up your eyes to him in this case. You only defiantly shake your fist at him, the fist which you have clenched because of your impatience and unwillingness to suffer. This will not turn out well for you.

If you were Christians you would stop threatening and resisting with fist and sword. Instead, you would continually abide by the Lord's Prayer and say, "Thy will be done," and, "Deliver us from evil, Amen" [Matt. 6:10, 13]. The psalms show us many examples of genuine saints taking their needs to God and complaining to him about them. They seek help from God: they do not try to defend themselves or to resist evil. That kind of prayer would have been more help to you, in all your needs, than if the world were full of people on your side. This would be especially true if, besides that, you had a good conscience and the comforting assurance that your prayers were heard, as his promises declare: "God is the Savior of all men, especially of those who believe," I Timothy 4[:10]; "Call upon me in the day of trouble, I will deliver you," Psalm 50[:15]; "He called upon me in trouble, therefore I will help him," Psalm 91[:15]. See! That is the Christian way to get rid of misfortune and evil, that is, to endure it and to call upon God. But because you neither call upon God nor patiently endure, but rather help yourselves by your own power and make yourselves your own god and savior, God cannot and must not be your God and Savior. By God's permission you might accomplish something as the heathen and blasphemers you are—and we pray that he will prevent that—but it will only be to your temporal and eternal destruction. However, as Christians or Evangelicals, you will win nothing. I would stake my life a thousand times on that.

On this basis it is now easy to reply to all your articles. Even though they all were just and equitable in terms of natural law, you have not been putting this program into effect and achieving your goals by patiently praying to God, as Christians ought to do, but have instead undertaken to compel the rulers to give you what you wanted by using force and violence. This is against the law of the land and against natural justice. The man who composed your articles is no godly and honest man. His marginal notes refer to many chapters of Scripture on which the articles are supposed to be based. But he talks with his mouth full of nothing, and leaves out the passages which would show his own wickedness and that of your cause. He has done this to deceive you, to incite you, and to bring you into danger. Anyone who reads through the chapters cited will realize that they speak very little in favor of what you are doing. On the contrary, they say that men should live and act like Christians. He who seeks to use you to destroy the Gospel is a prophet of discord. May God prevent that and guard you against him!

In the preface you are conciliatory and claim that you do not want to be rebels. You even excuse your actions by claiming that you desire to teach and to live according to the Gospel. Your own words and actions condemn you. You confess that you are causing disturbances and revolting. And then you try to excuse this behavior with the Gospel. You have heard above that the Gospel teaches Christians to endure and suffer wrong and to pray to God in every need. You, however, are not willing to suffer, but like heathen, you want to force the rulers to conform to your impatient will. You cite the children of Israel as an example, saying that God heard their crying and delivered them [Exod. 6:5–7]. Why then do you not follow the example that you cite? Call upon God and wait until he sends you a Moses, who will prove by signs and wonders that he is sent from God. The children of Israel did not riot against Pharaoh, or help themselves, as you propose to do. This illustration, therefore is completely against you, and condemns you. You boast of it, and yet you do the opposite of what it teaches.

Furthermore, your declaration that you teach and live according to the Gospel is not ture. Not one of the articles teaches anything of the Gospel. Rather, everything is aimed at obtaining freedom for your person and for your property. To sum it up, everything is concerned with worldly and temporal matters. You want power and wealth so that you will not suffer injustice. The Gospel, however, does not become involved in the affairs of this world, but seaks of our life in the world in terms of suffering, injustice, the cross, patience, and contempt for this life and temporal wealth. How, then, does the Gospel agree with you? You are only trying to give your evangelical and un-Christian enterprise and evangelical appearance; and you do not see that in so doing you are bringing shame upon the holy Gospel of Christ, and making it a cover for wickedness. Therefore you must take a different attitude. If you want to be Christians and use the name Christian, then stop what you are doing and decide to suffer these injustices. If you want to keep on doing these things, then use another name and do not ask anyone to call you or think of you as Christians. There is no other possibility.

True enough, you are right in desiring the Gospel, if you are really serious about it. Indeed, I am willing to make this article even sharper than you do, and say it is intolerable that anyone should be shut out of heaven and driven by force into hell. No one should suffer that; he ought rather to lose his life a hundred times. But whoever keeps the Gospel from me, closes heaven to me and drives me by force into hell; for the Gospel is the only means of salvation for the soul. And on peril of losing my soul, I should not permit this. Tell me, is that not stated sharply enough? And yet it does not follow that I must rebel against the rulers who do me this wrong. "But," you saw, "how am I supposed to suffer it and yet not suffer it at the same time?" The answer is easy. It is impossible to keep the Gospel from anyone. No power in heaven or on earth can do this, for it is a public teaching that moves about freely under the heavens and is bound to no one place. It is like the star that went in the sky ahead of the Wise Men from the east and showed them where Christ was born [Matt. 2:9].

It is true, of course, that the rulers may suppress the Gospel in cities or places where the Gospel is, or where there are preachers; but you can leave these cities or places and follow the Gospel to some other place. It is not necessary, for the Gospel's sake, for you to capture or occupy the city or place; on the contrary, let the ruler have his city; you follow the Gospel. Thus you permit men to wrong you and drive you away; and yet, same time, you do not permit men to take the Gospel from you or keep it from you. Thus the two things, suffering and not suffering, turn out to be one. If you occupy the city for the sake of the Gospel, you rob the ruler of the city of what is his, and pretend that you are doing it for the Gospel's sake. Dear friend, the Gospel does not teach us to rob or to take things, even though the owner of the property abuses it by using it against God, wrongfully, and to your injury. The Gospel needs no physical place or city in which to dwell; it will and must dwell in hearts. This is what Christ taught in Matthew 10[:23], "When they persecute you in one town, flee to the next." He does not say, "When they persecute you in one town, stay there and take over the town by force and rebel against the ruler of the town-all to the praise of the Gospel," as men now want to do, and are teaching. However, Jesus says, "Flee, flee straightaway into another, until the Son of man shall come." And in Matthew 23[:34] he says that godless men will drive his evangelists from town to town. And in II Corinthians 4[I Cor. 4:11] Paul says that we are homeless. And if it does happen that a Christian must, for the sake of the Gospel, constantly move from one place to another, and leave all his possessions behind him, or even if his situation is very uncertain and he expects to have to move at any moment, he is only experiencing what is appropriate for a Christian. For because he will not suffer the Gospel to be taken or kept from him, he has to let his city, town, property, and everything that he is and has be taken and kept from him. Now how does your undertaking conform to this? You capture and hold cities and towns that are not yours, and you will not let them be taken or kept from you; though you take and keep them from their natural rulers. What kind of Christians are these, who, for the Gospel's sake, become robbers, thieves, and scoundrels, and then say afterward that they are evangelicals?

On the First Article

"The entire community should have the power and authority to choose and appoint a pastor." This article is just only if it is understood in a Christian sense, even though the chapters indicated in the margin do not support it. If the possessions of the parish come from the rulers and not from the community, then the community cannot give these possessions to one whom they choose, for that would be robbery and theft. If they desire a pastor, let them first humbly ask the rulers to give them one. If the rulers are unwilling, then let them choose their own pastor, and support him out of their own possessions; they should let the rulers keep their property, or else secure it from the m in a lawful way. But if the rulers will not tolerate the pastor whom they chose and support, then let him flee to another city, and let any flee with him who want to do as Christ teaches. That is a Christian and evangelical way to choose and have one's own pastor. Whoever does otherwise, acts in an un-Christian manner, and is a robber and brawler.

On the Second Article

The pastor "shall receive out of this tithe...; the remainder shall be distributed to the poor and needy." This article is nothing but theft and highway robbery. They want to appropriate for themselves the tithes, which are not theirs but the rulers.' and want to use them to do what they please. Oh, no, dear friends! That is the same as deposing the rulers altogether. Your preface expressly says that no one is to be deprived of what is his. If you want to give gifts and do good, use your own possessions, as the wise man says [Prov. 3:9]. And God says through Isaiah, "I hate the offering that is given out of stolen goods" [Isa. 61:8]. You speak in this article as though you were already lords in the land and had taken all the property of the rulers for your own and would be no one's subjects, and would give nothing. This shows what your intention really is. Stop it, dear sirs, stop it! It will not be you who puts an end to it! The chapters of Scripture which your lying preacher and false prophet has smeared on the margin do not help you at all; they are against you.

On the Third Article

You assert that no one is to be the serf of anyone else, because Christ has made us all free. That is making Christian freedom a completely physical matter. Did not Abraham [Gen. l7:23] and other patriarchs and prophets have slaves? Read what St. Paul teaches about servants, who, at that time, were all slaves. This article, therefore, absolutely contradicts the Gospel. It proposes robbery, for it suggests that every man should take his body away from his lord, even though his body is the lord's property. A slave can be a Christian, and have Christian freedom, in the same way that a prisoner or a sick man is a Christian, and yet not free. This article would make all men equal, and turn the spiritual kingdom of Christ into a worldly, external kingdom; and that is impossible. A worldly kingdom cannot exist without an inequality of persons, some being free, some imprisoned, some lords, some subjects, etc.; and St. Paul says in Galatians 5 that in Christ the lord and the servant are equal. My good friend Urbanus Rhegius has written more adequately on this subject. If you want to know more, read his book.

On the Other Eight Articles

The other articles, which discuss the freedom to hunt game animals and birds, to catch fish, to use wood from the forest, their obligation to provide free labor, the amount of their rents and taxes, the death tax, etc., are all matters for the lawyers to discuss. It is not fitting that I, an evangelist, should judge or make decisions in such matters. I am to instruct and teach men's consciences in things that concern divine and Christian matters; there are books enough about the other things in the imperial laws. I said above that these things do not concern a Christian, and that he cares nothing about them. He lets anyone who will rob, take, cheat, scrape, devour, and rage—for the Christian is a martyr on earth. Therefore the peasants ought properly to stop using the name Christian and use some other name that would show that they are men who seek their human and natural rights rather than their rights as Christians. For obtaining their rights as Christians would mean they should keep quiet about all these matters and complain only to God when they suffer.

Dear friends, this is the instruction that you asked me to give you in the second document. Please remember that you have gladly offered to receive instruction on the basis of Scripture. So when this reaches you, do not be so ready to scream, "Luther flatters the princes and speaks contrary to the Gospel." First read and examine my arguments from Scripture. For this is your affair; I am excused in the sight of God and the world. I know well the false prophets who are among you. Do not listen to them. They are surely deceiving you. They do not think of your consciences; they want to make Galatians of you. They want to use you to gain riches and honor for themselves. Afterward, both you and they will be damned eternally in hell.

Admonition to Both Rulers and Peasants

Now, dear sirs, there is nothing Christian on either side and nothing Chrisitan is at issue between you; both lords and peasants are discussing questions of justice and injustice in heathen, or worldly, terms. Furthermore, both parties are acting against God and are under his wrath, as you have heard. For God's sake, then, take my advice! Take a hold of these matters properly, with justice and not with force or violence and do not start endless bloodshed in Germany. For because both of you are wrong, and both of you want to avenge and defend yourselves, both of you will destroy yourselves and God will use one rascal to flog another.

Both Scripture and history are against you lords, for both tell how tyrants are punished. Even the heathen poets say that tyrants seldom die a dry death, but are usually slain and perish in their own blood. Because, then, it is an established fact that you rule tyrannically and with rage, prohibit preaching of the Gospel, and cheat and oppress the poor, you have no reason to be confident or to hope that you will perish in any other way that your kind have always perished. Look at all the kingdoms that have come to their end by the sword—Assyria, Persia, Israel, Judah, and Rome. In the end they were all destroyed in the same way they destroyed others. Thus God shows that he is Judge upon earth and that he leaves no wrong unpunished. Therefore nothing is more certain than that this same judgment is breathing down your necks, whether it comes now or later, unless you reform.

Scripture and experience are also against you peasants. They teach that rebellion has never had a good end and that God always keeps his word exactly, "He that takes the sword will perish by the sword" [Matt. 26:52]. You are certainly under the wrath of God, because you are doing wrong by judging your own case and avenging yourselves and are bearing the name Christian unworthily. Even though you win and destroy all the lords, you will finally start tearing the flesh from one another's bones, like wild beasts. For because flesh and blood, not spirit, prevails among you, God will soon send an evil spirit among you, as he did to the men of Shechem and to Abimelech [Judg. 9:22–57]. See the end that finally comes to rebellion in the story of Korah, Numbers 16 [:31–35], and of Absalom [II Sam. 18:14–15], of Sheba [II Sam. 20:22], Zimri [I Kings 16:18], and others like them. In short, God hates both tyrants and rebels; therefore he sets them against each other, so that both parties perish shamefully, and his wrath and judgment upon the godless are fulfilled.

As I see it, the worst thing about this completely miserable affair is that both sides will sustain irreparable damage; and I would gladly risk my life and even die if I could prevent that from happening. Since neither side fights with a good conscience, but both fight to uphold injustice, it must follow, in the first place, that those who are slain are lost eternally, body and soul, as men who die in their sins, without penitence and without grace, under the wrath of God. Nothing can be done for them. The lords would be fighting to strengthen and maintain their tyranny, their persecution of the Gospel, and their unjust oppression of the poor, or else to help that kind of ruler. That is a terrible injustice and is against God. He who commits such a sin must be lost eternally. The peasants, on the other hand, would fight to defend their rebellion and their abuse of the name Christian. Both these things are great sins against God, and he who dies in them or for them must also be lost eternally, and nothing can prevent it.

The second injury is that Germany will be laid waste, and if this bloodshed once starts, it will not stop until everything is destroyed. It is easy to start a fight, but we cannot stop the fighting whenever we want to. What have all these innocent women, children, and old people, whom you fools are drawing with you into such danger, ever done to you? Why do you insist on filling the land with blood and robbery, widows and orphans? Oh, the devil has wicked plans! And God is angry; he threatens to let the devil loose upon us and cool his rage in our blood and souls. Beware, dear sirs, and be wise! Both of you are equally involved! What good will it do you intentionally to damn yourselves for all eternity and, in addition, to bequeath a desolate, devastated and bloody land to your descendants, when you still have time to find a better solution by repenting before God, by concluding a friendly agreement, or even by voluntarily suffering for the sake of humanity? You will accomplish nothing through strife and violence.

I, therefore, sincerely advise you to choose certain counts and lords from among the nobility and certain councilmen from the cities and ask them to arbitrate and settle this dispute amicably. You lords, stop being so stubborn! You will finally have to stop being such oppressive tyrants—whether you want to or not. Give these poor people room in which to live and air to breathe. You peasants, let yourselves be instructed and give up the excessive demands of some of your articles. In this way it may be possible to reach a solution of this dispute through human laws and agreements, if not through Christian means.

If you do not follow this advice—God forbid!—I must let you come to blows. But I am innocent of your souls, your blood, or your property. The guilt is yours alone. I have told you that you are both wrong and that what you are fighting for is wrong. You lords are not fighting against Christians—Christians do nothing against you; they prefer to suffer all things—but against outright robbers and defamers of the Christian name. Those of them who die are already condemned eternally. On the other hand, you peasants are not fighting against Christians, but against tyrants, and persecutors of God and man, and murderers of the saints of Christ. Those of them who die are also condemned eternally. There you have God's sure verdict upon both parties. This I know. Do what you please to preserve your bodies and souls, if you will not accept my advice.

I, however, will pray to my God that he will either reconcile you both and bring about an agreement between you, or else graciously prevent things from turning out as you intend. Nonetheless, the terrible signs and wonders that have come to pass in these times give me a heavy heart and make me fear that God's wrath has grown too great; as he says in Jeremiah, "Though Noah, Job, and Daniel stood before me, I would have no pleasure in the people." Would to God that you might fear his wrath and amend your ways that this disaster might be delayed and postponed a while! In any case, my conscience assures me that I have faithfully given you my Christian and fraternal advice. God grant that it helps! Amen.

"The Twelve Articles of the Swabian Peasants (February 27–March 1, 1525)." From *Readings in European History, A collection of extracts from the sources chosen with the purpose of illustrating the progress of culture in Western Europe since the German Invasions*, Vol. II, 94–99. Boston: Ginn & Company, 1904–1906.

"Martin Luther's Admonition to Peace." In *The Twelve Articles and Luther's Admonition to Peace*, translated and edited by Robert C. Schultz, in *Luther's Works*, Vol. 46, edited by Jaroslav Pelikan and Helmut T. Lehrmann, 8–43. Philadelphia: Fortress Press, 1967. © 1967 by Fortress Press. Used by permission of 1517 Media and Augsburg Fortress.

POST-READING PARS

1. Identify two words or phrases that Luther and/or the peasants used to galvanize their respective agendas.
2. Identify two features of the peasants' demands that characterize it as a political movement.

Inquiry Corner

Content Question(s):	Critical Question(s):
Outline the main points in Martin Luther's response while also identifying the shift in his tone between his two intended audiences.	Why do you think Luther reacted so strongly to the Twelve Articles? How do you think the peasants navigated being repudiated by someone they considered an inspiration?
Looking at the scriptural references in each piece, are there any commonalities in theme between the Twelve Articles and the Admonition for Peace?	
Comparative Question(s):	**Connection Question(s):**
How might the peasants' demands compare to other revolutions you are familiar with in terms of context and action?	In what ways do you see this type of dialogue between opposing viewpoints occurring in present-day cultural and social movements?

The editors and publisher gratefully acknowledge the permission granted to reproduce the copyrighted material in this book. Every effort has been made to trace copyright holders and to obtain their permission for the use of copyrighted material. The publisher apologizes for any errors or omissions in the list below and would be grateful if notified of any corrections that should be incorporated in future reprints or editions of this book.

Administration of Akbar (Ain-i Akbari): Abu'l-Fazl 'Allami (ibn Mubārak). Selections from *The Ain I Akbari*, translated by H. Blochmann, M.A., 44–45, 56–59, 153–56, 258–59, 277–79. Calcutta: Baptist Mission Press, G. H. Rouse, 1873. [Public Domain]

The Babylonian Talmud: Auerbach, Leo. "Tractate Peah." In *The Babylonian Talmud: In Selection*, 49–53. New York: Philosophical Library, 1944. [Public Domain]

Book of the City of Ladies: de Pizan, Christine. Selections from *The Book of the City of Ladies*, translated by Earl Jeffrey Richards, 3–7, 16, 18, 62–64, 254–57. New York: Persea, 1998. Reprinted by permission of Persea Books via The Permission Company.

Book of Margery Kempe: Kempe, Margery. Chapters 51 and 52. In *The Book of Margery Kempe*, translated by B. A. Windeatt, 159–67. New York: Penguin Classics, 1985. Reprinted by permission of Penguin Random House UK. Three thousand three hundred (3,300) words from *The Book of Margery Kempe* by Margery Kempe, translated by B. A. Windeatt. Copyright © B. A Windeattt, 1985, 1994.

Canons and Decrees of the Council of Trent: Selections from "Decree on Justification" and "Decree Concerning Purgatory." In *Dogmatic canons and decrees: Authorized translations of the dogmatic decrees of the Council of Trent, the decree on the Immaculate Conception, the Syllabus of Pope Pius IX, and the decrees of the Vatican Council*, 21–27, 29–33, 35–40, 45–46, 165–72. New York: Devin-Adair Company, 1912. Internet Archive. https://archive.org/stream/dogmaticcanonsanoounknuoft /dogmaticcanonsanoounknuoft_djvu.txt (accessed March 12, 2020).

The Canticle of the Creatures: (1225) In *Francis of Assisi: The Early Documents*, Vol. 1, edited by Regis J. Armstrong, J. A. Wayne Hellmann, and William J. Short, 113–14. Hyde Park, NY: New City Press, 1999. Reprinted by permission of New City Press.

Divine Stories: "The Story of Two Parrot Chicks." In *Divine Stories: Divyavadana*, translated by Andy Rotman, Vol. 1, 333–36. Boston: Wisdom Publications, 2008. "The Story of the Two Parrot Chicks." In *Divine Stories: Divyavadana, Part I*, translated by Andy Rotman. Translation copyright © 2008 by Andy Rotman. Reprinted with the permission of The Permissions Company, LLC on behalf of Wisdom Publications, wisdompubs.org.

A Dream of Splendors Past in the Eastern Capital: Used with permission of University of Hawai'i Press, from "Recollections of the Northern Song Capital." In *Hawaii Reader in Traditional Chinese Culture*, edited by Victor H. Mair, Nancy S. Steinhardt, and Paul R. Goldin, 408–412, 420–421. Honolulu: University of Hawai'i Press, 2005. Permission conveyed through Copyright Clearance Center, Inc.

Ganga Lahari: Panditaraja Jagannatha, and Sadasiva Sri. *Panditaraja Jagannatha's Gangalahari*, edited by Irma Schotsman. Delhi: NAG Publishers, 1999.

A Guide to the Bodhisattva's Way of Life: Shantideva. Selections from "Perfection of Meditation" and "The Perfection of Wisdom." In *A Guide to the Bodhisattva Way of Life (Bodhicaryavatara)*, translated by Vesna A. Wallace and B. Alan Wallace, 100–102, 115–27. Ithaca, NY: Snow Lion Publications, 1997. Reprinted by arrangement with The Permissions Company, LLC on behalf of Shambhala Publications Inc., Boulder, CO, www.shambhala.com.

History of the Wars and The Secret History:

Procopius. From "History of the Wars." In *Procopious: Volume I*. Loeb Classical Library, Vol. 48, translated by H. B. Dewing, 3–5, 219–223, 231–233. Cambridge, MA: Harvard University Press, 1914. [Public Domain]

Procopius. "Preface," "Justinian's Misgovernment," and "The Arrogance of the Imperial Pair" from *The Secret History*, translated by G. A. Williamson, 37–39, 94, 111, 192–194. New York: Penguin Classics, 1966. Copyright 1966 by G. A. Williamson. Two thousand two hundred (2,200) words from *The Secret History* by Procopius, translated by G. A. Williamson Copyright © G. A Williamson, 1966

Prokopius. "The Affair of Antonina," "Justinian's Appearance and Character," and "Theodora's Background," from *The Secret History*, edited and translated by Anthony Kaldellis, 5–7, 36–43. Indianapolis, IN: Hackett, 2010. Reprinted by permission of Hackett Publishing Company, Inc. All rights reserved.

Kalila and Dimna: Munshi, Nasrullah (Naòsr Allåah Munshåi). "The Lion and the Bull." Selections from *Kalila and Dimna*, translated from the Persian by Wheeler Thackston, 3–15. Indianapolis, IN: Hackett Publishing, 2019. Copyright © 2019 by

Hackett Publishing Company, Inc. Reprinted by permission of Hackett Publishing Company, Inc. All rights reserved.

Kebra Negast: *Kebra Nagast: The Queen of Sheba & her only son Menyelek; being the history of the departure of God & His Ark of the covenant from Jerusalem to Ethiopia, and the establishment of the religion of the Hebrews & the Solomonic line of kings in that country,* translated by E. A. Wallis (Ernest Alfred Wallis) Budge, 20–54. London, Boston: [etc.] The Medici Society, limited, 1922. https://archive.org/embed /queenofshebaheroobudgrich (accessed March 19, 2020).

Mishneh Torah: Maimonides. "Matnot Aniyim—Chapter 10." In *Mishneh Torah,* translated by Eliyahu Touger. Published and copyright by Moznaim Publications. https://www.chabad.org/library/article_cdo/aid/986711/jewish/Matnot-Aniyim -Chapter-10.htm, (accessed October 10, 2020).

Muqaddimah: Used by permission of Princeton University Press, from Khaldūn, 'Abd al-Rahman ibn, "The Introduction." In *The Muqaddimah,* edited by N. J. Dawood, translated by Franz Rosenthal. Princeton: Princeton University Press, 1958, 1967. Permission conveyed through Copyright Clearance Center, Inc.

The Ocean of Story: "Alankaravati." In *Somadeva: Tales from the Kathasaritsagara,* translated by Arshia Sattar, 106–30. New York: Penguin, 1994.

Oration on the Dignity of Man: Used by permission of University of Chicago Press. "Introduction" and "Oration on the Dignity of Man." In *The Renaissance Philosophy of Man* by Giovanni della Mirandola Pico, translated by Elizabeth Livermore Forbes and edited by Ernst Cassirer, Paul Oskar Kristeller, and John Herman Randall, 215–17, 223–27, 229–30, 233–35. Chicago: University of Chicago Press, 1948. Permission conveyed through Copyright Clearance Center, Inc.

Origins of Higher Education: Selections from *University Records and Life in the Middle Ages,* edited by Lynn Thorndike, 26–30, 39–40, 64–65, 78–80, 171–72, 237. New York: Columbia University Press, 1944. Copyright © 1944 Columbia University Press. Reprinted with permission of the publisher.

Pillow Book: Shonagon, Sei. From *The Pillow Book of Sei Shonagon,* translated by Ivan Morris, 21, 25–26, 34–39, 44–50. New York: Columbia University Press. Copyright © 1967, 1911. Reproduced with permission of Oxford University Press through PLSclear and Columbia University Press.

Poems of Kabir: In *Songs of the Saints of India,* translated by John Stratton Hawley and Mark Juergensmeyer, 53–59. New York: Oxford University Press, 1988. Reproduced with permission of the Licensor through PLSclear.

Poems of Mirabai: In *Songs of the Saints of India,* edited by J. S. Hawley and Mark Jeurgensmeyer, 134–35. New York: Oxford University Press, 1988. Reproduced with permission of the Licensor through PLSclear.

Popol Wuj (Preamble and Creation Narratives): Used with permission of University of Oklahoma Press. From *Popol Vuh: The Sacred Book of the Maya*, translated by Allen J. Christenson, 48–75. Norman: University of Oklahoma Press, 2007. Permission conveyed through Copyright Clearance Center, Inc.

Rule of Saint Benedict: Abbot of Monte Cassino Benedict of Nursia. "St. Benedict's Rule for Monasteries," translated by Leonard J. Doyle, 1–9, 13–20, 33–34, 41–42, 55–56. Project Gutenberg. Collegeville, MN: The Liturgical Press, St. John's Abbey. [Public Domain] https://www.gutenberg.org/files/50040/50040-h/50040-h.html (accessed March 13, 2020).

Scivias: Used with permission of Paulist Press. From *Hildegard of Bingen: Scivias*, edited and translated by Mother Columba Hart and Jane Bishop, 169–74. New York: Paulist Press, Abbey of Regina Laudis, 1990. Permission conveyed through Copyright Clearance Center, Inc.

Shahnameh: Firdawsi. "Sekandar Reaches a Land Where the Men Have Soft Feet and Kills a Dragon." In *Stories from the Shahnameh of Ferdowsi: Sunset of Empire*, translated by Dick Davis, 87, 91–95. Odenton, MD: Mage Publishers, 2004. Used by permission of Mage Publishers.

A Short Account of the Destruction of the Indies: De Las Casas, Bartolomé. Selections from "Prologue," "Preface," and "Hispaniola." In *A Short Account of the Destruction of the Indies*, translated by Nigel Griffin, 5–17. London: Penguin, 1992.

Song of the Lute: Po Chü-i. "Song of the Lute." In *The Columbia Book of Chinese Poetry: From Early Times to the Thirteenth Century*, by Burton Watson, editor and translator, 249–52. Copyright © 1984 Columbia University Press. Reprinted with permission of the publisher.

The Spiritual Exercises: Loyola. "To Have the True Sentiment Which We Ought to Have in the Church Militant." In *The Spiritual Exercises of St. Ignatius Loyola*, translated from *The Autograph* by Father Elder Mullan, 39. New York: P. J. Kennedy & Sons: 1914. [Public Domain]

The Travels: Battuta, Ibn. "Ibn Battuta Arrives at the City of Mali, Capital of the Kingdom of Mali." In *Ibn Battúta: Travels in Asia and Africa, 1325–1354*, translated by H. A. R. Gibb, 323–35. London: Broadway House, 1929. [Public Domain]

The Truth About Stories: King, Thomas. Excerpted from "'You'll Never Believe What Happened' is always a great way to start." In *The Truth About Stories: A Native Narrative*, edited by Thomas King, 10–21. Toronto: House of Anansi Press, 2003. © 2003. Reprinted by permission of House of Anansi Press [www.anansi.ca] and the U.S. Publisher the University of Minnesota Press.

Aesthetics: perception of beauty; principles governing appreciation of beauty; cultural aestheticism; **see also Music and Entertainment; Poetry**

Pillow Book   Song of the Lute

Agriculture, Land, and Food: crop production; use and access to land; food sourcing and preparation and cuisine; local food customs; medicinal herbs; trading involving; **see also Indigeneity**

Administration of Akbar   *Babylonian Talmud*
Dream of Splendors   *Popul Wuj*
Sunjata   *Travels*
Twelve Articles

Asceticism: physical and mental forms of self-denial for religious purposes; experience of; metaphors related to; criteria for; expected outcomes of; **see also Body; Pilgrimage**

Ganga Lahari   *Guide to the Bodhisattva Way*
Poems of Kabir   Poems of Mirabai
Rule of Saint Benedict   *Scivias*

Authority and Institution: kingship; church; governance; caste system; political institutions; heresy and orthodoxy; **see also Power Structures**

Administration of Akbar   *Book of Margery Kempe*
Canons and Decrees/Trent   *Kalila and Dimna*
Kebra Nagast   Origins of Higher Education
Othello   Poems of Kabir
Scivias   *Spiritual Exercises*
Sunjata   *Twelve Articles*

Body: sensuality; denial of; embodied experience; metaphors about; **see also Asceticism**

Guide to the Bodhisattva Way   Poems of Kabir
Poems of Mirabai   *Rule of Saint Benedict*
Scivias

Community: monastic; brotherhood; group identity; **see also Identity and Self**

Babylonian Talmud
Mishneh Torah
Rule of Saint Benedict

Guide to the Bodhisattva Way
Muqaddima

Cross-Cultural Encounters: through travel; through transmission of narratives; conflict and war; trade; pilgrimage; colonization; **see also Identity and Self; Power Structures**

Kalila and Dimna
Muqaddima
Shahnameh
Travels

Kebra Nagast
Othello
Short Account/Indies

Devotion: personal relation with deity; intimacy; surrender; union; **see also Mysticism; Pilgrimage; Religion; Ways of Knowing**

Deliverance from Error
Poems of Kabir
Vishnu Purana (Krishna)

Ganga Lahari
Poems of Mirabai

Education: literacy; instructive texts; university; curriculum; **see also Philosophy; Ways of Knowing**

Administration of Akbar
Book of the City of Ladies
Kalila and Dimna
Rule of Saint Benedict

Book of Margery Kempe
Divine Stories (Parrot Chicks)
Origins of Higher Education
Spiritual Exercises

Empire: founding of; expansion; colonization; enslavement; legacy building; administration of; accounts of court life; **see also Cross-Cultural Encounters; Epic; Indigeneity; Power Structures**

Administration of Akbar
Pillow Book
Short Account/Indies

History of the Wars
Shahnameh
Sunjata

Epic: oral tradition; legends; history of nation; a long poem; cultural identity; heroic adventures; derived from; **see also Empire; Myth and Legend; Narrative; Poetry**

Kebra Nagast

Shahnameh
Vishnu Purana (Krishna)

Ethics and Morality: how to live well; narrative ethics; moral stories; situatedness of; reflecting on morals; **see also Philosophy; Rituals and Practices**

Babylonian Talmud	*Book of the City of Ladies*
Deliverance from Error	*Guide to the Bodhisattva Way*
Kalila and Dimna	*Mishneh Torah*
Ocean of Story	*Othello*
Rule of Saint Benedict	*Truth About Stories* (Sky Woman)

Formations and Reformations: Renaissance; rebellion; revolution; organizational ethos; group identity; Protestant Reformation; Counter Reformation; **see also Humanism**

Administration of Akbar	*Canons and Decrees/Trent*
Canticle of the Creatures	*Kebra Nagast*
Muqaddima	*Othello*
Rule of Saint Benedict	*Sunjata*
Twelve Articles	

Gender: politics of; roles involving; power and agency; identity; **see also Women; Self and Identity**

Book of Margery Kempe	*Book of the City of Ladies*
History of the Wars	*Ocean of Story*
Pillow Book	Song of the Lute

Historiography: how to write history; methodology; writing about history

Administration of Akbar	*History of the Wars*
Muqaddima	*Shahnameh*

Humanism: celebration of humans; what it means to be human; renaissance; against individualism; **see also Formations and Reformations**

Administration of Akbar	*Guide to the Bodhisattva Way*
Oration on the Dignity of Man	*Othello*

Identity and Self: self-fashioning; self-definition; nature of self; exile; **see also Community; Cross-Cultural Encounters; Gender; Indigeneity**

Book of the City of Ladies	*Canons and Decrees/Trent*
Guide to the Bodhisattva Way	*Oration on the Dignity of Man*
Othello	*Short Account/Indies*
Song of the Lute	*Spiritual Exercises*

Indigeneity: indigenous perspectives; oppression of; silencing of; genocide; **see also Agriculture, Land, and Food; Empire; Orality; Ways of Knowing**

Popol Wuj	*Short Account/Indies*
Truth About Stories (Sky Woman)	

Islamic World: originating from; cultural sphere of influence of Islam

Administration of Akbar
Kalila and Dimna
Travels

Deliverance from Error
Muqaddima

Music and Entertainment: instrumental; singing; performance; dance; commercialization of; location of social bonding; cultural expression; **see also Aesthetics; Orality; Poetry**

Dream of Splendors
Poems of Kabir
Song of the Lute

Othello
Poems of Mirabai
Sunjata

Mysticism: Sufism; visions; experience of; tradition of mystical writings; **see also Devotion; Religion**

Book of Margery Kempe
Deliverance from Error
Poems of Kabir

Canticle of the Creatures
Oration on the Dignity of Man
Scivias

Myth and Legend: creation stories, mythologies, cultural identity; **see also Epic; Narrative**

Divine Stories (Parrot Chicks)
Popol Wuj
Sunjata
Vishnu Purana (Krishna)

Ganga Lahari
Shahnameh
Truth About Stories (Sky Woman)

Narrative: narrative ethics; storytelling; origin stories; creation myth; memoir; autobiography; fables; travelogue; **see also Epic; Myth and legend; Orality; Poetry**

Deliverance from Error
Kalila and Dimna
Othello
Popol Wuj
Travels

Dream of Splendors
Muqaddima
Pillow Book
Shahnameh
Truth About Stories (Sky Woman)

Nature and Sacred: connection between; values from; interdependence; reciprocity; animal imagery; **see also Spirituality**

Canticle of the Creatures
Ganga Lahari
Sunjata

Divine Stories (Parrot Chicks)
Popol Wuj
Vishnu Purana (Krishna)

Orality: oral tradition; oral narrative; oration; oral histories; performance of; **see also Epic; Indigeneity; Music and Entertainment; Narrative**

Kalila and Dimna
Oration on the Dignity of Man
Popol Wuj
Truth About Stories (Sky Woman)

Ocean of Story
Poems of Kabir
Sunjata

Philosophy: nature of reality; meaning of life; fundamental questions; epistemology; writing about; **see also Education; Ethics and Morality; Ways of Knowing**

Administration of Akbar   *Book of the City of Ladies*
Deliverance from Error   *Guide to the Bodhisattva Way*
Oration on the Dignity of Man   Origins of Higher Education

Pilgrimage: travel for; search for connection with divine; hajj; commerce; **see also Asceticism; Cross-Cultural Encounters; Devotion**

Book of Margery Kempe   *Ocean of Story*
Travels

Poetry: genre of composition; aesthetic; expression; rhythm; religious; lyric; **see also Aesthetics; Epic; Music and Entertainment; Narrative; Orality**

Canticle of the Creatures
Ganga Lahari   Poems of Kabir
Poems of Mirabai   *Sunjata*

Power Structures: interrogation of; enslavement; colonialism; revolution and rebellion; **see also Authority and Institutions; Cross-Cultural Encounters; Empire; Formation and Reformation; Religion**

Administration of Akbar   *History of the Wars*
Kebra Nagast   *Muqaddima*
Poems of Kabir   *Popol Wuj*
Short Account/Indies   *Spiritual Exercises*
Twelve Articles

Religion: organized belief systems; Christianity; Buddhism; Islam; Hinduism; teachings of; laws about; beliefs about afterlife; **see also Devotion; Mysticism; Power Structures**

Babylonian Talmud   *Canons and Decrees/Trent*
Deliverance from Error   *Divine Stories* (Parrot Chicks)
Ganga Lahari   *Guide to the Bodhisattva Way*
Kebra Nagast   *Mishneh Torah*
Oration on the Dignity of Man   Origins of Higher Education
Othello   Poems of Mirabai
Rule of Saint Benedict   *Spiritual Exercises*
Vishnu Purana (Krishna)

Ritual and Practice: compassion; meditation; contemplation; gift-giving; charity; prayer; reciprocity; relationality; sacrifice; **see also Ethics and Morality**

Babylonian Talmud   *Book of Margery Kempe*
Canticle of the Creatures   *Guide to the Bodhisattva Way*
Mishneh Torah   Poems of Mirabai
Sunjata   *Truth About Stories* (Sky Woman)

Spirituality: individual's exploration of the divine and/or sacred; outside the confines of organized religion; **see also Nature and Sacred**

Book of Margery Kempe   Canticle of the Creatures
Divine Stories (Parrot Chicks)   Poems of Kabir
Poems of Mirabai   *Popol Wuj*
Rule of Saint Benedict   *Scivias*
Vishnu Purana (Krishna)

Ways of Knowing: reading; learning; thinking; epistemology; Traditional Ecological Knowledge (TEK); transmission of information; **see also Devotion; Education; Indigeneity; Philosophy**

Book of the City of Ladies   *Deliverance from Error*
History of the Wars   *Kalila and Dimna*
Muqaddima   *Oration on the Dignity of Man*
Origins of Higher Education   *Othello*
Popol Wuj   *Scivias*
Truth About Stories (Sky Woman)

Women: by a woman; main character is a woman; women's history; women's perspective; **see also Gender**

Administration of Akbar   *Book of Margery Kempe*
Book of the City of Ladies   *Kebra Nagast*
Pillow Book   Poems of Mirabai
Scivias   Song of the Lute

*aashrama*s, 220

Abbasid Caliphate, 19

abbot, 302

Administration of Akbar (Ain- i Akbari) ('Al-lami), 171–73; The Imperial Harem, 174–75; The Imperial Kitchen, 175–77; The Manner in Which His Majesty Spends His Time, 177–79; Regulations for Admission to Court, 180–81; Regulations Regarding Marriages, 182–83, 183–84; Regulations Regarding the Wa'qi'ahnawis, 181–82

administrative report, genre. See *Administration of Akbar*

adventure, cherishing. See *Shahnameh*

aesthetics: *Pillow Book, The,* 240–51; "Song of the Lute," 263–68

Africa: Ethiopia, 39–41; *Kebra Nagast,* 42–61; *Mishneh Torah,* 63–71; *Muqaddima,* 72–80; Negus, 40; Southernization of, 22–26; *Sunjata* (Introduction), 81–82; *Travels, The,* 83–89

aggadah, 128

agriculture, 4, 11, 23, 30, 81, 133, 171, 183, 397: *Administration of Akbar,* 171–84; *Babylonian Talmud, The,* 127–33; *Dream of Splendors Past in the Eastern Capital, A,* 190–98; *Popol Wuj,* 102–16; *Sunjata* (Introduction), 81–82; *Travels, The,* 83–89. *See also* food; land

al-Ghazali, 134–37. See also *Deliverance from Error*

Al-Musta'sim, 20

al-Tabari, Muhammad, 19–20

"Alankaravati" *(Kathasaritsagara),* 219–21; *Anangaprabh's Curse Is Finally Over,* 237–38; *Anangaprabha's Last Husband,* 236–37; *Anangaprabha's Adventures Continue,* 233–35;

Jivadatta Is Released, 232–33; *Jivadatta Wakes Up,* 230–32; *Jivadatta Wins the Vidyadhari,* 229–30; *Naravahanadatta Falls In Love With Alankaravati,* 222–24; *The Princess Who Refused To Marry,* 227–29; *Sita's' Banishment,* 224–26

'Allam, Abu'l-Fazl, 171–73. See also *Administration of Akbar*

Americas: *Popol Wuj,* 102–16; *Short Account of the Destruction of the Indies, A,* 117–26; Southernization of, 26–33; *Truth About Stories: A Native Narrative, The,* 90–101

anchoress, 359

anchorites, 301

Aryabhata, 4

'asabiyya, 73

asceticism, 200, 302, 397; *Bodhicaryavatara,* 205–18; *Ganga Lahari (Waves of the Ganges River),* 199–204; Kabir poems/epigrams, 252–57; Mirabai poems, 258–62; *Rule of Saint Benedict* (Benedict), 301–17

Asia: *Administration of Akbar (Ain- i Akbari),* 171–84; *Babylonian Talmud, The,* 127–33; *Deliverance from Error,* 134–37; *Divine Stories (Divyavadana),* 185–89; *Dream of Splendors Past in the Eastern Capital, A (Dongjing meng hua lu),* 190–98; *Ganga Lahari (Waves of the Ganges River),* 199–204; *Guide to the Bodhisattva Way of Life, A (Bodhicaryavatara),* 205–18; *History of the Wars,* 138–52; Kabir poems, 252–57; *Kalila and Dimna,* 153–65; Mirabai poems, 258–62; *Ocean of Story, The (Kathasaritsagara),* 219–39; *Pillow Book, The,* 240–51; *Secret History, The,* 138–52; Southernization of, 2–13; "Song of the Lute," 263–68; *Vishnu Purana,* 269–73

Attila the Hun, 13

audience. See *Pillow Book, The*

Aurangzeb, Emperor, 8

authority, 18, 73, 253, 274–75, 337, 368, 397: *Administration of Akbar*, 171–84; *Book of Margery Kempe, The* (Kempe), 336–45; *Canons and Decrees of the Council of Trent*, 274–83; Kabir poems/epigrams, 252–57; *Kalila and Dimna*, 153–65; *Kebra Nagast*, 42–61; "Origins of Higher Education," 346–55; *Othello*, 356–58; *Spiritual Exercises*, 318–24; *Sunjata* (Introduction), 81–82

autobiography, genre, 134–35, 137, 337, 400. See *Book of Margery Kempe, The*; *Deliverance from Error*

avatars, 269

Aztec Empire, 28–29

Babylonian Talmud, The, 127–29; "Tractate Peah," 130–33

Bai, Jodha, 8

Bakr, Abu, 18

Bantu Migration, 22–23

Battuta, Ibn. See *Travels, The*

Benedict of Nursia (St.), 301–2

bhakti, 4, 199

Bhakti movement, 5, 252, 258–59, 270

Black Death, 2, 17, 21, 72

Bodhicaryavatara, 205–7; Chapter IX, 209–18; Chapter VIII, 208–9

body, 93, 127, 291: *Bodhicaryavatara*, 205–18; Kabir poems/epigrams, 252–57; Mirabai poems, 258–62; *Rule of Saint Benedict* (Benedict), 301–17

Book of Margery Kempe, The (Kempe), 336–37; Chapter 51, 338–39; Chapter 52, 340–45

Book of the City of Ladies, The (Pizan): Christine Asks Reason Whether God Has Ever Wished to Ennoble the Mind of Woman with the Loftiness of the Sciences; and Reason's Answer., 331–32; The End of the Book: Christine Addresses the Ladies., 332–34; Here Begins the Book of the City of Ladies Whose First Chapter Tells Why and for What Purpose this Book was Written., 327–28; Here Christine Describes How Three Ladies Appeared to Her and How the One Who Was in Front Spoke First and Comforted Her in Her Pain., 329–30; Here

Christine Tells How, Under Reason's Command and Assistance, She Began to Excavate the Earth and Lay the Foundation., 330–31

Book of the City of Ladies, The (Pizan), 325–26

Book of the Mat. See *Popol Wuj*

brahmins, 5, 154, 220–21

Buddha Maitreya, 9

Buddhism, 9–11, 127, 185–86, 205–6, 301

Byzantine Empire, 138–40

Caliphate of Cordoba, 16

Calvin, John, 17–18

Canons and Decrees of the Council of Trent, 274–75; Decree Concerning Justification, 276–80; Decree Concerning Purgatory, 280–81; On the Invocation, Veneration, and Relics of Saints, and on Sacred Images, 281–83

"Canticle of the Creatures," 284–86

Caribbean islands, 31–32

Catholic Reformation, 319

Central Asia, 1, 7, 9, 11; Southernization in, 2–4

Chandragupta I, 4

charity: *Babylonian Talmud, The*, 127–33; *Mishneh Torah*, 63–71

Charlemagne, 14–15

Cherokee, 30

Christianity, 13, 20, 23–24, 29, 103, 117, 274, 290, 302, 401

Chü-i, Po, 287–88. See also "Song of the Lute"

city life, 191. See *Dream of Splendors Past in the Eastern Capital, A* (*Dongjing meng hua lu*)

Columbus, Christopher, 21, 31

common ground, finding. See "Song of the Lute"

community, 154, 186, 200, 205, 253, 274, 302, 398: *Babylonian Talmud, The*, 127–33; *Bodhicaryavatara*, 205–18; and caste, 154; Islamic ummah, footnote 83; *Mishneh Torah*, 63–71; *Muqaddima*, 72–80; *Rule of Saint Benedict* (Benedict), 301–17; sangha/Buddhist, 186

conciliar, 274

concubine, 264

Constantine, Emperor, 13, 138–40, 275

Cortés, Hernán, 29

Counter Reformation, 319

court lady, life of. See *Pillow Book, The*

courtesan, 264

creation story, 90–93. See also *Truth About Stories: A Native Narrative, The; Popol Wuj*
creation narrative, genre, 103. See also *Popol Wuj*
creature. See Kempe, Margery
cross-cultural encounters, 398: *Kalila and Dimna,* 153–65; *Kebra Nagast,* 42–61; *Muqaddima,* 72–80; *Othello,* 356–58; *Shahnameh,* 166–70; *Short Account of the Destruction of the Indies, A,* 117–26; *Travels, The,* 83–89

Dar-al-slam, 84
darshan, 6, 270
Delhi Sultanate, 5–6, 7
Deliverance from Error (al-Ghazali), 134–37
Deutscher Bauernkrieg, 368
devotion, 4–5, 172, 199–200, 252, 258–59, 269, 398: *Deliverance from Error* (al-Ghazali), 134–37; *Ganga Lahari (Waves of the Ganges River),* 199–204; Kabir poems/epigrams, 252–57; "Krishna and Kaliya," 269–73; Mirabai poems, 258–62. See also knowing, ways of, mysticism, pilgrimage; religion
devshirme, 21–22
dharma, 185. See also *Divine Stories (Divyavadana),* 220
dialectic argumentation, 347
Diet of Worms, 368
din-i-ilahi, 172
disputation, 291
Divine Stories (Divyavadana), 185–86; Sukapotaka-Avadana, 187–89
doctors, 337, 348
Dream of Splendors Past in the Eastern Capital, A, 190–91; Avenues and Alleys at the Eastern Gate of Xiangguo, 192–94; Avenues and Alleys at the Southeastern Tower, 194–95; Streets and Alley Outside of the Gate of the Vermilion Bird, 195–96; Restaurants, 196–97; Wine, Food, and Fruits, 197–98

East Asia, Southernization in, 8–13
Ecumenical, 274
education, 128, 186, 290–91, 318, 325–26, 346–47, 360: *Administration of Akbar,* 171–84; *Book of Margery Kempe, The* (Kempe), 336–45; *Book of the City of Ladies,* 325–34; *Divine Stories,* 185–89; *Kalila and Dimna,* 153–65; "Origins of Higher Education," 346–55; *Rule of Saint Benedict* (Bene-

dict), 301–17; *Spiritual Exercises,* 318–24. See also knowing, ways of, philosophy
empire, 4, 8, 13–14, 22, 24, 26, 28–30: *History of the Wars,* 138–52; *Pillow Book, The,* 240–51; *Secret History, The,* 138–52; *Shahnameh,* 166–70; *Short Account of the Destruction of the Indies, A,* 117–26; *Sunjata* (Introduction), 81–82. See also cross-cultural encounters; epic; indigeneity; power structures
emptiness, 207
encomiendas, 118
English Revolution, 18
entertainment, 241, 259, 264, 356: *Dream of Splendors Past in the Eastern Capital, A,* 190–98; Kabir poems/epigrams, 252–57; Mirabai poems, 258–62; *Othello,* 356–58; "Song of the Lute," 263–68; *Sunjata* (Introduction), 81–82. See also aesthetics; orality; poetry
epic, genre, 81–82, 167, 220: "Krishna and Kaliya," 269–73; *Kebra Nagast,* 42–61; *Shahnameh,* 166–70; *Sunjata* (Introduction), 81–82. See also empire; myths; narrative; poetry
Epic of Sundiata, 24–25
ethics, 64, 291: *Babylonian Talmud, The,* 127–33; *Bodhicaryavatara,* 205–18; *Book of the City of Ladies,* 325–34; *Deliverance from Error* (al-Ghazali), 134–37; *Kalila and Dimna,* 153–65; *Kathasaritsagara,* 219–39; *Mishneh Torah,* 63–71; *Othello,* 356–58; *Rule of Saint Benedict* (Benedict), 301–17; *Truth About Stories: A Native Narrative, The,* 90–101. See also philosophy; rituals
Ethiopia, 39–41
Europe, Southernization of, 13–18. See also Mediterranean Europe; Northern Europe
Europeans, atrocities performed by, 26–33
Exurge Dominae, 368

fable, genre. See *Kalila and Dimna*
faith, term. See *Spiritual Exercises, The*
Fatimid Shi'ites, 17
feminism, term. See *Book of the City of Ladies*
Ferdowsi, Abdoqasem, 166–70. See also *Shahnameh*
Five Pillars of Islam, 18
flying cash, 11
folklore, genre, 39. See also *Ocean of Story, The*
food, 28, 32, 186, 191, 270, 285. See also agriculture; indigeneity

formations, 206; *Administration of Akbar,*
171–84; *Canons and Decrees of the Council of
Trent,* 274–83; "Canticle of the Creatures,"
284–89; *Kebra Nagast,* 42–61; *Muqaddima,*
72–80; *Othello,* 356–58; *Rule of Saint Benedict* (Benedict), 301–17; *Sunjata* (Introduction), 81–82. *See also* humanism
four noble truths, 186
Francis of Assisi (St.), 284–86. *See also* "Canticle of the Creatures"

Ganga Lahari (Waves of the Ganges River),
199–204
Gemara, 63–64, 128
gender, 81, 92, 104, 240–41,357, 360, 399: *Book of
Margery Kempe, The* (Kempe), 336–45; *Book
of the City of Ladies,* 325–34; *History of the
Wars,* 138–52; *Kathasaritsagara,* 219–39; *Pil-
low Book, The,* 240–51; *Secret History, The,*
138–52; "Song of the Lute," 263–68. *See also*
identify; women
Gengis Khan, 11
Ghana Empire, 24–25
goddess, idea of. *See Ganga Lahari (Waves of the
Ganges River)*
grace, term. *See Spiritual Exercises, The*
Great Anti-Buddhist Persecution, 10
Great Western Schism, 275
griots, 81
*Guide to the Bodhisattva Way of Life, A. See
Bodhicaryavatara*
Gupta Empire, 4, 5

Hagia Sophia, 14
hagiography, 258–59
Hajj, 84
halacha. *See Mishneh Torah*
halakha, 63–64, 128
harem, characterizing. *See Administration of
Akbar (Ain- i Akbari)* ('Allami)
Heian Period, 9
heretic, 337
Hildegard of Bingen, 359–60. *See also Scivias*
historical account. *See Muqaddima*
historiography, genre, 73, 399; *Administration of
Akbar,* 171–84; *History of the Wars,* 138–52;
Muqaddima, 72–80; *Secret History, The,*
138–52; *Shahnameh,* 166–70
History of the Wars (Procopius), 138–43

human dignity. *See Oration on the Dignity of
Man* (Mirandola)
humanism, 399; *Administration of Akbar,*
171–84; *Bodhicaryavatara,* 205–18; *Oration
on the Dignity of Man,* 290–300; *Othello,*
356–58. *See also* formations
humanities, 291
Hundred Years War, 17
hymn, genre. *See* "Canticle of the Creatures"

identity, 399; *Bodhicaryavatara,* 205–18; *Book
of the City of Ladies,* 325–34; *Canons and
Decrees of the Council of Trent,* 274–83; *Oration on the Dignity of Man,* 290–300; *Othello,*
356–58; *Short Account of the Destruction of the
Indies, A,* 117–26; *Spiritual Exercises,* 318–24;
"Song of the Lute," 263–68
Ignatius of Loyola (St.), 318–20. *See also Spiritual Exercises, The*
indigeneity: *Popol Wuj,* 102–16; *Short Account
of the Destruction of the Indies, A,* 117–26;
Truth About Stories: A Native Narrative, The,
90–101. *See also* community; cross-cultural
encounters; gender; indigeneity
indulgences, 275, 367
institutions, 346–47, 397; *Martin Luther's Admonition to Peace,* 367–90; *Twelve Articles,*
367–90. *See also* power structures
instructions, 92
Islam, arrival of, 24
Islamic world, 83–84, 346–48, 400: *Administration of Akbar,* 171–84; *Deliverance
from Error* (al-Ghazali), 134–37; *Kalila and
Dimna,* 153–65; *Muqaddima,* 72–80; Southernization of, 18–22; *Travels, The,* 83–89

Jagannatha, Panditaraja, 199–200. *See also
Ganga Lahari (Waves of the Ganges River)*
jatis, 5
Jenne-jeno, 24
Jesuits, 319
jizya, 172; tax, 19, 21
Joan of Arc, 17
Joara, establishing outpost at, 30–31
Justinian Code, 13
Justinian, Emperor, 13–14

K'awiil, Jasaw Chan, I, 27
Kabir, 252–53; poems/epigrams of, 254–57

Kabra Nagast: How King Solomon held intercourse with his son, 56–58; How Solomon asked His Son Questions, 58–59; How the King planned to send away his son wth the children of the nobles, 59–60; How they made the Son of Solomon King, 60–61

Kalila and Dimna (Munshi), 153–54; The Crow That Killed a Snake, 164–65; The Fox That Tried to Eat a Drum, 160–62; The Holy Man's Adventures, 162–64; The Lion and the Bull, 155–56; The Monkey That Pulled Out the Wedge, 156–60

Kamakura Period, 9

karma, 186

Kathasaritsagara, 219–21; "Alankaravati," 222–38

Kebra Nagast: Concerning how King Solomon swore to the Queen, 49–51; Concerning the Labourer, 45–46; Concerning the sign which Solomon gave the Queen, 51; Concerning the Three Hundred and Eighteen [Patriarchs], 48–49; How King Solomon sent to his son the commander of his army, 55–56; How Solomon gave Commandments to the Queen, 46–48; How the King held converse with the Queen, 44–45; How the King of Ethiopia travelled, 52–53; How the Queen brought forth and came to her own Country, 52; How the Queen came to Solomon the King, 43–44; How the Queen made ready to set out on her Journey, 42–43; How the young man arrived in his mother's country, 53–54; introduction, 39–41; section of, 42–61

Kempe, Margery, 336–37

Khaldun, Ibn. See *Muqaddima*

knowing, ways of, xvi, 402; *Book of the City of Ladies,* 325–34; *Deliverance from Error* (al-Ghazali), 134–37; *History of the Wars,* 138–52; *Kalila and Dimna,* 153–65; *Muqaddima,* 72–80; "Origins of Higher Education," 346–55; *Oration on the Dignity of Man,* 290–300; *Othello,* 356–58; *Popol Wuj,* 102–16; *Secret History, The,* 138–52; *Truth About Stories: A Native Narrative, The,* 90–101. See also devotion; education; indigeneity; philosophy

"Krishna and Kaliya," 269–73

kshatriyas, 5

Kublai Khan, 11

La Malinche, 29

land-pedagogies, 92

land, 13, 19, 22, 28–32, 92, 118, 166, 318. See also agriculture; food; indigeneity

Las Casas, Bartolome de, 117–18. See also *Short Account of the Destruction of the Indies, A*

legal code, genre. See *Babylonian Talmud, The*; *Mishneh Torah*

legend, genre. See *Divine Stories; Ocean of Story, The*

letter, genre. See *Deliverance from Error*

lila, 270

lingua franca, 84

lion, characterizing. See *Kalila and Dimna* (Munshi)

Little Ice Age, 32

Lollard, 337

Luther, Martin, 17–18, 275, 367–69

Ma, Empress, 12

Machu Picchu, 30

Madhyamaka, 206

magister, 347

Mahabharata, 5

Mali Empire, 24–25, 81–82. See *Travels, The*

Mansa Musa, Emperor, 25–26

Martin Luther's Admonition to Peace, 367–69; *Admonition to Both Rulers and Peasants,* 387–90; *On the First Article,* 386; *On the Other Eight Articles,* 387; *To the Peasants,* 376–85; *To the Princess and Lords,* 374–76; *A Reply to the Twelve Articles of the Peasants in Swabia,* 373–74; *On the Second Article,* 386; *On the Third Article,* 386–87

Mayans, 26–27

Mediterranean Europe: *Book of the City of Ladies,* 325–34; *Canons and Decrees of the Council of Trent,* 274–83; "Canticle of the Creatures," 284–89; *Oration on the Dignity of Man,* 290–300; *Rule of Saint Benedict,* 301–17; *Spiritual Exercises,* 318–24

memoir, genre. See *Dream of Splendors Past in the Eastern Capital, A*

memorandum, composing. See *Administration of Akbar (Ain- i Akbari)* ('Allami)

merit, term. See *Spiritual Exercises, The,* 318–24

Muhammad, 18

Ming dynasty, 11, 13, 32–33

Mirabai, 258–59; poems of, 260–62

Mirandola, Giovanni Pico della, 290–92. See
    also *Oration on the Dignity of Man*
Mishnah, 63–64, 128
Mishneh Torah, 63–65
mitzvah, 127
Moctezuma II, 28–29
Mongol synthesis, rejecting, 11–12
monks, 301
morality, 186, 206, 326. *See* ethics
Mughal Empire, 7–8
Muhammad, Abu Hamid. See *Deliverance from
    Error*
Munshi, Nasrullah, 153–54. See also *Kalila and
    Dimna*
Muqaddima (Khaldun), 72–73
music, describing, 8, 19, 82, 103, 172, 186, 259,
    264, 356. *See* entertainment; "Song of the
    Lute"
Muslim Spain, 20, 72
mystical encounters, 336
mysticism, 7, 20, 39, 72, 291, 295, 400; "Canticle
    of the Creatures," 284–89; *Book of Margery
    Kempe, The* (Kempe), 336–45; *Deliverance
    from Error* (al-Ghazali), 134–37; Kabir po-
    ems/epigrams, 252–57; *Oration on the Dignity
    of Man*, 290–300. *See also* devotion; religion
myths, 400; "Krishna and Kaliya," 269–73;
    Divine Stories, 185–89; *Ganga Lahari (Waves
    of the Ganges River)*, 199–204; *Shahnameh*,
    166–70; *Sunjata* (Introduction), 81–82. See
    also epic; narrative

Nalanda Mahavihara, 5
narrative, genre, 40, 81, 103, 153–54, 241, 259,
    400: *Deliverance from Error* (al-Ghazali),
    134–37; *Dream of Splendors Past in the East-
    ern Capital, A*, 190–98; *Kalila and Dimna*,
    153–65; *Muqaddima*, 72–80; *Othello*, 356–58;
    Pillow Book, The, 240–51: *Popol Wuj*,
    102–16; *Shahnameh*, 166–70; *Travels, The*,
    83–89; *Truth About Stories: A Native Nar-
    rative, The*, 90–101. See also *Divine Stories*;
    epic; myths; orality; poetry
nature, 79, 149, 240, 400: "Canticle of the
    Creatures," 284–89; "Krishna and Kaliya,"
    269–73; *Divine Stories*, 185–89; *Ganga
    Lahari (Waves of the Ganges River)*, 199–200;
    Popol Wuj, 102–16. *See also* spirituality
Negus, 40

nirguna bhakti, 252
nirvana, 186, 206
Northern Europe: *Book of the City of Ladies,
    The*, 325–35; *Book of Margery Kempe, The*,
    336–45; Martin Luther's Admonition to
    Peace, 367–90; "Origins of Higher Edu-
    cation," 346–54; *Othello*, 356–58; *Scivias*,
    359–66; *Twelve Articles, The*, 367–90
Northern Song dynasty, 10–11, 190

Ocean of Story, The. See *Kathasaritsagara*
Ojibwe, 31
orality, xvii: Kabir poems/epigrams, 252–57;
    Kalila and Dimna, 153–65; *Kathasaritsagara*,
    219–39; *Oration on the Dignity of Man*,
    290–300; *Popol Wuj*, 102–16; *Sunjata*
    (Introduction), 81–82; *Truth About Stories:
    A Native Narrative, The*, 90–101. See also
    epic; entertainment; indigeneity; narrative
Oration on the Dignity of Man (Mirandola),
    290–300
origin-myths, defining: *Kebra Nagast*, 42–61.
    See also creation story
origin narrative, genre. See *Sunjata*
Original Instruction, 91
"Origins of Higher Education," 346–48. *See
    also* "Rules of the University of Paris, 1215"
orthodox, 337
Orthodox (faith), 274
Othello (Shakespeare), 356–58
Ottoman Empire, 21–22

Pachacuti, 30
pack animals, 29–30
Panchatantra (Five Treatises), 153
papal bull, 368
penance, 284
personal opinion. See *Dream of Splendors Past
    in the Eastern Capital, A* (Dongjing meng
    hua lu)
philosophy, genre, 63, 72–73, 206, 291, 347, 401:
    Administration of Akbar, 171–84; *Bodhicary-
    avatara*, 205–18; *Book of the City of Ladies*,
    325–34; *Deliverance from Error* (al-Ghazali),
    134–37; *Oration on the Dignity of Man*,
    290–300; "Origins of Higher Education,"
    346–55. *See also* education; ethics; knowing,
    ways of
pilgrimage, 9, 18, 25, 84, 172, 275, 318, 336–37,

401; *Book of Margery Kempe, The* (Kempe),
336–45; *Kathasaritsagara,* 219–39; *Travels,
The,* 83–89. *See also* asceticism; cross-cultural
encounters; devotion
Pillow Book, The, 240–41; 11. The Sliding
Screen in the Back of the Hall, 243–46; 5.
Different Ways of Speaking, 242; 14. Hateful
Things, 246–50; 1. In Spring It Is the Dawn,
242; 6. That Parents Should Bring Up Some
Beloved Son, 242–43;
Pizan, Christine, 325–26. *See also Book of the
City of Ladies, The*
Pizarro, Francisco, 30
play, genre. *See Othello*
poetry, 401; "Canticle of the Creatures,"
284–89; *Ganga Lahari (Waves of the Ganges
River),* 199–204; *Guide to the Bodhisattva
Way of Life,* 205–18; Kabir, 252–57; Mirabai,
258–62; Shahnameh, 166–70; "Song of
the Lute," 263–68; *Sunjata* (Introduction),
81–82. *See also* aesthetics; entertainment;
epic; narrative; orality
Popol Wuj, 102–4; Animals, 109–11; Creation
of the Earth, 108–9; Creation of the Effigies
of Carved Woods, 112–13; Creation of the
Mud Person, 111–12; Fall of the Effigies of
Carved Wood, 114–15; Preamble, 105–7;
Primordial World, 107–8
power structures, 401; *Administration of Akbar,*
171–84; *History of the Wars,* 138–52; Kabir
poems/epigrams, 252–57; *Kebra Nagast,*
42–61; *Martin Luther's Admonition to Peace,*
367–90; *Muqaddima,* 72–80; *Popol Wuj,*
102–16; *Secret History, The,* 138–52; *Short
Account of the Destruction of the Indies, A,*
117–26; *Spiritual Exercises,* 318–24; *Twelve
Articles,* 367–90. *See also* authority; cross-
cultural encounters; empire; formations;
institutions; religion
predestination, term. *See Spiritual Exercises,
The*
prisca theologia, 291
Procopius. *See History of the Wars; Secret History, The*
Protestant Reformation, 17–18
prose, genre. *See Pillow Book, The*
proto-capitalism, 2
public opinion. *See History of the Wars; Secret
History, The*

puja, 270
Purana, 269–70. *See also Vishnu Purana*
*purana*s, 5

Queen of Sheba, 39–41. *See also Kebra Nagast*

rabbis, 128
rabbit, characterizing. *See Kalila and Dimna*
(Munshi)
Rajaraja I, 6
rajas, 5
rakshasa, 269
Ramayana, 5
Rashidun Caliphs, 18
reality TV, comparison to. *Pillow Book, The*
reciprocity-based Traditional Ecological Knowledge (TEK), 91–92
reciprocity, 92
Red Turban Rebellion, 11
reformation: *Martin Luther's Admonition to
Peace,* 367–90; *Twelve Articles,* 367–90
regulation, genre. *See* "Origins of Higher
Education"
relationality, 90
religion, 4–10, 17, 23, 29, 84, 103, 134–35, 154,
166, 171–72, 191, 253, 259, 291, 301, 319, 346,
357, 401; *Babylonian Talmud, The,* 127–33;
Bodhicaryavatara, 205–18; *Canons and
Decrees of the Council of Trent,* 274–83;
Deliverance from Error (al-Ghazali), 134–37;
Divine Stories, 185–89; *Ganga Lahari (Waves
of the Ganges River),* 199–204; *Kebra Nagast,*
42–61; "Krishna and Kaliya," 269–73; Mirabai poems, 258–62; *Mishneh Torah,* 63–71;
Oration on the Dignity of Man, 290–300;
"Origins of Higher Education," 346–55;
Othello, 356–58; *Rule of Saint Benedict*
(Benedict), 301–17; *Spiritual Exercises,*
318–24. *See also* devotion; mysticism; power
structures
religious/royal origin myth, genre. *See Kebra
Nagast*
renaissance: *Martin Luther's Admonition to
Peace,* 367–90; *Twelve Articles,* 367–90
Renaissance, 16–17
Renaissance humanism, 290
revolutions: *Martin Luther's Admonition to
Peace,* 367–90; *Twelve Articles,* 367–90
Rihla, 83

rituals, 9, 25, 220, 258; *Babylonian Talmud,*
    The, 117   331 *Bodhicaryavatara,* 205–18; *Book*
    of Margery Kempe, The (Kempe), 336–45;
    "Canticle of the Creatures," 284–89; Mirabai
    poems, 258–62; *Mishneh Torah,* 63–71;
    Sunjata (Introduction), 81–82; *Truth About*
    Stories: A Native Narrative, The, 90–101. *See*
    also ethics
rivers, characterizing. *See Ganga Lahari (Waves*
    of the Ganges River)
Roderic, King, 15
Rule of Saint Benedict (Benedict), 301–2; Chap-
    ter 5 On Obedience, 308–9; Chapter 48 On
    the Daily Manual Labor, 315–16; Chapter
    7 On Humility, 310–14; Prologue, 303–5;
    Chapter 6 On the Spirit of Silence, 309–10;
    Chapter 3 On Calling the Brethren for Coun-
    sel, 308; Chapter 33 Whether Monks Ought
    to Have Anything of Their Own, 315; Chapter
    24 What the Measure of Excommunication
    Should Be, 314; Chapter 23 On Excommuni-
    cation for Faults, 314; Chapter 2 What Kind
    of Man the Abbot Ought to Be, 305–8
"Rules of the University of Paris, 1215," 349–50;
    The condemnation of 1210; Banning of Aristo-
    tle's Works, 353; Courses in Arts, Paris, 353–54;
    Gregory IX on Books Offensive to the Catholic
    Faith, 1231, 353; Method of Lecturing in the
    Liberal Arts Prescribed, Paris, December 10,
    1355, 352–53; Proclamation of the Official of the
    Episcopal Court of Paris against Clerks and
    Scholars Who Go about Paris Armed by Day
    and Night and Commit Crimes: January 11,
    1269, 351; On the Vices of Masters by Alvarus
    Pelagius, 351–52

saguna bhakti, 252
salvation, term. *See Spiritual Exercises, The*
sangha, 186
sant, 252
sati, 259
scholasticism, 347
Scivias (Hildegard), 359–60. *See also* "Vision
    Three The Church, Bride of Christ and
    Mother of the Faithful"
Secret History, The (Procopius), 138–40, 143–52
Shahnameh (Ferdowsi), 166–67; Sekandar
    Reaches a Land Where the Men Have Soft
    Feet and Kills a Dragon, 168–70

Shakespeare, William, 356–58. *See also Othello*
Shantideva, 205–7. *See also Bodhicaryavatara*
shogun, 9
Shonagon, Sei, 240–41. *See also Pillow Book, The*
Short Account of the Destruction of the Indies,
    A (Las Casas), 117–18; Hispaniola, 123–25;
    Preface, 120–23; Prologue, 119–20
Sikhism, 253
silambam, 6
Silk Road, 1, 3, 6, 9, 20–22, 84
sinocentrism, 9
"Sky Woman Falling." *See Truth About Stories:*
    A Native Narrative, The
slang. *See Dream of Splendors Past in the Eastern*
    Capital, A (Dongjing meng hua lu)
slave labor, 26
sola gratia, 275
sola scriptura, 275
Solomon, King. *See Kebra Nagast*
Somadeva, 219–21. *See also Kathasaritsagara*
"Song of the Lute" (Chü-i), 265–68
South America, Southernization in, 29–30
South Asia: *Administration of Akbar (Ain-i*
    Akbari), 171–84; *Divine Stories (Divyava-*
    dana); Kabir poems, 252–57; Mirabai poems,
    258–62; Southernization in, 4–8; *Vishnu*
    Purana ("Krishna and Kaliya"), 269–73
Southern Song dynasty, 11, 190
Southernization, 1–2; Americas, 26–33; Central
    Asia, 2–4; East Asia, 8–13; Europe, 13–18;
    Islamic world, 18–22; South Asia, 4–8; sub-
    Saharan Africa, 22–26; term, 9
Spanish Inquisition, 17
Spiritual Exercises, The (Ignatius), 318–24
spirituality: *Book of Margery Kempe, The*
    (Kempe), 336–45; "Canticle of the Crea-
    tures," 284–89; *Divine Stories,* 185–89; Kabir
    poems/epigrams, 252–57; "Krishna and
    Kaliya," 269–73; Mirabai poems, 258–62;
    Popol Wuj, 102–16; *Rule of Saint Benedict*
    (Benedict), 301–17
Srivijaya, 5
Story of the Two Parrot Chicks, The. *See Divine*
    Stories (Divyavadana)
story, story within. *See* "Alankaravati"
    (Kathasaritsagara)
stories, genre. *See Ocean of Story, The*
storytelling, genre. *See Truth About Stories: A*
    Native Narrative, The

sub-Saharan Africa: Southernization of, 22–26
Sufi, 72
Sufism, 134–37
Sulh-i-kul, 172
Sultana, Razia, 7

Talmud, 64, 128
Teotihuacan, 27–29
text, critical reading of, 72–80
Theodora, Empress, 139
Theodosius, 13
Three Great Teachings of China, 10
Tokugawa Shogunate, 13
Torah, 63, 127
tragedy, genre. See *Othello*
travelogue, genre. See *Travels, See*
Travels, The (Battuta), 83–84; The court cere-
    monial of king Sulayman of Mali, 86–87; fes-
    tival ceremonial, 87–88; Ibn Battuta arrives
    at the city of Mali, capital of the kingdom of
    Mali, 85; Ibn Battuta judges the character of
    the people of Mali, 88; Ibn Battuta leaves the
    city of Mali, 89; Ibn Battuta meets the king of
    Mali, 85–86; The nakedness of the women,
    88–89; Their piety, 88
treatise, genre. See *Martin Luther's Admonition
    to Peace; Twelve Articles, The*
Tridentine, 319
Truth About Stories: A Native Narrative, The
    (King), 90–101
Twelve Articles of the Peasants, The, 367–69, 370–73
tzedakah, 64, 128–29

Umayyad Caliphate, 18–19
Urban, Pope, II, 17

vaishyas, 5
vernacular, 285
vidyadhara, 220
Viking Age, 14–16
Vinci, Leonardo da, 17
virtues. See *Administration of Akbar (Ain-i
    Akbari)* ('Allami)
Vishnu Purana. See "Krishna and Kaliya"
"Vision Three: The Church, Bride of Christ
    and Mother of the Faithful," 361–66

Wen of Sui, Emperor, 8–9
women, 402: *Administration of Akbar,* 171–84;
    Book of Margery Kempe, The (Kempe),
    336–45; *Book of the City of Ladies,* 325–34;
    Kebra Nagast, 42–61; Mirabai poems,
    258–62; *Pillow Book, The,* 240–51; "Song of
    the Lute," 263–68. *See also* gender
Wuzong, Emperor, 10

Xuanzang, 9

Yanga, Gaspar, 31–32
Yuan dynasty, 11
Yuan, collapse of, 11
Yuanlao, Meng, 190–91. See also *Dream of
    Splendors Past in the Eastern Capital, A
    (Dongjing meng hua lu)*

Zanj Rebellion, 19
Zeraim, 64, 128–29
Zetian, Wu, 9
Zicheng, Li, 13
Zoroaster, 166
zuihitsu, 240

CPSIA information can be obtained
at www.ICGtesting.com
Printed in the USA
LVHW070729060122
707997LV00007B/58